WPF in Action with Visual Studio 2008

WPF in Action
with Visual Studio 2008

COVERS VISUAL STUDIO 2008 SP1 AND .NET 3.5 SP1

ARLEN FELDMAN
MAXX DAYMON

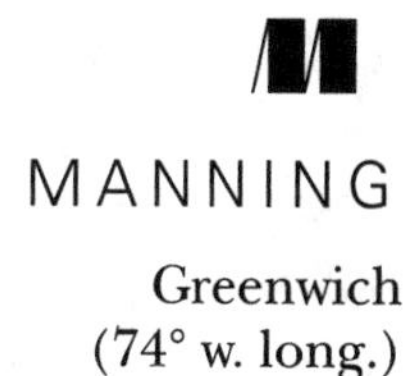

Greenwich
(74° w. long.)

For online information and ordering of this and other Manning books, please visit www.manning.com. The publisher offers discounts on this book when ordered in quantity. For more information, please contact:

Special Sales Department
Manning Publications Co.
Sound View Court 3B   Fax: (609) 877-8256
Greenwich, CT 06830   Email: orders@manning.com

Manning Publications Co.
Sound View Court 3B
Greenwich, CT 06830

Development Editor: Jeff Bleiel
Copyeditor: Andrea Kaucher
Typesetter: Dennis Dalinnik
Cover designer: Leslie Haimes

ISBN 1-933988-22-3
Printed in the United States of America
1 2 3 4 5 6 7 8 9 10 – MAL – 12 11 10 09 08

brief contents

PART 1 PAST, PRESENT, AND FUTURE 1

1 ■ The road to Avalon (WPF) 3
2 ■ Getting started with WPF and Visual Studio 2008 22
3 ■ WPF from 723 feet 41

PART 2 THE BASICS 63

4 ■ Working with layouts 65
5 ■ The Grid panel 94
6 ■ Resources, styles, control templates, and themes 119
7 ■ Events 147
8 ■ Oooh, shiny! 157

PART 3 APPLICATION DEVELOPMENT 177

9 ■ Laying out a more complex application 179
10 ■ Commands 191
11 ■ Data binding with WPF 209
12 ■ Advanced data templates and binding 253

13 ■ Custom controls 299

14 ■ Drawing 315

15 ■ Drawing in 3D 352

PART 4 THE LAST MILE 371

16 ■ Building a navigation application 373

17 ■ WPF and browsers: XBAP, ClickOnce, and Silverlight 390

18 ■ Printing, documents, and XPS 406

19 ■ Transition effects 427

20 ■ Interoperability 457

21 ■ Threading 474

contents

preface xvii
acknowledgments xix
about this book xxi
about the cover illustration xxv

PART 1 PAST, PRESENT, AND FUTURE 1

1 *The road to Avalon (WPF) 3*

1.1 The past and the present 4

Why Windows drawing is the way it is 5 ▪ How we currently create Windows UIs 7 ▪ Why the web is the way it is 9 ▪ How UI is created on the web 10

1.2 Why Avalon/WPF 11

Taking advantage of modern hardware 12 ▪ Using modern software design 13 ▪ Separating presentation logic from presentation 14 ▪ Making it simpler to code GUIs 15

1.3 Creating UI using WPF 16

Defining WPF UI with XAML 16 ▪ Defining WPF UI through code 17 ▪ Defining WPF UI with tools 18 ▪ Who does the drawing 19 ▪ Pixels versus vectors 19

1.4 Summary 20

2 ***Getting started with WPF and Visual Studio 2008 22***

2.1 Your grandpa's Hello, World! 23

Adding a button and button-handler to the window 25
Running Hello, World! 27 ▪ The TextBlock control 27

2.2 The application definition 30

Defining application startup in XAML 30
Why define the application in XAML? 31

2.3 A tour of WPF in Visual Studio 2008 34

The XAML designer 35 ▪ The Properties grid 38
Selection controls in Visual Studio 39 ▪ The Document Outline 39

2.4 Summary 40

3 ***WPF from 723 feet 41***

3.1 Where does WPF fit in Windows? 42

Red bits and green bits 42 ▪ Silverlight 43

3.2 Framework services 44

Base services 44 ▪ Media services 51 ▪ User interface services 55 ▪ Document services 56

3.3 Necessary and useful tools 58

Microsoft Expression family 59 ▪ Visual Studio 60
Other tools 60

3.4 Summary 61

PART 2 THE BASICS 63

4 ***Working with layouts 65***

4.1 The idea behind layout panels 66

4.2 The Canvas layout 68

Converting a Grid layout to a Canvas layout by modifying the XAML 69 ▪ Adding a Canvas to an existing layout 69
Using attached properties 72 ▪ Setting up a Canvas programmatically 73

4.3 The StackPanel layout 76

Adding scrolling support 80 ▪ The Expander control 81

4.4 The DockPanel layout 83

Defining a DockPanel in XAML 84 ▪ Setting up a DockPanel programmatically 85

4.5 The WrapPanel layout 86

4.6 Other layout options 88

Specialized layout panels 89 ▪ The FlowDocument 89

4.7 Summary 93

5 *The Grid panel 94*

5.1 Getting started with the Grid layout panel 95

Modifying the Grid 96 ▪ Grid specific properties 100

5.2 Using the Grid layout to build a calculator UI 101

Planning the calculator 101 ▪ Laying out the calculator 102 Tweaking appearance 104

5.3 The Grid and localization 107

5.4 UniformGrid 109

5.5 Making the calculator work 110

Handling operations 110 ▪ Genericizing the handlers 114

5.6 Summary 117

6 *Resources, styles, control templates, and themes 119*

6.1 Resources 120

Using standalone resource dictionaries 122 ▪ Using resources from code 124 ▪ Dynamic resources 125

6.2 Styles 131

Styles based on other styles 133 ▪ Implicitly applying styles 135

6.3 Control templates 136

Creating a control template 137 ▪ ContentPresenters 137 Template binding 138 ▪ Triggers 139

6.4 Themes 140

Using a specific theme 142 ▪ Changing themes from code 145

6.5 Summary 146

7 *Events 147*

7.1 Routed events 148

Bubbling events 149 ▪ Tunneling events 151

7.2 Events from code 154
handledEventsToo 155 ▪ Class events 156
7.3 Summary 156

8 ***Oooh, shiny! 157***
8.1 Glass buttons 158
Styling the text 162 ▪ Adding glow when over buttons 162
Handling the button click 164
8.2 Adding some simple animation 165
Animating button glow 165 ▪ Animating a color 168
8.3 Reflections 169
8.4 Transforms 173
8.5 Summary 174

PART 3 APPLICATION DEVELOPMENT 177

9 ***Laying out a more complex application 179***
9.1 Creating the Desktop Wiki Project 181
9.2 Nesting layouts 182
Preparing the layout for menus and toolbars 183
Adding menubars, statusbars, and toolbars... 184
9.3 Nested layouts 186
Adding the first Grid 187 ▪ Adding the second Grid 188
Using a StackPanel and Expander as navigation aids 189
9.4 Summary 190

10 ***Commands 191***
10.1 A brief history of commands 192
Windows Forms and simple event handlers 192
Son of MFC 193
10.2 The WPF approach 194
The Command pattern 194 ▪ WPF commands 195
10.3 Using the built-in system commands 196
ApplicationCommands 197 ▪ NavigationCommands 198
EditingCommands 198 ▪ Component and media commands 200

10.4 Handling commands 200

Handling a built-in command 200 ▪ Creating a custom command 201 ▪ Shortcuts and gestures 202

10.5 Command routing 203

10.6 A cleaner custom command implementation 204

Implementing a RoutedUICommand 204 ▪ Adding a CommandBinding 206

10.7 Summary 208

11 ***Data binding with WPF 209***

11.1 WPF data binding 210

11.2 ProcessMonitor: A simple binding example 212

Binding Data with XAML 212 ▪ Binding in code 217 Binding notation and options 219

11.3 Binding to XML 223

Creating the CVE Viewer application 225 ▪ Binding controls to XML 227 ▪ XPath binding notation 228 ▪ Path versus XPath 229 ▪ Understanding and using DataContexts 230 Master-Detail Binding 233

11.4 Binding to ADO.NET database objects 234

Creating a bookmark utility 236 ▪ Creating the simple DAL 236 Laying out the UI and creating data bindings 238

11.5 Binding to business objects 242

Creating a WikiPage business object 242 ObservableCollection 243 ▪ Create a model façade 244 Wiring business objects to presentation objects 246

11.6 Binding to LINQ data 250

11.7 Summary 252

12 ***Advanced data templates and binding 253***

12.1 Data converters 254

Formatting bound data with StringFormat 255 ▪ A number to formatted string data converter 259 ▪ Converter parameters 261

12.2 DataTriggers 263

12.3 CollectionViewSource 266

Sorting with CollectionViewSource 266 ▪ Programatically sorting with CollectionViewSource 268 ▪ Filtering with CollectionViewSource 270

12.4 Conditional templates 273

A more involved template 273 ▪ Conditionally using a template 275 ▪ Templates based on type 277

12.5 Validators 278

The ExceptionValidationRule 278 ▪ Custom ErrorTemplates 280 ▪ Custom validation rules 282

12.6 Model-View-ViewModel 283

12.7 Advanced binding capabilities 285

Hierarchical binding 285 ▪ MultiBinding 289 PriorityBinding 295

12.8 Summary 298

13 ***Custom controls 299***

13.1 Composing new user controls 301

Building a LinkLabel control 301 Testing the LinkLabel UserControl 304

13.2 Building custom controls 306

Building a control library 307 ▪ Create the new custom control 308 ▪ Create the default template for the control 310 Testing the control 312 ▪ Customizing a custom control with a template 313

13.3 Summary 314

14 ***Drawing 315***

14.1 Drawing with Shapes 317

Shapes in XAML 317 ▪ Stupid shape tricks 321

14.2 Creating the graphing control 323

Building the GraphHolder control 323 ▪ Graphing using shapes 327 ▪ Catching clicks 331 ▪ The downside of Shapes 332

14.3 Drawing with direct rendering 332

Recreating the graph control 333 ▪ Pluses and minuses of direct rendering 338

14.4 Drawing with Visuals 338

Control for display Visuals 339 ▪ Hit testing with Visuals 342 Adding labels to our graph 344

14.5 Drawings and Geometries 345

GeometryDrawing 348 ▪ Using Drawings 349

14.6 Summary 351

15 ***Drawing in 3D 352***

15.1 Lights, camera... 353

Models 354 ▪ Lights 357 ▪ Cameras 358

15.2 Graphing in 3D 359

15.3 3D Transforms 365

A 3D Transform in XAML 366 ▪ A 3D Transform in code 366

15.4 Summary 369

PART 4 THE LAST MILE 371

16 ***Building a navigation application 373***

16.1 When and where to use navigation applications 374

16.2 Creating a basic navigation application 375

Adding some navigation 378 ▪ Implementing dictionary lookup 379 ▪ Navigating programmatically 381

16.3 Page functions 384

Creating a Page function 384 ▪ Calling a page function 386

16.4 Summary 389

17 ***WPF and browsers: XBAP, ClickOnce, and Silverlight 390***

17.1 Building an XBAP 391

XBAP security 394 ▪ Deploying an XBAP 396 When to use XBAP 399

17.2 Using ClickOnce 400

Deploying a WPF application via ClickOnce 401 When to use ClickOnce 402

17.3 Using Silverlight 403

17.4 Summary 405

18 *Printing, documents, and XPS 406*

18.1 Printing flow documents 407

Setting up to print 408 ▪ Customizing the output 411 Printing asynchronously 413

18.2 Printing FixedDocuments 415

Adding some FlowDocument content to our FixedDocument 417 Matching resolution 420 ▪ Printing Visuals 421

18.3 XPS 422

Saving an XPS document to a file 422 ▪ The problem with images... 424

18.4 Summary 426

19 *Transition effects 427*

19.1 Building the World Browser application 428

The DictionaryLookup class 428 ▪ Working with the Application object 431 ▪ Our WorldListView user control 432 Populating the country list 433

19.2 Adding a simple transition 436

19.3 Building a generic transition control 439

Creating the transition control 439 ▪ Using the transition control 442 ▪ Defining a ControlTemplate for our control 443 Using the ABSwitcher 445

19.4 Adding some interesting transition effects 445

The fade effect 446 ▪ Wipe effect 448 ▪ Adding a selector for effects 453

19.5 Summary 454

20 *Interoperability 457*

20.1 Using Windows Forms controls in WPF 458

Using the Windows Forms DateTimePicker in WPF 458 Enabling Windows themes for Windows Forms control 461 What you can't do with embedded Windows Forms controls 462 Using your own Windows Forms controls 463 ▪ Popping up Windows Forms dialogs 464

20.2 Embedding ActiveX and C++ in WPF 466

Embedding ActiveX controls in WPF 466 ▪ Embedding C++ controls in WPF 468

20.3 Using WPF in Windows Forms 469

Using a WPF control inside of Windows Forms 469 ▪ Popping up WPF dialogs 472

20.4 Summary 473

21 ***Threading 474***

21.1 Moving slow work into a background thread 476

21.2 Asynchronous calls 479

21.3 Timers 480

21.4 Summary 481

index 483

preface

A number of years ago, the two of us worked at the same company and had to design a new form definition language for an entirely definitionally-driven system. The definitions were to be stored in XML. They had to be loosely bound to data definitions, and allow for complex behavior changes based on data. The individual elements of a form had their own properties, but also had to store properties that they didn't care about but that were relevant to higher-level layout mechanisms. We built this long before WPF was even a glimmer of a concept at Microsoft.

We'd like to pretend that Microsoft saw our brilliant design and decided to copy it when creating WPF, but that would be a lie, and we only lie when we're fairly sure that our facts can't be verified elsewhere.

Nonetheless, WPF does encapsulate all the basic design principles that we had for our form definition language, and then goes soaring off to leave our pitiful efforts in the dust. When we first started playing around with (extremely) early versions of what was then called Avalon, we had a lot of "duh, why didn't we do it that way" moments as well as, to be kind to our battered egos, a few "yeah, that's how *we* did it" moments.

We're both extremely comfortable in the Windows Forms (and the Windows SDK) world, so moving to WPF was both a happy and sad experience—sad in that we watched a lot of our hard-won knowledge become obsolete, but happy in that WPF made us way more productive, and let us do things quickly and easily that we would have just skipped with Windows Forms because they would have taken entirely too much effort.

Not that everything was a bowl of things that you like to keep in bowls—particularly with early betas and lack of documentation; we definitely spent time whining and banging our heads into walls. Overall, though, we are pretty happy with WPF, and are looking forward to where it's going to go in the future.

Fast forward a year or two, and one of us foolishly answered a phone call from Mike Stephens at Manning, asking about a completely different project. After many abject refusals, the conversation turned to WPF and the fact that there weren't many/any books out there that covered both WPF *and* Visual Studio 2008. Some slightly less abject refusals later, we suddenly discovered that we'd signed a contract to produce said book and have it ready in time for the release of Visual Studio 2008.

The astute reader might check when VS 2008 came out and the published date on this book and realize that we didn't quite make our original deadline. But, rather than laziness on our part, this really speaks to our timing genius—we managed to completely revise the book to take into account the many changes in Visual Studio 2008 SP1, which was released not long before these words were typed.

The goal of this book is to provide a practical guide to building WPF applications using Visual Studio 2008 SP1. It isn't intended to replace the MSDN reference material, but to provide guidance on how to get started and what you need to know to be productive in WPF. Productive is a relative term, of course—WPF has a lot of cool capabilities that can enhance your apps in many ways—and suck up all your available time with tweaking. It's up to you whether you can really ship your application without that flaming drop-shadow…

acknowledgments

This book wouldn't exist if it were not for a conversation many months (years? decades?) ago with Mike Stephens at Manning on an entirely different topic. Whether this warrants thanks or not remains to be seen, but we do have to thank him for being a great person to work with and for being incredibly patient with us as we watched deadlines sail majestically by (and for having a great sense of humor).

We also have to thank our fantastic editor Jeff Bleiel, and our original editor Douglas Pundick who left for reasons entirely unrelated to us (we hope). Also, thanks to the rest of the production team at Manning: Andrea Kaucher, Mary Piergies, Maureen Spencer, Karen Tegtmeyer, Dennis Dalinnik, Dottie Marsico, Tiffany Taylor, Leslie Haimes, Gabriel Dobrescu, and Ron Tomich.

We'd like to thank these reviewers for their valuable feedback on the manuscript during the various stages of development. Their insights and comments helped make it much, much better: Tim Sneath, Beatriz Costa, Patrick Long, Lester Lobo, Don Burnett, Andrew Konkol, Alessandro Gallo, Bryce Darling, Frank LaVigne, Nishant Sivakumar, Rama Krishna Vavilala, Barry Elzel, Joe Stagner, Ben Constable, David Barkol, Cal Schrotenboer, Oliver Sturm, Scott Pugh, Nick Kramer, Scott Baldwin, Dave Corun, Mark Mrachek, Riccardo Audano, Darren Neimke, Jeff Maurone, Michael Feathers, Doug Warren, Radhakrishna M.V., Jon Skeet, Tomas Restrepo, Berndt Hamboek, Aleksey Nudelman, Andrew Stopford, John Price, and Curt Christianson.

We also have to thank the legion of reviewers who took the time to review early versions of the manuscript on the Manning Author Online forum and who helped test drive the code. A big shout-out also goes to the WPF blogging community who were running into and through issues that had us stymied, and who gave us a number of ideas and insights.

At Microsoft, we have to first thank Luke Hoban, who was not only willing to answer irritating questions but also to bother all sorts of other people on our behalf to answer irritating questions. Thanks also to Mark Boulter, The Program Manager/Tech Lead on the .NET Client Team, for answering pages of questions while trying to get not one but *two* massive products out the door. Sam Bent on the data binding team spent several days confirming that we had hit real bugs, and were not insane. Well, not just insane. Charlie Calvert and Kevin Moore also gave us a hand, which we appreciate.

In the category of blatant friend abuse, we have to thank our blog-compatriot at www.exotribe.com, Tim Binkley-Jones, for being a sounding board and for eventually ending up doing our technical review, as well as David Russell for general guinea-pig services (and who probably now knows more about WPF than either of us. Sigh).

We also have to thank our wives—Tami Wandell and Adriana Wood—for not murdering either of us in our sleep, an act which would have been entirely warranted.

Finally, we would like to thank Microsoft for creating WPF—without which this book would have been a lot more confusing, and much less likely to have been published.

about this book

This book is designed to give you a working knowledge of Windows Presentation Foundation (WPF). The assumption is that the reader is already a .NET developer with some familiarity with other UI technologies (WinForms, MFC, HTML) but is new to WPF. In particular, the book focuses on using WPF with Visual Studio 2008, which we believe is the primary tool that most WPF developers will use, although we still spend *some* time talking about other available tools.

Throughout the book, your authors have injected some measure of their twisted humor, and have been known, on occasion, to resort to irony and sarcasm. We truly love WPF, but we also try not to take anything too seriously—and we hope that it makes reading yet another technical book just that little bit less gnaw-your-own-leg-off boring.

Roadmap

This book is broken down into four main parts. Part 1 is mostly about history and overviews. Chapter 1 starts this off by explaining how drawing in Windows and on the web got to where they are today, and the general way in which WPF addresses some existing problems. Chapter 2 is the first chance to get your feet wet with some simple WPF code, and also provides a guided tour of WPF-specific features of Visual Studio 2008. Chapter 3 provides a reasonably detailed look at what WPF is made of, as well as various surrounding technologies and acronyms that are likely to cross your path.

Part 2 covers the core concepts and technologies of WPF, primarily through an extremely brilliantly thought-out example application (OK, OK, a calculator). Chapter 4 is all about layouts and the general laying out of content in WPF. In chapter 5, we introduce the most complex of the layouts—the Grid—and use it to rough in the calculator example. Chapter 6 demonstrates how to control the look of an application via the use of resources, control templates, and themes. In chapter 7, we cover the new eventing model of WPF. Finally, in chapter 8, we pull out all the stops to make the calculator sexy and demonstrate some of the hotness that is WPF.

Part 3 focuses on building real-world applications. In chapter 9, we show how to build the framework for a complex application, including menus and toolbars. Chapter 10 demonstrates WPF command routing. Chapter 11 shows how to hook up data to WPF applications via data binding, including pulling data from databases, XML, or objects in general. Chapter 12 continues the binding conversation with more advanced types of binding and with the use of data templates to control the way data is handled. We also explain the new Model-View-ViewModel pattern.

Chapter 13 is about building custom controls in WPF—either one-off combinations of controls, or standalone controls designed to be distributed. In chapter 14, we demonstrate various ways of doing drawing in WPF, and in chapter 15, the last chapter of part 3, we extend that to the third dimension.

Part 4 covers some additional topics likely to be relevant to developing WPF apps. Chapter 16 demonstrates building navigation applications—apps with back/forward and hyperlinking support, which is built into WPF. In chapter 17, we take the navigation application and demonstrate how it can be hosted inside a browser via the use of XBAP. We also demonstrate ClickOnce deployment with a WPF application and touch (briefly) on Silverlight—a third way in which WPF can take to the web.

Chapter 18 is all about printing and documents. WPF has extensive support for printing and for transferring content around via XPS. In chapter 19, we take a break from the boring stuff and demonstrate how to add slick transitions to your applications. We also talk a fair amount about designing an application to support effects. Chapter 20 is about using other stuff with WPF, such as Windows Forms and WPF, and using WPF with Windows Forms. Finally, chapter 21 covers threading, including the new WPF Dispatcher, and timers.

Throughout the text, we've also sprinkled various tips and nags on WPF, UI design, and whatever else we felt like at the time. The book is *generally* designed to be read from start to finish, but you can certainly jump around to different topics and use the various chapters for reference as needed.

Code

This book contains a number of examples written in C# and/or in XAML. Although we did most of the work using the Professional version of Visual Studio 2008, you can do *almost* everything here using Visual Studio 2008 Express, which can be downloaded for free from Microsoft at www.microsoft.com/express. We've tried to indicate when particular capabilities require one of the for-money versions. All the source code for the book (and a few additional examples) can be downloaded from www.manning.com/WPFinAction or from our blog at www.exotribe.com.

The following conventions are used throughout the book:

- Courier typeface is used to denote code samples, as well as elements and attributes, method names, classes, interfaces, and other identifiers.
- Code annotations accompany many segments of code. Certain annotations are marked with bullets such as ❶. These annotations have further explanations that follow the code.

Author Online

The purchase of *WPF in Action with Visual Studio 2008* includes free access to a private forum run by Manning Publications where you can make comments about the book, ask technical questions, and receive help from the authors and other users. You can access and subscribe to the forum at www.manning.com/WPFinAction. This page provides information on how to get on the forum once you are registered, what kind of help is available, and the rules of conduct in the forum.

Manning's commitment to our readers is to provide a venue where a meaningful dialogue among individual readers and between readers and authors can take place. It isn't a commitment to any specific amount of participation on the part of the authors, whose contributions to the book's forum remain voluntary (and unpaid). We suggest you try asking the authors some challenging questions, lest their interests stray!

The Author Online forum and the archives of previous discussions will be accessible from the publisher's website as long as the book is in print.

There are a number of good WPF resources out on the web, including:

- The authors' blog, which covers a number of topics (including WPF), at www.exotribe.com
- Microsoft's windowsclient.net, which is a good place for general WPF (and WinForms) articles
- The WPF team blog at wpf.netfx3.com/blogs/presentation_bloggers
- The blog of Tim Sneath, a Technical Evangelist at Microsoft and the creator of the famed WPF New York Times Reader, at http://blogs.msdn.com/tims
- Beatriz Costa's blog, which is the place to go for data binding info, at www.beacosta.com/blog

About the authors

ARLEN FELDMAN has been developing software professionally for over 20 years, and has been a Windows developer for the last 14. He was chief architect for the award-winning HEAT software product, and has been working with .NET since its earliest days, including working with Microsoft on the direction of .NET, the C# language, and Visual Studio, as a member of the C# customer council. Arlen specializes in architecting and building metadata-driven applications, particularly focusing on the usability issues of such systems. Because of an accident involving rogue metadata retrieval, his brain is now a five-dimensional hyper-cube.

Arlen is the author of *ADO.NET Programming* (Manning, 2003), and is currently the Chief Architect for Cherwell Software, builders of .NET-based support solutions. He lives in Colorado Springs, Colorado.

MAXX DAYMON learned BASIC (on a Commodore VIC-20) before he learned English. His extremely eclectic background has given him experience with virtually every type of personal computer and a whole host of different industries; he's considered an expert in the back-end to the front-end of application design. To say that he's somewhat obsessed with human factors engineering would be like saying that Ghengis Kahn kind of liked fuzzy hats.

Maxx is MCPD Certified for both Windows and web development, and has been working with .NET since its preview releases. Maxx is currently a Software Architect at Configuresoft, a leading developer of configuration-management and compliance software.

About the title

By combining introductions, overviews, and how-to examples, the *In Action* books are designed to help learning and remembering. According to research in cognitive science, the things people remember are things they discover during self-motivated exploration.

Although no one at Manning is a cognitive scientist, we're convinced that, for learning to become permanent, it must pass through stages of exploration, play, and, interestingly, retelling of what is being learned. People understand and remember new things, which is to say they master them, only after actively exploring them. Humans learn *in action*. An essential part of an *In Action* book is that it's example-driven. It encourages the reader to try things out, to play with new code, and explore new ideas.

There is another, more mundane, reason for the title of this book: our readers are busy. They use books to do a job or solve a problem. They need books that allow them to jump in and jump out easily and learn just what they want just when they want it. They need books that aid them *in action*. The books in this series are designed for such readers.

about the cover illustration

The figure on the cover of *WPF in Action with Visual Studio 2008* is captioned "Henri, Seigneur de Metz." A seigneur was a medieval lord, who was granted power and privilege by the King, as well as large tracts of land which he, in turn, then leased to others. Metz today is the capital of Lorraine, a district in northeastern France.

The illustration is taken from the 1805 edition of Sylvain Maréchal's four-volume compendium of regional and historical dress customs. This book was first published in Paris in 1788, one year before the French Revolution. Each illustration is finely drawn and colored by hand. The colorful variety of Maréchal's collection reminds us vividly of how culturally apart the world's towns and regions—as well as its inhabitants—were centuries ago. You could tell where they lived and what their station in life was by their dress alone.

Dress codes have changed since then and the diversity by region and class has faded away. It is now hard to tell apart the inhabitants of different continents, let alone different countries, towns, or regions. Perhaps we have traded cultural diversity for a more varied personal life–certainly for a more varied and fast-paced technological life.

At a time when it is hard to tell one computer book from another, we at Manning celebrate the inventiveness and initiative of the computer business with book covers based on the rich diversity of regional life of many centuries ago, brought back to life by Maréchal's pictures.

Part 1

Past, present, and future

Before we get into the nuts and bolts of WPF, we think it's important to explain where WPF came from and why. That is the topic of chapter 1, "The road to Avalon (WPF)." This background will help developers using existing technologies—Windows or web—understand the whys and wherefores of WPF and, in particular, some of the bigger differences.

We'll also explain where WPF fits in the grand scheme of things (at least relative to the latest version of .NET) and provide a breakdown of the technology and tools that make up WPF. That's the topic of chapter 3, "WPF from 723 feet." This overview will provide a framework for understanding how all the bits and pieces tie together and, if nothing else, will provide the keywords you'll need when searching Google!

Part 1 isn't entirely devoid of code. In chapter 2, "Getting started with WPF and Visual Studio 2008," we'll provide an obligatory (if much reviled) Hello, World! to give you an idea of what WPF development looks like. That chapter also includes a tour of Visual Studio 2008, focusing on the features built specifically to support WPF.

1 The road to Avalon (WPF)

This chapter covers:

- A brief history of Windows drawing
- A briefer history of web UI design
- The underlying theory and purpose of WPF
- Some slightly intemperate comments about Microsoft's marketing department

When the development team at Microsoft started to work on their brand-new framework for developing user interfaces, they used the code name *Avalon.* Avalon, in British mythology, is the island where King Arthur was taken under the care of the Lady of the Lake—until the time when he will return. The name conjures up images of user interfaces with glimmering water and misty backgrounds.

The *marketing* department at Microsoft, whose job it is to make technology appealing to the masses, decided that a better, more appealing name would be *Windows Presentation Foundation* (WPF). Ah, well. If the name isn't particularly appealing, the technology certainly is.

Building user interfaces (UIs) is an often underappreciated facet of development. We, the authors of this book, have architected systems, large and small, dealing with everything from the database, security, and communication, all the way to the UI. It's hard to say that one part of the infrastructure of a system is more or less important than any other. To the user, the interface *is* the application. It doesn't matter how brilliantly you build stored procedures or how carefully you make sure your communications are secure. If the UI is poor, the application is poor. Period.

That's where WPF comes in. WPF is the latest Microsoft technology for building rich Windows applications. *Rich* is one of the terms used to differentiate Windows applications from browser applications.[1] They're also sometimes called smart applications or (usually if you're a web developer) fat applications. In this respect, WPF can be seen as the latest in the line of technologies including the Windows SDK, MFC, and Windows Forms. WPF does include several other technologies, which we'll discuss in more detail in chapter 3; but, when you get right down to it, WPF is mostly about building Windows applications.

This book isn't only about how to use WPF—it's also about how to use WPF *well.* Throughout the book, we provide suggestions on best practices and good UI design.

This first chapter explains some of the motivations for building WPF in the first place, and provides an extremely high-level view of how WPF works. But, before we get to that, we want to provide some historical context, explaining some existing technologies and comparing them to WPF. We take this approach partially to help bridge the gap between how you currently go about building UI and how it's done in WPF. We also believe strongly in the maxim that those who don't remember the past are condemned to repeat it. (And it was painful enough the first time through.)

1.1 The past and the present

Up until now, developing for Windows and for the web required a completely different set of tools and technologies. This is hardly surprising considering the target and genesis of each, but as times have changed, there has been a huge demand for Windows-like tools for the web and web-like tools for the desktop.

The results have been, shall we say, mixed.

Bringing functionality from one platform to the other has generally involved tacking additional functionality semi-randomly onto existing tools and technologies—sort of like mounting an oven on the top of your SUV so that you can have snacks while you drive. WPF, on the other hand, has the advantage of being built from the ground up with this problem in mind. It can address the needs of its target domain and learn the lessons from all the other frameworks and technologies that have grown up in the last few years.

WPF is primarily a technology for building Windows applications, but it also has a web story and a document-format story. All these stories fall under the aegis of *presentation*—presenting content to a user, whether via a rich application, a browser, or a piece of paper.

---

[1] Although a new term has started floating around—RIA for *Rich Internet Application*—when we use the term *rich*, we're specifically talking about non-browser applications.

The *Foundation* part of Windows Presentation Foundation comes in because WPF is the base for presentation-based applications, just as Windows Communication Foundation (WCF) is the base for communication between applications. The names may be a tad on the pretentious side, but for those of us who survived the alphabet soup of Microsoft DNA, it isn't too bad.

WPF had the opportunity to start from scratch and learn lessons from earlier technologies. Two of the strongest influences on WPF were existing Windows development methods and web development—and by influence, we mean "let's not do *that* ever again."

To understand how revolutionary WPF is, we should look at how Windows development and web development came into being and how they exist today. You're probably already somewhat familiar with the details of one or both technologies, but we'll try to highlight their genesis and some of the specific issues that WPF addresses.

1.1.1 Why Windows drawing is the way it is

Time passes strangely in the computer world. We talk about last year's technology being obsolete and only fit for the rubbish heap. At the same time, we end up having to do things in certain ways because of decisions made decades ago. Windows first came out in 1985, and Windows 3.0 (the first popular version) came out in 1990. Despite the many enhancements and new versions, some of that early Windows code is still floating around behind the scenes; and, more scarily, the *patterns* of that code are still around, like some sort of design virus, even when the code itself has been replaced. Figure 1.1 shows a screen shot from Window 3.x. Although it looks quite different than Windows XP or Vista, it *is* easily recognizable as a forebear.

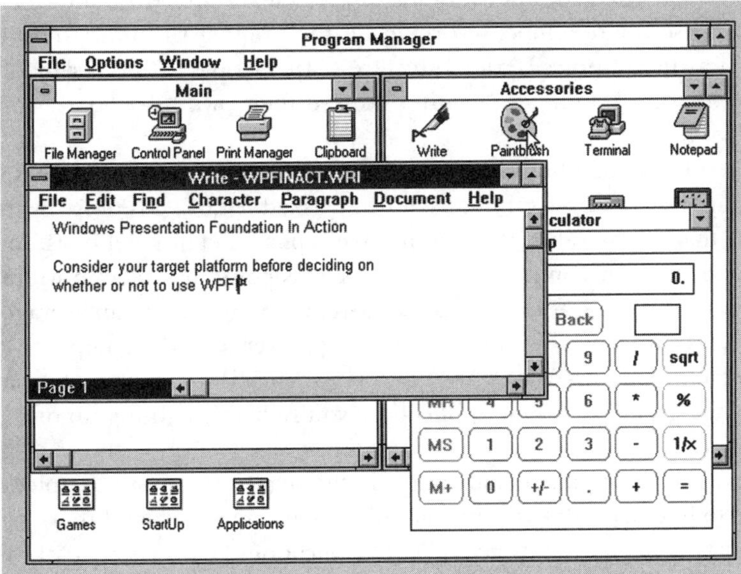

Figure 1.1 Although Windows 3.x came out more than 15 years ago, it has an influence on the UIs of today.

Drawing/painting in Windows is one area where those original decisions have a strong influence. Think back to the computer you were using in 1985. In the fledgling PC world, 4.77 megahertz (note the *m*) machines were all the rage, and 640K was more memory than anyone would ever need.[2] The machine on which this text is being written is about twenty-thousand times faster and has around two-thousand times more memory (although, sadly, it takes much longer to boot than our machines from 1985). It's important to our story to note that those fancy 640x480 256-glorious-color VGA cards didn't come out until 1988.

Even with all those limitations, the Windows designers attempted to think ahead by making things as abstract as possible. You didn't code directly to the screen's memory but to a *device context*, which might be the screen or a printer. Instead of plotting everything directly to the screen, you created brushes, fonts, and pens, and worked with handles that abstracted them slightly (although woe betide anyone who had more than five declared at one time). Windows—and the controls within windows—were even represented by object-oriented*ish* structures called classes, and referenced by pointers, **H**andles to **WiND**ows (HWNDs).

All this history matters today because, up until WPF, nearly every drawing technology on Windows has sat on top of this design. MFC, for example, was a thin wrapper. .NET Windows Forms, which is much more robust, does a lot to hide the complexity and the arcane rules of working with the low-level libraries. Even with Windows Forms, the original design occasionally leaks through. Why, when you draw a line, does it end one pixel shy of where you said? Because HP was a big customer of Microsoft, and their plotters needed the pens to stop short to avoid getting a noticeable blob at corners. Why do the rules for disabled text differ from the rules for regular text? Because the developers working on the original UI library didn't want to wait around for the Graphics Device Interface (GDI) people to add disabled text support to their `TextOut()` function, so they created their own `DrawText()` function. It goes on and on.

The biggest legacy of all this is the *philosophy* of drawing. Each window is responsible for drawing itself and refreshing itself when asked. Drawing is done by using various methods that set the value of different pixels on a pixel-by-pixel basis. And all the drawing is done by your computer's processor. This point may seem obvious, but it's not. In this day and age, graphics cards are extremely powerful. In an average gamer's PC, the graphics card may have more computing power than the computer itself. Yet, when you write a Windows Forms application, as Mark Boulter[3] says, no matter how complicated the graphics in your application, you're barely lighting up one diode on your graphics card.

WPF is an almost complete departure from this legacy. It's *almost* complete because WPF still has to interact with existing technologies at some level, and there's still a single HWND lurking below the surface of WPF applications. The existence of this HWND

[2] Bill Gates supposedly made this claim in 1981, although he denies it!

[3] The Program Manager/Technical Lead on the .NET Client Team

has some implications for WPF development, particularly when interacting with non-WPF code. But, as you'll see throughout the rest of this book, WPF is a new beast, built from the ground up. It takes the best ideas from Windows drawing, web presentation, DirectX, and modern graphics theory, with only a minimal thread tying it to the limitations of the technology and ideas that have ruled GUI development for the last 20 years.

To see exactly how far we've come, we should look at how existing Windows applications work.

1.1.2 How we currently create Windows UIs

When you look at a Windows Forms application (or an MFC or ATL application, or even one written using C and doing low-level message handling) you're looking at some number of windows. If you see a dialog with some text, a text box, and a couple of buttons, you're probably looking at five windows—one for the dialog, one for the text, one for the text box, and one for each of the buttons.

Each of those windows is responsible for painting itself and responding to messages. Messages might be things like "the mouse has moved over me" or "I just got focus." For some windows, such as buttons, Windows (capital W) knows what to do and automatically provides basic handling. For others that do their own things or have special behaviors (for example, a button that looks like glass), the applications are responsible for handling everything themselves.

The fact that each window is responsible for painting itself is important. If you drag something over the top of the dialog and then move it, Windows doesn't remember what that dialog looked like. Instead, it sends a message to the dialog, and to each window within the dialog, telling them each to repaint themselves. The major reason why Windows works that way is that there isn't enough memory to store the bits representing each separate pixel on all the possible overlapping windows.

To be consistent with this approach, when a window wants to change the way it looks, it doesn't just repaint the bit of the screen that it occupies. For example, consider what happens when you click a button. When the mouse is pressed, the button has to be drawn in a depressed (or happy but pushed) state. Instead of painting over that bit of the screen, this is more or less what happens (figure 1.2):

Figure 1.2 To have a control change state, you have to force it to redraw itself, as with these buttons shown before and during a click.

1. The user clicks the mouse over the button.
2. The button detects the mouse-down.
3. The button Invalidates the bit of the screen it occupies, telling Windows that it needs to be repainted.
4. Windows (at some point in the future) sends a Paint message to the application, telling it to repaint part of itself.
5. The application passes the message to the button.
6. The button draws a depressed version of itself.

There are two important points to remember about the way Windows UI works:

- Each window is constantly redrawing itself—when it's first created, when it's covered and then reexposed, or when something about the look-and-feel needs to change.
- Controls are responsible for receiving messages from Windows and handling them appropriately. These messages are pretty low-level—"the mouse moved over me," "focus has changed from me," and so on. Windows Forms does some wrapping to make handling these messages as painless as possible, but rest assured, messages are zipping merrily back and forth behind the scenes. If you want to customize behavior or look-and-feel, even in Windows Forms, you need to know a lot about handling messages.

Finally, there's the drawing itself. When the application is told to paint something, it works with a device context (wrapped in a `Graphics` object in Windows Forms). The device context/`Graphics` object is an abstraction so that the same code can paint to a printer, to different screens, to a bitmap, and so on. A good (but not entirely accurate) way to think of the device context is as a surface on which you can draw.

Drawing is a matter of calling various methods for things like rectangles, shapes, or text. This is much like painting in a drawing program. Once you draw a circle on a device context, it's no longer a circle, but a bunch of dots with color values. The same thing happens with drawing lines, dots, or even text—although text is special because graphics cards and printers work better if they know that they're printing text instead of dots. But for all practical purposes, the text is just dots as far as any interface that you can get to is concerned.

If you've used fancy layout programs like CorelDRAW or Visio, you know that you can click circles, for example, and move them around. The drawing program is doing all the work, including determining whether your click was inside the circle or outside it (which can get complicated with more complex shapes) and telling Windows to redraw the parts of the screen where the circle was and where the circle has moved to.

The way in which classic Windows draws is very different from the Visio approach, bringing us to one final important point:

- In classic Windows applications, everything you see, as far as Windows is concerned, is a bunch of colored dots.

This statement is a ridiculously high-level overview of how classic Windows UIs are created; but, when we talk about the way in which WPF handles drawing, you should remember these three important points to see how different WPF is.

Programming Windows UI is often about figuring out *how* to do things. At the same time that Windows development was maturing, the World Wide Web came into being. On the web, everything was about *what* you wanted to say, with the details of presentation left to the browser. As the web developed, more and more effort went into controlling *how* that content was presented.

1.1.3 Why the web is the way it is

In 1990, around the time Windows 3.0 was being released, Tim Berners-Lee was busy creating the World Wide Web. Originally designed to author and disseminate documents, the web has grown into a multipurpose platform far beyond its original roots. Through many incremental advances, the web has become an application platform, although it's still fundamentally document-centric. The evolution of the web into an application platform is a testament both to the flexibility of the system and to the creativity of the developers who write applications for it.

HTML is the means by which web content is created and displayed. Early HTML was mostly *semantic*. Semantic HTML is HTML in which the tags describe the structure and meaning of the content, not the way it's presented. For example, rather than declaring the font, size, and style of text as you might do in a word processor, you declare the text as being a header, paragraph, a citation, and so on. The web client software then determines the appropriate font, size, and style to render. This is particularly relevant because control of the presentation of documents by the document authors wasn't a primary concern, and even something to be avoided.

Then something happened that turned all of this on its head. War was declared!

THE FIRST GREAT BROWSER WAR

In the mid-1990s, seeing the potential of the web, Marc Andreessen and Jim Clark formed Mosaic Communications Corporation (later to become Netscape). When excitement around the web grew, it eventually caught the roving (Sauron-like) eye of Microsoft, who then entered with their own web browser, Internet Explorer. The increasingly tense competition resulted in a number of design decisions that would simultaneously advance and drag down web development for years.

The first casualty was the erratic and uncontrolled expansion of HTML. To gain favor, Netscape and Microsoft both added tags to HTML that would describe, not only what a given block of text was for, but also how to format the text. The most egregious, shark-jumping example of these additions would have to be Netscape's inclusion of the `<blink>` tag. (And shame on you if you ever used it.)

At the same time Netscape and Microsoft were battling it out, developers were piling onto the HTML bandwagon. In wild-west style, people were staking claims and figuring out what worked and using it, even if it only worked because of an accident or side effect of that week's browser release.

TOO LATE FOR CONFORMANCE

By the time standards were starting to get nailed down, it was already too late. Too many people were relying on the side effects. The solution? Make *conformance* optional. An HTML document could violate the rules[4] of HTML, and browsers would simply do their best to display the document. The ability to render invalid HTML even became a selling point. A great deal of energy today goes into browser development to

[4] The rules around the HTML document structure are defined by a metalanguage called SGML, but even that wasn't true until HTML 2.0.

make invalid documents display correctly. (Browsers to this day have things like *quirks mode* and, we kid you not, *almost-standards mode*)

In the last few years, there has been some improvement with the introduction of Cascading Style Sheets (CSS). With CSS, the content to be rendered (in the HTML) is separated from the instructions as to how it should be rendered (in the CSS). In addition to making things simpler, this approach provides significantly more control over how content is rendered.[5] HTML with CSS is an example of the concept of *separation of concerns*, which we'll touch on throughout this book.

As with existing Windows technology, the WPF team looked thoroughly at how UI works on the web, so it's worth spending time talking about this ourselves.

1.1.4 How UI is created on the web

The basis for any true web application[6] is HTML. HTML provides for UIs indirectly through a subset of native platform controls. This control support was originally provided to enable form-based documents with fillable fields. By design, a limited subset of controls is exposed by HTML for this purpose (figure 1.3). One important goal of HTML is to be usable across a wide variety of platforms and devices, and that goal tends to gravitate toward the lowest common denominator of the platforms of interest. The lack of controls can be problematic for developers. In particular, we've seen the lack of tree controls, combo boxes, and calendar controls cause many Windows developers confusion and grief when first introduced to web development.

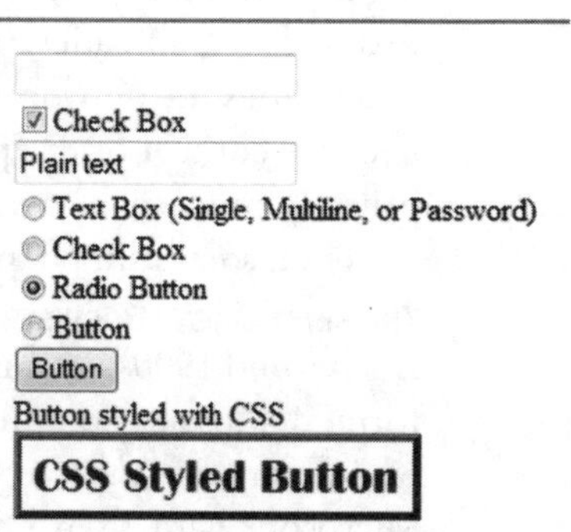

Figure 1.3 The set of available native controls in HTML is limited. This image shows most of them.

Though not essential, JavaScript is the second tool in the web UI designer's toolbox. JavaScript is an object-oriented[7] (OO) scripting language that enables use of the events on HTML elements and controls and allows behavior to be overridden to an extent, providing a much richer user experience. Without JavaScript, web UIs are extremely limited and largely only support the form-submission model from HTML, where controls may either contain information (text box, radio button, check box), send information to a server (via form button), or abandon a view entirely (by leaving the page).

---

5 For a CSS tour-de-force, visit www.csszengarden.com. We haven't seen a better site for demonstrating the power of CSS as a theming device.

6 For the purposes of this discussion, a web application is one that doesn't rely on any platform-specific technologies such as ActiveX or Flash, which should be considered to be Windows or Flash applications delivered via HTTP.

7 Few statements in the book have generated more comments in the forums and from reviewers than this. Yes, JavaScript is an object-oriented language, although it's rarely used as such.

The third major tool, CSS, provides the developer with the ability to fine-tune the look and behavior of the UI. CSS is used to define the way content should be presented by providing styles that are applied to various elements. The degree to which the presentation can be altered lies within the constraints of CSS itself. Prior to widespread support of CSS, web-based interfaces (and documents, for that matter) tended to include an obscene number of tables to influence the layout of the UI. Like HTML, CSS is oriented around the formatting of documents and tends to center around page-layout instructions.

To summarize, we want to emphasize two important points for web UI development:

- *Web UI is described using HTML and CSS.* The browser then follows a set of internal rules to create the UI from the descriptions given to it. Describing what you want, rather than specifically coding it, is the basis of declarative programming. This approach can be extremely powerful, as it greatly simplifies UI design and allows for dynamic UIs.
- *A web developer doesn't have direct control over the UI.* Through use of HTML, CSS, and JavaScript, the web developer influences the UI, but ultimately, the browser has the final word. If CSS doesn't support a text style you want, you can't add it. If, for example, CSS didn't support ~~strikethrough~~, you're pretty much out of luck (barring some ugly image-based hack). Contrast this with native UI development in which the developer may choose to take over virtually any aspect of presentation and behavior of a UI element.

Some web application frameworks overcome, in varying degrees, many of the limitations discussed—albeit with considerable effort. The best of these frameworks typically create an entire presentation layer based on JavaScript, many generic HTML `<div>` and `<span>` tags, and extensive use of CSS. Although the results can be impressive, the downside of this approach is that a tremendous amount of power is dedicated to providing a user experience on par with Windows 3.1.

Now, imagine a markup language with the simplicity and declarative style of HTML, but expressly designed for describing applications rather than documents. Imagine a framework that uses the massive power of modern Graphics Processing Units (GPUs) to provide the next generation user experience. Enter Windows Presentation Foundation.

1.2 Why Avalon/WPF

Why did Microsoft decide that it was time to completely re-create the way in which UIs were built? In many ways, the last two sections provide a lot of reasons—the technology behind Windows UI is creaking. The technology behind web UI is being tortured into something that can be used for building applications. Both have some powerful capabilities and concepts, but the two certainly don't play well together.

Microsoft had big goals for Windows Vista, their new flagship OS. Sadly, a lot of these goals have been missed, such as Windows Future Storage (WinFS), the SQL Server-based replacement for the NTFS filesystem. As far as presentation is concerned, WPF delivers on most of its promises (and doesn't even require Windows Vista).

Obviously, some of the impetus for a new graphical system is market driven. Anyone who has any familiarity with Macintosh OS X knows that it's extremely slick, both to use and to code. Although Apple's market share is pretty small[8] in comparison, Microsoft knows a good idea when they see it. Even if keeping up with the Jobses was one of the driving factors behind the decision to create WPF, there were also a lot of specific technical goals, as follows:

- *To use modern hardware*—Hardware has changed a lot in the last decade or two, but taking advantage of the hardware requires extremely specialized coding. WPF should make use of the underlying hardware by default.
- *To use modern software design*—When the graphic subsystem of Windows was first created, things like OO development, patterns, and garbage collection were either nonexistent or bleeding edge. WPF should be built using modern software design and easy to access by programmers who use modern software design.
- *To separate presentation from presentation logic*—WPF should allow programmers to develop the look-and-feel of an application independently from the logic that makes it work.
- *To simplify coding*—Doing simple things is pretty easy, but WPF should make doing complex, formerly painful things relatively easy as well.

We'll dig a little deeper into each of these goals.

1.2.1 Taking advantage of modern hardware

Earlier, we talked about how little advantage most Windows applications take of the super-powered graphics cards in most of today's PCs. Prior to WPF, to do any sort of serious graphical UI, you were required to use DirectX or Open Graphics Library (OpenGL). It's ironic that programming games required doing some of the most unpleasant types of programming. Making the standard library for Windows UI take advantage of current and future graphics cards was important.

But modern hardware refers to more than the graphics card. For example, tablet PCs are becoming popular (well, *more* popular), and handheld devices in general are everywhere. Handling their specialized input easily was important—which is where Ink comes in. Ink is the technology that provides support for writing directly on screens and converting that writing into text. WPF applications can get input from Ink, merging it with standard mouse and keyboard input so that your applications work reasonably, even if not built for tablets.

Modern display devices also needed to be addressed. Multiple monitors are now much more common, and high-definition displays will be the norm in the near future. Even today, many machines ship with their dots per inch (DPI) set to 120, instead of the standard 96 DPI to which most applications have been developed. Windows Forms

[8] Apple's handicap is its size, whereas Microsoft's is its size.

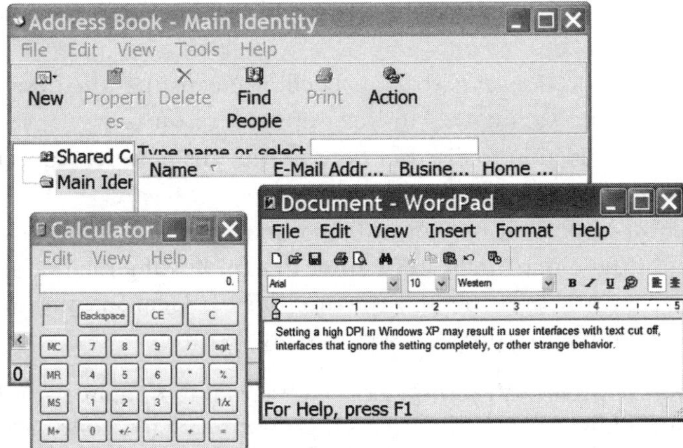

Figure 1.4 Most applications don't handle DPI changes elegantly. These are Windows programs running at a higher DPI, with various poor side effects. Vista handles higher DPI settings better than XP but still has issues; for example, old toolbars tend to be tiny.

and other technologies play tricks to try to make things look the same when changing DPI. But it doesn't work all that well. It's not uncommon for applications to wrap text strangely or have oddly sized text when running at an alternative DPI (figure 1.4). These approaches don't take advantage of the better equipment; instead of having a sharper UI, the UI just gets smaller.

If Microsoft's own applications don't handle DPI changes well, what chance do we have? To date, the most common solution has been to request that users not use the fancy new modes of their equipment—not a popular workaround.

WPF is built on top of Direct3D, which can take advantage of the features of current and new graphics cards as they come out. As you'll see, it also has a clean approach for the DPI problem. WPF uses *device independent pixels* (DIPs). There are always 96 pixels to an inch. If the DPI setting of the target device changes, everything is automatically scaled up or down. The main reason that 96 was used is that most current hardware uses 96 DPI. Also, it's easy to scale from 96ths of an inch to 72nds of an inch, which is what most fonts use.

1.2.2 Using modern software design

It's a little odd to describe object-oriented programming (OOP) as modern, given that it's been around since the '70s. It wasn't until much later that the concepts and technology caught up with the promise of the early days. Windows Forms is OO, and MFC is—um—MFC has things called classes. Both MFC and Windows Forms are wrappers on low-level technology, and the underlying mechanisms have a lot of influence on the higher-level design. Also, the non-OO stuff underneath peeks its head out rather more than is desirable. WPF was built OO from the ground up.

The WPF API is also completely *managed*, and almost all of WPF itself is written with managed code. This is a major change for Windows. For the first time, there's no underlying C interface that you can call directly—the managed code *is* the code. Some advantages to going managed are, as follows:

- Managed WPF code operates extremely smoothly with applications that are also managed.
- Having a model that relies on garbage collection means that the design of the framework isn't driven by the need to clean up after resources.
- Being able to use reflection to discover behavior means powerful tools that can pick up new capabilities automatically.
- Possibly the most important benefit of being managed is avoiding the serious security issues of the older C APIs. It's harder to exploit vulnerabilities, and you can also safely run WPF over the web (picture this on Amazon.com) and know that the code is limited to a properly secure sandbox.

NOTE Managed code is Microsoft's term for code designed to operate with the .NET Common Language Runtime (CLR). Before managed code, a program was compiled directly to a machine-understandable format and did what it liked. Now programs are compiled into an intermediate language (called, cleverly, Intermediate Language) that's processed by the CLR at runtime. It's beyond the scope of this book to go into a detailed explanation of why managed code is a good idea and how it works in detail, but it does provide a huge number of advantages including security, garbage collection, interoperability between languages, reflection, better multiple target support, and extra dessert on Tuesdays.

Being managed is hardly the only modern thing about WPF. The framework makes use of best practices and patterns developed over the last umpteen years. WPF isn't hampered by limitations that no longer exist (640K, anyone?).

1.2.3 Separating presentation logic from presentation

Hard as it is to admit, most programmers are not artists. That isn't to say we don't try; given six or seven hours, we can come up with a 16x16 toolbar button that's almost (but not quite) recognizable. Design has become harder as resolutions and user expectations have increased (figure 1.5). Microsoft has recognized this difficulty and has built WPF with the explicit idea that a developer will make things work, but a UI designer will make things look nice. In WPF, the graphic designer can take the description of the UI and make it pretty without (we hope) breaking the behavior.

Figure 1.5 Which one requires an artist? Users have a much greater expectation for pretty UIs these days.

The downside to this theory is that many companies don't bother with a UI designer, so developers are still responsible for the look-and-feel of many applications.[9] We think it will be a long time before most companies have the resources to create the desired separation of responsibilities suggested by Microsoft. Fortunately, the default behavior for UI is reasonably sane with Visual Studio. The problem is

---

9 Although the design of WPF and Windows Vista may cause this to change.

that, although Windows Forms was flexible, there was a limit on how horrible a UI could be developed. With WPF, the opportunities for crimes against good taste have expanded exponentially.

One major benefit of separating the look-and-feel from the behavior is in prototyping UIs. Often, if a company does have a graphic artist, he'll create mock-ups in tools like Photoshop or Flash. The mock-ups may be pretty, but they have two big problems. First, Photoshop can create pictures of *anything*. WPF is flexible, but replicating an artist's painted vision can be, shall we say, difficult. Second, the prototype is a throwaway; it has nothing to do with the real application. With WPF and XAML, the graphic designer can build his mock-up using tools that create real WPF UI elements. The developer can take that UI and make it work. If things need to change, the mock-up just has to be updated—a necessary task anyway because it's now part of the application.

1.2.4 Making it simpler to code GUIs

This is one of those sections that can get you into a lot of trouble. WPF *does* simplify the development of UIs. In particular, it makes it easier to do things that would have previously been extremely difficult and required an extensive knowledge of underlying APIs. But in some respects, programming with WPF will make some things *harder*!

The reason for this interesting contradiction isn't so much WPF itself, but the broader target of applications. It's still possible to build a dialog by dragging a bunch of controls onto a form, positioning them in a way that looks nice, and then going forward. But if you want that form to adapt properly when the display device is at a different DPI setting or automatically adjust when terminology changes or be set up properly for your graphic artist to work out the ideal look-and-feel, you'll have to spend more time upfront planning and setting up your UI elements.

In addition, WPF and Windows Vista will raise the bar on what's considered acceptable UI. The tools keep improving, but so do the targets. For example, a few years ago (okay, a decade or so ago), features such as toolbars, context menus, and drag-and-drop, weren't expected. Now, they're considered basic functionality. An application that doesn't take advantage of the richness of WPF will, in a few years, stand out starkly. We have to do more work to provide the basics.

Even so, WPF does make it easier to do most things. There's also a great deal of tool support, both within Visual Studio and with tools like Expression Blend for graphic designers. The tools will also improve with time, and third-party tools are already available.

Overall, WPF has done a good job of addressing all of these goals and a host of lesser goals including animation support, 3D drawing, style support, and a consistent printing model. As you'll see as we move forward, there are literally dozens of other advantages to WPF.

So, what is involved in building a WPF application? In the next chapter, we'll show a more complete example, but we first want to talk about the building blocks and tools involved in creating a WPF application.

1.3 Creating UI using WPF

In many respects, developing WPF UI is much more like building web UI than native Windows development. WPF development is more about "what do I want" than "how do I make it work." You start by defining the elements that make up your UI and go from there. There are also two (and one-half) different ways in which you can specify what you want. One way is by writing code to create the various elements and appropriately associate them. The other way is by using XAML. The remaining *one-half* is to use the designers and tools such as those in Visual Studio or Blend.

In the next sections, we'll talk about how to define UI in WPF, and then we'll talk about WPF's approach to rendering that UI.

1.3.1 Defining WPF UI with XAML

XAML (pronounced *zammel*) is an acronym for e**X**tensible **A**pplication **M**arkup **L**anguage and is an XML-based specification for defining UIs.[10] Although XAML was created specifically for WPF, it's possible that, in the future, it might be used for defining UI for other things. It wouldn't be too far-fetched, for example, to see some version of XAML replace HTML![11]

Using XAML, you can describe what your user interface should look like. This is technically called a *declarative* programming model. WPF will take that definition and convert it into real elements on the screen. For example, let's look at the canonical (albeit somewhat dull) Hello, World! example (listing 1.1).

Listing 1.1 Hello, World! in XAML

```
<Page
   xmlns="http://schemas.microsoft.com/winfx/2006/xaml/presentation">
  <StackPanel>
    <Label>Hello, World!</Label>
  </StackPanel>
</Page>
```

If you'd like to see what it looks like (it will be a big surprise, we assure you), there's a great utility program called XAMLPad that comes with the Windows SDK. It should be on the SDK menu, under Tools. Run XAMLPad and type in the example into the window at the bottom. You should see something like figure 1.6.

The XML here is validated by a schema, which is referenced in the `xmlns` attribute in the first line. The schema enforces the correctness of the XAML. The enforcement of the schema goes extremely deep; XAML documents are *strict* XML. Every tag (for example, `StackPanel` or `Label`) and attribute (for example, `Margin` or `FontSize`) must correspond to a valid .NET type or property. If a tag has the wrong case or an unknown

---

[10] Technically, *XAML* can also be used for other technologies, such as defining workflows, but its *raison d'être* is for designing UI via WPF. In fact, XAML used to stand for eXtensible *Avalon* Markup Language, (remember: Avalon was the code name for WPF), but they changed it to Application because Avalon wasn't going to be the public name.

[11] What *is* far-fetched would be the W3C accepting a standard patented by Microsoft, and using it…

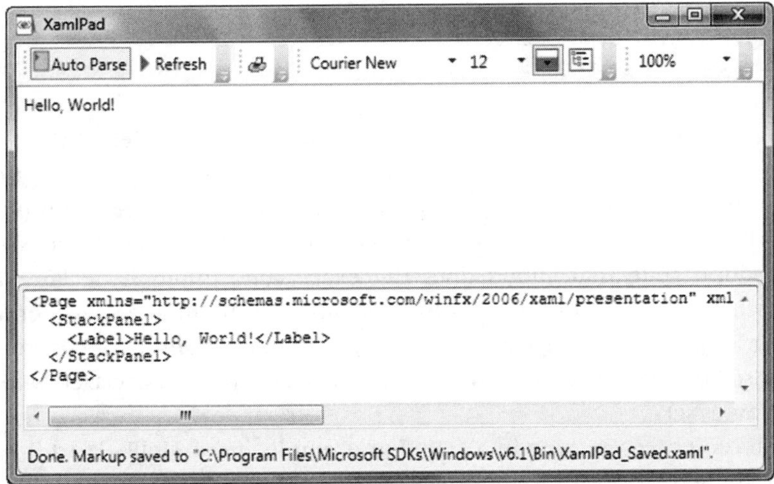

Figure 1.6 Hello, World! in XAMLPad. XAMLPad is a utility that can immediately render XAML as you type.

attribute is used, the resulting XAML won't work. The benefit of this validation is that XAML won't ever fall into the black hole of quirks, incompatibilities, and haphazard development of HTML.

There are a fair number of other markup languages for designing user interfaces, such as MXML (Adobe Flex), XUL (Mozilla/Firefox), and GladeXML (GNOME/Linux). Given the ubiquity of Windows, it's likely that XAML will quickly become the most widely deployed of these languages.

1.3.2 Defining WPF UI through code

You don't have to use XAML to define UI elements. You can write code to define your UI, much as you did with Windows Forms. This is the classic *imperative* programming model that we all know and love. Alternatively, you can mix and match—define the basics in XAML, but have some elements added in code. The following code does exactly the same thing as the XAML in listing 1.2.

Listing 1.2 Hello, World! in code

```
Window window1;
Page page1;
StackPanel stackPanel1;
Label label1;

public Procedural()
{
  window1 = new Window();
  page1 = new Page();
  stackPanel1 = new StackPanel();

  label1 = new Label();
  label1.Content = "Hello, World!";
```

```
    stackPanel1.Children.Add(label1);
    page1.Content = stackPanel1;
    window1.Content = page1;
}
```

One thing should be immediately obvious: The declarative model (XAML) is much more concise and easier to read. Declarative programming recognizes that domain-specific problems (such as creating a UI) generally operate in a well-known and prescribed fashion. Think about creating a form using Windows Forms. The designer creates procedural code that always does the exact same thing: It declares a set of controls, sets the relevant properties on them, and adds them to each other as necessary. Using XML to create a declarative UI language, the parenting of controls can be implied based on the hierarchy of the XML, and each control is declared with the relevant attributes set.

But you can't do everything in XAML. For example, if our Hello, World! had put a button on the screen, you could, using XAML, completely change the way the button looks and even make it do things like change color when the mouse moves over it. But if you want the button to do something useful when the user clicks it, you have to add code somewhere.

Also, some things that can be done in either code or XAML are easier to read in code. You'll see this as we go through various examples. The nice thing is that you have the choice.

In this day and age, we don't necessarily expect to have to write presentation code from scratch; rather, we rely on tools.

1.3.3 Defining WPF UI with tools

We said that there are two and one-half ways to build user interfaces in WPF. The first two are declarative (XAML) and imperative (coding). In all probability, much of your work will be done using the *half*—Microsoft's nifty tools for graphic designers, such as Visual Studio 2008 and Microsoft Expression Blend.

Visual Studio has a WPF form designer that's similar to the one for Windows Forms. But by switching to a declarative model, the tools can become much better and more reliable. Prior to XAML, typical UI development involved a delicate editing dance between the developer and IDE. Unfortunately, things could get out of hand (shorthand for "the bloody designer ate my form again") if the design view and code view got out of sync. Partial classes were added to .NET 2.0 largely to support the IDE writing UI and web code. The core problem is that the imperative model doesn't fit well with the UI designer concept. Declarative models work extremely well—so well that working on the UI and code independently is now not only possible but a reasonable and recommended approach.

Now that the look-and-feel of the UI can be defined in XAML, linked only by references to the code, it becomes much easier to have different tools (such as Expression Blend) for graphic designers that let them play with look-and-feel without messing up the underlying code, and vice versa.

Unfortunately, there's a reason why we called using tools only *half* a method. WPF is so flexible, and the tools are new enough, that there are severe limits to what they can do. You'll probably find yourself dropping into XAML often. We hope that, as the tools mature, this will become less necessary, but it's unlikely that the tools will ever be able to handle *everything* that WPF can do.

No matter how you choose to build your user interface—via XAML, code or with the use of the provided tools—you still end up with a description of how your UI should look. It's then up to WPF to figure out how to present that UI and make it behave appropriately.

1.3.4 Who does the drawing

As you may have noticed, XAML is a lot like HTML. Rather than specifically turning on dots on the screen when you're told that you need to repaint, you describe what you want and get out of the way. Unlike HTML, you have extreme control over the way in which everything is rendered.

When using WPF, you describe the look-and-feel and the behavior of the UI. WPF then takes care of making all that work. Then, you only have to worry about dealing with application behavior. If you, via XAML, say that you want a video to show up on a button whenever the user moves the mouse over it and then have the button change color, WPF takes care of it for you. You don't have to watch for mouse move events to start and stop the video, manage the state of the button, and so on.

You *can* look for and handle the low-level messages about mouse moves and other messages, but the situations where you have to are rarer. WPF has an extremely powerful event model for dealing with the types of events that you do care about, which we'll discuss later in great detail.

WPF works with your graphics card under the hood, offloading the heavy lifting of drawing. This cooperation means that you can have a significantly more complex UI that runs much more smoothly than a relatively simple Windows Forms application that has to do the drawing, handle input, and do the dishes, as well as all the application-specific work.

We said that you describe the UI to WPF. This approach goes all the way from complex control trees, right down to low-level drawing.

1.3.5 Pixels versus vectors

We haven't discussed straight drawing much yet. When talking about classic Windows, we pointed out that you're drawing dots on a surface. If you draw a circle, it gets turned into a set of dots. Nothing in the system is aware that those dots make up a circle. This approach is called *immediate mode* drawing.

WPF, on the other hand, remembers what you've drawn. If you describe a circle, to WPF it *is* a circle and can receive events and be scaled as a circle. This is part of how WPF can do what it does—it doesn't have to store each separate pixel and ask for more information when sizes change. It only has to know a center point and a radius. This is called *retained-mode* drawing. Conveniently, modern graphics cards know how to draw circles too, so WPF can pass that information to the card to do the work.

But screens these days *don't* know how to draw circles. Everything eventually does get turned into dots, but it's done at the last point of contact, not the first, and that makes a huge difference. Interestingly, monitors used to be able to draw vector-based images (although circles were pushing it). If you ever played some of the old video games like Asteroids or Battle Zone, those games did everything by constantly redrawing vectors to the screen.

1.4 Summary

In the section about Windows and web UIs, we brought up a number of important points about the ways in which each work. Now that we've also talked about how WPF works, we'd like to revisit those points and compare the old and new worlds:

- In classic Windows, the application is responsible for drawing itself whenever it's told to do so. In WPF, the application describes how the UI should look and then lets WPF do all the drawing work. Even if you decide to do the rendering for a specialized control yourself, you don't have to keep doing it. WPF will ask your custom control to render (literally calling the `OnRender` method on your control), you do the drawing once, and then WPF handles it from there, unless you specifically indicate that something has changed and that you want to render the control differently. This approach is referred to as *retained-mode* drawing, and we'll go into much more detail about this topic when we talk about drawing.
- In classic Windows, the application receives low-level messages from the OS. The application must appropriately handle the messages to change appearance and so forth, and to determine that an event that relates to the application logic has taken place. (For example, the mouse was pushed down and then released while over the button so that's treated as a click.) In WPF, the low-level stuff is taken care of. You only have to worry about events that relate to application logic, and WPF provides lots of support for making handling application-level events even easier.
- In classic Windows, you draw dots on a surface. The dots are just dots with no semantic meaning. In WPF, you draw shapes, and WPF intrinsically understands that they're shapes.
- On the web, UI is described by HTML, just as WPF UI is described by XAML. Unlike HTML, XAML is strongly typed and validated, so the description is reliable and consistent.
- On the web, you're extremely limited as to what you can control as far as the UI is concerned. In WPF, you have control over *everything*.
- Falling between the two sections, for both classic Windows and the web, the look-and-feel and the behavior of the UI are tightly coupled. In WPF, you can completely divorce the two so that a graphics designer builds the look-and-feel and a developer makes the application operate.

Any one of these points would be enough to make WPF significantly superior. In addition, you'll discover dozens of other smaller advantages to WPF throughout the book. As we go through different facets of WPF, we'll revisit these points to highlight advantages (and potential pitfalls) of the WPF approach.

In the next chapter, we'll provide a simple demonstration of using WPF with Visual Studio, and we'll also tour Visual Studio 2008 and its WPF-specific features. After that, in chapter 3, we'll discuss all the various technologies that make up and surround WPF.

2 Getting started with WPF and Visual Studio 2008

This chapter covers:

- Building a simple WPF application
- Targeting different versions of the .NET runtime
- The joy of `TextBlocks`
- A guided tour of Visual Studio 2008
- Why Kernighan and Ritchie won't return our phone calls

We have a confession to make. We *hate* Hello, World! applications. When we first started this book, we decided categorically that we were not going to put one in—particularly not one that looks almost identical to one you might have built in any other Windows presentation medium for the last decade.

However…

We need to accomplish a few things before we can move on to the interesting stuff. First, we need to go through the basic steps for creating a project in the environment to make sure that everything is set up and building correctly. Second, we want to talk about some options related to applications with WPF, and doing that with something simple is more straightforward. Finally, we want to point out the various features of Visual Studio 2008 for working with WPF.

Ignoring our cursing of Kernighan and Ritchie for starting the practice in the first place, we present a Hello, World! application for your edification and enjoyment.

2.1 *Your grandpa's Hello, World!*

Creating a WPF application in Visual Studio is pretty much the same as creating a Windows Forms application. In fact, the process is similar enough that it's easy to create the wrong type of application—Visual Studio still contains complete support for Windows Forms applications. This is a mistake that we, the authors, make continuously when we're not paying attention. As you can see in figure 2.1, it's easy to confuse the two.

If you want to follow along, run Visual Studio 2008, and create a new project of type Windows Application (WPF) as shown in figure 2.1.

By the way, notice that in the upper-right corner of this dialog is a combo box that says .NET Framework 3.5.[1] A new feature of Visual Studio 2008 allows you to target different versions of the .NET Framework. This is incredibly handy because it means that

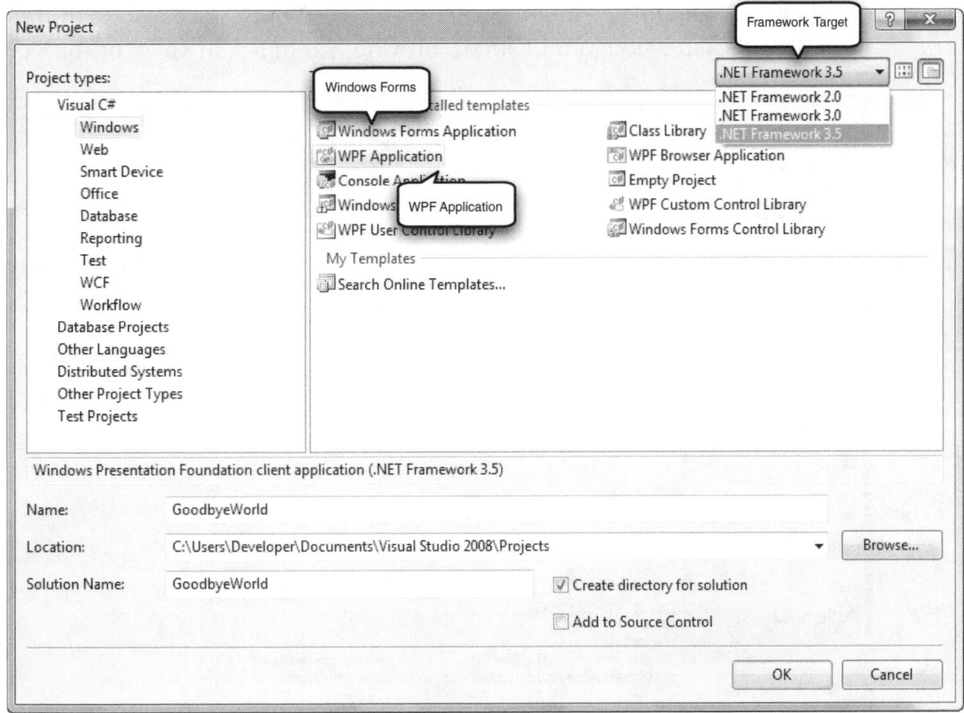

Figure 2.1 Creating a new WPF Windows project via the New Project dialog in Visual Studio

---

[1] If you're using the Express version of Visual Studio, this combo box isn't shown, but you can still change the target platform in the Project Properties page.

you can use the latest tools even when building old applications. You have the following options:

- *.NET 3.5*—The version of .NET that ships with Visual Studio 2008. New projects should generally use this. Technically, the latest version of Visual Studio ships with .NET 3.5 *SP1*, but this difference should rarely be an issue because anyone who has .NET 3.5 will probably already have received 3.5 SP1 via Windows Update.
- *.NET 3.0*—The version of .NET that ships with Windows Vista. If you want to target Vista development without requiring a .NET install, this is what you should choose. Note that a 3.5 application *will* run on Windows Vista without installing .NET 3.0—right up until the point where you use something that's only available in 3.5.
- *.NET 2.0*—The version of .NET associated with Visual Studio 2005. Use this for backwards compatibility. If you select it, a number of options will go away.

For the moment, let's leave this set to .NET Framework 3.5. If everything is working correctly, you should get a window that looks something like figure 2.2.

There are a couple of interesting things here. Notice the two tabs in the editor—Design and XAML. Design and XAML provide two different views of the same thing.

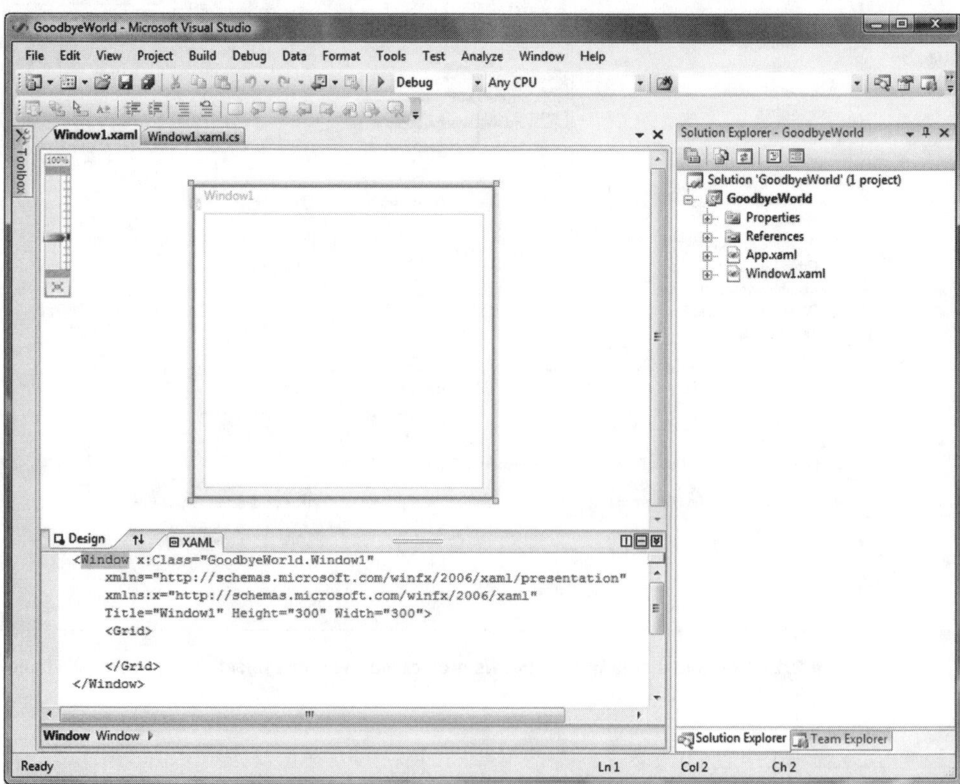

Figure 2.2 A new WPF Windows application

XAML is the raw XAML that describes the UI. Design is how that XAML will be rendered. Changing one of these windows changes the other.

You may also notice the file Window1.xaml.cs in the Solution Explorer. This file contains any implementation code needed for Window1—what Microsoft calls the *interaction code.* To open the file, you right-click in the Designer and select View Code, or expand the Window1.xaml node in the Solution Explorer to access it directly. An example of interaction code is putting a button onto a window—if you add an event handler for the button being clicked, the definition for the button and the information about the event will be stored in the XAML file, but the implementation for handling the click will be in the cs file. We'll show this whole process in the next section.

2.1.1 Adding a button and button-handler to the window

Adding a button to a window is as simple as dragging a button from the toolbox (in the Controls section) onto the window. Let's do this, and then double-click the button. This action creates the default event handler for the button. Inside of the click method, we just put in a call to `MessageBox`, as shown in listing 2.1.

Listing 2.1 Handling a button click

```
protected void button1_Click(object sender, RoutedEventArgs e)
{
  MessageBox.Show("Please don't click this button again");
}
```

Now, if you move between the two different views, you have the visual Design view shown in figure 2.3.

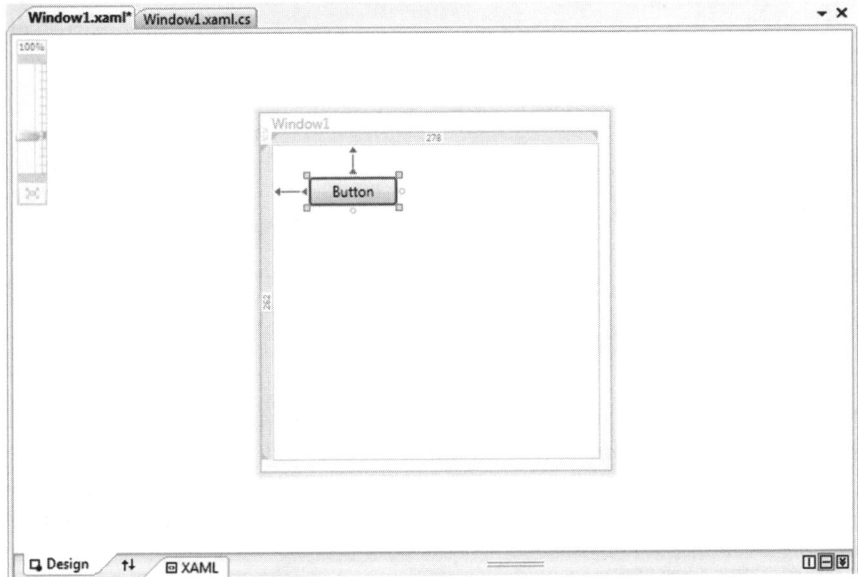

Figure 2.3 Hello, World! Design view. This is a drag-and-drop editor for WPF controls.

The contents of the XAML tab will look like listing 2.2.

Listing 2.2 Hello, World!—XAML view

```
<Window x:Class="GoodbyeWorld.Window1"
    xmlns="http://schemas.microsoft.com/winfx/2006/xaml/presentation"
    xmlns:x="http://schemas.microsoft.com/winfx/2006/xaml"
    Title="GoodbyeWorld" Height="300" Width="300">
  <Grid>                                                    ❶  ❷
    <Button Height="23" Click="button1_Click"
       HorizontalAlignment="Left" Margin="38,35,0,0" Name="button1"
       VerticalAlignment="Top" Width="75">Button</Button>
  </Grid>
</Window>
```

The `Grid` element ❶ defines the *layout* of the window. By default, a new window is set up to use a `Grid` layout. Because the `Grid`, also by default, only has one row and one column, it acts like a precisely positioned layout. Most of the properties of the button are self-explanatory. Notice that the `Click` event attribute ❷ specifies the method in the code file that handles the `Click` event. (You can right-click the event handler name in the XAML to navigate to the handler if you want to.)

Finally, the contents for the Source tab (slightly edited for space) are shown in listing 2.3.

Listing 2.3 Hello, World!—Source view

```
using System.Windows;
...a bunch of other using statements...

namespace GoodbyeWorld
{
  /// <summary>Interaction logic for Window1.xaml</summary>
  public partial class Window1 : System.Windows.Window
  {
    public Window1()
    {
      InitializeComponent();
    }

    protected void button1_Click(object sender, RoutedEventArgs e)
    {
      MessageBox.Show("Please don't click this button again");
    }
  }
}
```

Other than the massive number of using statements,[2] one of the first things to notice is that this is a *partial* class. Windows Forms did this as well (starting with .NET 2.0), separating the code that generated the UI from the implementation code. But with Windows Forms, the code for generating the form was another code file. With

[2] Of which only `System.Windows` is used by the sample code!

WPF, there's only the XAML file. The compiler generates the other part of the partial class at compile time. It also generates the `InitializeComponent()` method called by the constructor.

2.1.2 Running Hello, World!

If you hit Ctrl-F5, the application will be compiled and run. You should get a window with a button. Go ahead, hit the button. We'll wait. Exciting, wasn't it? If you're running on Vista, you'll see something like figure 2.4. On XP, it will be the old XP-style message box.

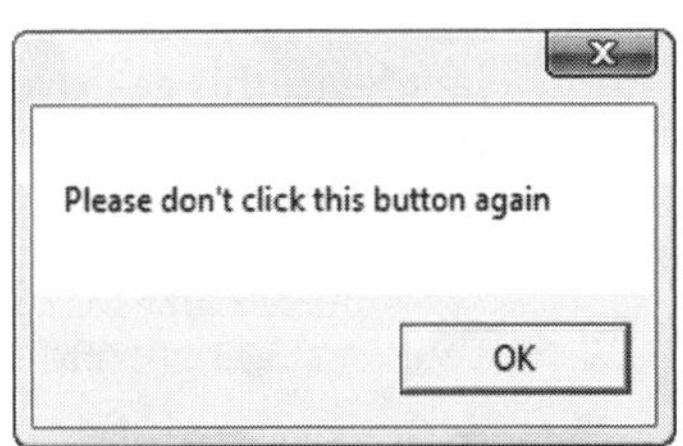

Figure 2.4 Pressing the button. Note that this is how the message box looks under Windows Vista. If you're using XP, it will look like the old-style message box.

So far, we haven't done anything particularly special. As we get deeper and deeper into WPF, you'll start to see the capabilities that differentiate WPF from older technologies—both in the way that applications are built and in the capabilities that they have. In the next section, we'll add an additional control to the Hello, World! application that will provide a glimpse of WPF's power.

2.1.3 The TextBlock control

To get an idea of the power of WPF, we'd like to add a `TextBlock` control to the application. The `TextBlock`, as its name implies, is a control that lets you put a block of text onto a window. But because of the compositional nature of WPF, the `TextBlock` control can do so much more.

If you're following along, go ahead and drag a `TextBlock` onto the window beneath the button. Just as with a `Label`, you could go to properties and enter a value into the `Text` property. This will work, but completely misses the power of the `TextBlock`. Instead, we want to set the `TextBlock`'s *Content*. The `Content` property isn't available in the properties list because, as you'll see later, the content can be virtually anything—and there's no reasonable property editor for that. If you look at the XAML, you'll see something like:

```
<TextBlock Margin="50,123,108,118" Name="textBlock1" />
```

We just want to set the content to be some simple text, which will go into the `TextBlock` element. The existing XML element is closed—the / before the closing > is the XML way of indicating an element with no content. Using the closing slash is equivalent to

```
<TextBlock Margin="50,123,108,118" Name="textBlock1"></TextBlock>
```

The `TextBlock` tag is still empty, but now we have a place to put content—between the opening `TextBlock` and the closing `/TextBlock` tags. You can delete the slash and then type the closing tag, or you can cheat and delete both the slash and the closing >. Then, when you retype the > character, the editor will automatically create a closing tag for you! Either way, after you have a closing tag, go ahead and enter some text like the following:

```
<TextBlock Margin="50,123,108,118" Name="textBlock1">Hello,
  World</TextBlock>
```

By setting the content to a string, we get something that looks pretty much like a label—in this case with the text *Hello, World.* But you can also do some more complex things in the XAML.

```
<TextBlock FontSize="16" Name="textBlock1" VerticalAlignment="Center"
   HorizontalAlignment="Center"><Bold>Goodbye</Bold> world, hello
   <Italic>Mars!</Italic></TextBlock>
```

Note that you can set the `FontSize` and the vertical and horizontal alignment. The thing that you could *not* have done in Windows Forms is easily mark part of the text as bold and part as italic.

```
<Bold>Goodbye</Bold> world, hello
   <Italic>Mars!</Italic>
```

If you're used to web development, this seems like no big deal. However, for Windows Forms developers, it is ridiculously hard to do things like this properly (see figure 2.5).

Figure 2.5 A `TextBlock` with font styles. Doing this in Windows Forms is *really* hard.

There is one caveat to using the `TextBlock`—handling whitespace. Let's go back to the `TextBlock`, and add some additional spaces after *hello.*

```
<TextBlock FontSize="16" Name="textBlock1"
   VerticalAlignment="Center"
   HorizontalAlignment="Center">
<Bold>Goodbye</Bold> world, hello     <Italic>Mars!</Italic></TextBlock>
```

If you run again, you'll see that the extra space has been ignored (figure 2.6).

Goodbye world, hello *Mars!*

Figure 2.6 Where have all the spaces gone?

Notice that all the extra spacing has disappeared. This is probably less of a surprise to web developers than to Windows developers. XAML, like XHTML, uses *normalized* spacing. All whitespace around tags (including carriage returns, spaces, and tabs) is reduced to a single space. This is a compromise between the needs to have whitespace in content and the rules for XML that allow it to be formatted in any way. For example, this version of the preceding XAML is exactly equivalent:

```
<TextBlock
  FontSize="16"
  Name="textBlock1"
  VerticalAlignment="Center"
  HorizontalAlignment="Center">
  <Bold>Goodbye</Bold>
```

```
    world, hello
    <Italic>Mars!</Italic>
  </TextBlock>
```

If the spaces in the text were taken into account, the result would be quite different. Normalized spacing is a pretty good compromise but can sometimes cause unexpected results.[3]

Fortunately, there's a simple way to tell XML to preserve the white space around tags.

```
<TextBlock FontSize="16" Name="textBlock1" VerticalAlignment="Center"
  HorizontalAlignment="Center" xml:space="preserve">
  <Bold>Goodbye</Bold> world, hello   <Italic>Mars!</Italic> </TextBlock>
```

Goodbye world, hello   *Mars!*

Figure 2.7 A `TextBlock` with whitespace preserved

One caution: For the book, we had to wrap this text to fit. If you put the linebreaks into the code, they would be preserved. Assuming you keep everything on one line, the results should look like figure 2.7.

For Windows Forms people, at least, this is pretty cool. In Windows Forms, you have the following three choices for creating this text:

- *Create three label controls, set their font styles individually, and then position them to emulate space.* If the text changed or the resolution was different or you wanted to localize the text and so on and so forth, you'd be out of luck.
- *Create a custom control and define your own markup for specifying fonts.* Aside from this being a lot of work, you'd also have to rely on the notoriously inaccurate methods for measuring the width of text (so that you could figure out where to put the next word).
- *Use the RTF control.* This is extremely heavy, and you'd end up spending a lot of time making it look like text instead of an edit control, and you'd have to work with RTF to get the text the way you wanted.

And this is only an example to show how tasks that used to be painful are now simple. You can go even further with WPF. For example, what if you wanted a rectangle in the middle of the text?

```
<TextBlock FontSize="16" Name="textBlock1" VerticalAlignment="Center"
  HorizontalAlignment="Center" xml:space="preserve">
  <Bold>Goodbye</Bold> world,
  <Rectangle Width="20" Height="20" Fill="Blue"/> hello
  <Italic>Mars!</Italic></TextBlock>
```

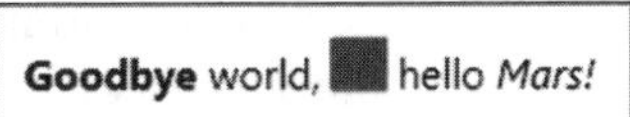
Goodbye world, hello Mars!

Figure 2.8 We now have a rectangle in the middle of the text.

We shove the definition for a rectangle into the middle of the text and—voilá—figure 2.8!

This is where you start to see the real power of composition—although, arguably, you probably won't have many situations where you need to put shapes

[3] An example of normalized spacing surprises was ASP.NET 1.1; the editor wrapped lines, causing spaces to be added in the middle of literal text.

into your text. The point is that whatever you need to accomplish, you can invariably get the desired results by building up, or *composing*, a description in XAML. The engine does all the heavy lifting for you.

This is pretty much as far as we want to go with Hello, World! We do need to talk about one last thing. Hello, World! is a window inside of an application, primarily written as a definition. But what about the definition of the application itself?

2.2 The application definition

Up to this point, we've only had to write one line of code—the call to bring up the message box when the button is pressed. Arguably, a few lines of autogenerated code were also in the xaml.cs file, but they were just put there as a placeholder for future implementation.

But what about the startup code for the application itself? At some point, when a program is run, Windows has to have some code to *run* that tells it to display the dialog and other stuff. When you execute a program, Windows looks for a function in your executable either called `Main()` or `WinMain()`. In .NET, you have a static method called `Main()`. This method usually sets some values, creates a new form, and tells it to run. Well, with WPF, even *that* can be defined in XAML!

In the next two sections, we'll talk about how an application is defined in XAML and why it's done this way.

2.2.1 Defining application startup in XAML

If you look in the Hello, World! application, in the Solution Explorer, you'll see a file called App.xaml and its companion implementation file App.xaml.cs. If you look in App.xaml.cs, you'll see that it's an empty shell. The application definition is all in the XAML file, as shown in listing 2.4.

Listing 2.4 Defining an application in XAML

```
<Application x:Class="GoodbyeWorld.App"
  xmlns="http://schemas.microsoft.com/winfx/2006/xaml/presentation"
  xmlns:x="http://schemas.microsoft.com/winfx/2006/xaml"
  StartupUri="Window1.xaml">      <-- StartupUri specifies
  <Application.Resources>             window to start

  </Application.Resources>
</Application>
```

Aside from providing references to the appropriate namespaces and providing a place to put resources (the `Application.Resources` tag), the important item here is the `StartupUri` attribute. It tells WPF what window to start up. You can also provide other attributes here—like the following:

```
ShutdownMode="OnLastWindowClose"
```

This attribute sets the application property `ShutdownMode`, specifying that the application should stop running when the last application window is closed.

NOTE XML is case-sensitive. If you put `Shutdownmode` or `ShutDownMode`, the attribute won't be recognized, and you'll get a compile-time error.

You can also set properties or do other application startup in code. The `Application` tag specifies a handler for the `Startup` event (the same way you caught the event for the button click).

```
<Application x:Class="GoodbyeWorld.App"
  xmlns="http://schemas.microsoft.com/winfx/2006/xaml/presentation"
  xmlns:x="http://schemas.microsoft.com/winfx/2006/xaml"
  StartupUri="Window1.xaml" Startup="Application_Startup">
```

If you type `Startup=`, IntelliSense gives you the option to create a `<New Event Handler>`. If you hit the Enter key, a name is automatically assigned, and the event handler is created. If you right-click the handler, you can select Navigate To Event Handler to be taken to the code (listing 2.5). We add the line of code in the method.

Listing 2.5 Handling the `Startup` event in code

```
protected void Application_Startup (object sender,StartupEventArgs e)    ❶
{
  this.ShutdownMode = ShutdownMode.OnLastWindowClose;    ❷
}
```

`StartupEventArgs` ❶ provides the list of command-line arguments to the application. If you want, you can launch a different window based on arguments or do any other application setup. In this case, we only set the `ShutdownMode` property ❷. Doing this here provides the identical result as defining the value in the XAML.

2.2.2 Why define the application in XAML?

There are a number of reasons for going to a XAML-based application definition, instead of putting the initialization and launch code in a `Main()` method. First, you could argue that it's simpler to change a definition instead of modifying code.[4] Working with definitions is also more familiar to web developers who are used to config files. Second, by relying on the compiler to take the XAML and generate the appropriate hunk of code, it gives some flexibility back to Microsoft to change behavior without breaking code. Three bigger reasons for using XAML are declarative programming, Windows Vista, and navigation hosting.

DECLARATIVE PROGRAMMING

Every application has certain characteristics that are basically the same. It used to be that every developer had to build a message loop that was essentially identical—likewise, the startup code for applications. Until recently, the model was to autogenerate the code but allow it to be modified. Because there might be slight differences in implementation, there had to be a hook for that.

---

[4] Or you could argue the opposite. Real programmers like code. In fact, we'd prefer to write everything in assembler. No, directly in binary code. And having 0s *and* 1s is overkill. We just need 1s!

Ideally, you don't need startup code; you need a place to tell the system what special behavior you want. The application XAML is the perfect place to do that. In reality, the amount of code involved in application startup is pretty minimal, but the idea of doing everything declaratively—that is, describing *what* you want the system to do rather than *how* it should be done—is the direction of WPF, and .NET development in general. The future is now.

WINDOWS VISTA

WPF can run under Windows XP or Windows Server 2003, but it was *built* for Windows Vista. A number of WPF features only work when running under Vista (like direct access to the glass look-and-feel, which you can see in figure 2.9). Also, WPF can take advantage of the more advanced graphics card support behind Vista, making Vista smoother, prettier, and shinier.

NAVIGATION HOSTING

We are used to building applications either for Windows *or* the web, but WPF blurs the distinction in several ways. The Hello, World! application we built was defined as a `Window` but could've easily been defined as a `Page`. WPF has built-in support for page-based applications, including automatic handling for navigating between pages and

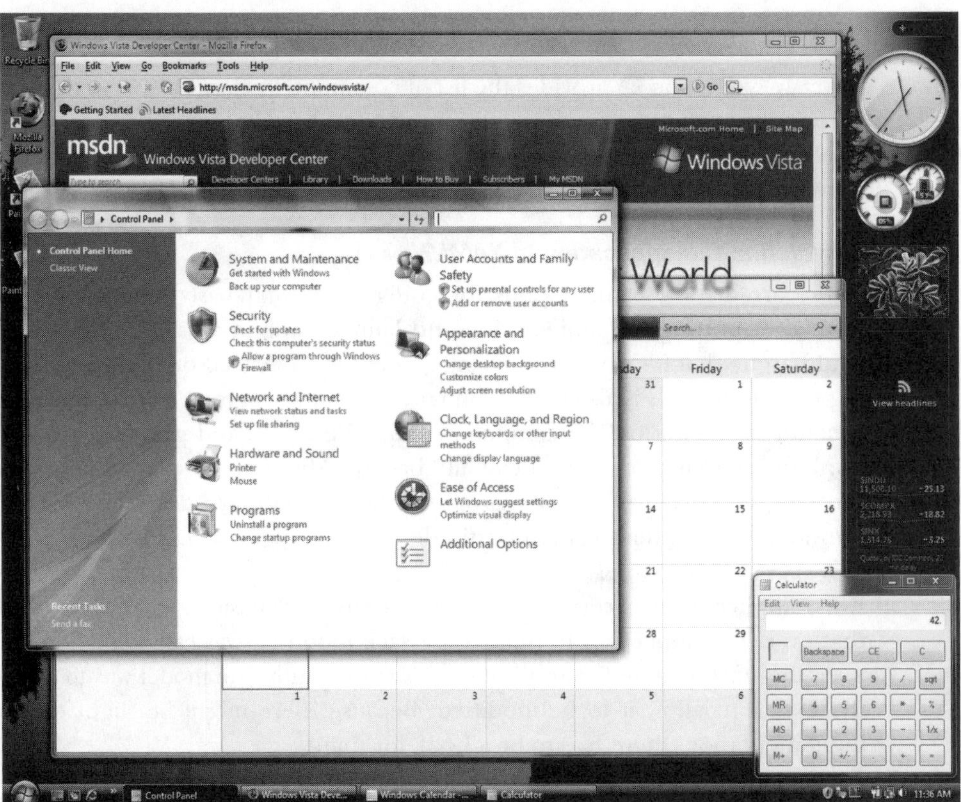

Figure 2.9 The glass theme in Windows Vista makes the borders and titles of the windows slightly transparent.

back-and-forward navigation. By default, if you set up a page-based application, you automatically get a toolbar with web-style navigation buttons (figure 2.10).

To get this behavior, we change the main element from `Window` to `Page` and the base class of the supporting code. We also specify that the startup item for the application is a page instead of a window. So we change

```
StartupUri="Window1.xaml"
```

to

```
StartupUri="Page1.xaml"
```

Figure 2.10 Hello, World! as a navigation-style application

All the back-forward handling, and navigation (if you had hyperlinks, they could reference other pages), is provided by the application. To be more precise, it's provided by the appropriate *`NavigationService`*—the default application-based navigation service. And, because the application is declared as XAML and not code, it's easy for other navigation services to provide different but comparable functionality. We'll go into detail about navigation-style applications in chapter 16.

One of the coolest *alternative* navigation services comes by way of a technology called **X**AML **B**rowser **AP**plication, or XBAP. You can take the same page and put it into a browser (figure 2.11).

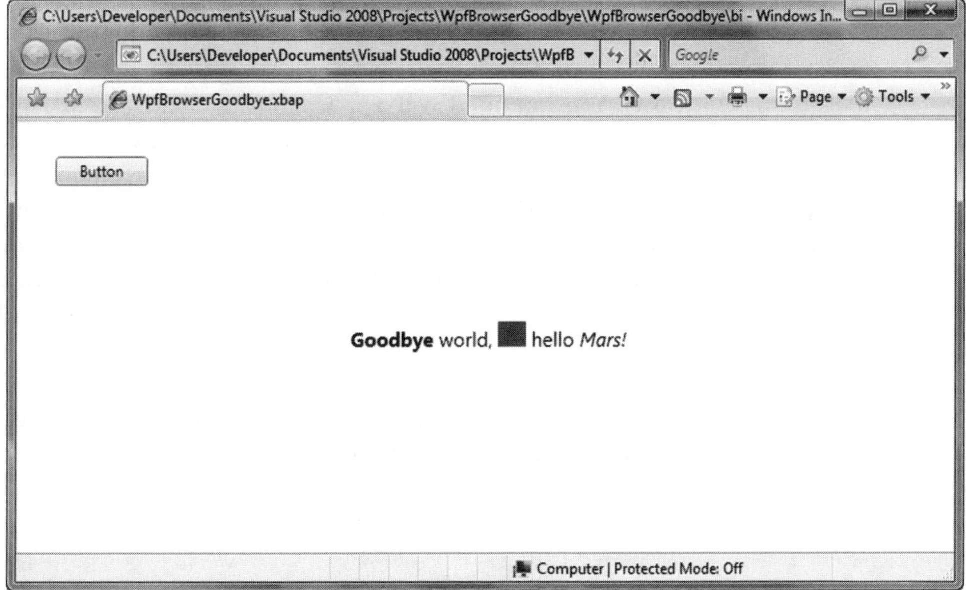

Figure 2.11 Hello, World! in a browser—how cool is that?

This isn't a re-creation of the page in HTML. This is *exactly* the same page with the same code, running hosted within Internet Explorer—not only that, but the application XAML is also identical! XBAP takes advantage of an enhanced version of the existing ClickOnce technology that became available with .NET 2.0. For security reasons, limitations are placed on what's permitted within a hosted XAML application. By default, the application is run with the permission given to applications in the Internet Zone.[5] For example, you can't do the following:

- Interact with the filesystem, registry, or other resources of the host machine (except in some limited ways)
- Pop up child windows (such as dialogs)
- Interact with the web browser via script

Even so, you *can* do an awful lot; and, if your environment is one where applications can be given greater trust, you can do even more. Also, XBAPs aren't limited to Internet Explorer—Firefox supports XBAP too. Another technology, called Silverlight, even lets you use WPF on the Mac using Safari or Firefox. We'll talk more about XBAP and Silverlight in chapter 17.

We've talked quite a bit about how to get started with WPF, as well as application options with WPF, but this book isn't only about WPF; it's about using WPF with Visual Studio 2008. Visual Studio 2008 is the primary tool you'll most likely use when working with WPF, and it has a number of nice features for doing so. In the next section, we'll do a flyby and hit on the major ones.

2.3 A tour of WPF in Visual Studio 2008

Believe it or not, WPF has been around for a while. It shipped as part of Windows Vista in January of 2007, and several of the utilities and system components of Vista make use of it. But using WPF hasn't been entirely practical, largely because there were few tools to make it easier. You *can* build WPF applications by writing XAML in notepad and manually compiling everything, but it isn't fun or straightforward.

Now Visual Studio 2008 is available, and that makes a huge difference. Finally, building WPF applications is as straightforward as building Windows Forms or MFC apps. There's one caveat: The Windows Forms and MFC tools have been around for a while and have had a chance to mature. The WPF tools are still relatively new, and there are definitely some holes to be filled. Even so, WPF, with Visual Studio 2008 SP1, is now ready for primetime.

This section will highlight some of the primary tools in VS 2008 for working with WPF. We'll also point out where some of the duct tape is hiding and things that we know the VS team is improving for the next version.

---

[5] The default security context in Internet Explorer for evil, untrusted websites where most of us spend what is supposed to be the productive part of our days.

2.3.1 The XAML designer

By far the most important WPF tool in Visual Studio 2008 is the XAML designer—the combination control that lets you edit XAML directly or the visual representation of that XAML. Figure 2.12 shows the designer.

When the designer comes up, it defaults to show two different panes: the Design pane and the XAML pane.

THE DESIGN PANE

The Design pane shows the visual representation of a XAML file and automatically changes to reflect any changes to the raw XAML. It's fully interactive, so you can drag elements from the Toolbox. It's also synchronized with the XAML pane, so if you select something in the Design pane, it's automatically selected in XAML, and vice versa.

One issue with the Design pane is that it only renders legal XAML. If you break the XAML, you'll either get a message at the top of the screen telling you that your

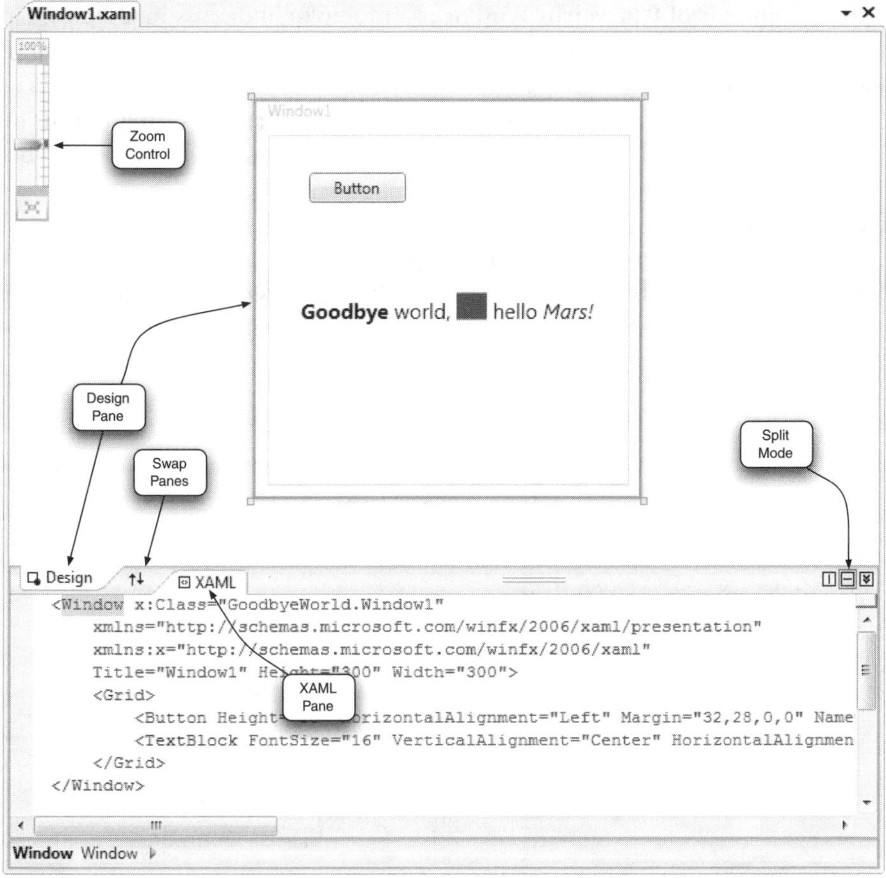

Figure 2.12 The Visual Studio XAML editor. We've labeled a few of the more interesting elements.

"document contains errors that must be fixed before the designer can be updated," or, in very serious cases, you'll get a big "Whoops" message up above until you correct your problem. If you do get the error message, clicking it will take you to the Error List, which will tell you what's wrong. Most of the time, though, the designer does a good job of reflecting what's going on.

The Design pane also features a Zoom control in the upper-left corner, which allows you to zoom in and out on your current element. This feature can be handy when you're working on a large window that doesn't quite fit or trying to line up items that you can't quite see in regular mode. The Zoom takes advantage of the vector nature of WPF, so there are no pixilation effects; the control gets bigger or smaller (figure 2.13). It's also a good way to make sure that you haven't done something to break DPI independence!

The designer has similar autoposition and autosize features to the Windows Forms editor, where controls can be automatically snapped to reasonable places relative to other controls, although there are differences because of the different positioning/layout behavior of WPF versus WinForms, a topic we'll discuss in a later chapter. The positioning is also a little slicker than with WinForms—as well as snapping to reasonable places, you also get snapping based on the margins of other controls and a display telling you the number of pixels between close-by items, In addition to context menus, you also get little handles that let you pull up control-specific behavior—again, pretty similar to WinForms.

THE XAML PANE

Because the semantics of XAML are so flexible, many things can't be done directly in the designer. As each new version of the editor comes out, more holes are filled, but there are things that will probably never be available via property editors. You'll have to do some things directly in XAML.

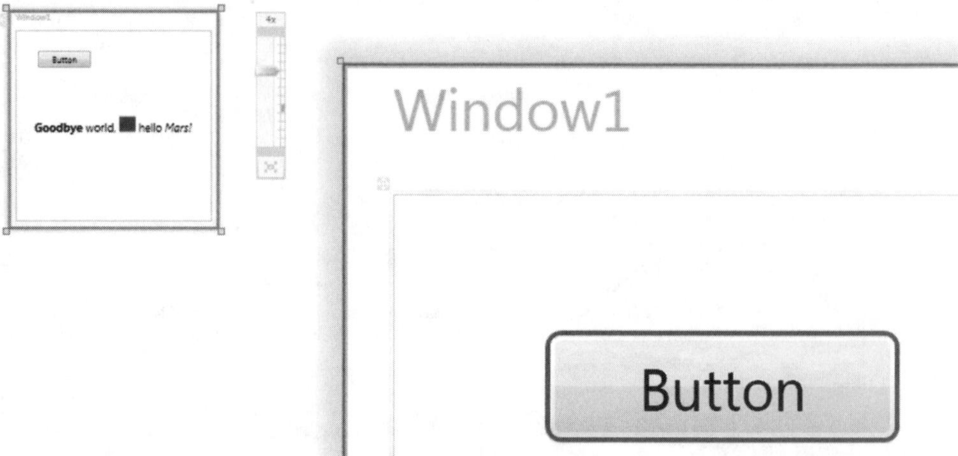

Figure 2.13 When you zoom in and out in the editor, the quality of the various elements is maintained because drawing in XAML is based on vectors, rather than on bitmaps.

It would be a mistake to dismiss the XAML editor as only a place to type raw XML. Probably almost as much work has gone into the XAML editor as the designer for one major reason: IntelliSense support. We started working with XAML back when there was no Visual Studio release, and we used a generic XML editor. Believe us when we say the difference is like night and day.

The XAML editor is good at providing the list of available child tags and attributes and attribute values; this isn't trivial because, as we said, XAML is flexible. The editor also manages to catch a large number of errors immediately. It does more than verifying that you're following the schema; it keeps track of the code and makes sure that there aren't illegal mismatches. The XAML editor also generates code stubs automatically for things like event handlers.

If we had the choice between either a 10-times-better visual editor with the requirement to use a regular XML editor or the XAML editor in Visual Studio, we'd take the XAML editor.

Now, with all of that said, the editor is still missing some things. One of the most serious is something to help with binding (see chapter 11). Microsoft assures us that this will be addressed in a future release.

SPLIT MODES

Although it isn't a major feature, one nice thing about the editor is that you can move the panes so that they're split vertically instead of horizontally, or you can have either the XAML or Design views take up the entire editor, swapping between the two by using the tabs. This is nice if you're about to do a bunch of edits to the XAML and don't want to wait for the Design view to catch up. Figure 2.14 shows the different modes.

If you want to, you can also swap the panes so that, for instance, the XAML is at the top and the Design view is at the bottom. One thing that the editor doesn't currently have good support for is multiple monitors. We'd love to be able to have the XAML on one monitor and the Design mode on the other. A cute workaround is to split the panes vertically and then stretch Visual Studio across both screens.

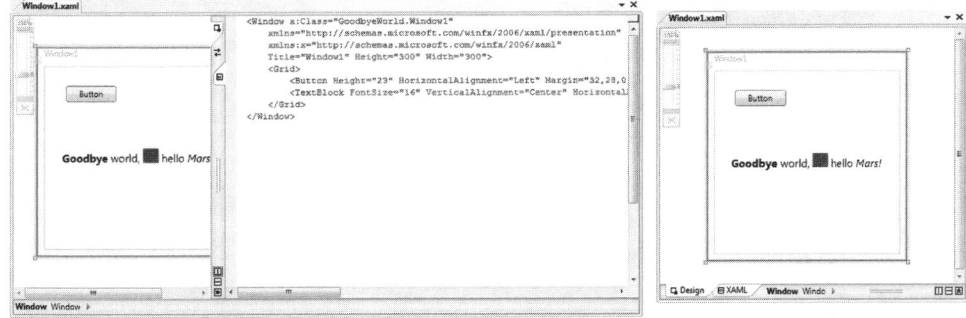

Figure 2.14 The designer lets you change the orientation of the panes or lets you collapse the panes so that only one is visible at a time.

2.3.2 *The Properties grid*

Just as with Windows Forms, you can change the various properties of the currently selected control(s) via the Properties grid. Similarly, there's a list of events and event handlers. But WPF has made a few changes (figure 2.15).

These may seem like minor things, but the WPF Properties grid displays a preview of the currently selected control in the upper-left corner. Also, the name of the current control is now right at the top. The reason we like this change is that it's much easier to make sure you're editing what you think you're editing.

Another cool thing they've added to the Properties grid is a Search control that lets you narrow down the properties that are shown. For example, if you type TA, the property list will be limited to those properties that contain the text *TA* (*Ta*g, *Ta*bIndex, Horizon*Ta*lAlignment). If you type *TAB*, the list will be narrowed down to Is*Tab*Stop and *Tab*Index. Having spent a lot of time searching up and down the property list for a particular property, we think the developer who added this should get a raise and a corner office.

On the downside of the WPF property editor, not all the properties have the elegant editors that they used to have; often you have to type a string, get an error, and then try again. For example, you can choose a named web color from a drop-down, but there's no color preview and no support for custom or system colors. Also, WinForms

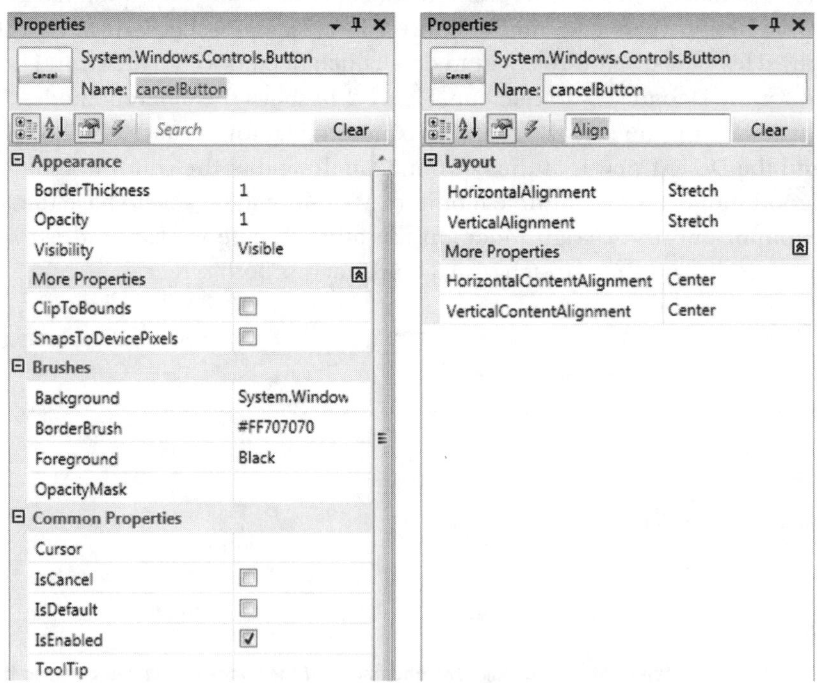

Figure 2.15 The WPF Properties grid. It's similar to the Windows Forms Properties grid but adds a preview feature and a search option, as well as moving the name of the selected control up to the top.

displayed help text for the selected property or event, but all you get with WPF is a tooltip that tells you the type of the property.

One thing that's missing—deliberately—from the Properties grid is the combo box that Windows Forms had listing all the controls on the form. Although the ability to select a control without having to click it was handy, the implementation wasn't great. The combo box usually wasn't wide enough, and it was easy to pick the wrong control. In WPF, which uses composition to build up complex layouts, it would've been inadequate. At the same time, being able to find the proper control whose property you want to edit is important—so important that there are at least four different ways to do it!

2.3.3 Selection controls in Visual Studio

When you want to get to the properties of a particular control, one simple way is to click the element within the XAML. This both selects the control in the Design view and sets that control as current in the property editor.

If you don't want to search through the XAML but have a number of overlapping elements, you can right-click an element in the visual designer, and choose Select. This gives you access to all the controls currently under your cursor (figure 2.16).

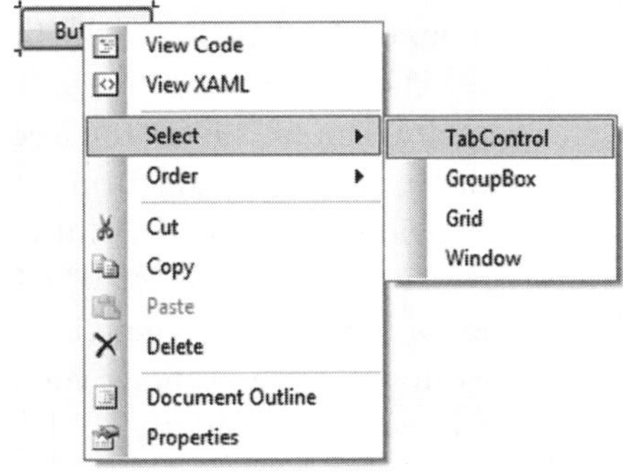

Figure 2.16 The Context menu's Select option lets you choose any of the controls under your current location.

Another way of selecting is also pretty cool. At the bottom of the XAML designer is a Path control that shows the currently selected element and lets you move to the element's ancestors (figure 2.17).

Figure 2.17 Path control shows the currently selected element and all the element's ancestors.

This control is easy to miss, but it's a gem. First, each ancestor is a hyperlink that takes you to that element. Second, you get a little preview of the control so that you can easily see which control you're floating over, and finally, the left/right buttons on the left let you move through a history of your selections.

The final selection tool is equally cool: the Document Outline.

2.3.4 The Document Outline

The Document Outline is a tree view of all the elements on the window (figure 2.18).

We have to admit—we love the Document Outline. Particularly when you get into layout, being able to see what's owned by whom is invaluable, and it's a great way of selecting controls that might not be easily accessible. When you click an item in the Document Outline, you get a preview (again, easier to make sure you have the right

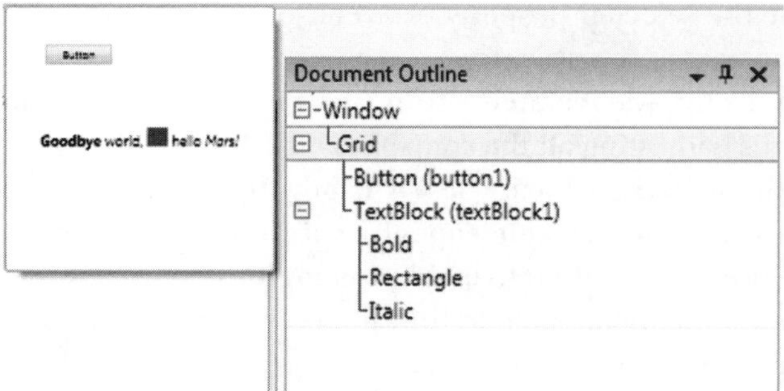

Figure 2.18
The Document Outline. A preview of the currently selected item is automatically generated.

thing selected). Also, what you select in the Outline is automatically selected in the designer and in XAML, and once selected, the context menu on the designer lets you jump to the XAML or to the properties for the element.

The one downside is that the Document Outline is read-only. We'd love to be able to drag controls from the Toolbox onto the Outline and to rearrange controls right there using drag-and-drop. The VS developers agree with us, so we hope to see that functionality in the near future.

These are the major WPF features in Visual Studio 2008 SP1, although there are a lot of behind-the-scenes changes to add support. The nice thing is that, when you're writing WPF applications, you're still writing .NET code; all the existing framework and tools are there, along with the other new features of .NET 3.x like LINQ and WCF.

2.4 Summary

This chapter gives the most basic taste of WPF and Visual Studio 2008 and shows the pieces that make up a simple WPF application. XAML provides the definition of the look-and-feel and the details of the application, and then code provides the behavior—although the behavior of the accursed Hello, World! application isn't exactly impressive.

Visual Studio 2008 is one of the most important tools you'll use when building WPF applications, but it isn't the only one. There are a number of tools and technologies that are related to WPF that you should at least be aware of, and we will cover these in the next chapter. Don't worry, though—we will start getting into some more significant, useful (and pretty) applications in the near future.

WPF from 723 feet[1]

3

This chapter covers:

- How WPF fits into Windows
- All the various components and layers of WPF
- Microsoft and third-party WPF tools
- What Microsoft has learned from Homeland Security

Think about how, prior to WPF, you might have approached an application with respect to the user interface, multimedia, and document lifecycle. You might have chosen Windows Forms to implement most of the UI, perhaps calling out to Adobe Flash for the multimedia aspects, and using PDF or proprietary file formats to handle the documentation artifacts. You may also have used Microsoft's Windows Media Player components or Apple's QuickTime to embed video content for tutorials or how-tos in your application. With WPF, Microsoft addresses all these concerns with a single, unified base technology.

One of the implications of this is that WPF is pretty extensive—extensive enough that a quick glance won't tell you what's there and where to find it. The main

---

[1] From 10,000 feet you can't really read the screen.

purpose of this chapter is to provide an overview of all the pieces that make up WPF, including many of the new acronyms. We'll discuss many of these pieces in much greater detail throughout the rest of the book, but we think it's important to have a mental framework for the whole technology.

We'll also discuss a number of tools that are relevant to WPF development. Although this book is focused almost exclusively on the use of Visual Studio 2008 with WPF, you should be aware of these other tools and know when they might be appropriate for you to use.

Before we get to all of that, we want to start by explaining where and how WPF fits into .NET and Windows.

3.1 Where does WPF fit in Windows?

WPF is one of the four pillars of .NET 3.x (the other three being Workflow Foundation, Windows Communication Foundation, and Windows CardSpace). One particularly subtle but important note about .NET 3.x is that its release marks the first time that the managed code world is a part of the primary Windows SDK. This is a tipping point in the relationship between .NET and what's been considered the native Windows platform, rather than a wrapper around native code. WPF is a core part of Windows from Vista forward and is available as an add-on to Windows XP and Windows Server 2003.

3.1.1 Red bits and green bits

Microsoft designed the .NET 1.0 and .NET 2.0 frameworks to be able to be installed side by side. In theory, this capability was a good idea, but it caused various manageability problems and concerns about what would happen when, say, .NET 8.0 came out and was installed side by side with seven previous versions (and their service packs). .NET 3.0 and .NET 3.5 take a different path. Although this explanation is something of an oversimplification, you can think of 3.0 as a superset of 2.0 that includes a number of *new* things (like WPF) and some *changes* to the existing 2.0 framework—changes that Microsoft assures us are safely backwards compatible. Likewise, 3.5 is a superset of 3.0 with some (equally backwards compatible) changes to 3.0 and to 2.0. The 3.5 Service Pack 1 just tweaks the 3.5 assemblies and is pushed out (*drizzled* is the word that Microsoft uses) via Windows Update; anyone who has 3.5 *should* have 3.5 SP1, so it doesn't really affect the picture. Figure 3.1 shows the relationship between the different versions and the new components.

As scary as the backwards compatibility story sounds, Microsoft has come up with a fairly good plan to make everything work, complete with a color coding system (à la Homeland Security)! The bits[2] that make up the framework are broken down as follows:

- *Green bits*—New for the version. For example, WPF was new for 3.0, and so it was safe for them to drop entirely new assemblies in (green == safe).
- *Red bits*—Changed in the existing code for the new version. For example, for 3.5, WPF was no longer new, so any changes became riskier and had to be handled with caution (red == dangerous).

---

[2] All the cool kids (particularly at Microsoft) refer to code as *bits*.

Figure 3.1 Rather than being a complete replacement, .NET 3.0 adds capabilities on top of the existing .NET 2.0 foundation. .NET 3.0 takes everything that already exists in .NET 2.0 and adds additional capabilities to it. Likewise, .NET 3.5 adds on to 3.0. The green bits are new and considered safe, whereas extra caution must be taken when modifying red bits—changes to existing code that have to be backwards compatible.

How good an idea is this? It's hard to say for sure, but it was obvious that the side-by-side approach wasn't going to work for the long term. Also, Microsoft has demonstrated a great deal of ability in maintaining backwards compatibility in the past, so we're willing to give them the benefit of the doubt—for the moment.

3.1.2 *Silverlight*

A discussion of the makeup of WPF wouldn't be complete without talking about Silverlight. Whereas WPF is designed for building rich, Windows applications, Silverlight is targeted at building browser-based rich internet applications, or RIAs. Silverlight combines a stripped-down version of the .NET Framework and WPF and not only runs in Internet Explorer but also supports Firefox and Safari on the Mac. Microsoft is also supporting Moonlight—an effort to support Silverlight on Linux/UNIX platforms.

Silverlight is very obviously designed to be a competitor to Adobe Flash, and Flash is a good model to consider when thinking about the sort of things that Silverlight is designed to do. Although this book is definitely *not* a book about Silverlight, much of what you learn about XAML is directly applicable (just as much of what you know about building .NET applications is applicable to building .NET Compact Framework applications).

Silverlight only contains a portion of the capabilities of WPF, but both are based on the same code and the same framework. In the next section, we'll talk about the pieces that make up the WPF framework.

3.2 Framework services

At the highest level, WPF is made of two main parts: the WPF Engine and the WPF Framework. The WPF Engine deals with rendering graphics, as well as detecting and enabling the accelerated features on various GPUs. The Engine has both managed and unmanaged components, whereas the Framework is almost entirely managed. The Framework is what you, as a developer, work with, and is divided into four primary service areas (table 3.1).

Table 3.1 The four primary services provided by the WPF Framework are the base, media, document, and user interface services.

Area	Description
Base services	The base services provide the infrastructure for the rest of the WPF Framework. These services include XAML, the property and eventing systems, and accessibility.
Media services	Media integration finally brings true multimedia support to the entire application development space. These services include 2D and 3D rendering, special effects, professional typographical support, audio, video, animation, and the composition engine.
User interface services	The user interface services are roughly equivalent to Windows Forms. These services provide the controls, layouts and data binding, as well as nonvisible application services and application deployment support.
Document services	Document services include packaging and layout. These services provide a subset of the full XAML specification tailored specifically to paginated documents.

We'll look at each of these services in more detail.

3.2.1 Base services

Base services are the fundamental services that the rest of the WPF Framework is built upon. The WPF base services include XAML, the Dependency Property System, input and events, and accessibility.

XAML

One of the more powerful aspects of web UI development is the declarative model with which it's designed. XAML brings the best of declarative user interface definitions from web development and combines it with an application—rather than document—focused architecture.

XAML is nothing more than an XML representation of CLR types. Anything that can be done in XAML can be written using .NET code as well.[3] As we discussed in

[3] Well, almost anything. The XAML compiler can convert some obscure things to code that *you*, as someone who isn't a framework developer, cannot.

chapter 1, the declarative model saves a lot of time by providing boilerplate code but also gives the flexibility to do things a little differently if necessary. Table 3.2 shows the relative simplicity and savings gained by taking a declarative approach to describing a UI.

This example demonstrates how much XAML can reduce the length of UI code by making simplifying assumptions about how UI is generally created. In the vast majority of cases, UI is created by defining a set of controls, relating them to each other in a

Table 3.2 XAML can be much more concise than the equivalent imperative code. Because we're taking all the default behavior for adding the controls, XAML lets us leave out all the declarations and overhead of the C# version.

Declarative using XAML	Imperative using C#

<pre><Window>
  <StackPanel>
    <TextBox>One</TextBox>
    <TextBox>Two</TextBox>
    <TextBox>Three
          </TextBox>
  </StackPanel>
</Window></pre>
	<pre>namespace ImperativeExample
	{
	 public class MyApp: Application
	 {
	   private Window window1;
	   private StackPanel panel1;
	   private TextBlock textBlock1;
	   private TextBlock textBlock2;
	   private TextBlock textBlock3;
	
	   protected override void
	        OnStartup(StartupEventArgs e)
	   {
	     base.OnStartup(e);
	
	     window1 = new Window();
	     panel1 = new StackPanel();
	     textBlock1 = new TextBlock();
	     textBlock2 = new TextBlock();
	     textBlock3 = new TextBlock();
	
	     textBlock1.Text = "One";
	     textBlock2.Text = "Two";
	     textBlock3.Text = "Three";
	
	     panel1.Children.Add(textBlock1);
	     panel1.Children.Add(textBlock2);
	     panel1.Children.Add(textBlock3);
	     window1.Content = panel1;
	     window1.Show();
	   }
	
	   [STAThread]
	   public static void Main()
	   {
	     Application app = new MyApp();
	     app.Run();
	   }
	 }
	}</pre>

hierarchical fashion, and displaying them. Because this process is almost always the same, the declarative approach internalizes these common operations and leaves only the specifics to define.

In XAML, you don't have to declare variables for the controls, to instantiate them, or explicitly parent them to each other. In the cases where some special logic *is* desired, you can write code to handle your special case.

Some might argue that developers don't need to understand XAML because the tools can hide the details and complexity of creating UI. A similar argument has been made for browser developers, yet as long as the tools have been around, the need to understand HTML certainly hasn't gone away. Likewise, the need to understand XAML won't go away for WPF developers. Furthermore, the first few versions of the tools still require a lot of trips to XAML to do anything substantial, and the tools may *never* expose some of the more esoteric capabilities. XAML is a language you'll want to become very familiar with.

Although XAML has the benefits of a well-defined XML schema, many of the things you'll do with XAML involve attribute and element values that are outside the scope and control of the schema. XML schemas can enforce that an attribute *has* a value, but it can't enforce that the attribute is *correct*. Fortunately, Visual Studio 2008 is a big help here because it can help make sure that attributes have legal values.

DEPENDENCY PROPERTY SYSTEM

In the design of WPF, the architects made a conscious decision to favor properties over methods and events. A property-centric framework lends itself well to declarative programming and allows for extensive reuse of boilerplate code.

The property-centric focus of WPF requires richer properties than the CLR provides by default. A CLR property is nothing more than syntactic sugar to wrap `get_X()` and `set_X()` methods for underlying fields. WPF needs more functionality from properties, including dependencies, two-way notification, optional inheritance, sparse storage, composition, and attached properties.

The *dependency* mechanism of the property system allows for interested parties to automatically be notified when a particular property has changed. For example, if the `Font` property is changed on a window, all of its children that use that font need to be notified about the change to refresh their display (figure 3.2).

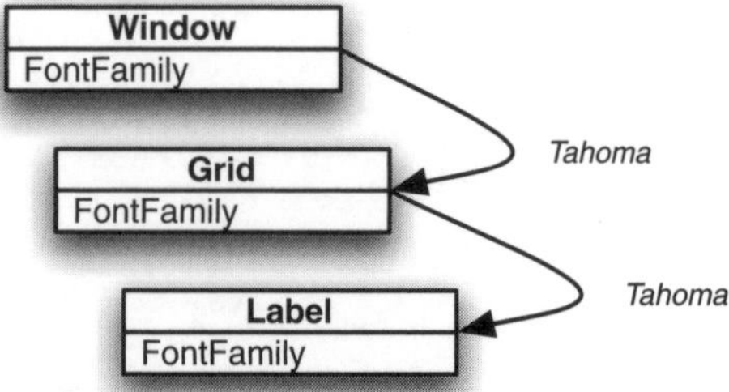

Figure 3.2 Changing the `FontFamily` on the Window notifies dependent children of the change so that they can act on the change as well. In this case, a user's preference of font is automatically carried through the application.

Two-way notification enables properties to publish and subscribe to events based on established dependencies between properties. If a property is inherited from a parent container, a change to the parent's property will notify its dependents. One of

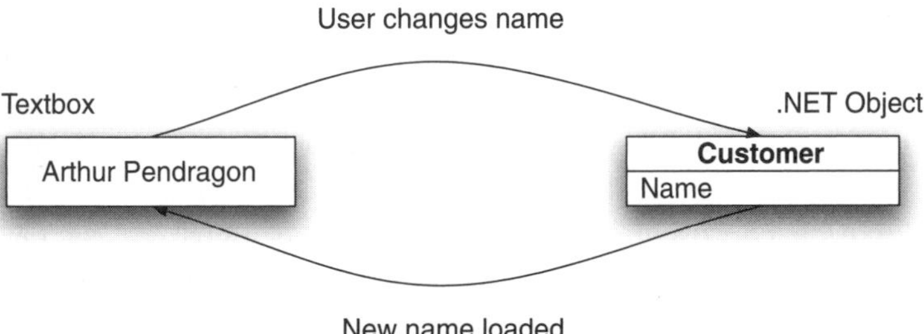

Figure 3.3 With dependency properties, any UI elements can subscribe to the changes made on a data model to reflect the latest state of the system, and the data model is easily and quickly updated from the UI.

the most common operations for a UI is to reflect the state of data from a data model in a graphic control, and when the user changes the value in that control, to persist the data back to the model. With two-way notification and dependency properties, setting up this behavior becomes a trivial exercise for any control. As seen in figure 3.3, if anything changes the value of the data, the control's property is notified and updated, and when the user changes the value of the control, the model is updated.

Compositional and *optional inheritance* provide the ability for controls to pick up property values and behavior from their *owners*. These types of inheritance are quite different than normal inheritance, where items can come from a parent class but not arbitrarily from an owner. A control can choose to override a particular property (say, the font to use), but if it chooses not to do this, then it automatically gets the property from its parent (perhaps, the form the control is on). Composition is the way in which WPF user interfaces are built—by combining or *composing* the UI out of various separate elements.

Compositional inheritance versus class inheritance

Speaking of compositional inheritance, this is a great time to point out the distinction between the classic OO inheritance you typically see in C++ and C# and the type of compositional inheritance we'll often be talking about in WPF. When you think of classic inheritance, you might think of a `Label` control deriving from a `ContentControl` control deriving from a `Control`. The visual properties of the `Control` are inherited and used by the `Label` through classic inheritance. If the font of the `Control` is changed, the `Label` inherits the behavior. Although class inheritance is certainly present and widely used in WPF, there's also a great deal of compositional inheritance. Through composition, the `Label` can inherit other properties from entirely unrelated controls that it's composed with, such as a `Window` or `Style` object. `Label` isn't derived from `Style`, but if you combine (through composition) a `Label` with a `Style`, you get different behavior. This type of inheritance is important for theming, consistency, and greater flexibility with a minimum of programming effort and code.

The WPF Property System also addresses the issue of *how many* properties tend to get associated with UI controls. If you've done much with Windows Forms or third-party controls, you've dealt with dozens or even hundreds of properties on any given control. Most of the time, the majority of these properties will be inherited or defaulted in some way, but every instance of the control carries the *entire* set of properties with it (the properties of the control, the properties of the control's parent, the parent's parent, and so on). *Sparse property storage* allows WPF controls to carry only those properties set explicitly by the developer, creating a far more efficient model for a UI with hundreds of individual controls.[4]

Another compositional pattern in WPF is seen with *attached properties.* Think about docking. In the past, each control with docking support exposed a number of properties around docking. WPF also has the concept of docking, but docking in WPF doesn't require each individual control to support it. The `DockPanel` has a number of properties around docking behavior (left, right, full, and so on). Controls that are children of the `DockPanel` can *attach* these properties to themselves to describe how they should behave in the docking system, even though the controls themselves don't care or even know about the property values at all! It's the `DockPanel` *itself* that maintains the dock-specific property data associated with each of the various controls. When the `DockPanel` goes to lay out its children, it checks internally for each child control to see if it has a `Dock` value stored for it.

By using attached properties, developers can come up with their own layout concepts and allow layout specific properties to be set on controls that have no knowledge of the new system. In figure 3.4, the `Label` control knows nothing about docking from its inheritance chain but is able to set a docking-specific property as defined by the `DockPanel` and, from the XAML at least, it looks like the `Label` was dynamically given a new property.

The last topic of the Property System we'll discuss is the *property expression.* You can think of a property expression as the bit of code that determines how to get a value for

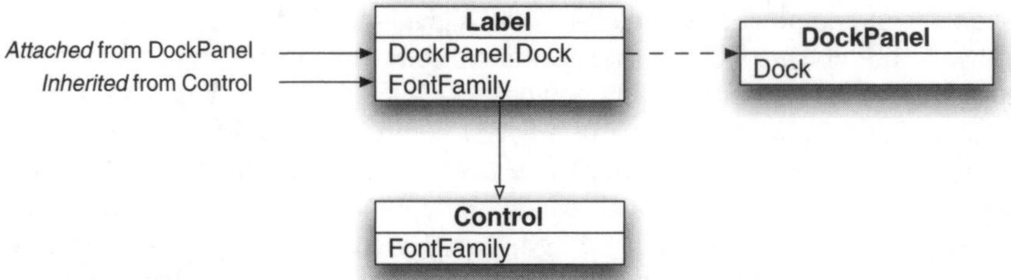

Figure 3.4 In this example, the `Label` object has two properties: `FontFamily` and `DockPanel.Dock`. `Label` is derived from `Control` and gets the `FontFamily` property from there. Label is *not* derived from `DockPanel` in any way—it's contained within the `DockPanel`. It's still legal to set the `DockPanel.Dock` property on the `Label`, The property will only be used by the `DockPanel`.

[4] .NET 2.0 started along this road with the use of *ambient properties.*

a property and what to do when that property's value changes. Property expressions enable many of the behaviors we just discussed—styling, compositional inheritance, default values, and so on. For example, a property expression is used to decide what background color to use when drawing a control. Is the control using the defaults (and if so, what's the default?) set from a style, or is it explicitly defined? The property expression defines the order in which these decisions are applied. Property expressions also support the changing of property values in data binding, and inheritance of properties between objects.

We've barely touched on the WPF Property System, and you can see how complex properties have become. Properties are extremely powerful and important throughout WPF, and understanding how they work is critical to understanding WPF. As we develop applications, we'll definitely be looking at these mechanisms and how they work in more depth.

INPUT AND EVENTS

Eventing in WPF was obviously influenced by the web, and is much richer than the traditional Win32/WinForms model. In a traditional WinForms event, only explicit subscribers are notified when an event is fired. If you want to pass a standard event on, you must write specific code to do so. WPF introduces a new type of .NET event called a *routed event*. Like the web event model, routed events can automatically tunnel down and bubble up the visual tree. As compared with the OO parent-child relationship through class definitions, the visual tree describes the parent-child relationship of controls as composed in the UI. Figure 3.5 shows the path of events bubbling and tunneling through a hierarchy of controls.

To discuss routed events, we must clarify the difference between implementation inheritance relationships and compositional relationships. In figure 3.5, the `Button` is the child of the `DockPanel`, which is the child of the `Grid`. In this case, the relationship described by the visual tree describes how the event will propagate. Contrast this to how an event is handled in a class hierarchy, where the `Button` may override the parent (superclass) control's event handler. In effect, you must think about events both from a classic inheritance perspective, as well as from a compositional approach. The three types of routed events in WPF are:

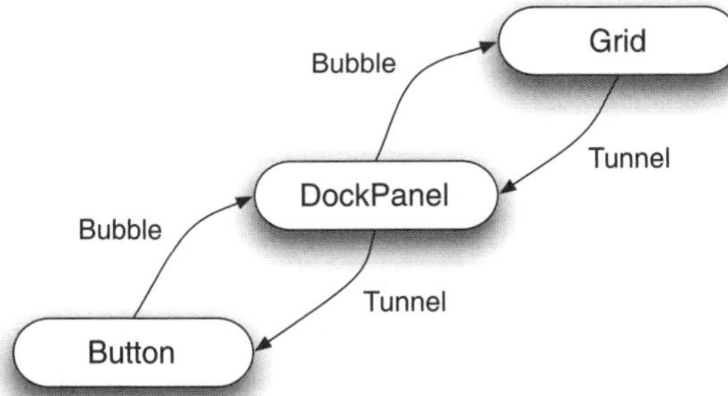

Figure 3.5 Routed events may bubble and tunnel through the visual tree. In this example, an event starts at the `Grid` and tunnels the events down to the `Button`, and the `Button` bubbles the events back up to the `DockPanel` and then the `Grid`.

- *Bubble events*—Bubble *up* the tree to the root node at the top. The naming convention for bubbled events is the event name such as *Click*. Event bubbling allows each control to respond in turn to the various events that can occur.
- *Tunnel events*—Tunnel *down* from the root of the visual tree. The naming convention for this type of event is *Preview* plus the event name, such as *PreviewClick*. As you may have surmised, a control higher up the tree can potentially hide an event from the element that generated it.
- *Direct events*—Operate as traditional events do. Only the specific control is notified; parents and children aren't. As discussed previously, if this were a `SpecialButton` that derived from `Button`, it would still be able to take part in the event via an overridden event-handler method of the base `Button` class.

Without routed events, controls would need to manually call other related controls; each control in the chain would have to support the event, or the bubble/tunnel would stop. Because composition is so prevalent throughout WPF, being able to rely on event tunneling and bubbling is an important aspect of the system's flexibility. Like properties, events in WPF are greatly enhanced, allowing controls to respond to events without any special work to propagate the notifications.

ACCESSIBILITY

Accessibility is about making it possible for people with various disabilities to use systems that they otherwise wouldn't be able to access. In 1998, the U.S. Congress amended the Rehabilitation Act. This act now requires federal agencies to ensure information technology systems be accessible to people with various forms of disabilities and any systems purchased by the federal government be the same. The laws created by this amendment are commonly referred to as *Section 508*. Both the web and Windows already have specific Section 508 accessibility support to enable screen readers, Braille output, high contrast, programmatic control of UI elements, and so on.

Accessibility doesn't just benefit the disabled. Programmatic control of UI elements allows for script and test automation. Keyboard access ensures that power users aren't held up by switching to and from the mouse constantly.[5] Display scaling and zooming is useful to a normal-sighted audience in a presentation or pair-programming exercise. Software that supports alternative input can support new input systems like Tablet PC Ink without changing a single line of code. Even if Section 508 support isn't a specific goal, developing toward an accessible UI is good for everyone.

WPF enhances accessibility in a number of ways. One of the most obvious immediate advantages is that people with low vision are able to seamlessly scale WPF UI to whatever clarity they need. WPF has also been built with accessibility in mind, so every control and aspect of the framework is enabled for accessibility.

The WPF base services—XAML, the property and eventing systems, and accessibility support—make up the core shell of WPF upon which everything else is based. You might be forgiven if you're already going cross-eyed at this point. We promise that

[5] Yes, we are that lazy.

once you get out of theory and into implementation, the value of all this stuff will be evident. Before we get to that, we need to cover the higher-level services, starting with media services.

3.2.2 Media services

Media services are concerned with audio, video, imaging, animation, and so on. Media services encompass all that you'd expect from a multimedia API, and a bit more. Many of the components in the media services layer support the type of presentation normally done with a product such as Adobe Flash, through custom code, or through interoperability to individual multimedia controls.

Overall, the media services layer brings true multimedia development to mainstream UI creation, while avoiding the often Frankensteinian complexity of incorporating disparate media technologies. It also allows much finer-grained integration of media functionality into UI controls than existing technologies tend to allow. The media services are comprised of drawing (2D), typography, audio/video, WPF Imaging Components (WIC), 3D rendering, animation, bitmap effects, and the composition engine.

DRAWING (IN 2D)

2D drawing in WPF is a considerable leap from previous frameworks. In fact, the 2D elements of XAML are comparable to full-featured Scalable Vector Graphics (SVG), a format created to describe complex vector drawings. Complex 2D XAML drawings can be created in specialized software for the specific purpose of graphic design, or programmatically created by a developer. We'll explore 2D drawing in detail in chapter 14, but for now, it will suffice to say that the 2D API is rich enough to be the basis for dedicated drawing software.

TYPOGRAPHY

WPF gives a much needed boost to typography. Although typography has long been available via specialized applications, WPF brings it to all applications, enabling the best the OpenType format offers. Various controls have been available to edit and display rich text, but full typographic support has never been available across the board. WPF brings rich, professional typographic support across the entire framework.

Some of the advanced features of OpenType available to the entire framework include ligatures, swash variants, superscript, subscript, and small caps. Some of these capabilities are demonstrated in figure 3.6.

Ligatures: ff, fi. New Style numerals: 80386

No ligatures: ff, fi. Old Style numerals: 80386

Figure 3.6 WPF has access to advanced OpenType features. In the top line, ligatures are enabled. (Note how ff and fi are joined together.) The rest of the first line is fairly ordinary. In the second line, swash alternative capitals are on. (note the *N* in *No* and S in *Style*), and numbers are using an old style offset pattern (note the 3).

By the way, if you install the Windows SDK, you get several OpenType fonts to play with in one of the samples. Look in the following directory:

```
\Program Files\Microsoft SDKs\Windows\v6.1\
  Samples\WPFSamples.zip\GraphicsMM_Text\OpenTypeFontsSample\xaml\fontlibrary
```

These fonts were designed by a company called Ascender. For more information, look at their website at http://www.ascendercorp.com/WPF_fonts.html.

AUDIO/VIDEO

Traditionally, audio is not something that comes to mind when thinking about UI frameworks. Audio's inclusion in WPF is an example of multimedia becoming a first-class citizen in the user experience for Windows applications. As previously mentioned with typography, when adding audio and video in a Windows application, you had to use some embedded component that invariably took longer to integrate and debug than the rest of the application took to write. The video content rarely integrated smoothly, and you were severely limited in how you could tie it in.

Combined with the acceleration afforded by modern GPUs, the audio/video capabilities of WPF provide a platform where media integration is more and more practical. The value of this can be seen on Apple's OS X, where the GPU power is available across the entire UI framework through Quartz and Quartz Extreme, and applications take extensive advantage of it.

Some of the obvious uses of a/v include tutorials and training videos, but many more subtle uses of this power exist. For example, think of the (nicer) menu systems on DVDs or the screens in kiosk-style applications. Video brushes could be applied to a set of buttons to select from a set of vacation packages in a kiosk-style application. Another example of a tasteful use of video is the header of the Copy Files dialog in Windows Vista. Small, simple videos can communicate to the user the nature of activity being performed by the system.

WINDOWS IMAGING COMPONENT (WIC[6])

For a long time, dealing in anything other than bitmap (.bmp) images was a chore in Windows because supporting any other format required various third-party components—or a lot of home-grown code. GDI+ (and .NET in general) alleviated this somewhat with an extended set of supported file formats, but WPF finally nails this problem by providing a rich, extensible imaging API. You former Amiga users can rest easy now that the Windows equivalent of the Amiga Datatype system has arrived—well, at least the *imaging* aspect of it has arrived.

WIC provides several managed and unmanaged components for encoding and decoding images, color transforms, pixel format conversion, scaling, and clipping.

THE 3RD DIMENSION

Although most of WPF is designed around two dimensions, under the hood, it makes extensive use of Direct3D. This has made it easy for WPF to provide support for working in 3D, although currently only a subset of 3D capabilities is directly available. WPF's 3D support is useful for visualizations and lighter duty gaming. (Think along the lines of chess, mahjong, solitaire—not Halo 3.) A potential business use would be an integrated 3D map of an office building, showing the path you might take to find a conference room or emergency exit. Another good example of 3D in day-to-day applications

---

6 Also, also wic!

is Eric Sink's furniture construction application.[7] Product visualization is another potential aspect of integrated 3D support, allowing users to explore their content.

Unfortunately, a lot of 3D has resulted in horribly unusable interfaces. There are definitely challenges in making the 3D capabilities increase usability and efficiency. Many attempts at adding 3D to file and document management make us want to run screaming back to the physical world where we at least have more precise control. Years ago there was a movie about bringing dinosaurs back to life. The most terrifying part of the movie was when a UNIX 3D filesystem interface went horribly wrong…or maybe the dinosaur experiment went horribly wrong. In any case, it was all very horrifying to see.

THE 4TH DIMENSION: ANIMATION

In the early days of Windows, *animation* referred to the *two* states an object might have. Later on, file operations in Explorer gained simple animations of papers being tossed between folders, duplicated, and otherwise manipulated in all their eight-frame glory—even the animation support of Windows Forms centers around the animated GIF or performing some ugly interop to external components with varying degrees of success.

WPF supports animation to the degree that today's hardware deserves. Rather than providing specific frames, the WPF animation model takes direction on what should be where and how it should get there. The WPF animation engine then does the job of calculating how to achieve the animation with the hardware and resources available. On lower-end machines, an animation might result in five frames over five seconds, whereas a top-of-the-line system may have fifty frames in the same amount of time.

Animation is another one of those wonderful capabilities that can greatly enhance a UI by providing visual cues and affordances or destroy an otherwise respectable application with overzealous use.

BITMAP EFFECTS

Bitmap effects allow WPF interfaces to be altered after the fact by low-level filters that enhance or change the UI in some way. Some of the effects supported out of the box include bevel, blur, glow, and drop shadow. Although these effects are pretty cool, they're one of the few parts of WPF which uses unmanaged code. This is relevant because *some* of the effects are software rendered, which can have a significant impact on performance. Prior to SP1, all the effects were usually software rendered, but now the most commonly used effects—blur and drop shadow—are hardware rendered.

COMPOSITION ENGINE

Prior to WPF, UI graphics were generally rendered directly to the frame buffer (video card) memory. If an application obscured another application's window and you moved it, the obscured application would be asked to draw the area that was covered. Also, when the controls drew themselves, they didn't know anything about the pixels behind them. In figure 3.7, if you moved the window of App2, App1 would have to redraw itself in the area exposed by the movement, and App2 would have to

---

[7] http://sawdust.com/p1/index.html

redraw the area revealed after moving out from under App3.

In WPF, rather than drawing to the frame buffer directly, each application draws to a *surface*. WPF then takes care of all the mechanics of *composing* the final presentation without requiring the applications to get involved. Vista takes this even further. The Vista Desktop Window Manager (DWM) can handle surfaces with different DPI levels and different contrast levels. As seen in figure 3.8, by using composition, entirely new approaches to desktop management are afforded without any need for the applications to specifically support or be aware of them.

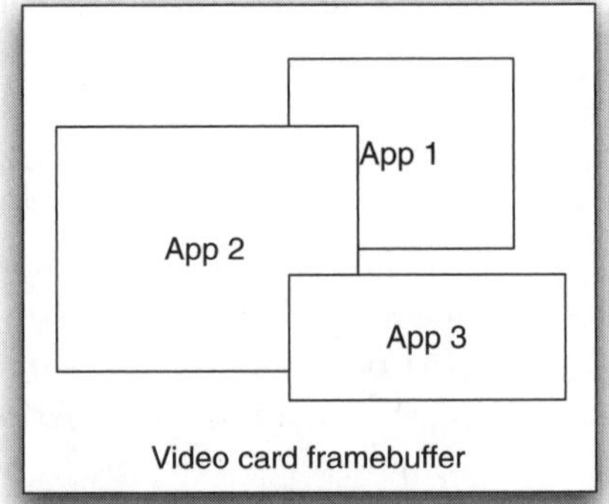

Figure 3.7 Applications are drawn directly into the frame buffer of the video card.

Drawing in WPF is much lighter-weight than Win32 drawing, at least for the CPU. The GPU performs many of the drawing operations directly on the graphics card, so the CPU is free to spend more time on application logic and processing. Furthermore, unless you're interoperating with legacy UI, WPF isn't limited by scarce Windows resources such as handles.

In WPF, you're given a surface to work with (although you're unaware of this 98% of the time). Typically, this is a DirectX surface; and, depending on the OS, it may be directly in the frame buffer, or it may be rendered offscreen. The important point is that, like the `DeviceContext` of the past, you don't know where you're drawing; you deal with your application's surface and let the engine composite it in an appropriate manner for the environment.

All the elements we've discussed so far have been fairly low level. When it comes to application development, there are certain elements that you expect to find—controls and layout, for example. These lie in the domain of user interface services.

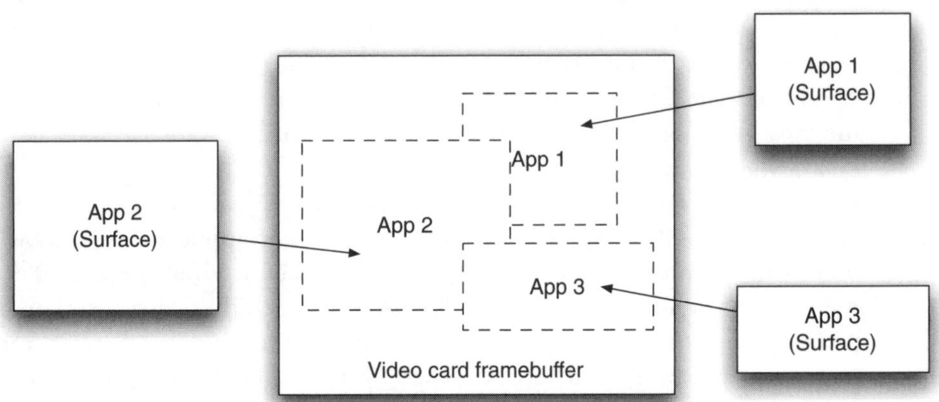

Figure 3.8 Composition allows more flexibility than drawing directly.

3.2.3 User interface services

We've seen quite a bit so far without talking about UIs directly. If you were looking for the successor to Windows Forms (and then some), this layer contains most of the classic functions of a UI framework—application services, deployment, controls, styles, layout, and data binding. Like the Document-View architecture of MFC, WPF provides a lot more around the application framework than WinForms did. If you have an MFC background, you might notice some of the application framework support coming back as well.

Application services

We previously saw in table 3.2 how encoding the logic and plumbing common to almost every application results in a tremendous reduction of code (and, therefore, maintenance cost) of UI. Typically, you'll specify what type of application you want, and WPF will generate the plumbing for you. Some of the application services of WPF provide lifetime management, navigation infrastructure, and application resources. The application services also provide the event model that replaces the old Windows message pump.

Deployment

WPF has considerable changes and improvements to the deployment process. In particular, web deployment of smart applications is a first-class citizen in WPF. A major difference between targeting an application for web deployment versus installer-based deployment is in the much more restricted security environment the web model entails. Other than security, the difference between WPF web applications and standalone applications is minimal.

In the web deployment model, applications are packaged as XBAPs and run in a sandbox, which by default provides limited access to local resources and doesn't permit unmanaged code. Browser-based WPF applications can't run offline, so access to the deployment site is necessary to execute the application.

Standalone applications potentially have full trust and are ideal for applications that are being migrated from unsafe/unmanaged code or for applications used offline. Standalone applications may also be deployed over the web using ClickOnce. When a user browses to a standalone application, it will be installed on the end user's system and may be executed offline as well.

Controls

What is a UI without controls? If anything is fundamental to a user interface (besides the user), it would have to be the controls. Controls are the basic unit of interaction for any graphic interface. Most of the usual suspects are all present (for example: buttons, tab controls, labels), as well as some new entries (such as layout containers, flow document, and document viewers).

In previous frameworks, changing the look of a control required a developer to write a custom control and take over the entire drawing process. Unlike previous controls, WPF controls are extremely malleable. Altering a control's appearance is built in and fundamental to WPF. In fact, most WPF controls have no visible component at all;

they draw based on the themes and styles in effect at the time they're rendered. Controls are also extremely composable. In the legacy Windows UI, adding graphic treatment to a control frequently required a developer to implement owner-drawing code. The level of effort to add a simple embellishment wasn't justified.

STYLES

Think of WPF Styles as being analogous to CSS on the web (except not in a bizarre made-up language). Styles are the means by which UIs are themed. Styles and themes (a collection of styles) are pervasive and supported throughout WPF. You can (and should) define the styles completely separately from the controls, providing an extremely custom look for your application or allowing the system-wide theme to define the exact look.

LAYOUT

In traditional Win32 UI development, there was little concept of layout. In general, you placed controls where you wanted them, and the entire design surface was based on absolute positioning of UI elements. Windows Forms added rudimentary layout concepts of anchoring and docking but lacked full layout support (and fairly horrible performance for anything remotely complex). The web does Windows Forms one better by providing three forms of layout: document flow, table, and absolute positions (via Positional Cascading Style Sheets, or CSS-P). Java UI programmers know all about layout managers, and may be happy to know that WPF finally brings the concept to Windows development. Microsoft provides a collection of built-in layout managers with WPF and, as importantly, allows developers to create their own layout strategies.

DATA BINDING

The purpose of virtually any UI is to present some sort of underlying data model. In WinForms, data binding was often used to connect some sort of dataset to a control, typically a grid or list, and automatically render the results. The purpose of data binding in WPF remains the same but becomes far more powerful.

Data binding in WPF involves two things: a target and a source. A data binding target is any dependency property on a control. Given that most properties in WPF are dependency properties, this means that almost anything in WPF can be bound to a data source. The aptly named source of the data binding is where the data comes from. The source can be *any* of a number of things including any public property, any CLR object, as well as specialized data sources such as DataSets and XML. Throughout the book, we'll use data binding extensively to develop our working applications.

The services we've looked at so far (base, user interface, and media services) are the sorts of services you'd expect to find in a new presentation library. Less obvious is the inclusion of document services in WPF.

3.2.4 Document services

Presentation isn't limited to presenting content on a screen for a user. It also includes the ability to create and share documents—either by printing them, or by packaging them in a format that can be transferred to other users. In WPF, document services address printing, packaging, and document lifecycle. The centerpiece of the document services layer is the XML Paper Specification (XPS), which is defined as a subset of XAML.

XML Page Specification (XPS)

XPS is Microsoft's entry into the paginated document format. XPS describes paginated data in a cross-platform portable XML document. If you think this sounds a lot like PDF, you'd be right. One interesting point is that XPS is available to systems without .NET 3.x installed; the XPS viewer doesn't use .NET 3.x because it's an independent XAML engine, making the format reasonably portable. The specification is available via the ECMA for third-party implementations.

WPF has several different controls that allow for easily displaying XPS documents, depending on your need—from lightweight to a complete editor with searching. The standalone viewer generally comes up in your browser and has the various tools that you'd expect, including searching, zooming, and printing. Figure 3.9 shows an XPS document.

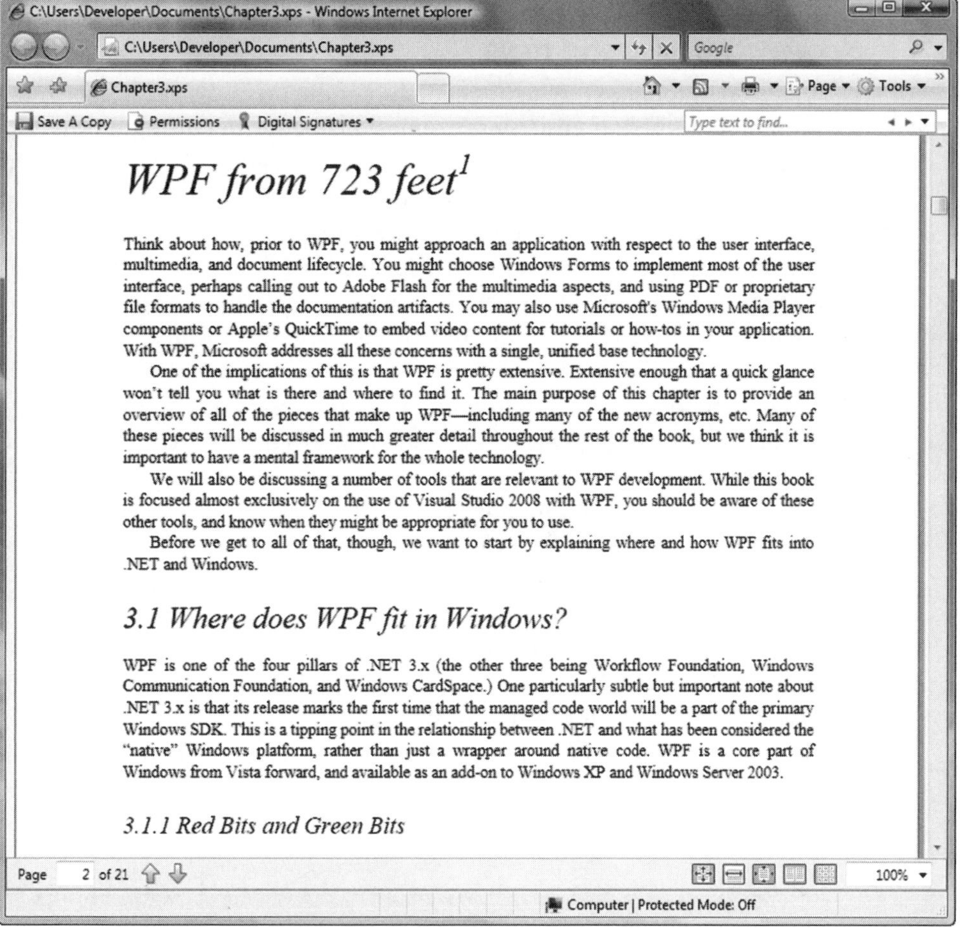

WPF from 723 feet[1]

Think about how, prior to WPF, you might approach an application with respect to the user interface, multimedia, and document lifecycle. You might choose Windows Forms to implement most of the user interface, perhaps calling out to Adobe Flash for the multimedia aspects, and using PDF or proprietary file formats to handle the documentation artifacts. You may also use Microsoft's Windows Media Player components or Apple's QuickTime to embed video content for tutorials or how-tos in your application. With WPF, Microsoft addresses all these concerns with a single, unified base technology.

One of the implications of this is that WPF is pretty extensive. Extensive enough that a quick glance won't tell you what is there and where to find it. The main purpose of this chapter is to provide an overview of all of the pieces that make up WPF—including many of the new acronyms, etc. Many of these pieces will be discussed in much greater detail throughout the rest of the book, but we think it is important to have a mental framework for the whole technology.

We will also be discussing a number of tools that are relevant to WPF development. While this book is focused almost exclusively on the use of Visual Studio 2008 with WPF, you should be aware of these other tools, and know when they might be appropriate for you to use.

Before we get to all of that, though, we want to start by explaining where and how WPF fits into .NET and Windows.

3.1 Where does WPF fit in Windows?

WPF is one of the four pillars of .NET 3.x (the other three being Workflow Foundation, Windows Communication Foundation, and Windows CardSpace.) One particularly subtle but important note about .NET 3.x is that its release marks the first time that the managed code world will be a part of the primary Windows SDK. This is a tipping point in the relationship between .NET and what has been considered the "native" Windows platform, rather than just a wrapper around native code. WPF is a core part of Windows from Vista forward, and available as an add-on to Windows XP and Windows Server 2003.

3.1.1 Red Bits and Green Bits

Figure 3.9 An XPS document in the viewer is embedded inside of Internet Explorer.

Like PDF documents, an XPS document can be as simple or as complex as required. A companion technology to XPS is Open Packaging, which is used for storing and transmitting XPS documents.

OPEN PACKAGING

The 2007 Microsoft Office System introduced the Open Packaging Conventions (OPC), which is also a part of WPF. Open Packaging is a set of conventions around the use of XML, zip archives, resources, and metadata for document interchange. Like XPS, this format is also being standardized through the ECMA.

Open Packaging is designed to provide a generic way of storing all the various resources that might make up a document, including images and fonts. Open Packaging can be used without XPS, but XPS uses Open Packaging for documents.

Now that we've seen an overview of the base, media, user interface, and document services provided in WPF, let's take a look at some helpful tools that make development of WPF applications easier and more efficient.

3.3 Necessary and useful tools

Without a good tool box, trying to meet the product requirements that your CEO happily promised at the last customer forum is analogous to cutting down a mighty tree while armed with a very unhappy herring.[8] The fundamental purpose of software is to create tools that increase the reliability, accuracy, and speed of some manual process. Yet many times, we neglect to create or use tools in our *own* process of creating software. It's strange, but we run into developers all the time who claim that they have no need of specialized tools—they have Notepad, after all. In our opinion, these developers are implying that what they do for a living is a waste of time.

We're more in line with the idea of the "lazy" developer who will spend three days building a tool to avoid having to spend five minutes doing something every day. The even lazier developer hopes that someone else will spend three years building a tool that will save five minutes.

Microsoft has created a number of tools to make our lives easier (okay, programmers in general, but we mostly care about ourselves here). They've also gone a step further by making sure that the framework exists for other companies to provide tools as well.

The principal tool from Microsoft for developers to work with WPF is Visual Studio 2008. In addition, they've created a series of applications under the general name of *Expression.* One of these tools—Expression Blend—is specifically designed to work with XAML and WPF, and another—Expression Design—can be used to export XAML images. None of the other Expression applications have anything to do with WPF or XAML, but you'll likely see them grouped together, so we've provided some quick definitions.

---

[8] The CEO bought you that herring, and he expects you to make good use of it.

3.3.1 Microsoft Expression family

The Microsoft Expression family of products introduces tools aimed not at the developer, but at the supporting roles around the developer, including graphic designers, designer-developers, and human factors engineers. The assumption is that an entire team is now involved in the building of applications, of which the classic developer is a part. The two primary tools are:

- *Expression Blend*—The primary tool for designers and human factors engineers to participate in the development workflow. Blend is also unique in among the Expression line because it's written with WPF. Any resemblance to Adobe Flash is *not* coincidental. Blend is definitely in the Flash space and, with Silverlight, may prove to be a significant challenger. Although Adobe Flash and its new framework, Flex, work toward providing a web-application development platform, Microsoft is combining a significantly more mature and complete backend to WPF to create a compelling answer to Flash/Flex. Figure 3.10 shows the Expression Blend designer.
- *Expression Design*—The basis of Microsoft's vector and graphics editing tools for WPF. Expression Design started life as Creature House Expression, a vector graphics editor. In 2003, Microsoft acquired the product, company, and developers.

Figure 3.10 Expression Blend is a more designer-oriented way of building WPF applications. It's definitely more of a tool for artists and designers than for developers.

Microsoft has added raster image capabilities and XAML export, although XAML isn't the native format. Expression Design is roughly in a similar market as Adobe Illustrator (at the low end), Photoshop, Inkscape, and CorelDRAW/PhotoPaint.

In addition, the following Expression tools are only vaguely related to WPF:

- *Expression Web*—Primarily an HTML/ASP.NET authoring system. It's slated to replace FrontPage as Microsoft's professional web-design tool.
- *Expression Media*—Primarily a tool for managing images and other media. It does have the ability to export directly to Silverlight via a plug-in called Expression Encoder.
- *Expression Encoder*—A tool for encoding audio and video for use with Silverlight.
- *Expression Studio*—The combined package of Expression products: Web, Design, Blend, and Media.

3.3.2 Visual Studio

As you might expect (if for no other reason than the cover of the book), Visual Studio is the primary tool that we'll be using to develop and demonstrate WPF. Visual Studio 2008 was the first version that provides support for WPF, although there were some experimental Community Technology Previews (CTPs) available as plug-ins for VS 2005. This book primarily uses Visual Studio 2008 SP1, which has added a number of fixes and improvements.

The WPF editor within Visual Studio handles the basics fairly well, and this definitely speeds up WPF development. That said, with the scope of WPF and the fact that it's so new, there are still a lot of things that the designer *can't* do. As we go through the book, we'll point these things out and demonstrate workarounds as necessary.

By the way, you don't need the full-blown $12,000 Team Edition of Visual Studio to work with WPF. Visual Studio Express is available at no cost and also supports WPF.

3.3.3 Other tools

Some other tools from the Microsoft SDK are also useful as you develop WPF applications. These are some that we use daily.

XAMLPad

XAMLPad is a fantastic tool included with the Windows SDK to test WPF markup that really shows off the power of a declarative approach to UI work. XAMLPad combines a validating XAML text editor with a real-time preview of the resulting UI. You can run a number of the simpler examples in the book in XAMLPad without having to create an entire Visual Studio project.

UI Spy

UI Spy gives managed code developers a tool to externally inspect and manipulate UIs. This tool can also be used to verify programmatic accessibility.

THIRD-PARTY TOOLS

XAML opens up the opportunities for third-party tools to join the development workflow. You should definitely have a validating XML editor to work with XAML. There are also a number of third-party, XAML-aware tools such as ZAM3D by Electric Rain and Aurora by Mobiform Software. For a great list of available WPF related tools, check out Mike Swanson's tools page at

http://blogs.msdn.com/mswanson/articles/WPFToolsAndControls.aspx

3.4 Summary

WPF is a massive framework. It provides a complete toolset for presentation layer development with a great deal of capability and power, and will certainly enable new UI ideas that were previously too time-consuming or difficult to create. By emphasizing a declarative model, tools should become more reliable than the traditional code generation approach employed by the WinForms designers, and will also allow third parties to join the WPF process through an XML contract via XAML.

Aside from being large, WPF is also extremely ambitious. It aims to provide a toolkit for completely replacing the way that Windows UI is developed. Although WPF is already capable, the first few releases can't possibly address every possible contingency. We'd argue that, until there's feedback from real-life implementers, it's generally not wise to even try. But it's critical to have a framework that can be extended and expanded, and Microsoft has definitely done a good job laying groundwork for the future.

These first three chapters have tried to provide some context for WPF, starting with the motivations behind WPF, some simple examples, and ending, in this chapter, with a description of the parts of the WPF framework and the available toolset. This overview provides a general framework for the more specific elements discussed throughout the rest of the book. Starting with the next chapter, we'll get into the real nuts and bolts of using WPF.

Part 2

The basics

So far we've been long on theory and short on code. Well, that's all about to change. In the next five chapters, we're going to build a real, working application in WPF—a calculator.

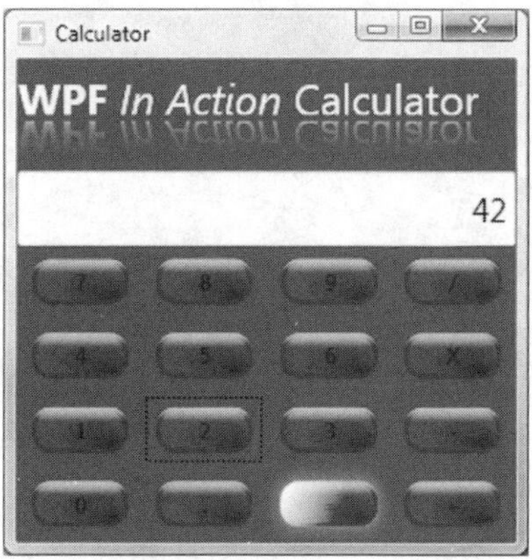

The calculator demonstrates the basics of WPF development.

Granted, what you were looking for in your life was probably *not* another calculator implementation, but the calculator is good for covering the core concepts of WPF. Before we get to the calculator, in chapter 4, "Working with layouts," we'll discuss ways of laying out WPF applications. Then, in chapter 5, "The Grid panel," we'll introduce the most powerful layout control in WPF and use it to build the calculator.

Chapter 6, "Resources, styles, control templates, and themes," will demonstrate how you can use the style mechanisms of WPF to make the calculator a little prettier (although we'll pass through several phases of *uglier* on the way).

In chapter 7, "Events," we'll show the new event capabilities of WPF (such as bubble-up and tunnel-down events) that make the calculator more responsive.

Finally, in chapter 8, "Oooh, shiny!" (our favorite chapter of the entire book), we'll demonstrate how to soup up the calculator by adding glass buttons that glow when you press them and some reflections and other effects.

4 Working with layouts

> ***This chapter covers:***
> - Laying out controls with `Panels`
> - The different layout panels in WPF
> - The `FlowDocument`
> - Things named poorly in order to confuse and confound

Starting in the next chapter, we're going to build a calculator. We know it's boring and all, but it demonstrates a lot of concepts relative to WPF, and is a simple enough example that the implementation details won't get too much in the way of what we're doing. As with any application, one of the key elements is figuring out how to handle the layout of the various controls. Unlike in previous MS frameworks, the idea of *layout* is a concrete concept in WPF, and there are a number of predefined layouts.

The most powerful layout is the `Grid` layout, which is big enough to warrant its own chapter (chapter 5). Before we get to that, we'll explain the idea behind layouts and demonstrate a number of the other built-in WPF layouts. We'll also talk a bit about some controls and concepts that aren't technically layouts but have much to do with laying out content.

4.1 The idea behind layout panels

Suppose you wanted to build something like the calculator from figure 4.1 using Windows Forms. You would probably start dragging controls onto a form and then use the various alignment tools to line everything up. Of course, if you decided that you wanted the buttons to be a different size, you'd have to resize the buttons and then re-lay them out. If you wanted the controls and buttons to automatically resize based on the size of the parent, then things would get difficult. You could write custom code to do the resizing, or you could attempt to use docking and anchoring, adding lots of different, layered panels. Either of these approaches *might* work, but the form would be hard to edit and would draw slowly.

Figure 4.1 The simple version of the calculator example that we'll start to build in the next chapter. It uses the `Grid` layout.

In WPF, you *can* drag controls onto a form and position them by hand, but there's a far better way—layout panels. Layout panels let you define how you want things to be arranged. You put your content into the layout and let it handle all of the work of positioning and sizing your controls. There are also various generic properties to control the behavior of the layout, and each layout also has its own specific properties.

All layout panels have a collection of children. The management of these children is handled by the base class for all the panels (called, cleverly enough, `Panel`), so adding and removing children is identical from panel to panel, although, as you'd expect, the way in which the children are handled is different for each type of panel. `Children` can be anything—controls, objects, even other layout panels. It's up to the layout panel to figure out the best way to arrange the contained items. This can be simple, such as just stacking its children one-on-top-of-the-other, or complicated, involving a grid of rows and columns to hold different items.

NOTE If you're familiar with Windows Forms, you'll know that `Panel` is also the name of a Windows Forms class. There's no relationship between the two. In fact, a lot of WPF classes have exactly the same name as Windows Forms classes. You'll rarely run into problems, though, because of the different namespaces—`System.Windows.Forms` for Windows Forms and `System.Windows.Controls` for WPF. The place where you're most likely to run into trouble is when looking things up in Help. In the Help file, you'll have to make sure you're looking at the `System.Windows.Controls` version of a control and not the Windows Forms version *or* the web form version, which also has the same name!

There are five main layout panels available, as well as some custom ones for special purposes. Table 4.1 shows each of the major layout panels.

Each of these different layouts is designed to serve a different purpose, although there's a lot of overlap. In particular, the `Grid` layout can provide the same functionality as a `StackPanel`, `DockPanel` or even a `Canvas`. As we'll show in the next few sections,

Table 4.1 The major layout panel types

Layout name	Description	Example
`Canvas`	A `Canvas` is most like a standard form from Windows Forms. You provide the specific location and size for controls, and that's where they stay. This is obviously the most flexible layout, but gives you the least help.	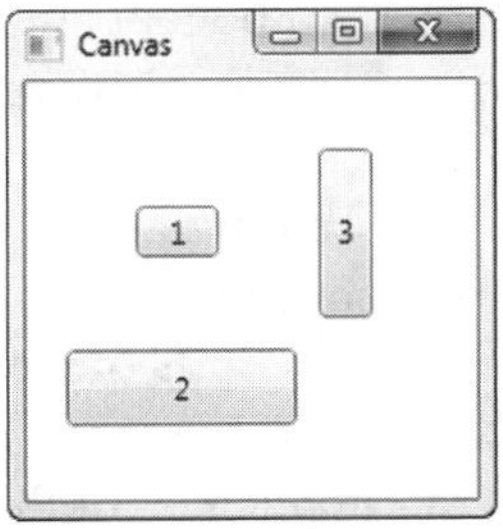
`StackPanel`	A `StackPanel`, as the name implies, takes all your content and puts it into a stack, one item above another or one item to the right of the next, depending on whether the panel is stacked horizontally or vertically. The example shows how the calculator might be reimagined using a stack panel.	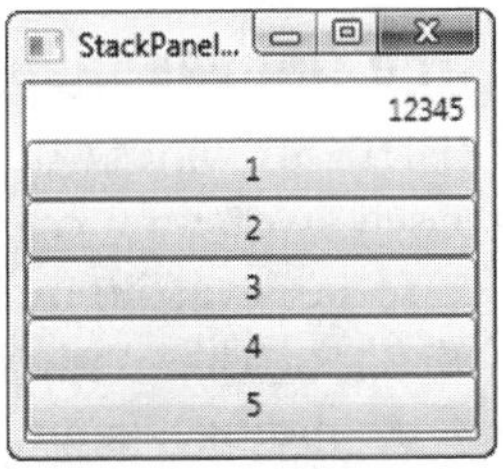
`DockPanel`	A `DockPanel` lets you arrange items against the edges of the window. This is close to the way in which docking works in Windows Forms—you specify docking for controls, and those controls are put against the appropriate edge. As you can see from the example, it's probably not the most appropriate layout to use for our calculator.	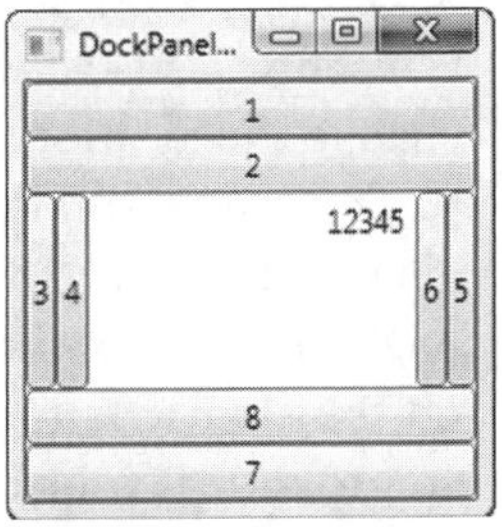
`WrapPanel`	The `WrapPanel` works sort of like word wrap in a word processor. As many items as possible are put in a line. When there's no more space, the next item is pushed onto the next line, and so on. Once again, not exactly perfect for our calculator.	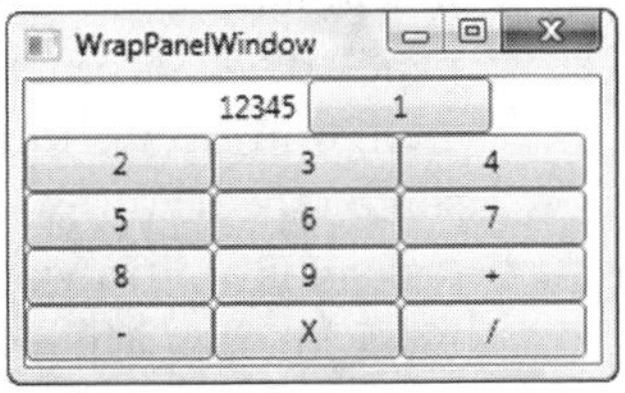
`Grid`	The `Grid` layout is the most complex of the layouts, and the most powerful. A `Grid` can have any number of rows and columns, and content can be placed into individual cells or span multiple cells. This is similar to the table layout in HTML. The example shows our calculator. The heading (WPF In Action Calculator) and the current value text box span several columns. Each button is in an explicit column and row. Chapter 5 will show how the calculator layout was created.	

there are reasons to use each of the different types of layout. The different layouts are also designed to be used together. For example, the main part of your application might use a `DockPanel` to arrange the big pieces but, within that, a `StackPanel` for one component and a `Grid` for another.

You can also create your own custom layout panel if you so desire, by deriving from `Panel` and overriding the methods that handle the measuring and laying out of children. It's also likely that third-party companies will start to provide specialized layout controls.

Each of the next sections goes through each type of layout container in detail. We start with the `Canvas` because it's the simplest. While discussing the `Canvas`, we'll also talk about a lot of things that apply to the other layouts as well.

4.2 The Canvas layout

There are times when you want to set up all or part of the UI of your application precisely—you want control X to be at a particular point with a particular size, and shape Y to be at a different point. For example, your application is some form of visual designer (like Visio), or you are representing data graphically (like a chart), or you are building a game. In these cases, you'll probably want to use the `Canvas` layout.

The `Canvas` is a fixed-position layout—where you drop your controls is where they stay. The `Canvas` doesn't ever change the location or size of the controls (figure 4.2).

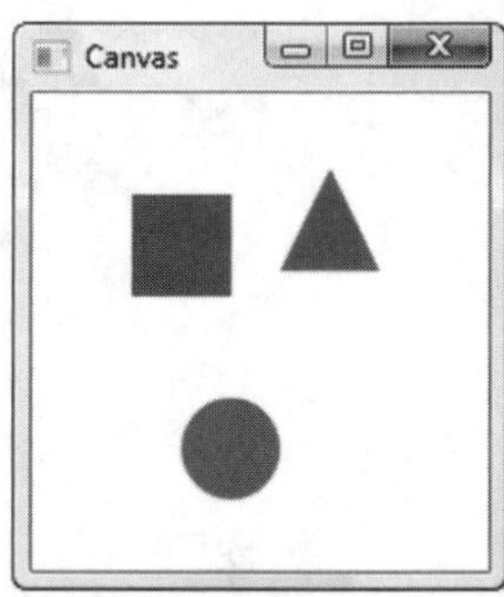

Figure 4.2 One reason to use a `Canvas` layout might be if the user can drag on items. For example, a simple drawing program might allow shapes to be dragged onto a `Canvas`.

Sometimes you may want to set up your UI quickly, dragging controls onto the panel and aligning them, the way you might have done with Windows Forms or with MFC. You *can* do this, but we strongly recommend that you don't. This approach may initially be quicker, but you'll end up with a much more brittle UI than if you use an appropriate layout panel. It will save you time up front but cost you later.

If you do decide to use a `Canvas` layout, it does have some nice features. To use them, you first have to set up a `Canvas` layout to work with. You might think, based on its behavior, that when you create a new `Window`, it's set up as a `Canvas` layout; after all, you drag on controls, and they stick where you put them. But it's a trick, a lie, a con—the default layout for a new `Window` (or `Page`) is a `Grid`!

Earlier, we mentioned that the `Grid` is flexible enough to provide the functionality of other layout mechanisms. In this case, the controls are being positioned within a `Grid` with a single row and a single column, and margins are set to emulate positioning. This automatic behavior is clever because it allows the same editor to support layout-managed editing and also fixed*ish* positioning layout. It's also problematic because the editor can't necessarily tell when you're trying to put something into a properly layout-managed space versus when you are trying to fix-position something.

So, how do you set up the editor to work with a `Canvas`? It would be nice if the editor had a simple way to switch the top-level layout to use any particular layout, but it doesn't. You have two ways to make a `Window` use a `Canvas`: edit the XAML directly or put a `Canvas` inside the `Grid` cell.

Because there are so many layout options, it's expected that developers will have to go back and forth between the editor and the XAML for a number of operations. This is in contrast to the Windows Forms editor, which worked on the (faulty) assumption that the autogenerated code wouldn't be touched by the developer.

4.2.1 Converting a Grid layout to a Canvas layout by modifying the XAML

When you look at the XAML for a new Window, you'll see a `Grid` tag already in place:

```
<Grid>
</Grid>
```

The tag is empty because there's no content and no setup for the grid. To switch to a `Canvas`, we delete the `Grid` tags and add a `Canvas` tag:

```
<Canvas>
</Canvas>
```

Now we can drag controls onto the `Canvas`, and they'll stick where we put them. Of course, it *is* more likely that you'll be adding items to a `Canvas` programmatically; we'll show how to do that later.

Note that for all the other non-`Grid` layouts, if you want to use them as top-level controls, you'll have to make a similar change. It's usually easier to leave them inside the existing `Grid` control.

4.2.2 Adding a Canvas to an existing layout

It's fairly unlikely that you'll want the top-level of your `Window` to be a `Canvas`; it's far more likely that you'll have a `Canvas` inside a different layout. For example, you may use docking for your application layout, but have a panel in the middle that shows precisely positioned items, as in figure 4.3.

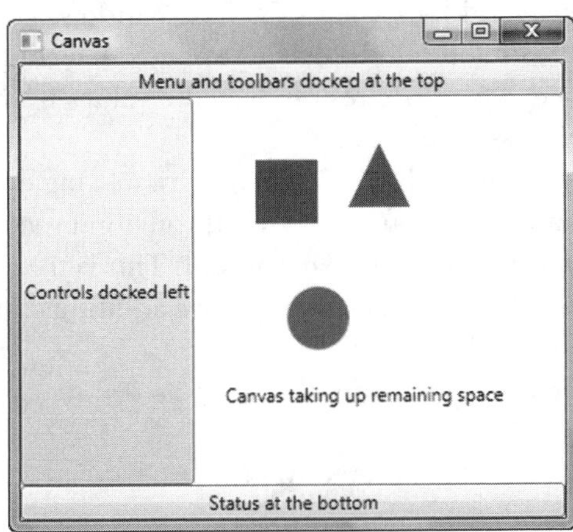

Figure 4.3 Controls around the edges use a `DockPanel` layout; the `Canvas` in the middle allows for precisely positioned items.

The easiest way to add a Canvas to a layout is to drag a Canvas control from the control palette. If you drag it onto the empty Grid control, it would ideally take up all the available space (based on properties that we'll talk about later). But for the purposes of discussing the Canvas, it doesn't matter if it takes up all the space, so long as it's big enough to work with.

Go ahead and drag a couple of Buttons (or other controls) onto the Canvas (something like figure 4.4).

Listing 4.1 shows what the XAML looks like after dragging on the controls. Extra credit will be awarded if you get your Buttons to stop in exactly the same spots as ours.

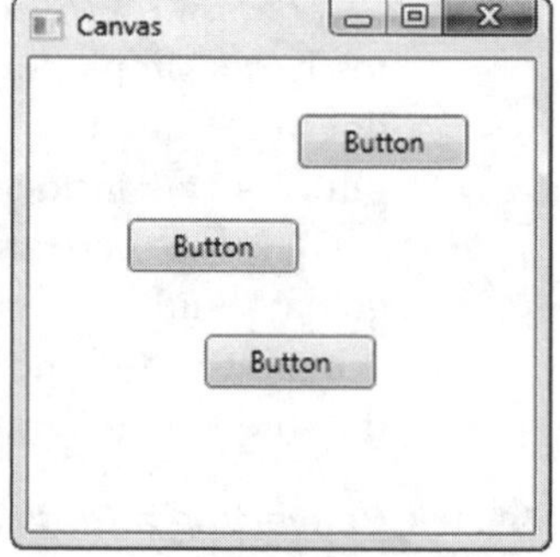

Figure 4.4 We dragged a few Buttons onto a Canvas. Their positions are fixed.

Listing 4.1 XAML for dragged-on Buttons

```
<Window x:Class="CanvasTest.Window1"
    xmlns="http://schemas.microsoft.com/winfx/2006/xaml/presentation"
    xmlns:x="http://schemas.microsoft.com/winfx/2006/xaml"
    Title="Canvas" Height="244" Width="242">
  <Canvas>
    <Button Canvas.Left="119" Canvas.Top="24"
        Height="23" Name="button1" Width="75">Button</Button>
    <Button Canvas.Left="44" Canvas.Top="69"
        Height="23" Name="button2" Width="75">Button</Button>
    <Button Canvas.Left="78" Canvas.Top="119"
        Height="23" Name="button3" Width="75">Button</Button>
  </Canvas>
</Window>
```

The XAML for the Buttons is pretty reasonable—Left, Right, Width, Height, Name, and the text to display inside the element. You may notice something odd about the way that the Left and Top properties are defined, but we'll get to that in a moment.

Right now the Width and Height are set to default values by the editor. What happens if we remove the XAML for Width and Height? If this were Windows Forms, the Buttons would disappear, but in WPF, something different happens. We could either delete the XAML for the Width and Height attributes or clear the values in the property editor. Either way, the result looks like figure 4.5.

Instead of disappearing, the Buttons have shrunk until they're just big enough to hold their content. This behavior is standard throughout WPF. If you don't specify a particular size, then controls will generally be sized to their content. This is true with layouts other than the Canvas, except that the other layouts also have additional influence on the size of the controls, as you'll see in the next sections.

You can do other things to the Buttons' properties that have an influence on their sizes. Figure 4.6 shows the result of some of these options.

Listing 4.2 shows the updated XAML that generated figure 4.6.

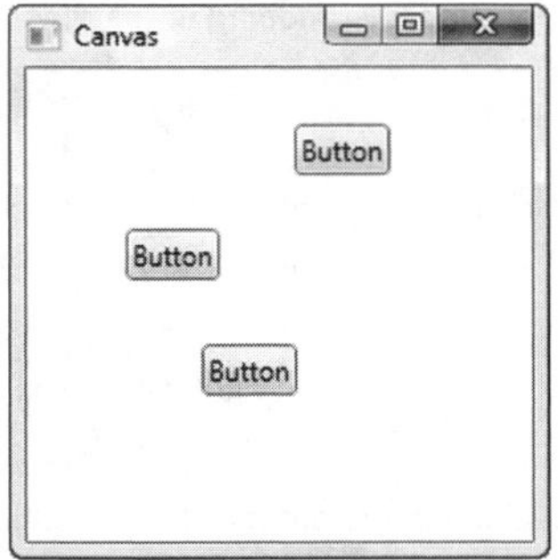

Figure 4.5 If we remove the `Width` and `Height`, controls are automatically sized based on their contents.

Figure 4.6 `Buttons` gone wild—with some additional properties.

Listing 4.2 XAML for `Canvas` with additional properties set

```
<Canvas>
  <Button Canvas.Left="119" Canvas.Top="24" Name="button1"     ❶ Sets Width and Height
      Width="70" Height="23" >Button</Button>
  <Button Canvas.Left="44" Canvas.Top="69"                     ❷ Adds more text
      Name="button2" >Button2 is quite wide</Button>
  <Button Canvas.Left="78" Canvas.Top="119" Name="button3"     ❸ Adds padding
      Padding="10 2" >Button</Button>
/Canvas>
```

As you can see, all the `Buttons` are now different sizes. In each case, the sizing has been accomplished in a different way. For button1 ❶, we set the width and height. If the text didn't fit, it would be truncated. For button2 ❷, we make the text longer. The `Button` automatically increases its size to accommodate the new text. In some scenarios, this is desirable. In others, such as when you have a stack of `Buttons` that should all be the same size, it's quite annoying.

For button3 ❸, we add *padding*. `Padding` is another property present on all controls. It says, "Add this much space (in pixels) around the contents of this control." Note the way in which the value for `Padding` is specified:

```
Padding="10 2"
```

You'll see this notation wherever multiple values need to be specified. In this case, the padding is set to 10 pixels on the left and right, and 2 pixels on the top and bottom. For the `Padding` property, you can specify 1, 2, or 4 different values. Table 4.2 shows the different options.

The values here are space-delimited, but you can also comma-delimit them if you prefer:

```
Padding="10,2,12,4"
```

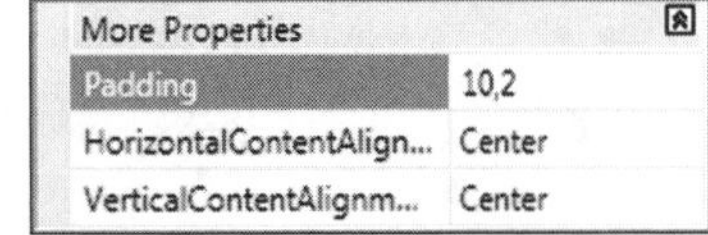

Figure 4.7 You can set padding in the XAML editor or in the property designer. The editor defaults to comma-delimiting the values.

Figure 4.7 shows how the value will appear if you set it through the designer.

Table 4.2 Different ways for providing multiple values for properties like padding or margins

Value	Meaning
`Padding="10"`	The same value will be used for all sides—`Left`, `Right`, `Top`, and `Bottom`. In this case, 10 pixels of padding will be placed on each side of the control's content.
`Padding="10 2"`	The first value (10) will be used for the left and right sides. The second value (2) will be used for the top and the bottom.
`Padding="10 2 12 4"`	All four values are explicitly specified in the order of `Left` (10), `Top` (2), `Right` (12), and `Bottom` (4). If you have a web development background, you should note that the order here is different.

Properties like `Padding`, `Width` and many of the other properties that show up in the Properties grid are pretty straightforward. Not all WPF properties work the same way though…

4.2.3 Using attached properties

You may have noticed an interesting thing about the property values in listing 4.2. Properties such as `Width` and `Padding` look like regular XML attributes. But the `Left` and `Top` properties' notation is a little different:

```
<Button Canvas.Left="40" Canvas.Top="40" >
```

`Button` does *not* have properties for `Left` and `Top`. Unlike Windows Forms, which assumed that everything has an explicit location, the working assumption for WPF is that the *parent* is responsible for the placement of each control. You'll see this with the other layout types. In the case of a `Canvas`, each control has to have its explicit location set. Because it is the `Canvas` layout that requires this information, it is up to the `Canvas` layout to handle this information.

In "classic" XML (that is, XML that could be validated by a Schema), you'd normally have to introduce an element around each child to specify the properties specific to the parent—something like listing 4.3.

Listing 4.3 A way to set properties for `children` (but *not* supported by WPF)

```
<Canvas>
  <CanvasItem Left = "40" Top="40">
    <Button>Button1</Button>
  </CanvasItem>
</Canvas>
```

This approach would work but is quite verbose, particularly when you have a lot of nested items. It also implies a hierarchy that doesn't really exist. Rather than requiring more verbose XML and making `Canvas` follow a structure that it probably doesn't need, XAML introduces a notation that allows properties that belong to the parent to be defined on the child, via the use of the *dot* notation:

```
<Canvas>
  <Button Canvas.Left="40" Canvas.Top="50">Button1</Button>
</Canvas>
```

This should be read as "When you add the Button to the Canvas, tell the Canvas that the Button should be positioned at Left 40 and Top 40." These properties are called *attached properties* because they're attached to the child to which they refer, even though they belong to the containing control (the Canvas in this case). You'll see this notation throughout XAML for all sorts of properties. You just need to remember that properties with dots in the middle are really setting values that are used by the containing control. The nice thing is that, when you're editing the properties of the control in the property editor, attached properties are displayed as part of the set of the control's properties (figure 4.8).

⊟ Layout	
Canvas.Left	40
Canvas.Top	50

Figure 4.8 The property editor displays attached properties as part of the set of the control's properties.

In the case of the Canvas, there are only 4 attached properties: Left, Right, Top, and Bottom. These properties don't act precisely as you'd expect. Rather than providing an explicit location, they specify the *distance* from the particular edge. So, if you set Left to 40, the left edge of the control will be 40 pixels from the left edge, but if you set Right to 40, the right edge will be positioned 40 pixels away from the right edge (figure 4.9).

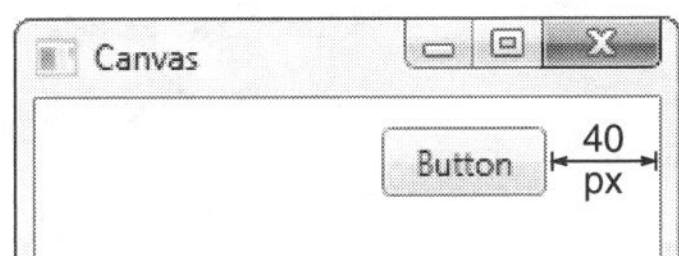

Figure 4.9 If you set Canvas.Right, the control will move with the right edge of the parent.

The nice thing about setting the Right value is that the control will move with the right edge of the parent control, so if you resize, it will move with the edge. This is sort of like anchoring in Windows Forms. Unlike anchoring, you cannot set both the Left and the Right values and have the control automatically expand. If you set both Left and Right, then the Right value will be ignored. Similarly, if you set both Top and Bottom, Bottom will be ignored.

It would be nice if this worked the way you'd expect—sticking to both edges and expanding when the parent changes size. We suspect that the reason it doesn't *might* be to discourage people from using the Canvas for building forms instead of more appropriate layouts. We considered hiring a private investigator to trail behind the WPF team with cameras to figure it out, but our publisher wouldn't spring for the expense.

Attached properties aren't used only for the Canvas; they're used throughout WPF and by most of the other layouts as well. It's the standard way for WPF to provide properties on a child that are important to the parent.

4.2.4 Setting up a Canvas programmatically

If you're using the Canvas the way it's designed to be used, you'll rarely be dragging controls onto the editor. You are much more likely to have code that adds items directly. All the different layout controls allow their properties and children to be set programmatically. The `Canvas` will almost always be set programmatically.

To demonstrate how to programmatically add controls and set their properties, you first need to set up a place for the code. In a real application (as you'll see later), this could happen based on a button click or part of some other initialization. For our purposes, you'll add the controls as part of the initialization of the Window.

We want to add the controls right after the XAML has been processed. We could do this in two different ways. The first would be to put the code in the constructor of the class. If you create a new `Window` and go the Window1.xaml.cs file, you'll see a constructor with a call to the method `InitializeComponent()`, as in listing 4.4.

Listing 4.4 Placing code to run after initialization in constructor

```
public partial class Window1 : System.Windows.Window
{
  public Window1()
  {
    InitializeComponent();

    // You could put your code right here
  }
...
```

`InitializeComponent()` calls a method automatically created by the compiler when it compiles the XAML file. This method does all the work described in the XAML defined in Window1.xaml. In the example, it creates the `Canvas` and then adds the three `Buttons`. At the moment, the XAML file is empty, so initialization is minimal.

The second way to execute code after initialization is to catch the `Loaded` event. This event is triggered after the `Window` has been set up. To do this, we need to add a reference to the event in the XAML and then put the event handler in the code file. Listing 4.5 shows the XAML with the reference to the `Loaded` event.

Listing 4.5 XAML for a `Window` that has registered for the `Loaded` event

```
<Window x:Class="Layouts.Window1"
    xmlns="http://schemas.microsoft.com/winfx/2006/xaml/presentation"
    xmlns:x="http://schemas.microsoft.com/winfx/2006/xaml"
    Title="Layouts" Height="300" Width="300" Loaded="Window_Loaded">
    <Canvas Name="canvas1">     <-- (1) Names Canvas
    </Canvas>
</Window>
```

Notice that we manually change the default `Grid` to a `Canvas`. We also give the `Canvas` a name (1) by defining a value for the `Name` attribute. Why do we do this now, when we didn't earlier? Earlier, we didn't need to talk to the `Canvas`. Everything we wanted to do was defined in the XAML, and the items in the `Canvas` knew they were part of it because they were nested inside of its XML tag. Now, we're going to programmatically add things to the `Canvas`, and to do that, we need a way to reference it. The name we give it will end up as the name of a member of the `Window1` class that we can reference, as you'll see in a moment.[1] Note that virtually all XAML elements can be given names.

We also add the `Loaded="Window_Loaded"` attribute value. When the `Loaded` event is fired, the `Window_Loaded` method in Window1 will be called. You can see the format of the event handler in listing 4.6, along with the implementation for adding all the controls.

Listing 4.6 Catching `Loaded` event and programmatically adding controls

```
Button button1 = null;      ❶
Button button2 = null;
Button button3 = null;

private void Window_Loaded(object sender, RoutedEventArgs e)     ❷
{
  button1 = new Button {Content="Button", Width=70, Height=23};     ❸
  Canvas.SetLeft(button1,119);       ❹
  Canvas.SetTop(button1,24);
  canvas1.Children.Add(button1);    ❺

  button2 = new Button {Content="Button2 is quite wide"};     ❻
  Canvas.SetLeft(button2,44);
  Canvas.SetTop(button2,69);
  canvas1.Children.Add(button2);

  button3 = new Button {Content="Button"};     ❼
  Canvas.SetLeft(button3,78);
  Canvas.SetTop(button3,119);
  button3.Padding = new Thickness(10,2,10,2);     ❽
  canvas1.Children.Add(button3);
}
```

Because we didn't define any of our `Buttons` in the XAML, we create our own declarations for them ❶. If we *had* created them in the XAML and given them names, we could have referenced them by those names.

The declaration for the event handler ❷ follows the standard pattern for *routed* events. Many WPF events look like this, although there are certainly a number of exceptions where special handling is required. We'll talk about `RoutedEventArgs` when we talk about events in more detail in chapter 7.

Creating a control and setting its properties is pretty much the same as with Windows Forms. We create a new instance ❸, and set values for properties such as `Width` or `Content`. The code uses *object initializers*. This is a new feature of .NET 3.0 that lets you assign values to members of an object when you declare it. It would have been just as legal (but more verbose) to have a separate line to set each property.

One noticeable difference in this code from Windows Forms is that, instead of setting a `Text` property for the text to display, we set the `Content` of the control. As you'll see, *content* can be text, nested controls, or any object.

[1] It also gives the Canvas a greater sense of self-worth. How would you like it if everyone just went around calling you *Person*, instead of by your name?

When setting the `Left` and `Top` positions in XAML, it more or less looked like we were setting properties on the `Button`, even though we knew that the properties belonged to the `Canvas`. When we're writing code, we can no longer hide this fact ❹. The `Button` does *not* have a `Left` or `Top` property. You may notice, though, that we're not exactly setting the `Left` on the `Canvas` (canvas1) either; we're calling a static method on the `Canvas` class called `SetLeft()`.

`SetLeft()` takes the `Control` and the value for `Left` as arguments, but note that it doesn't take a reference to the `Canvas`. It's *decorating* the `Button` with some information that doesn't mean anything to the `Button`. When the `Canvas` looks at the `Button`, it looks at that decoration and says, "Aha, this `Button` wants to be positioned 119 pixels from the left edge." You'll see this throughout WPF—property values that don't belong to a control are nonetheless *attached* to the control for another control's consumption.

Finally, we add the `Button` to the collection of `Children` for the `Canvas` ❺. All the layout `Panels` have a `Children` collection to contain the controls they own. We then add the other two `Buttons` ❻, ❼ with slightly different property values. Note that the `Padding` property ❽ takes a `Thickness` object that holds values for each edge.

If you now run the application, you'll get something like figure 4.10.

Figure 4.10 The `Canvas` layout with child elements added programmatically

Note that this looks *exactly* the same as figure 4.6. This could be because we figured we could get away with copying and pasting the same screenshot, but it's *mainly* because there's no functional difference between the XAML approach and the programmatic approach.

In a real-world example, it's unlikely that you'd only create standard controls to add to a `Canvas`. It's more likely that you'd respond to events and method calls and dynamically create appropriate content. The way you'd do this is much the same as you see here.

Even though the `Canvas` layout panel is the simplest of the panels to understand, we've spent more time talking about it than we'll spend on the other layout panels. We spent so much time on this panel because we wanted to talk about and show the mechanisms *behind* the panels. No matter how complex the layout, these concepts won't change. But each of the following layout panels does have its own set of properties and behaviors.

4.3 The StackPanel layout

Sometimes, the name of a class pretty much tells you all you need to know about it. The `StackPanel` is a panel that stacks things. Well, now for the next section…

Okay, so maybe a few more details.

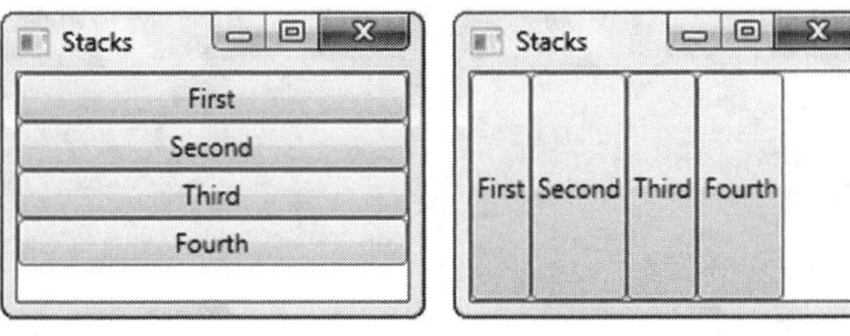

Figure 4.11 `StackPanel` **oriented vertically and horizontally**

As with the other layout panels, the `StackPanel` has a collection of `Children` that it literally shoves one after the other. You set the orientation to either horizontal or vertical to control where the items go (figure 4.11).

You might use the `StackPanel` if you have a series of controls with a set width or height that you want to show up in a row. For example, you might use `StackPanel` when you have a series of controls in a side panel (like the *accordion control* in Microsoft Outlook—you can expand/contract sections for mail, calendar, tasks, and so on). The controls can all change size, and the other controls will automatically be moved to accommodate the space.

Another scenario might be an options dialog where you have a series of subcontrols. Additional controls can be added easily; and, once again, if the size of a particular control changes, the rest of the display will adapt.

Figure 4.12 shows a dialog that could be built using stack panels. A horizontally oriented stack panel could hold the selector control on the left and another stack-panel on the right. That stack panel would hold all the other controls such as the authentication and user-information controls.

If you need another control, it can be added to the stack without requiring any special handling. Figure 4.13 shows the way the dialog from 4.12 might be constructed using stack panels.

NOTE One major advantage that WPF has over Windows Forms is that the *cost* of having multiple layers of panels and controls is considerably lower. With Windows Forms, each `Panel` and each `Control` would be associated with a Window handle. The more layers, the more handles, the more resources, and the worse the performance. With WPF, there's no such overhead.

Figure 4.13 shows one of several ways you could accomplish this same layout. As you'll see, the `DockPanel` or the `Grid` or some combination could also be used. To set the orientation, we select the panel and change the `Orientation` property in the Properties grid (figure 4.14).

To add controls to the `StackPanel`, we drag them from the toolbox. When we added controls to the `Canvas`, the default behavior was for the controls to take up the minimum space, although we could change that by explicitly setting the width, padding, and so on. You may have noticed in figure 4.11 that the default behavior for controls in the `StackPanel` is different; in the direction of stacking, controls behave the same way—taking up the minimum space—but in the other direction, the control is

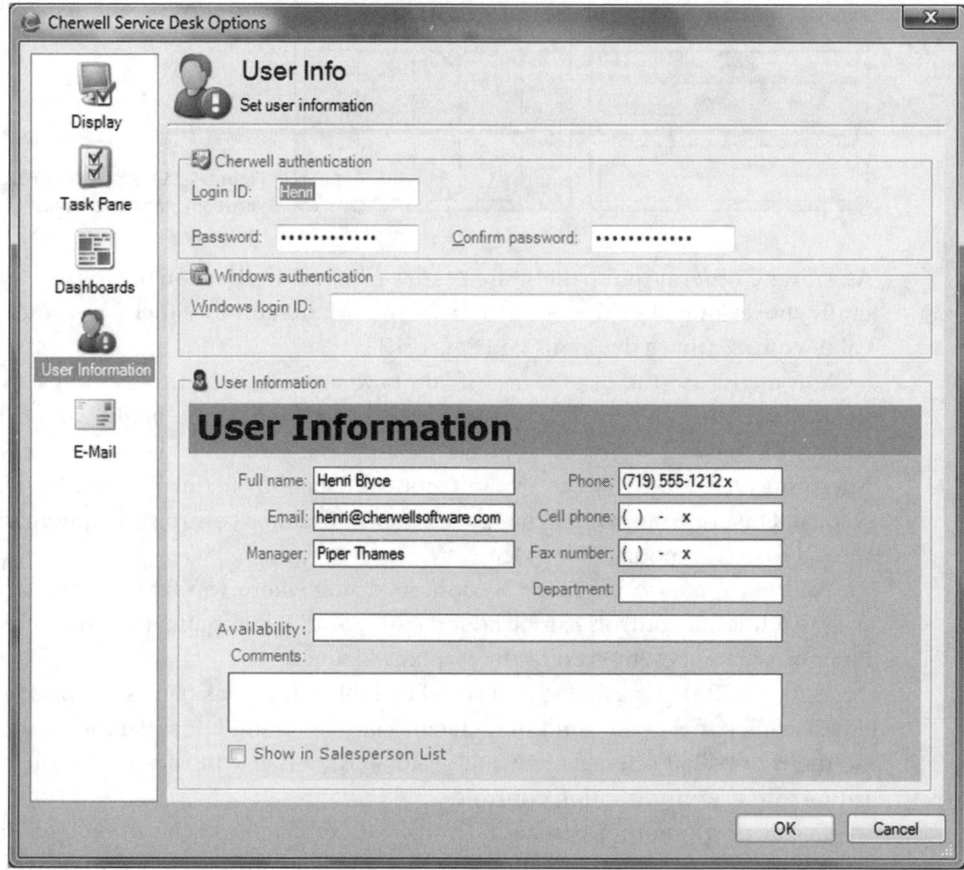

Figure 4.12 An example of an option dialog with multiple stacked items. The different authentication sections and the user information are each independent controls stacked one above the other.

stretched to take up the maximum amount of space, so long as we don't provide an explicit width or height to limit it.

As before, we can change the behavior by setting properties on the controls. Figure 4.15 shows the `StackPanel` when some properties are explicitly set on the controls.

Listing 4.7 is the XAML for figure 4.15. We can set all these properties in the Properties grid or directly in XAML.

Listing 4.7 XAML for `StackPanel` with various attributes set

```
<StackPanel Orientation="Vertical">
  <Button Width="200">First</Button>                              ❶
  <Button HorizontalAlignment="Left">Second</Button>              ❷
  <Button Padding="10 4">Third</Button>                           ❸
  <Button Margin="20 20">Fourth</Button>                          ❹
  <Button Padding="10 4" HorizontalAlignment="Right">Fifth</Button>
  <Button HorizontalAlignment="Stretch">Sixth</Button>            ❺
</StackPanel>
```

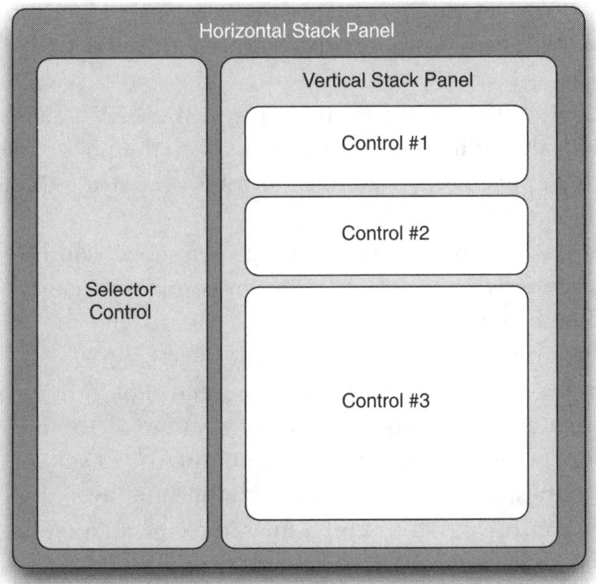

Figure 4.13 This is one way in which stack panels could be used to set up a dialog like that in figure 4.12

If you look at all the attributes, you'll see that *none* of them use the dot notation (such as `Canvas.Left`). We make all the behavior changes by setting properties available on the controls themselves. The `StackPanel` automatically takes these properties into account when laying out the controls. We've highlighted some of the specific properties.

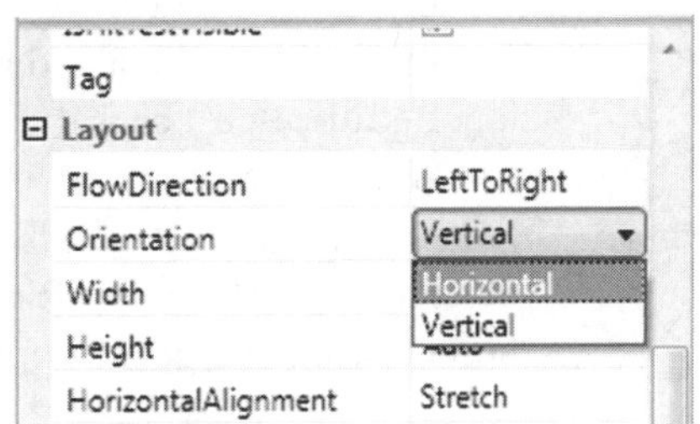

Figure 4.14 Setting the `StackPanel` orientation in the Properties grid

On the first control, we set an explicit width ❶. The layout panel still tries to stretch the control (because `Stretch` is the default alignment), but it can't quite reach all the way across now. The control appears centered but with the specified `Width` of `200`.

On the second control ❷, we set `HorizontalAlignment` to `Left`, rather than letting it default to `Stretch`. The `HorizontalAlignment` property tells the containing layout how it would prefer to be positioned. Because the control is now left-justified, it takes on its default sizing behavior.

Figure 4.15 `StackPanel` with some values set explicitly on the controls

As you've probably guessed, there's also a `VerticalAlignment` property. Because of the current orientation of the `StackPanel`, setting `VerticalAlignment` would have no effect. If the orientation were set to Horizontal, the VerticalAlignment property value would become meaningful. These properties can cause different behavior on other layouts.

Here ❸ we set padding, as we did when working with the Canvas layout. As you can see, although the vertical padding has an obvious impact, the horizontal padding doesn't show up. It *is* being applied, but then the control is stretched to fill the space, so you can't see any meaningful effect.

We've not yet seen the Margin property ❹, but it's present on all controls. Whereas padding is used to set space *inside* a control, the margin controls spacing around the control. The margin was meaningless when using the Canvas, but the StackPanel automatically adds 20 pixels on each side of the control.

Margins are unbelievably handy. If you look at the screen shot in figure 4.12, you can see space between each of the sections. With Windows Forms,[2] you'd either have to add a spacing control between each section (meaning the use of yet another Window handle) or include extra space in each control. To adjust the spacing, you'd have to modify each and every control and, if you used the same control in more than one place, you'd have to have the same spacing—or add nasty hacks. With WPF, we just set the margin and sit back while the appropriate layout handles everything for us.

Here ❺ we explicitly set the horizontal alignment to Stretch, which means that the layout panel should make the control take up all available space in the horizontal direction. Because Stretch is the default, it looks like it would if we had said nothing at all.

Using the StackPanel is easy, and you can see how it would work for layouts like that shown in figure 4.12. But it's possible that not all the controls in the stack will fit into the available space. Right now, if we reduce the size of the window, the bottom-most controls will get chopped off. A scrollbar here would be lovely.

4.3.1 Adding scrolling support

Adding scrolling is easy, and, once you get used to the idea of control composition, fairly intuitive. We simply put the StackPanel (or anything else we want to automatically scroll) inside a ScrollViewer, as shown in listing 4.8.

Listing 4.8 Adding scrolling to a WPF element with ScrollViewer

```
<ScrollViewer>
  <StackPanel Orientation="Vertical">
    <Button Width="200" >First</Button>
    <Button HorizontalAlignment ="Left">Second</Button>
    <Button Padding="10 4">Third</Button>
    <Button Margin="20 20">Fourth</Button>
    <Button Padding="10 4" HorizontalAlignment="Right">Fifth</Button>
    <Button HorizontalAlignment="Stretch">Sixth</Button>
  </StackPanel>
</ScrollViewer>
```

2 As it happens, Windows Forms controls *do* have a Margin property. Unfortunately, it's almost universally ignored.

We know we keep harping on this, but the idea of composition is extremely powerful and core to the whole makeup of WPF. In the past, you might have expected `StackPanel` to have some scrolling options, but every single container control would have to have the same options. Sure, there could be a base class; but, if everything had to be derived from that, you'd end up with duplicate properties everywhere and be limited to a single derivation tree.

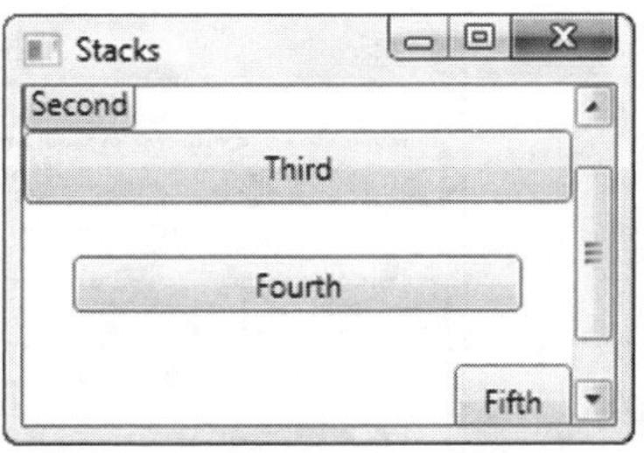

Figure 4.16 Adding a `ScrollViewer` around the `StackPanel` automatically adds scrolling behavior.

Composition does away with all of that. `ScrollViewer` handles scrolling. Nothing else has to care. We wrap it and forget it. Figure 4.16 shows the `Buttons` with a scrollbar.

By default, a `ScrollViewer` adds a vertical scrollbar that's always present but no horizontal scrollbar. This works well for the current example but would be less useful if we had set the orientation to horizontal. It is also slightly annoying that a scrollbar is displayed even if there is enough space for everything (figure 4.17).

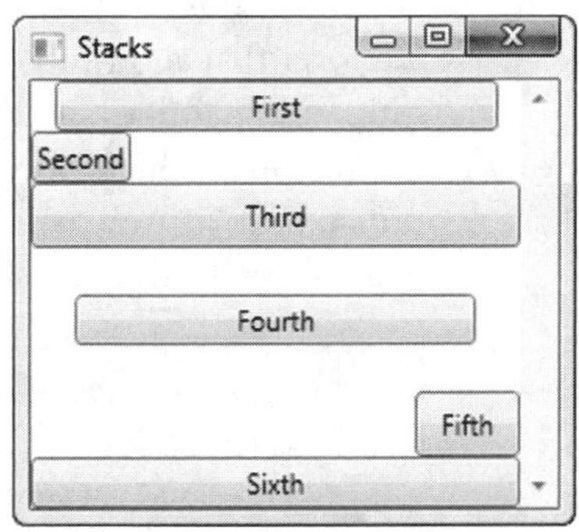

Figure 4.17 The scrollbar shows up even if it's not needed—at least it's disabled, though.

Fortunately, it's trivial to make the scrollbar only show if it's needed (figure 4.18).

Selecting Auto makes the scrollbar show only if it's needed. Similarly, to have a horizontal scrollbar and no vertical is also easy. Here it is in XAML:

```
<ScrollViewer VerticalScrollBarVisibility="Hidden"
  HorizontalScrollBarVisibility="Auto">
```

We could also explicitly set the size of ScrollViewer and programmatically control it.

While we're talking about dealing with space management, it might be nice to take a brief detour and talk about a fairly handy control that lets the user hide and show pieces of content as desired—the Expander control.

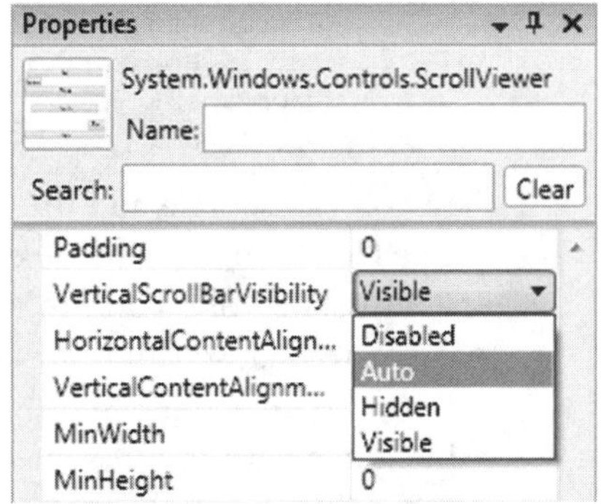

Figure 4.18 Setting the vertical scrollbar's visibility

4.3.2 The Expander control

Earlier, we suggested that one place to use a `StackPanel` is with expanding panels—when the panels expand or contract, everything else changes size automatically. The WPF team has been nice enough to provide an expanding/contracting control which makes this behavior easy to demonstrate. (We assume they put it in for the convenience of the

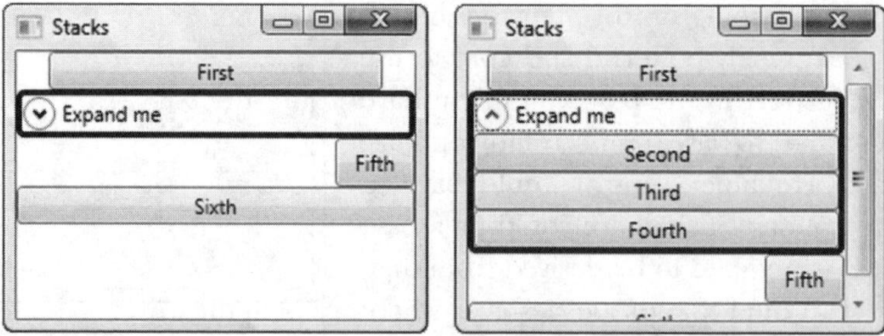

Figure 4.19 Expander shown unexpanded and expanded

authors of this book.) The Expander control works similarly to the sections in Windows Explorer that allow you to show or hide different sections. Figure 4.19 shows our sample with an Expander bar added.

We put a thick border around the Expander so it would be easier to see. Also notice that, as well as moving everything down, we got our automatic scrollbar after expanding. Listing 4.9 shows the XAML for the Expander.

Listing 4.9 Expander added to `StackPanel`

```
<ScrollViewer VerticalScrollBarVisibility="Auto">
  <StackPanel Orientation="Vertical">
    <Button Width="200" >First</Button>
    <Expander Header="Expand me"
        BorderThickness="3" BorderBrush="Black">      ❶ Adds Expander
      <StackPanel>                                   ❷ Adds panel in Expander
        <Button>Second</Button>
        <Button>Third</Button>
        <Button>Fourth</Button>
      </StackPanel>
    </Expander>
    <Button Padding="10 4" HorizontalAlignment="Right">Fifth</Button>
    <Button HorizontalAlignment="Stretch">Sixth</Button>
  </StackPanel>
</ScrollViewer>
```

As you can see, we add the definition for an `Expander` panel into the `StackPanel` ❶. The Header defines the text that appears at the top of the section. We also set the border thickness and color to make the content a little easier to see.

Note that we can't put the buttons directly inside the `Expander`. As with *most* controls, the `Expander` can only contain one thing: its contents. If we want to add multiple items, we have to put something inside the `Expander` that can hold some number of other things. The `StackPanel`, as with all the other layout panels, can hold multiple items, so we can add another `StackPanel` ❷.

The `StackPanel` itself solves some specific layout scenarios, but it's quite flexible. It *could* be used, for example, to build a calculator. You should be able to see how this would work—one vertical `StackPanel` containing a number of vertical `StackPanels` for the buttons. It wouldn't be easy, but it would be possible. In the next section, we will talk about the DockPanel. The DockPanel can be used to solve some of the same problems but in a different way. As with the StackPanel, the DockPanel, while flexible, is designed to handle a different set of scenarios.

4.4 The DockPanel layout

A DockPanel is useful when you want to position various elements on the edges of your window. For example, you might put a menu and a toolbar at the top, an explorer bar at the left, and a status bar at the bottom. The remaining space would contain the main content with which the user interacts. As with a StackPanel, if you put a series of items on the same side, they will stack one after the other. In fact, if you add all the items at the top or the left, the behavior will be similar to that of a StackPanel.

Similar but not identical. The big difference is that a StackPanel keeps taking up space as you add more items (the reason we added a scrollbar), whereas a DockPanel tries to constrain all its content in the available space. Figure 4.20 shows what happens when we take some of the content from the example StackPanel and put it into a DockPanel, but with everything docked to the top.

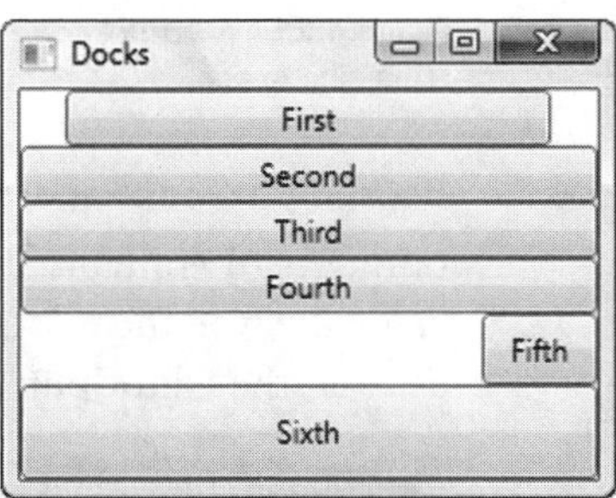

Figure 4.20 By default, a `DockPanel` tries to use up the available space.

Notice that the Sixth button has been expanded to fill the remaining available space. By default, the last control always takes up all the remaining space, although you could change that behavior by setting the LastChildFill property:

```
<DockPanel LastChildFill="False">
```

If LastChildFill is turned off (it defaults to True), then the last control is docked like any other control, and nothing fills any remaining space. If you do this and then set the Sixth button to be docked to the top, then the result would look similar to a StackPanel; but, if you want that type of behavior, the StackPanel is obviously a better fit. Also, notice that the properties we'd set previously for some of the controls are applied on the DockPanel as well—properties such as Width, Padding, and HorizontalAlignment.

Of course, the more common use of a DockPanel is to lay out a number of different controls on different edges of the screen, as seen in figure 4.21.

If you were brave, you could probably emulate all this docking with the use of a series of nested StackPanels, but the DockPanel is rather more appropriate. Let's see how all of this is defined.

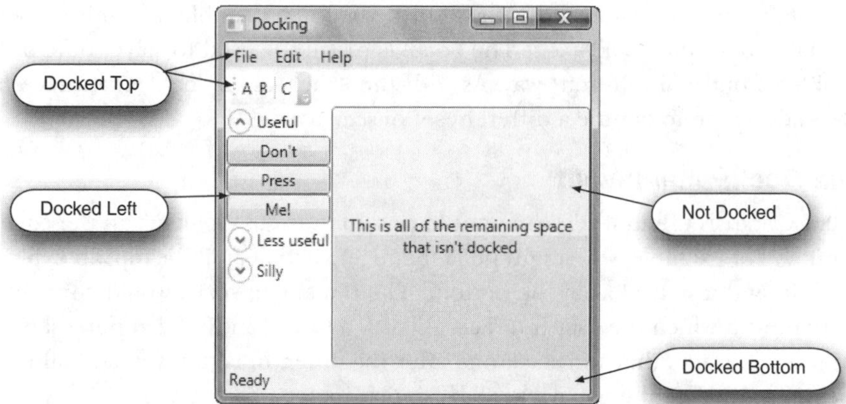

Figure 4.21 A `DockPanel` with items docked to most sides and a control in the remaining space

4.4.1 Defining a DockPanel in XAML

Listing 4.10 contains the XAML for the layout shown in figure 4.21. We can either manually type the XAML or use the editor, although we'd have to clear some properties that the editor puts into place.

Listing 4.10 XAML for a `DockPanel` with a number of real-looking controls

```
<DockPanel x:Name="dockPanel1">
  <Menu DockPanel.Dock="Top">                         <- Docks menu at top
    <MenuItem Header="_File"/>
    <MenuItem Header="_Edit"/>
    <MenuItem Header="_Help"/>
  </Menu>
  <ToolBarTray Background="White" DockPanel.Dock="Top">   <- Docked top
    <ToolBar Band="1" BandIndex="1">                  <- Toolbar tray holds toolbar
      <Button>A</Button>
      <Button>B</Button>
      <Separator/>
      <Button>C</Button>
    </ToolBar>
  </ToolBarTray>
  <StatusBar DockPanel.Dock="Bottom">                 <- Docks status bar at bottom
    <StatusBarItem>
      <TextBlock>Ready</TextBlock>
    </StatusBarItem>
  </StatusBar>
  <StackPanel DockPanel.Dock="Left">                  <- StackPanel with several expanders on left
    <Expander Header="Useful">
      <StackPanel>
        <Button>Don't</Button>
        <Button>Press</Button>
        <Button>Me!</Button>
      </StackPanel>
    </Expander>
```

```
    <Expander Header="Less useful"></Expander>
    <Expander Header="Silly"></Expander>
  </StackPanel>
  <Button Padding="10 10">
    <TextBlock TextWrapping="Wrap" TextAlignment="Center">This is all
       of the remaining space that is not docked</TextBlock>
  </Button>
</DockPanel>
```

Control takes up remaining space and isn't docked

Once again, we're setting properties on the controls that don't belong to the controls themselves, but are used by the parent:

```
DockPanel.Dock="Top"
```

Dock is also an attached property, as we talked about when discussing the Canvas in section 4.2.3, and can be set to Top, Bottom, Left, or Right. The order in which the controls are listed is also important. For example, if we put the status bar *after* the StackPanel on the left that's designed to look like an explorer bar, we'd get a result like that in figure 4.22.

Figure 4.22 If we order controls differently in a DockPanel, we'll get different results.

See how the status bar no longer goes all the way across the bottom. WPF has some nice support for menus, toolbars, and the like. We'll see much more of this in chapter 10.

We can also add items to a DockPanel programmatically.

4.4.2 *Setting up a DockPanel programmatically*

Setting up the DockPanel programmatically is similar to the way we set up the Canvas. Listing 4.11 shows some code added to the Loaded event handler of the Window that adds a right-docked control.

Listing 4.11 Adding a control to DockPanel programatically

```
protected void Window_Loaded(object sender, RoutedEventArgs e)
{
  Button buttonRight = new Button{Content = "Right"};
  DockPanel.SetDock(buttonRight, Dock.Right);          ❶ Sets Docking
  dockPanel1.Children.Insert(0,buttonRight);           ❷ Adds control
}
```

To make this work, we register for the Loaded event in the Window:

```
Loaded="Window_Loaded"
```

We could also have gone to the Events page of the properties editor and double-clicked the Loaded event to have our handler be automatically created.

On the DockPanel, there are similar methods to the Canvas.SetLeft method. In particular, SetDock ❶ is a static method on Canvas that sets the dock side.

To add the control to the DockPanel, we put it in the Children collection ❷. We give the DockPanel the name of dockPanel1 by adding a Name="dockPanel1" attribute to the XAML. Although we could Add the Button to the Children collection, we instead call Insert and force the Button to be at the beginning. We do this because the order within the collection changes the docking behavior, as you saw earlier.

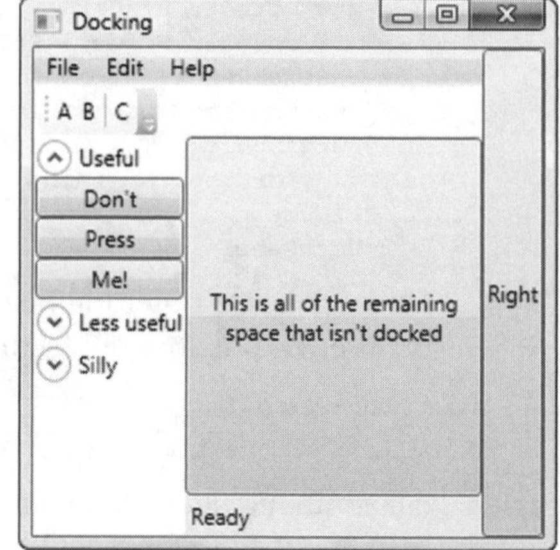

Figure 4.23 A complex demonstration of docking with the DockPanel. Everything was done in XAML except adding the Right control.

Figure 4.23 shows the DockPanel with the new, added Button.

It would be possible to build the calculator with a DockPanel, but boy, would it hurt. It might make sense to use a DockPanel if, for example, you want to add a menu to the top of the calculator and some extra slide-out advanced functionality. The display and buttons for the calculator are best left to a different type of layout. In most applications, you'll likely use multiple layouts together.

The next section introduces the WrapPanel layout. The WrapPanel is probably the most specific of the standard layouts and would, arguably, be the hardest to use to build the calculator—unless you really like strange wrappy calculators.

4.5 The WrapPanel layout

As the name implies, the WrapPanel wraps its children, sort of like word wrap in a document. It shoves as many things on a line as possible and then moves the next item to the next line. A good example of this type of functionality is Photoshop's control palette. The palette contains a series of tools, and as you size the palette, the palette's contents get moved around, as in figure 4.24.

The XAML for a WrapPanel is pretty straightforward—just the WrapPanel tag and its list of children.

Figure 4.24 All the Buttons are in a WrapPanel. As the available space changes, the Buttons wrap accordingly.

```
<WrapPanel>
  <Button Width="30">A</Button>
  <Button Width="30">B</Button>
  ...
  <Button Width="30">P</Button>
</WrapPanel>
```

We can also have the WrapPanel wrap vertically instead of horizontally:

```
<WrapPanel Orientation="Vertical">
```

This snippet gives the expected result shown in figure 4.25.

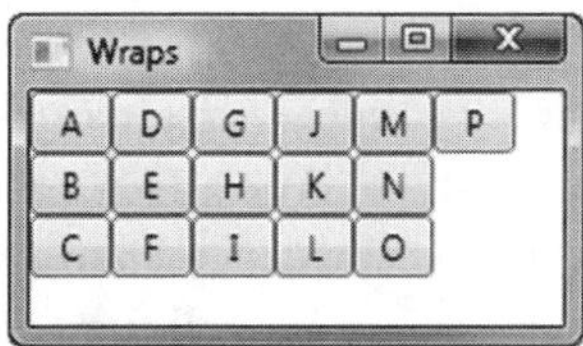

Figure 4.25 WrapPanel with vertical orientation

By default, each item takes up the amount of space that it desires based on its content, margins, padding, and so on. But the WrapPanel lets us specify the amount of space that *every* item should take up. If the space specified is bigger than the items would be, the items are placed appropriately in the space (based on the alignment properties). If, on the other hand, the items don't fit, they will be cut off. For example, if we specify a width for all items (using the ItemWidth property), the Buttons will all get cut off. Here's the XAML:

```
<WrapPanel ItemWidth="20">
```

And figure 4.26 shows the results.

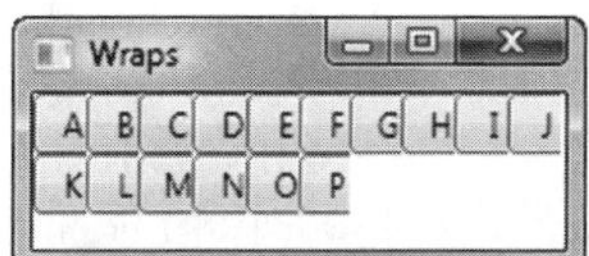

Figure 4.26 Limiting all items to less space than they require

Kind of a neat effect, but probably not that desirable. The XAML in listing 4.12 sets the spacing to a larger value, but also sets some options on the Buttons to show the effects. The results are shown in figure 4.27.

Listing 4.12 Specifying Width and Height for items and then setting different properties

```
<WrapPanel ItemWidth="40" ItemHeight="40">           ❶
  <Button Width="30">A</Button>                     ❷
  <Button Padding="10 10">B</Button>              ❸
  <Button Padding="30 30">C</Button>                ❹
  <Button Margin="10 10">D</Button>                      ❺
  <Button HorizontalAlignment="Right">E</Button>        ❻
  <Button HorizontalAlignment="Left" >F</Button>            ❼
  <Button HorizontalAlignment="Stretch">G</Button>              ❽
  <Button Width="30" VerticalAlignment="Top"          ❾
     HorizontalAlignment="Left">H</Button>
  <Button Width="30" VerticalAlignment="Bottom"       ❿
     HorizontalAlignment="Right">I</Button>
  <Button Width="60" Height="60">J</Button>           ⓫
  <Button Width="30">K</Button>
...
  <Button Width="30">P</Button>        ⓬
</WrapPanel>
```

Every item will be provided with exactly 40 pixels of width and height ❶. The properties on each Button determine how that space is used.

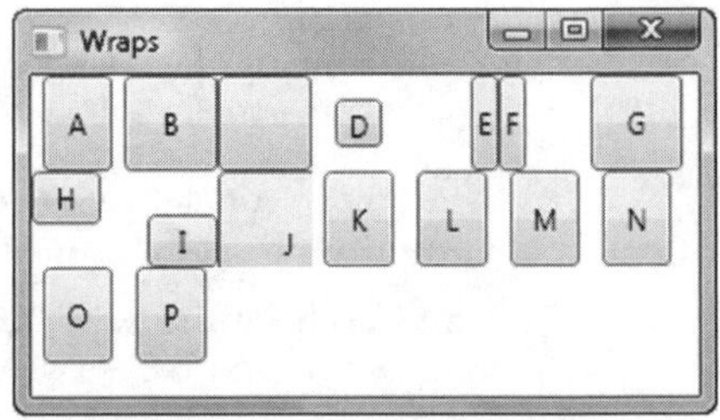

Figure 4.27 The results from listing 4.12. Setting the space to use for each item and then setting properties.

We explicitly set the width of the `Button` ❷. Because the width is less than the space provided, space appears on either side of the `Button`.

We add padding around the content ❸. This makes the `Button` almost fill the available space.

We add a lot more padding ❹. Because the `Button` is still just taking up the available 40x40 space, the text is pushed off of the `Button`, so it appears blank.

We add a margin around the `Button` ❺, shrinking its size.

We tell the `Button` to be aligned horizontally to the right ❻, moving the `Button` to the right edge of the space.

We tell the `Button` to be aligned horizontally to the left ❼, moving the `Button` to the left edge of the space.

We tell the `Button` to stretch horizontally ❽, making it take up the entire width. This is the default behavior.

By setting the vertical and horizontal alignment ❾, we move the `Button` to the upper-left corner of the available space.

This ❿ is similar to the previous `Button`, except that we move the `Button` to the lower-right corner.

By explicitly setting the width and height to values greater than the available space ⓫, the `Button` no longer fits in the provided space and so is cut off.

The last `Button` ⓬ isn't fancy—a truly boring button.

We'd like to keep talking about the `WrapPanel` (and, if we were paid by the word, we probably would). But that's pretty much all there is to say. When we started out, we didn't think that there were that many uses for the `WrapPanel`, but it has turned out to be surprisingly useful. For example, we often use it to hold the content within `ListBoxes` when we want to show several different values. If the `ListBox` is wide enough, the items all fit on one line, but if not, each item wraps onto a second line.

There is one more major layout panel—the `Grid`. It has a large number of options, so we moved it to its own chapter, chapter 5. (We *are* paid by the chapter.)

But, before we get to that, we want to talk about a few more layout-type things. The next section covers some items that don't exactly fit into our discussion of layout panels but are, nonetheless, related to laying out content.

4.6 Other layout options

In addition to the `Grid` panel, which we'll spend most of chapter 5 discussing, a handful of other controls fall roughly into the categorization of *layout*. They either are specialized panels of one sort or another or provide layout-like functionality. We'll start by (briefly) talking about some of the specialized layout panels that exist for specific scenarios, and then we'll talk about the FlowDocument, which isn't a layout panel, per se, but a mechanism for laying out content in the manner of a word processor.

4.6.1 Specialized layout panels

In addition to the panels we've discussed, there's also a handful of other layout panels, which are all extremely specialized. Some things also have names that would *imply* that they're layout panels, but they are often unrelated.

Of the ones that are layout panels, you'll see things like TabPanel and VirtualizingStackPanel. These are primarily used by specific controls. For example, TabPanel handles the tabs that appear above a TabControl, wrapping or scrolling them as appropriate. VirtualizingStackPanel is a special control used by controls like ListBoxes to hold all the child items.

Back in the olden days (last year), the idea that you'd use a control that *held* controls representing each item in a ListBox would have caused serious laughter. The performance hit would have caused trouble somewhere around item 20. No longer—composition in WPF is so lightweight as to make it completely practical. Even so, you may have noticed the *Virtualizing* in VirtualizingStackPanel. That's because, with data binding, you might not want to create a control for every row of your one-million-row database.[3] There are also some pretty nifty features related to VirtualizingStackPanel, such as the ability to recycle containers that aren't on the screen or to defer scrolling until the user releases the scrollbar.

We're not going to go into any real detail on these other panels—just enough to let you know that they're there and you *might* want to use them for specialized purposes. More often you'll end up using them indirectly, via the controls they support.

You may also see, in your travels, reference to something called InkPanel. This is called InkPanel to confuse you because it isn't a layout panel—it's a control designed to collect input from users of tablet PCs. *Ink* is the tablet PC entry system.

Finally, you can also create your own layout panels. If you have a specific scenario, it isn't terribly hard to create a panel with its own rules and behaviors. But that's beyond the discussion of this chapter.

We do want to cover one other control in some detail—the FlowDocument. It works completely differently than all the layout panels we've discussed so far and, ostensibly, has a completely different purpose. But its purpose in life is to handle the layout and presentation of rich content, and for this reason, we think that this is a good place to mention it.

4.6.2 The FlowDocument

Rich application developers tend to look down a little on browser application developers. After all, Windows developers have the full power of the machine at their disposal, whereas browser developers are limited to whatever the browser is willing to expose.

---

[3] Stamps, movies, tooth collection, whatever—who are we to judge?

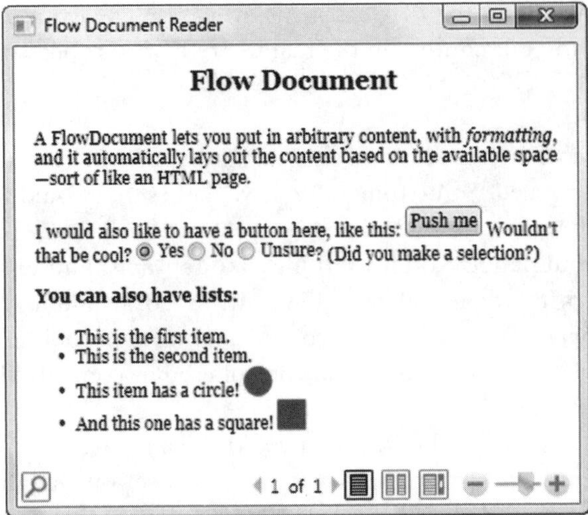

Figure 4.28 An example of a `FlowDocument` with some arbitrary content

For that reason, it's irritating to rich Windows application developers when there's something that can be done in a browser that's *really* difficult to do in rich applications.

One thing that's trivial in a browser and a royal pain in Windows is building document-flow-like UIs—a user interface where everything fills in the available space, wraps and flows like, well, a web page. Figure 4.28 shows an example of a `FlowDocument`.

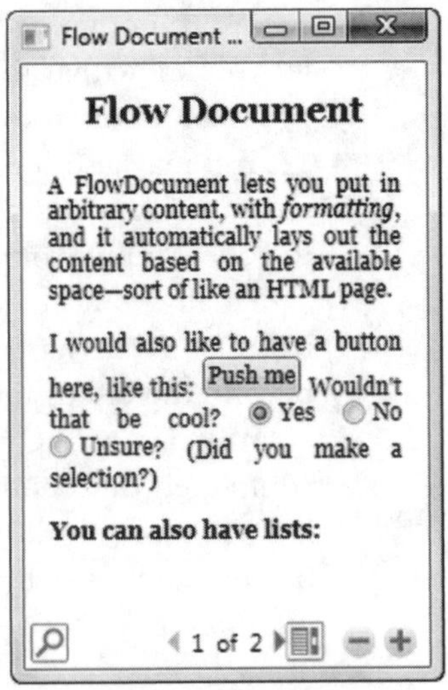

Figure 4.29 `FlowDocument` shrunk down

You can put text, formatting, controls, lists, drawing, and just about anything else in a `FlowDocument`. If you resize the available space (figure 4.29), the content will automatically be recalculated.

As you can see, it automatically repaginates. Also notice that there's a page count on the automatic toolbar that appears at the bottom. This is pretty cool—it lets you zoom in and out, change between different views, and move between pages, much like print preview. This isn't a coincidence. There's also a search feature (the magnifier on the left)—all for free.

Listing 4.13 shows the XAML for the `FlowDocument` shown in figures 4.28 and 4.29. We pretty much have to use XAML for this. The editor doesn't help at all with `FlowDocuments`, although that will hopefully change in the future (much the way that editors work directly with HTML today).

Listing 4.13 XAML for `FlowDocument` in previous figures

```
<FlowDocumentReader>
 <FlowDocument FontSize="12" xml:space="preserve">
```

1 Reader holds document

2 Preserves whitespace

```
    <Paragraph TextAlignment="Center" FontSize="18">        <-3 Places content in
      <Bold>Flow Document</Bold></Paragraph>                   Paragraph tag
    <Paragraph>A FlowDocument lets you put in arbitrary content,
      with <Italic>formatting</Italic>, and it automatically lays out the
      content based on the available space - sort of like an HTML
      page.</Paragraph>
    <Paragraph>I would also like to have a button here, like this:
      <Button>Push me</Button> Wouldn't that be cool?   <-
      <RadioButton IsChecked="True">Yes</RadioButton>     4 Adds controls
      <RadioButton>No</RadioButton> <RadioButton>Unsure</RadioButton>?
      (Did you make a selection)?</Paragraph>
    <Paragraph><Bold>You can also have lists:</Bold></Paragraph>
    <List>
      <ListItem><Paragraph>This is the first item</Paragraph></ListItem>
      <ListItem><Paragraph>This is the second item</Paragraph></ListItem>
      <ListItem><Paragraph>This item has a circle! <Ellipse Fill="Red"
        Width="20" Height="20"></Ellipse></Paragraph></ListItem>
      <ListItem><Paragraph>And this one has a square! <Rectangle
        Fill="Blue" Width="20" Height="20"></Rectangle>
        </Paragraph></ListItem>
    </List>
  </FlowDocument>
</FlowDocumentReader>
```

You can't just shove a `FlowDocument` directly into XAML. Instead, you have to put it into one of several container controls provided by WPF. In the example, we use a `FlowDocumentReader` ❶, which is a fairly rich document container—it provides the search, paging, and zoom controls.

You may remember the discussion on whitespace from chapter 3. The `FlowDocument` doesn't quite behave like regular XAML. By default, it does *not* use normalized spacing but automatically removes spacing around tags. Setting space to be preserved ❷ gives us a much better result but also means that we can't wrap lines. If you take the version of the listing as wrapped for the book, it gets seriously ugly.

All the content we put into a `FlowDocument` has to be inside of some sort of a container, such as a `Paragraph` ❸ or a `List`. `Paragraph` is a lot like a `TextBlock`, and we can add items in a similar way. `FlowDocument` also has support for tables, sections, and other word-processy things.

As with a `TextBlock`, we can add controls ❹. In this example, we add a button and some radio buttons. Later on, we add some shapes as well. To the layout manager, it's all the same.

One of the really, really cool things about WPF—something that we can't emphasize enough[4]—is that the whole system is based on composition. In the past, you might have bought a third-party control that let you deal with rich text, or, if desperate, made use of the built-in RTF control in Windows. That control did its own thing. Here, you have a control that lets you arbitrarily embed any type of control within it and handles it appropriately. More than that, the `FlowDocument` is held in a container

[4] Although you may feel that we've come close.

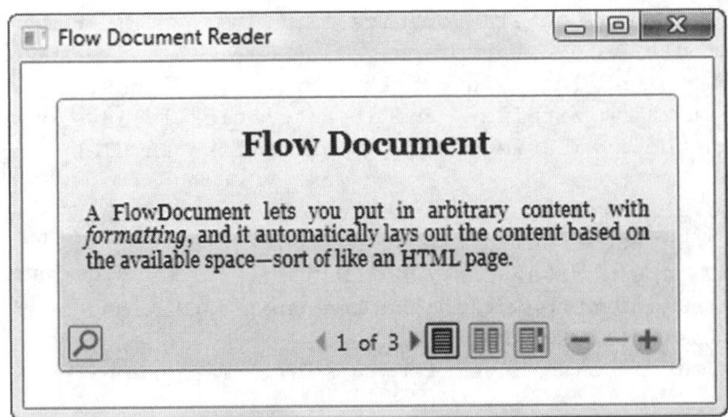

Figure 4.30 Controls can be composed with one another arbitrarily, such as putting a `FlowDocument` on a `Button`.

that's also a control, like any other, and can be used as one. Figure 4.30 shows the `FlowDocument` as the content of a (quite large) `Button`.

This was accomplished by putting in a panel (in this case a `DockPanel`), then a `Button`, and then putting the `FlowDocument` within it, as you can see in listing 4.14.

Listing 4.14 Embedding a `FlowDocument` within a `Button` within a `DockPanel`

```
<DockPanel>
  <Button Padding="20" Margin="40">
    <FlowDocumentReader>
      <FlowDocument FontSize="12" xml:space="preserve">
        <Paragraph TextAlignment="Center" FontSize="18">
          <Bold>Flow Document</Bold></Paragraph>
...other content here...
      </FlowDocument>
    </FlowDocumentReader>
  </Button>
</DockPanel>
```

There are also some issues to consider when controls are combined in this way. For example, the `FlowDocument` is a control that expects input, as is the `Button`. If you try clicking the `Button` over the area where the `FlowDocument` is located, you'll end up interacting with the `FlowDocument` instead.

The danger of creating custom behavior

The ability to compose controls arbitrarily is a double-edged sword. Just because you *can* do something doesn't mean that it makes good UI. In particular, you should avoid presenting users with completely unfamiliar controls in places where they're unexpected. That said, there are some places where this capability might make things clearer. For example, adding a slider to a button that controls what the button does *might* be a good way of making the behavior of the button clearer, but you have to weigh whether it will require additional dexterity of the user and whether the UI will be clearer by putting the slider next to the control (see figure 4.31)

Figure 4.31 The `Button` with the slider is cooler, but which is more usable?

We'll return to the `FlowDocument` in later chapters. One place where the `FlowDocument` really shines is when we want to print, which we will cover in chapter 18. The important thing to know is that it's an option for laying out content.

4.7 Summary

If you have come from the Windows Form or Windows SDK world, where you could just drag stuff onto a form and be done with it, all of this layout kerfuffle may seem like a major pain. In some respects, it is—particularly when you're first creating a UI. But the more you play around with your UI, and the more options you want to support, the more layout will make your life easier. In fact, once you get used to it, you may find, as we did, that using layout panels can be quicker than dragging and aligning controls.

We've yet to discuss one major layout panel in detail—the one that, frankly, you'll probably use more than any other—the `Grid`. A lot of concepts that applied to the other layouts also apply to the `Grid`. In chapter 5, we'll show you the `Grid`, and we'll use it to build our first real application.

5 The Grid panel

This chapter covers:

- The `Grid` layout
- Localizing with the `Grid`
- The `UniformGrid`
- Turning your $2000 computer into a $5 pocket calculator

So far we've spent a lot of time talking about all the different layout controls available—except the one that you're likely to use much of the time! The `Grid` panel control is the most powerful and, except for the `Canvas` which has no real rules, the most flexible. The `Grid` *can* be used to emulate the behavior of many of the other layout options, but it's easier to use the more appropriate layout panel.

Aside from being the default layout used by Visual Studio, the `Grid` is a good layout for things like dialogs with a number of interactive controls (text boxes, radio buttons, and so on). The `Grid` panel can also behave like a `Canvas` "explicit position" control with pseudo-docking abilities—although using the `Grid` in this way loses some of the advantages of layout.

This chapter will cover the `Grid` control fairly thoroughly, demonstrating how to use the `Grid` layout to lay out the calculator. So, why are we building a calculator?

After all, the operating system has one, and it's certainly not the most exciting application ever. The answer is that a calculator is complex enough to make use of a number of WPF capabilities and simple enough that the implementation won't get in our way or require a bunch of pages of code to make it work. The calculator also lends itself well to a `Grid`, although, as you'll see, the `Grid` is a good layout for many standard forms and dialogs.

5.1 Getting started with the Grid layout panel

The `Grid` layout, as its name implies, lays out controls in a grid, with rows and columns. Children can be placed within specific cells or can cross between cells. When you create a new Window, it automatically creates a new `Grid` panel. In fact, let's do that now—create a new WPF application. The application will come up with a default Window1 window that has a `Grid` on it. The `Grid` has exactly one row and one column, so you'd be forgiven for mistaking it for a blank `Canvas`. The `Canvas`-like behavior is taken a step further if you drag a control (such as a `Button`) onto the form—it stays where you drop it (figure 5.1).

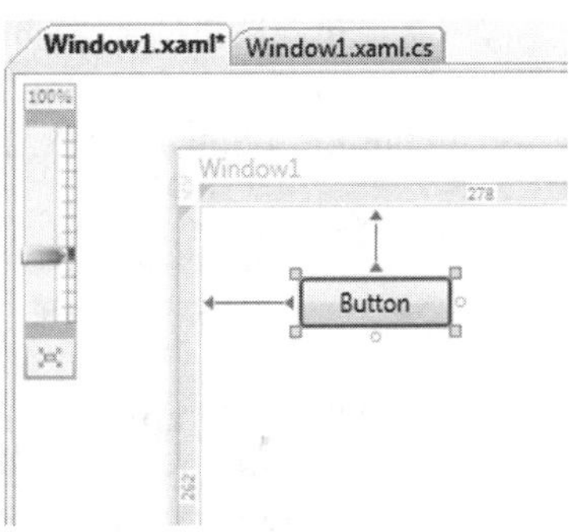

Figure 5.1 When we drop a control on the `Grid` editor, it acts as though it has been precisely positioned.

The short lines that appear between the left edge of the window and the button, and the top edge and button, indicate a type of anchoring. If you move closer to the right edge, you'll get a line there indicating that you're anchored to that edge, and so on. You click the little circles to anchor to the associated edge, or the triangles to unanchor.

As we mentioned earlier, this behavior is a sort of con, and it's a con that might cause you all sorts of problems down the road. It seems as though the Visual Studio developers wanted people to use layouts but were afraid that most wouldn't be bothered, so the `Grid` editor is a hybrid. It *emulates* fixed-position (`Canvas`) layout, but also acts as a `Grid` layout. If this were a `Canvas` layout, the XAML would look something like this:

```
<Canvas>
  <Button Canvas.Left="61" Canvas.Top="34"
    Width="75" Height="23">Button</Button>
</Canvas>
```

This provides the location and size of the `Button` in a fairly easy-to-follow format. Because we're using the `Grid` layout, though, the XAML looks like this:

```
<Grid>
  <Button Height="23" Margin="61,34,0,0" Name="button1"
    VerticalAlignment="Top" HorizontalAlignment="Left"
    Width="75">Button</Button>
</Grid>
```

Behind the scenes, the editor is using the `Height`, `Width`, `Alignment`, and `Margin` properties to force the `Button` to be positioned where it was dropped on the `Grid`. The editor does a nice job with this. If, for example, we want the button to stretch with the screen, we click the little circle on the right (figure 5.2).

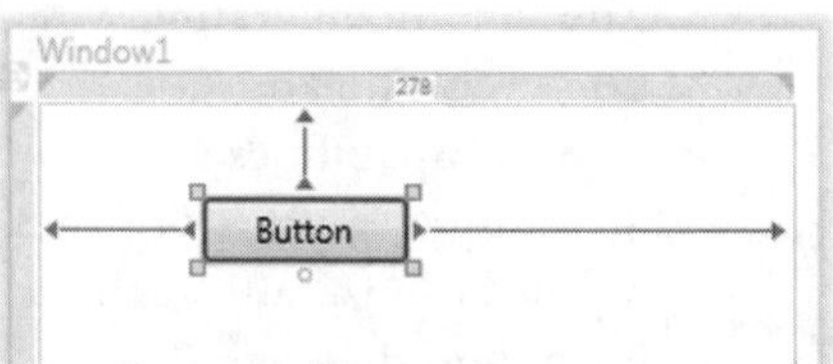

Figure 5.2 The `Button` is now anchored to the left and right edges. The arrows running from button to the sides indicate the edges against which the button is anchored.

See the line stretching to the right edge. Now when the window gets wider, so will the button. Look at the XAML for this change:

```
<Grid>
  <Button Height="23" Margin="61,34,142,0" Name="button1"
     VerticalAlignment="Top">Button</Button>
</Grid>
```

Looking for an `Anchor="Left,Right"` property? It's not there. Instead, the editor removes the `HorizontalAlignment` and the `Width` properties and sets the right margin to 142. This works. (In fact, it works rather more smoothly than Windows Forms anchoring.) But it isn't remotely intuitive. You can figure out what's going on outside the editor, but it's tricky. And if you want to make your own changes, you'll likely do a lot of head-scratching and experimenting to get the settings right.

There's another downside to this automatic `Grid`-panel behavior. When you start using the `Grid` *as a grid*—when you've added multiple rows and columns—you almost always want items to take up all the space within their individual cells (or have a particular margin). Unfortunately, the editor is busy trying to figure out clever margins and spaces, so it's a bit trickier to use the `Grid` layout in the way it's intended.

5.1.1 Modifying the Grid

When you do want to use the `Grid` "properly," you can either use the editor or directly edit the `Grid`'s XAML. In our experience, it's likely that you'll end up doing both—using the editor to roughly get the right things in place and then editing the XAML to get rid of extraneous attributes and set things the way you'd like. This is true when setting up the basic row/column layout and also when adding items to the layout.

ADDING ROWS AND COLUMNS TO A GRID

We can add rows and columns either using the editor or directly via XAML. To use the editor, we click the top of the grid, and a thick border appears with a number at the top and a number at the left side. These numbers indicate the width and height of the current cell. If we click somewhere on the top, a column separator appears, allowing us to drag it back and forth and position it as we prefer (figure 5.3).

Note the small numbers above each column indicating its size. Now that there's a separator, there are two column definitions, as you can see if you look at the XAML:

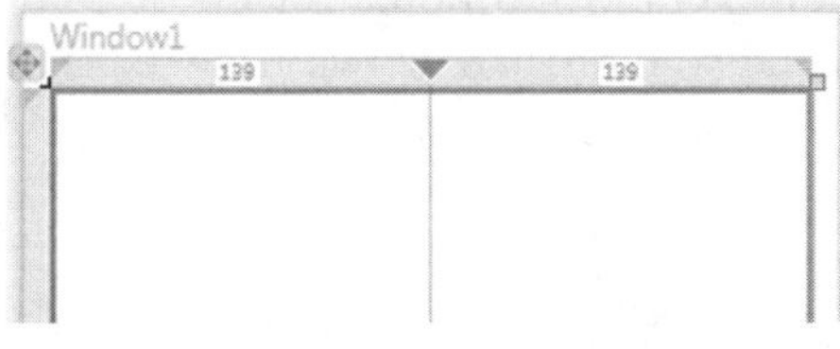

Figure 5.3 Clicking on the Grid control's header adds a separator, creating two separate column definitions.

```
<Grid>
  <Grid.ColumnDefinitions>
    <ColumnDefinition Width="146*" />
    <ColumnDefinition Width="146*" />
  </Grid.ColumnDefinitions>
</Grid>
```

The `146` is the number of pixels, but notice the `*` after each number? That's the editor being clever. This asterisk notation is used to imply a *part* of the available space. With the asterisk, the width of the column automatically changes proportionally to the leading number. Because the numbers in front of each column are the same, each column gets exactly half of the space available. In fact, we can change the values to make this a little more obvious:

```
<Grid>
  <Grid.ColumnDefinitions>
    <ColumnDefinition Width="0.5*" />
    <ColumnDefinition Width="0.5*" />
  </Grid.ColumnDefinitions>
</Grid>
```

This change has no effect on the width of the columns. If we make the entire window bigger, each column continues to take up half of the available space. This mechanism works in a similar manner to an HTML table, although the notation is more flexible. If we *don't* want the width to change, we can specify an explicit number of pixels:

```
<Grid>
  <Grid.ColumnDefinitions>
    <ColumnDefinition Width="146" />
    <ColumnDefinition Width="146" />
  </Grid.ColumnDefinitions>
</Grid>
```

With this change, the columns are now exactly 146 pixels each and don't change size when the parent does. Alternatively, we can mix the two formats. The following XAML makes the first column stay the same size, but makes the second column take up all remaining space:

```
<Grid>
  <Grid.ColumnDefinitions>
    <ColumnDefinition Width="146" />
    <ColumnDefinition Width="*" />
  </Grid.ColumnDefinitions>
</Grid>
```

We can specify other values to create different proportional relationships. For example, the following XAML makes the second column take up twice the space as the first:

```
<Grid>
  <Grid.ColumnDefinitions>
    <ColumnDefinition Width="1*" />
    <ColumnDefinition Width="2*" />
  </Grid.ColumnDefinitions>
</Grid>
```

Figure 5.4 shows the result.

To determine the percentage of the space used by a column using this notation, we take the number in front of the asterisk and divide it by the *total* of all the numbers in front of all the asterisks. The total in the example is 1 + 2 = 3, so the first column takes up one-third and the second takes up two-thirds. Amazing how first grade math comes in useful again.[1]

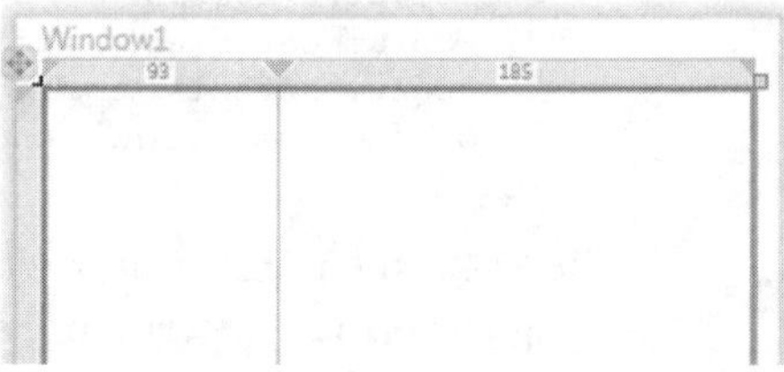

Figure 5.4 The asterisks in the column widths make the sizes proportional, so column 2 takes up twice the space as column 1.

You can either drag all the columns onto the grid and then manually edit them, or you can add them directly to the XAML. (It's often easier to add the first one via the editor and then do the rest in XAML by copying.) You can also edit the `Columns` property in the Properties grid by clicking the … button next to ColumnDefinition (figure 5.5).

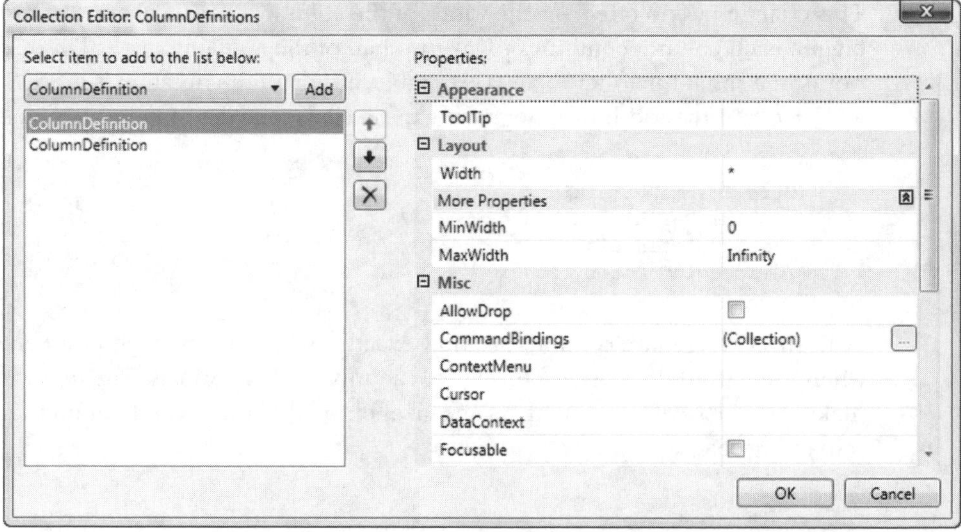

Figure 5.5 You can edit the column (and row) definitions in the interactive editor.

[1] Also very useful when making bets while playing poker.

As you've probably guessed, adding rows is exactly the same, except you click the left edge instead of the top of the grid, and you have to turn your head sideways to read the little numbers. Here's the XAML for a grid with two rows and two columns:

```
<Grid>
  <Grid.RowDefinitions>
    <RowDefinition Height="*" />    ❶
    <RowDefinition Height="*" />
  </Grid.RowDefinitions>
  <Grid.ColumnDefinitions>
    <ColumnDefinition Width="*" />
    <ColumnDefinition Width="*" />
  </Grid.ColumnDefinitions>
</Grid>
```

Note that an asterisk by itself `"*"` ❶ is equivalent to 1*.

ARRANGING CONTENT IN THE GRID

Having an empty grid is fun and all, but unless you can put some content into it, it isn't very useful. If you're following along, go ahead and drag a `Button` into the lower-right square (figure 5.6).

As you can see, the editor is trying to be helpful again by automatically figuring out margins to keep the control where you dropped it. But if you're using a `Grid` layout, chances are that you want the `Grid` to do the laying out, rather than relying on fixed positioning. The main thing you need to do to fix this is to set the `Margin` property to `0`, although if you've done any playing, you may have to set a few other properties, as shown in table 5.1.

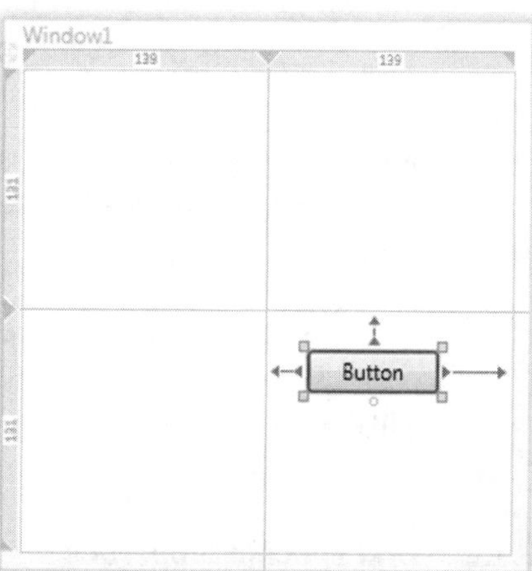

Figure 5.6 Dragging content into a cell of a `Grid` doesn't entirely do what we'd like.

Table 5.1 Properties that need to be changed to make a control take up the entire cell

Property	Value
`Height`	`Auto`—Tells the control to figure out its height based on content and layout, rather than a fixed value
`Width`	`Auto` (Should already be set to this)
`VerticalAlignment`	`Stretch`—Takes up all the available space.
`HorizontalAlignment`	`Stretch`
`Margin`	`0` (The main way in which the editor positions controls within a grid cell)

Width	Auto
Height	Auto
HorizontalAlignment	Stretch
VerticalAlignment	Stretch
Margin	0

Figure 5.7 All the properties you need to set to make a control take up an entire grid cell are grouped together in the Layout section of the editor.

Fortunately, all these properties are together in the Layout section of the Properties grid (figure 5.7), so it's not too tough to set them all in one go.

When you've done all that, you should have something that looks like figure 5.8.

If you look at the XAML, you'll see the following:

```
<Button Grid.Row="1" Name="button1"
  Grid.Column="1">Button</Button>
```

Although, if you've set and then unset some properties, it may look like this:

```
<Button Grid.Row="1" Height="Auto"
  Margin="0,0,0,0" Name="button1"
   VerticalAlignment="Stretch"
  Grid.Column="1">Button</Button>
```

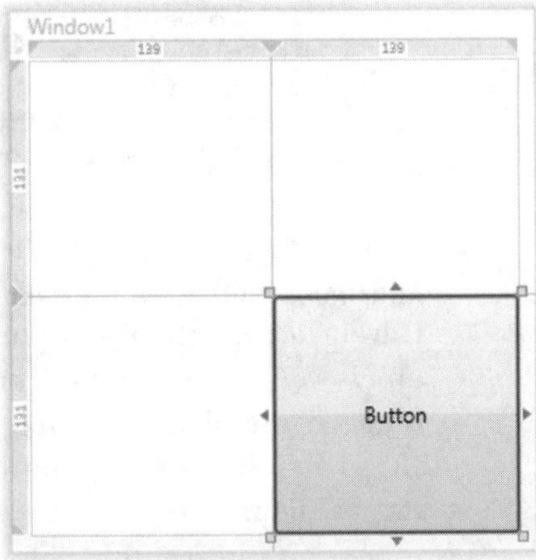

Figure 5.8 Making content take up all available space

This is equivalent to the first example, but it shows default values for some additional properties.

5.1.2 *Grid specific properties*

A couple of properties we haven't discussed yet are `Grid.Row` and `Grid.Column`. As you've probably surmised, these specify which row and column the item should go into. These are attached properties, like `Canvas.Left` on the `Canvas` and `DockPanel.Dock` on the `DockPanel`. The values are 0-based, so specifying 1 means that you want to put something into the second row or column.

If you ever want to drop content into a cell and be done with it, these would be the only properties that you'd need. But suppose you want content to be contained within more than one cell? For example, in the calculator, if we had only buttons, we could easily shove them into the appropriate cells, but we also have some header text and the output display going all the way across the calculator (see figure 5.9).

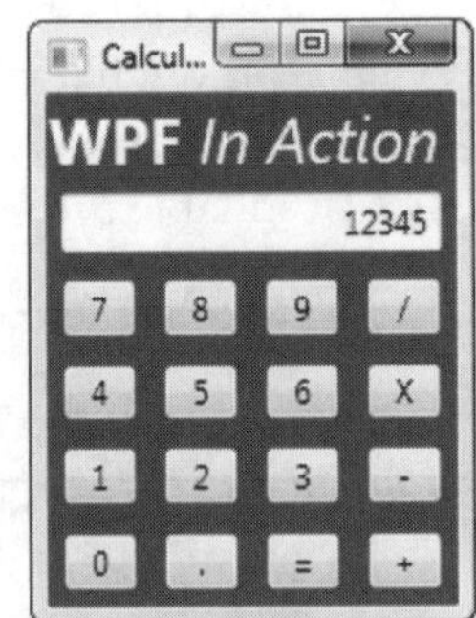

Figure 5.9 The header text and the output display for the calculator go all the way across the `Grid`.

It's easy to do this with a grid. All you have to do is to tell the control to span multiple cells:

```
<Button Grid.Row="0" Name="button1" Grid.Column="0"
   Grid.ColumnSpan="2">Button</Button>
```

`ColumnSpan` says that the content should span this many columns. Note that we moved the button to the upper-left cell so that there's space for the button to expand. The span starts with the specified cell and moves over as many additional cells as specified in the `ColumnSpan` attribute (minus one for where it started). Figure 5.10 shows the results.

At the risk of belaboring the point—To make the content span multiple rows, we specify a value for the `RowSpan` attribute:

```
<Button Grid.Row="0" Name="button1" Grid.Column="0"
  Grid.RowSpan="2">Button</Button>
```

The result is shown in figure 5.11.

Figure 5.10 The button spans two columns.

Figure 5.11 The button spans two rows.

We can also span both columns and rows. This isn't particularly interesting yet, we admit, but in the next section we'll make use of all these properties to build the initial calculator UI. This will, no doubt, send you into paroxysms of excitement.

5.2 Using the Grid layout to build a calculator UI

It seems like we've been hinting about this calculator thing for a long time now. We're finally going to start building it! Rather than jumping nostrils-first into the XAML, though, let's first do a little bit of planning.

5.2.1 Planning the calculator

With Windows Forms or MFC, you'd probably have just started dragging buttons onto a form—and be done by now. But if you decided you wanted to change the way your buttons looked, you'd have had to spend quite a bit of time fiddling around. With

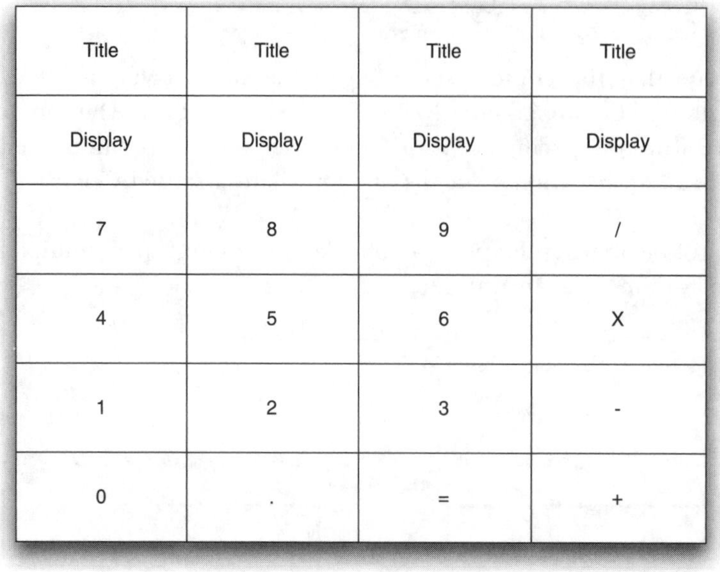

Title	Title	Title	Title
Display	Display	Display	Display
7	8	9	/
4	5	6	X
1	2	3	-
0	.	=	+

Figure 5.12 This is one possible way to lay out the calculator on a grid.

WPF, the planning up front takes more time, but changing things later will usually be quite a bit easier.

If you look at a simple calculator, with the standard numbers 0-9, the four standard operators, and an equals button, you can probably visualize how that would go onto a grid. But we went ahead and sketched it out on the grid before creating the control. It's probably overkill in this example, but, with more complicated UIs, a few sketches on a whiteboard up front can save a bunch of time later. A sketch for the calculator looks something like figure 5.12.

As you can see, we have six rows and four columns. We want the title and the display to span all four columns. Each button is in a cell by itself. We can start with all the rows and columns being the same size, although later on we might want the display to be a little narrower. Because the calculator is fairly simple, the up-front planning doesn't take long, but it will save some time when we set up the layout.

5.2.2 Laying out the calculator

We're finally ready to start creating some XAML. If you want, you can use the Window1 window that WPF creates when you create a new WPF application, or you can create a new window called *Calculator.* If you do the latter, you need to change the startup URI in App.xaml to point to the right place.

You can use the editor to set up the rows and columns, add the buttons, and then edit the XAML to get rid of extraneous attributes. Listing 5.1 shows the XAML for our first rough attempt.

Listing 5.1 Creating a calculator laid out in XAML

```
<Grid>
  <Grid.RowDefinitions>            Defines six rows
    <RowDefinition />
    <RowDefinition />
    <RowDefinition />
    <RowDefinition />
    <RowDefinition />
    <RowDefinition />
  </Grid.RowDefinitions>
  <Grid.ColumnDefinitions>         And four columns
    <ColumnDefinition  />
    <ColumnDefinition  />
    <ColumnDefinition  />
    <ColumnDefinition  />
  </Grid.ColumnDefinitions>
  <TextBlock Grid.Column="0" Grid.Row="0" Grid.ColumnSpan="4" FontSize="24"
    VerticalAlignment="Center">
    <Bold>WPF</Bold> <Italic>In Action</Italic> Calculator
  </TextBlock>                     TextBlock with header text spans four columns
  <TextBox Name="textBoxDisplay" Grid.Column="0" Grid.ColumnSpan="4"
     Grid.Row="1" VerticalContentAlignment="Center"
     HorizontalContentAlignment="Right">12345</TextBox>              ❶
  <Button Grid.Column="0" Grid.Row="2" Name="button7" >7</Button>
  <Button Grid.Column="1" Grid.Row="2" Name="button8" >8</Button>    ❷
  <Button Grid.Column="2" Grid.Row="2" Name="button9" >9</Button>
  <Button Grid.Column="3" Grid.Row="2" Name="buttonDivide" >/</Button>
  <Button Grid.Column="0" Grid.Row="3" Name="button4" >4</Button>
  <Button Grid.Column="1" Grid.Row="3" Name="button5" >5</Button>
  <Button Grid.Column="2" Grid.Row="3" Name="button6" >6</Button>
  <Button Grid.Column="3" Grid.Row="3" Name="buttonTimes" >X</Button>
  <Button Grid.Column="0" Grid.Row="4" Name="button1" >1</Button>
  <Button Grid.Column="1" Grid.Row="4" Name="button2" >2</Button>
  <Button Grid.Column="2" Grid.Row="4" Name="button3" >3</Button>
  <Button Grid.Column="3" Grid.Row="4" Name="buttonMinus" >-</Button>
  <Button Grid.Column="0" Grid.Row="5" Name="button0" >0</Button>
  <Button Grid.Column="1" Grid.Row="5" Name="buttonDecimal" >.</Button>
  <Button Grid.Column="2" Grid.Row="5" Name="buttonEquals" >=</Button>
  <Button Grid.Column="3" Grid.Row="5" Name="buttonPlus" >+</Button>
</Grid>
```

In addition to setting up the `TextBox` ❶ to span four columns, we also set its value to 12345, so it can be easily seen. Obviously, when we make the calculator work for real, this value will be the current calculated value.

If you notice, each button has a row and a column specified ❷. These are attached properties that the `Grid` panel uses to figure out where to place each control. We've also customized each `Button`'s name. This step isn't strictly required but makes referring to the controls from code easier, if we want to do that later.

If you run the program at this point, without doing much more than dropping a bunch of controls onto a form, you have something that looks remarkably close to a calculator (figure 5.13).

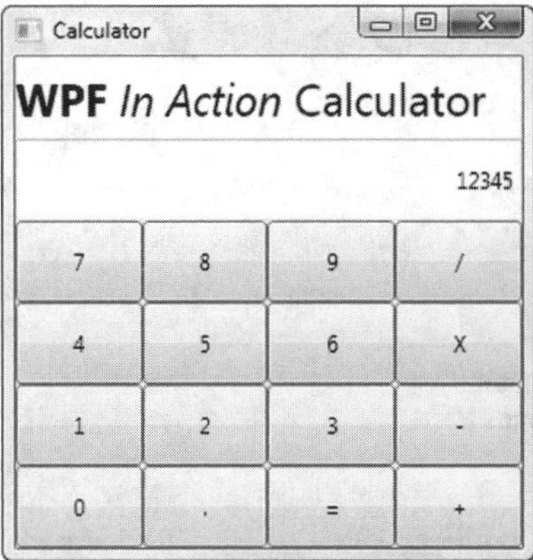

Figure 5.13 This is a first pass at creating a calculator using a `Grid` layout to hold the various buttons and controls.

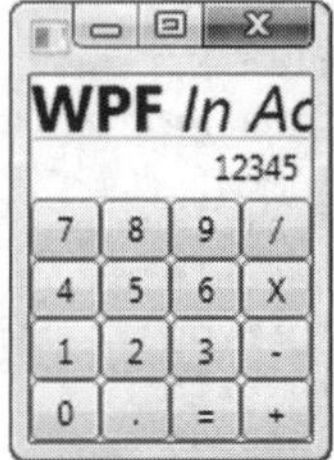

Figure 5.14 Iddy-biddy calculator. Note that, except for the fonts, everything is automatically scaling.

Also, because of the use of the `Grid` layout, the calculator automatically handles sizing—whether we stretch the dialog or whether we constrain the whole grid in some other container. Figure 5.14 shows the calculator shrunk down.

As we'll demonstrate in the next section, you can also use all the other formatting options you've seen.

5.2.3 *Tweaking appearance*

We already have something that looks much like a calculator, but we can improve the look-and-feel with a few simple tweaks. For example, we can put some margins around the display and the buttons to make things more appealing (listing 5.2). Note that the easiest way to do this is to select all the buttons in the editor, and then set the `Margin` in the Properties grid.

Listing 5.2 Adding margins around text display and buttons

```
<TextBox Name="textBoxDisplay" Margin="5" Grid.Column="0"
   Grid.ColumnSpan="4"
  Grid.Row="1" VerticalContentAlignment="Center"
  HorizontalContentAlignment="Right">12345</TextBox>
<Button Grid.Column="0" Grid.Row="2" Margin="5" Name="button7">7</Button>
<Button Grid.Column="1" Grid.Row="2" Margin="5" Name="button8" >8</Button>
...
<Button Grid.Column="3" Grid.Row="5" Margin="5" Name="buttonPlus" >+</
   Button>
```

This addition gives a slightly more attractive output, as shown in figure 5.15.

We've truncated listing 5.2, but we added the same margin value to every single button—a pain. If we want to change the value (say to 10 pixels instead of 5), we have to go through and update every margin statement—even more of a pain. Fortunately, there are several ways in which we can define those margins generally and have them apply to the buttons, via the use of styles and control templates. That's the topic of chapter 6, so we won't spend much time tweaking the look-and-feel of the buttons at the moment.

There are a few things that we'd like to show you to give a hint about what you can do cosmetically with WPF and also to demonstrate some more variants on XAML. For a start, let's change the background of the calculator to blue and the title text to white (so that it's easier to read on the blue):

```
<Grid Background="Blue">
...
    <TextBlock Foreground="White"
  Grid.Column="0" Grid.Row="0"
       Grid.ColumnSpan="4" FontSize="24"
  VerticalAlignment="Center">
      <Bold>WPF</Bold> <Italic>In
  Action</Italic> Calculator
    </TextBlock>
...
```

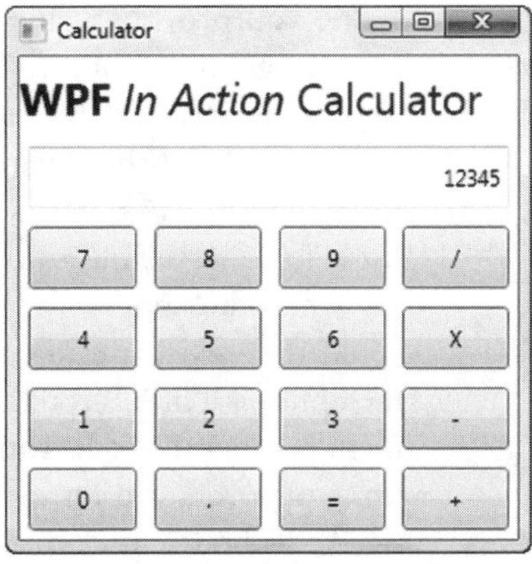

Figure 5.15 Adding margins to the button

Simple enough—we set the `Background` property of the entire grid to `Blue` and the `Foreground` property on the TextBlock to `White`. These, by the way, are from the web list of colors that you might recognize from HTML or the color selector from Windows Forms. We can also specify colors in Hex:

```
<Grid Background="#0000FF">
```

is equivalent to

```
<Grid Background="Blue">
```

The # notation expects either three or four two-digit hex numbers to follow it. Three values represent the Red, Green and Blue values for an RGB color (#RRGGBB). Four values add a preceding Alpha value for transparency (#AARRGGBB). Figure 5.16 shows the blue calculator.

Although the calculator is more colorful in blue (If you aren't coding along, you can see the results with a pair of 3D glasses—just look through the blue side. You might also want to keep them handy for chapter 15 on drawing in 3D where we make extensive use of the red side.), the main reason we wanted to show you this was to talk about properties like `Background`. The format (`Background="Blue"`) is a shorthand for

Figure 5.16 This calculator is blue, even though it looks gray in black-and-white!

```
<Grid>
  <Grid.Background>
    <SolidColorBrush>Blue</SolidColorBrush>
  </Grid.Background>
  ...
</Grid>
```

When you provide a single color value, the XAML interprets this to mean that you want a solid brush of that particular color for the entire background. If you want to do something more elaborate, you have to use the more verbose format. You may be familiar with brushes from Windows Forms or SDK programming. The idea is that you set up your brush the way you want to use it (think: dipping it in blue paint) and then use it to paint various things such as the background of a control.

When the concept of brushes was first created, the metaphor was good.—a brush could have a texture (a pattern) and a color. Brushes have evolved since then, so the metaphor is a little stretched but still mostly works. Now, for example, you can have gradient brushes that start with one color and change to another, image brushes that paint using pictures, or even specialized brushes that paint using controllable surfaces.

We'll show many more examples using more complex painting and brushes as we go, but let's look at an example of using a radial gradient brush. (A linear gradient brush starts at one point with one color and goes to another point with another color, whereas a radial gradient starts at one point and radiates outwards to a secondary color.) Here's the XAML:

```
<Grid.Background>
  <RadialGradientBrush>
    <GradientStop Offset="0" Color="Blue"/>
    <GradientStop Offset="1"  Color="White"/>
  </RadialGradientBrush>
</Grid.Background>
```

Here there are only have two gradient stops, but you can add as many as you like. You can also set where the center of the gradient starts and a whole host of other options. Figure 5.17 shows the calculator with the gradient (although it's a little hard to see under the buttons).

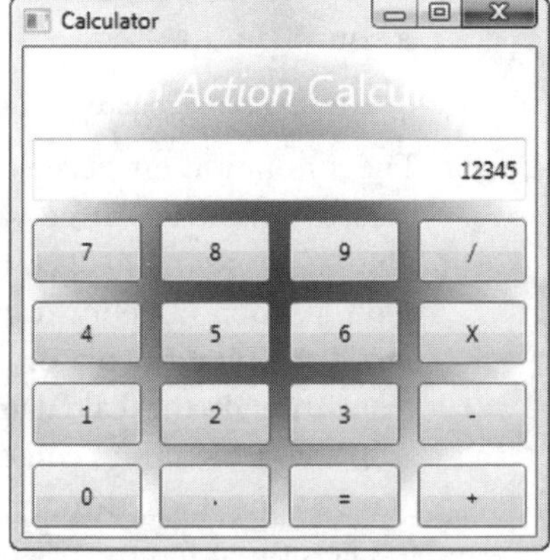

Figure 5.17 Calculator with a radial gradient

Throughout XAML, properties often have a shorthand and a verbose way of being expressed. There's also a whole notation for referring to resources and data in properties. For example, if we want the gradient color to be based on the desktop color, we write:

```
<Grid.Background>
  <RadialGradientBrush>
    <GradientStop Offset="0"
      Color="{DynamicResource {x:Static SystemColors.DesktopColorKey}}"/>
    <GradientStop Offset="1"  Color="White"/>
  </RadialGradientBrush>
</Grid.Background>
```

That whole mess for the `Color` attribute says something to the effect of "tie the color of the gradient stop to the `DesktopColor` system color, and dynamically update it if the color changes." It's a little ugly,[2] but the automatic power is quite something. In chapter 6, we'll talk more about the property system, which is a powerful mechanism tied to properties that lets you do some really cool things such as automatically animating properties without writing code or binding the value to resources or properties of objects. But we did want to give you a glimpse of it now.

One last comment on the editor: The editor lets you set a control to use a particular color, but if you want to do anything fancier (a gradient, for example), you have to drop down to XAML.

5.3 The Grid and localization

One major advantage of using the `Grid` layout versus dumping controls onto a WinForms Form is evident when you translate your application into other languages. If you spend some time up front, you can make your UI so that, once the strings have been localized, your UI automatically adapts to other languages.

We're not going to go extremely deep into localization here, but we do want to show some features of the `Grid` panel that are handy for localized applications. We'd use the calculator to demonstrate this, but because it already handles scaling pretty well, we'd have to break it to make the point (and that would be silly). Instead, we'll create a simple dialog in a more likely scenario (figure 5.18).

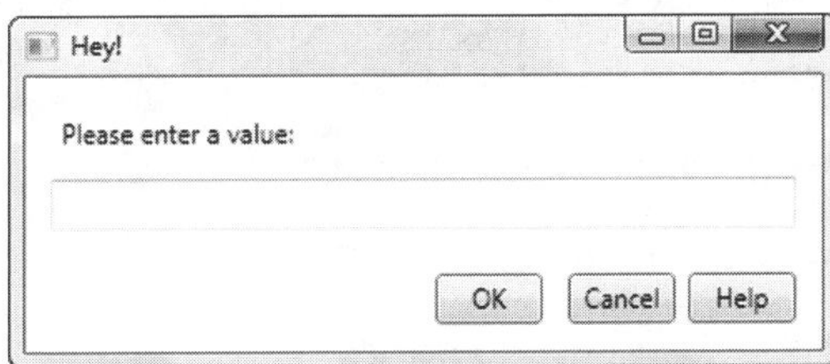

Figure 5.18 A dialog in English. Nothing to worry about.

So far, so good. But what happens if we translate the strings in this dialog to another language such as German, which tends to be a lot more verbose? Take a look at figure 5.19.

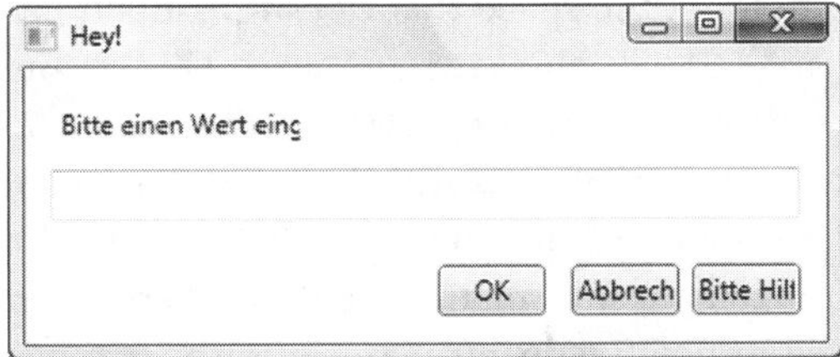

Figure 5.19 When we translate to German, the label and the text are cut off. We're cheating a bit to make our point because the Help button reads *Please Help* in German. The Germans are nothing if not polite.

As you can see, the text is truncated on the label and on the buttons. The default behavior of controls is to fit their content, provided you don't force a size. We could remove the `Width` from the label and the buttons (figure 5.20).

[2] Okay, it's very ugly.

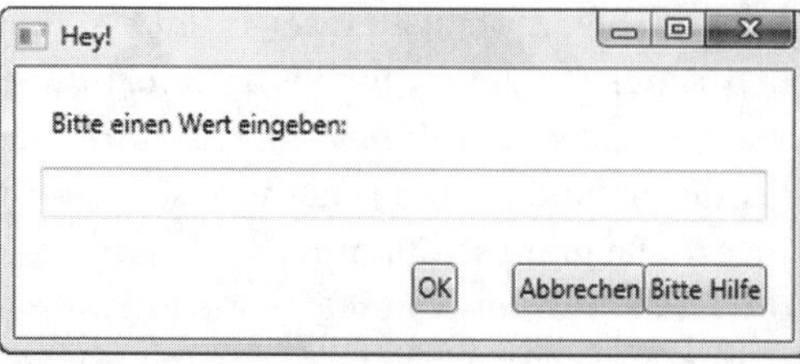

Figure 5.20 Without `Width` being set, the label now works, but the buttons—not so much.

As you can see, the buttons are now big enough, but this is hardly the result we want. We want the buttons to be big enough and to be spaced appropriately, and ideally, we want all the buttons to be the same size, instead of having a tiny OK button and a huge Abbrechen button. Fortunately, a feature of the `Grid` is designed to handle this situation—`SharedSizeGroups`. We can indicate that a set of columns (or rows) should all be the same size. Listing 5.3 shows the XAML for a `Grid` for the buttons. (The `Grid` itself also has to be in some form of layout, such as a `StackPanel`.)

Listing 5.3 Using `SharedSizeGroups` to make buttons the same size

```
<Grid Grid.Row="1" IsSharedSizeScope="True">          <-- (1) Enables sharing
  <Grid.ColumnDefinitions>
    <ColumnDefinition />                                <-- (2)
    <ColumnDefinition Width="Auto" SharedSizeGroup="A"/>   <-- (3) Shares sizing
    <ColumnDefinition Width="Auto" SharedSizeGroup="A"/>
    <ColumnDefinition Width="Auto" SharedSizeGroup="A"/>
  </Grid.ColumnDefinitions>
  <Button Grid.Column="1" Margin="3,0" Name="button1"     (4)
       Height="23" VerticalAlignment="Center" >OK</Button>
  <Button Grid.Column="2" Margin="3,0" Name="button2"
       Height="23" VerticalAlignment="Center">Abbrechen</Button>
  <Button Grid.Column="3" Margin="3,0" Name="button3"
       Height="23" VerticalAlignment="Center">Bitte Hilfe</Button>
</Grid>
```

Sharing sizing between columns or rows isn't enabled by default (for performance reasons). We have to turn it on by setting the `IsSharedSizeScope` to `true` (1). Then we define four columns—the first to hold all the space that doesn't contain `Buttons` (2) and the next three for each `Button` (3). We set the `Width` to `Auto`. This means that the column should be sized based on its content, but we also set the `SharedSizeGroup` property to the same value on each of the columns with buttons. The name can be anything (within reason)—it just has to be the same between the shared columns.

For each of the `Button` definitions (4), you'll see that we have a) specified the column it will appear in, b) gotten rid of any fixed width, and c) given it a margin—so that the `Buttons` won't be crammed up against each other. We also set the `VerticalAlignment` to `Center` so that the `Buttons` are vertically centered within the `Grid`.

When the layout manager sizes the columns, it first figures out the size of the largest button, based on its text, margin, and other properties. It then makes all the columns in the shared size group that size. Figure 5.21 shows the resulting dialog.

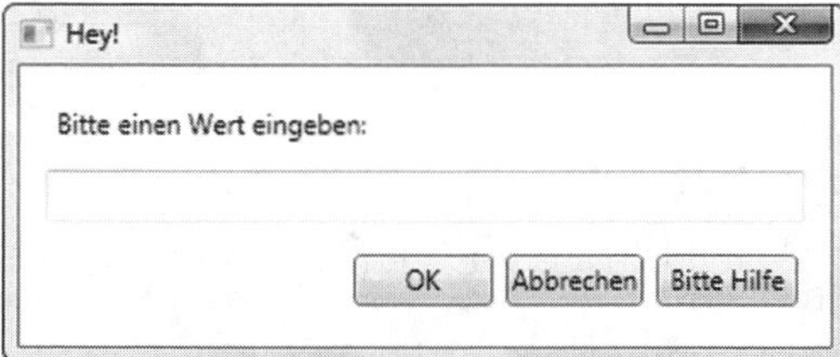

Figure 5.21 The buttons are all the same size, based on the size of the largest button. We could add some padding to the buttons to make them a little nicer.

The WPF team spent a lot of time thinking about localization, and a lot of built-in features support it. For example, we can make your entire window size itself based on its contained content, if it happens to get bigger or smaller, by adding `SizeToContent="WidthAndHeight"` to our window element.[3] We can also give all our elements unique IDs so that a Satellite resource assembly can replace all our strings based on the current language.

NOTE When you write .NET code, you put that code into an assembly. That assembly will also contain various resources such as all your strings. When you localize, you put your localized resources into a *satellite assembly*. If your main assembly is called MyCode.dll and you localize for Brazilian Portuguese, you'd have a satellite assembly called MyCode.pt-BR.dll; or, if you wanted to translate from American into English, you'd have an assembly called MyCode.en-UK.dll.

Unfortunately, the Visual Studio team didn't have time to wrap this for Visual Studio 2008, so we end up having to manually edit project files and run command-line utilities. Still, we expect that this issue will be addressed in the not-to-distant future.

5.4 *UniformGrid*

What makes the `Grid` layout so useful is its flexibility, but there are times when you don't need anything so complex. WPF has a much simpler grid control that can occasionally be useful. We already discussed several specialized layout panels in the previous chapter. The `UniformGrid` is another, but we wanted to wait to introduce it until we had discussed the real `Grid`. The `UniformGrid` is a simple grid where we just specify the number of rows and columns that we want:

```
<UniformGrid Name="uniformGrid1" Rows="2" Columns="2">
```

All the rows and the columns are exactly the same size. Also, we can't specify the location of content explicitly. The first child we add goes in the first cell, the second in the second cell and so on. For example, the XAML

```
<UniformGrid Rows="2" Columns="2">
  <Button>Button 1</Button>
  <Button>Button 2</Button>
```

[3] Although if you don't plan well, the results might not be what you expect!

```
    <Button>Button 3</Button>
    <Button>Button 4</Button>
</UniformGrid>
```

gives an output something like figure 5.22.

We could have used the UniformGrid for the buttons of our calculator, although we would then also have had to use an additional layout mechanism for the rest of the controls. In general, we prefer the flexibility of the Grid, but sometimes a UniformGrid is all that's needed.

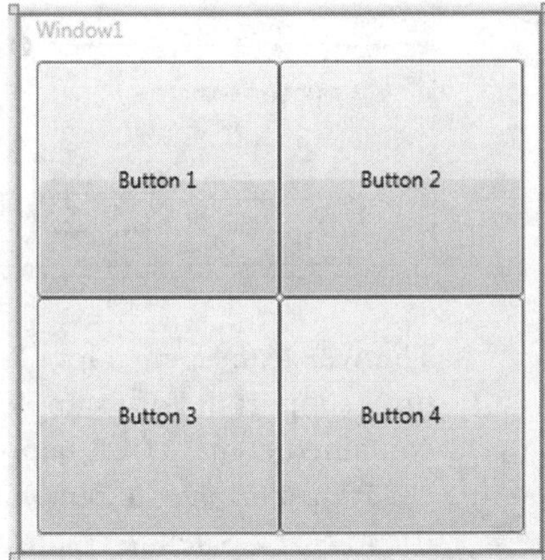

Figure 5.22 Controls in a UniformGrid. The controls are put into cells based on the order they are added. Each row is the same height, and each column the same width.

5.5 Making the calculator work

At this point, we have something that looks like a calculator, but it isn't particularly useful. At some level, we don't really care—this is a book on WPF, not Math 101. But a little bit of our souls cries out when we see an application that doesn't do something. More importantly, implementing a WPF application brings up some specific issues—such as hooking into events and tying application-specific values to XAML.

The nuts-and-bolts implementation for the calculator we're providing here is relatively naïve. If you're the sort of person who likes to break things, you can certainly find things that won't work;[4] but, if you follow along, you'll have a calculator that does something calculatory.

5.5.1 Handling operations

A good place to start with the calculator is with the various operations we want to support. Because we're lazy, the calculator can only do four things: add, subtract, multiply, and divide. For convenience, we'll define an enum with all the operators:

```
public enum Operator
{
  None,
  Plus,
  Minus,
  Times,
  Divide,
  Equals
}
```

Note the inclusion of equals as an operator because we have to handle the equals button somewhat as if it's an operator. We put this enum at the top of the Window1.xaml.cs file, within the namespace for the class. We could create a new file—and, if

[4] Although this probably says more about you than about the calculator…

this was production code, we'd suggest that—but putting it in the same file will work for now.

Inside of the Window1 class, we also need to create a few member variables:

```
private Operator lastOperator = Operator.None;
private decimal valueSoFar = 0;
private bool numberHitSinceLastOperator = false;
```

Table 5.2 explains what each variable is for.

Table 5.2 Member variables used in the `Calculator` class

Member variable	Purpose
`lastOperator`	If you think about how a calculator operates, when you hit an operator (or equals), the calculator executes the last operator hit between the value entered before the last operator, and the currently entered value. We use `lastOperator` to hold the operator that was last entered. If the user hits *1 + 2 =*, the last operator will be + at the point when the user hits =.
`valueSoFar`	This variable holds the value entered before the last operator was hit. For 1 + 2 =, the value so far will be 1 before = is hit, and 3 after it's hit.
`numberHitSinceLastOperator`	This Boolean is used to determine if the last key hit was an operator versus a number.

Now, we need a method to handle the execution of operators. This method, shown in listing 5.4, takes the operator just hit as an argument but executes the last operator.

Listing 5.4 `ExecuteLastOperator` method

```
private void ExecuteLastOperator(Operator newOperator)
{
  decimal currentValue = Convert.ToDecimal(textBoxDisplay.Text);     ❶
  decimal newValue = currentValue;

  if (numberHitSinceLastOperator)     ❷
  {
    switch (lastOperator)
    {
      case Operator.Plus:
        newValue = valueSoFar + currentValue;     ❸
        break;
      case Operator.Minus:
        newValue = valueSoFar - currentValue;
        break;
      case Operator.Times:
        newValue = valueSoFar * currentValue;
        break;
      case Operator.Divide:
        if (currentValue == 0)     <-- Handles divide-by-zero problems
          newValue = 0;
```

```
        else
          newValue = valueSoFar / currentValue;
        break;
      case Operator.Equals:           ❹
        newValue = currentValue;
        break;
    }
  }
  valueSoFar = newValue;              <-- Remembers result as value so far
  lastOperator = newOperator;         <-- Remembers operator as new last operator
  numberHitSinceLastOperator = false;
  textBoxDisplay.Text = valueSoFar.ToString();   <-- Puts value so far back into text box
}
```

We get the current entered value by converting the value stored in the text box into a number ❶.

This check ❷ is here to handle the situation of a user hitting an operator and then hitting another operator without entering a number in between. Because the calculator is so cheesy, we could have let this go, but it's pretty easy to handle. The behavior this check gives us is that, if a user hits two operators in a row, we forget about the first one and use the second one.

For each operator, we take the old value (the value so far) and the current value from the TextBox and apply the operator appropriately ❸. We treat equals ❹ as another operator. The operation we apply is to take the current value and make it the old value.

We also need a method to handle digits. Listing 5.5 shows this fairly simple method.

Listing 5.5 The `HandleDigit` method

```
private void HandleDigit(int digit)
{
  string valueSoFar = numberHitSinceLastOperator ?
                                  textBoxDisplay.Text : "";
  string newValue = valueSoFar + digit.ToString();

  textBoxDisplay.Text = newValue;
  numberHitSinceLastOperator = true;
}
```

All this method does is add the digit to the right of the text in the text box. If this is the first digit hit after an operator, it first clears the existing text. Note that this is a fairly naïve implementation—it doesn't handle overflows, and you could hit a bunch of zeros before typing a number, for example. But as we said, the point isn't to make the perfect calculator; it's to get the thing working.

We need one final method—to handle the decimal point. The method for this is shown in listing 5.6.

Listing 5.6 `HandleDecimal` method

```
private void HandleDecimal()
{
```

```
    string valueSoFar = numberHitSinceLastOperator ?
                                        textBoxDisplay.Text : "";
    string newValue = "";

    if (valueSoFar.IndexOf(".") < 0)
    {
        if (valueSoFar.Length == 0)
            newValue = "0.";
        else
            newValue = valueSoFar + ".";
    }
    else
        newValue = valueSoFar;

    textBoxDisplay.Text = newValue;
    numberHitSinceLastOperator = true;
}
```

This method is similar to the `HandleDigit` method, except that it handles a few special situations such as if the user hits the decimal before hitting a digit or if the user hits the decimal more than once.

So, now we have all these fancy methods to make the calculator work—except that we don't currently call any of them. We need to catch the clicks of the various buttons and provide methods to be called. For the moment, we'll create a different method for each digit and each operator button. Listing 5.7 shows the calculator XAML with the `Click` attribute set, although we pulled the other attributes (`Grid.Column`, `Grid.Row`, and `Margin`) off of the XML for readability.

Listing 5.7 Click handlers for each `Button`

```
<Button Name="button7" Click="OnClick7">7</Button>
<Button Name="button8" Click="OnClick8">8</Button>
<Button Name="button9" Click="OnClick9">9</Button>
<Button Name="buttonDivide" Click="OnClickDivide">/</Button>
<Button Name="button4" Click="OnClick4">4</Button>
<Button Name="button5" Click="OnClick5">5</Button>
<Button Name="button6" Click="OnClick6">6</Button>
<Button Name="buttonTimes" Click="OnClickTimes">X</Button>
<Button Name="button1" Click="OnClick1">1</Button>
<Button Name="button2" Click="OnClick2">2</Button>
<Button Name="button3" Click="OnClick3">3</Button>
<Button Name="buttonMinus" Click="OnClickMinus">-</Button>
<Button Name="button0" Click="OnClick0">0</Button>
<Button Name="buttonDecimal" Click="OnClickDecimal" >.</Button>
<Button Name="buttonEquals" Click="OnClickEquals">=</Button>
<Button Name="buttonPlus" Click="OnClickPlus">+</Button>
```

If you thought it was tedious adding all those attributes, now you need to add a handler for each one. If you don't care about the names of the methods so much, you can double-click each button in turn. Listing 5.8 shows the add button handler, the decimal button handler, and a handler for one of the digits. The other handlers are virtually the same, except that they pass a different operator or digit.

Listing 5.8 Calculator click handlers

```
private void OnClick7(object sender, RoutedEventArgs e)
{
  HandleDigit(7);
}

private void OnClickDecimal(object sender, RoutedEventArgs e)
{
  HandleDecimal();
}

private void OnClickPlus(object sender, RoutedEventArgs e)
{
  ExecuteLastOperator(Operator.Plus);
}
```

Other than changing the default text for the `TextBox` to 0 instead of 12345 (and a whole bunch of cutting and pasting), that's all that's needed to make the calculator operate. If you've been coding along, go ahead and run the calculator. It should now do more calculator-like things (figure 5.23).

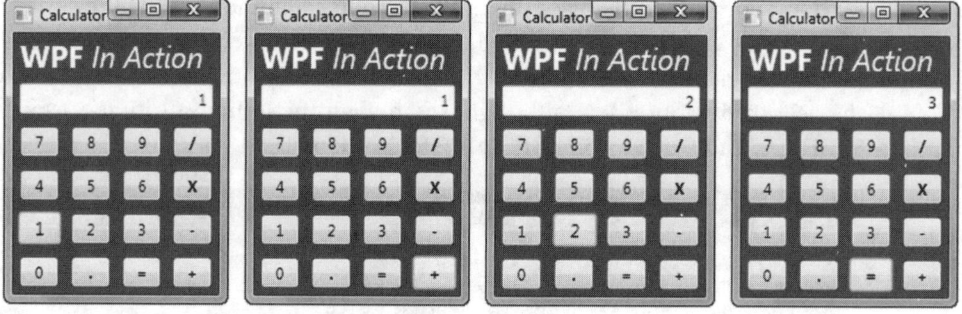

Figure 5.23 The calculator in action

Pretty snazzy, eh? Having to create all those separate handlers was kind of irritating, though. We're programmers—which means that we're lazy—which means that we'll go to any amount of effort to avoid spending a few minutes copying and pasting. To avoid this annoyance, we can make the handlers more generic.

5.5.2 *Genericizing the handlers*

We can eliminate the handlers in several different ways. For example, we could write a generic digit handler that figured out which digit was hit based on the text of the button (listing 5.9).

Listing 5.9 Generic digit handler

```
private void OnClickDigit(object sender, RoutedEventArgs e)
{
  Button btn = sender as Button;
```

```
    int digit = Convert.ToInt32(btn.Content.ToString());
    HandleDigit(digit);
  }
```

Because the first argument sent to the click event handler is the button itself (although it's sent as a generic `sender`), we can get the content of the button, convert it to a string, and then to an integer. We then pass that value to the `HandleDigit` method. Now, we can make all the digit buttons call the generic handler:

```
<Button Name="button7" Click="OnClickDigit">7</Button>
<Button Name="button8" Click="OnClickDigit">8</Button>
<Button Name="button9" Click="OnClickDigit">9</Button>
...
```

This approach is better because we only have a single handler to worry about now, but we still have to put in a click handler for every single button (although if we type `Click=` in the XAML, we can choose the existing handler from the context menu). In the next two chapters, we'll show two different approaches for avoiding hooking up individual handlers—by using a style in chapter 6 and through alternative ways of catching events in chapter 7.

It's easy to convert the numeric text into a digit, but not so easy with the operator buttons. We could do a couple of ugly things, such as comparing the text on the button:

```
if(string.Compare(sender.Content.ToString(),"=") == 0)
  HandleOperator(Operator.Equal);
...
```

Or, being slightly less dependent on arbitrary text, we could check for a specific button:

```
if(sender == buttonEquals)
  HandleOperator(Operator.Equal);
...
```

But neither of these solutions is particularly clean. What would be nice is if we could associate an object with the button that we could check with the handler. Fortunately, as with Windows Forms, controls have a `Tag` property, which is ideal for this. We can put in an on-load handler for the `Window`:

```
<Window x:Class="Calculator.Window1"
    xmlns="http://schemas.microsoft.com/winfx/2006/xaml/presentation"
    xmlns:x="http://schemas.microsoft.com/winfx/2006/xaml"
    Title="Calculator" Height="300" Width="300" Background="Transparent"
    Loaded="Window_Loaded">
```

And in the handler, we can associate an appropriate value with each button:

```
private void Window_Loaded(object sender, RoutedEventArgs e)
{
  buttonPlus.Tag = Operator.Plus;
  buttonMinus.Tag = Operator.Minus;
  buttonTimes.Tag = Operator.Times;
  buttonDivide.Tag = Operator.Divide;
  buttonEquals.Tag = Operator.Equals;
}
```

Now we can make all the operator buttons call a generic `OnClickOperator` method:

```
private void OnClickOperator(object sender, RoutedEventArgs e)
{
  Button btn = sender as Button;
    if(btn.Tag != null)
    {
      Operator op = (Operator)btn.Tag;
      ExecuteLastOperator(op);
    }
}
```

One issue with this method is that we're setting the tag in code away from where we define the buttons. It would be better if we could set the tag in the designer. In the designer, we can easily set the tag to be a string (figure 5.24).

Figure 5.24 It's easy to set the `Tag` property to a string.

And then we can modify the `OnClickOperator` to convert it into an `Operator` enum value:

```
private void OnClickOperator(object sender, RoutedEventArgs e)
{
  Button btn = sender as Button;
  if (btn.Tag is string)
  {
    Operator op = (Operator)Enum.Parse(typeof(Operator),
                                        btn.Tag.ToString());
    ExecuteLastOperator(op);
  }
}
```

This code will work, and it puts the definition of the operator with the definition of the button—a much cleaner process. One drawback is that, as we're storing a string, it's easy to mistype something or have something mismatch if the enum changes. Because the value is a string, the error won't show up at compile time and will only blow up when the user hits the button with the problem.

NOTE Some purists dislike the use of the `Tag` property and suggest that other approaches are more appropriate—such as creating a derivation of `Button` that has an appropriate property to store the value of the `Tag`. We respectfully disagree. Programming always involves trade-offs, but we always incline to the trade-off that provides the simplest, most easily maintainable code. Using the `Tag` property is a little ambiguous, but creating additional classes every time we want to store additional properties can dramatically increase code complexity.

It isn't too hard to store the real enum value in XAML because XAML can reference any CLR type. But before we can do that, we have to reference the namespace that contains the `Operator` enum. To do this, we have to map the C# namespace to an XML namespace. We do this in the main element for the calculator's `Window`:

```
<Window x:Class="Calculator.Window1"
    xmlns="http://schemas.microsoft.com/winfx/2006/xaml/presentation"
    xmlns:x="http://schemas.microsoft.com/winfx/2006/xaml"
    xmlns:local="clr-namespace:Calculator"
    Title="Calculator" Height="300" Width="300" Background="Transparent"
    Loaded="Window_Loaded">
```

The important line here is the one that starts with `xmlns:local=`. What this says is "map the XML namespace called *local* to the .NET Calculator namespace." Because we aren't adding a reference to a particular assembly, it's assumed that we mean the namespace in the current assembly. We don't have to type this whole line. Once we type the equals sign, we can select the namespace from the IntelliSense drop-down menu.

Using *local* as the namespace for the local code is a convention. It now means that we can reference classes from the Calculator namespace in XAML. For example, to reference the `Operator` enum, we could write:

```
local:Operator
```

Now, you might think that we could update the XAML for each button to reference the right value:

```
<Button Name="buttonEquals" Tag="local:Operator.Equals"/>
```

But this doesn't work. The XAML compiler has no way to tell that we mean to reference a class, rather than a string that looks like one. Instead, we have to use a special notation. We won't go into a lot of detail about this now, but it's a notation you'll become painfully familiar with in the next few chapters. When we want to reference a static property (an enum value can be considered a static property of the enum, at least as far as XAML is concerned), we use curly braces to tell XAML that we're trying to get a value (versus setting a string) and `Static` to indicate that we want the static value:

```
<Button Name="buttonEquals" Tag="{x:Static local:Operator.Equals}"/>
```

This XAML is equivalent to the code in the `Window_Loaded` method:

```
buttonEquals.Tag = Operator.Equals;
```

The `Tag` property is set to the enum value, and the click handler can cast it to an `Operator` value to use it.

You'll be seeing the namespace references and the curly-brace notation over and over again throughout the rest of the book. It's so fundamental that we think it's worth emphasizing whenever we get the chance.

5.6 Summary

We chose to use a calculator for our utility sample because it shows the power of the `Grid` layout. The speed with which you can lay out fairly complex sets of controls, and have them automatically size and scale, is impressive.

We spent two chapters on layout because it's such a key component of WPF. No matter what you're doing, deciding on a layout approach is almost always going to be one of your first steps.

By taking advantage of the Grid layout and basic properties, we managed to put together a UI that looks like a calculator in no time. We even spent a little time making the calculator act like a calculator as well.

The next chapter will focus on the look-and-feel of the calculator via the use of styles and control templates. Then, in chapter 7, we'll come back to events and look at some different approaches to handling behavior.

6 Resources, styles, control templates, and themes

This chapter covers:

- Resources
- Styles
- Control templates
- Themes
- The similarities between Windows XP and a certain children's program

Even the title for this chapter is exhausting. It isn't as bad as it sounds, though—all these topics are related. Styles let you combine a set of attributes together and give them a name. You can then apply that style to an element (such as a control). Control templates are special styles that apply to the look-and-feel and behavior of controls. Resources are blobs of content that you can store in your XAML. They relate to the other topics because styles are stored in resources, and control templates are just types of styles. A theme is a collection of styles that control the look-and-feel of an entire application, such as the Aero theme, which is the default for Windows Vista.

The topics in this chapter also form much of the basis for one of the key capabilities of WPF—the ability to easily separate UI from behavior. A graphic artist can provide a theme, a collection of styles and templates stored as resources that can be referenced by your code or can even override behavior of particular types of controls. The artist can edit these properties without touching code, and vice versa. You could give your XAML to your artist and let them edit that while you keep the supporting code separate, but that's more risky. It would be too easy for important properties or handlers to go missing.

But we're getting ahead of ourselves. We first need to talk about resources and how to use them, before worrying about letting other people play with them. We'll return to the calculator for this—first for a little abuse, but later to improve the way it looks.

6.1 Resources

At the most basic level, resources are nothing more than values stored in a dictionary. Generally, you provide a key and get back some sort of object. You most often define resources directly within XAML, as shown in listing 6.1.

Listing 6.1 A simple `Window`-level resource

```
<Window.Resources>
  <SolidColorBrush x:Key="myBrush" Color="Red" />
</Window.Resources>
```

These resources are in a `Window.Resources` element because they belong to our main window. Resources can be associated with any framework element or framework content element. These elements include things like controls, so, in theory, you can associate resources with each and every control you define. But you're more likely to associate resources with higher-level items such as `Windows`, `Pages`, or even the application itself. Listing 6.1 defines a resource with the key `myBrush` set up to paint with the solid color red.

> **`FrameworkElement` and `FrameworkContentElement`**
>
> It isn't easy to give a one sentence definition for a framework element—other than to say that it's the base class for a lot of the visual elements of WPF, such as `Window`, `Panel`, and `Control`. `FrameworkElement` is itself derived from `UIElement`, which provides the most basic support for mouse and keyboard events and layout support. `FrameworkElement` then extends this by adding support for styles, data binding, dynamic properties, and a number of other things. Most important for this section is that it adds support for resources.
>
> `FrameworkContentElement` comes from a different derivation tree, but also provides resource support. The `Content` classes are used by things like `FlowDocument`, where you can put together documents. Things like `Paragraphs` and `Lists` are `FrameworkContentElements`.

Now that we have a resource defined, we can reference it from within our XAML like this:

```
<Button BorderBrush="{StaticResource myBrush}" ...>7</Button>
```

The blob of text inside the `BorderBrush` attribute is one of the special markup extension notations used by XAML—a shorthand for specifying how to find a value that would be extremely cumbersome if it had to follow the standard rules of XML. This markup should be read as "Find the static resource called `myBrush` and set the `BorderBrush` to its value." A static resource is one that doesn't change, as opposed to a dynamic resource that can (we'll discuss dynamic resources in the near future). Figure 6.1 shows the calculator with the 7 button with a red border. Because the book is in black and white, it may not be too easy to see!

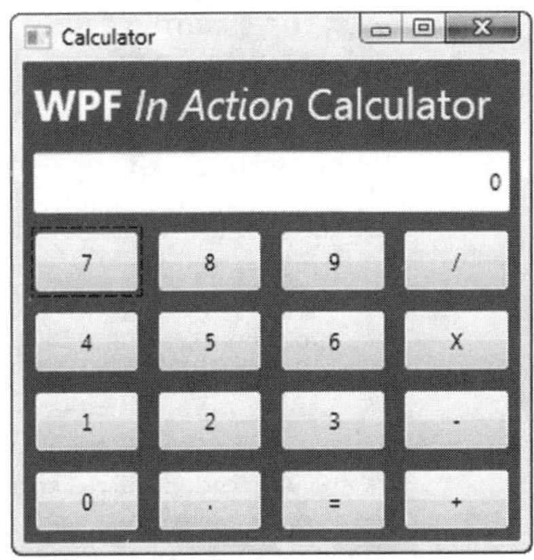

Figure 6.1 The 7 button uses a resource-based brush to set its border.

By moving the definition of the brush into a resource and referencing it, we've already made the UI slightly easier to modify. Each button could have set its border to use `myBrush`, and then you could be able to change the border style of all the buttons at once. This is handy, but it has several drawbacks. For one, you'd have to go through and set up each of these properties on each button manually. Also, the only properties that you could change in this way are ones that you happened to have thought to pull out and put into resources. As you'll see later, styles will let you work around both of these issues. Styles, in fact, are just another type of *thing* you can shove into a resource dictionary.

But, before we get to styles, we still need to discuss a number of other things about resources in general. For example, how does the system locate resources? The button can have its own resources but, in this case, does not. (In fact, the button does have a resource dictionary, but it's empty.) The answer is that WPF automatically steps up the ownership chain until it finds the requested resource. Figure 6.2 shows the search order from the example.

As you might imagine, resources are only available to objects at or below the level where they're defined, so the `Window` couldn't access resources that belong only to the

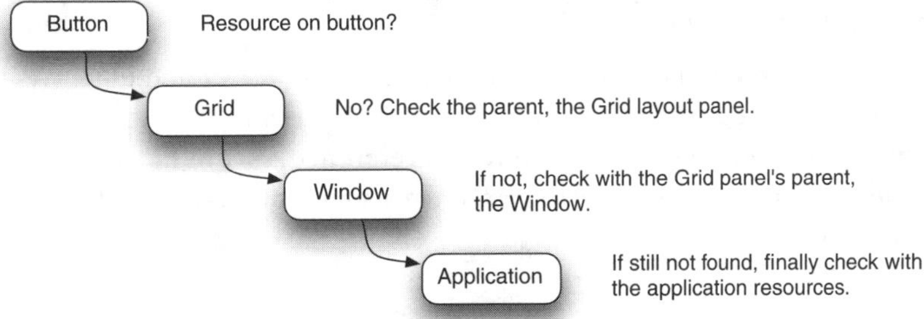

Figure 6.2 WPF searches for resources in the object, and then steps up through parents until it finds the referenced resource.

`Grid`, for example.[1] Also, unlike in code, order matters. The XAML that defines your resources must be found before the place where it's referenced. The format for the resources is the same, no matter where it's defined. For example, we could move the brush up to the application:

```
<Application x:Class="Calculator.App"
  xmlns="http://schemas.microsoft.com/winfx/2006/xaml/presentation"
  xmlns:x="http://schemas.microsoft.com/winfx/2006/xaml"
  StartupUri="Window1.xaml"
  >
  <Application.Resources>
    <SolidColorBrush x:Key="myBrush" Color="Red" />
  </Application.Resources>
</Application>
```

By defining a resource at the application level, it will be available to everything in the application. If you're sure you want everything to see the resource, this is a good choice, although there will be a slight performance hit. Also, there can be side effects of doing this. If this was a control template, for example, that template would apply everywhere in the application, whereas you might only want to use it on a particular `Window`.

In addition to embedding resources directly in your XAML files, you can also create standalone resource dictionaries and reference those dictionaries as needed.

6.1.1 Using standalone resource dictionaries

A resource dictionary is just an XML file that contains a `ResourceDictionary` element. We can create one by adding a new project item (figure 6.3).

Listing 6.2 shows the solid-color brush moved into a new standalone resource dictionary.

Listing 6.2 Standalone resource dictionary

```
<ResourceDictionary xmlns="http://schemas.microsoft.com/winfx/2006/xaml/
   presentation"
    xmlns:x="http://schemas.microsoft.com/winfx/2006/xaml"
    >
  <SolidColorBrush x:Key=" myBrush" Color="Yellow"/>
</ResourceDictionary>
```

Creating resource dictionaries is pretty easy and also a pretty good idea. We can create multiple styles and resources and then reference them in multiple projects as needed. To use the resources, we do have to put in a reference, sort of like a `using` statement in C# code. Listing 6.3 shows how to reference a single standalone resource dictionary from within the `Window`.

---

[1] At least not automatically. You could write code at the `Window` level that asked the `Grid` for a resource directly.

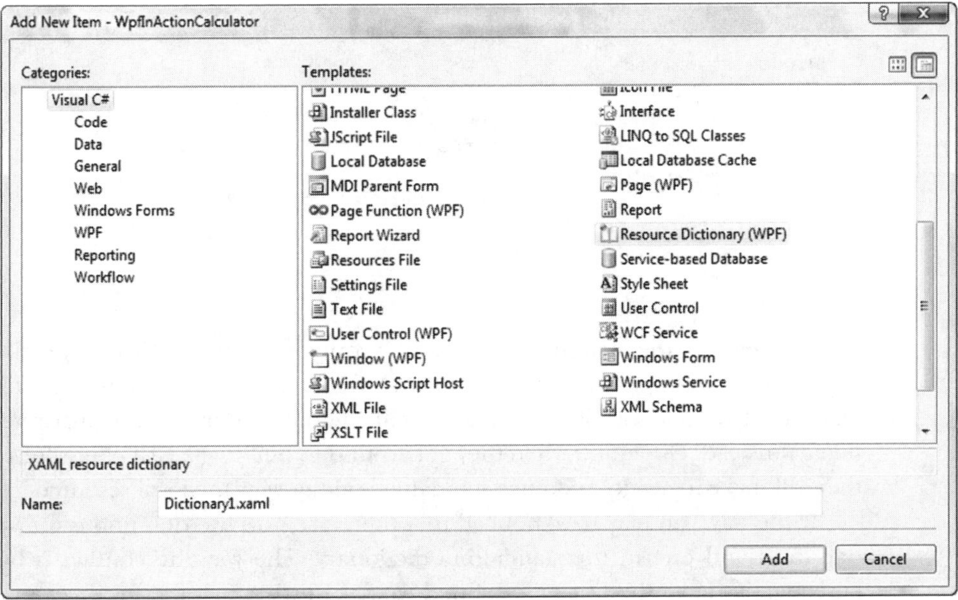

Figure 6.3 Adding a new resource dictionary to our project

Listing 6.3 Referencing a single resource dictionary

```
<Window.Resources>
  <ResourceDictionary Source="Dictionary1.xaml"/>
</Window.Resources>
```

This works, but it only allows a single reference. We can't, for example, also reference Dictionary2. Worse, we also can't reference one dictionary and have other local resource definitions. Fortunately, we can create a *merged dictionary*, which combines the contents of multiple dictionaries into one. Listing 6.4 shows how to include multiple standalone dictionaries.

Listing 6.4 Referencing multiple standalone dictionaries

```
<Window.Resources>
  <ResourceDictionary>
    <ResourceDictionary.MergedDictionaries>
      <ResourceDictionary Source="Dictionary1.xaml"/>
      <ResourceDictionary Source="Dictionary2.xaml"/>
    </ResourceDictionary.MergedDictionaries>
  </ResourceDictionary>
</Window.Resources>
```

The `MergedDictionaries` tag allows for any number of dictionaries to be referenced and then merged together. A dictionary can be a reference to a standalone dictionary or can be a dictionary declared directly in the XAML. The latter is how we go about including references to standalones combined with local resources, as you can see in listing 6.5.

Listing 6.5 Referencing a standalone dictionary and local resources

```
<Window.Resources>
  <ResourceDictionary>
    <ResourceDictionary.MergedDictionaries>
      <ResourceDictionary Source="Dictionary1.xaml"/>
      <ResourceDictionary>                                          ❶
        <SolidColorBrush x:Key="myBrush" Color="Red" />
      </ResourceDictionary>
    </ResourceDictionary.MergedDictionaries>
  </ResourceDictionary>
</Window.Resources>
```

You can see how the second dictionary only contains resources ❶ including the brush we've been working with. This notation is a little bulky, and it would be nice if Microsoft had provided some sort of reference tag that could be put inside a regular resource dictionary instead. Hopefully, when they get around to building a GUI editor for resources, they will make it easy to reference standalones along with the local resources.

By the way, you may have noticed that there are now two definitions for `myBrush`—one local and one in the standalone dictionary. The way the conflict is handled is fairly egalitarian—the last one defined wins. In listing 6.5, the local version is listed second, so the border will be red. If we turn around the XAML

```
<ResourceDictionary.MergedDictionaries>
  <ResourceDictionary>
    <SolidColorBrush x:Key="myBrush" Color="Red" />
  </ResourceDictionary>
  <ResourceDictionary Source="Dictionary1.xaml"/>
</ResourceDictionary.MergedDictionaries>
```

then we'd get the yellow version defined in Dictionary1.

6.1.2 Using resources from code

Anything we can do in XAML, we can also do in code.[2] XAML is a shortcut to code—the appropriate objects get constructed based on the XAML, and then their code is executed. This is true for resources as well. The resource dictionary is available for each object, and can be referenced and modified as needed. Let's start with accessing existing resources.

Resources are available via the `Resources` property of framework elements and framework content elements. Resources are exposed as a collection, so we can add, iterate, and do other collection-y things. But, when we look for resources, we generally don't hit the collection directly. We use the `FindResource` method instead:

```
button9.BorderBrush = (Brush)FindResource("myBrush");
```

This method searches resources in the same way as if we had put the declaration in XAML. It searches the local resources first, then steps up the chain to the parent, and

[2] Although there are a few things that would be *really* painful to do in code.

so on. If it fails to find the resource, then it throws an exception—the same as the XAML version. If we don't want the code to throw an exception if it fails to find the resource, there's another version of `FindResource` called `TryFindResource`:

```
button9.BorderBrush = (Brush)TryFindResource("myBrush");
```

This version returns null if the resource isn't found. If null isn't a supported value for the particular property, then we end up with an exception anyway. For brushes in general, this isn't a problem—null means that the value isn't set, so go with the default behavior.

Adding and updating resources is as simple as updating any dictionary. For example, to change the `myBrush` brush to a different color, we write:

```
this.Resources["myBrush"] = new SolidColorBrush(Colors.Green);
```

The *this* in this case is the `Window`, so we're updating the `Window`'s resources. We could as easily update the resources for the `Grid` or one of the buttons. By the way, it's pretty easy to update the `Application`'s resources as well—the `Application` object has a static property that exposes the current application:

```
Application.Current.Resources["myBrush"] = new
  SolidColorBrush(Colors.Green);
```

One caveat here is that we're updating a specific resource dictionary. So, if the brush you're using is in the application and you set the value on the `Window`'s resource dictionary, you end up with two different versions of the brush at two different levels. This may or may not cause problems, depending on your goals.

In the examples so far, we've retrieved values from the resource dictionary and set a property as a one-off thing. It's more important to update the proper resources if you want properties to change dynamically when the resource value changes.

6.1.3 Dynamic resources

Much of the time, when you set the value of a property, you're done. The background is going to be blue, so you set the background to blue. But there are times when it isn't a one-off thing. For example, suppose you want to set the background based on a user preference. In yon olden days, when the user changed the preference, the fastidious programmer would write code to step through all the UI and update the value, or destroy the UI elements and re-create them with the new color.[3]

To plan for a lot of such changes, you might build some sort of dictionary for looking up colors. You could then update the dictionary and tell all the UI elements to redraw themselves, causing them to look up the new color. Because all the built-in elements wouldn't know about your dictionary, you'd have to build support code to pass on values, and you'd have to make sure that every color that might change was appropriately redirected. Quite a bit of work.

---

[3] The lazy programmer would tell the user to restart the application, but the rest of us would be required to heap scorn upon such an approach.

Now that WPF is here, you don't have to mess around with any of that. You can still set properties to specific values, but you can also set a property's value to depend on the value of something that might change. If your background points at a particular resource dictionary, by changing the value in that dictionary, anything that references that value can be set to automatically change.

The Property System

You might think that there is a member variable behind each property you set on a control or other WPF object. Given the number of properties available, though, even if each variable only took up 4 bytes, each control would end up eating a fair amount of memory, and that memory would be used even if you never set the value away from the default.

Instead, each WPF object has its own dictionary of property values. This way, objects only use memory when the property has been set, a much more efficient approach. The Property System also provides a whole bunch of other capabilities, including the automatic retrieval of parent values and the ability to handle dynamic properties that change automatically when their dependency changes.

Attached properties also depend on the use of this dictionary. The property dictionary can hold property values even if the particular control doesn't understand what they're for (like `Dock.Left`).

Because WPF handles properties in a consistent way, it's easy to set up this dynamic behavior. Let's take the border example from before, where we referenced a brush from a resource:

```
<Button BorderBrush="{StaticResource myBrush}" ...>7</Button>
```

The use of `StaticResource` means that the value for the brush will be retrieved once and then used from that point forward. When the XAML is read, the system immediately retrieves the value for `myBrush`, sets the border appropriately, and then forgets about it. If we change *static* to *dynamic*, we get different behavior:

```
<Button BorderBrush="{DynamicResource myBrush}" ...>7</Button>
```

`DynamicResource` is fancier. When the system goes to handle this XAML, it doesn't assign a value immediately; instead, it puts in an expression. That expression isn't evaluated until the value is needed. This is an important distinction: The `DynamicResource` is lazy-loaded, so the item referenced doesn't have to exist at the point when the XAML is read. With a `StaticResource`, if the item referenced doesn't exist when the XAML is read, an exception is thrown. In the case of the example, that's not a problem, but the resource could be something you create at runtime (maybe it's a user preference). The same approach is used for data binding, where it's less likely that the data is available before the XAML is read.

The behavior of a `DynamicResource` goes further than lazy loading. Instead of having a value assigned to the property, a connection is made such that, if the referenced value changes, the property also changes with it. Let's modify the calculator so that one button uses a static resource and one a dynamic:

```
<Button BorderBrush="{DynamicResource myBrush}" ...>7</Button>
<Button BorderBrush="{StaticResource myBrush}"  ...>8</Button>
```

Now, we can add some code to the `OnClickOperator` (from the last chapter) method to change the brush when the user hits any operator button (listing 6.6). This might seem like a silly example. Okay, this is a silly example. But, if we took it a little further, it could be made into a nice little UI hint—it isn't always obvious that the user has hit the button and the color change could be used to indicate the last button pressed.

Listing 6.6 Changing `Brush` when user hits an operator

```
private void OnClickOperator(object sender, RoutedEventArgs e)
{
  Button btn = sender as Button;
  OperatorHolder holder = btn.Content as OperatorHolder;
  ExecuteLastOperator(holder.Operator);

  this.Resources["myBrush"] = new SolidColorBrush(Colors.Gray);
}
```

All we're doing here is updating the `Window's` `myBrush` resource to be a gray brush instead of the red brush we already had. Note that we aren't doing anything to tell the system to redraw the buttons or update their values, yet the dynamically set button gets updated anyway (figure 6.4). Notice also that the static button's color doesn't change.

If you want to set up a dynamic property value via code, it's fairly straightforward. Instead of setting the property value directly, you have to use a special method on the control, called `SetResourceReference`. For example, if we want the 9 button to use the brush dynamically, we'd do the following:

```
button9.SetResourceReference(Button.
   BorderBrushProperty,"myBrush");
```

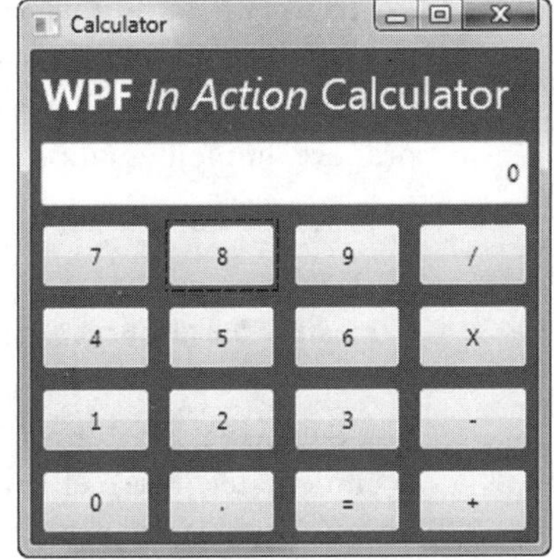

Figure 6.4 The border around the 7 button changes automatically when we update the resource. The color around the 8 button doesn't because it uses a static resource reference.

This sets the button's border color to the value in `myBrush`, and that value is updated whenever the `myBrush` resource changes. Notice that we're passing `Button.BorderBrushProperty` as the property to set. This is a dependency property, and we'll explain what that means in the next section.

DEPENDENCY PROPERTIES

Although not all properties on controls and other WPF elements are dependency properties, the vast majority are. A *dependency property* is a property that participates in the WPF Property System. We're sure you're used to properties exposing a backing member variable, like this:

```
private Color backColor;

public Color BackColor
{
  get {return backColor;}
  set
  {
    backColor = value;
    Invalidate(); // Force repaint
  }
}
```

This certainly works, but if you think of all the properties available for controls, that's a lot of member variables. Even if each variable only takes up, say, 4 bytes, you're potentially talking about hundreds of bytes for each control—whether or not the value is ever set. This might not be a big deal for the average dialog, but WPF uses composition for everything. Each `ListBox` entry, for example, is a control that can contain controls. A few hundred bytes for each item can quickly add up to a huge memory footprint.

To work around this, WPF takes a different approach to properties. There's a dictionary of property values associated with each object. The dictionary only has entries for property values that have been set. If you could look inside the real `BackColor` property implementation,[4] you'd see something much more like this:

```
public Color BackColor
{
  get {return (Color)GetValue(BackColorProperty);}
  set {SetValue(BackColorProperty,value);}
}
```

The `GetValue` and `SetValue` methods are accessing the dictionary of properties. This is immediately more efficient because it's much more likely that you'll only set three or four properties (or none, for that matter). The official name for this is sparse storage. Each property takes up a little more space, but overall, the savings are enormous. But the benefits don't stop there.

Because the implementation of properties is a dictionary, it's possible to put things into that dictionary that aren't understood by the object directly. For example, suppose a control is within a `DockPanel`. The dictionary can hold a `DockLocation` property, with a value like `Dock.Left`. This is meaningless to the control itself but useful to the parent. This is how attached properties are implemented.

The generic nature of the dictionary of properties also makes it easy for other things to set properties without necessarily understanding what they're doing. This is how styles can set properties. The style has a setter that says, "Set arbitrary property X

[4] As it happens, Microsoft has released the source code for .NET, so you *can* look at the implementation if you want to!

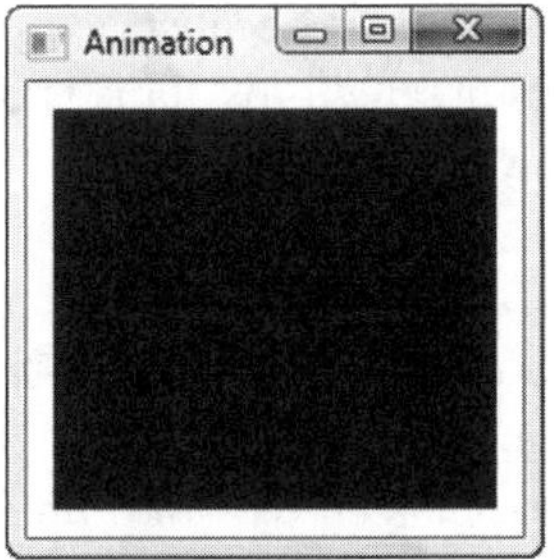

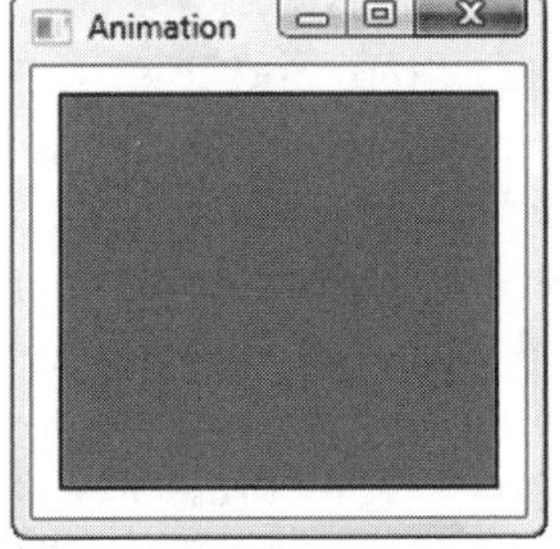

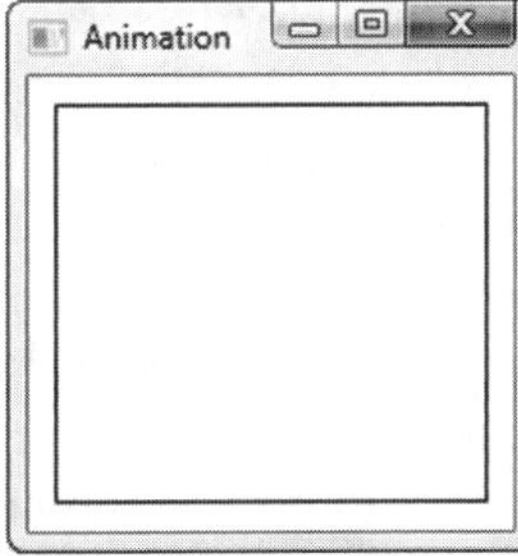

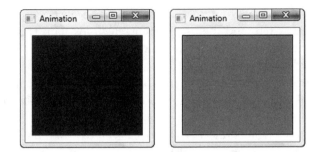

Figure 6.5 Because of the generic mechanisms within the WPF Property System, it's easy to automatically animate a property. In this case, the rectangle's color is automatically fading from black to gray to white, back to gray and finally back to black.

to value Y." The same mechanism can set the background color, the foreground color, or any other property with a color value, without having to resort to reflection tricks. This approach is also used for animation. A property's value can be animated over time without any particular regard to what the animation does (figure 6.5).

On top of the value of the property dictionary, several other services are provided by the Property System. For one thing, it's possible for a property to get its value from its parent within the tree of objects. For example, if the font is set on a `Window`, all the children can automatically pick up that font without having to explicitly set it. They pick up these values from the visual tree, rather than just from the derivation tree. Another set of capabilities that the Property System provides are data binding and dynamic properties.

In the previous section we set up the border color to be dynamically tied to a value from a resource—you get this capability for free on any dependency property. This same basic mechanism can be used to arbitrarily tie a property to a data source, which we'll demonstrate in chapter 11.

In general, properties are exposed via standard get/set methods. There's also a static property for each dependency property, named, by convention, as *propertyname-Property*. From the example for the `BorderBrush`, the static property is named `BorderBrushProperty`. This static value is of type `DependencyProperty` and performs double duty—it's the key into the property dictionary, and it also holds information about the behavior of the property. In chapter 13, we'll create some custom controls that have their own dependency properties, so you'll be able to see what options are available.

This section has a lot of text without much code, but understanding what is going on under the hood with properties will pay off when we start talking about styles. Before we get to that, there's one last thing to mention about resources: dynamically using system colors and other system resources.

REFERENCING NON-RESOURCES FROM XAML

You can reference things other than resources in XAML. For example, in WPF there's a class called `SystemColors` that has things, like the current `Window` background color, foreground color, and so on, from system settings. This class isn't a resource, but it's still possible to reference these colors from XAML. This is good because a good UI will play nice with the operating system and the user's color selections. This is especially important for users who have vision problems and rely on high-contrast modes to be able to read their screens.

Technically, hooking up to `SystemColors` makes use of binding. Binding is the underlying technology used to tie data sources to data users. A data source could be a database or an XML document or a particular property on a class. You'll be unsurprised to learn that pulling data from a resource is a specialized type of binding. Binding is the primary topic for both chapters 11 and 12.

We're bringing it up briefly because we're talking about referencing colors, and the discussion would be pretty incomplete if we didn't mention accessing system colors. Because we're referencing the `SystemColors` class, rather than a resource, the syntax is different. If we want to tie our background, for example, to the default `Window` background color, we do the following:

```
<Rectangle Fill="{x:Static SystemColors.WindowBrush}" />
```

You may recognize this notation from the previous chapter, where we referenced the value from a value from the `Operators` enum. What this says is to tie the rectangle's `Fill` color to the value stored in the `SystemColors.WindowBrush` property. The reason for the different syntax is that we're setting the `Fill` color to come from the static property on the `SystemColors` object, which is different from setting the `Fill` based on a value in a resource dictionary.

You could equally tie this to a property of one of your own classes. You'd first have to make that class available via a namespace in your XAML, again as we did with the `Operators` enum. `SystemColors` is available because it's referenced by one of the standard XAML namespaces already.

Setting the property in the way shown will work, but there's a problem. If the user changes the system colors while the application is running, the rectangle's fill color *won't* change. That's because the value has been set statically. If we want it to change dynamically, we have to set up a dynamic association and, you guessed it, the notation is slightly different again:

```
<Rectangle
    Fill="{DynamicResource {x:Static SystemColors.WindowBrushKey}}" />
```

There's a lot going on here. First off, we're back to the `DynamicResource` statement of yore, but instead of providing the name of a resource, we use the curly-brace notation to indicate that the value we want to bind to is coming from elsewhere. Second, and this is easy to miss, notice that instead of `WindowBrush`, we're referencing `WindowBrushKey`. The `SystemColors` class has a second property for each color, with the word *Key* appended. We aren't binding to the color, but to the key which can be used to find the color.

This is an example where the added flexibility of WPF really makes things more complicated. In Windows Forms, most controls automatically handled changing color when the system changed color. This was all done behind the scenes. Granted, it was painful for the Windows Forms developers to make it work, but that is, as they say, their problem. Also, there were a few controls that didn't behave properly, and it was often a pain to handle the exceptions. Even so, there was a fairly reasonable 80% solution that required almost no effort on the part of the average coder.

Now, if you want to do something that used to be simple, you have to spew some fairly icky-looking XAML. We hope that in the next version of Visual Studio the designer will hide some or all of this, but at the moment, it seems like a step backward.

Overall, the Property System makes our lives much easier, and the resource mechanism is flexible and straightforward. The real power comes in when you start playing with styles.

6.2 Styles

If you've worked much with the web or created any complex word-processing documents, the concept of styling should be familiar to you. A style represents a series of properties that can be applied to items. On the web, Cascading Style Sheets (CSS) can be used to control the look-and-feel of pages by formatting their content. In a word processor, styles can be applied to sections of text or paragraphs. When the style is applied, it can set the font, spacing, and various other properties.

The buttons on the calculator provide a perfect example of a situation where a style would be useful. Right now we have a margin defined for each button that's always the same. Because of some of the experiments, the border of a couple of the buttons uses a color, but not all of them. If we set up a style for the buttons, then we can change all the buttons to use it; and then we can tweak the style and have it automatically change all the buttons. Listing 6.7 shows the resource section for the `Window`, including the old brush that we were using for borders, and also a new button style.

Listing 6.7 Style for calculator buttons

```
<Window.Resources>
  <SolidColorBrush x:Key="myBrush" Color="Red" />
  <Style x:Key="CalcButtonStyle" TargetType="Button">
    <Setter Property="Margin" Value="5"/>
    <Setter Property="BorderBrush" Value="{DynamicResource myBrush}"/>
  </Style>
</Window.Resources>
```

The `x:Key` is the "name" of the style. This is how we'll reference the style later. All styles (like all resources) have to have a name, although, as you'll see later, there are situations where the name (or the key) is implied. The `TargetType` is the type of control you want the style to apply to. You don't have to specify the target type, but if you don't, you have to provide more information for the setters. For example, we're setting the `Margin` property. Because `TargetType` is set to `Button`, this is effectively setting the `Button.Margin` property. If we hadn't specified a target type, then we'd have had to fully qualify the setter's property:

```
<Setter Property="Button.Margin" Value="5"/>
```

Or, if we want to use the style more generally, we can use the following:

```
<Setter Property="Control.Margin" Value="5"/>
```

Then this style will work with anything derived from `Control`. Setters pretty much do what their name implies; they set a property on the styled control to the specified value. Once again we see the benefits of the Property System—even though the style itself knows nothing about the target object, it's trivial for it to set the property.

By the way, it's perfectly legal to provide setters in a style that don't apply to all the targets. For example, suppose we want to use the same style for both text boxes and buttons. We could specify a `MaxLength` property setter in the style:

```
<Style x:Key="ButtonOrTextBox" TargetType="Control">
  <Setter Property="Margin" Value="5"/>
  <Setter Property="BorderBrush" Value="{DynamicResource myBrush}"/>
  <Setter Property="TextBox.MaxLength" Value="100"/>
</Style>
```

If we use this style with a `TextBox`, the maximum length is set to 100. If we use this style with a `Button`, because a `Button` doesn't have a `MaxLength` property, the setter doesn't do anything.

To use the style, we provide a value to the `Style` property of the target control:

```
<Button Grid.Column="0" Grid.Row="3"
   Style="{StaticResource CalcButtonStyle}"
   Name="button4" Click="OnClickDigit">4</Button>
```

The syntax for the `Style` property is the same as for any other resource reference. In this case, we're saying that we want the style to be set statically to the `CalcButtonStyle` resource. We could go ahead and set all our buttons to use the style, and get rid of all the margin and border properties. Then we could, for example, change the margin to be 10 instead of 5 in one place, and have it change all the buttons (figure 6.6).

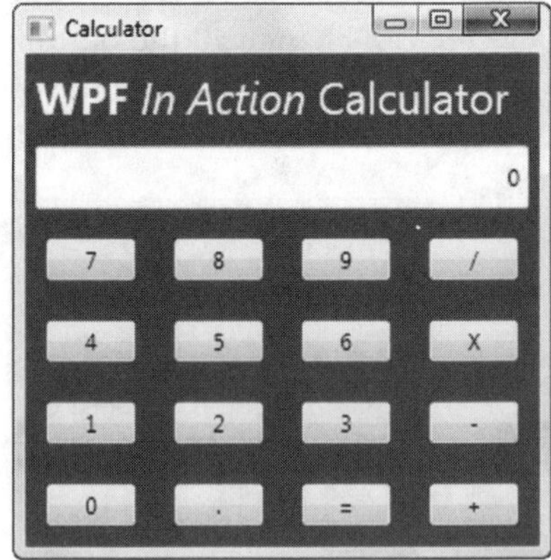

Figure 6.6 We've applied a style to all the buttons that sets the margins and the border color.

In addition to properties, the buttons also have something else in common—events. All the digits call a common handler for processing, as do all the operators. It might be nice if we could add the event handler to the style so that we wouldn't have to specify it for every single button. Adding an event handler to a style is similar to adding a property. We add an `EventSetter`:

```
<Style x:Key="CalcButtonStyle" TargetType="Button">
  <Setter Property=" Margin" Value="10"/>
  <Setter Property="BorderBrush" Value="{DynamicResource myBrush}"/>
  <EventSetter Event="Click" Handler="OnButtonClicked"/>
</Style>
```

This does exactly what you'd expect—every button using this style automatically calls the `OnButtonClicked` method when the user clicks the button. Although the event handler works, it doesn't entirely fit in with the calculator. We have a different handler for digits than for operators. Also, we're mixing two different things here—look-and-feel and behavior. We're back to the scenario where changing the appearance might break the way things work. We recommend that you use events in styles only for presentation handling (for example, if you want to customize the presentation of a control based on an event taking place). In chapter 7, we'll show you better ways of handling events without sticking them in styles.

6.2.1 Styles based on other styles

Sometimes, you might have multiple items that are similar, but have some minor differences. For example, you might want all the buttons to have the same margins and basic properties but a different border color for operators than for digits. Ideally, you'd have a basic style that has the common attributes in it and then specialized styles that contain the differences. For example, we can do this via the use of the `BasedOn` property of a style, as shown in listing 6.8.

Listing 6.8 Two styles derived from a base

```
<Window.Resources>
  <SolidColorBrush x:Key="myBrush" Color="Red" />
  <Style x:Key="CalcButtonStyle"  TargetType="Button">    <-- Original style
    <Setter Property="FrameworkElement.Margin" Value="10"/>
    <Setter Property="BorderBrush" Value="{DynamicResource myBrush}"/>
  </Style>
  <Style x:Key="DigitButtonStyle"
             BasedOn="{StaticResource CalcButtonStyle}"    ❶
     TargetType="Button">
  </Style>
  <Style x:Key="OperatorButtonStyle"
             BasedOn="{StaticResource CalcButtonStyle}"    ❷
    TargetType="Button">
    <Setter Property="BorderBrush" Value="Green"/>         ❸
    <Setter Property="FontWeight" Value="UltraBold"/>
  </Style>
</Window.Resources>
```

`DigitButtonStyle` ❶ is derived from, or *based on*, the `CalcButtonStyle`. The value for the `BasedOn` attribute is the same as for any other static resource reference. Because `DigitButtonStyle` is based on `CalcButtonStyle`, it automatically contains all the setters from `CalcButtonStyle`, as well as its own properties. At the moment, `DigitButtonStyle` doesn't provide any specialized behavior; it's only a placeholder. We also create an `OperatorButtonStyle` derivation ❷ with different setters.

Notice that the `OperatorButtonStyle` provides a setter for the `BorderBrush` ❸. As you'd expect, the version in the derived style overrides the value in `CalcButtonStyle`, so the border for the operator buttons is green. We also set the `FontWeight` to be

UltraBold to make them stand out. We could've just used Bold, but why be bold when you can be ultra bold!

NOTE *EventSetters in derived styles.* You might think that you can override EventSetters in the same way you override property setters. But event setters work differently. If you have a setter in the base and in the derived version, both methods are called. Properties have a single value, whereas events can have any number of subscribers. You could argue as to whether this is good or not. For some events, you might always want to get a notification, no matter what the child does with it. For others, you might want to provide default behavior that can be overwritten. We would have suggested that they add an Overridable property to control this behavior, but we (probably for good reasons) aren't in charge.

To get the styles to show up appropriately, we have to make sure that the right buttons have the right styles. Digits look like this:

```
<Button Grid.Column="0" Grid.Row="3"
   Style="{StaticResource DigitButtonStyle}" Name="button4">4</Button>
```

And operators like this:

```
<Button Grid.Column="0" Grid.Row="3"
   Style="{StaticResource OperatorButtonStyle}"
   Name="buttonTimes">X</Button>
```

Figure 6.7 shows the calculator with the new styles applied. As you can see, the operators have the different style.

Styles are just resources, so we access them from code the same way we access any other resource:

```
button1.Style =
   (Style)FindResource("DigitButtonStyle"
   );
```

Simple enough. One caveat is that, once a style has been applied, it can no longer be changed—so you can't update the style's properties and have it automatically change all the styled items. But you can switch between different styles by changing the value of the Style property.

If you don't want to have to set the style for every single button, you can easily write code that steps through all the buttons and assigns the style programmatically. But there's another way that you can have a style automatically apply to controls.

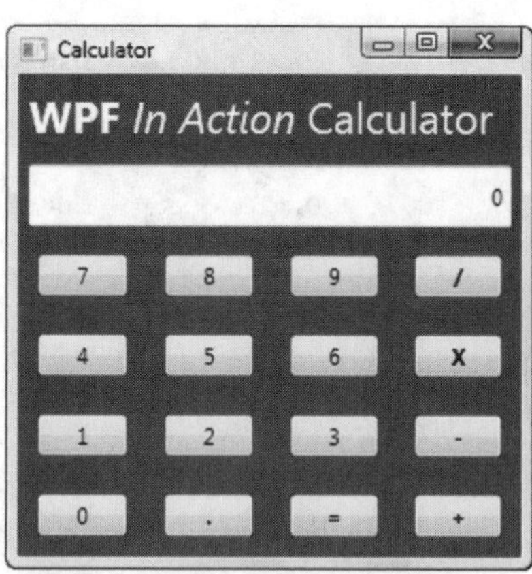

Figure 6.7 We explicitly used a different style for the operators to differentiate them from the digits. The operator style has bolded text and a green border (although that is hard to see in black and white—but we are not bitter about that—not at all.)

6.2.2 *Implicitly applying styles*

When we created our styles before, we gave them a key and a target type. The key is the name by which you reference the style to use it with controls. But if you exclude the key from a style, the system assumes you want to automatically apply the style to all objects of the target type. For example, the following style has a `TargetType` of button, but no key:

```
<Style TargetType="Button">
  <Setter Property="FrameworkElement.Margin" Value="10"/>
  <Setter Property="BorderBrush" Value="{DynamicResource myBrush}"/>
</Style>
```

Because there's no key, this style is automatically applied to all the buttons below the resource. If this style is defined at the `Window` level, all the buttons on the `Window` pick up this style. If you define the style at the `Grid`-panel level, only buttons in the `Grid` get it; and, if you define it at the `Application` level, every single button in the application picks up the style—unless a different button style is applied at a lower level. Controls pick up the style defined closest to them, so a style on the button overrides one on the `Grid`, which would override one on the window, and so on.

Earlier, we said that styles, like any other resource, have to have a key such as `DigitButtonStyle`. This is sort of a cheat because there's no explicit key. Instead, WPF figures out a name automatically. If we need to reference this style, we can reference it by that implicit name:

```
{x:Type Button}
```

The name is the type turned into a key. We can reference the style in XAML like this:

```
<Button Style="{StaticResource {x:Type Button}}" />
```

Although in this case, it would be a silly thing to do because the style is automatically going to be applied to all buttons. A more reasonable example would be using this notation in a based-on clause to derive a new style from it.

If you're coding along and have gone to all the effort of referencing your custom styles for each button, you can go ahead and take all those references out and, instead, create a single style that applies to them all automatically.

This won't quite work for the calculator, will it? There's a different style for operators than for digit buttons. Well, there are a couple of possible solutions. For one thing, we could pull the generic elements into the style that's applied to every button and then override the specific properties we want to be different:

```
<Button Grid.Column="2" Grid.Row="5" BorderBrush="Green"
   FontWeight="UltraBold"
    Name="buttonEquals">=</Button>
```

We explicitly set the `Brush` and the `FontWeight`. The `Brush` was also set by the style, but the local setting automatically overrides the style. This is true of properties in general—setting a property on an item directly always beats setting a property via a style.

This would work, but it means that a bunch of the buttons would be hardcoded instead of based on a style. Instead, we could derive the style for the operators from the generic style:

```
<Style x:Key="OperatorButtonStyle"
         BasedOn="{StaticResource {x:Type Button}}"
         TargetType="Button">
  <Setter Property="BorderBrush" Value="Green"/>
  <Setter Property="FontWeight" Value="UltraBold"/>
</Style>
```

Notice the use of the implicit name for the automatic button style. Now, we can make the operator buttons use this style. Here's the XAML for a digit button and for an operator button:

```
<Button Grid.Column="0" Grid.Row="3" Name="button4">4</Button>
<Button Grid.Column="0" Grid.Row="3"
   Style="{StaticResource OperatorButtonStyle}" Name="buttonTimes">X</
  Button>
```

Notice that `button4` doesn't reference a style at all. It's automatically using the implicit button style without having to do anything. For the operators, though, we have to explicitly use the `OperatorButtonStyle`. Because an object can only have one style at a time, the `buttonTimes` uses the operator style, overriding the implicit style.

This approach is better still—at least we only have to provide styles for 5 of the 16 buttons. This is one of those cases where it might be better to explicitly use a style for every button. Implicit styles work better when there's a generic look-and-feel always implied. When there are divergent styles for similar items, explicit references are generally better.

Speaking of which, you can do more with styles than setting a few properties. You can also override the control's template to completely change the look-and-feel of a control.

6.3 Control templates

As strange as it may sound, controls in WPF are look-less. They have defined behavior but no appearance. This gives ultimate flexibility because you can completely control the way that a control is presented. If you had to define the way every single control looked before you could use it, you wouldn't be terribly productive. You don't have to do this, though, because every control has a default control template—a definition of how the control should be displayed.

The default control template controls how the button should be drawn in its normal state, as well as in special states such as mouse over, clicked, that sort of thing. The default templates are defined as part of themes and so can be different depending on the currently selected theme—we'll talk about that later. Although you can override the template for an individual control, you'll more often create a style that overrides the look-and-feel.

6.3.1 *Creating a control template*

One of the properties of a control is its template, which defines how it looks and behaves in general. We say *in general* because the template still takes some directing. For example, the template might say that the control has a rectangle as its background, but the color or fill of that rectangle might be overridden by any particular control.

Because the template is a property, it can be set as part of a style. In fact, this is the most common way of defining a new control template. For example, we can modify the `Button` style to change all the buttons into ellipses (listing 6.9).

Listing 6.9 Style that makes buttons ellipses

```
<Style x:Key="CalcButton"  TargetType="Button">
  <Setter Property="Template">                          ❶ Sets template property
    <Setter.Value>
      <ControlTemplate TargetType="Button">
        <Ellipse Fill="LightGreen" />                   ❷ Sets content to ellipse
      </ControlTemplate>
    </Setter.Value>
  </Setter>
  <Setter Property="Control.Margin" Value="10"/>
</Style>
```

All we're doing here is setting the `Template` property ❶ via the style. In this case, we set the content to be a light green ellipse ❷. When the code is run, any controls that use this style replaces their control templates with the template here (figure 6.8).

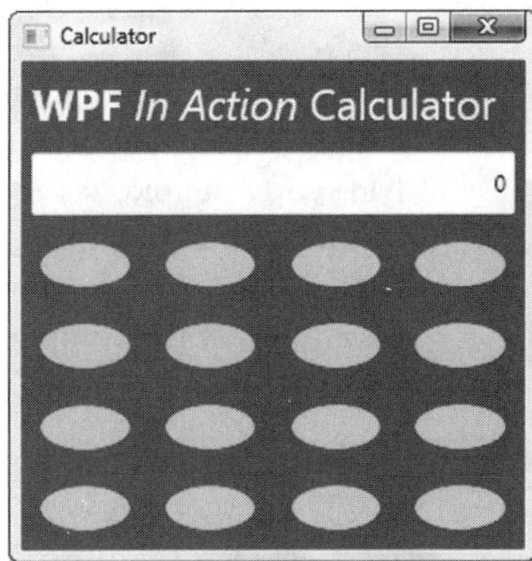

Figure 6.8 We've replaced the `Button` style to use an ellipse. Unfortunately, we've now lost the text from the buttons.

Depending on how late you were up last night, you may or may not notice a slight problem with the calculator. In fact, there are several problems. Aside from the obvious—there's no longer text on the buttons—the buttons no longer act like buttons. There are no visual clues when you move over the button or click the button. The buttons *do* still work, though—you can click them and do calculations—provided you have a good memory for where the various digits and operators are located.

6.3.2 *ContentPresenters*

To make the text show up again, we need to tell the system where to put that content. Fortunately, this is pretty easy. There's a special framework element called a `ContentPresenter`. When you put a `ContentPresenter` into a control template, WPF shoves the control's content wherever the content presenter says. As always, there's a wrinkle. A template can only hold a single framework element. You can put an ellipse there, or a rectangle, or any one thing, but you can't put an ellipse and a rectangle or, most importantly for our purposes, an ellipse *and* a content presenter.

This is the same issue you have when you're adding controls anywhere. Most places only support a single control, but that single control can be anything—including a layout panel. And a layout panel can hold any number of children. For simplicity, let's use a `Grid` layout panel (because this is the default) without adding any rows or columns so that it behaves like a `Canvas`, but with more support for positioning. Here's the XAML for the `ControlTemplate` (the rest of the style definition is unchanged):

```
<ControlTemplate TargetType="Button">
  <Grid>
    <Ellipse Fill="LightGreen"/>
    <ContentPresenter HorizontalAlignment="Center"
                      VerticalAlignment="Center"/>
  </Grid>
</ControlTemplate>
```

By adding the `Grid`, we can add two controls; the ellipse and the `ContentPresenter`. The `ContentPresenter` has both horizontal and vertical alignment set to center, so the content will be centered. Now if we run the calculator, we get our text back (figure 6.9).

It is worth mentioning that the content presenter presents whatever content the button had. For example, if we were drawing pictures on the buttons, or had other embedded controls, they would count as the content and would appear where the content presenter said. This is a key mechanism behind composition.

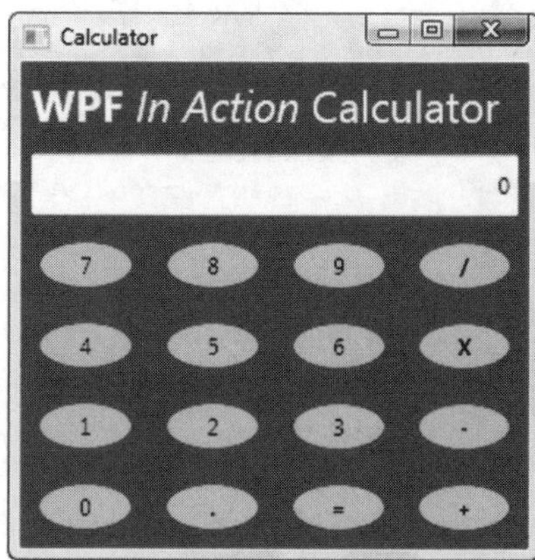

Figure 6.9 By using a content presenter, we now get the text to show up on the ellipse buttons.

6.3.3 Template binding

In the example so far, we've hardcoded the color for the buttons to a fairly ugly shade of green. If you wanted to add a border, you could also hardcode that, say, to the red used for the button border. You also have another option—you can bind any of the properties to the value set on the control. If there's code already setting a particular color on the button, you can use that color in the control presenter. For example, we already went to some effort to set a border brush for different controls. Let's use that to set the border around the ellipse. We just have to change the line in the XAML that draws the ellipse:

```
<Ellipse Fill="LightGreen" Stroke="{TemplateBinding Control.BorderBrush}"/>
```

`Stroke` is the property on an ellipse that controls the outline color. We're using the curly-brace notation again; but this time, instead of binding to a resource, we're binding to a property of the template—the border brush. The buttons now pick up the brush that's set on each button and use that to draw the outline of the ellipse. Figure 6.10 shows the results.

We can't say that this has improved the appearance of the calculator, but it's at least doing what we told it to do. But we still have the problem of the buttons not reacting like buttons. We'd at least like the buttons to change color or something when the user clicks them.

Figure 6.10 The ellipse border is now picking up the brush set for each individual button. It may be hard to see, but digits have a red outline, whereas operators have a dark green outline.

6.3.4 Triggers

We can make the buttons react to the user by adding triggers to the control template. A trigger does something when an event occurs or a property value changes. We aren't going to go into a huge amount of detail about triggers at this point But we *will* give you a simple example. Listing 6.10 sets a trigger on the `IsPressed` state of the `Button`.

Listing 6.10 Trigger on `IsPressed` state of `Button`

```
<Style x:Key="CalcButton"  TargetType="Button">
  <Setter Property="Template">
    <Setter.Value>
      <ControlTemplate TargetType="Button">
        <Grid>
          <Ellipse x:Name="theEllipse" Fill="LightGreen"          ❶
              Stroke="{TemplateBinding Control.BorderBrush}"/>
          <ContentPresenter HorizontalAlignment="Center"
                            VerticalAlignment="Center"/>
        </Grid>
      <ControlTemplate.Triggers>                              ❷
        <Trigger Property="Button.IsPressed" Value="True" >
          <Setter TargetName="theEllipse"
                  Property="Fill" Value="Yellow"/>      ❸
        </Trigger>
      </ControlTemplate.Triggers>
    </ControlTemplate>
   </Setter.Value>
  </Setter>
```

We went ahead and gave our ellipse a name—`theEllipse` ❶. We did that because the trigger needs to be able to reference the thing to change, and an easy way to do this is by name. If the template was more complex, we could give names to any element we want to change.

We then added a collection of triggers ❷ to the template. We could have any number of triggers, checking for things like focus changes, or mouse over; but, in this case, we only have the one. The trigger itself ❸ watches the `IsPressed` property on the control. The trigger fires when the value of the property becomes true (when the button is pressed). What the trigger does is controlled by setters—much like a general style setter. It finds the target object to change (`theEllipse`) and sets the `Fill` property to `Yellow`.

We don't have to worry about unsetting the color when the button is released. By default, WPF takes care of that for us—restoring the properties to their original values. Figure 6.11 shows the calculator with one of the buttons being pressed.

It isn't perfect, but at least there's some reaction when the button is pressed, providing an affordance to the user. In chapter 9, we'll play around with making this behavior a little fancier.

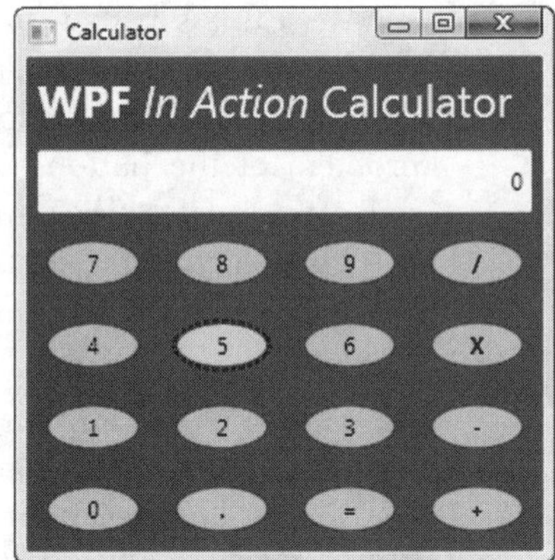

Figure 6.11 The 5 button is being pressed, triggering a color change.

> **Affordances**
>
> Affordances are characteristics of interfaces that provide clues and guidance to users. The classic example of an affordance is a doorknob. Because you see a knob on a door, you get a clue that you can manipulate the door. But if, instead of opening the door, it gives you, say, a million-volt electric shock, it would be a poor affordance—implying one capability but providing another.
>
> Many UIs go the way of the million-volt electric shock by not clearly providing guidance to the user as to how to manipulate things and whether they're being successful. This is particularly troublesome because computer UI isn't natural to begin with. Providing feedback on things like button clicks is important because the feedback lets users know they're successfully operating within the virtual environment.

Styles and control templates are extremely powerful. In addition to some of the capabilities we've shown so far, you can even add things like animation based on styles, which we'll demonstrate in chapter 8. To take styles to their logical conclusion, you can create a series of related styles for different types of controls and build them into a theme.

6.4 Themes

When Windows XP first came out, we thought it looked like a cartoon—big green buttons, blue gradients, curved edges everywhere. The Microsoft usability engineers apparently knew what they were doing,[5] because now, a few years later, the formerly sharp-looking Windows 2000 now looks dowdy and old. The new look-and-feel of Windows XP was driven by themes. The default Luna theme even has three versions—the

---

[5] One of us had the opportunity of sitting down with one of the Microsoft usability engineers. She had advanced degrees in computer science *and* psychology.

default blue, the futuristic silver (Metallic, shown in figure 6.12), and the slightly nauseating green (Homestead).

Unfortunately, the implementation of themes was, shall we say, ugly. The themes had to work with existing applications that knew nothing about themes, as well as allow new applications to take advantage of the themed elements. In addition to its Byzantine coding style, it was also very much tied to the Win32 HWND model. This fact is quite relevant to our current topic because WPF *isn't*. When you run a WPF application, the main frame of your window is still a `Window` as far as Windows is concerned, and the theme code can paint the title bar and the borders of your window. But everything *inside* your window is WPF-only, and it isn't possible (or particularly desirable) for the Windows theme code to do any of the drawing.

Fortunately, where implementing themes in classic Windows was a nightmare, WPF is built around the idea of styling. And what is a theme but a collection of styles? Providing a theme for WPF is as simple as building a resource dictionary and referencing it. Unfortunately, WPF doesn't rule the world (yet), so WPF applications are caught between the Windows themes and WPF styles.

The WPF team worked (hacked?) around the problem by implementing a series of WPF styles that mimic all the common Windows themes. When your WPF application

Figure 6.12 Windows XP with the Metallic version of the Luna theme and the default background image. Does anyone else think that hill looks like something out of the *Teletubbies*?

starts up, WPF figures out which Windows theme is running and then loads one of its own themes that matches the look-and-feel around it. That way, your application looks like other running applications—provided you're using one of the standard Windows themes. This approach has already broken down to some extent. Microsoft shipped a new theme to go with the release of the Zune—called the Zune theme. WPF doesn't know about it, so WPF applications running under the Zune theme revert to the classic Windows 2000 look-and-feel. (So far, though, we haven't heard complaints from either of the people who bought Zunes.)

6.4.1 *Using a specific theme*

You don't have to rely on the automatic behavior for choosing a theme. If you want to, you can explicitly use one of the existing themes (or a theme built by someone else). You reference a theme more or less the same way that you reference any other standalone resource dictionary. The only difference is that you have to reference the theme via the assembly that contains it, and you have to use the assembly's complete name, including its strong key token. Listing 6.11 shows the resource section from a window that references the new Windows Vista Aero theme.

Listing 6.11 Referencing the Vista Aero theme

```
<Window.Resources>
  <ResourceDictionary Source="/PresentationFramework.Aero, Version=3.0.0.0,
       Culture=neutral, PublicKeyToken=31bf3856ad364e35
       ;component/themes/aero.normalcolor.xaml" />
</Window.Resources>
```

This code references an assembly that Microsoft provides called `PresentationFramework.Aero`, which contains the theme. The `Version`, `Culture`, and `PublicKeyToken` are all part of the fully qualified strong name of the assembly. (Theme assemblies have to be strongly named.) The theme itself is a resource dictionary stored in the resource component/themes/aero.normalcolor.xaml. Figure 6.13 shows an XP dialog with a few controls and with the theme explicitly set to use Aero.

Figure 6.13 Even though this window is running on Windows XP (note the XP-style title bar and border), the theme has explicitly been set to use the Windows Vista Aero style.

The window in figure 6.13 is running on Windows XP, but the controls look how they would when running on Windows Vista. You can't see it in the picture, but the controls have all sorts of little animations as well. For example, when you click a check box, the check slowly fades in. The bits drawn by Windows directly—the title bar and the border—still look like the style for Windows XP.

> **When to use a different theme**
>
> In general, it's a good idea for applications to be consistent with their operating environment. When applications look (or, worse, work) in a different manner than the rest of a user's applications, it makes it harder for the user to adapt.
>
> Sometimes it's okay to vary from this, within reason. The look of an application can be one of its selling points, and building a theme for your applications is perfectly fine—so long as it's consistent within itself and reasonably consistent with other applications. For example, in figure 6.13, the controls are using a different style, but there's no question that a button is a button or a text box is a text box.
>
> It's also sometimes easier and quicker to build an application if you can rely on particular elements. For example, if you have a number of graphics on the page, having to create a different version of each graphic that looks good with green controls or blue controls or silver controls can be extremely onerous.

Microsoft provides support for six different themes. Table 6.1 shows how to reference them and what they look like. We do need to warn you that manually switching between the built-in themes is considered a no-no by Microsoft. They claim the right to change the references at any time, although we think this is unlikely.[6]

Table 6.1 WPF-supported themes

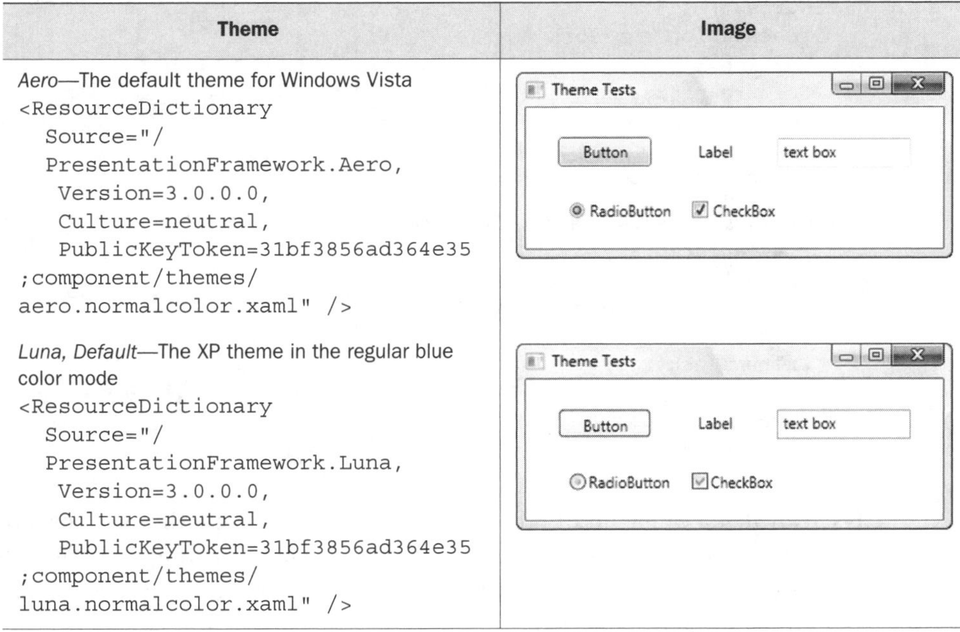

Theme	Image

Aero—The default theme for Windows Vista
`<ResourceDictionary`
`  Source="/`
`  PresentationFramework.Aero,`
`   Version=3.0.0.0,`
`   Culture=neutral,`
`   PublicKeyToken=31bf3856ad364e35`
`;component/themes/`
`aero.normalcolor.xaml" />`
	Theme Tests
	Button Label text box
	RadioButton CheckBox

Luna, Default—The XP theme in the regular blue color mode
`<ResourceDictionary`
`  Source="/`
`  PresentationFramework.Luna,`
`   Version=3.0.0.0,`
`   Culture=neutral,`
`   PublicKeyToken=31bf3856ad364e35`
`;component/themes/`
`luna.normalcolor.xaml" />`
	Theme Tests
	Button Label text box
	RadioButton CheckBox

[6] In fact, there are a couple of scenarios where you really need to be able to reference the existing assemblies explicitly—for instance, if you want to extend an existing style.

Table 6.1 WPF-supported themes *(continued)*

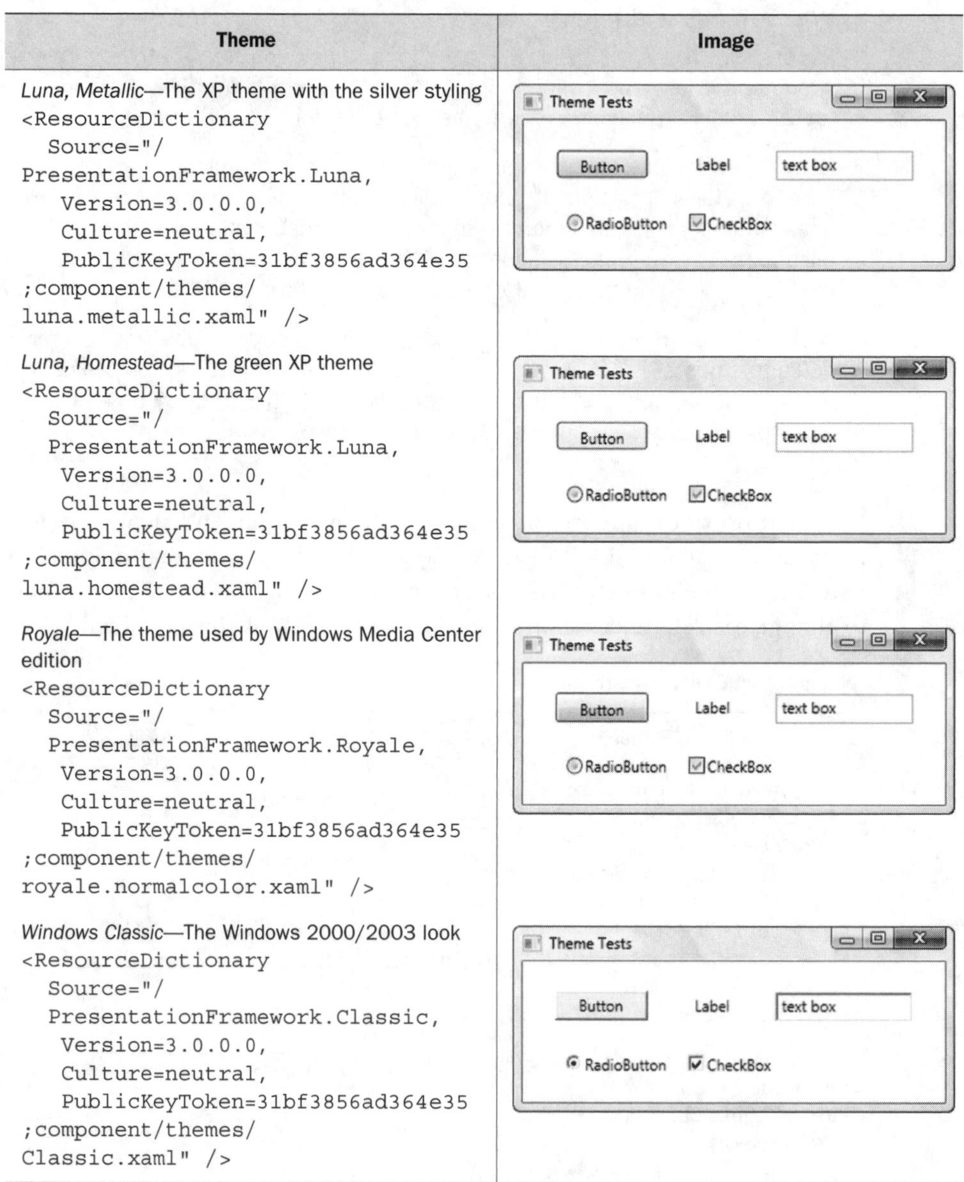

Theme	Image

Luna, Metallic—The XP theme with the silver styling
`<ResourceDictionary`
`Source="/`
`PresentationFramework.Luna,`
`Version=3.0.0.0,`
`Culture=neutral,`
`PublicKeyToken=31bf3856ad364e35`
`;component/themes/`
`luna.metallic.xaml" />`	

Luna, Homestead—The green XP theme
`<ResourceDictionary`
`Source="/`
`PresentationFramework.Luna,`
`Version=3.0.0.0,`
`Culture=neutral,`
`PublicKeyToken=31bf3856ad364e35`
`;component/themes/`
`luna.homestead.xaml" />`	

Royale—The theme used by Windows Media Center edition
`<ResourceDictionary`
`Source="/`
`PresentationFramework.Royale,`
`Version=3.0.0.0,`
`Culture=neutral,`
`PublicKeyToken=31bf3856ad364e35`
`;component/themes/`
`royale.normalcolor.xaml" />`	

Windows Classic—The Windows 2000/2003 look
`<ResourceDictionary`
`Source="/`
`PresentationFramework.Classic,`
`Version=3.0.0.0,`
`Culture=neutral,`
`PublicKeyToken=31bf3856ad364e35`
`;component/themes/`
`Classic.xaml" />`	

It's likely that a whole lot of other themes will be available either for download or for sale in the near future. You can also create your own by creating a resource dictionary in an assembly (although you must strongly sign the assembly). But we're not going to go into the specific details here.

6.4.2 Changing themes from code

As well as setting the theme via XAML, it's easy to change the theme programmatically. You could, for example, allow your users to choose a theme for your application from either the system or custom theme assemblies. You could also programmatically set a default theme if the appropriate theme wasn't found, although the code to do this would be tricky (and, frankly, is something that WPF should support directly).

To set a theme in code, you have to load the resource dictionary from its assembly and then make it your resource dictionary. Listing 6.12 changes the theme for the `Window` to the Aero theme.

Listing 6.12 Changing the theme to Aero

```
Uri uriToTheme = new Uri("/PresentationFramework.Aero,
     Version=3.0.0.0,Culture=neutral,
     PublicKeyToken=31bf3856ad364e35
     ;component/themes/aero.normalcolor.xaml",UriKind.Relative);

object theme = Application.LoadComponent(uriToTheme);
this.Resources = (ResourceDictionary)theme;
```

In this code, we create a URI that points to the resource. You may notice that the contents of the URI are exactly the same as the XAML we used to point to the theme. Then we load the theme and literally replace the `Window`'s resources with the loaded resources.

In fact, just for fun, we hooked up the button on the form to a method that cycled between different themes. Clicking the button was way more fun than it should have been. We really should get out more.

Although this code works, there are a couple of issues. First of all, we're changing the `Window`'s resources instead of the entire application's. This is an easy fix—we just change where we store the resources, and what we update:

```
Application.Current.Resources = (ResourceDictionary)theme;
```

Now, when you click the button, every control in the entire application changes (so long as it isn't overridden with a custom style). The second problem is a little trickier; when you replace the `Resources` collection on the window or the app, you're blowing away any of your own local resources. This was fine when the entire `Window`'s resources were pointing at the theme, but more of a problem when you're merging multiple dictionaries. Fortunately, the problem is also the solution; instead of replacing the entire resource dictionary, you can work with the merged dictionary.

For example, suppose we have a theme reference and a reference to a local resource dictionary:

```
<Window.Resources>
  <ResourceDictionary>
    <ResourceDictionary.MergedDictionaries>
      <ResourceDictionary Source="/PresentationFramework.Classic,
        Version=3.0.0.0, Culture=neutral, PublicKeyToken=31bf3856ad364e35
```

```
        ;component/themes/Classic.xaml" />          <- Reference to Classic theme
      <ResourceDictionary Source="MyLocalResources.xaml"/>   <- Reference to some local resources
    </ResourceDictionary.MergedDictionaries>
  </ResourceDictionary>
</Window.Resources>
```

This is nothing new, except that one of the merged resource dictionaries is coming from a system theme assembly. Now, instead of replacing the entire `ResourceDictionary`, we can update the `Resource`'s collection of merged dictionaries:

```
if(this.Resources.MergedDictionaries.Count > 0)
  this.Resources.MergedDictionaries[0] = (ResourceDictionary)theme;
```

This changes the theme reference, while leaving our local resources alone. You may notice that we're relying on the specific position of the theme reference in the `MergedDictionaries` collection. Unfortunately, there's no built-in way to tell which is a theme resource dictionary and which is the local collection. To the system, there's no real difference. You could try a few tricks such as storing a particular resource in your own resource dictionaries that wouldn't be present in the system ones. You could also check the `Source` property of the `ResourceDictionary`, which contains the URI, to look for system references.

The nice thing about themes is that they're nothing special—they're resource dictionaries that have been shoved into their own assemblies. The power of this is that you don't have to do anything different to work with a system theme, your own theme, or your own locally-defined resources.

6.5 Summary

Sometimes, when you look at a piece of code or a design, you see an element of elegance. Even with the most complex systems, that elegance tends to come from a simple, clean idea that has been well executed. We wouldn't want to imply that everything about WPF is that way,[7] but both the Property System and the resource mechanisms of WPF have that core simplicity that makes them flexible and powerful. If you think about it, they're both built around simple dictionaries, yet they empower the rest of the system.

But the real world intrudes. The simple cores can't do everything, particularly when working with existing systems. That's how you end up with duplicate (Windows/WPF) theme mechanisms or a bunch of different ways to refer to different types of things in XAML. Nevertheless, the approach to properties, styles, and resources in WPF seems superior to any of the competing mechanisms we've seen so far, and much of that is due to its core simplicity.

The event system in WPF is also simple yet flexible. It addresses some of the issues of events in Window Form implementations, as well as some of the unique issues that WPF, by its compositional nature, creates for itself. The next chapter will go into detail about the event system.

---

[7] After all, *we* didn't write it. Everyone knows that only their own code is truly perfect.

7 Events

This chapter covers:

- Bubble-up events
- Tunnel-down events
- Handling events even when they've already been handled
- Class-level events
- Clever ways to annoy your users

If you've used both MFC and Windows Forms, you'll know that the event model in Windows Forms was a major improvement over the message-map model used by MFC. Controls in Windows Forms exposed events that could be subscribed to by code that cares, and that code was called when appropriate. The classic example is a user clicking a button, resulting in the appropriate handler being called. Many other events work in the same way.

Classic Windows Forms events did have some issues. The most problematic was that the code that cared about the event either needed to have direct access to the event generator, or the event had to be manually passed up the chain. For example, picture a button on a user control on a form in an application. If the application needs to know about the event, the application either needs to know about the button (breaking encapsulation), or the button needs to tell the user control, which needs to tell the form, which needs to tell the application—which is a pain in the neck.

WPF adds an additional complication—composition. Before WPF, a radio button was just a radio button—a control that had behavior. With WPF, you can think of a radio button as a series of shapes joined together cooperatively (a circle, a dot to indicate checked, the text, the focus rectangle, and so on). Each of these needs to know what's going on in some manner; which "bit" of the control gets the click that eventually generates an event can vary. If you had to subscribe to an event on the circle, the dot, *and* the text in order to determine if someone had clicked the radio button, it would get seriously tedious. This nesting can be taken arbitrarily further—the circle for the radio button could be replaced with a 3D animation, itself made up of different elements.

To address these and other issues, WPF has a number of new (and very cool) event-based capabilities. The most powerful and useful of these are *routed events*, the primary topic of this chapter.

7.1 Routed events

In a classic .NET event, an interested party has to directly subscribe to an event in order to be notified. For non-UI code, this makes a lot of sense. After all, there's no particular way for regular code to know who else might care and what legitimate rules may exist for passing events to other objects. With UI, events have a pretty clear path—below the top level, each control is owned by another control. When you look at the XAML for a `Window`, the natural nesting of items defines that path. In Visual Studio 2008, you can look at the document outline for our calculator (figure 7.1), for example, by selecting View > Other Windows > Document Outline from the menu.

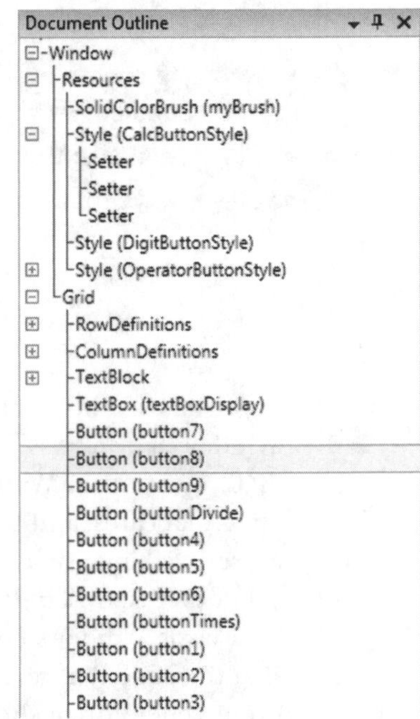

Figure 7.1 The Document Outline for the calculator shows the natural tree of controls.

Notice how the `Window` holds the `Grid` which, in turn, holds the various text controls and all the buttons. It would be fairly natural to expect that, if a button click wasn't handled by the button itself, perhaps the `Grid` or the `Window` might handle it.

Routed events give us this capability. An event can be defined to bubble up to its parents in the element tree. Events can also be defined to tunnel down, which is the exact opposite. If the `Window` doesn't handle the event, then the `Grid` is given the chance, and then, finally the children are given a shot (figure 7.2).

The decision of an event's *routing strategy*—whether an event should bubble up or tunnel down—is made when the event is defined. `Click`, for example, is a bubble-up event, so it can be caught by elements higher up in the element tree. `PreviewDragEnter` is a tunnel-down event sent when a user drags something over a `Window`. If the highest level doesn't want to handle it, a lower level can be asked, and so on. There's also one additional routing strategy: direct. Direct events work pretty much like standard .NET events. A direct event can only be handled by subscribing to the specific element that raises it.

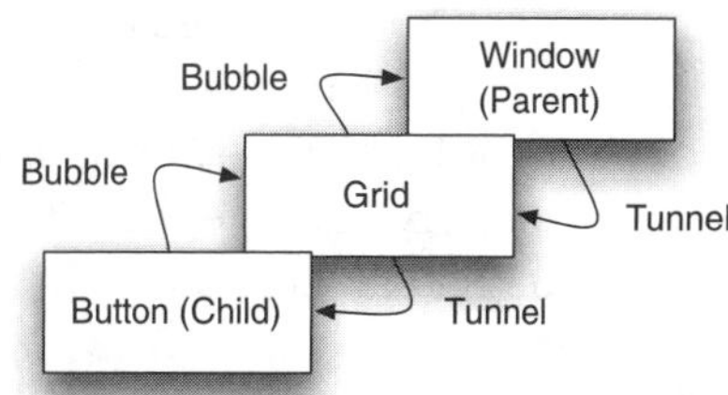

Figure 7.2 Events can be set up to bubble up to their parents in the element tree or tunnel down to their children.

Routing events follow a similar pattern, and are implemented in a similar way, to properties in the WPF Property System. We associate events with objects that don't know what they're for. We'll demonstrate this in the next section.

7.1.1 Bubbling events

Wouldn't it be nice if, in our calculator, we didn't have to specify a handler for every single button? Well, because the `Click` event on a button is a bubble-up event, we can remove all the individual `Click="OnClick"` handlers from the buttons and, instead, put a single handler on one of the higher-level containers such as the `Window` or the `Grid`:

```
<Grid Button.Click="OnAnyButtonClick">
```

We have to manually add the event handler—the Properties grid list of events will only show us those events that are directly exposed by the `Grid`. If the Properties grid had to show all the events of all the children, it would get quite messy (although a tree that showed children and their events might not be a bad UI).

Anyway, the `Button.Click` handler does exactly what you'd expect—it waits to be told that a button has been clicked and then calls the `OnAnyButtonClick` method. It gets called if any button contained within the `Grid` is clicked. Just as with attached properties, we have to be more explicit in our declaration because `Grid` doesn't expose a `Click` event—we have to say `Button.Click` instead of just `Click`. Let's look at the implementation of `OnAnyButtonClick` (listing 7.1).

Listing 7.1 `OnAnyButtonClick` implementation

```
private void OnAnyButtonClick
              (object sender, RoutedEventArgs e)      ❶ Routed event arguments
{
  Button btn = e.OriginalSource as Button;            ❷ Event originator
  if (btn.Tag is Operator)                            ❸ Determines the button type
    OnClickOperator(e.OriginalSource, e);
  else
    OnClickDigit(e.OriginalSource, e);
}
```

As we've mentioned before, instead of the old, dowdy `EventArgs` that used to be passed, routed events pass a `RoutedEventArgs` object ❶ instead. `RoutedEventArgs` have several useful properties, including the `OriginalSource` property ❷ that contains the object that originally generated the event. The original source has to be passed because the object handling the event is no longer required to be the object generating the event. If we were to look at the sender, we'd see that it's the `Grid` rather than a button.

Now we have a problem, though. Before, we simply hooked up a different handler for operators than for digits, so we knew that the proper event handler would end up being called. Now, the same handler is responsible for both types of buttons, so we need to determine if the button is an operator or a digit.

In this case, we're relying on the fact that we're storing an `Operator` in the `Tag` of operator buttons ❸. This approach isn't super elegant, but it works. For a more complex implementation, we might have created a custom object and associated an instance with each button that made it clear which was which. Our cheap implementation looks for an `Operator` in the `Tag`. If it's an `Operator`, we assume the button is an operator. Otherwise, we assume it's a digit. We then call the appropriate handler for each. Because we're being cheap, we didn't bother creating methods that just took the button, but we could have done that too.

Those of you who are paying close attention will have noticed that there's one button we aren't handling—the decimal point, which is neither a digit nor an operator. We could put another case in the `OnAnyButtonClick()` handler, something like:

```
if (btn == buttonDecimal)
  HandleDecimal();
else if (btn.Tag is String)
  ...
```

But it seems odd to add in a single case here, when we could simply leave the handler in place for the decimal button:

```
<Button Name="buttonDecimal" Click="OnClickDecimal">.</Button>
```

The `OnClickDecimal()` method handles the decimal click as before. The only problem is that we now have the `OnAnyButtonClick()` handler in place. Unlike properties, events aren't overridden; instead, all specified handlers are called. When the user hits the decimal point, the `OnClickDecimal()` method properly handles the decimal point, and then `OnAnyButtonClick()` assumes that the decimal is a digit and calls the `OnDigit()` method, which will snort milk out of its nose and crash.

Fortunately, WPF has a simple and elegant way of handling this situation. Once a handler has handled an event, it can say so, stopping it from doing any more bubbling. We can modify the `OnClickDecimal()` handler to indicate that it has handled the event by setting the appropriate property on the `RoutedEventArgs`:

```
private void OnClickDecimal(object sender, RoutedEventArgs e)
{
  HandleDecimal();
  e.Handled = true;
}
```

Setting the `Handled` property to `true` stops the event from bubbling any further. The same property prevents additional tunneling, as you'll see in the next section. We're now handling all our buttons in a much more elegant way even if, from a user's perspective, nothing has changed. In the next section, we'll do something that adds functionality to our long-suffering utility.

7.1.2 Tunneling events

When you think about it, making a calculator that looks like a real, physical calculator is a little bit silly. Although it has the advantage of instant recognizability, making the user use a mouse to click buttons in rough mimicry of what he could do far more quickly with his finger on a real calculator isn't the best UI strategy—particularly if the user has a perfectly serviceable keyboard with a numeric keypad and (presumably) a perfectly serviceable finger.

If we're going to make a UI that looks like a real-world object, the least we can do is make it possible for the user to *also* use his numeric keypad or other keys on his keyboard.

To do this properly, we'll make use of a different type of event—a tunneling (or tunnel-down) event. Now, it may seem greedy to want yet another type of event, considering that, before WPF, we didn't even have bubbling (or bubble-up) events; but, if you look at how implementing this functionality works using bubble-up events, you'll see where the need to tunneling comes in.

An event called `KeyDown` is triggered when a key on the keyboard is pressed, and a matching `KeyUp` when the key is released. Conceptually, these events are familiar to you if you've used Windows Forms, MFC, or the raw Windows SDK. If you're familiar with those older technologies, you'll also now probably experience a slight twinge of pain that goes by the name of *focus*.

In Windows, only one widget at a time has focus, and that widget is the one that Windows thinks you're most likely working with—the one that, for instance, sends all keyboard events. For example, if you click the 2 button on the calculator, you notice that it gets a little dotted square around the button to let you know that the 2 button has focus. When you press a keyboard button (say, 3), the keystroke is sent to the 2 button, which happily ignores it.

This is where WPF events can shine. We don't care what has focus, so long as it's somewhere on the calculator—we want to catch keys and act appropriately when they're hit.

We could do exactly the same thing we did earlier with the `Click` event and catch it on the `Grid`. In that case, if the 2 button has focus and the user hits another number, the event first gives the 2 button a shot of handling it and then passes it up the chain. But what would happen if the text box where we're displaying our results has focus (figure 7.3)?

Using a bubble-up event, we hit the 2 button, set focus to the `TextBox`, and then hit the number 3 one time. The `TextBox` gets the first chance at the event and handles it normally. Then our handler catches it at the `Grid` and inserts it at the end. Obviously, we could have made the TextBox read-only, but in some situations, we might want to allow direct editing (for example, to allow the user to clear the value).

What we need is a chance to handle the event before the TextBox. So, instead of waiting for an event to bubble up from where it originated in the hopes that we're the first to handle it, we want to be the first to catch it before it gets given to some nasty control that might do something unspeakable to it before we have our chance.

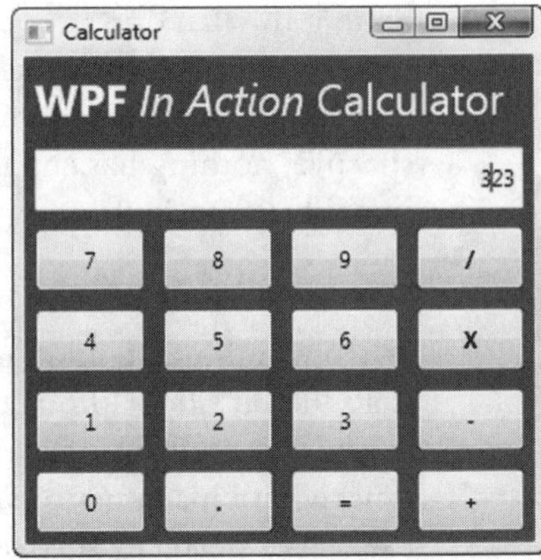

Figure 7.3 Using a bubble-up event when focus is on the text box causes a bad side effect—the text box gets the keystroke and enters the key, and then our handler gets it and handles the key properly.

With many input events (keyboard, mouse, Ink, and so on), in addition to the bubble-up event, there is also a second event that, rather than bubbling up, tunnels down, starting with the top of our visual tree and working down to the control with focus. For the keyboard, these events are called PreviewKeyDown and PreviewKeyUp. It's a convention for tunnel-down events to be prefixed with the word *Preview* and to have a matching bubble-up event without the word *Preview* to allow for complete flexibility. All the higher-level controls have a chance to preview the event and handle it if they see fit. If it isn't handled, then the regular bubbling event is fired and bubbles up until it *is* handled. Table 7.1 shows how a keystroke is routed if not handled.

Table 7.1 Routing of a keyboard event

User hits the 3 key >	
	Window is sent the PreviewKeyDown event.
	Grid is sent the PreviewKeyDown event.
	Focused button is sent the PreviewKeyDown event.
	Focused button is sent the KeyDown event.
	Grid is sent the KeyDown event.
	Window is sent the KeyDown event.
	Window is sent the PreviewKeyUp event.
	Grid is sent the PreviewKeyUp event.
	Focused button is sent the PreviewKeyUp event.
	Focused button is sent the KeyUp event.
	Grid is sent the KeyUp event.
	Window is sent the KeyUp event.

Of course, if any of the handlers mark the event as handled, it isn't sent to any of the remaining handlers.

NOTE Even though the tunnel-down and bubble-up events are paired, they *are* two separate events. The `RoutedEventArgs` sent to the `PreviewKeyDown` and to `KeyDown` are two different objects. Marking `PreviewKeyDown` prevents `KeyDown` from being fired purely because of logic built into the event handler and not because of generic behavior related to paired events. Usually, this behavior is consistent, but it's possible for the behavior to be different for some events.

To handle the keyboard, we want to catch the `PreviewKeyDown` event at the `Grid` level:

```
<Grid Button.Click="OnAnyButtonClick" PreviewKeyDown="OnKeyDown">
```

Then we need to define the `OnKeyDown` handler (listing 7.2).

Listing 7.2 OnKeyDown handler

```
private void OnKeyDown(object sender, KeyEventArgs e)        ❶ Key event arguments
{
  if((e.Key >= Key.D0) && (e.Key <= Key.D9))                ❷ Regular keyboard digit
  {
    int digit = (int)(e.Key - Key.D0);
    HandleDigit(digit);
  }
  else if ((e.Key >= Key.NumPad0) && (e.Key <= Key.NumPad9))   ❸ Numeric keypad digit
  {
    int digit = (int)(e.Key - Key.NumPad0);
    HandleDigit(digit);
  }
  else
  {
    switch (e.Key)                                          ❹ Handles other keys
    {
      case Key.Add:
        ExecuteLastOperator(Operator.Plus);
        break;
      case Key.Subtract:
        ExecuteLastOperator(Operator.Minus);
        break;
      case Key.Divide:
        ExecuteLastOperator(Operator.Divide);
        break;
      case Key.Multiply:
        ExecuteLastOperator(Operator.Times);
        break;
      case Key.OemPlus:
      case Key.Enter:
        ExecuteLastOperator(Operator.Equals);
        break;
      case Key.Decimal:
        HandleDecimal();
        break;
```

```
        }
    }
    e.Handled = true;     <-- ❺ Marks event as handled
}
```

We aren't going to go into a huge amount of detail about the method itself, but there are a few things worth noting. First, we're getting a `KeyEventArgs` ❶ instead of a `RoutedEventArgs`. `KeyEventArgs` is derived from `RoutedEventArgs` but adds a few additional details (like the key that's hit). We check to see if the key hit is a digit ❷ or a numeric keypad digit ❸ based on the enum value, and then convert to a digit and call the digit handler. It's kind of cool that we can easily tell digits and operators apart without worrying about scan codes, but it's also a pain that there's no easy way to ask: "Is this a digit?" Then we look for other keys ❹—operator, decimal, and so on—and handle them appropriately.

Finally, we mark the event as handled ❺—no matter what. For our calculator, we're saying that we want the final word on all keystrokes and don't want anything else to handle keys. We could be a bit more flexible and only mark the event as handled if we, you know, handle it, but this way we don't allow any extraneous, unplanned keyboard behavior.

This is a pretty low-level way of handling keystrokes. There is another mechanism in WPF that we could use—we could associate keystrokes with `Commands`. Whereas events tend to be more low level (mouse moved, key was hit), `Commands` are more like the options you see on a menu or toolbar, such as Save or Print. Often with `Commands`, you don't care whether a command came from a menu, toolbar, hot-key, or somewhere else, and the command mechanism in WPF is built to handle these scenarios. We'll demonstrate that mechanism in chapter 10. But there are still many situations where you'll want to do things at the lowly event level.

One thing that we've left out is making the buttons provide feedback when the associated key is detected. This would be a nice affordance, but because the appearance of the digit in the output provides some feedback, we lazed out on that.

So far we've defined all our events via XAML; but, in the real world, there are often situations where you want or need to subscribe to events via code, such as when you're dynamically creating controls.

7.2 Events from code

As with properties, and WPF in general, anything you can do in XAML, you can also do in code, although the reverse isn't always true. If you want to subscribe to a routed event on the object that exposes it, you can use the traditional event subscription mechanism:

```
button1.Click += new RoutedEventHandler(OnButton1Clicked);
```

This is fine if you want to directly subscribe to the object that contains the event, but it won't work if you want to catch the event at a higher level. `Grid`, for example, doesn't have a `Click` event exposed, and it wouldn't make much sense for it to do so because it isn't a button. Nor could `Grid`, `Window`, or any of the containing classes practically expose all the possible events of all possible children.

Instead, you can call a method called `AddHandler` to indicate your interest in an event. This method takes a `RoutedEvent` which is generally available as a static member on the class that exposes the event. This parallels the Property System mechanism.

For example, let's add a handler to our top-level `Window` to catch the `Click` event, as well as the beep every time a user clicks a button. You might want to do this, say, if you really hate your users. A good place to do this would be in the `Window_Loaded()` handler. (In your code, make sure you've subscribed to the `Loaded` event on the `Window`.)

```
private void Window_Loaded(object sender, RoutedEventArgs e)
{
  AddHandler(Button.ClickEvent, new RoutedEventHandler(OnAnyClickOnForm));
}
```

`Button.ClickEvent` is the static `RoutedEvent` for the `Click` event that lets the system hook into the appropriate event. The second argument is the handler for the method we want to call, which plays a beep:

```
private void OnAnyClickOnForm(object sender, RoutedEventArgs e)
{
  System.Media.SystemSounds.Beep.Play();
}
```

Go ahead and run the calculator. As you click the buttons, if everything is working, you should get really annoyed. Note that using the keyboard doesn't cause the beep. We're explicitly dealing with the button clicks. Something odd that you may notice: You get a beep for *almost* all the buttons, but not the decimal point. Strange, no?

Actually, it isn't that strange. We already have a handler for the decimal point, and that handler marks the event as `Handled`. It needs to do this to stop the generic grid-button handler from getting confused. Fortunately, there's a nice, simple fix.

7.2.1 handledEventsToo

Sometimes a property or parameter has a name that pretty much tells you everything you need to know. `handledEventsToo` is a flag you can specify if you want to handle the event too, even if it has been marked as handled. The flag is a parameter on the `AddHandler` method—we pass `true` as a third argument to have the handler be called even if another handler has marked the event as handled:

```
AddHandler(Button.ClickEvent,
               new RoutedEventHandler(OnAnyClickOnForm),true);
```

Now, when we run the code, we get a nice, irritating beep even when the decimal point is clicked. By the way, we have to set this flag via the `AddHandler` call; there's no way to set it via XAML.

This code catches all buttons clicks that belong to the object and objects below on the visual tree. Sometimes, you want to catch an event for all instances of that object. There's a way of doing that too.

7.2.2 *Class events*

WPF allows you to register for an event for all instances of a particular class. For example, you could catch the `Click` event for all buttons, no matter where they are. There are several advantages to this approach versus putting a handler at the top-level control. One is that this handler is called *first* before all the specific handlers, so you have the first crack at dealing with the event. Another is that it avoids cluttering up the top-level object and lets you encapsulate the handlers more appropriately—particularly useful with your own custom controls. Also, it's a little bit faster because it doesn't have to navigate the tree.

You have to register for class events in a static constructor. The following code registers for the `ClickEvent` on all buttons:

```
static Window1()
{
  EventManager.RegisterClassHandler(typeof(Button), Button.ClickEvent,
     new RoutedEventHandler(ClassButtonHandler));
}
```

Here, we specify the type of the class for which we're registering, the specific event and the method to call. The method (`ClassButtonHandler`) looks much like any other routed event handler, except that it has to be static:

```
private static void ClassButtonHandler(object sender, RoutedEventArgs e)
{
  System.Media.SystemSounds.Beep.Play();
}
```

If you're following along, make sure that you remove the `OnAnyClickOnForm` registration and handler before you run this code or clicking buttons might lead to temporary two-beep insanity.

By the way, you could also mark the event as handled here, in which case none of the other handlers will be called, unless they've set `handledEventsToo` to `true`.

7.3 *Summary*

When we start talking about custom controls, we'll need to look into how events are implemented and new events are defined. Overall, the event system is fairly nice, and the ability to bubble-up and tunnel-down is extremely handy.

We've improved the calculator by adding keyboard support and made it more annoying by adding beeps when you click keys. But the calculator is still pretty plain vanilla. Given all the hype about WPF, we should be able to make the calculator a lot cooler—and that's the subject of the next chapter.

8

Oooh, shiny!

This chapter covers:

- Layered effects
- Animation
- Transforms
- A poor attempt at counting the dimensions of a page

Unless you build games or screensavers for a living, chances are that your applications are, well, a little boring. After all, they have work to do, and it's pretty hard to justify spending an extra month adding flare and élan to that time-sheet entry program. WPF is as much about those time-sheet programs as anything else—as merely the next generation technology for building applications.

But WPF has another side as well—it isn't all about property systems and layout composition—WPF is hot! Or at least it can be. This chapter shows how you can add some glitter to your applications. Some things are easy, and others tricky—but still considerably easier than they would've been before WPF. As you'll see, half the problem is figuring out how to approach a problem; the solutions themselves tend to be relatively easy to implement once the approach has been figured out.

Some people, including many people at Microsoft, will say that Visual Studio isn't the appropriate tool for creating effects like the ones shown in this chapter. The new model is to have a graphic artist use a tool like Expression Blend to do the fancy stuff while the developers toil in an underground bunker doing all the boring "application" work.

From our perspective, there are several problems with this model. First of all, this is a book about using WPF with Visual Studio 2008, so going off into Expression Blend would be quite a departure from the topic of the book. But, more practically speaking, we don't have a graphic designer, and we know that most development shops don't either. Expression Blend is an artist's tool and isn't remotely intuitive to developers.[1] Unless you do have the resources to have a dedicated graphic designer, switching between paradigms for development isn't necessarily a good idea.

Anyway, enough of our ranting. In this chapter, we'll give our long-suffering calculator a makeover. We'll give it some snazzy-looking glass buttons that glow when pressed, and also use a simple transform to create a cool reflection effect (and also talk about some other transform options). Although we'll be covering a number of different, unrelated technologies here, the thing that brings them together (other than their general shininess) is that they're all about how you can combine some simple underlying capabilities to create some impressive effects.

There is a serious side to this chapter as well. For commercial software, having a modern, sexy look-and-feel can have a significant impact on customer impressions and, therefore, on sales. For non-commercial software, a good looking application, rightly or wrongly, is less likely to be thought of as buggy, so users tend to try to solve problems themselves before blaming the software.

That means you can spend more time making the application shiny and ignore all those bugs that keep deleting the user's data.

8.1 Glass buttons

There's something about glass that looks modern and cool. Some operating systems understand that and make their buttons look like glass from the get-go. Well, that's fine and all, but if everyone has glass buttons, then what makes your application special? The lack of built-in glass buttons in Vista is obviously there to give programmers the opportunity to make their own applications stand out by implementing the effect themselves.

Figure 8.1 Calculator with glass buttons. The 6 is glowing because it has focus.

So, we'll start punching up the calculator by giving it glass buttons (figure 8.1). In fact, a lot of the chapter is given over to glass buttons because

[1] Developers who do web development will have less trouble here because Expression Blend isn't a million miles away from some web-development or Flash tools.

they're relatively time-consuming, but we'll also demonstrate several interesting capabilities along the way.

There are a lot of different ways to draw glassy buttons, and many of them are likely better looking than our way, but ours has the advantage of being (relatively) simple to create, scales easily, and is easy to recolor. Users of Expression Blend with some artistic talent can create some stunning effects. But we specifically want to create our effects inside Visual Studio.

So, our effects *are* created entirely using Visual Studio. Unfortunately, the designer gives you almost zero help here—you pretty much have to edit XAML directly to do this. At least XAML does have IntelliSense, so it isn't all bad. Also, the Visual Studio team has made the property editor work on items that you select in the XAML. For example, if you click a `Rectangle` XAML element, the property window shows its properties and allows them to be changed.

The glass-button look is based on a `ControlTemplate` just like we used in chapter 6. To get started, let's set up a basic lozenge-shaped button by creating a `ControlTemplate` with a rounded rectangle (listing 8.1).

Listing 8.1 Lozenge-shaped button

```
<Window.Resources>
  <Style TargetType="Button">    ❶
    <Setter Property="Template">
      <Setter.Value>
        <ControlTemplate TargetType="Button">
          <Grid Margin="3">    ❷
            <Rectangle Fill="Purple" RadiusX="10" RadiusY="10"/>    ❸
            <ContentPresenter HorizontalAlignment="Center"
                              VerticalAlignment="Center"/>    ◁ Where content goes
          </Grid>
        </ControlTemplate>
      </Setter.Value>
    </Setter>
  </Style>
</Window.Resources>
```

If you're coding along, this code goes into the calculator code from where we left it at the end of the chapter 7 (or, if you didn't bother with the event code, from the end of chapter 6). Depending on how fastidious you've been, this XAML will either go into the `Resources` section of Window1.xaml or Calculator.xaml. The XAML itself should all be fairly familiar from chapter 6. The style ❶ doesn't have a name but does have a target type of `Button`, so the style is automatically applied to all buttons on the `Window`. The `ControlTemplate` can only hold a single *thing*; but, because we need to have multiple *things*, we have the `ControlTemplate` holding a `Grid` layout ❷, which holds multiple children. A `Grid` with one cell and one column (the default) is quite convenient for multiple items that sit on top of each other. We've also taken the opportunity to set a margin to give some space around our shape.

The *lozenge* ❸ is a rectangle with rounded corners. Finally, we provide a place to shove the content of the buttons—the numbers, operators, and so on—by putting in a `ContentPresenter` and telling it to center whatever content the buttons have. Figure 8.2 shows the final result.

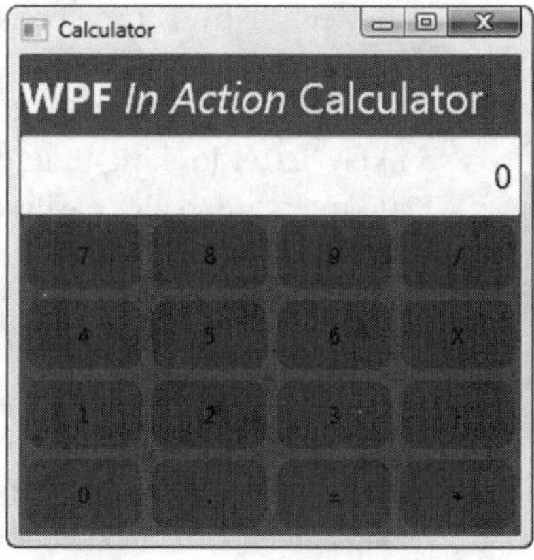

Figure 8.2 The calculator with lozenge-shaped "Barney" buttons

We now have the desired shape. Notice how much like glass the buttons *don't* look? You probably can't tell from the picture, but with the purple shade, it looks a bit like the buttons are cut out of Barney's hide. The trick to making the buttons look glassy is in layers and transparency. Figure 8.3 shows all the layers that make up our particular glass effect.

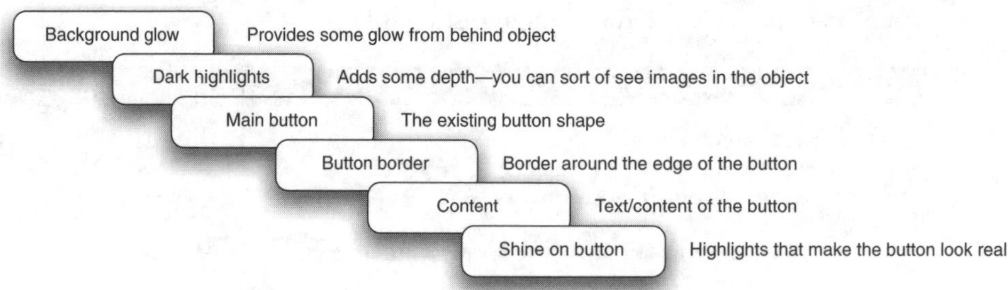

Figure 8.3 The layers that make up the glass button

Obviously, most of these layers are somewhat transparent, or you wouldn't see much. Listing 8.2 shows the XAML for all these layers. We've excluded the resource and style tags and are just showing the layout grid and its contents.

Listing 8.2 All layers for glass button

```
<Grid Margin="3">
  <Rectangle x:Name="backGlow" Fill=                  ❶
   "#FFEE08" RadiusX="10" RadiusY="10"/>
  <Rectangle x:Name="backDark" RadiusX="10" RadiusY="10">     ❷
    <Rectangle.Fill>
      <RadialGradientBrush GradientOrigin="0.9,0.9">
        <GradientStop Color="Black" Offset="0"/>
        <GradientStop Color="Black" Offset="0.1"/>
        <GradientStop Color="Transparent" Offset="0.8"/>
      </RadialGradientBrush>
    </Rectangle.Fill>
  </Rectangle>
  <Rectangle x:Name="mainButton" Fill="Purple" Opacity="0.75"    ❸
                    RadiusX="10" RadiusY="10"/>
  <Rectangle x:Name="mainButtonBorder" Stroke="Purple"
```

```
                  StrokeThickness="2" RadiusX="10" RadiusY="10"/>  ❹
  <ContentPresenter HorizontalAlignment="Center"
                  VerticalAlignment="Center"/>       ❺
  <Rectangle x:Name="buttonTopShine" Grid.ColumnSpan="3"
                  RadiusX="10" RadiusY="10">         ❻
    <Rectangle.Fill>
      <LinearGradientBrush StartPoint=
       "0,0" EndPoint="0,1" Opacity="0.8">     ❼
        <GradientStop Color="White" Offset="0"/>
        <GradientStop Color="Transparent" Offset="0.3"/>
      </LinearGradientBrush>
    </Rectangle.Fill>
  </Rectangle>
</Grid>
```

The XAML mirrors the diagram from figure 8.3. The glow is accomplished by creating a rounded rectangle the same size as the button ❶ but with a bright yellow color (#FFEE08). This hex color code is somewhat brighter than just Yellow, albeit harder to read.

The next element is a *dark object* ❷. Again, it's another rounded rectangle, but instead of being a solid color, it uses a radial gradient that starts out black and then goes to transparent. By having two gradient stops that are black, we get a slightly bigger dark area before the gradient drops off. We also set the origin of the object at 0.9,0.9, putting it toward the lower-right corner. You can play with all these numbers to try and get slightly different effects.

Next is our button ❸. The only change is to make it somewhat translucent by setting its `Opacity` to 75%. Otherwise, we wouldn't be able to see the glow or the dark highlights behind it. Next we have the border for the button ❹. We could make a border on the button directly, but the button is slightly transparent, and we want the border to be solid. Immediately after that, we have our button content ❺. We put it behind the shine to try and make it seem a little bit buried. In a moment, we'll also change the content slightly to make it look like it's further behind the surface.

Finally, we have the button shine ❻. This is what makes the nice glow at the top of the button. Again, it's a rounded rectangle with a gradient, although this time, the gradient is linear. We set the `StartPoint` and `EndPoint` of the gradient ❼ to make it be vertical. We also set the transparent gradient offset at 30%; in effect, we have a white-to-clear gradient at the top 30% of the shape.

You can spend a lot of time tweaking all these values, playing with different gradients, and so on. In fact, that's precisely how we achieved our effect. Figure 8.4 shows the result of all these changes.

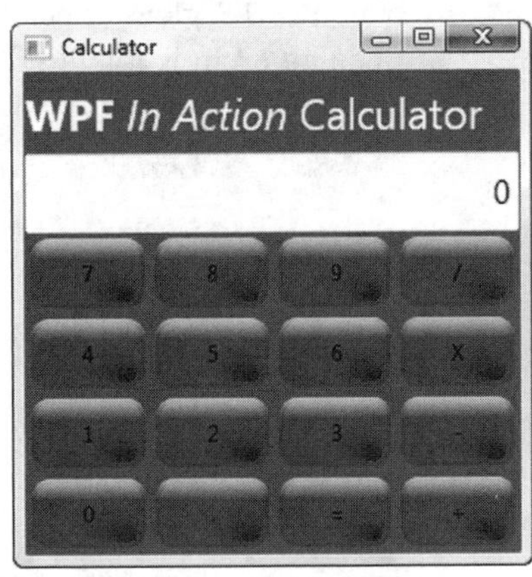

Figure 8.4 Calculator with glassy buttons but no effects

This isn't bad, but there are a few things missing. For one thing, the text on the buttons is a little lackluster. Also, the buttons don't react to anything. If you move over the buttons or click the buttons, they just lie there looking pretty, even though the click events do happen and the calculator does work. Without feedback, the buttons feel wrong. We'll rectify these issues in the next few sections.

8.1.1 Styling the text

This one is pretty easy. All we're going to do is make the text a bit transparent and also bold it to make it more visible. This will make it seem as though the text is within the buttons instead of on top. We add a couple of additional setters to our style.

```
<Setter Property="FontWeight" Value="Bold"/>
<Setter Property="Foreground" Value="#AF000000"/>
```

The font weight is pretty self-explanatory. For the foreground, we set the font color to black, but a slightly transparent version of black. The # format is #AARRGGBB, where AA is the alpha value, followed by the values for red, green, and blue. FF is fully opaque, and 00 is fully transparent. So our black is only slightly transparent. Figure 8.5 shows the results.

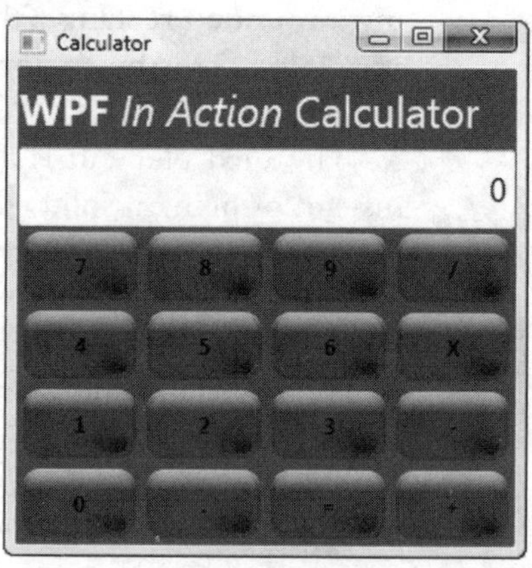

Figure 8.5 Text on the buttons is slightly transparent to make the text look like it's floating within the buttons.

The effect is subtle but, we think, nice. Now, on to something a little flashier.

8.1.2 Adding glow when over buttons

When the user is over a button, we'd like it to glow slightly. We could do this in a couple of ways. The easiest would be to make use of the built-in WPF glow effect by setting a property when an event is triggered (listing 8.3).

Listing 8.3 Adding a glow

```
<ControlTemplate.Triggers>
  <Trigger Property="Button.IsMouseOver" Value="True">
    <Setter Property="BitmapEffect">
      <Setter.Value>
        <OuterGlowBitmapEffect GlowColor="Violet" GlowSize="10"/>
      </Setter.Value>
    </Setter>
  </Trigger>
</ControlTemplate.Triggers>
```

The `ControlTemplate.Triggers` section needs to be added within the `ControlTemplate`. We put it right under the `</Grid>` element. The effect is triggered when

`IsMouseOver` is `true`. So, when the mouse is over the button, the `BitmapEffect` property is set. `BitmapEffect` allows one of a number of built-in effects, such as drop-shadows, embossing, and—the one we're using—outer glow. Violet is used as a bright version of the button's purple color. Figure 8.6 shows the glow effect.

This isn't too bad—it creates a pretty effect. But even though there's a glow around the button, the button itself isn't glowing. There are also some issues with the bitmap effects.

Figure 8.6 Glow on the 6 button as the user moves over it

NOTE *WARNING.* Although the bitmap effects are pretty cool, some of them come with a cost—they aren't efficient. They cause everything around them to suffer as well because WPF usually tries to do everything on the graphics card, but the bitmap effects are often done in memory. As a result, the whole area has to be rendered in memory—which is much, much slower. The blur and drop-shadow effects are hardware rendered, but the other effects (including glow) are generally software rendered. In fact, on Windows XP, these other bitmap effects are always rendered in memory. On Vista, if you have the right graphics card and the stars are appropriately aligned, then they *might* be rendered on the graphics card, but there are no guarantees. Use these effects sparingly; and, if performance becomes an issue, drop them like a pretty, glowing hot potato.

Another way we can make a glow effect is by adding a highlight to the button when the mouse moves over—like the highlight at the top of the button, but only visible sometimes. We can do this easily by adding a new highlight. This highlight will be completely transparent until the mouse moves over, at which time it will show up. Here is yet another layer to add to our XAML. This one comes right after the top highlight (`buttonTopShine`):

```
<Rectangle x:Name="buttonHoverGlow" Opacity="0" RadiusX="10" RadiusY="10">
  <Rectangle.Fill>
    <LinearGradientBrush>
      <GradientStop Color="White" Offset="0"/>
      <GradientStop Color="White" Offset="0.1"/>
      <GradientStop Color="Transparent" Offset="0.6"/>
    </LinearGradientBrush>
  </Rectangle.Fill>
</Rectangle>
```

Yes, yet another rounded rectangle with a gradient. This rectangle uses another linear gradient, but we aren't setting the end points, so it will have the default angle. How do you determine the values for the stop offsets? You play with the values until they look right. Even though you can't edit the properties in the property editor, the designer shows the changes as they're made in the XAML, so it's pretty easy to experiment. Notice that the `Opacity` of this rectangle is 0, meaning that it's invisible. To make it show up, we add another `Setter` to our `IsMouseOver` trigger. For the moment, we left the outer glow bitmap effect as well because it's pretty, and our calculator is simple enough that we don't mind spending a few cycles on it. For a real application, we'd probably either implement the outer glow ourselves in some manner or live without it.

```
<ControlTemplate.Triggers>
  <Trigger Property="Button.IsMouseOver" Value="True">
    <Setter Property="BitmapEffect">
      <Setter.Value>
        <OuterGlowBitmapEffect GlowColor="Violet" GlowSize="10"/>
      </Setter.Value>
    </Setter>
    <Setter TargetName="buttonHoverGlow" Property="Opacity" Value="1"/>
  </Trigger>
</ControlTemplate.Triggers>
```

The `Setter` references our new shape by name and sets the `Opacity` to 1, which is completely opaque (although, because the object is partially transparent, it's still see-through in places). Figure 8.7 shows a button with the hover glow and the bitmap outer glow.

We think this looks pretty cool. Now, when the user moves over the button, it's pretty obvious. The last thing to handle is when the user clicks the button.

Figure 8.7 Now button 6 has the hover glow showing as well as the outer glow.

8.1.3 Handling the button click

It's pretty obvious when the user is over a button, but clicking still has no visual effect. A simple but effective approach is to change the color of the button from purple to a lighter purple so that it looks like it's glowing even more. We can do this easily by adding another trigger for when the `IsPressed` property becomes true:

```
<Trigger Property="Button.IsPressed" Value="True" >
  <Setter TargetName="mainButton" Property="Fill" Value="Violet"/>
</Trigger>
```

All we are doing here is changing the color of the button from Purple to Violet, which, we're reliably informed, is a lighter shade of purple. While the button is pressed, the color changes to be brighter, as you can see in figure 8.8.

Notice that we still have our glow and the white highlight. By definition, if the button is being clicked the mouse is also over the button, so we get the combination of effects. You could also override effects if you wanted to. For example, you could make the outer glow bigger when the button is pressed. The definition in the second handler would override the first, and you'd get a brighter glow.

We're not quite done with the glow. Impressive though it is, it's pretty static. We can make it nicer by adding some simple animation.

Figure 8.8 Button gets brighter when it's clicked.

8.2 Adding some simple animation

If a thing is worth doing, it's worth overdoing. One thing that we don't like about the glow on our button is the speed it starts to glow—a glow should spread, not suddenly be there. You'd think that light traveled at the speed of, well, uh…we just think it would look better.

So far, with all our event triggers, we have set a property to a different value and relied on the handlers to automatically set it back when we left. But we can also launch an animation when the trigger is fired.

8.2.1 Animating button glow

In yon olden days, if you wanted to animate something in your UI, you had a choice between a number of fairly bad options: You could play a canned animation—an AVI or an animated GIF—or you could create it yourself, using Windows timers and a lot of playing.

WPF has animation support built in that takes advantage of the Property System. For example, suppose you want a background color to change from red to green over a period of time. WPF has its own built-in timing mechanism and, because the properties are generic, can automatically set the value of the background color to all the colors in between, starting with red, going through shades until it gets to green, breaking down the duration into some number of time slices to make the change. It doesn't care what it's changing; it's setting a value in a property, but changing that property automatically updates the UI with the change.

Right now, when the user moves over one of our buttons, we change the opacity of our hover glow from 0 (invisible) to 1 (fully visible). Instead of changing the value immediately, we can start an animation that changes the value from 0 to 1 over a period of time.

We'll set up the animation to start when the mouse enters the space of the button. We need a real event to trigger our animation, rather than depending on the state of a flag (`IsMouseOver`). You can set animations to trigger when the state of `IsMouseOver` changes, but this way you'll see some additional options. Listing 8.4 shows the code to make the `Opacity` change when the mouse first moves over the button.

Listing 8.4 Animation when mouse enters our button

```
<EventTrigger RoutedEvent="Button.MouseEnter">
  <EventTrigger.Actions>
    <BeginStoryboard>
      <Storyboard>
        <DoubleAnimation Storyboard.TargetName="buttonHoverGlow"
            Storyboard.TargetProperty="Opacity" To="1"
            Duration="0:0:0.1" />
      </Storyboard>
    </BeginStoryboard>
  </EventTrigger.Actions>
</EventTrigger>
```

The `EventTrigger` ❶ is a trigger fired when an event takes place. It can be added to the Triggers collection along with the existing property-based triggers. By the way, make sure you remove the setter from the `IsMouseOver` trigger, or the animation will act strangely.

```
<Setter TargetName="buttonHoverGlow" Property="Opacity" Value="1"/>
```

(Take this line out to avoid strange problems.)

Now we have a collection of actions to take ❷ when the event is triggered. We want to launch a storyboard ❸. Storyboards are the details of an animation. Picture the preparation for a big Hollywood movie, where they draw out what happens first, then next, and so on. Same idea, except that in an animation storyboard you are instructing WPF what to do. Our storyboard is simple since it only contains one thing, but it could be arbitrarily complex (make the object visible, then change its color, then make it spin around, and so on).

The content of our storyboard is a `DoubleAnimation` ❹. The name doesn't imply that it will do everything twice—rather it indicates that the property whose value is being animated is of type `double`. `Opacity` is a number. If we were animating a color, we'd be using a `ColorAnimation` here, and so on. We tell the animation what object we want to change (`TargetName`), and what property (`Opacity`). We also specify a value for `To`, the final value we want the `Opacity` to be set to, as well as the `Duration`, the amount of time we want the animation to take. The format is hours:minutes:seconds, so we're specifying a duration of a tenth of a second. You may wonder why we have a `To` value and not a `From` value. We'll explain that in a moment.

If you go ahead and run the application now, you get half of the behavior we want—when you move the mouse over a button, the glow appears slowly over a tenth of a second. But when you move off the button, the glow doesn't go away. Figure 8.9 shows the calculator after we've floated over a few buttons.

If you're coding along, you'll see the nice fade-up of the glow effect. In the book, of course, you can't because we couldn't convince the publisher to spring for four-dimensional paper. We couldn't even get them to go with color and had to fight to get both black *and* white.

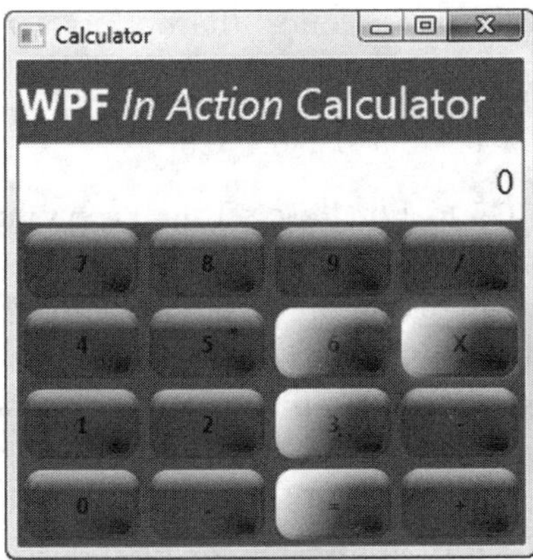

Figure 8.9 Thanks to our animation, the glow on the buttons shows up slowly, but it doesn't go away. We need to add another animation effect to make the glow go away when the mouse is no longer over the button.

The way to make the glow go away is to add another animation that gets executed when the mouse leaves the button. It's similar to the existing one, except that it sets the `Opacity` to 0 instead of 1. We also made the duration a bit longer because a fading glow tends to last longer than a rising one:

```
<EventTrigger RoutedEvent="Button.MouseLeave">
  <EventTrigger.Actions>
    <BeginStoryboard>
      <Storyboard>
        <DoubleAnimation Storyboard.TargetName="buttonHoverGlow"
           Storyboard.TargetProperty="Opacity" To="0" Duration="0:0:0.25"/>
      </Storyboard>
    </BeginStoryboard>
  </EventTrigger.Actions>
</EventTrigger>
```

We could put up another picture here, but it would look exactly like figure 8.7 because of the boringly three-dimensional nature of the publishing industry. Once again, we specify a `To` value but no `From` value. `DoubleAnimation` supports a `From` value, so you might think that the `MouseEnter` animation would have values like this:

```
From="0" To="1"
```

And the `MouseLeave` animation the opposite:

```
From"1" To="0"
```

This would work—it would set the `Opacity` to 0 when it first started (which is where it was, so no big deal) and then animate the value until equal to 1. But there's one situation where the animation wouldn't behave as desired. Suppose the user moves the mouse over the button and then moves off before the animation is finished? It's hard to see the problem when the duration is a tenth of a second, but imagine that the animation was running over 10 seconds. Assuming the user moves over the control and then moves off after each second, the opacity would look like this:

0.0 0.1 0.2 0.3 0.4 0.5 0.6 0.7 0.8 0.9 1.0 0.9 0.8 0.7 0.6 0.5 0.4 0.3 0.2 0.1 0.0

But if the user moves off of the button after five seconds, the opacity would look like this:

0.1 0.2 0.3 0.4 **0.5 1.0** 0.9 0.8 0.7 0.6 0.5 0.4 0.3 0.2 0.1 0.0

Notice how the value suddenly jumps from 0.5 to 1.0? If we set the `From` value of the leaving animation, it will set the starting value immediately when the user starts to leave. We don't see this when we let the first animation finish, but it's fairly noticeable when the animation is only half-finished. Fortunately, WPF handles this situation nicely if we exclude the `From` value. If `From` isn't specified, then the `From` value is assumed to be the current value in the control, and everything becomes nice and smooth.

There are lots of little things you can do with this simple animation. For example, you could make the glow wait a moment before appearing (or disappearing). You could make animations repeat some number of times, or indefinitely. Using the `AutoReverse` property, you could make the animation automatically return the property to its original state. The Property System is incredibly powerful, but, unfortunately, we can only scratch the surface here. We will provide *one* more example—this time a color change.

8.2.2 Animating a color

The buttons are reacting nicely now, but we also allow users to enter values via the keyboard. When the value changes in the text box at the top of the calculator, you can tell because, well, the value has changed. But we can add some emphasis by having the text in the text box change color whenever its value changes.

Instead of creating a style, we're going to define this behavior directly on the `TextBox` element. Generally, you'd define something like this in a style, but you should be aware that you can do all these things directly and there are situations where that makes sense—for instance, if the behavior is something that needs to happen even if styles are changed.

Listing 8.5 shows the XAML for the `TextBox` with all the handling for the event and the animation.

Listing 8.5 Animating text color

```
<TextBox FontSize="18" Name="textBoxDisplay" Grid.Column="0"          ❶
     Grid.ColumnSpan="4" Grid.Row="1" VerticalContentAlignment="Center"
     HorizontalContentAlignment="Right">0      ❷
  <TextBox.Triggers>
    <EventTrigger RoutedEvent="TextBox.TextChanged">      ❸
      <EventTrigger.Actions>
        <BeginStoryboard>
          <Storyboard>
            <ColorAnimation Storyboard.TargetName="textBoxDisplay"     ❹
                 Storyboard.TargetProperty="Foreground.Color"
                 To="Gold" Duration="0:0:0.2" AutoReverse="True"/>
          </Storyboard>
        </BeginStoryboard>
```

```
      </EventTrigger.Actions>
    </EventTrigger>
  </TextBox.Triggers>
</TextBox>
```

The `TextBox` definition ❶ is pretty much unchanged except for increasing the font size to make it more obvious that it's changing (and to make it look better). We put the collection of `Triggers` ❷ right below the `TextBox` definition and define a trigger for whenever the text changes ❸. The `ColorAnimation` ❹ looks similar to the `DoubleAnimation` from before, except that our `To` value is a color instead of a number. We also specify `AutoReverse` to tell the system to restore the color back to its original value when the animation is done.

Once you get the hang of these types of animations, they end up being fairly simple. The trickiest thing tends to be figuring out the `Target` property. For example, here we're specifying the `Color` property of the `Foreground` property via the dot notation.

Figure 8.10 shows the results of this code, caught mid-flash.

We'll revisit animation in (a little) more detail in chapter 19, but it's a topic that could easily make up its own book. Before we leave the calculator, there's one more effect we'd like to demonstrate.

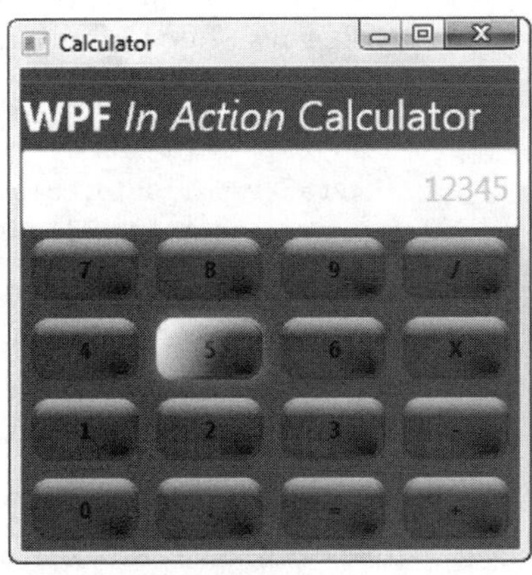

Figure 8.10 Display caught mid-flash by our lightning reflexes

8.3 Reflections

The header for our calculator is okay, but kind of boring. Even with knowing that having bold and italic text mixed in a regular block of text would've been quite painful without WPF, it still isn't that cool. What would be nice is if we could do something that would be really hard to do without WPF or evil hackery—for example, having our header look like it has a reflection like in figure 8.11.

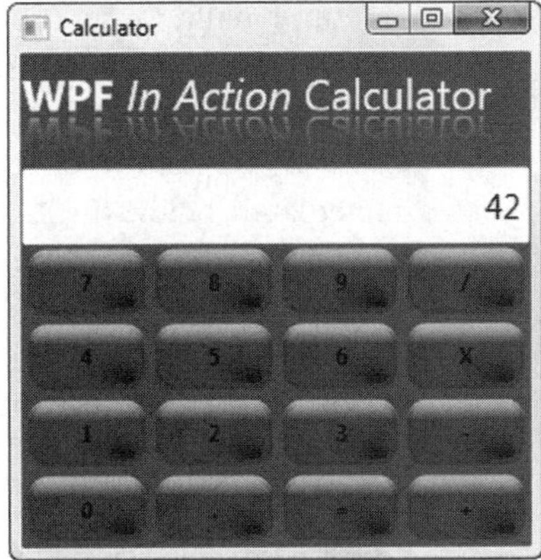

Figure 8.11 Really cool header with reflected text

The purpose of this section isn't only to demonstrate some of the things that WPF makes fairly easy but also to introduce a few new concepts and ideas. Before we get to that, we first need to make the space for our header bigger and set up a space to hold the reflection. The easiest way to give more space is to increase the size of the row in the `Grid` that holds the title. We could add another row to the `Grid` to hold the reflection, but then we'd have to go through and change all our controls and buttons, and there's no easy way to do that. (Hint, Microsoft: an insert row/column feature would be awfully nice.) Anyway, we'll set up the row to be one-and-a-half times bigger than all the other rows.

```
<Grid.RowDefinitions>
  <RowDefinition Height="1.5*" />
  <RowDefinition />
  <RowDefinition />
  ...
```

Now, for a place to put the reflection. Right now, the first row only contains the `TextBlock`. We'll replace that with a `StackPanel` and then put the `TextBlock` in the `StackPanel` first, followed by a `Rectangle` to hold the reflection. We'll also set a few properties while we're in there (listing 8.6).

Listing 8.6 Preparing for reflection

```
<StackPanel Grid.Column="0" Grid.Row="0" Grid.ColumnSpan="4"      ❶
        VerticalAlignment="Center">
  <TextBlock Height="25" x:Name="titleBlock" Foreground="White"     ❷
        FontSize="24" HorizontalAlignment="Left">
     <Bold> WPF</Bold> <Italic>In Action</Italic> Calculator
  </TextBlock>
  <Rectangle Height="25"/>     ❸
</StackPanel>
```

We create a `StackPanel` ❶ and set its grid positioning to be what we formerly used for the `TextBlock`—Row 0, Column 0, spanning all four columns. Then we put the `TextBlock` into the `StackPanel` ❷, but we have to make a few changes. First, we set the foreground color to white and give the block a name (which we'll use later). Next, we set an explicit height for the `TextBlock` so that the text fills the control from top to bottom. Finally, we set the horizontal alignment to left so that the `TextBlock` is only as wide as the text it contains, instead of stretched all the way across the available space.

We also add a `Rectangle` ❸ to the `StackPanel`. By the nature of the `StackPanel`, it exists immediately below the `TextBlock`, although you won't currently see anything because it has no fill or border. We also set the `Height` explicitly, to be the same as the `TextBlock`. Figure 8.12 shows the way the top of the calculator now looks.

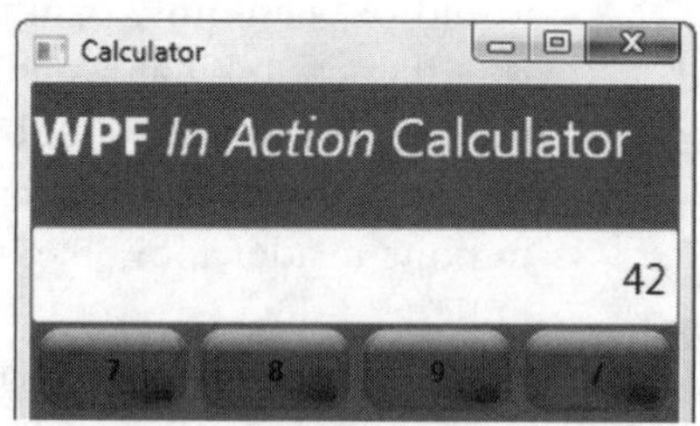

Figure 8.12 We've added space for the reflection underneath the title text, but haven't yet put anything interesting there to fill the space.

Not too bad, but now we need to put something into our empty rectangle. We've used solid brushes and various gradients before to paint the background of something. Now we're going to use another type of brush called a `VisualBrush`.[2]

[2] *`Visual`* is the base class for everything in WPF that can be drawn, so a `VisualBrush` can paint with anything you can draw in WPF.

The `VisualBrush` is very cool. It takes the content from whatever it's pointing to and uses that to paint with. So, if we point it at the `TextBlock`, it will use the image of the `TextBlock` to paint with. We could use that for any type of painting, but we only want to make the background of our rectangle be painted with the visual image from the `TextBlock`. It's fairly easy to do.

```
<Rectangle Height="25" >
  <Rectangle.Fill>
    <VisualBrush Visual="{Binding ElementName=titleBlock}"
          Stretch="None" AlignmentX="Left" />
  </Rectangle.Fill>
</Rectangle>
```

We specify the fill in the usual way, except we use a `VisualBrush`. The `Visual` property points to the source of the visual to display. This could literally come from anywhere, but we're binding it to the `titleBlock` element (our `TextBlock`). We'll discuss this notation in more detail in the chapter on binding (chapter 11), but for now, just recognize that this says, "Get your content from the thing called `titleBlock`." We also set the following properties on the `VisualBrush`:

- *`Stretch="None"`*—Tells the `VisualBrush` to keep the content its original size. By default, a `VisualBrush` stretches its content to fill the available space. A `VisualBrush` can also be set to tile its contents—which would also be bad.
- *`AlignmentX="Left"`*—Tells the `VisualBrush` to start painting the content at the left edge instead of centering the content.

It might be a good idea to play with some of the different values for `Stretch` and `Alignment` to see what happens if they aren't set this way. With the current settings, we get something that looks like figure 8.13.

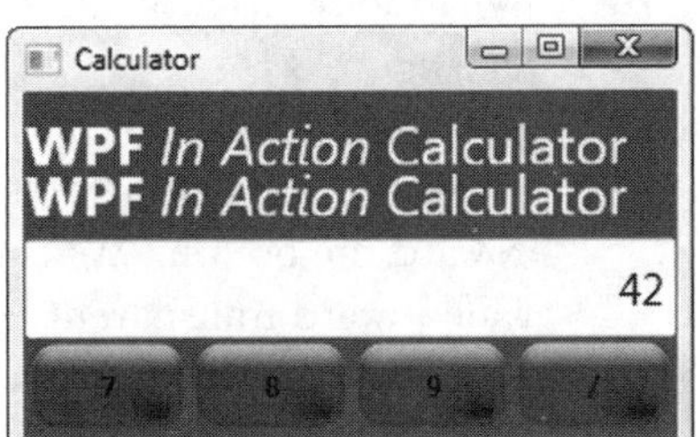

Figure 8.13 We're now populating our rectangle with the contents of the `TextBlock`.

Well, so far, so good, but as you may have noticed, our reflection is the wrong way up, in that it's currently the right way up. We need to flip it over. We can do this with a transform. Transforms are various operations—including scaling, moving, skewing, and rotating—that can be applied to virtually any element in WPF. You can also do fancy higher-math matrix transforms, although for the unprepared they're apt to make your brain explode. We'll talk about all the different transforms available in the next section, but for the moment, we're going to use only one: the scale transform. Scaling is usually used to make things bigger or smaller; but, by using a negative value, it can also be used to flip something over, such as our text.

```
<Rectangle Height="25" >
  <Rectangle.Fill>
    <VisualBrush Visual="{Binding ElementName=titleBlock}"
```

```
            Stretch="None" AlignmentX="Left" >
        <VisualBrush.Transform>
          <ScaleTransform ScaleX="1" ScaleY="-1.1" CenterY="12.5"/>
        </VisualBrush.Transform>
      </VisualBrush>
    </Rectangle.Fill>
  </Rectangle>
```

We're setting the transform property on the brush, but we could also set a similar property on other elements as well. For example, we could've set the `LayoutTransform` property of the rectangle to get the same effect. The transform takes the following properties to control its behavior:

- *`ScaleX="1"`*— Stretches, shrinks, or flips the content along the X-axis. In our case, we don't want change the scale at all. 1 means multiply everything by 1, doing nothing.
- *`ScaleY="-1.1"`*— -Stretches, shrinks, or flips content along the Y-axis. Here, we want to flip the content over. To do that, we would choose -1. But we also want our reflection to be a little taller than the original image, so we use -1.1. Read this as multiplying everything by -1.1 in the Y direction.
- *`CenterY="12.5"`*—Controls where we want the flip to be centered. Because we know our image is 25 pixels high, we've selected the exact middle. If we'd chosen a different center, the image would still be flipped but would be moved up or down based on the center. Again, experiment with this to see what it does.

What does this look like? Something very much like figure 8.14.

Figure 8.14 Our upside-down text is now the right way up!

The last step for the reflection effect is to make the reflection look like it's disappearing toward the bottom. We can do this by making it fade toward transparent. But there's no particular element that we can make fade (we're already using a brush with our visual content). Instead, we can use something called an opacity mask. This property specifies how an element (such as our rectangle) sets its visibility. You provide a brush to use for the mask. Where the brush is solid, the element is solid; where the brush is transparent, the element is transparent. If we use a solid brush with a partially transparent color, the entire element will be partially transparent. If we use a gradient brush (as we intend to do) the transparency of the element will vary with the gradient.

```
<Rectangle.OpacityMask>
  <LinearGradientBrush StartPoint="0,0" EndPoint="0,1">
    <GradientStop Offset="0" Color="Black"></GradientStop>
    <GradientStop Offset="0.2" Color="#7F000000"></GradientStop>
    <GradientStop Offset="1" Color="Transparent"></GradientStop>
  </LinearGradientBrush>
</Rectangle.OpacityMask>
```

We put this below the close of the `Rectangle.Fill` element. Note that we're specifying our start and end points the same way we did for the top shine on the buttons so that our gradient goes top to bottom. Then we go from full solid to slightly transparent to fully transparent. Again, we played with the values until they looked pleasing. The specific color we use isn't important; only the transparency value of the color is used by the mask. Now we finally have our finished reflection (figure 8.15).

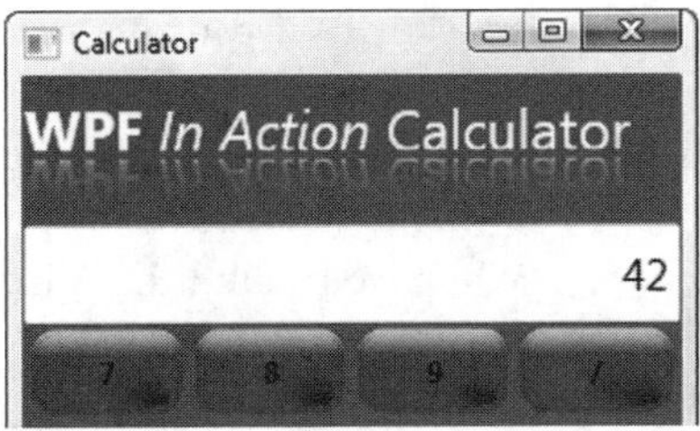

Figure 8.15 Our finished reflection

That should pretty much do it, although, honestly, we could go on tweaking the visuals forever. For example, we could use a Skew transform as well to make the reflection go off at a slight angle, and then animate the skew so that the image floats gently back and forth, and then...well, you get the point. Transforms are extremely powerful, and WPF has built-in support for all the standard ones.

8.4 Transforms

We used the Scale transform to flip over our text. WPF supports a number of different transforms, and they can be used against most elements. Table 8.1 shows the effects of the different transforms supported by WPF. In each case, the gray A shows the original position of the transform.

There are two additional transforms: `TransformGroup`, which allows for multiple transforms to be combined, and `MatrixTransform`, which lets you do more advanced

Table 8.1 WPF 2D Transforms

Effect	Transform
	`ScaleTransform`—Changes the size of the object. In this case, we've shrunk the object by 60% in each direction.
	`TranslateTransform`—Moves the object. We've moved the object over by 20 pixels and down by 20 pixels.
	`RotateTransform`—Rotates the object. The A has been rotated here by 110 degrees.
	`SkewTransform`—Skews the object by a specified angle. This sort of allows for a 3D-like effect.

transforms if you're a math wonk. The property you set to control the transform differs depending on what type of element you're transforming and how and when you want the transform to be done. With the `VisualBrush` on the calculator, the `Brush` has a single `Transform` property. On things like controls, there are multiple properties. When we rotated the A in the example, we used a `LayoutTransform`.

```
<Label VerticalAlignm.nt="Center"
       HorizontalAlignment="Center" FontSize="100" Foreground="Blue">
  <Label.Content>A</Label.Content>
  <Label.LayoutTransform>
    <RotateTransform Angle="110"/>
  </Label.LayoutTransform>
</Label>
```

`LayoutTransforms` are applied when the layout is calculated. The A was rotated, and then, because the label was centered horizontally and vertically, the rotated A was centered. The `LayoutTransform` was fine for all our examples except for the Translate transform because the transform moved the A, and then the layout engine proceeded to re-center it for us. Instead, for the Translate, we used a `RenderTransform`:

```
<Label VerticalAlignment="Center"
       HorizontalAlignment="Center" FontSize="100" Foreground="Blue">
  <Label.Content>A</Label.Content>
  <Label.RenderTransform>
    <TranslateTransform  X="20" Y="20"/>
  </Label.RenderTransform>
</Label>
```

`RenderTransforms` are applied when the object is *rendered*, independently of layout, so the transform wasn't hidden by the centering options. Being able to provide rendering options is handy if you want effects that ignore the layout—for example, if you wanted a button to rotate when the user clicked it, you wouldn't want it to be constrained to the location where layout puts the button, and you wouldn't want the layout engine to constantly rearrange all the other elements around the rotating button.

There's another set of transforms that, although similar, are used when working with 3D elements. We'll see those in chapter 15.

8.5 Summary

This chapter was a lot of fun to write—in the real world, you often don't get the chance to play with cool effects while deadlines are looming. We did, though, have several serious reasons for covering what we did here.

First, we wanted to provide a taste of the power of WPF. None of the things we did here was particularly hard, yet the results were far beyond what could have easily been accomplished without WPF. We also wanted to introduce, albeit briefly, a bunch of concepts: complex styles, event triggers, animation, visual brushes, transforms, and so on. This chapter was obviously not a detailed examination of any of these topics, but it should at least give you an idea of where to start looking when you have a particular goal in mind.

Second, we wanted to talk about some of the dangers of WPF. Aside from the obvious—that you can get sucked into spending all your time trying to get an effect right instead of doing real work—there are two more dangers. One is procedural; there are a lot of different ways to get to a particular result in WPF, but it's also easy to end up going a long way down the wrong road. Make sure that you make frequent copies of your code while you're experimenting because you may find that bits of approaches will often be helpful. Also, if you get stuck, spend some time thinking about what you're trying to accomplish. WPF will help you if you go with the flow and get in your way continuously if you fight it. If something seems really hard, you may be going the wrong way.

The other danger of WPF we were trying to demonstrate is that it lends itself to cuteness. Just because you *can* do some sort of effect doesn't mean it's necessarily a good idea. For example, feedback on our buttons definitely made sense. Having a header that takes up a massive amount of space in our utility purely because it looks cool? Well, it was a small application, so not too big a deal, but in a full-screen application full of data—not so much.

Make sure you think about the balance between cool, cute, and useful. When in doubt, go with useful!

This is the last chapter focusing on the calculator. We will miss the thing. Although the last thing most people need in their life is another calculator implementation, it was a great sample for the topics we covered throughout this section: layouts, resources, styles, and events. It also lent itself well to being turned into an Xmas tree for this chapter. In fact, Microsoft ships a calculator sample to demonstrate some similar concepts, and we can honestly say that ours is a lot better looking.

All the concepts that we've covered through Part 2 (except, perhaps, the shiny bits) are the necessary building blocks for almost any application. In Part 3, we'll move into the areas related to more real-world application development, such as commands and data binding.

Part 3

Application development

Sad to say, most of the day-to-day work we all do is less about zip-lining across the Grand Canyon, and more about hooking up real-world applications. The nature of those applications differs from place to place, but there are a lot of common threads. In part 3, we'll talk about the WPF capabilities designed to help build these applications, and also show a number of examples. Although we obviously couldn't have very deep implementations on any of the examples, we've tried to make them as real-world*ish* as we could, and, where possible, at least vaguely useful.

The first chapter in part 3, chapter 9—"Laying out a more complex application"—goes through the up-front work of designing a WPF application. It also introduces our first new application, a Desktop Wiki for note taking.

This application appears in several chapters, including chapter 10—"Commands," which explains the unified approach to commands (like File >Print) within WPF—and chapter 11—"Data binding with WPF." Data Binding is such a large topic, that it spills over into chapter 12—"Advanced data templates and binding," which covers more advanced binding capabilities and controlling the display of data. Both of these chapters introduce several other sample applications.

The last three chapters are a little more low level. Chapter 13—"Custom controls"—shows how to build reusable controls and components. Chapter 14—"Drawing"—and chapter 15—Drawing in 3D"—demonstrate how to add drawing to your applications, using a graphing application as an example.

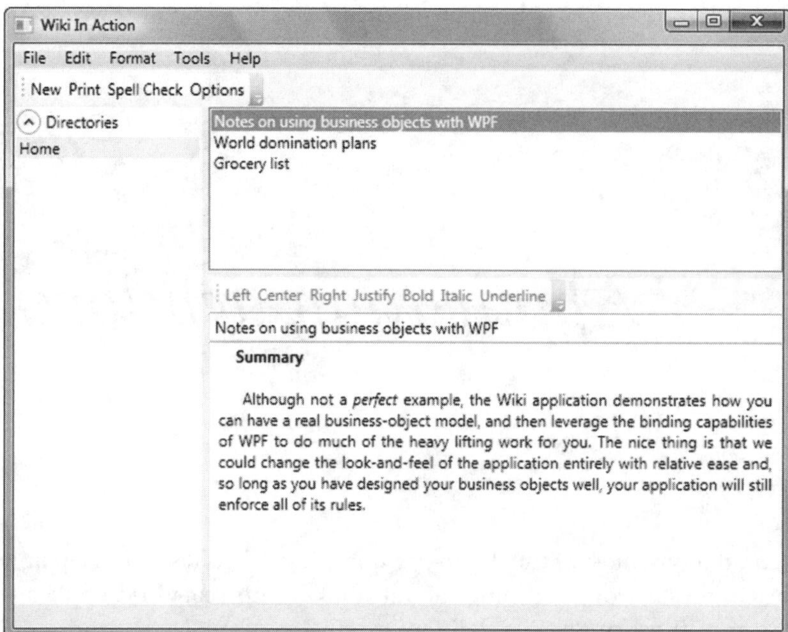

The Wiki in Action application is used to demonstrate more advanced application concepts such as command routing and binding.

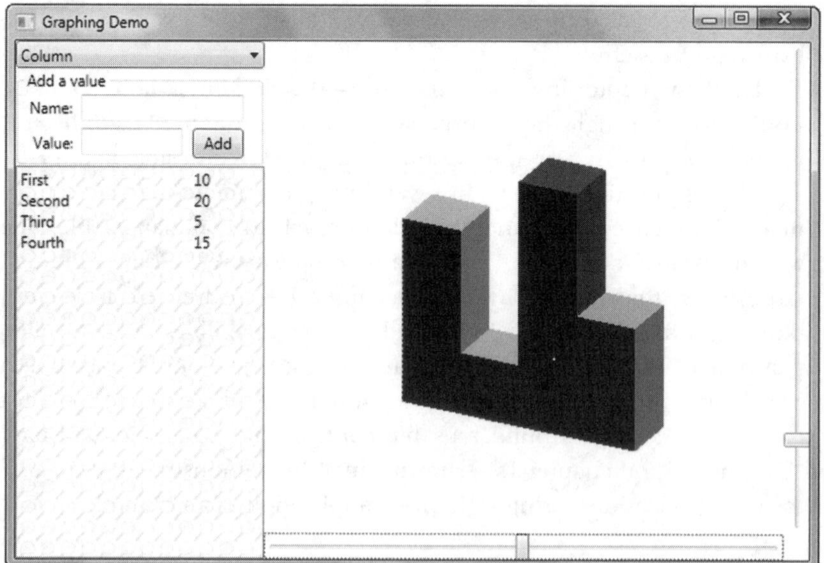

The graphing application demonstrates several low-level drawing mechanisms including drawing in 3D.

9 Laying out a more complex application

This chapter covers:

- Planning a WPF application
- Layering multiple layouts
- Setting up menus and toolbars
- The reason fast-food restaurants always give you 5 million napkins

It's no secret that many applications are based on design concepts users are already familiar with. Some of this approach is purely practical—users can't be expected (and typically don't want) to learn significantly different ways of interacting with every program they use. Changing the fundamental building blocks of an application is a sure way to create some disenchantment with your users, and WPF gives a dangerous[1] level of ability to do that.

WPF certainly provides the ability to easily create applications with completely novel presentations, and we're sure that's going to happen. Depending on what you're creating, that may be something you want to look into; but there are only a few companies with the market penetration to successfully drive entirely new

[1] Maybe *dangerous* is a little strong, but then, if you're writing a UI for a nuclear power plant or tanker navigation system, maybe it isn't.

design approaches, and when they do, they tend to spread like wildfire. We can't count how many times we've heard an executive or manager ask for a Money-like interface; and within weeks of the first Ribbon, every component vendor in the market had a Ribbon-like UI to offer. By the way, Microsoft has finally added a Ribbon control to Visual Studio 2008. It didn't ship with SP1, but, as of late 2008, it should be available as a download.

In this chapter, we're going to walk you through designing and laying out a more complex application—a Desktop Wiki[2] application that allows for entering and searching information. The application will have a number of the "classic" application items—menus, icons, and toolbars—but with a less traditional wiki back-end. This will give us the opportunity to explore the process involved with creating applications in WPF.

Particularly when designing a layout-manager-based UI, we find it useful to sketch some ideas on a whiteboard, notebook, napkin, or whatever else happens to be within marking distance. Even with XAMLPad, we aren't going to be able to accomplish quickly some of what we can accomplish in the sketch (figure 9.1). It's surprising how many people skip this step.

You may notice a certain resemblance to a popular email client and just about every RSS newsreader ever made. This isn't accidental. Because of this common design, we won't need to explain the expected behavior too much, and users should be able to start using the application right away.

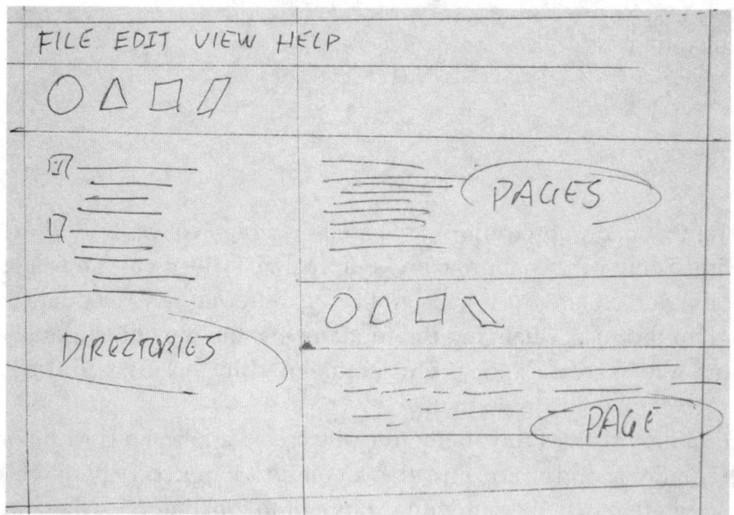

Figure 9.1 We worked hard to create a (very) rough sketch of our proposed UI.

2 If you haven't heard of wikis, you should check out Wikipedia (http://www.wikipedia.com) for more information and an example of a large, successful wiki.

9.1 Creating the Desktop Wiki Project

Now that we have our really elegant design (presumably approved by marketing and product management), we can get started building it. In previous chapters, we've bounced back and forth between the visual designer and the XAML view. Although we'll still do that elsewhere in the book, for this chapter, we're going to do everything that we can in the visual designer to demonstrate that it is both possible and practical.

If you want to follow along, start by creating a new .NET Framework 3.5 WPF Application Project called *Desktop Wiki*. This brings you to an empty `Window` called *Window1* with an empty `Grid` of one column by one row.

Pardon the rant, but it seems rather obvious that we don't want something called Window1 and probably never will. Nonetheless, Visual Studio has seen fit to create the files Window1.xaml, Window1.xaml.cs, and has named our class Window1, and probably registered it with the local sheriff's office. (For some reason, we're required to register at the sheriff's office whenever we visit a new city—not sure why.) The first order of business is to simply delete it.[3] Now that we have a clean slate, right-click on the Desktop Wiki solution in the Solution Explorer and select Add/Window (figure 9.2).

Now Visual Studio does the right thing and asks what to call this thing. Ours is called *WikiWindow.xaml*. Then, select Add. Now there's only one thing to fix: Like the `Main` method defines the entry point in a traditional C/C++/C# program, the `StartupUri` defines the entry point of a WPF application, so we need to open up App.xaml and find the `StartupUri` attribute and change it to our new `Window` (listing 9.1).

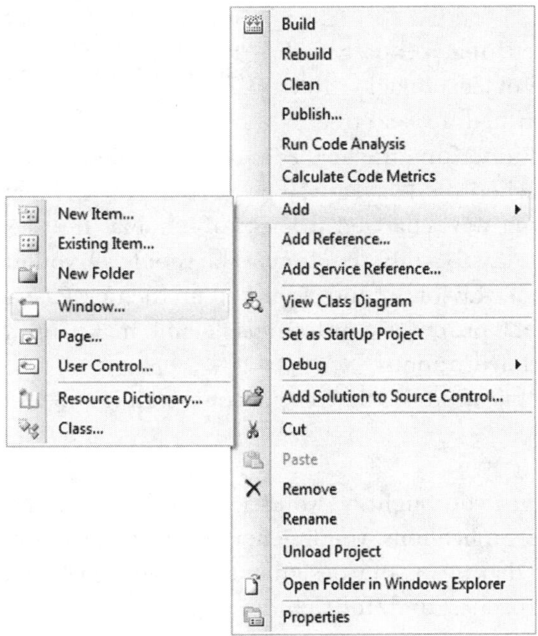

Figure 9.2 To add a new Window, right-click on the Desktop Wiki solution and choose add a new `Window` to the project.

[3] If you have a nice refactoring tool such as CodeRush!, ReSharper, or C# Refactory, you might go ahead and just rename it, but our approach is to delete the thing and create the new window that we want.

Listing 9.1 App.xaml

```
<Application x:Class="Desktop_Wiki.App"
    xmlns="http://schemas.microsoft.com/winfx/2006/xaml/presentation"
    xmlns:x="http://schemas.microsoft.com/winfx/2006/xaml"
    StartupUri="WikiWindow.xaml">
    <Application.Resources>

    </Application.Resources>
</Application>
```

Changes StartupUri="Windowl.xaml" to StartupUri="WikiWindow.xaml"

This is the one thing that we *must* do in XAML. After this, everything else will be via the visual designer—we promise. The next step is to set some reasonable properties for the new window. First, right-click the titlebar of the `WikiWindow` and select the Properties menu item. Find the Title property and change it to Wiki In Action (figure 9.3).

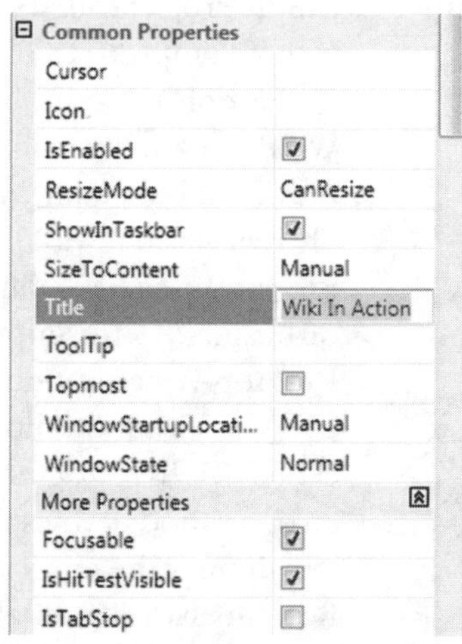

Figure 9.3 Use the Properties editor to change the `Title` attribute of the `WikiWindow` class.

You should keep one important point in mind when using the Properties window. Once you edit a property, it sets that property explicitly in the XAML. For example, while watching the XAML view, check the item `Topmost` and then uncheck it. When you check `Topmost`, it adds an attribute of `Topmost` set to `True`; when you uncheck it, it changes the value to `False`, but left the attribute in.

Once a property is touched, that property will always be explicitly set on the object. Imagine how frustrating this would be if you had a visual tree of hundreds of WPF elements, all inheriting the `FontFamily` as specified by the `Window`, but someone inadvertently touched the `FontFamily` property on an element halfway through and, in a well meaning way, changed it back to Tahoma. If at some later point, you changed the `FontFamily` to a different font at the root level, you might pull your hair out trying to figure out why some controls picked up the new face and some didn't. If you do accidentally set a property away from its default, make sure you clear it out of the XAML to avoid such frustrations.

Now that we have a basic application, it's time to put some stuff into it.

9.2 Nesting layouts

If you're new to layout managers, you might be wondering which layout manager to choose. Except for very simple applications, you'll generally use many layout managers and combine them in ways that meet your design and behavior goals. This isn't a far cry from the previous approaches; and, for web developers, it's standard operating procedure.

> **Menus, icons, and toolbars**
>
> In some circles, menus are falling out of favor. One big member of that circle appears to be Microsoft. Looking at Office 2007, MSN Messenger, or Internet Explorer 7, one thing you *won't* see are a lot of menus.[4] Menus do have a few drawbacks. Like any UI element, menus can end up holding more information than they can reasonably support. When this happens, some users may consider the menus overwhelming and may find it difficult to understand them. Menus certainly can be abused; submenus can be particularly difficult to use, especially with every increasing level of depth. Poorly organized menu structures can irritate users and prevent them from finding the functions they need. At the same time, some people really *love* menus. Some use menus as a discovery tool to explore what's possible in an application. Menus also offer a known geography of features that users can memorize, allowing them to become comfortable and efficient in an application. Menus that present options in a clear and consistent manner can be a great benefit as well.
>
> From our standpoint, menus have proven to be useful, and a not insignificant number of users are fairly upset with the trend away from menus, so we think covering both approaches is appropriate. We'll leave it to you to decide how far you want to go with it.

In our application, the layouts are nested, mirroring the structure of the XAML, so we'll have to start from the outside and work toward the center. Because we're going with a more traditional look, the first thing we need to do is structure the menus and toolbars.

9.2.1 Preparing the layout for menus and toolbars

If you don't have the toolbox open, select View/Toolbox to bring it up. If you don't see a set of controls, click in the middle of the `WikiWindow` and they should appear.

The first thing we need is a `DockPanel`. The `DockPanel` will control the position of the menu bar, status bar, and hold the main layout panel of our application. Expand the Common section of the Toolbox to get a `DockPanel` and drag it to the WikiWindow (figure 9.4).

Adding the `DockPanel` doesn't behave quite as we'd like. As you can see in figure 9.5, the designer positions a small rectangle in the middle of the `Grid` element, using margins to control position and size.

This is fairly easy to correct; go to the XAML view and delete all the attributes of the `DockPanel` or set the margin to 0 in the property editor.

```
<DockPanel Margin="130,107,112,110" Name="dockPanel1" />
```

---

[4] Well, that isn't strictly true. Windows Live Messenger hides all the menus behind a single icon on the titlebar area; pressing the Alt key exposes the menu in IE 7, and there are many context menus throughout the applications. But the writing is on the wall.

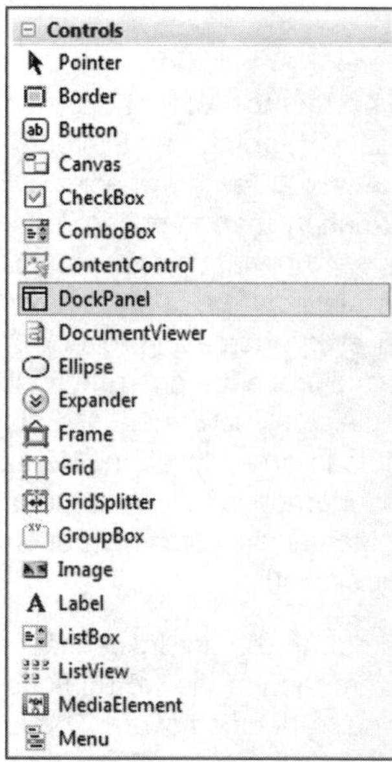

Figure 9.4 The WPF `DockPanel` can be found in the Common Containers section of the `ToolBox`.

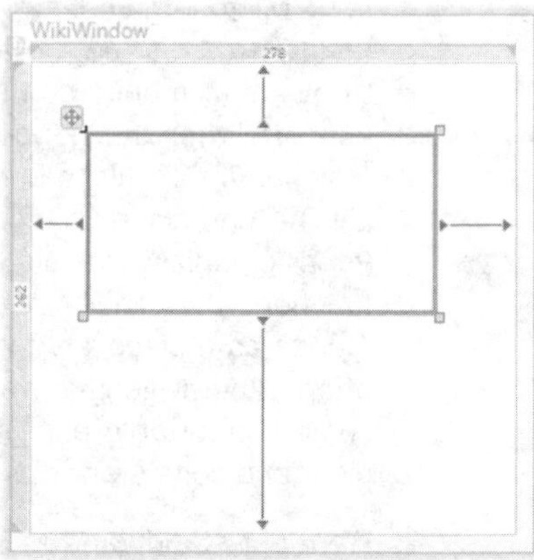

Figure 9.5 By default, the `DockPanel` is positioned uselessly in the main window.

Now that we have a `DockPanel` on top of a `Grid`, this is a good time to note that Visual Studio 2008 has a number of ways to select the various elements in your WPF classes. Typically, you click the element you want and interact with it. As you start nesting controls, that isn't as easy as it sounds. Clicking the middle of the form selects the `DockPanel`, and clicking the window edge selects the `Window`, but how do you select the `Grid`?

Aside from selecting the XAML, there are three primary methods: A context-menu click on any element above the desired element, the Document Outline window, and the location bar. Figure 9.6 shows all three methods at once.

Not all of these are new ways of selecting UI elements in the designer, but these methods become far more important with the deeply nested hierarchies in WPF. It isn't uncommon to have five or ten elements on top of each other in a deeply composed design.

9.2.2 *Adding menubars, statusbars, and toolbars…*

Now that the `DockPanel` is set up, we're ready to add the menus and toolbars. In the Toolbox, open the section titled Controls and find the Menu item. Drag the Menu over to the newly created `DockPanel`. Note that the menu now has an attached property from the `Dock` called `DockPanel.Dock`. Set this property to `Top`. Now we need some menu items. Click the … button next to Items in the property editor. This will bring up an interactive dialog where you can add and edit the commands. Go ahead and just add the top-level menu items for File, Edit, Format, Tools and Help. For the moment, we're just going to set the Header Text—the text to display for the menu—and the Name for each `MenuItem`. Figure 9.7 shows the interactive menu editor.

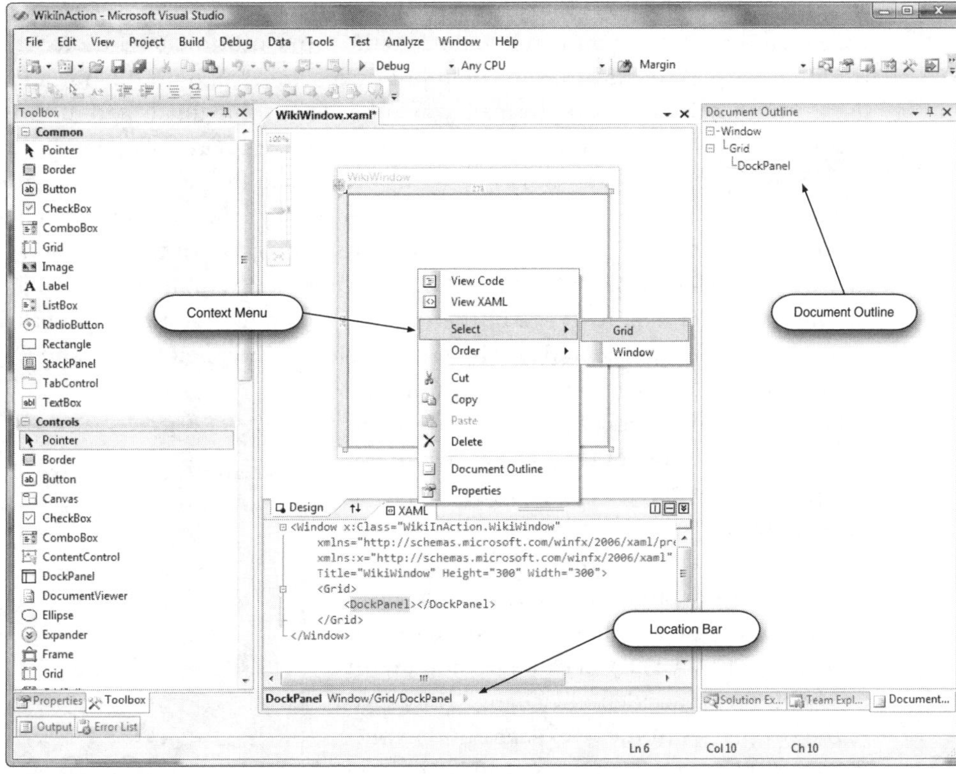

Figure 9.6 There are three methods to select obscured elements.

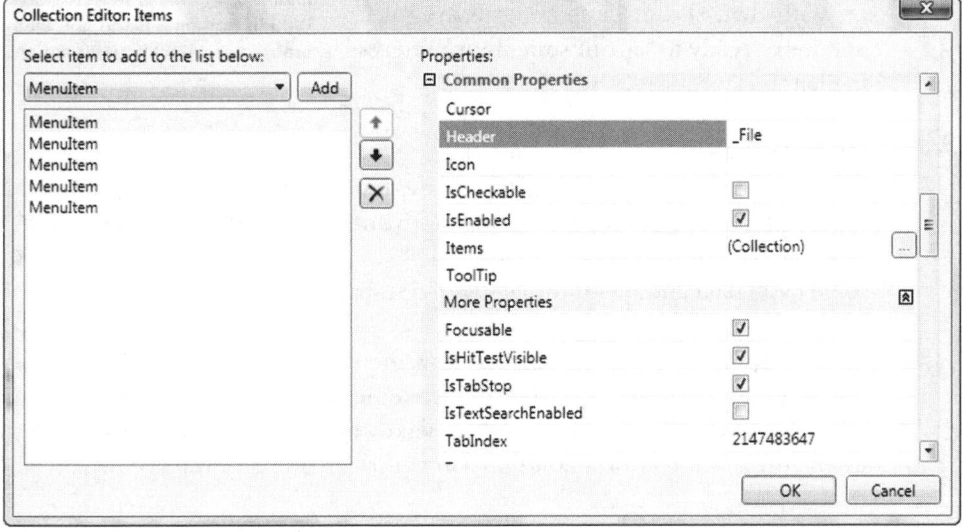

Figure 9.7 The interactive Menu Item editor. We're just setting the Name and the Header text for the moment.

Next up is the toolbar. `ToolBars` are a little special—we need a `ToolBarTray` to host it. Drag on a `ToolBarTray`, and set it to dock to the top. Unfortunately, the `ToolBar` editor is a little persnickety. Ideally, you could just drag a `ToolBar` onto the tray and go from there, but that doesn't work. Instead, you either have to manually add the `ToolBar` via XAML or click the … button next to `ToolBars` in the `ToolBarTray`'s properties and hit Add. This approach doesn't work for adding `Buttons` to the `ToolBar`—The Add button in the `Items` collection editor isn't enabled (probably because you can put arbitrary controls onto a `ToolBar`). In this case, you have to drop down to XAML and manually insert `Button` elements inside of the `ToolBar`. Once you've done this, though, you *can* hit the … button next to `Items` in the Properties grid and edit the properties on the added buttons. Go ahead and add buttons for New, Print, Spell Check, and Options.

The `StatusBar` is going to be fun when we get to data binding. Drag a `StatusBar` over and dock it to the bottom of the window. We're not going to put anything on the `StatusBar` yet, so leave it blank.

Finally, add a `Grid` as the last element of the `DockPanel`. By default, the last child of a `DockPanel` fills it, (You may have noticed there's no `Dock` property of `Fill`.) Because we don't want this behavior to accidentally change on us, go to the properties of the `DockPanel` and explicitly set `LastChildFill` to `True`. If all is well, you should have something that looks a lot like figure 9.8.

Figure 9.8 This is what we have so far for Wiki In Action; a menu, a toolbar, and a status bar, all waiting for action.

With that, all our basic controls are set up and we're ready to lay out some more interesting parts.

9.3 Nested layouts

In our sketch, we have a navigation bar extended from the top to the bottom on the left (the label navigation area), and a horizontal split in the view on the right (a classic summary on top, details on bottom view). In HTML, you might think about creating some table data and table row tags with `colspan` and `rowspan` attributes, and in HTML that would probably be a good idea.[5]

Back in chapter 5, we discussed how the `Grid` panel pushes the responsibility of defining the spanning into the child elements. In the calculator, we went ahead and spanned the elements, but that makes our design a bit brittle. What happens when you add a row or a column? Do you really want to track how and where each

---

[5] Well, actually, it would be a horrible idea if you were using a table to control the layout. You should use styled divs and spans to control your layout, but XAML is layout markup, not document markup, so using the `Grid` is perfectly ok.

item should span? We're going to avoid that whole mess by creating a two-cell grid split vertically to divide our labels from our summary-detail view, and we'll use another grid split vertically to divide the summary items from the detail items.

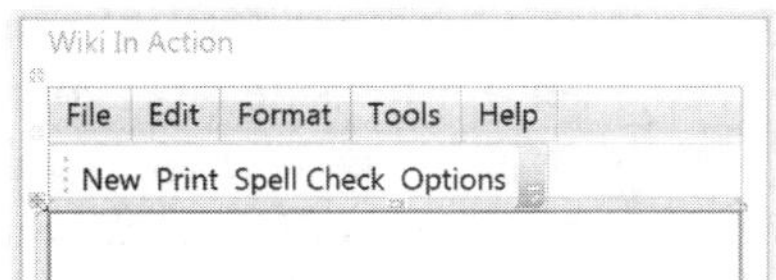

Figure 9.9 We zoomed the Wiki In Action window 200% to make it easier to see the `Grid` margin adornments.

9.3.1 *Adding the first Grid*

To create the columns, select the `Grid` to bring up the designer adornments. A light blue margin appears above the `Grid` specifying the current width of the single column in the `Grid`, as shown in figure 9.9.

We need three columns in all: one column each for the navigation side and summary/detail, and one column for the splitter. You can quickly create columns by putting the pointer in the light blue margin area above the grid and clicking. For now, let's divide the area evenly; we'll fine tune the columns in a minute. Do this twice to have three columns as shown in figure 9.10.

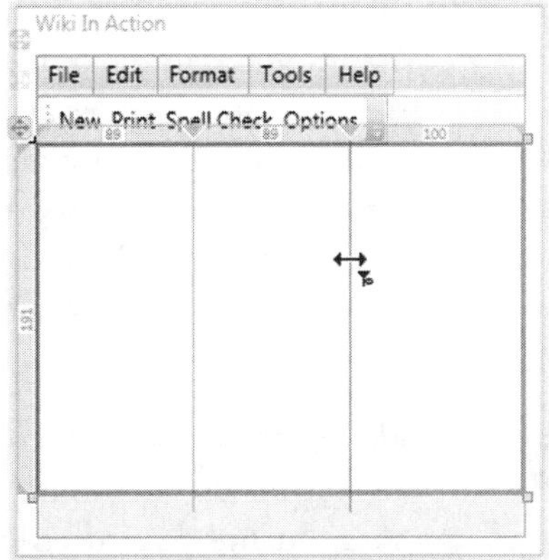

Figure 9.10 Here's the Wiki In Action window after multiple columns are created.

The next thing we need from the `Grid` is splitter behavior. In the pre-WPF days, the splitter was a complicated thing, and if you added things in just the wrong way, you lost your splitter content in the designer. Because WPF is focused around layout managers, splitter behavior is little more than tweaking a panel to respond to sizing changes at runtime. Also, whereas splitters were designed around docking behavior prior to WPF, splitters are an aspect of the `Grid` layout.

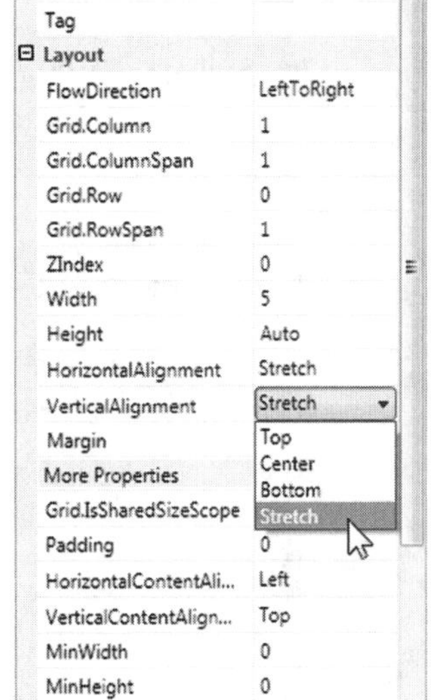

Figure 9.11 The `GridSplitter` properties that need changing are in the Layout section of the Properties Grid.

To get our first splitter, go to the Toolbox and under the section Controls select the `GridSplitter` and drop it in the middle column. Unfortunately, the default properties of our splitter aren't very useful, so we'll need to tweak them. First, erase the `Margin` and `Name` properties. The `Margin` is unnecessary, and we don't need a name for this splitter. Next, because this is a vertical splitter, set the `HorizontalAlignment` to `Center` and the `VerticalAlignment` to `Stretch`. Finally, set the `GridSplitter`'s `Width` to `5` (figure 9.11).

That should do it for the `GridSplitter` itself. Now we need to tune our columns. For our left-side label column, specify a width of 1* and a `MinWidth` of 50 and, for the right-side column, a `Width` of 2* and, again, a `MinWidth` of 50. As you may remember from chapter 5, this notation results in a nice one-third to two-thirds split between the navigation area and data area. This also ensures that we can't lose either column by shrinking it down too far.

This brings us to the column hosting the `GridSplitter`. Because we've already explicitly set the `GridSplitter`'s width, all we need to do with this column is set its width to `Auto`, and the column will simply size to whatever the splitter control is set to. That should tighten up the middle column to the `GridSplitter`; we've now finished a basic Explorer-style navigation window, as shown in figure 9.12.

If you're following along (and haven't already), now would be a good time to run the project and see the splitter in action, as it were. The first thing you may notice is that the behavior is much more sensible than the splitter from the WinForms days, and as you move the splitter and resize the window, the relative size behavior is followed.

9.3.2 Adding the second Grid

We still need our summary-detail view, so go back to the toolbox and get another `Grid`, but this time drag it into the right column of the interface. Like we just did, erase the `Margin` and `Name` properties and create three *rows* this time. The only difference from what we did previously is that we click along the left edge of the `Grid` to create the rows (figure 9.13).

We need another splitter control, too, so drag a `GridSplitter` to the middle row and erase the `Margin` and `Name`, but set the properties slightly inverted as compared with the vertical splitter. For a horizontal splitter, set `HorizontalAlignment` to `Stretch` and set `VerticalAlignment` to `Center`; rather than setting the `Width`, set the `Height` to `5`.

Figure 9.12 The Wiki In Action window now has the finished Explorer-style split using the `Grid` and `GridSplitter` elements.

Figure 9.13 We need three rows in the data area of the application on the nested `Grid` element.

Finally, we need to adjust the rows as we did for the columns; but, instead of a one-third to two-thirds split, we'll do an even half and half. Again, as before with an ever so slight twist: Set the `Height` to `1*` and the `MinHeight` to `50` for both the top and bottom rows and the middle row's `Height` to `Auto`. That's all we need for the `Grids`—now to fill in a little detail for the navigation.

9.3.3 Using a StackPanel and Expander as navigation aids

The last thing we need to do is create the Favorites and All Labels groups for our navigation area—a look-and-feel common to the Windows environment. You can see variations of this in the Task Pane of folders, the Outlook bar, and the Microsoft Money sidebar. Two panels provide the behavior we need for this: The first is the `StackPanel`. The `StackPanel` arranges elements next to or above each other, automatically growing or shrinking as necessary. The second is the `Expander`. As you've seen previously, the `Expander` shrinks and grows depending on whether you want to see what's in it or not. In the web environment, this ability isn't very exciting—the flow layout model of web pages lends itself well to reformatting automatically; but, for rich client development, this is a powerful combination, and something that used to require a fair bit more effort than it does now.

Back to the Toolbox, and we're almost done! The `StackPanel` is with the rest under Common, so drag one over to the left column and delete the `Margin` and `Name` properties (again…) and that's all we need to do. Next drag a couple of `Expanders` over to the newly created `StackPanel`. We want a clean slate, so delete all the attributes Visual Studio created, and you should have a set of stacked `Expanders`. To see them work, we can put some fake data in, so open properties, set the Header for the first to Favorites and the second to All Labels, and set `IsExpanded` to `True` for both `Expanders`.

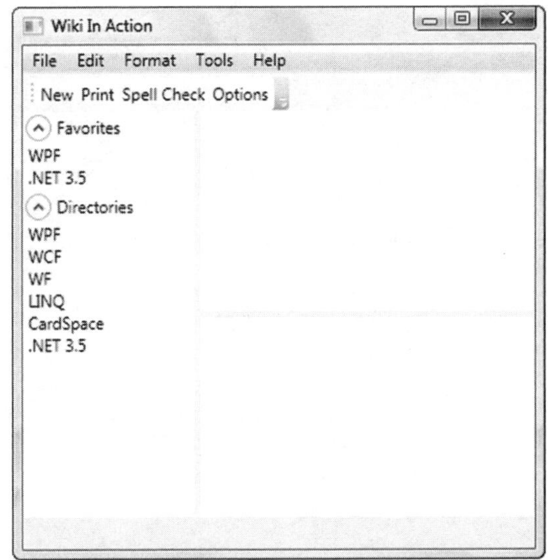

Figure 9.14 Voila! Here's the final Wiki In Action application window.

Finally, so we can see the `Expanders` work, let's add a `ListBox` to each `Expander` and some text to each `ListBox`. If all goes well when you run the application, you should have something a lot like figure 9.14, with working expanders and splitters that's ready to hook up to some business logic.

At this point, we've combined a `DockPanel`, `StackPanel`, and multiple `Grids` and `Expanders` to create a resolution-independent UI. It personally took us less than

20 minutes, and we even had to write about it while we were doing it! Now it's time to think about making this UI do something…

9.4 Summary

Except for truly trivial applications or, perhaps, simple dialogs within other applications, you'll invariably build your UI by combining multiple different layouts together. The power of this technique is unmistakable, but we can't stress enough how important preplanning is here. If you don't think through your basic design up front, you'll end up doing a lot of tedious cutting, pasting, and correcting.

So far, we haven't hooked up any actual functionality to our presentation, and that's exactly how it should be. In the next chapter, we'll explore WPF's built-in command routing to add both custom and system commands for our wiki, and show how to hook them to our presentation layer. The benefits of keeping presentation separate from business logic will become even more apparent later, but unlike the calculator, we aren't going to leak any business logic back into this application's UI.

10 Commands

This chapter covers:

- Approaches to command handling
- The command pattern
- System commands
- Custom commands
- Us gesturing at our application and our application gesturing back

In the last chapter, we created a simple application shell, but it doesn't *do* anything. In this chapter, we'll look at how WPF approaches the interaction between the presentation and business logic, and implement some custom business logic as well. Unlike the calculator, the implementation of the wiki in this chapter will show how WPF applications *should* be hooked together—no cheating by putting business logic in the UI.

Fortunately, WPF provides a lot of tools to accomplish a properly separated business logic layer—although, like Windows Forms, you can easily slide into allowing business logic in the UI. Even though commands are nothing new to Windows development, WPF marks the official introduction of commands into the .NET world (and about time too). This isn't to say we can't all create our own command models in .NET; but, without a common model to work around, this can lead to some pretty horrible-looking code when trying to integrate many third-party components, all taking similar but slightly varying approaches to the problem.

10.1 A brief history of commands

To some people, the WPF command model will appear a bit heavy and complex, so we'll go through a brief bit of history about commands and demonstrate why a small investment in the command pattern does pay off over time. The commanding system of WPF is based on both the Command pattern and the MFC command model.

10.1.1 Windows Forms and simple event handlers

In Windows Forms, a common (and unfortunate) approach for connecting the UI to trigger behavior in the application was through event handlers. This has two bad side effects:

- Business logic leaked into the presentation tier.
- The UI was required to drive the application, making automation and service-orientation an expensive retrofit.

Imagine adding a print command to an existing Windows Forms application.[1] You might have some code that starts out innocently enough:

```
private void printButton_Click(object sender, EventArgs e)
{
  document.Print();
}
```

Invariably the code isn't going to remain this simple. Over time, you'll add security checks, make sure the document is valid, and run it through some process. It's probably going to end up looking a lot more like this code:

```
private void printButton_Click(object sender, EventArgs e)
{
    if (document != null)
    {
      if (!SecurityManager.IsTrue(PrintingPermission))
        throw new SecurityException( Resources.PrintingNotPermitted);

      PrintTemplate template = new PrintingTemplate(document);
      template.Print();
    }
    else
    {
        MessageBox.Show(Resources.NoDocumentToPrint);
    }
}
```

At this point, we have a problem. Actually, we have two problems. The first is that our business logic now lives in the UI. Some form class somewhere is deciding whether or

[1] Or imagine adding an implementation to a WPF calculator…

not it's OK to print a document. If we want to print from somewhere besides the print button, perhaps from a menu, we're likely to either miss this security check, or we'll end up copying and pasting code–a serious offense.

The second problem is that, at some point, someone is going to want to use automation to tell the application to print, or a customer is going to want to use an API to control the application, and the only API we now have is the UI. We also have a fair number of other minor problems cropping up, such as, if we throw a security exception and want to retry printing after the user enters credentials, we lose the original requests, and the users must set everything up again as they want. If this were a different type of command, such as cut or paste, we wouldn't have any way to undo that operation either.

Again, via `RoutedEvents`, WPF has full support for this model, as you've seen in the calculator and other examples. In fact, if you *do* use events for handling commands, the ability to bubble up and tunnel down makes it superior to the WinForms model because you can at least move your handlers up a few levels. But it isn't recommended for any but the most trivial of applications.

10.1.2 Son of MFC

If you have any experience with MFC, you'll undoubtedly notice that the WPF command model is heavily influenced by it. Given that this is a book on WPF, we won't go into a tremendous amount of detail on the MFC implementation. If you're familiar with MFC, consider this a refresher or, if not, an interesting bit of trivia.

Command routing in MFC was based around the idea of the Message Map. At a low level, everything in Windows is driven by messages. If the user clicks the mouse, a `WM_LBUTTONDOWN` is sent to the application, followed by a `WM_LBUTTONUP`. (The *L* is for the left button). If part of the screen needs to be repainted, a `WM_PAINT` message is sent. And, if a command needs to be executed, such as something from a classic Windows menu, a `WM_COMMAND` message is sent.

In MFC, the trick was to make sure that the appropriate code got called when one of these messages was sent. This was generally done by putting a Message Map in the file, with entries for each message and command to be handled.

```
BEGIN_MESSAGE_MAP(CMyClass, CFrameWnd)
ON_LBUTTONDOWN()
ON_WMPAINT()
ON_COMMAND(IDC_DoSomething, OnDoSomething)
ON_COMMAND(IDC_DoSomethingElse, OnDoSomethingElse)
END_MESSAGE_MAP()
```

All the capitalized terms in a message map are C++ macros—at compile time this block got turned into a hunk of code that generated a static array in the class that mapped messages to a bit of code that mapped to a pointer to each function. The IDC_DoSomething values were defined as particular numbers. If you wanted to add a command, you would create a new value defined in a constants file, and implement the appropriate method in your class. When the command was executed (for example, the user clicked a toolbar button), MFC would convert it into a message, and Windows would route it to the appropriate application window, which would then each check its static arrays of commands and call the appropriate methods.

The best that could be said for this approach is that it (mostly) worked and was fairly fast. The real fun came when you wanted to handle enabling and disabling commands—for example, if you wanted to gray out toolbar buttons. During idle processing (maybe 10 to 20 times a second), a `WM_UPDATE_COMMAND` message would be sent for every single command on the toolbars asking if they should be enabled or grayed out. So, 10 to 20 times a second (or more) each of these methods would be called saying, "Should I gray this one out now? How about now? How about now?" Invariably, some junior coders would end up putting in a database query in one of these handlers, and suck the entire bandwidth for the Eastern Seaboard whenever their applications ran.

Unlike MFC, *every* element and control in WPF can have commands, and many already understand existing system commands. Also, although the process is similar, the implementation varies greatly (and for the better) by using events and objects instead of macros and message maps. If you know the MFC commanding system, you may get a sense of déjà-vu as we go through WPF commands.

10.2 The WPF approach

Now that we've talked about some of the historical influences on WPF commands, we'll talk about how WPF handles them. Like many modern command models, the WPF model has been *influenced* by the classic Gang-of-Four (GoF) Command pattern, so let's start there.

10.2.1 The Command pattern

The WPF approach to commands is definitely related to the traditional Command pattern, but there are some issues with the classic pattern, and the WPF design takes this into account.

In a nutshell, the idea behind the Command pattern is to encapsulate a method call and its parameters so that you can treat the method call itself as an object in the system.

This leads to interesting possibilities such as easily implemented undo, script automation, and macro capabilities all for free (free as in "after you've spent the time implementing the pattern itself").

Things that cause commands to be executed—menus, toolbars, and so on—have a reference to a `Command` object. The `Command` object knows how to do whatever it's supposed to do via the `Execute()` method. If undo is supported, then it also keeps track of how to reverse what it does. The menus and toolbars only have to know to call the `Execute()` method. Anything else that needs to execute commands—ribbons, macro-languages, and so on—gets a reference to the appropriate `Command` and to call `Execute()`.

There are some issues with this pattern. For one thing, it can be fiddly trying to create a distinct `Command` class for every different command. Also, strangely enough, it can cause encapsulation issues—if you have a series of related commands that rely on a particular infrastructure, you don't want to break up the execution code across a whole bunch of helper objects.

The WPF infrastructure *does* allow for a classic implementation of the Command pattern, but that isn't the default way WPF implements command handling. Nonetheless, WPF does make use of certain facets of the pattern. It's important to keep in mind that the patterns are more guidelines than implementation advice, so the precise implementations will vary.

10.2.2 WPF commands

WPF command handling has elements from all three of the previous models. Following the Command pattern, there *is* an object that represents each command. Instead of there being a different type of class for each command, the commands are static instances of one or two preexisting classes. Like MFC, there are command generators and subscribers; but, instead of requiring a painful mapping function, the tie-ins are more like the WinForms event model.

Think about our earlier printing example. In Windows Forms, we called `document.Print()` from the `OnClick` handler of a button control to print our document. In WPF, we still catch the command in an event, but the command is encapsulated, so we can send it on to someone else to handle or handle it right there if appropriate.

In WPF, if you want a print command, you'll really have an object called *PrintCommand*, although it will probably only be an instance of a class called *RoutedCommand*—you don't have to create a whole new custom class. The things that can cause a command to be executed—menus, toolbars, and so on, referred to as the *command sources*—are associated with those commands.

In the places where you want to catch the command, you create a *command binding*. This is usually a bit of XAML (a little bit like the MFC Message Map) that says which command you care about and what method in your code to call when the command is received.

Multiple different classes can have command bindings to the same command. For some commands this is silly—you only want to implement one About box handler, for example. For others, like cut and paste, you want the current control (or something acting on its behalf) to be the one that handles the command. The class that handles the command is called the *command target*. You can specify a particular command target to always be used. If you don't, then the control that currently has focus is the target. If the current control doesn't handle the command, then it bubbles up until something finally does handle it (for example, Control, Layout, Window, Application). Figure 10.1 shows the different pieces that come together to handle a command.

Before we dive deeper into the routing model and custom commands, we'll warm up by hooking in some existing system commands. This will get our application doing something *very* quickly. After that, we'll take a look at the WPF command implementation (so that we can start adding our own custom commands), going into depth on the specific types of commands in WPF and how to register for and handle commands.

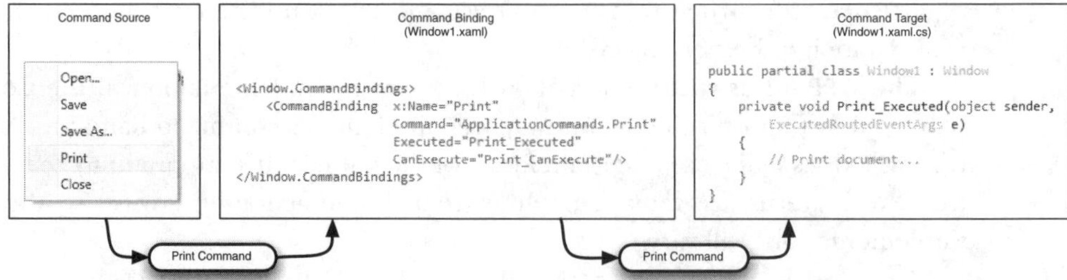

Figure 10.1 Handling a command in WPF. A command source (the menu) is associated with the appropriate Command object (`PrintCommand`). When a source goes to execute the command, the routing mechanism determines the appropriate target. The command binding in that target (in this case, our main `Window`) specifies how the command should be handled. Here it indicates that an appropriate method in the command target should be called.

10.3 Using the built-in system commands

WPF ships with many (156 at last count) commands built in, and many of the various elements of WPF already respond appropriately to them; in many cases, wiring commands is sinfully trivial. The commands are divided into five categories and are defined in the classes described in table 10.1.

Table 10.1 Categories of built-in `Commands`

Command class	Description
`ApplicationCommands`	The category contains various commands you might expect in any sort of productivity application, as well as the high-level general purpose commands such as activating a context menu, closing the document or application, and so on.
`NavigationCommands`	Commands in this class primarily support the Navigation model that we'll be looking at later. For the most part, if you aren't using the WPF Navigation model, you won't be interested in these.
`EditingCommands`	These are what they sound like: commands around editing behavior. Interestingly, some commands you'd expect to find here, like cut, copy, and paste, are in `ApplicationCommands`.
`ComponentCommands`	Probably the least obvious, this set of commands relates to interaction with UI components—movement through the component and to other components.
`MediaCommands`	If you plan on integrating audio, video, or that sort of thing, `MediaCommands` will come in useful.

Each of these classes has a number of static properties—one for each of the commands. If we were using the classic Commands pattern, this would be a threading issue, but because the classes are only being used for routing, this isn't a big deal. If you do decide to implement your own command strategy, the statics are something to keep in mind.

10.3.1 *ApplicationCommands*

Like many types in .NET, most of the commands are extremely well named; it's pretty obvious what they're intended for without further explanation. `ApplicationCommmands` is the set of commands that you'd likely encounter in an application. Here's what is in `ApplicationCommands`:

- `New`, `Close`, `Save`, `SaveAs`
- `Cut`, `Copy`, `Paste`, `Delete`, `SelectAll`
- `Print`, `CancelPrint`, `PrintPreview`
- `Properties`
- `Find`, `Replace`
- `ContextMenu`
- `NotACommand`[2]

We haven't yet created any data storage for our wiki pages, but if we drop a `RichTextBox` below the splitter on the right, we can hook up some of the application commands right away. Because they'll do something, we're going to hook up the cut, copy, and paste commands right now.

ADDING CUT, COPY, PASTE, AND DELETE SUPPORT

The menu items are already created, but they don't do anything yet. If you're following along, open your WikiWindow.xaml, and we'll add this functionality remarkably quickly with the following steps:

1. Right-click the Edit menu (in the application, not the Visual Studio edit menu).
2. Select Properties.
3. Click the ellipses next to the `Items` property.
4. Add the commands and set the `Command` property for each item as described in table 10.2.

Table 10.2 Command assignments for `MenuItems`

MenuItem	Command property
Cut	`ApplicationCommands.Cut`
Copy	`ApplicationCommands.Copy`
Paste	`ApplicationCommands.Paste`

Once you're finished, your XAML should look like this:

```
<MenuItem Header="_Edit">
  <MenuItem Header="Cut" Command="ApplicationCommands.Cut" />
  <MenuItem Header="Copy" Command="ApplicationCommands.Copy" />
  <MenuItem Header="Paste" Command="ApplicationCommands.Paste" />
```

---

2 Yes, there's really a NotACommand command…

```
    <MenuItem Header="Delete" Command="ApplicationCommands.Delete" />
  </MenuItem>
```

Go ahead and run the application and type some things into the text box. Not only do cut, copy, and paste all work now, you may also notice that they enable and disable correctly depending on whether or not the `RichTextBox` control is active and whether or not it has a selection. Now tell your boss you need a couple more days to implement the feature and catch up on all those movies you've been missing.

By the way, we're fully qualifying the names here (`ApplicationCommands.Cut` and so forth); but, for the built-in commands, it's also legal to just say `Cut` because the `Command` property has a converter that knows the built-in commands and can automatically find them by their shortened name. (The WPF developers were careful to avoid any dupes in the built-in commands.) When you implement your *own* commands, you do have to fully qualify them.

10.3.2 NavigationCommands

If you were writing a web browser, you'd probably find what you need in `NavigationCommands`. These commands include `BrowseForward`, `BrowseBack`, `Favorites`, `History`, and so on. We aren't going to be using any of these commands in this particular application, but we could use them, for instance, in the navigation application we build in later chapters.

10.3.3 EditingCommands

Think about creating a word processor and you've got a good idea of what lives in the `EditingCommands` class. There are *many* commands in this class, including commands such as `SelectUp`, `SelectRight`, `ToggleCenter`, `MoveUpLine`, `MoveToDocumentStart`, `MoveToDocumentEnd`, and the list goes on. These commands are a lot more interesting; if you think about our `RichTextBox`, it's a lot like a miniature word processor. It stands to reason that it probably implements many of these commands (and it does), so we can hook these up quickly and turn our `RichTextBox` into a respectable control.

We don't need to add a lot right now, but it would be good if we had alignment (left, right, justify, and center), text effects (bold, underline, italic)—and that's probably enough. This time we'll hook the commands up to the toolbar we created above the `RichTextBox`.

As we mentioned earlier, you can't add buttons through the toolbar's properties, but you can put buttons in place in XAML (put in seven), then open the Collection Editor (figure 10.2) for the toolbar by clicking the ellipsis button of the `Items` property. Set the properties for each button to represent the commands we want to have on our `RichTextBox` (table 10.3).

On each `Button`, we set the `Command` to the respective command in the `EditingCommands` class. After the properties have been set, the XAML looks like this:

```
<ToolBar>
  <Button Command="EditingCommands.AlignLeft">Left</Button>
  <Button Command="EditingCommands.AlignCenter">Center</Button>
```

```
    <Button Command="EditingCommands.AlignRight">Right</Button>
    <Button Command="EditingCommands.AlignJustify">Justify</Button>
    <Button Command="EditingCommands.ToggleBold">Bold</Button>
    <Button Command="EditingCommands.ToggleItalic">Italic</Button>
    <Button Command="EditingCommands.ToggleUnderline">Underline</Button>
</ToolBar>
```

That's it! Because the `RichTextBox` element already understands all these commands, it will enable them when it has focus, and our text editor has some nice functionality very quickly. In some ways, the real advantage we get from using these built-in commands is the direct support built directly into the `RichTextBox`. If we had a simple text control that didn't *implement* any of these commands, it would still take a great deal of effort to implement everything `EditingCommands` already has to

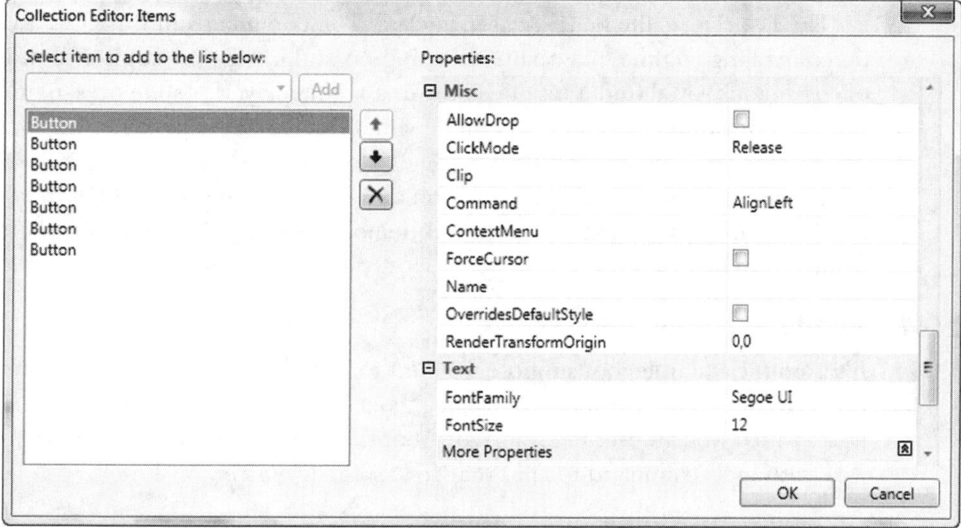

Figure 10.2 The Collection Editor displays a list of elements you can add to other framework elements as well as a property editor.

Table 10.3 Command assignments for toolbar above the `RichTextBox`

MenuItem	Command property
Left	`EditingCommands.AlignLeft`
Center	`EditingCommands.AlignCenter`
Right	`EditingCommands.AlignRight`
Justify	`EditingCommands.AlignJustify`
Bold	`EditingCommands.ToggleBold`
Underline	`EditingCommands.ToggleUnderline`
Italic	`EditingCommands.ToggleItalic`

offer.[3] This counts as another advantage of the command mechanism—the fact that a large number of .NET controls are already command aware, and third-party controls are also likely to support the default commands out of the box.

10.3.4 Component and media commands

There are two more built-in command classes, but we're not going to hook them up right now. The first is the `ComponentCommands` class. These commands are all centered around scrolling, moving, and selecting objects in the UI. Certainly interesting, but the keyboard bindings are already hooked up for most of the controls, so we can tab through, page up, page down, and so on. The majority of the `ComponentCommands` are bound through the keyboard or accessibility devices, not directly exposed by menus or buttons.

The last class is the `MediaCommands` class. The commands in this class are focused on controlling volume, play, pause, turning on and off the microphone, and the sort of commands you'd find a lot of use for in a media player or slide presentation application. If we added the ability to embed video clips in our wiki pages, we could find a good use for this set of commands.

So far, we've put some commands on a menu and allowed the built-in controls to handle them. In the next section, we'll demonstrate how to handle one of the commands ourselves.

10.4 Handling commands

It's a simple example, but suppose we want to hook up the About box on our application. There's no `ApplicationCommands.About`, but there *is* an `ApplicationCommands.Help`, which we can use. Let's add an About... menu item on the Help menu in the wiki, setting its command to `ApplicationCommands.Help`.

10.4.1 Handling a built-in command

To handle the command, we have to create a binding to that command. In a UI class (anything derived from `UIElement` or `ContentElement`), it's easy to do this via XAML. For example, if we want to handle the command in our main window, we could add the binding shown in listing 10.1.

Listing 10.1 Adding a command binding to our main window

```
<Window.CommandBindings>
  <CommandBinding Command="ApplicationCommands.Help"
                  Executed="HelpExecuted"/>
</Window.CommandBindings>
```

The `Command` is the command we want to handle, and the `Executed` attribute points to the handler in our code, which looks like this:

---

[3] Feel free to implement the other 50 or so `EditingCommands` if you so desire.

```
private void HelpExecuted(object sender, ExecutedRoutedEventArgs e)
{
  MessageBox.Show("Welcome to WikiInAction");
}
```

The `ExecutedRoutedEventArgs` has some useful things in it, such as the `Command` object and the `Source` of the event. It also has a `Handled` property that, like a `RoutedEvent`, is used to make sure that no one else handles the command after us. Figure 10.3 shows the menu and the command in action.

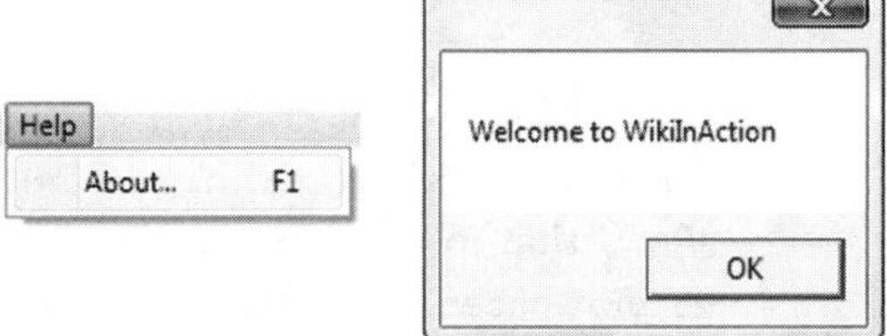

Figure 10.3 Our About menu option in action. Notice the F1 shortcut appearing on the menu.

Nothing to it. We could have used an event to get a similar effect because we're handling the command in the same class where we have our menu defined, but commands are a *lot* more flexible, as you saw with the `RichTextBox`, and as you will in our future examples.

You may have noticed that the menu added an F1 shortcut to our About... menu item. It did this because the built-in Help command has an associated *keyboard gesture* that it automatically hooks up. If you hit F1 in the application, you'll also see the About box. We'll talk more about gestures and keyboard shortcuts in a moment. But we don't really want F1 to bring up the About box—that's an artifact of using the built-in Help command. It would be better if we created our own.

10.4.2 Creating a custom command

Creating a command and referencing it is easy. At the moment, we're going to implement the command right in our `Window` class, although that's a bad thing to do from a code separation standpoint. Don't worry, though—we'll show how to do this more cleanly in the next section.

To create the command, we have to create our own instance of a `RoutedCommand` object. Like the built-in commands, we'll make this static. We put the following line into the `Window1` class:

```
public static RoutedCommand About = new RoutedCommand();
```

We're creating a public static variable here—really this should be a property exposing a backing field, but this will work fine for now. The next thing is to put our command on the menu; but, before we can do that, we have to worry about namespaces—our `Window` doesn't know about our code yet. By now, you should know the drill—add the *local* namespace into the main `Window` tag:

```
xmlns:local="clr-namespace:WikiInAction"
```

Now we can use our command on the menu:

```
<MenuItem Header="About..." Command="local:WikiWindow.About" />
```

Other than the namespace reference, this looks like any other command reference, although the fact that we're referencing it from `WikiWindow`, instead of a commands class of some sort, is pretty ugly. To bind to the command, we do almost what we did before, although the notation for using our own commands isn't quite as simple:

```
<CommandBinding Command="{x:Static local:WikiWindow.About}"
                           Executed="AboutExecuted"/>
```

We use the special notation to bind to a static member of our class. This notation would also work for all the built-in commands, but they have special handling which allows that to be skipped. We also rename our handler `AboutExecuted`, instead of `HelpExecuted`, to be more accurate.

When you run, you should get *almost* exactly the same behavior as before. The one difference is that we no longer have the F1 shortcut showing up on our menu. If you *do* want to add a shortcut key, that's also pretty straightforward.

10.4.3 Shortcuts and gestures

One of the properties of a `RoutedCommand` is a collection of *InputGestures*. *Gesture* is a generic term for something that the user can do that elicits a response from the computer.[4] Examples might be the user hitting Alt-F5 or clicking the right mouse button while holding down the Ctrl key. We wouldn't be surprised if, in the future, gestures also include special mouse moves—for example, if you swoop the mouse to the left, you get a control palette, and if you swoosh to the right, it goes away.

We've worked on computers that have gesture software installed that does this sort of thing. It's definitely an acquired taste. A better example, that doesn't rely on superhuman mouse control, is Apple's iPhone that uses various motions to do things like zoom and scroll. Many laptops now have similar (although slightly less cool and trendy) touchpad options.

Anyway, the much simpler gesture we're interested in is the user hitting a key—say, F3—to execute our command. All we have to do is to add the appropriate gesture to our static `Command`, and the easiest place to do that is in a static constructor:

```
static WikiWindow()
{
  About.InputGestures.Add(new KeyGesture(Key.F3));
}
```

The `KeyGesture` class also lets us specify modifier keys (Shift, Alt, Ctrl). In fact, if we want to use a key like the letter *A*, we have to specify modifiers—you aren't allowed to hook up regular input keys as gestures.

If you run the application again, you'll notice that F3 now appears next to the About menu item (figure 10.4) and that hitting F3 brings up the About box.

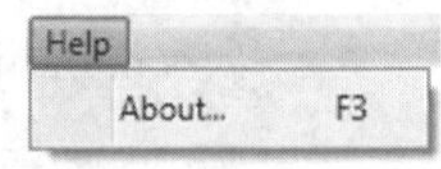

Figure 10.4 Our new F3 shortcut shows up next to the menu item.

This is a much superior way of handling shortcuts. Because the shortcut is associated with the command instead of the menu item, we could add the command to multiple places and

[4] We were going to put a joke in here, but that hardly seems necessary.

not have to worry about it executing multiple times. In fact, we don't have to have the command on a menu (or other selector control) at all—even if we remove About from the menu, F3 will still bring it up.

Because `InputGestures` is a collection, there can also be more than one for a particular command. For example, if we also want Ctrl-right-mouse-double-click to bring up the About box (why not?), we write this:

```
About.InputGestures.Add(new KeyGesture(Key.F3));
About.InputGestures.Add(new
     MouseGesture(MouseAction.RightDoubleClick,ModifierKeys.Control));
```

Now you can either hit F3 or double-click the right mouse button while holding down the Ctrl key to show the About box. Of course, this type of operation would only appeal to Emacs users. Let's reign things in a bit and talk about how commands work under the hood and how they should be handled in a real application.

10.5 Command routing

Arguably, the most interesting and powerful concept of the WPF Command implementation is the command routing process. Command routing enables at least two important things:

- The UI element that triggers a process is completely separated from the objects that perform the actions. This enables much more loosely coupled designs.
- Elements and classes can enlist in command processing without explicitly knowing how or whom to pass commands on to. UI controls can respond to commands visually to give additional cues to the user about what happens. For example, a window could flash after a snapshot command is executed to indicate to the user that a capture took place. Used sparingly, these kinds of cues can greatly enhance understanding of what the application is doing for the user.

Microsoft has obviously spent a lot of time thinking through their approach to command handling, and it's incredibly flexible. Although, as always, we have some complaints (which we'll discuss later), overall we're pretty happy with the approach. The next section goes into the implementation in some detail.

The following three major types represent commands in WPF:

- `ICommand`
- `RoutedCommand`
- `RoutedUICommand`

`ICommand` is the base interface for all commands. Technically, `ICommand` is generic enough that it can be used regardless of whether you're using WPF or not, and is the interface you'd extend to support your own non-UI related back-end commanding systems (for example, if you wanted your web services to use commands as well). The `ICommand` interface follows the traditional GoF pattern closely with an `Execute` method, a `CanExecute` method, and also a `CanExecuteChanged` event.

Notably absent is the `Undo` method. A bit disappointing... To have commands without building in `Undo` is like getting one of those RC cars that only turns in reverse. Anyhow, this almost immediately calls for an `IUndoableCommand` interface, or an `Undo` command. We suppose it wouldn't be any fun if Microsoft solved *everything* for us. Interestingly, some of the controls support undo internally, but don't expose any standard mechanism for dealing with it.

The `RoutedCommand` class could be called the *WPF* implementation of `ICommand`. It's called `RoutedCommand` because this class is designed to support the WPF framework `RoutedEvents`, as well as the tunneling and bubbling of commands throughout the visual tree. Anything that has `CommandBindings` (which happens to be every WPF class derived from `UIElement` and `ContentElement`) is a potential direct or indirect command receiver of these types of commands. Most of the time, when we're talking about commands, we're referring to `RoutedCommands`.

`RoutedUICommand` is derived from `RoutedCommand`, and adds a `Text` property that's useful for presenting localized text for display in a UI. Every command defined in WPF has its `Text` property set, so the built-in commands even come with their own labels. Obviously from a localization standpoint, this is a real time-saver and just kinda nice to have.

As far as structure goes, WPF commands aren't quite singletons. By definition, a singleton prevents more than a single instance of a particular class from being instantiated. WPF commands are all instances of `RoutedUICommand`,[5] and we can create instances of those classes willy-nilly.

The approach for ensuring a single `Copy` command, for example, is to create a well-known static instance library class (`ApplicationCommands`, in this case) and put a property on it for a `Copy` command instance. As long as everyone agrees to call `ApplicationCommands.Copy`, they'll all be sure to be dealing with the same command. Likewise, with our `About` command, all code that wants to use it must refer to the instance in the `WikiWindow` class. This isn't ideal (in fact, it's downright ugly). In our next example, we'll provide a much cleaner implementation of a custom command.

10.6 A cleaner custom command implementation

We can go pretty far with the built-in set of commands, but if we wanted, for some crazy reason, to add some custom functionality to our application, we'd like a clean way to do it. One thing that we'd like to do, for example, is provide a way of turning the currently selected text in our wiki into a new link. We checked—there's no built-in command for that.

10.6.1 Implementing a RoutedUICommand

In a traditional wiki, a link is created by Pascal-casing a word. For example, if you were to write `RoutedCommand`, it would become a link automatically because .NET classes are Pascal-cased by the same convention. It's also useful (and arguably more friendly) to

---

[5] They are often instances of `SecureUICommand`, which is a `RoutedUICommand` with some Permission stuff sprinkled on, but that's a secret type we don't get to use!

select some text and turn it into a document link, and we want to create a command to do that.

Because we're a rich client with a Rich (with a capital R) text box, we may also want to handle our wiki conventions beyond simple character conventions. We need the following characteristics from this command:

- The command should be unavailable when no text is highlighted.
- The command text should display a portion of the text to turn into a link when text is selected.
- Only text selected in the `RichTextBox` for editing pages should make the command available.

CREATING A STATIC CLASS TO HOLD THE COMMAND

The first step is to give our command a new home. Instead of shoving the command into our main window as we did before, we'll follow the pattern established by WPF and create a static command class, with our command as a member. To do this, we add a new class to the WikiInAction project, call it `WikiCommands`, and add the code from listing 10.2.

Listing 10.2 Our custom commands class

```
using System.Windows.Input;

namespace WikiInAction
{
  public static class WikiCommands
  {
    private static RoutedUICommand createLinkFromSelection;     ❶ Our command

    static WikiCommands()
    {
      createLinkFromSelection = new RoutedUICommand(     ❷ Initializes the command
              "Create Link from Selection",
              "CreateLinkFromSelection",
              typeof(WikiCommands));
    }

    public static RoutedUICommand CreateLinkFromSelection     ❸ Command property
    {
      get { return createLinkFromSelection; }
    }
  }
}
```

We have a static `RoutedUICommand` ❶ to hold the single instance of the command. Unlike our previous example, this is a private member variable, and we're exposing the command as a property ❸. Because we're using a property, we *could* lazy-initialize the command—only create it when it's needed—but we'd have to make sure the code was thread-safe and so on; because we don't have many commands, we're keeping it simple.

The initialization of our command is being done in the static constructor for our class ❷. Although not strictly required, we're passing several arguments to the constructor—default descriptive text for the command, a name for the command, and the class that's registering the class.

Now that we've got our custom command, we need to figure out how to hook it up and make it work with a control that's never heard nuthin' 'bout no wikis.

10.6.2 Adding a CommandBinding

Every `UIElement` and `ContentElement` in WPF (which is essentially everything you can see and much of what you can't) can receive a command. Obviously, our `RichTextBox` *knows* commands, but it doesn't know *our* command. We're going to graft our command on after the fact. Now we could be lazy and graft it onto the main `Window` element—after all, the command will bubble up and eventually reach the `RichTextBox`. But that's pretty inefficient because we know that it's the only control that will be involved in this command.

PUTTING THE COMMAND ON THE MENU

If you're following along and didn't add the namespace earlier, go ahead and add the following now:

```
xmlns:local="clr-namespace:WikiInAction"
```

Otherwise, you won't be able to reference our class. As we saw before, adding it to the menu is trivial. Add a menu item as follows:

```
<MenuItem Header="Make Link"
  Command="local:WikiCommands.CreateLinkFromSelection" />
```

This is the same notation we used before, but it's much clearer because we're referencing `WikiCommands` instead of the generic `WikiWindow`. Note that ours is added on the Edit menu.

BINDING THE COMMAND TO A CONTROL

The command is available, but nobody cares about it (sniff). Until someone cares, it will never be available (because nobody will ever respond to the `CanExecute` method). This is the part where we bind it up to the `RichTextBox` (listing 10.3).

Listing 10.3 Binding the command to the `RichTextBox`

```
<RichTextBox>
  <RichTextBox.CommandBindings>    ❶                        Binds to our ❷
    <CommandBinding                                              command
     Command="{x:Static local:WikiCommands.CreateLinkFromSelection}"  <-
                Executed="CreateLinkFromSelectionExecuted"            ❸
                CanExecute="CreateLinkFromSelectionCanExecute"/>    <-
  </RichTextBox.CommandBindings>                                      ❹
</RichTextBox>
```

We bind the command to the `RichTextBox` ❶ instead of to the `Window` because we only want the command to be available for the `RichTextBox`. Again, we have to use the `Static` notation to reference our command ❷. We have a handler for when the command is `Executed` ❸, but we also have a handler for the `CanExecute` property ❹. This handler is how we'll enable and disable the command.

ENABLING AND DISABLING THE COMMAND

There are two factors involved in enabling and disabling a command. The first is the current target. Because we didn't explicitly specify a target on the menu, the target is the currently focused control. Because no other control than the RichTextBox has a handler for CreateLinkFromSelection, the command is disabled until the RichTextBox gets focus. At that time, WPF calls our registered CanExecute method to see if the command should be enabled. Note that, if we hadn't specified a CanExecute method, the presence of an Executed method would be enough to convince WPF that the command should be available.

The second factor is the behavior of the CanExecute method. We said that we only want this command available if something is selected in the RichTextBox. Because we can't easily change the RichTextBox code, we define the handlers in our custom window class. This is a simple bit of code to ensure our command isn't called when nothing can be done about it (listing 10.4).

Listing 10.4 CanExecute handler

```
public void CreateLinkFromSelectionCanExecute(object sender,
                                    CanExecuteRoutedEventArgs args)
{
  RichTextBox wikiEditor = sender as RichTextBox;              ❶ Bound control
  args.CanExecute = !wikiEditor.Selection.IsEmpty;          ❷
  args.ContinueRouting = false;        ❸
  args.Handled = true;            ❹
}
```

The control that the command is bound to is passed to our handler as the sender ❶. Because we bound to the RichTextBox, that's what is passed. The main thing we have to do in this method is set the CanExecute flag on the passed event arguments ❷. *True* means the command should be allowed, and we're setting the value based on the convenient method on the RichTextBox that tells us if any text is selected.

We next set a flag to indicate that there's no point continuing to route the request to any other handlers because we've handled it here ❸. Doing this isn't really required in this case, but might if there were a higher-level handler. Finally, we set the Handled flag to true ❹. This is inherited from RoutedEventArgs, and it isn't strictly necessary to set it, except for some very weird scenarios.

Figure 10.5 shows the Create Link from Edit menu item enabled and disabled as we change focus to and from the RichTextBox.

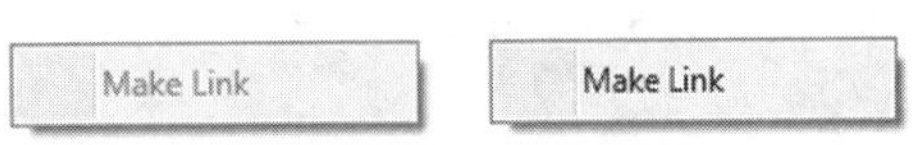

Figure 10.5 If the RichTextBox doesn't have focus, the Make Link option is grayed. Once it has focus, it must also have a selection to be enabled.

One thing you might *not* expect is that, when the selection in the RichTextBox changes, the menu item also automatically enables and disables—yet, we aren't doing anything to make this happen! The first horrible thought might be that, like MFC, WPF is continuously calling our handler. Don't worry, though—nothing so extreme is going in.

Instead, many of the built-in controls automatically notify the command handling framework when things that commonly effect commands change. These include the selection in controls, which is why our selection is updating the menu. Commands are also updated when focus changes or after any command has finished being executed.

This automatic behavior is a pretty good balance between convenience and performance. Unlike MFC, you aren't constantly having all your handlers called, but you also don't have to worry about manually enabling/disabling items as you did in WinForms. If a situation arises where you want to manually force commands to be refreshed, you can call the following:

```
CommandManager.InvalidateRequerySuggested();
```

Which is, in fact, what all those other controls are doing. This method forces all the commands to be reevaluated.

10.7 Summary

Command handling was a major missing piece from Windows Forms, and we're happy that WPF hasn't let it slide. Using the command model buys a lot of flexibility in applications, so going that little extra bit further is worth it over allowing your business logic to start filling up event handlers. Our one big grumble is that, to use the built-in handling, we have to be in a class derived from `UIElement`, and we'd like to be able to implement commands in a completely standalone way. But this isn't too big a price to pay, considering that commands *do* primarily originate from the UI.

The Make Link handling we've shown here is a good example of the command infrastructure, even though we haven't made it do anything. Although we probably won't get as far as making the page links work, the version of the wiki application on our website has this implemented if you'd like to see it.

Our wiki application is shaping up pretty well, but this rather nagging problem has come up. We haven't hooked up any data to this application, and we have no behavioral model to act upon. Even if we type some gibberish and highlight it, there's nothing we can do with it.[6] We're going to have to add some sort of back-end to this application.

Fortunately, that happens to be the topic of the next chapter. We aren't going to spend a lot of time making anything fancy; the point of the chapter will be to understand data binding, not how to write a wiki storage engine, but we're going to end up with one at the end.

---

6 We suppose we could put up a message box. If that would help, go ahead and put a `MessageBox.Show` in the handler. Feel better?

11 Data binding with WPF

This chapter covers:

- Binding to objects
- Binding to XML
- Binding to ADO.NET
- Binding to LINQ
- Binding spells for system daemons

Now that we have a user interface and a way to drive it, we need to put some data behind it—otherwise, it isn't likely to be terribly useful. Before we get to modifying the Desktop Wiki application, we first want to explore data binding more generally; the easiest way is to build some small utilities that will make use of data binding. Once we've done that we'll return to the wiki and give it some data. The first example we'll show is a process monitor (figure 11.1). It binds to the list of processes currently running on the system. This first version of the process monitor is relatively ugly, but we'll return to it in chapter 12, where we'll make it *really* ugly.

Next, we'll demonstrate binding to XML with our Common Vulnerabilities and Exposures (CVE) viewer. As you'll see, binding to XML in WPF is extremely easy. Binding to ADO.NET data, such as from a `DataTable`, will be demonstrated using a simple Bookmark application. We'll also talk a bit about binding to data returned from a

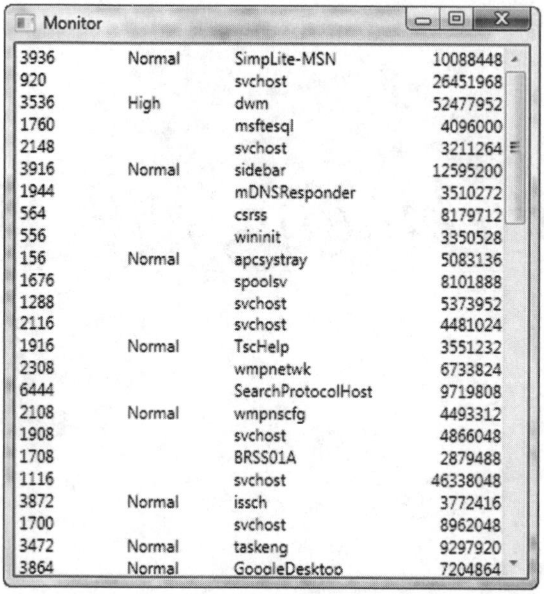

Monitor

3936	Normal	SimpLite-MSN	10088448
920		svchost	26451968
3536	High	dwm	52477952
1760		msftesql	4096000
2148		svchost	3211264
3916	Normal	sidebar	12595200
1944		mDNSResponder	3510272
564		csrss	8179712
556		wininit	3350528
156	Normal	apcsystray	5083136
1676		spoolsv	8101888
1288		svchost	5373952
2116		svchost	4481024
1916	Normal	TscHelp	3551232
2308		wmpnetwk	6733824
6444		SearchProtocolHost	9719808
2108	Normal	wmpnscfg	4493312
1908		svchost	4866048
1708		BRSS01A	2879488
1116		svchost	46338048
3872	Normal	issch	3772416
1700		svchost	8962048
3472	Normal	taskeng	9297920
3864	Normal	GoogleDesktop	7204864

Figure 11.1 The Process Monitor application demonstrates binding to a collection returned by a method call.

LINQ query. Finally, we'll get back to the Desktop Wiki application that allows various notes to be entered, categorized, and stored.

The idea behind data binding isn't all that complex. Given that essentially all applications are some sort of user interface over some kind of data, the problem of connecting that data to the interface is one that virtually every application must handle. This is precisely the problem that data binding addresses—connecting data instances to user interfaces quickly and in a way that requires a minimum of effort and code. As usual, the devil lies in the details.

For the longest time, every application had its own approach for tying data to UI. Over time, different frameworks have tried to genericize the problem—with various degrees of success. Windows Forms became the first Microsoft UI technology to have a solid data binding model by baking binding deep into the framework. WPF takes this even further. Data binding has the status of a first-class citizen in WPF, and support is pervasive and flexible.

In Windows Forms, certain properties of certain objects were set up to allow data binding, and only that limited subset of properties supported binding. In WPF, *almost* every property you can think of can be bound—certainly every property that participates in the Property System. Some of the examples of this may seem silly, but this ubiquitous support provides enormous opportunities for making the UI subtly (or not) reflect the user's data.

11.1 WPF data binding

Before we get into any examples, it's worth going over some terminology that we'll be using throughout. Three important elements that make up data binding in WPF are:

- `Source`—The authoritative data, the *stuff* we want to display.
- `Target`—The object that will reflect the data in some manner, such as a control that displays values or changes color based on the values and so on.
- `Binding`—The rules around how the data will be reflected. For example, is the source or target read-only? Does the source change? When does it change? How often does it change? Is the source a list? Is the target a list?

You can think of the `Binding` as the bridge between the `Source` and the `Target`. Particularly when using XAML, you define the `Binding` as the value of the property on the target—something like:

```
<TextBlock Text="{Binding Path=ProcessName}"
```

The important part is determining where your data is coming from—the binding source.

BINDING SOURCES

There are four sources that WPF can bind to out of the box. These four sources are broad enough that they cover virtually any type of *thing* you'd care to bind to. They are the following:

- *CLR objects*—Individual objects or collections.
- *ADO.NET data types*—`DataTable`, `DataView`, `DataSet`, and so on. There's also direct support for binding to LINQ to SQL.
- *XML data*—Via `XPath` or LINQ to XML.
- *`DependencyObjects`*—WPF objects that participate in the WPF property system.

You might look at the first item on the list and say that *all* these sources are CLR objects, and that would be true. In more practical terms, the binding system has increasing support to bind to objects as they implement and use various existing and new interfaces. For ordinary CLR objects that don't implement any WPF interface or pattern, the binding capabilities are more limited; not all binding modes are supported, for example. But, WPF *can* do at least simple binding against *any* .NET object—which is pretty cool.

Support for binding against ADO.NET objects obviously continues. Although .NET 3.5 adds some types to `System.Data`, the existing .NET 2.0 types aren't replaced, so WPF binds to the same `DataSet`, `DataTable`, and so on, that Windows Forms binds to.

Binding to XML is done via the `XmlDataProvider` class, which can point to an XML file or URI, an `XMLDocument`, or can contain XML directly.

The native WPF data binding mode uses the `DependencyObjects` and `DependencyProperties` that are pervasive throughout the entire WPF framework. As you'll see, using the native approach yields the most flexibility and benefits.

BINDING MODES

There are four binding modes in WPF: `OneTime`, `OneWay` (to target), `OneWayToSource`, `TwoWay`, and `Default`. We know what you're probably thinking—that we can't count. You're suspicious because we listed five items. Default isn't a mode per se—it figures out the most appropriate of the other modes to use. Table 11.1 describes the different modes in a little more detail.

Table 11.1 Binding modes

Mode	Description
`OneTime`	`OneTime` does just as the name implies; it copies the source data value to the target of the data binding operation once. The advantage here is performance because, once the data is copied, the framework can forget that the binding exists. For data sources that aren't expected to change during the execution of the program (like the operating system version or, perhaps, certain machine configuration settings) or where manually forcing the binding to update is reasonable, this may be the best mode to bind with.
`OneWay`	There are two `OneWay` modes. `OneWay` (or more precisely: `OneWay`*`ToTarget`*) never tries to write the value back to the source. For the cases when you want to expose some underlying data in the UI, but the data is read-only or otherwise not meaningful to modify, `OneWay` is the one true way. `OneWay` is the most common `OneWay` binding mode.
`OneWayToSource`	The cases for `OneWayToSource` are rare, but when you need it, it's nice to have. Whenever the binding target changes, `OneWayToSource` copies the data to the source, effectively making this a reverse binding. `OneWayToSource` allows data binding with a target that isn't a `DependencyProperty`.
`TwoWay`	`TwoWay` represents the common business logic scenario in which you have some business data to load and reflect in the UI; when the data is changed in the UI, the changes are automatically propagated back to the business object. This mode saves a lot of manual updating of values to and from data objects.

Not setting the binding mode and setting it to `Default` have the same effect. In either case, the target `DependencyProperty` is examined, and the system automatically selects the most appropriate mode. In our first example, the `ProcessMonitor`, we're presenting a read-only list of values, so our binding will be `OneWay`.

11.2 ProcessMonitor: A simple binding example

Our first binding example is like a little `TaskManager`, in that it shows a list of all the processes; it's also unlike `TaskManager`, in that you can't do anything with the list of processes—like shutting things down. Figure 11.2 shows what the final application will look like.

To follow along, create a new WPF Application called `ProcessMonitor`. Then, create a new `Window` called Monitor.xaml. This is our main window, so you'll need to update the `StartupURI` in App.xaml to point to Monitor.xaml instead of Window1.xaml. If you're feeling especially tidy, you can go ahead and delete Window1.xaml—it's kind of annoying anyway.

With that done, we're ready to get started.

11.2.1 Binding Data with XAML

The first thing we need is some data. It turns out that `System.Diagnostics` has a class for manipulating process information called, cleverly enough, `Process`. `Process`

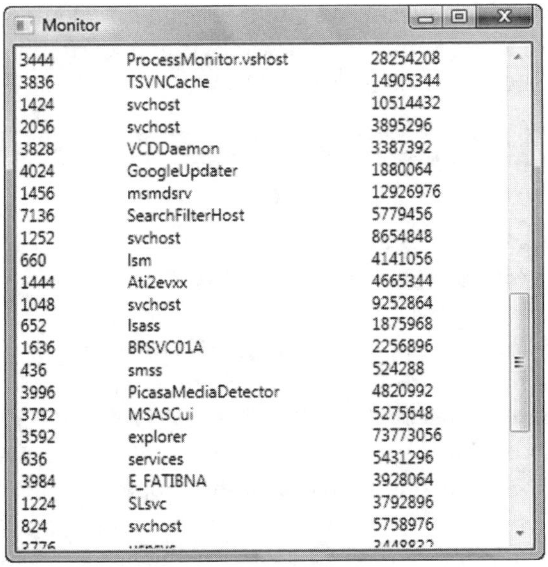

Figure 11.2 `ProcessMonitor` uses data binding to tie a list of processes to a `ListView`.

has a static method, `GetProcesses`, on it that gives back an array of `Processes`. Sounds perfect.

BINDING A LIST SOURCE TO A LIST TARGET

Because we have a list of data for the source, we'll also want a list control to show it. We drag a `ListView` over from the Toolbox, remove the automatically created `Margin` attribute, and split the tag because we're going to be doing some XAML surgery soon.

```
<ListView Name="listView1">
</ListView>
```

Now we need access to that `Process` class from the XAML. This class is available in the `System.Diagnostics` namespace of the `System` assembly, so we add the assembly via the XML namespace using statement `xmlns:diag="clr-namespace:System.Diagnostics;assembly=System."` The `Window` tag should look like this:

```
<Window x:Class="ProcessMonitor.Monitor"
        xmlns="http://schemas.microsoft.com/winfx/2006/xaml/presentation"
        xmlns:x="http://schemas.microsoft.com/winfx/2006/xaml"
        xmlns:diag="clr-namespace:System.Diagnostics;assembly=System"
        Title="Monitor" Height="400" Width="400">
```

WPF provides two classes to help bind data: `ObjectDataProvider` and `XmlDataProvider`. These classes are derivations of `DataSourceProvider`. This is the class that we'd extend if we want to expose some custom form of data that isn't supported in the way we want. We'll try the `XmlDataProvider` a little later, but for this task, we need the `ObjectDataProvider`. These classes are adapters that WPF uses to bind to particular types of data, and are designed so that they can be described declaratively in XAML. They also allow asynchronous binding so that the UI can operate while data is being loaded.

Setting up an ObjectDataProvider is easy. We give it enough information to get to the data we need, and declare it as a resource somewhere in the XAML. In this case, we'll create the resource in the Grid element (listing 11.1).

Listing 11.1 Binding to the process list of the Process object

```
<Grid.Resources>
  <ObjectDataProvider x:Key="processes"                  ❶
                      MethodName="GetProcesses"          ❷
                      ObjectType="{x:Type diag:Process}"/>    ❸
</Grid.Resources>
```

We use the key *processes* ❶ so that we can reference the resource later. Because the goal is to bind from the array returned from a method on that object, not the object itself, we need another attribute to specify the MethodName to call—in this case, GetProcesses ❷. If we wanted to bind to a static property instead of a static method, we wouldn't have specified a MethodName, but the name of the property we wanted later on when doing the binding.[1]

Finally, we need to use a markup extension ❸ to specify the Process class *type*, as opposed to an instance of a class. The x:Type indicates that we're passing a type, and diag:Process specifies the Process class. This is equivalent to the C# code typeof(Process).

Now that we've created our ObjectDataProvider, the next step is to bind to it.

SETTING UP BINDINGS

There are slight differences in the way you bind for different controls—primarily related to the way in which the data will be used. For a TextBlock, we'd most likely bind to the Text property. For the ListView, the property to specify the source of the items is called ItemsSource because it's the source for the list of items. Because we declared our resource in XAML, we can add an ItemsSource attribute like this:

```
<ListView Name="listView1"
  ItemsSource="{Binding Source={StaticResource processes}}">
```

We set the ItemSource property using the XAML's special binding notation. We'll go into the binding notation in a lot more detail later, but we'll talk you through what we're doing right here. The curly-brace notation indicates that some form of reference is going on. {Binding} means that we're doing data binding. This will create, behind the scenes, an object of type Binding. For the Binding to be useful, it needs to have some properties set, and the particular property we're setting is the Source property.

Fortunately, the curly-brace notation allows nesting because we want to set the value of the Source property to reference the *processes* resource we created earlier. This uses the StaticResource reference that we've been seeing for a while now.

---

[1] In fact, as you've seen in previous chapters, we can bind to a Static property without using an ObjectDataProvider at all, using the {Static *class.property*} notation.

Debugging bindings

Given the declarative nature of WPF, debugging can be frustrating. When data binding works, it's lovely; but, when it doesn't, it can be an extremely frustrating experience. Fortunately, there's at least some help. By default, if there's a binding problem, *some* information will be written to the output window. You can increase the amount of information written out via WPF's support for debugging bindings. It isn't a debugger in the traditional sense because you can't step through the XAML to see what's happening, but it will write out a bunch of extra information about what's going on when you run.

To enable debug assistance, you need to add another reference to the XAML. Add the following namespace on the `Window` element:

```
xmlns:debug="clr-namespace:System.Diagnostics;assembly=WindowsBase"
```

When you want to debug a particular binding, you can add a `tracelevel` to the statement, like this:

```
ItemsSource="{Binding Source={StaticResource processes},
                        debug:PresentationTraceSources.TraceLevel=High}"
```

Now when you run, a whole host of useful messages will be written to the output window, telling you step-by-step what's happening during the bind. It isn't guaranteed to help, but it's better than guessing!

The `ListView` now has a scroll bar as shown in figure 11.3. But the `ListView` itself is empty—the data is there, but we still can't see it.

The problem is that we have an array of `Process` objects, but the `ListView` has no idea how we want them displayed. We need a template. ASP.NET developers should feel right at home here because WPF templates are similar to ASP.NET templates. Visual Studio 2008 doesn't have a template editor, so it's time to expand the XAML editor.

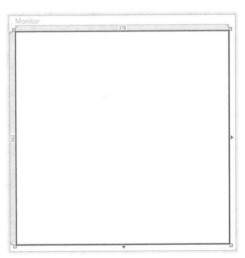

Figure 11.3 The window shows evidence of data with a scrollbar, but nothing is showing up.

To explain what we want to see and how we want to see it to this `ListView`, we need to create a `DataTemplate` describing it. `ListView` has a property called `ItemTemplate` that lets us tell the control how we want our data displayed. We add the following XAML within the `ListView` tag:

```
<ListView.ItemTemplate>
  <DataTemplate>
    <TextBlock Text="{Binding Path=ProcessName}"/>
  </DataTemplate>
</ListView.ItemTemplate>
```

Here we use the expanded form of a XAML property setter to declare and instantiate a `DataTemplate` object that contains a single `TextBlock`. The `Text` property of the `TextBlock` is bound to a property called `ProcessName`. `Path` references the particular property that we want to access. Because we aren't specifying a `Source` this time, the binding mechanism assumes that we want to bind to whatever object we have available—in this case, the `Process` object in the current row of the `ListView`. Once the designer refreshes, the process names should be on the system as in figure 11.4.

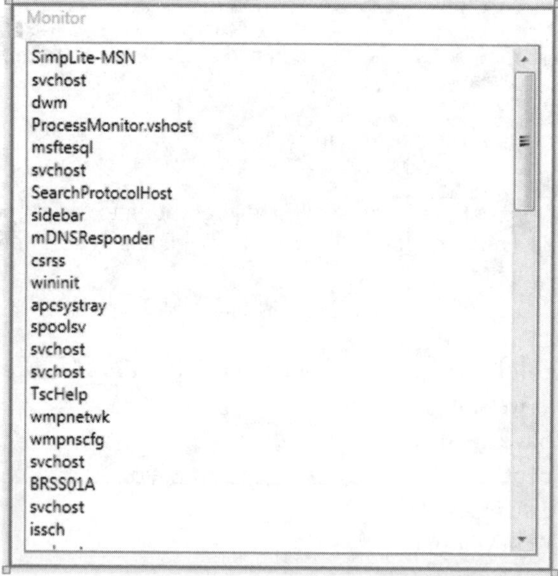

Figure 11.4 With a `DataTemplate` in place, the `ListView` now shows our running processes.

Now we're getting somewhere, but the name of the process by itself isn't overly interesting. It would be nice to have the ID and, perhaps, the `WorkingSet` as well. The `Process` class has a lot of properties, so we should hook up at least a couple more (listing 11.2).

Listing 11.2 `DataTemplate` that pulls multiple properties from data source

```
<ListView.ItemTemplate>
  <DataTemplate>
    <WrapPanel>                        ❶
      <TextBlock Text="{Binding Path=Id}" MinWidth="80" />
      <TextBlock Text="{Binding Path=ProcessName}" MinWidth="180" />
      <TextBlock>
        <TextBlock.Text>
          <Binding Path="WorkingSet" />    ❷
```

```
        </TextBlock.Text>
      </TextBlock>
    </WrapPanel>
  </DataTemplate>
</ListView.ItemTemplate>
```

As you can see, the `DataTemplate` can be as complex as we like. For example, here we're using a `WrapPanel` ❶. We could just as easily use a `Grid` or other layout, put in drawings, set colors and backgrounds, and so on. In chapter 12, we'll demonstrate some more elaborate data templates.

You may also notice that, although we're using the string notation (called the `MarkupExtension`) for two of our `TextBlocks`, for the third one, we're using a slightly different notation ❷. The two are functionally equivalent. Whereas the `MarkupExtension` is more compact, the expanded `Binding` element is easier to read and allows you to do a few things you can do only with the longhand notation.

In any case, now we've got some nice data in figure 11.5.

If we were to carry on with this application, we'd probably prefer a more flexible set of views with columns, sorting, and grouping.

Now that we've got all the data binding figured out using XAML, how would we do it with code?

11.2.2 Binding in code

So far, all the binding we've done has been through XAML. Sometimes binding in code is necessary or simpler. If you want to bind against instances that are controlled and exposed via a strong business logic layer, you'll probably want to bind in code. XAML bindings prefer XAML declarations and tend toward statics and widely shared

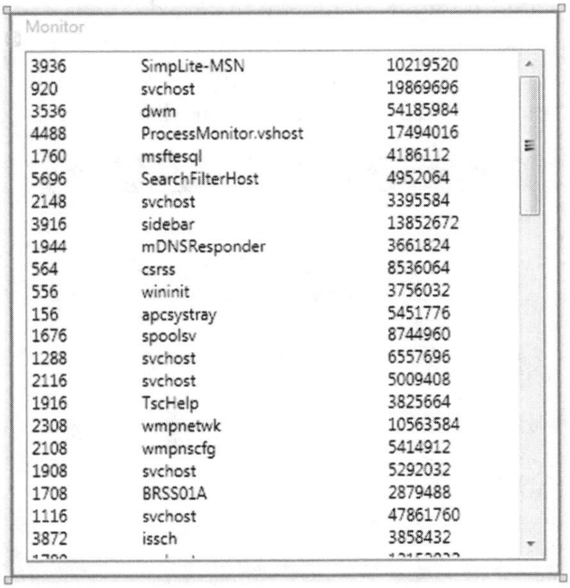

Monitor

3936	SimpLite-MSN	10219520
920	svchost	19869696
3536	dwm	54185984
4488	ProcessMonitor.vshost	17494016
1760	msftesql	4186112
5696	SearchFilterHost	4952064
2148	svchost	3395584
3916	sidebar	13852672
1944	mDNSResponder	3661824
564	csrss	8536064
556	wininit	3756032
156	apcsystray	5451776
1676	spoolsv	8744960
1288	svchost	6557696
2116	svchost	5009408
1916	TscHelp	3825664
2308	wmpnetwk	10563584
2108	wmpnscfg	5414912
1908	svchost	5292032
1708	BRSS01A	2879488
1116	svchost	47861760
3872	issch	3858432

Figure 11.5 With a more sophisticated template, we get more appealing results.

instances, which may be contrary to threading or isolation goals. In any case, we can do everything we just did in code.

First, we remove everything we just did (or save it off and start a new project). The XAML should look like this:

```
<Window x:Class="ProcessMonitor.Monitor"
        xmlns="http://schemas.microsoft.com/winfx/2006/xaml/presentation"
        xmlns:x="http://schemas.microsoft.com/winfx/2006/xaml"
        Title="Monitor" Height="400" Width="400">
  <Grid>
    <ListView Name="listView1">
      <ListView.ItemTemplate>
        <DataTemplate>
         <WrapPanel>
            <TextBlock Text="{Binding Path=Id}" MinWidth="80" />
            <TextBlock Text="{Binding Path=ProcessName}" MinWidth="180" />
            <TextBlock>
              <TextBlock.Text>
              <Binding Path="WorkingSet" />
              </TextBlock.Text>
            </TextBlock>
          </WrapPanel>
        </DataTemplate>
      </ListView.ItemTemplate>
    </ListView>
  </Grid>
</Window>
```

Notice that, although we've removed all the binding, we left the `ItemTemplate` in place. Given that the `ItemTemplate` is all about how to display our data, it makes sense to leave it in XAML. The `DataTemplate` does have specific bindings to specific properties; but, if they aren't found, they'll simply fail quietly. In fact, although it's possible to create a `DataTemplate` with code, it's fairly tricky and somewhat discouraged.

Anyway, on to the code. We right-click Monitor.xaml and select View Code and then create a new method called `BindProcessesToListView` (listing 11.3).

Listing 11.3 Binding in code

```
public Monitor()
{
  InitializeComponent();
  BindProcessesToListView();      <-- Calls method to create Binding
}

private void BindProcessesToListView()
{
  ObjectDataProvider provider = new ObjectDataProvider();      (1)
  provider.ObjectType = typeof(Process);
  provider.MethodName = "GetProcesses";

  Binding binding = new Binding();      (2)
  binding.Source = provider;
  binding.Mode = BindingMode.OneWay;
```

```
    PresentationTraceSources.SetTraceLevel(binding,
                                    PresentationTraceLevel.High);    ❸

    listView1.SetBinding(ListView.ItemsSourceProperty, binding);      ❹
}
```

The code here mostly mirrors what we did in XAML. First, we create the `ObjectDataProvider` ❶, pointing it to the `Process` object and the `GetProcesses` method. Next, we create the `Binding` object ❷. The data source for the `Binding` is the `ObjectDataProvider` we just created. We also specify that the binding is only going to go one way—from the `DataProvider` to the `ListView`.

We also enable debug tracing ❸ to write out information for us about what's going on the binding. Finally, we associate the binding to the `ListView`'s `ItemsSource` property ❹.

Binding performance

Under the hood, binding to CLR uses a lot of reflection, and wherever there's reflection, there are potential performance problems. Fortunately, Microsoft's API philosophy of "make the simple things simple and make the complex things possible" is in full force here. In the simple case, the framework gets `Type` and `Property` descriptors on the CLR objects and sets up the binding appropriately. In the case where performance is more critical, .NET and WPF provide the following interfaces (neither of which is new to WPF) to increase binding speed:

- *`ICustomTypeDescriptor`*—Provides a way for the binding code to find out about the object and its properties without using reflection. If you haven't used binding in the past due to performance or functionality limitations, this is an interface you'll want to get cozy with.
- *`INotifyPropertyChanged`*—Provides an interface to implement a custom scheme for notifying the property system that the source data has been updated. WPF native `DependencyProperties` already provide this notification logic (although they don't use `INotifyPropertyChanged`).

In most cases, you'll probably find that you don't even need these optimizations, but if you do, it's nice to know that they are there.

If you run this code, it will look exactly like figure 11.5.

11.2.3 Binding notation and options

Binding is used all over the place in WPF. It's used to get data, as we've seen, but it's also used in tons of other things such as sizing (to bind the width of one control to the width of another control), animation (to get to the properties that are being animated), and control templates (to tie pieces of the template to specific properties).

The great thing is that the binding notation is really flexible. The downside is that the binding notation is really flexible. WPF hasn't been out for very long. We suspect that, if all the time spent debugging and fixing bindings could be harnessed, we would have, as a species, solved global warming and world hunger, and figured out a way of getting your food delivered before the toast gets cold.

The source of a binding can be broken down into two things: where the data is coming from and what bit of data you want from there. The *where* can be one of four different things (table 11.2).

Table 11.2 Where the data comes from in a `Binding`

Property	Description
`Source`	You use `Source` when you want to bind to a particular object. Invariably, that object is defined as a resource, so the notation looks like this (from our `ListView` example): `<ListView Name="listView1" ItemsSource="{Binding Source={StaticResource processes}}">`
`ElementName`	You use `ElementName` when you want to bind to a property on some other *element* in your UI. For example, if there were a control called *someListBox* and you wanted a `TextBox` to be the same color as the list box, you'd write this: `<TextBox Background="{Binding ElementName=someListBox, Path=Background}" />`
`RelativeSource`	`RelativeSource` is used when you don't know the specific element you want to reference, but you know where that element is *relative* to where you are now—that is, relative to the element that you're currently binding. There are several different modes for `RelativeSource` that control its behavior.

Mode	Behavior
`FindAncestor`	In this case, the `RelativeSource` is the first ancestor element that meets a particular condition. You can specify the ancestor you want based on how many levels up it is. `{Binding RelativeSource={RelativeSource FindAncestor, AncestorLevel=2}}` This statement says to find the element two levels up from where you are (parent's parent). Or you can specify that you want the first element of a particular type. `{Binding RelativeSource={RelativeSource FindAncestor, AncestorType={x:Type GroupBox}}}` This says find the first parent element of type `GroupBox`. You can also combine `Level` and `Type`—you could bind to the third parent of type `GroupBox`, for example.

Table 11.2 Where the data comes from in a `Binding` *(continued)*

Property	Description	
`RelativeSource` *(continued)*	`Self`	This is used to bind to a property on the current element. For example, suppose that you want to set your border color to be the same as your text color, you'd do something like this: `<TextBox BorderBrush= {Binding RelativeSource= {RelativeSource Self}, Path=Foreground} />`

	`TemplatedParent`	This is a special reference used when you're defining `ControlTemplates` or `DataTemplates`.
		When you're writing a control template (for example), there are two different places where you might want to bind—to something in the control that's *using* the control template or from something in the control template itself.
		For example, you might have a control template that defines the look-and-feel of a button. The content of the template might well be driven off of the data associated with the button, but the control template can have several animations that need to depend on properties in the template. The notation for `TemplatedParent` is as follows:
		`{Binding RelativeSource= {RelativeSource TemplatedParent}, Path=somethingInTemplate}`
		We aren't showing a real-world example here because it would be meaningless without an entire template and an example, but we make use of this capability in the chapter on transition effects. To give you an idea of how well used this version of `RelativeSource` is, there's a custom notation for it.
		`{TemplateBinding somethingInTemplate}`
		This notation does almost exactly the same thing. (We've run into few situations where only one or the other works.)

	`PreviousData`	`PreviousData` is only used when you're binding to something like a `ListBox` that has a currently selected item and a previously selected item. As you can guess, `PreviousData` returns the *last* selected value before the current value. This might be used to display history or if you want to build a transition from the old value to the new value. `{Binding RelativeSource={Relative Source PreviousData},Path=Value}`

Table 11.2 Where the data comes from in a `Binding` (continued)

Property	Description
Nothing	No, there isn't a property called *nothing*. If you don't specify a `Source`, `RelativeSource`, or `ElementName`, their absence means something to the binding code—that the data will be determined based on the *data context* of the current item. We'll talk about data contexts in a lot more detail later, but they're explicitly or implicitly set locations to retrieve data. If the data context isn't set for a particular element, then that element determines it based on its parent.

Once you've figured out where you're getting your data, you can use the `Path` property to specify the path to the bit of data in that object. If you exclude `Path`, then you're binding to the entire object. (For example, if you want to bind a `ListBox` to a collection, you want the entire collection.) Otherwise, `Path` can point to a property or indicate the path to data in more complex ways. Here are some examples:

- `Path=SelectedItem`
- `Path=SelectedItem.Tag`
- `Path=SelectedItem.Tag[30]`
- `Path=SelectedItem.Tag[30].Name`
- `Path=SelectedItem.Tag[30].(Parent.Element).Name`

If you think that this is scary, you should try debugging some of the code we've written that uses stuff like this. The point that we want to make is that `Path` is *very* flexible and has a rich syntax. In practice, if you're doing things like some of the worst examples here, you might want to reconsider your design. (Often, you can create a simple intermediate object in code that will make most of this nastiness go away.)

Binding also has several other features. For example, we can specify a converter that can take the value returned by the binding and change it to be something else.

```
{Binding Path=ActualWidth,Converter={StaticResource AddPadding}}
```

The `AddPadding` resource points to an object that implements the `IValueConverter` interface—a simple interface with only the two methods `Convert` and `ConvertBack` (and no one ever bothers implementing the `ConvertBack` method). The `AddPadding` resource looks like this:

```
<Window.Resources>
  <local:AddPaddingValueConverter x:Key="AddPadding"/>
</Window.Resources>
```

Where `local` is the namespace for our local code. The `AddPaddingValueConverter` looks something like this:

```
public class AddPaddingValueConverter: IValueConverter
{
  public AddPaddingValueConverter () {}
```

```
    public object Convert(object value, Type targetType,
         object parameter, System.Globalization.CultureInfo culture)
    {
      double d = System.Convert.ToDouble(value);
      return d + 20;
    }

    public object ConvertBack(object value, Type targetType,
         object parameter, System.Globalization.CultureInfo culture)
    {
      double d = System.Convert.ToDouble(value);
      return d - 20;
    }
  }
```

See, nothing to it! But now, when the value is retrieved from the `ActualWidth` property, it's passed to the converter, and 20 is added to the value that's used. Even though we've shown all the different properties that you can set on a binding, we're only scratching the surface on binding notations and options. You'll be seeing many, many examples both throughout this chapter and throughout the book. For example, the next section talks about binding to XML.

11.3 Binding to XML

We're not sure. Our track record with technology is somewhat hit-and-miss, littered with Betamax tapes and Amiga computers, but we've had a look at this whole XML thing, and we think it has a chance of catching on. No promises, though.

Seriously, XML is everywhere now, and WPF supports binding directly to XML objects, as we'll demonstrate in this section. For this exercise, we wanted to push the binding system, so we found some nice, large XML examples.

MITRE is a federally funded research lab. One of the projects MITRE works on is called the Common Vunerabilities and Exposures (CVE) list. This list provides a single source to identify and describe vulnerabilities and exposures in computer systems, and it so happens that the list is published as an XML file. The latest version of the XML, as of this writing, weighed in at around 30MB. That sounds like a nice chunk of XML to give the binding engine to chew on. In effect, the XML is going to be our model.

But even for something like a web browser, an intermediate object model[2] is generally used to encapsulate behavior. For all but the simplest applications, using a *data format* as the abstraction for your model is almost certainly a lousy idea. If we were to write an application around CVEs, like a CVE editor for instance, we'd build business objects with interactive behavior, and the details of how we stored it would be invisible from the UI.

That all being said, sometimes a light wrapping over XML or SQL is all you need. Along those lines, we're going to create a little application to view the data in these XML files (figure 11.6).

---

2 If you were writing an XML editor, these would be ideal domain objects.

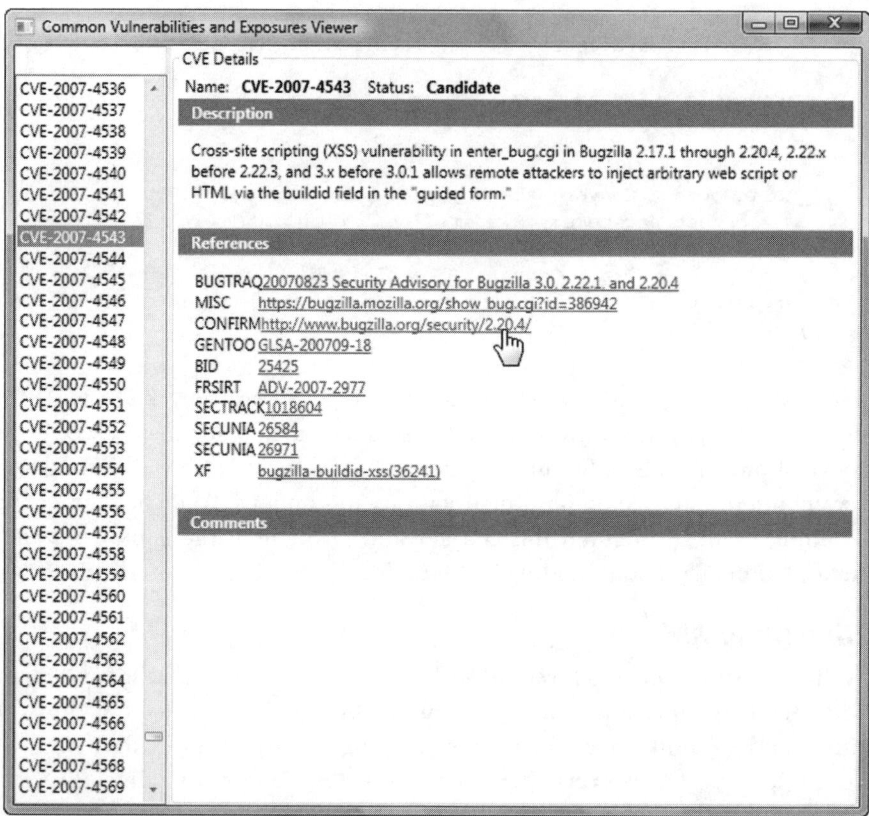

Figure 11.6 The finished CVE Viewer utility

The CVE XML also provides some nested data, which is something we're after for this example. Before we get too far, though, we need the XML data file—the CVE list from MITRE. The main site for CVE is located at

http://cve.mitre.org/

and the CVE list downloads are available at

http://cve.mitre.org/data/downloads/index.html

There are three files: *All*, *CANs*, and *Entries*. The Entries file is smaller (about 2MB), whereas the All and CANs files are closer to 30MB. For the purpose of this exercise, we want to see how the data binding holds up under some pressure, so we downloaded the All file (allitems.xml) for our experiment. Feel free to choose the smaller file if you desire. Here's a sample entry from the allitems.xml:

```
<cve>
  <item type="CVE" name="CVE-1999-0002" seq="1999-0002">
    <status>Entry</status>
    <desc>Buffer overflow in NFS mountd gives root access to remote
      attackers, mostly in Linux systems.</desc>
```

```
    <refs>
      <ref source="CERT">CA-98.12.mountd</ref>
      <ref source="BID" url="http://www.securityfocus.com/bid/121">121</ref>
      <ref source="XF">linux-mountd-bo</ref>
    </refs>
  </item>

  "A billion more items here"
</cve>
```

NOTE There's one problem with the way that the CVE files are set up. Inside the `<cve>` tag, there are references to various namespaces that cause .NET's XML parser to have problems. To simplify matters, the easiest thing to do is to remove the namespace references and reduce the main cve tag down to `<cve>`.

We'll be displaying the list of items in the lefthand column, and the details from the various tags on the right.

11.3.1 Creating the CVE Viewer application

Once we have the files, we create a new WPF Application project called *CVE Viewer*, delete Window1.xaml as usual, create a new window called CveViewer.xaml, and point the `StartupUri` to it. The layout here is going to be a bit more involved than the `ProcessMonitor`, so we need to do a bit more setup than we did before. The final layout appears in figure 11.7.

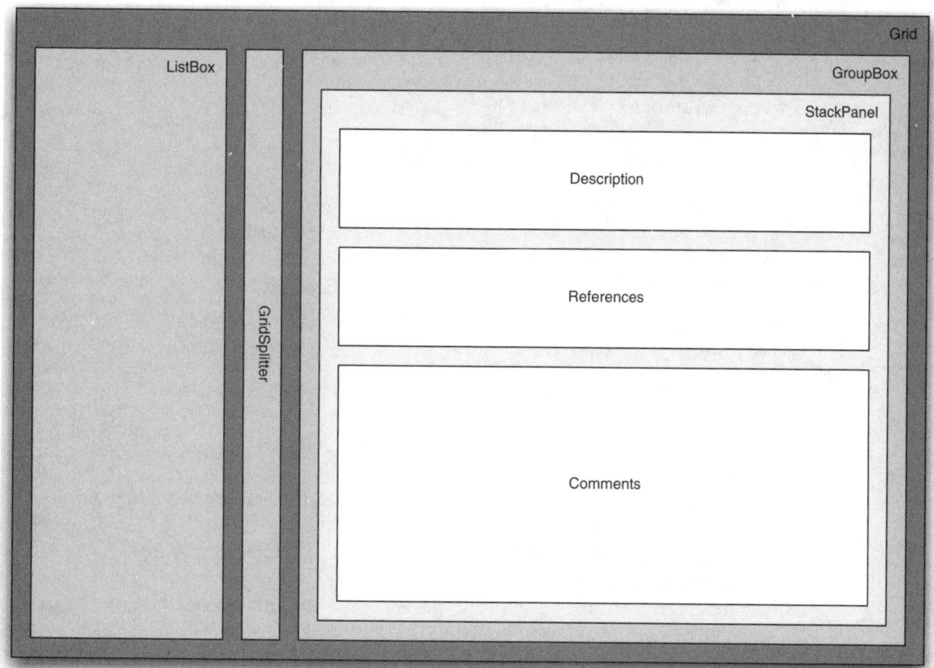

Figure 11.7 The basic layout of the CVE Viewer application

To set up this layout, we do the following:

1. We divide the grid into three columns with widths of 120, 5, and 1*.
2. In the first column, we create a `DockPanel`.
3. We add a `TextBox` followed by a `ListBox` in the `DockPanel`.
4. In the second column, we add a `GridSplitter`. Although the CVE names are currently a predictable width, we don't want the app to behave poorly if more verbose names are used.
5. In the third column, we add a `GroupBox`.
6. In the `GroupBox`, we want some areas for description, references, and comments. We add a `StackPanel`, and then add the controls shown in listing 11.4.

The `StackPanel` is going to give us the document effect for this part of the UI, and we'll style the `TextBlock` elements to look like headers. We also need a `TextBlock` element and some `ListBoxes` to display the nested lists of data for references and comments. Listing 11.4 shows the XAML for the layout, along with the controls we need.

Listing 11.4 XAML for CVE Viewer

```
<Window x:Class="CVE_Viewer.CveViewer"
    xmlns="http://schemas.microsoft.com/winfx/2006/xaml/presentation"
    xmlns:x="http://schemas.microsoft.com/winfx/2006/xaml"
    xmlns:debug="clr-namespace:System.Diagnostics;assembly=WindowsBase"
    Title="Common Vulnerabilities and Exposures Viewer"
    Width="600" Height="400">
 <Grid>
   <Grid.ColumnDefinitions>
     <ColumnDefinition Width="120" />
     <ColumnDefinition Width="3" />
     <ColumnDefinition Width="1*" />
   </Grid.ColumnDefinitions>

   <DockPanel>
     <TextBox Name="filter" DockPanel.Dock="Top" />
     <ListBox Name="listBox1" />
   </DockPanel>
                                              Controls on left
   <GridSplitter Grid.Column="1"
       VerticalAlignment="Stretch" HorizontalAlignment="Stretch" />   Splitter

   <GroupBox Grid.Column="2" Header="CVE Details">   Detail data
    <StackPanel>
     <WrapPanel>
       <Label Height="23">Name:</Label>
       <Label FontWeight="Bold" Height="23" MinWidth="100" />   (1)
       <Label Height="23">Status:</Label>
       <Label FontWeight="Bold" Height="23" MinWidth="80" />
     </WrapPanel>
     <TextBlock FontSize="12" FontWeight="Bold" Background="SteelBlue"
         Foreground="White" Padding="10,2,2,2">Description</TextBlock>   Banners are wide blue TextBlocks
     <TextBlock TextWrapping="Wrap" Margin="10,10,10,20" />
     <TextBlock FontSize="12" FontWeight="Bold" Background="SteelBlue"
         Foreground="White" Padding="10,2,2,2">References</TextBlock>
```

```
        <ListBox Margin="10,10,10,20" BorderThickness="0" />
        <TextBlock FontSize="12" FontWeight="Bold" Background="SteelBlue"
            Foreground="White" Padding="10,2,2,2">Comments</TextBlock>
        <ListView Margin="10,10,10,20" BorderThickness="0" />
      </StackPanel>
    </GroupBox>
  </Grid>
</Window>
```

You may notice that there are a number of controls that don't have any value ❶. That's because we're going to eventually bind their values to our source XML.

11.3.2 Binding controls to XML

For the next task, we're going to use the `XmlDataProvider`. Like the `ObjectDataProvider`, the `XmlDataProvider` allows simple XAML-based declaration of XML resources for use in a WPF application. In this case, we're going to declare it as a resource on the top-level `Window` element. Also, we need to bring in a namespace to enable the `PresentationTraceSources` attribute on the `Window` element itself.

```
xmlns:debug="clr-namespace:System.Diagnostics;assembly=WindowsBase"
```

Now, we'll add the `XmlDataProvider` to the `Window` element (listing 11.5).

Listing 11.5 Adding the `XmlDataProvider`

```
<Window.Resources>
   <XmlDataProvider x:Key="cve"
                    Source="X:\Path\to\allitems.xml"          ❶
                    XPath="/cve/item"                     ❷
                    IsAsynchronous="False"                    ❸
                    IsInitialLoadEnabled="True"                  ❹
                    debug:PresentationTraceSources.TraceLevel="High"
                    />
</Window.Resources>
```

If you're coding along, make sure that you specify the correct path to the XML file in the `Source` attribute ❶. There are a few interesting attributes on this `DataProvider`. `IsAsynchronous` enables asynchronous loading of the XML document ❸. We also tell the provider to automatically load the XML when the window is created using the `IsInitialLoadEnabled` attribute ❹. The last line enables debugging on the provider to make our lives easier later.

This is pretty much all we have to do to make the XML available to our application. We could've, just as easily, pointed the provider to a valid URI, or brought in an `XmlDocument` or `XmlReader`. One attribute we haven't mentioned, though, is the `XPath` attribute ❷.

`XPath` is a standard for defining selections within XML. The standard is maintained by the W3C and is one of the most common ways of selecting items from within an XML document. The particular expression here, `/cve/item`, says to select all the `item` elements underneath the root cve element. This is our initial data set.

11.3.3 XPath binding notation

In the previous section, we used `Path` to specify the specific property we wanted to bind to. With the `XmlDataProvider`, `Path` is still in play, but an additional property, called `XPath`, is going to be more interesting. The first binding we want is on the lefthand side `ListBox`. This will display all the CVEs in the XML data source:

```
<ListBox Name="listBox1"
  ItemsSource="{Binding Source=
    {StaticResource cve}}">
```

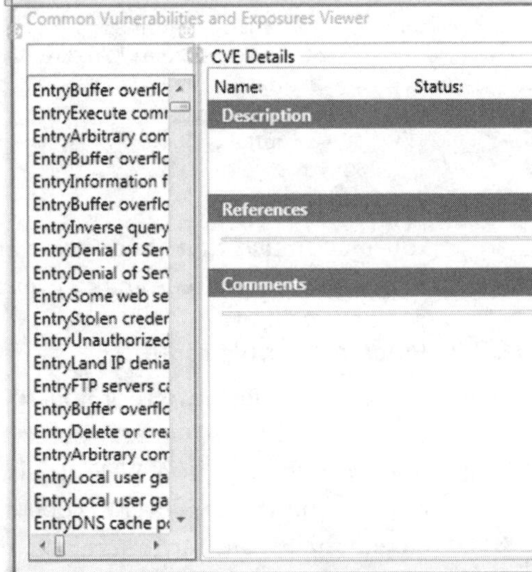

Figure 11.8 The binding is executed in real time against our data in the editor. It only looks like a bunch of errors because it's, well, a list of a bunch of errors.

So far, the only difference between the object binding and XML binding is the configuration of the data source. You may also notice in the designer that our `ListBox` now contains items from the live XML file. This can certainly be annoying at times, especially if the UI binds to a remote data source at design time. At the same time, it's rather convenient to see the effects of binding without having to run the program (figure 11.8).

NOTE If your list is empty, make sure you removed the namespaces from the `<cve>` tag.

Now we've got a rather ugly list because it's a list of the `InnerText` of the `XmlElements`. In the list on the left, we want the values from the name attributes of each item tag. As we did before, we need to set up a `DataTemplate`. We enter the following XAML within the `ListBox` tags:

```
<ListBox.ItemTemplate>
 <DataTemplate>
  <TextBlock Text="{Binding XPath=@name}" />
 </DataTemplate>
</ListBox.ItemTemplate>
```

`@name` is the `XPath` syntax to request an attribute called `name` from within the current element. Figure 11.9 shows the `ListBox` after the template has been defined.

Figure 11.9 Now that we have a `DataTemplate`, the `ListBox` data is much more readable.

Much better—now our list is a lot more sensible. This is a good time to take a closer look at what's happening between the source (the `XmlDataProvider`) and the target (the ListBox) in this example. XML is a particularly good medium for exploring the relationship between sources and targets.

With this setup, the XPath we specified in the XmlDataProvider is exposing the XML document as a collection of XmlElements—the XPath defines the set of item nodes under the root cve node. Our *source* is a collection of XmlElements of type item. Because ListBoxes can handle collections, all is well.

But, if we wanted to, we could change the source by removing the XPath expression. If you're following along, go ahead and remove the XPath="/cve/item" attribute from the XmlDataProvider. The list in the designer is now empty. The reason is that, without any XPath, the XmlDataProvider provides the root element (the cve element) of the document. The ListBox attempts to display a collection with one item in it, but because the cve element doesn't have a name attribute, it doesn't display anything at all.

To fix this, we can modify the ItemsSource attribute of the ListBox:

```
<ListBox Name="listBox1"
   ItemsSource="{Binding Source={StaticResource cve}, XPath=/cve/item}">
```

We've got elements again because we're now telling the ListBox to bind to the specified XPath *within* the data provided by the data source. This change gets us back to the same data we had before.

All we're demonstrating here is that, particularly with the power of XPath, there's no single, right way to accomplish any particular binding. It's the binding itself that understands both sides of the relationship and does the mapping, so you can convert the source into a list of XmlNodes and take them as the default binding, or have the target do the job by applying an XPath to something XPathable.

Now let's take a look at how you use Path versus XPath.

11.3.4 Path versus XPath

Both Path and XPath provide a way to reference the bit of data we want out of our current item, but they have somewhat different applications. For example, you can think of our ListBox as showing a list of XmlNodes. We use the XPath notation to select the name attribute from each of those nodes. But XmlNode is an object with properties. If we wanted to access the value of a property of the XmlNode *object* (ignoring the fact that it happens to hold XML), we could use the Path notation. For example, if we wanted to get the OuterXml (a property of XmlNode), we could do it by specifying the following:

```
<TextBlock Text="{Binding Path=OuterXml}" />
```

This is something that would be hard to do using XPath.

If you're coding along, you should have a list showing each ref XML item in the list. Among other things, this happens to be a convenient way to quickly visualize which XML elements are bound in a particular context and what's available on them. When we first set up the XML bindings, we bound to the OuterXml everywhere to watch as the context of the data changed. Before we head to the next section, the binding needs to be set back to using XPath.

```
<TextBlock Text="{Binding XPath=@name}" />
```

One thing that might not be entirely clear is how the binding knows what to execute the Path or the XPath *against.* The way this works is based on the current DataContext, which is what we'll cover next.

11.3.5 Understanding and using DataContexts

Whenever you specify a binding, you implicitly set up a data context. A data context is the data source at any given visual element, and it's used by every subsequent element up the tree until it changes. For example, the ListBox's data context is the collection of elements returned from the XmlDataProvider. Because the ListBox is designed to work with lists, it automatically doles out each element in the collection to each list item, so the data context for an individual item in the ListBox is the element from the collection.

We'll take this a little bit farther by hooking up some of the controls in the right-hand pane—the details from the currently selected item in the list box. UIElements all have a DataContext property that specifies where they'll go looking for data if no explicit source is specified as part of a Binding operation. We *could* set the DataContext on each of the controls that we want to bind; but, because the DataContext is inherited, if we set it on the GroupBox that holds all the controls, they'll automatically have the same context.

```
<GroupBox.DataContext>
  <Binding ElementName="listBox1" Path="SelectedItem" />
</GroupBox.DataContext>
```

This says that the DataContext for the GroupBox (and its children) is the SelectedItem property on the listBox1 ListBox control. Now, when we bind the individual elements, we only have to specify the binding *relative* to that data context. Figure 11.10 shows a visual representation of this. If we had an even deeper hierarchy, we could repeat this process ad nauseam.

We have four labels set up across a WrapPanel to show the name and status of each item as we click it. Without defining any sources on the Label controls themselves, we can specify Path or XPath bindings as if we specified the XML element. We add the following Content tags to the Labels:

```
<WrapPanel>
  <Label Height="23">Name:</Label>
  <Label FontWeight="Bold" Height="23" Content="{Binding XPath=@name}"
         MinWidth="100" />
  <Label Height="23">Status:</Label>
  <Label FontWeight="Bold" Height="23" Content="{Binding XPath=status}"
         MinWidth="80" />
</WrapPanel>
```

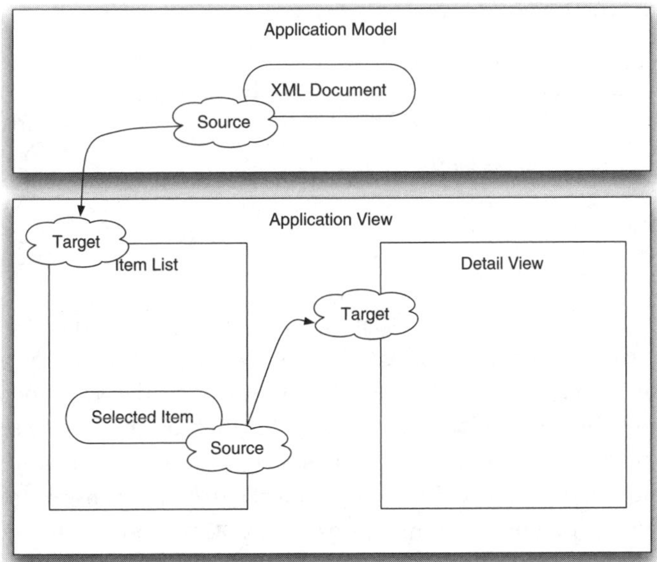

Figure 11.10 Because a binding target can be a source as well, the detail view can bind to the `SelectedItem` of the UI list, rather than working out how to track the active item in the XML source itself.

We bind the first label to the value from the `name` attribute and the second label to the value of the `status` element. (Because there's no @ sign in front of *status*, `XPath` interprets that to mean that we want the contents of a child element.) Directly after the `WrapPanel`, we can now bind our description as well.

```
<TextBlock Margin="10,10,10,20" TextWrapping="Wrap"
   Text="{Binding XPath=desc}" />
```

Because there's no selected item in the designer, the property will be null, and we won't see anything as we set all these up. But when you run the application, you should be able to click through the list and see the name, description, and status fields all populated. When the `SelectedItem` changes, the `Binding` we set on the `DataContext` property of the `GroupBox` catches the `PropertyChanged` event fired from the first `ListBox` and sets the `DataContext` accordingly. When the `DataContext` changes, the subsequent controls are then notified, and all the bindings we just defined are reevaluated and updated. Beautiful.

The next thing we want to do is to populate the `ListBox` that shows all the *refs* from the item xml. The *refs* are references to relevant data about the particular problem, and most of them include URLs to more detailed documentation. Listing 11.6 shows the XAML for binding the `ListBox` in the middle-right to the list of refs.

Listing 11.6 Binding to the list of refs

```
<ListBox ItemsSource="{Binding XPath=refs/ref}"                    <-- Binds to list of refs (1)
  "Margin="10,10,10,20" BorderThickness="0" BorderBrush="Transparent">
 <ListBox.ItemTemplate>
   <DataTemplate>
     <WrapPanel>
```

```
        <TextBlock MinWidth="50" Text="{Binding XPath=@source}" />    ❷ Source from under ref
        <TextBlock>
          <Hyperlink NavigateUri="{Binding XPath=@url}"    ❸
           RequestNavigate="Hyperlink_RequestNavigate">
           <TextBlock Text="{Binding Path=InnerText}" />
          </Hyperlink>
        </TextBlock>
      </WrapPanel>
    </DataTemplate>
  </ListBox.ItemTemplate>
</ListBox>
```

A fair amount is going on here, so we'll take it slow. First of all, we set the `ItemsSource` for the `ListBox` to use the `XPath` "refs/ref" ❶. Because we're inside the `DataContext` set on the `GroupBox`, this `XPath` is relative to that and so returns all the *ref* elements under the *refs* element under the current item (no, really). Further, because we're setting the `Source`, we're implicitly setting a new `DataContext` that applies to all the items in the `ListBox`. Any binding that we do within an item is relative to the current ref object.

The first control we put in our template is a `TextBlock` bound to the `source` attribute ❷. This is an attribute on ref elements. The next thing we want to do is create a hyperlink based on the data in the ref tag ❸. This is tricky because not everything inside a `Hyperlink` can be directly bound. Let's take the pieces one at a time.

```
NavigateUri="{Binding XPath=@url}"
```

This first piece is the easy one—we want the value from the `URL` attribute in the ref to be the location to which the hyperlink navigates us.

```
RequestNavigate="Hyperlink_RequestNavigate"
```

This is just an event handler. The `Hyperlink_RequestNavigate` method gets the `NavigateUri` from the passed `Hyperlink` and then does a `Process.Start()`. We haven't bothered showing the code, but it's in the online version.

```
<TextBlock Text="{Binding Path=InnerText}" />
```

Because we can't bind to the contents of a `Hyperlink` directly, we have to put something *inside* the `Hyperlink` to display the text we want to display. We're putting a `TextBlock` inside the `Hyperlink` (which is inside a `TextBlock`) so that we can bind the `TextBlock`'s `Text` property. Notice that we're using `Path` instead of `XPath` here because we want the `InnerText` of the `XmlElement`.

The binding for the comments `ListView` is pretty similar, albeit simpler (listing 11.7). We're using a `ListView` instead of a `ListBox` to demonstrate that there's no particular difference in the approach for binding to different list controls.

Listing 11.7 Binding the list of comments

```
<ListView ItemsSource="{Binding XPath=comments/comment}"    ❶ Collects all comments from item
  Margin="10,10,10,20" BorderThickness="0" >
  <ListView.ItemTemplate>
    <DataTemplate>
```

```
        <TextBlock Text="{Binding Path=InnerText}"/>
      </DataTemplate>
    </ListView.ItemTemplate>
  </ListView>
```

❷ Binds comment text—nothing fancy

At this point, we have a functional CVE viewer that binds XML remarkably fast. With the XML support in WPF, creating custom editors for XML is extremely easy and can be used to mitigate the pain of manually editing XML configuration files.

11.3.6 Master-Detail Binding

As you saw in figure 11.10, the list is driven from the data source, but the detail view is driven off of the list, rather than the data. From the user's perspective, this is irrelevant, but there are certainly situations where you want to make sure that what the user is viewing is tied to the data and not a selected control (for example, if there are multiple controls that can potentially control the current record). Also, from a purist's perspective, it's more correct to tie to data if possible (although not, perhaps, as simple).

The nice thing is that WPF data binding has automatic handling for master-detail binding. If you bind a list data source to a list control, as we've done in our previous example—tying the list of `Items` to the `ListBox`—then the list control shows a list of values. If you bind a *non-list* control to a list, like a `TextBox`, the binding mechanism automatically associates the binding with the *current* record in the list. Instead of doing this:

```
<GroupBox.DataContext>
  <Binding ElementName="listBox1" Path="SelectedItem" />
</GroupBox.DataContext>
```

We could do this:

```
<GroupBox.DataContext>
  <Binding Source="{StaticResource cve}"/>
</GroupBox.DataContext>
```

(provided we change the `XPath` tag in the `XmlDataProvider` back to `XPath="/cve/item"`).

Our individual controls are now bound to exactly the same thing as the list. If you run the application with this binding, you'll notice two things. First of all, the controls on the right of the application will all be populated even before you select a record in the list; second, changing the current selection in the list does *not* change what's displayed on the right.

So, the cool thing is that the binding code automatically knows what to do as far as figuring out how to hand the current record to all our controls on the right. The reason we have data automatically is that the binding automatically assumes that the first record is the selected record. The downside is that, because we're no longer binding to the selected item in the `ListBox`, we need to somehow let the binding know that the "current" record has changed when the value changes in the `ListBox`. We easily do this by setting a property on the `ListBox`.

```
<ListBox Name="listBox1"
         ItemsSource="{Binding Source={StaticResource cve}}"
         IsSynchronizedWithCurrentItem="True">
```

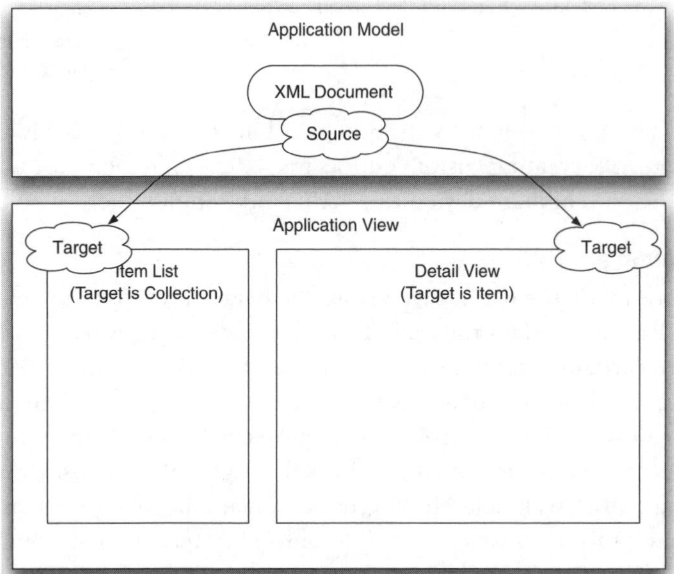

Figure 11.11 It's perfectly legal to bind controls that can only handle a single item to a multiple-item data source. The master-detail support in WPF Binding automatically associates those controls with the currently selected item.

`IsSynchronizedWithCurrentItem` tells the `ListBox` to update the binding source with the currently selected item—assuming that the binding source is one that can handle that (which is most). Now, if you run, everything will work as it did before, except that you'll be tied to the data source for the current item, rather than the `ListBox`. Figure 11.11 shows how this binding is working.

Both approaches (binding to the selected item in a list or relying on master-detail support to automatically bind to the data source) produce the same results. For simple UI, the first approach makes it easier to see what's going on, whereas the second approach is more "correct." For more complex situations, this correctness can often help make things work a little more cleanly.

We've covered a lot of ground so far—not only the theory behind binding, but also the specifics related to binding to static properties and to XML. We'll soon be returning to our Desktop Wiki application, but before we do, we have an example for binding to ADO.NET.

11.4 Binding to ADO.NET database objects

OK, so we need to talk.

WPF lets you bind data directly from a database to your UI. We're going to show you how to do that. We have to do this because a) there *are* situations in which this is an appropriate thing to do and b) it's a scenario you will see in many places. We really, really, *really*[3] would like to encourage you to think carefully before you do. Although

[3] Really, really, really…

we may sound (or be) OO bigots, we'd like to point out that many of the "magical" things that WPF does involve nothing more than applying good OO design.

Many applications today are written directly to a database. They have either no business objects or have things that *look* like business objects[4] but only ferry data blobs from the database to the UI and back again. Some of the signs that you aren't gaining the benefits of OO design are "business objects" that are nothing more than get/set methods for a set of properties, and a presentation layer with SQL strings, `SqlConnection`, and `SqlCommand` objects floating through it.

What is a business object?

Business objects are often misunderstood. For the sake of discussion, we need to clarify what we mean when we say *business object*. In the terms of C# programming, any instance of a class is an object. This definition is so broad as to have little meaning in practical use. In terms of OO *design*, an object encapsulates both the data and behavior of an entity that has meaning to your application. For example, imagine a business object that represents an employee. The employee has a first name, last name, and title.

One of the behaviors around the business object might be that the employee's title can't change without an associated `Approval` business object, which itself has a rule that it can only be created by an employee with a higher title. In this case, the `Title` property of the `Employee` class has code to ensure that only permitted title changes are made. Now imagine that the `Employee` class is only a set of simple getter and setter methods. This is called a *Data Transfer Object*, or DTO, and requires the presentation layer (or other code such as a web service layer) to check for the approval itself, comparing titles, and so on. This is an example of unencapsulated behavior, and the risk of another bit of code changing the object without following the rules, or following slightly different rules, is high.

By putting the rules with the data itself, it isn't possible to change the employee's title without the rules being enforced uniformly. Because database objects are essentially data transfer objects, using them makes it terribly easy to update the data without the safety and consistency of encapsulation.

That all being said, some simple applications do little more than present data from a database (or XML) and write it back; in these cases, binding UI directly to ADO.NET objects may be the best approach.[5] One example where this makes sense is if you need to show a list of available business objects—it may be inefficient to create a collection of instances of each business object, so you may populate a list of employees directly from a `DataTable`. To do anything with an employee, you'd create the business object

4 Martin Fowler calls this an Anemic Domain Model.

5 No, we don't really mean it.

as needed, by passing a DataRow from the list to a factory method on the business object. In fact, this is going to be our first example.

11.4.1 Creating a bookmark utility

To demonstrate binding to data, we want to show data that would make sense as something stored in a database. Our example will be a simple bookmark manager. Bookmarks could well be stored in a database—particularly if multiple users can store their own bookmarks and if the bookmarks need to be available to multiple machines. Because we aren't writing a book about database access, we're only going to create a mock database by creating some DataTables and DataSets programmatically. To emphasize proper separation of the data layer, this will all be done using a simple Data Access Layer (DAL). Even though we're pretending, our *binding* code will be identical to the binding code we would use if the DAL was really pulling the data from a database.

We'll get started by creating a new WPF application called Librarian.

11.4.2 Creating the simple DAL

There are some wonderful books on ADO.NET.[6] This isn't one of them. As such, we won't be going too much into the DAL code other than to explain how to hook it up to WPF. The DAL class creates a DataSet with two DataTables, and exposes the DataTable through a property—not unlike the sort you'd get back from an SQL database. If there's no existing XML file, the DAL populates a few sample bookmarks and saves the entire thing to an XML file, which is loaded on subsequent executions of the program. If you haven't downloaded the code, you'll have to create a new class called Library and enter the code from listing 11.8.

Listing 11.8 Library class that's a fake Data Access Layer

```
public class Library : INotifyPropertyChanged      ❶
{
  private DataSet library;
  private int bookmarkIdentity = 0;
  private string libraryFilename = "bookmarks.library";

  public Library()
  {
    CreateDataSource();

    if (!File.Exists(libraryFilename))
    {
      CreateDefaultBookmarks();
      Save();
    }
    else
    {
      Load();
```

[6] We might recommend *ADO.NET Programming* by Arlen Feldman, also from Manning.

```
  }
}
                                                 ❷ Datasource has
private void CreateDataSource()             <─┘    two DataTables
{
  library = new DataSet("Librarian");

  DataTable bookmarks = new DataTable("Bookmarks");
  bookmarks.Columns.Add("Id", typeof(Int32));
  bookmarks.Columns.Add("Title", typeof(string));
  bookmarks.Columns.Add("Uri", typeof(string));
  bookmarks.Columns.Add("Category", typeof(string));
  bookmarks.Columns.Add("LastMod", typeof(DateTime));

  DataTable identity = new DataTable("Ident");
  identity.Columns.Add("Name", typeof(string));
  identity.Columns.Add("Count", typeof(Int32));

  library.Tables.Add(bookmarks);
  library.Tables.Add(identity);
}                                             Access
                                              to data
public DataTable Bookmarks               <─┘
{
  get { return library.Tables["Bookmarks"]; }
}

public void AddBookmark(string name, string url, string category)
{
  Bookmarks.Rows.Add(new object[]
       { bookmarkIdentity++, name, url, category, DateTime.Now });
  library.AcceptChanges();
  NotifyPropertyChanged("Bookmarks");       ❸
}

#region DataStore operations      ❹

private void CreateDefaultBookmarks()
{
  library.Tables["Ident"].Rows.Add(new object[]
       { "bookmarks", bookmarkIdentity });

  AddBookmark("Manning", "http://www.manning.com/", "Books");
  AddBookmark("Cherwell", "http://www.cherwellsoftware.com/", "Sites");
  AddBookmark("Exotribe", "http://www.exotribe.com/", "Sites");

  library.AcceptChanges();
}

public void Load()
{
  library.ReadXml(libraryFilename, XmlReadMode.ReadSchema);
}

public void Save()
{
  library.AcceptChanges();
  library.WriteXml(libraryFilename, XmlWriteMode.WriteSchema);
}

#endregion
```

```
    #region INotifyPropertyChanged Members    ❺

    public event PropertyChangedEventHandler PropertyChanged;

    private void NotifyPropertyChanged(String propertyName)
    {
      if (PropertyChanged != null)
        PropertyChanged(this, new PropertyChangedEventArgs(propertyName));
    }

    #endregion
  }
```

Note that rather than using the `ObjectDataProvider`, we implement the `INotifyPropertyChanged` ❶ interface on our DAL. The `INotifyPropertyChanged` interface exposes a single event that WPF subscribes to in order to know when to update data bound values ❺. All we have to do is fire this event (`PropertyChanged`) to tell subscribers what has changed, as we do in the `AddBookmark` method ❸. This is the same interface used by `ObjectDataProvider` and `ObservableCollection`—see, no magic—the data source just pops up its hand to say when its data has changed.

Beyond this, the code is pretty straightforward. We have code to create the `DataTables` ❷ and set up some default values ❹, as well as to load and save the `DataSet` to disk.

To make our DAL available to the entire application, we open App.xaml and add the local namespace.

```
xmlns:local="clr-namespace:Librarian"
```

And under the `Application.Resources` tag, we add:

```
<Application.Resources>
  <local:Library x:Key="library" />
</Application.Resources>
```

Now that we have a DAL, we can lay out our UI and bind it. Because we've covered many of the fundamentals, we're going to focus on specifics around database bindings. Because we're using a DAL component, we'll use the `ObjectDataProvider` to create our DAL as we did with the CLR binding examples.

11.4.3 Laying out the UI and creating data bindings

We're going to do a simple UI for this piece, with a master-detail form. We create a brand-new WPF application called BookmarkLibrary, blow away `window1`, and create a new `Window` called BookmarkLibrary.xaml (and update the `StartupUri`). Next, we delete the `Grid` element and create a `DockPanel`, with `LastChildFill` set to `True`.

```
<DockPanel LastChildFill="True">
</DockPanel>
```

We're going to use a number of `DockPanels` to design our detail view. This will ensure proper scaling to high DPI monitors and maximize usable text input areas given any window size. Figure 11.12 shows the layout we're shooting for.

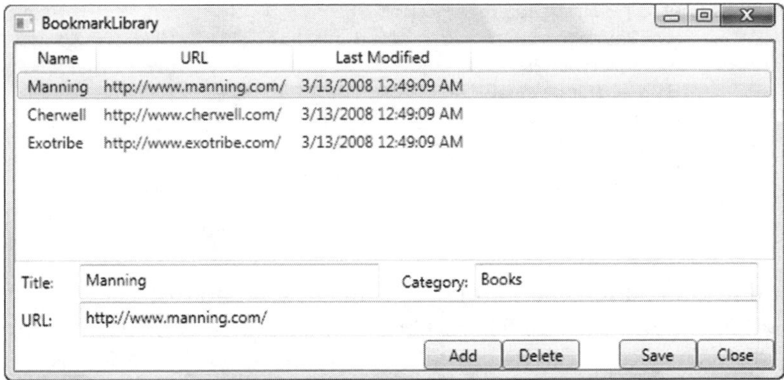

Figure 11.12 Layout of the bookmark application. The list at the top shows all of the bookmarks, and the pane at the bottom shows the details of the current row.

Unfortunately, most of this will require XAML surgery. We could drag these controls all in using the designer, but achieving the result would take a lot of trips to the property editor. Listing 11.9 shows the XAML for the `BookmarkLibrary` class.

Listing 11.9 XAML for `BookmarkLibrary` class

```
<DockPanel LastChildFill="True">
  <Grid DockPanel.Dock="Bottom"
     DataContext="{Binding ElementName=bookmarks, Path=SelectedItem}">   ❶
    <Grid.ColumnDefinitions>
      <ColumnDefinition Width="1*" />
      <ColumnDefinition Width="1*" />
    </Grid.ColumnDefinitions>
    <Grid.RowDefinitions>
      <RowDefinition Height="1*" />
      <RowDefinition Height="1*" />
    </Grid.RowDefinitions>
    <DockPanel Grid.Column="0" Grid.Row="0">
      <Label MinWidth="50" DockPanel.Dock="Left" Content="Title:" />
      <TextBox Text="{Binding Path=Title}" />     ❷
    </DockPanel>
    <DockPanel Grid.Column="1" Grid.Row="0">
      <Label MinWidth="50" DockPanel.Dock="Left" Content="Category:" />
      <TextBox  Margin="0,0,10,0" Text="{Binding Path=Category}" />
    </DockPanel>
    <DockPanel Grid.Column="0" Grid.Row="1" Grid.ColumnSpan="2">
      <Label MinWidth="50" Content="URL:"/>
      <TextBox Margin="0,0,10,0" Text="{Binding Path=Uri}"/>
    </DockPanel>
  </Grid>

  <ListView Name="bookmarks"
     ItemsSource=
        "{Binding Source={StaticResource library}, Path=Bookmarks}">    ❸
    <ListView.View>
      <GridView>
```

```
        <GridViewColumn Header="Name"
            DisplayMemberBinding="{Binding Path=Title}"/>      ❹
        <GridViewColumn Header="URL"
            DisplayMemberBinding="{Binding Path=Uri}"/>
        <GridViewColumn Header="Last Modified"
            DisplayMemberBinding="{Binding Path=LastMod}"/>
      </GridView>
    </ListView.View>
  </ListView>
</DockPanel>
```

The first thing to realize about this listing is that it's backwards! The first control, the `ListView` ❸, is listed second. That's because we want it to take up the remaining space in the `DockPanel`. Note that order of elements in WPF often matters; be careful when you're using Z-Order controls in the designer because Z-Order and functionality are *both* controlled by element ordering—we think this is quite a serious issue because it mixes two sometimes opposing purposes.

Let's talk about the second thing first—the `ListView` ❸ lets us present a list of data with some number of columns. It's amazingly easy to bind to the `DataTable`. The `Source` is our `library` object that we add to the `Application` object. By referencing it there, an instance is automatically created. The `Path` points to the `Bookmarks` object exposed on the `Library` class instance, which returns our Bookmarks `DataTable`.

The `ListView` has a `GridView` that defines its columns, and we have columns for the Name, URL, and the Last Modified Date/Time. As you can see, each `GridViewColumn` definition has a property called `DisplayMemberBinding` ❹. We're setting the `Path` to the name of the column in the `DataTable` we want to reference. Because we aren't specifying a `Source`, the source is automatically the current row in the `Grid`, and the `DataTable` is capable of taking the name and returning the right bit of data. Simple.

Binding to the controls at the bottom (but listed first in the XAML) is also fairly straightforward. The `Grid` control we put together to hold the controls ❶ has its `DataContext` set, which provides the `DataContext` to all its children. It points to the `ListView` (bookmarks) because we want to tie it to the list's `SelectedItem`, which is set as the path.

The individual `TextBoxes` are bound to elements by specifying the column name again ❷. The default binding is two-way, so editing the text in the `TextBoxes` automatically updates the `DataTable` and, therefore, the `Grid`.

If you're coding along and want to add support for the various buttons at the bottom of the control, you can add the following XAML for them at the top of the `DockPanel`, before the `Grid` with the `DockPanels`:

```
<StackPanel Orientation="Horizontal" DockPanel.Dock="Bottom"
                                          FlowDirection="RightToLeft">
  <Button MinWidth="60" Content="Close" Click="Close_Click" />
  <Button MinWidth="60" Content="Save" Click="Save_Click" />
  <Button MinWidth="60" Content="Delete" Margin="30,0,0,0"
                                       Click="Delete_Click" />
  <Button MinWidth="60" Content="Add" Click="Add_Click" />
</StackPanel>
```

Most of the XAML is for spacing, and so on. Notice that there are handlers for the `Click` event on each button.[7] Listing 11.10 shows the event handlers from the BookmarkLibrary.xaml.cs file.

Listing 11.10 Handlers for button click events

```
private void Close_Click(object sender, RoutedEventArgs e)
{
  Close();    <— Closes the app
}

private void Save_Click(object sender, RoutedEventArgs e)
{
  Library library = (Library)FindResource("library");
  library.Save();    <— ❶
}

private void Delete_Click(object sender, RoutedEventArgs e)
{
  DataRowView row = (DataRowView)bookmarks.SelectedItem;    ❷
  row.Delete();
}

private void Add_Click(object sender, RoutedEventArgs e)
{
  Library library = (Library)FindResource("library");
 library.AddBookmark("New Bookmark", "url", "");    ❸
}
```

Clicking Save calls the `Save()` method on the `Library` class ❶. The `library` instance was defined in XAML, but we can call it from code with no problem by calling `FindResource`. The `Delete` method ❷ gets the currently selected row and calls its `Delete()` method, which marks the row as deleted. Even though we don't explicitly create a `DataView`, the binding operation does it for us. The `DataView` implements the `PropertyChanged` event.

The `Add` button handler calls the `AddBookmark` method on the `library` object ❸, which adds a new row with some placeholder data to the `DataTable` and fires the `PropertyChanged` event. This is how the `Grid` knows to update itself.

Because we have two-way binding throughout, we don't have to do anything special other than save the XML out at the end. All our updates to the detail view are automatically done to the `DataRows` themselves (or sometimes through the `DataView`, which is directly tied to the `DataTable`). It's so easy that you can see how easy it is to fall into the trap of the missing business logic layer. Because WPF has such rich data binding capabilities with objects, there's little reason not to use business objects, and we'll look into that next.

---

7 We should really be using commands, but this takes up less space in the book!

11.5 Binding to business objects

If you've made it this far, give yourself a pat on the back because we're almost to the end. WPF support for binding to business objects is terrific and the right choice for our Wiki application. Go ahead and reload the Wiki application from chapters 9 and 10. Much like the previous example, we're going to create our own model to get access to the data; but, rather than exposing a data layer directly to the UI, we're going to expose a business object layer. First, we'll need some business objects.

11.5.1 Creating a WikiPage business object

Our first business object will be a `WikiPage`. A `WikiPage` will have a name and a `FlowDocument` associated with it. Because the `FlowDocument` isn't directly serializable, we have to use the `XamlReader` and `XamlWriter` classes to support serialization (listing 11.11).

Listing 11.11 `WikiPage` business object

```
[Serializable]
public class WikiPage
{
  public WikiPage()
  {
    Document = new FlowDocument();
  }

  public WikiPage(string name)
  {
    Name = name;
    Document = new FlowDocument();
  }

  private string pageName;
  public string Name
  {
    get { return pageName; }
    set { pageName = value; }
  }

  private FlowDocument document;
  internal FlowDocument Document        ❶
  {
    get { return document; }
    set { document = value; }
  }

  public string XamlDocument        ❷
  {
    get { return XamlWriter.Save(Document); }
    set
    {
       using (MemoryStream stream =
                new MemoryStream(Encoding.UTF8.GetBytes(value)))
       {
         Document = (FlowDocument)XamlReader.Load(stream);
```

```
            }
        }
    }
}
```

Other than the serialization section, this looks like a fairly standard Data Transfer Object (DTO). Don't worry—we'll be adding business logic to it a little later. Normally, we'd probably implement custom serialization to handle the document data; but, in this case, we're taking advantage of the fact that the XML serializer serializes public properties. By making our `FlowDocument` an internal property ❶, the XML serializer bypasses it. (We could use the Binary serializer to serialize even private fields, but we wouldn't have a human readable data file, which we want to be able to see the effects of the `XamlWriter`.)

The `XamlDocument` property ❷ *is* public and so is serialized. Notice that it's of type string, and we have some code to convert the document back and forth to a string. This version exists to make it easy to save the data, whereas the `FlowDocument Document` property is what we use for binding.

This is good enough for now; it stores our wiki pages and gives us a place to put our wiki page data. Now we need a model façade[8] to expose to the presentation layer. The heart of that façade will be an `ObservableCollection`.

11.5.2 ObservableCollection

Our wiki has a concept of directories—we want to provide categories for our various wiki pages such as home, work, school, and so on. We will use an `ObservableCollection` to hold our `WikiPage` objects. An `ObservableCollection` is a generic collection that implements the `INotifyCollectionChanged` and `INotifyPropertyChanged` interfaces. An `ObservableCollection` is handy for binding because the collection fires events when it's modified. Rather than deriving from `ObservableCollection`, we'll compose it into our next custom business object, `PageDirectory` (listing 11.12).

Listing 11.12 `PageDirectory` business object

```
[Serializable]
public class PageDirectory
{
  public PageDirectory() { }
  public PageDirectory(string name)
  {
    Name = name;
    pages = new ObservableCollection<WikiPage>();    <-- Creates WikiPage collection
  }

  private string collectionName;
  public string Name
  {
    get { return collectionName; }
```

[8] The façade pattern presents a single unified interface that represents an entire subsystem.

```
    set { collectionName = value; }
  }

  private ObservableCollection<WikiPage> pages;
  public ObservableCollection<WikiPage> Pages          <-- Exposes WikiPage collection
  {
    get { return pages; }
    set { pages = value; }
  }
}
```

At the moment, the PageDirectory is pretty simple—it only has a name and the collection of WikiPages. We expose the WikiPage collection in order to be able to bind to it. We have limited control over what's added and when, but we could rectify that by using a more involved collection, or by subscribing to the events on the collection and preventing unwanted operations (such as adding a page with the same name as an existing page).

11.5.3 Create a model façade

Now that we have our business objects, we need a model façade. The façade is a single point of entry for the presentation layer to deal with our business layer, and can be created easily as a resource in the XAML. This is like our Library class from before, but will use ObservableCollections of business objects rather than ADO.NET objects. As with the Library class, we will need to implement our own INotifyPropertyChanged interface, although the ObservableCollections we will be hosting implement the interface themselves, so we don't need to do anything special with them (listing 11.13).

Listing 11.13 The Wiki façade

```
[Serializable]
public class Wiki : INotifyPropertyChanged
{
  private string wikiDataFile = "wikiPages.xml";

  public Wiki()
  {
    if (!File.Exists(wikiDataFile))          <-- 1 Creates default file on first run
    {
      CreateDefaultDirectory();
      Save();
    }
    else
    {
      Load();          <-- 2 Or loads existing file
    }
  }

  private void CreateDefaultDirectory()
  {
    wikiDirectories = new ObservableCollection<PageDirectory>();
    wikiDirectories.Add(new PageDirectory("Home"));
  }
```

```
private ObservableCollection<PageDirectory> wikiDirectories;
public ObservableCollection<PageDirectory> Directories        <-- 3 Collection of directories
{
  get { return wikiDirectories; }
}

private PageDirectory currentDirectory;
public PageDirectory CurrentDirectory        <-- 4 Currently selected directory
{
  get { return currentDirectory; }
  set
  {
    currentDirectory = value;
    NotifyPropertyChanged("CurrentDirectory");
  }
}

public void AddPage()        <-- 5 Adds new page to directory
{
  CurrentDirectory.Pages.Add(new WikiPage("New Page"));
}

public void AddDirectory()        <-- 6 Adds new directory
{
  PageDirectory newDirectory = new
         PageDirectory(Guid.NewGuid().ToString());
  Directories.Add(newDirectory);
  CurrentDirectory = newDirectory;
}

public void Load()        <-- 7 Loads from XML file
{
  XmlSerializer serializer = new
         XmlSerializer(typeof(ObservableCollection<PageDirectory>));
  using (FileStream stream = new FileStream(wikiDataFile, FileMode.Open))
  {
   if (stream.CanRead)
   {
    wikiDirectories =
     (ObservableCollection<PageDirectory>)serializer.Deserialize(stream);
    NotifyPropertyChanged("Directories");
   }
  }
}

public void Save()        <-- 8 Saves to XML file
{
  XmlSerializer serializer =
         new XmlSerializer(typeof(ObservableCollection<PageDirectory>));
  using (FileStream stream = new FileStream(wikiDataFile,
                                            FileMode.Create))
  {
    serializer.Serialize(stream, wikiDirectories);
  }
}

public event PropertyChangedEventHandler PropertyChanged;        <-- 9 Property Change event
```

```
    private void NotifyPropertyChanged(String propertyName)
    {
      if (PropertyChanged != null)
        PropertyChanged(this, new PropertyChangedEventArgs(propertyName));
    }
  }
```

The `Wiki` object represents the core of our application. When first instantiated, it either creates a default, empty `Wiki` ❶ or loads existing data ❷. It contains a collection of `PageDirectory` objects ❸ where each directory contains some number of `WikiPages`. It also keeps track of the currently selected directory ❹.

For functionality, the `Wiki` object allows a new page to be added to the current directory ❺ or an entirely new directory to be created ❻. Because we're exposing default collections, the caller of the code could violate our business rules, and that's something that we would address in a more fleshed-out example.

The `Wiki` object also can read ❼ and write ❽ itself out to an XML file. This might be a reasonable representation for a single-user application, or it might need to pass a representation of itself to a DAL for storage in a database. Again, in a more fleshed-out example, the `Wiki` object wouldn't know about how it was stored—it would pass a representation to the code that does.

We also implement the `INotifyPropertyChanged` interface and expose the `PropertyChanged` event ❾ to let subscribers know when something has changed.

We're on the home stretch now. All we need to do is tie our business objects to the UI.

11.5.4 Wiring business objects to presentation objects

As we did with the Library, we need to make our Wiki business layer available to the presentation. Figure 11.13 shows what's bound to whom.

Before we can bind to the business objects, we need to create an instance. We'll do this via XAML. In App.xaml, we add the local namespace (as with previous examples) and the following resource:

```
<Application.Resources>
  <local:Wiki x:Key="wiki" />
</Application.Resources>
```

This causes a new instance of the `Wiki` business object to be instantiated at application scope. We can locate it in the code via the key *wiki* and store a local reference. The first thing we need to bind is the list of directories on the left side of the browser (listing 11.14). Because we did everything through the designer in chapter 9, we never really looked at the XAML. The `ListBox` we're referencing here is the *All Labels* `ListBox` that we added under the second `Expander`.

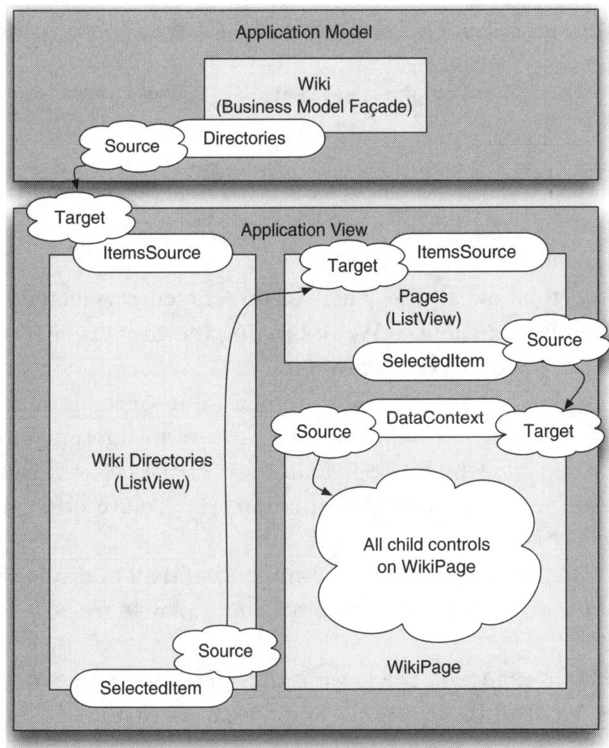

Figure 11.13 The various bindings used within the Wiki application. This is much like the CVE bindings, but taken down another level. Also note that `DataContext` is defined as *both* a source and target of data binding.

Listing 11.14 Binding the list of directories

```
<ListBox Name="WikiDirectories" BorderThickness="0"
   ItemsSource=
   "{Binding Source={StaticResource wiki}, Path=Directories}">    ❶
  <ListBox.ItemTemplate>
    <DataTemplate>
      <TextBlock Text="{Binding Path=Name}" />    ❷
    </DataTemplate>
  </ListBox.ItemTemplate>
</ListBox>
```

We're binding the entire list to the `Directories` property of the `Wiki` object instance ❶. We also create a `DataTemplate` for the `ListBox` so that we can bind each entry in the list to the `Name` property of the directory ❷.

Next, the list of pages in the directory needs to be bound. Before we can do that, we need a control to hold the list. Just drag a `ListView` into the upper-right cell of the `Grid` and make it take up all of the available space (by deleting the margin tag). Then, we add the XAML shown in listing 11.15.

Listing 11.15 Binding the list of pages

```
<ListView Name="pageList" ItemsSource=
    "{Binding ElementName=WikiDirectories, Path=SelectedItem.Pages}">    ❶
  <ListView.ItemTemplate>
    <DataTemplate>
      <TextBlock Text="{Binding Path=Name}" />    ❷
    </DataTemplate>
  </ListView.ItemTemplate>
</ListView>
```

The ListView is supposed to show all the pages in the currently selected directory from the WikiDirectories list on the left. We're binding the ListView to the WikiDirectories' SelectedItem property ❶. Because the WikiDirectories list is a list of PageDirectory objects, that's what SelectedItem returns. But we're binding to a list, and PageDirectory itself isn't a list but *contains* one. We have to reference the Pages collection of the PageDirectory, which is our collection of WikiPages. Notice how nicely the binding notation lets us handle this situation. (There are other situations where it isn't so friendly.)

And we're again using a DataTemplate to determine what data to display from the WikiPage. For the moment, we're only going to bind the display to the Name property of the WikiPage ❷.

Earlier we just had a RichTextBox in the lower-right cell of the Grid. Now, we want to add a few more things. We'll add a DockPanel and a TextBox to hold the title of our page. We'll insert the XAML around the original RichTextBox; but, if you want to, you can do this with the editor. Listing 11.16 shows the XAML for our changes *and* the binding to set the text in the TextBox to show the title of the currently selected page. We'll worry about the RichTextBox later.

Listing 11.16 Binding the WikiPage properties

```
<DockPanel LastChildFill="True">
  <DockPanel.DataContext>
    <Binding ElementName="pageList" Path="SelectedItem" />    ❶ Sets data context
  </DockPanel.DataContext>
  <TextBox DockPanel.Dock="Top" Name="wikiTitle"
    HorizontalAlignment="Stretch" Text="{Binding Path=Name}" />    ❷ Binds name
  <RichTextBox Name="activePage"
     DataContextChanged="activePage_DataContextChanged">    ❸
  </RichTextBox>
</DockPanel>
```

Much of this code is what you'd expect. We're setting the DataContext on the DockPanel to the SelectedItem on the pageList ❶. When the currently selected page changes, all the items in the DockPanel are updated. For example, we're binding the page's title TextBox control to the Name property of the WikiPage ❷. For the RichTextBox we use for editing, we have to do something different ❸.

The problem is that the Document property on RichTextBox isn't a bindable property. This is *probably* because it has to do a lot of conversion back and forth between the RichTextBox's internal representation and the FlowDocument representation. But this puts us into a bind.[9] Not to worry, though—all dependency objects have an event called DataContextChanged, which is fired whenever the value in the data context is, well, changed. We can catch that event and write a bit of code to set and retrieve the document (listing 11.17).

Listing 11.17 DataContextChanged event handler

```
private void activePage_DataContextChanged(object sender,
                                   DependencyPropertyChangedEventArgs e)
{
  RichTextBox wikiEditor = sender as RichTextBox;

  WikiPage page = e.NewValue as WikiPage;          <-- ❶ NewValue is new DataContext
  if (page != null)
  {
    wikiEditor.Document = page.Document;     ❷
  }
}
```

The DependencyPropertyChangedEventArgs that are passed to the event handler tell us what the old DataContext was and what the new Context now is ❶. Because we have a list of WikiPages, we know that the context will be a WikiPage. All the code has to do is set the current document in the RichTextBox ❷.

Now, you might be wondering why we don't have to retrieve the value from the RichTextBox first and put it into the old WikiPage. The reason is that the RichTextBox is just holding a reference to that document—the same reference held by the old WikiPage—so it's automatically up-to-date. Now you might further be wondering, if that's the case, why Microsoft didn't make the Document a dependency property. We wonder that too.

Figure 11.14 shows the Wiki application in action.

Although not a perfect example, the Wiki application demonstrates how you can have a real business-object model, and then leverage the binding capabilities of WPF to do much of the heavy lifting for you. The nice thing is that you could change the look-and-feel of the application entirely with relative ease and, so long as you've designed your business objects well, your application will still enforce all its rules.

All the binding sources that we've discussed so far are data sources that could have existing before .NET 3.x. There is an additional way that you might get data that *is* new.

[9] Did you catch that? We're clever.

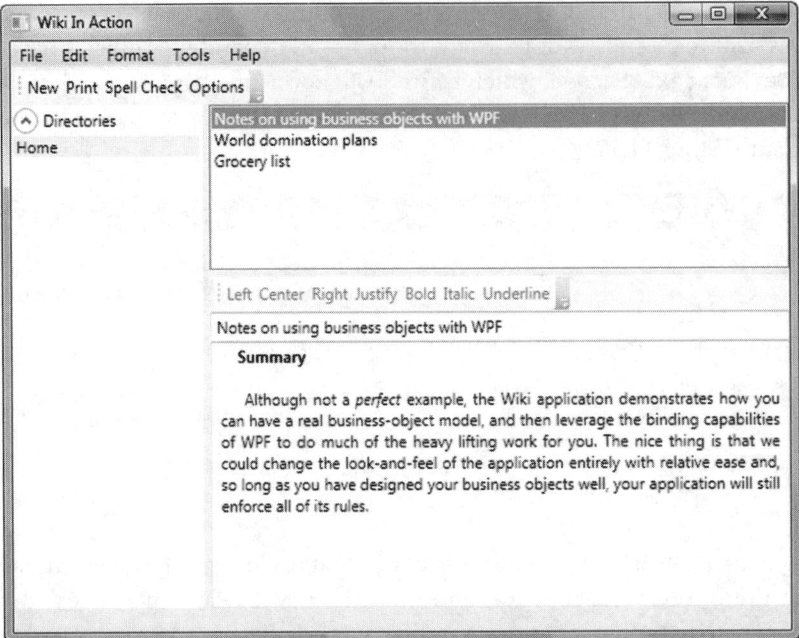

Figure 11.14 The Wiki application. Binding is being used to tie most of the elements together.

11.6 Binding to LINQ data

One of the new features of .NET 3.x is LINQ, which stands for **L**anguage **IN**tegrated **Q**uery, and adds querying capabilities directly to .NET. For instance, if we have a collection of values, such as

```
string[] zoo = { "Elephant", "Ant", "Duck", "Aardvark", "Donkey",
                                        "Anteater", "Antelope", "Newt"};
```

we can now write a query right in C# to, say, return all the animals whose name starts with the letter A and put the items into alphabetic order.

```
var results = from a in zoo
              where a[0] == 'A'
              orderby a
              select a;
```

There are also special providers that are part of LINQ, the two most important being LINQ to SQL, or DLINQ—which allows querying against SQL databases—and LINQ to XML, or XLINQ—which allows queries against XML data. LINQ is a move toward adding functional programming constructs into .NET. But both functional programming and LINQ in general are well beyond the scope of this book.

We do want to mention that you can bind to LINQ data (and by extension SQL or XML data) from WPF fairly easily because LINQ is built around the `IEnumerable<type>`

interface. Binding to LINQ data is as simple as binding to any other collection. For example, suppose we have an object called `AnimalView` that has a property called `JustTheAs` that returns the results of our previous query.

```
class AnimalView
{
  string[] zoo = { "Elephant", "Ant", "Duck", "Aardvark", "Donkey",
                                              "Anteater", "Antelope", "Newt"};

  public IEnumerable<string> JustTheAs
  {
    get
    {
      return from a in zoo
                       where a[0] == 'A'
                       orderby a
                       select a;
    }
  }
}
```

We could then bind a `ListBox` to the results from that collection pretty easily. We'd create a static instance of our object as a resource.

```
<local:AnimalView x:Key="zoo"/>
```

And then we bind as normal.

```
<ListBox Name="listBox1"
   ItemsSource="{Binding Source={StaticResource zoo},Path=JustTheAs}" />
```

WPF neither knows nor cares that the data came from LINQ. It just happily displays the data from the collection (figure 11.15).

Aardvark
Ant
Anteater
Antelope

Figure 11.15 The data from binding to a LINQ result. WPF is unaware that the data came from LINQ—it's just another collection.

If we were using LINQ to SQL, the collection would probably be of useful entities (customers, for example), and we could use binding and data templates to pull whatever data we liked. If we were using LINQ to XML, we would get back `XElement` objects and could work with them via an `XmlDataProvider`. (The `XmlDataProvider` understands `XElements` as well as `XmlElements`.)

There *is* one downside to binding to results that come back from LINQ. You generally get back an `IEnumerable` collection, which does *not* implement the `INotifyCollectionChanged` interface. If items are added or removed from results (or, more likely, from the underlying data store that the query was run against), the binding won't know about it and so won't be updated. This is a pretty serious limitation. The most common workaround is to create a wrapper object that implements the interface itself and watches the data source to check for changes, but this is kind of a pain.

There are also several people/groups who are working on a more LINQ*ish* solution. One good example is by an Australian developer, Paul Stovell. He's working on something called *SyncLINQ* that, by adding an additional term to a LINQ query, makes the result support synchronization. He has also added the ability to do asynchronous queries and several other cool things. We definitely recommend checking this out.

Obviously, this isn't meant to be a detailed exploration of LINQ, but before we moved on, we wanted to at least make sure you were aware that a) you can bind to LINQ results and b) it's no more complicated than binding to anything else.

11.7 Summary

Binding is a big topic because it's completely pervasive in WPF—it's used for tying data to UI, for tying elements of the UI to each other, and even for animation. The idea at Microsoft is to go beyond thinking of binding as a service that you occasionally use, and get to the point where binding is the core glue of your applications.

In many ways, the WPF binding system makes this possible—it's incredibly robust, flexible and *fast*, and has built-in support for binding to databases, XML, collections, or any object you want to expose to it. Also, once you get comfortable with the notation, you'll discover that a single line of XAML can replace a ton of regular code and, similarly, make your UI data-sensitive and responsive in ways that wouldn't have been practical in most applications.

All this power has a downside as well. When you start doing more complex bindings, it can be hard to debug when things don't work, even with the trace mechanism in place. Also, it's so easy to bind directly to data that you may find yourself building applications where your business logic seeps (or floods) into the UI. Fortunately, it's pretty easy to handle both these situations—and in the same way. Don't be afraid to build some helper, business logic, or façade objects. These can expose the objects to bind in ways that are much simpler to access, and can provide the appropriate locations to put your business logic.

We're not done with data binding yet. In the next chapter, we're going to explore some more advanced binding scenarios. We're also going to show how we can make data drive the look-and-feel of an application via the use of data templates.

12 Advanced data templates and binding

This chapter covers:

- Data templates
- `StringFormat`
- Sorting and filtering data
- Validating data
- Model-View-ViewModel
- Hierarchical, multiple, and priority binding
- Making your computer sound like Tinky Winky

The idea of data binding has been around in one form or another for a long time. Arguably, the WPF model is better in many respects, but something that *really* makes WPF binding shine (sometimes literally) is the ability to create complex templates that control the way data is displayed, based on that data, via data templates. There were some simple examples in the previous chapter, but we're going to get a lot fancier (figure 12.1).

While we're about it, we're also going to show some additional binding capabilities such as binding to hierarchical data, doing virtualized binding, and even binding to more than one thing at a time.

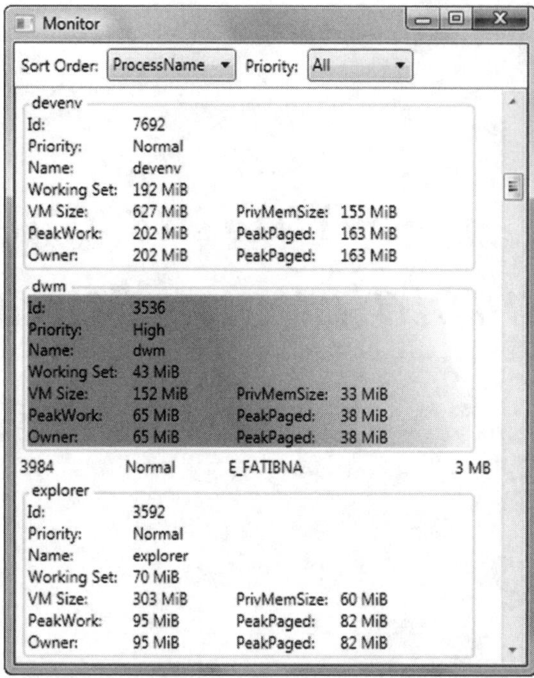

Figure 12.1 The Process Monitor application from the last chapter, but with a much fancier template for displaying the tasks as cards, as well as nicer displays for numbers. High priority tasks are shown in red, and the user can choose how to sort the items and filter them based on priority—all done with data templates and features of binding.

It's easy to think of binding as just another tool in the toolkit that you use when you need it; but, in many ways, binding in WPF is more a philosophy than a tool. In fact, Microsoft has developed a new variant of the Model-View-Controller pattern, called Model-View-ViewModel, that's entirely dependent on a fully featured binding engine such as the one in WPF. We'll provide a brief description of this pattern, and where it is appropriate to use it.

That's pretty deep, though. Before we get to that, we're going to concentrate on demonstrating some of the visual goodness of WPF data templates.

12.1 Data converters

A data converter is a chunk of code that converts one value into another. For example, we can take a number like 3723264 and convert it to 3 MiB, or we could take the same number and, via some algorithm, convert it to a color. Data converters add a huge amount of power to what you can do with XAML; XAML will do simple conversions for you—for example, a number to a string, a string to a particular enum. But, for anything beyond the simple, you need a custom converter.

In this section, we're going to return to one of the examples from the previous chapter—the Process Monitor. When last we left our hero, he was languishing with an appallingly ugly and hard-to-read UI (figure 12.2).

Now, one thing that we could do to improve things is to use columns, as we did with the book list application. But, that will limit us later, so we're going to stick with

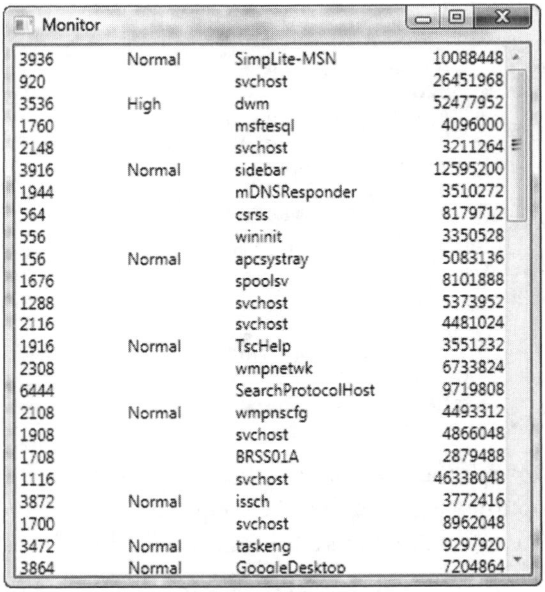

Figure 12.2 The Process Monitor is currently fairly ugly. We aren't going to help matters.

our current approach. There are still several other things that we can do to improve our look-and-feel. For example, the memory size is pretty hard to read as a huge number. Let's try fixing that up first.

12.1.1 Formatting bound data with StringFormat

Often, when you have some data, you can make it look much better by adding some simple formatting. For example, the memory size would be easier to read if it had commas. Via the use of `StringFormat`, this type of formatting is very easy to do (listing 12.1).

Listing 12.1 Using `StringFormat`

```
<TextBlock>
  <TextBlock.Text>
    <Binding Path="WorkingSet" StringFormat="N0"/>
  </TextBlock.Text>
</TextBlock>
```

Note that we've gone back to the version of the Process Monitor that's bound in XAML rather than in code. All we have to do is add a `StringFormat` to the binding of the `WorkingSet`. `StringFormat` uses the same format as `String.Format`, so `N` indicates that a number should be displayed using *Number* format, which gives us the number with commas separating thousands. The `0` after the `N` indicates that we don't want to display any decimal places (figure 12.3).

You can use any of the standard formatting options for numbers here. Table 12.1 shows the standard number formatting options.

Table 12.1 Number formatting options

Format	Description	Example	
C	Currency format	`"C"`	`$258,048.00`
D	Decimal format	`"D6"`	`00258048`
E	Scientific	`"E"`	`2.580480E+005`
F	Fixed-point	`"F"`	`258048.00`
G	General (default)	`"G"`	`258048`
N	Number	`"N"`	`258,048.000`
X	Hexadecimal	`"X"`	`3F000`

You aren't limited to a single formatting option. As with `String.Format`, you can put in additional text and other options. For example, we could add the word *bytes* after the display to indicate units. The format requires a little more work in that case, but as you'll see, the format is basically the same as when formatting strings in code.

```
<Binding Path="WorkingSet" StringFormat="{}{0:N0} bytes"/>
```

Because we're providing more than just a format, we have to specify where the value should appear in the string; in this case, we use `{0}`. The `:N0` after the `0` indicates the formatting to use on the number. The word *bytes* will be displayed in the string as expected. One thing that you've probably noticed is the {} in front of the string. This is a special escape notation required in order to not confuse the parser into thinking

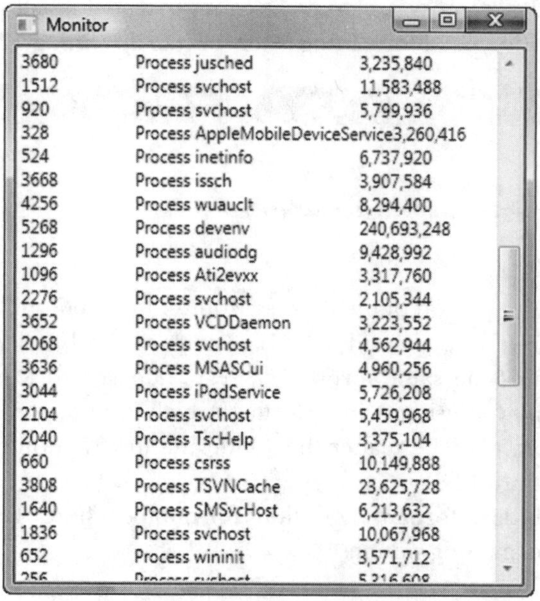

Figure 12.3 The memory display is now formatted with commas.

Figure 12.4 The memory display now indicates the units in use.

that the use of curly braces for the format is an indication of a binding or something like that. You generally only need to do this if the placeholder (the {0}) is at the beginning of the string. In fact, you can also just put in a blank space, which also seems to satisfy the parser. Figure 12.4 shows the results of our line of code.

Because we've used the expanded format for binding the `WorkingSet`, we're obviously setting the `StringFormat` as an attribute on the `Binding`. The same options are all available if we use the `MarkupExtension` notation.

STRINGFORMAT WITH THE MARKUPEXTENSION NOTATION

As you'll recall from the previous chapter, the `MarkupExtension` notation for binding allows us to specify the binding inline. For example, we could write our binding to `WorkingSet` like this:

```
<TextBlock Text="{Binding Path=WorkingSet}/>
```

We can still specify a `StringFormat` by adding an additional clause to the `Binding`.

```
<TextBlock Text="{Binding Path=WorkingSet,StringFormat=N0}" />
```

This will give us the same results as shown in figure 12.3. But, to get the results from figure 12.4, where we include the units (bytes), it's a little trickier. Here's the format:

```
<TextBlock Text="{Binding Path=WorkingSet,StringFormat=\{0:N0\} bytes}" />
```

The format is *almost* the same, but notice that we have to escape the curly braces. Note that the escaping format is different here—a leading slash versus a leading {}. In this context, the {} would cause the parser even more woes. We're a little sad about the different formats for escaping the curly braces; but, because the original releases of WPF didn't have support for `StringFormat` at all, we'll take what we can get.

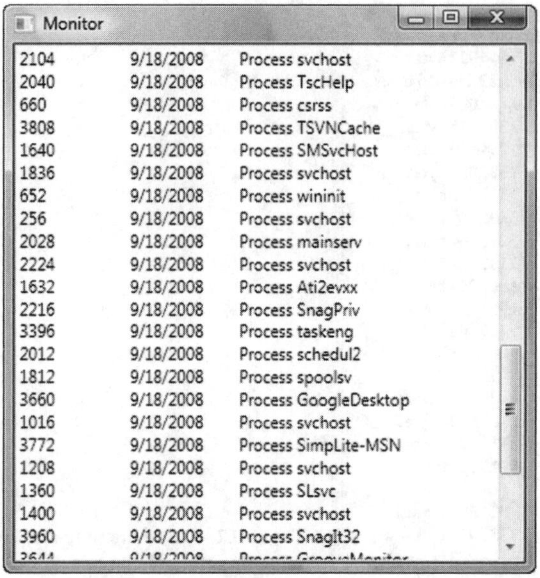

Figure 12.5 The `StartTime` of the `Process` is now shown, formatted to show the short version of the date.

FORMATTING OTHER DATA TYPES

String formatting isn't limited to numeric data types. You can also format other data types such as `DateTime`. For example, `Processes` have a `StartTime` property that we can add to the display.

```
<TextBlock Text="{Binding Path=StartTime,StringFormat=d}" />
```

The `d` format indicates that we want the short date format. Figure 12.5 shows the results.

`DateTimes` support a large number of formats. Table 12.2 shows a few of the more common.

Table 12.2 A few `DateTime` formatting options

Format	Description	Example
D	Short date	7/4/2008
T	Short time	5:16 PM
D	Long date	Friday, July 04, 2008
F	Full date and time	Friday, July 04, 2008 5:16:11 PM

As well as `DateTimes`, you can format any other data type using the appropriate formats, including strings—if, for example, you want to include text in front of or behind the string, you write the following:

```
<TextBlock Text="{Binding Path=ProcessName,StringFormat=Process \{0\}}" />
```

This puts the word *Process* in front of the name of each process.

StringFormats, as you can see, are fairly flexible. But, there are definite limits to what you can do with them. If you want to do some form of calculation against the displayed value, or any sort of specialized parsing, you have to use a data converter.

12.1.2 A number to formatted string data converter

A data converter is just a little lump of code for doing a conversion. You need a converter if you want to do some form of conversion or formatting that's beyond the capabilities of StringFormat. To create a data converter, you create a class that implements the IValueConverter interface. Listing 12.2 shows the code for a converter that takes a number of bytes and produces a string version of the number using IEC notations.

Listing 12.2 NumberToFormattedTextValueConverter

```
using System;
using System.Windows.Data;

namespace ProcessMonitor
{
  public class NumberToFormattedTextValueConverter: IValueConverter
  {
    public object Convert(object value, Type targetType,
          object parameter, System.Globalization.CultureInfo culture)
    {
      Int64 size = System.Convert.ToInt64(value);
      size = size / 1024;

      if (size < 1024)
        return size.ToString() + " KiB";
      else
        return (size / 1024).ToString() + " MiB";
    }

    public object ConvertBack(object value, Type targetType,
          object parameter, System.Globalization.CultureInfo culture)
    {
      throw new NotImplementedException();
    }
  }
}
```

❶ Implementing IValueConverter interface
❷ Convert method
❸ Value passed as an object
❹
❺ Non-implemented convert method

Our converter has to implement the IValueConverter interface ❶ so that WPF knows what to do with it. IValueConverter has two methods: Convert ❷ and ConvertBack ❺. The Convert method takes an object and returns an object—it's up to us to make sure that the right thing is passed and passed back. Because we know that the number being passed will be a number, we can convert the passed value directly to an integer ❸.

The rest of the code in the Convert method takes that number and does some simple formatting—either setting it to return a number of kibibytes or mebibytes—and then returns the appropriate string ❹. You may notice that we haven't bothered to implement the ConvertBack method ❺. In theory, this method would be able to take a value in the IEC format (for example, 3 MiB) and return the number of bytes, although this would be a lossy transaction because we don't have all the decimal places. In practice, though, we only need to be able to convert back if we're using some form of two-way binding—for example, if we were putting the value into a text box that could be edited by a user and set back to our data source. Because that isn't the case here, we won't bother with the implementation. Over time you'll see that a large number of value converters don't bother to implement `ConvertBack`.

Kibibytes, Mebibytes, and IEC

The terms kilobyte and megabyte are familiar, but over time their meanings have become a little bit confused. How big is a kilobyte? Most computer people would say that it is 1024 bytes, but the notation *k* is also commonly used to mean 1000. Likewise, 10M could be 10 x 1024 x 1024 (10,485,760), or it could mean 10 million (10,000,000). Often this isn't a big deal, but there are situations were the odd 485,760 bytes might be important. When you get to the gigabyte or terabyte level, the difference between the two interpretations is pretty impressive.

To work around the dual-meaning issue, a group called the IEC (the International Electrotechnical Commission—you may not have heard of them, but they've been around for more than 100 years) came up with a new notation. The notation basically adds an *i* to the existing terms (KB becomes KiB, MB becomes MiB, and so on), and has a new set of names (Kibibyte, Mebibyte) and these terms *always always always* refer to power-of-two values. A Kibibyte is 1024, and a Mebibyte is 1,048,576. (The *bi* in the names is there to indicate base-2.)

The notation hasn't yet gained a great deal of acceptance. Despite the fact that we're using the notation here, we're still on the fence as to whether it's really needed and whether or not it's just a tad pretentious. But, because there have been several lawsuits against drive manufacturers shipping, for example, a 256 MB flash drive that only had 244 MiBs of memory (because of the conversion), the terminology may become more relevant. The biggest downside of the notation is that, when you're using it, you tend to sound like a Teletubby.

Now that we have our converter, we need to put it to use. In XAML, we need to create a named instance of the converter—which we do as a resource.

```
<Window.Resources>
  <ObjectDataProvider x:Key="processes" MethodName="GetProcesses"
           ObjectType="{x:Type diag:Process}" />
  <local:NumberToFormattedTextValueConverter x:Key="numberToText" />
</Window.Resources>
```

If you're following along, don't forget to add the local namespace referencing the application. Now we can go ahead and update the binding for our size to use the converter.

```
<TextBlock Name="workingSet" MinWidth="60" TextAlignment="Right">
  <TextBlock.Text>
    <Binding Path="WorkingSet64"
         Converter="{StaticResource numberToText}" />
```

```
    </TextBlock.Text>
</TextBlock>
```

We could also have used the following inline notation:

```
<TextBlock Name="workingSet" MinWidth="60" TextAlignment="Right"
  Text="{Binding Path=WorkingSet64,
              Converter={StaticResource numberToText}}"/>
```

This approach is more concise, but it's harder to read. In either case, we get the results we want (figure 12.6). You might also notice that we've added a `MinWidth` and a `Right TextAlignment` so that our values will line up on the right edge.

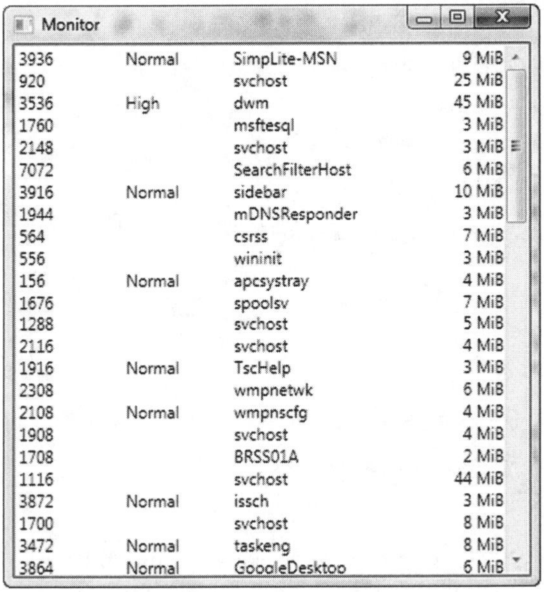

Figure 12.6 The size display now uses our value converter to go from a huge number to an easier-to-read IEC notation.

This is definitely a step in the right direction. We're also pretty taken with the whole Kibibyte-Mebibyte thing, but others may not like it. It might be nice if choosing between the two formats was an option.

12.1.3 Converter parameters

Our `NumberToFormattedTextValueConverter` takes a number and gives us back a string in IEC format. But, some people might not like that format, and might want to use something more traditional. We could accommodate that wish by writing multiple converters (`NumberToIecValueConverter`, `NumberToSiValueConverter`, and so on), but it would be nice if we could use the same converter and pass a parameter for the format to use. In fact, we can do just that—one of the values passed to the `Convert` method of `IValueConverter` is called `parameter`. We can modify our `Convert` method to look at that value and use it (listing 12.3).

Listing 12.3 Convert method with parameter

```
public object Convert(object value, Type targetType,
     object parameter, System.Globalization.CultureInfo culture)
{
  Int64 size = System.Convert.ToInt64(value);
  string units = (parameter != null) ? parameter.ToString() : "IEC";   ← ❶ Get parameter

  switch (units)
  {
    case "IEC":                                    ← IEC version
      size = size / 1024;
      if (size < 1024)
        return size.ToString() + " KiB";
      else
        return (size / 1024).ToString() + " MiB";

    case "BINARYSI":                               ← Binary SI version
      size = size / 1024;
      if (size < 1024)
        return size.ToString() + " KB";
      else
        return (size / 1024).ToString() + " MB";

    case "SI":                                     ← SI version
      size = size / 1000;

      if (size < 1000)
        return size.ToString() + " KB";
      else
        return (size / 1000).ToString() + " MB";
  }
                                                   ❷ Bad value passed
  return "Bad Param";                              ←
}
```

The main thing we're doing is checking the passed `parameter` and, if it isn't null, converting it to a string ❶. If it is null, we default to the IEC format. Otherwise, our switch statement checks the type and does the appropriate conversion. If some other value were passed, we'd return a value indicating that the parameter wasn't legal ❷.

This code could be significantly more elegant and could handle a bad parameter better, but you get the point. We can now specify the parameter to pass in our XAML.

```
<TextBlock.Text>
  <Binding Path="WorkingSet64" Converter="{StaticResource numberToText}"
    ConverterParameter="SI"/>
</TextBlock.Text>
```

Or, we could use the following inline notation:

```
<TextBlock Name="workingSet" MinWidth="60" TextAlignment="Right"
  Text="{Binding Path=WorkingSet64,
    Converter={StaticResource numberToText},ConverterParameter=BINARYSI}"/>
```

Either way, we can pass IEC, BINARYSI or SI. Figure 12.7 shows the three different versions side by side.

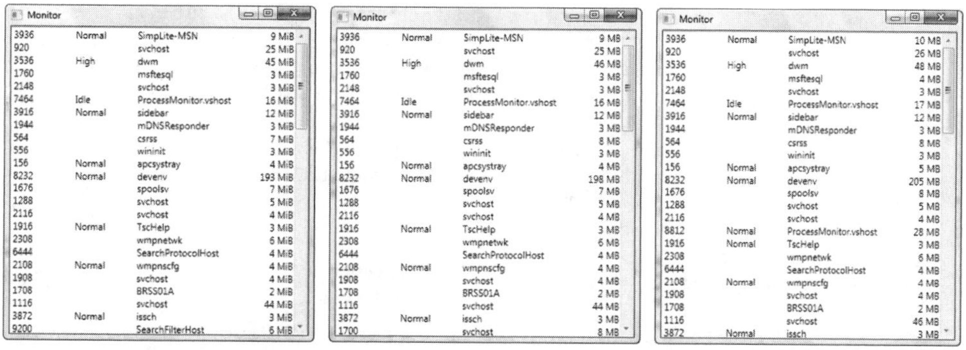

Figure 12.7 Via the use of a `parameter`, we can specify whether the display should use (respectively) IEC, BINARYSI, or SI units. Notice that the figures for the first two are pretty similar, but that, despite using the same units, there's quite a big difference between the BINARYSI and SI units. This is pretty much why the IEC standard was suggested.

Pretentious or not, the IEC units are much clearer than the Système International d'Unités (SI) units—notice the 11MB difference for Dev Studio (devenv) from the binary SI version to the standard SI version. The nice thing about `parameters` with value converters is that they can make the same converter much more powerful and flexible.

As time goes on, you'll tend to build up a fairly extensive library of data converters for various purposes. An example that we didn't include here, but is available with the downloadable code, is a converter that takes the size and returns a color—that's more or less red depending on how big the value is—that could be used for the text color, or the background, or anything you like. You'll see other examples of converters throughout the book, and later in this chapter, you'll also see converters that work with multiple values.

`Converters` and `StringFormats` aren't the only ways of changing/controlling the display of data. We can also cause the display to change based on some value, via the use of data triggers.

12.2 DataTriggers

In earlier chapters, we demonstrated *triggers*—using them, for example, to make a control glow when the mouse moved over it. A `DataTrigger` is similar, except that, as its name suggests, it's triggered based on a data value of some kind. For example, if a particular threshold is passed, then your text turns red—that sort of thing.

For an example, we'll go back to the Process Monitor. Processes have a priority—high, medium, low, and so on, so let's put a red gradient behind high priority processes to make them stand out (listing 12.4).

Listing 12.4 Priority `DataTrigger`

```
<ListView.ItemTemplate>
 <DataTemplate>
   <WrapPanel Name="wrapPanel1">
```

Names our panel

```
        <TextBlock Text="{Binding Path=Id}" MinWidth="80" />
        <TextBlock Text="{Binding Path=PriorityClass}" MinWidth="80" />
        <TextBlock Text="{Binding Path=ProcessName}" MinWidth="140" />
        <TextBlock Name="workingSet" MinWidth="60" TextAlignment="Right">
          <TextBlock.Text>
           <Binding Path="WorkingSet64"
            Converter="{StaticResource numberToText}"
    ConverterParameter="SI"/>
          </TextBlock.Text>
        </TextBlock>
      </WrapPanel>
      <DataTemplate.Triggers>
        <DataTrigger Binding="{Binding Path=PriorityClass}" Value="High">
          <Setter TargetName="wrapPanel1" Property="Background">
            <Setter.Value>
              <LinearGradientBrush>
                <GradientStop Color="Salmon" Offset="0" />
                <GradientStop Color="Salmon" Offset="0.4" />
                <GradientStop Color="White" Offset="1" />
              </LinearGradientBrush>
            </Setter.Value>
          </Setter>
        </DataTrigger>
      </DataTemplate.Triggers>
    </DataTemplate>
  </ListView.ItemTemplate>
```

❷ Collection of triggers

❸ Triggers on high priority

❹ Sets background

We've included the XAML for the entire `ListView` template to make what's happening clearer. The first change we make is to give our panel a name ❶. We need to do this so that we can refer to it from our trigger. Our `DataTemplate` has a collection of triggers ❷, although we only have one. The trigger itself ❸ has two attributes: the `Binding`—this provides the data we want to trigger off of—and the `Value`—the value that we want to compare the result to.

In our example, we're binding to our data source's `PriorityClass`, which will be High, Medium, Low, and so on. Our trigger will fire if the binding value is an exact match for the value `"High"`. If the condition is met, then some number of setters will be executed, just as with a control template. In this case, we're setting the `Background` property of our wrap panel ❹ to be a linear gradient brush that goes from salmon to white. Why salmon? Because catfish are really ugly.

Anyway, figure 12.8 shows our trigger in action.

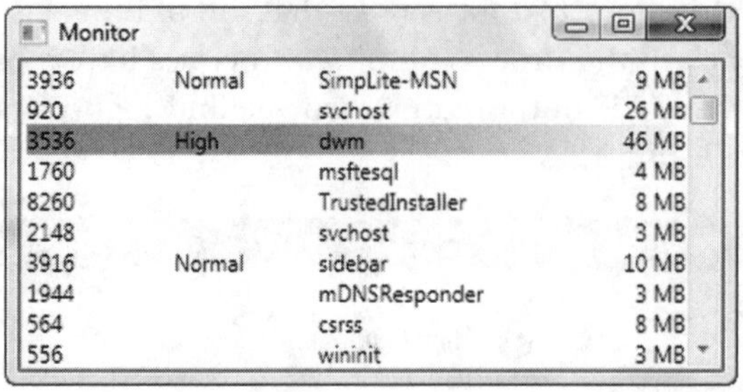

Figure 12.8 Our `DataTrigger` puts a red-to-white gradient behind all the processes that have a high priority.

The fact that you can only do a single comparison for a trigger may seem like a serious limitation, but it truly isn't much of one because the `Value` is provided via a binding, and bindings, as you've seen, can use converters. For example, if we want to highlight rows that have a memory size greater than a certain size, we can create an `IsLargeValueConverter` that checks for a particular value and returns `true` if the size is reached. Listing 12.5 shows what such a converter might look like.

Listing 12.5 `IsLargeValueConverter`

```
using System;
using System.Windows.Data;

namespace ProcessMonitor
{
  public class IsLargeValueConverter : IValueConverter
  {
    public object Convert(object value, Type targetType,
          object parameter, System.Globalization.CultureInfo culture)
    {
      Int64 convertedValue = System.Convert.ToInt64(value);      ❶ Value to check

      Int64 threshold = 1000;
      if (parameter != null)
        threshold = System.Convert.ToInt64(parameter);      ❷ Value to check against

      return (convertedValue > threshold);
    }

    public object ConvertBack(object value, Type targetType,
          object parameter, System.Globalization.CultureInfo culture)
    {
      throw new NotImplementedException();
    }
  }
}
```

This value converter takes the value passed in ❶ and compares it against the value passed as a `parameter` ❷ to see if it's big or not. This is one of those converters that goes well in a library because it can be used for lots of different situations. To use it, all we have to do is create an instance in resources.

```
<Window.Resources>
  ...
  <local:IsLargeValueConverter x:Key="isLarge" />
</Window.Resources>
```

And then we change our trigger to use it.

```
<DataTrigger Binding="{Binding Path=WorkingSet64,
   Converter={StaticResource isLarge},ConverterParameter=20000000}"
   Value="true">
```

The binding now uses our converter; 20MB (the SI version) is our threshold. Because our converter returns either `true` or `false`, we're checking for a return value of `true`. The setter is the same one we've been using. Figure 12.9 shows the results.

Monitor

2108	Normal	wmpnscfg	4 MB
1908		svchost	4 MB
1708		BRSS01A	2 MB
1116		svchost	46 MB
3872	Normal	issch	3 MB
1700		svchost	8 MB
3472	Normal	taskeng	9 MB
3864	Normal	GoogleDesktop	6 MB
4060	Normal	SnagIt32	28 MB
9280		SearchFilterHost	7 MB
1100		svchost	70 MB
504		csrss	4 MB
1880		mainserv	5 MB
2076		sqlwriter	4 MB
3848	Normal	jusched	3 MB
1876		sqlservr	13 MB
4040	Normal	Launchy	15 MB
2660		taskeng	4 MB
884		svchost	6 MB
3836	Normal	TSVNCache	20 MB
1424		svchost	10 MB
9544	Normal	ProcessMonitor.vshost	28 MB
2056		svchost	3 MB
3828	Normal	VCDDaemon	3 MB

Figure 12.9 Our new data trigger puts a gradient behind rows whose sizes are at least 20MB.

If we wanted to be *more* clever, instead of calling our converter `IsLargeValue`, we could call it something like `CompareValues` and have it return -1, 0, or 1 (or `"smaller"`, `"equals"`, `"bigger"`) depending on the comparison. In fact, this is the sort of thing that we wish they'd built into the framework because it's so likely to be useful.

There are also other options for data triggers. For example, there's a `MultiDataTrigger` that only fires when a number of comparisons are true. Setters can also be as complex as you like and can include triggering storyboards and animations. These capabilities aren't that useful with our static data; but, if the values could change behind us (say, if we bothered to make the display refresh), then having an animation fire when a threshold is crossed or a particular value becomes true, could be quite useful. Because we've talked about triggers when used with control templates, we won't go into them in detail here.

We aren't sure that the gradient improves the appearance of our display, but it at least provides some useful feedback. Thanks to our IEC converter, the value is also a lot easier to read. One thing we haven't addressed, though, is the order of our data in the list.

12.3 CollectionViewSource

Right now, our list view is bound directly to the list of processes from the `Processes.GetProcesses()` method, so the list is in the order that the data is provided. If we want to sort the data, then we need to put something between the list view and our data source—something that will let us control the order of our data. That is precisely what the `CollectionViewSource` object is for.

12.3.1 Sorting with CollectionViewSource

At its most basic, a `CollectionViewSource` has two things: a `Source`—where to get the data—and a `SortDescription`—details of how to sort the data. These details include the name of the property to sort by, and the direction (`Ascending` or `Descending`). Actually, there's a collection of `SortDescriptions`, so it's possible to define fairly complex sorts.

Once a `CollectionViewSource` has been created, the display (for example, our list) can be pointed at the `CollectionViewSource` instead of the raw data. The `CollectionView` will provide the data in the appropriate order. We can create a `CollectionViewSource` instance in XAML as a resource. But, we first have to add a new namespace to our header. This isn't for the `CollectionViewSource`; it's for the `SortDescription`, without which the `CollectionViewSource` is useless but which is, for some reason, in a different namespace. If you're following along, go ahead and add the following namespace declaration to the main `Window` tag:

```
xmlns:scm="clr-namespace:System.ComponentModel;assembly=WindowsBase"
```

Now we can create our `CollectionViewSource` object (listing 12.6).

Listing 12.6 Creating a `CollectionViewSource` object in XAML

```
<Window.Resources>
  <ObjectDataProvider x:Key="processes"
        MethodName="GetProcesses" ObjectType="{x:Type diag:Process}" />   ❶ Our original data source

  <CollectionViewSource x:Key="processesView"
                Source="{StaticResource processes}" >   ❷ CollectionViewSource pointing to data
    <CollectionViewSource.SortDescriptions>
      <scm:SortDescription PropertyName="ProcessName" />   ❸ Sort order
    </CollectionViewSource.SortDescriptions>
  </CollectionViewSource>
  ...
</Window.Resources>
```

No matter what we do, we still need our original data source—the list of processes ❶. This is unchanged. But, we now create a `CollectionViewSource` with the key `"processesView"` ❷. The `CollectionViewSource` has a `Source` property that references the processes' data provider. Note that the resources have to be defined in order—you can't reference the processes' provider until it has been defined.

The `CollectionViewSource` has a collection of `SortDescriptions`, and we have a single `SortDescription` ❸. The description has a `PropertyName` property that specifies the property in the data source to use for ordering. We could have also specified a Direction attribute to, for example, reverse the order. We could have also added additional `SortDescriptions` if we wanted to sort by more than one property.

The last step is to make our list point at the `CollectionViewSource` instead of directly at the processes' data source.

```
<ListView Name="listView1"
          ItemsSource="{Binding Source={StaticResource processesView}}" >
```

That's it. Now, when we run, the list will ask the `CollectionViewSource` for data. The `CollectionViewSource` will ask the processes' data source for data, retrieve it, order it

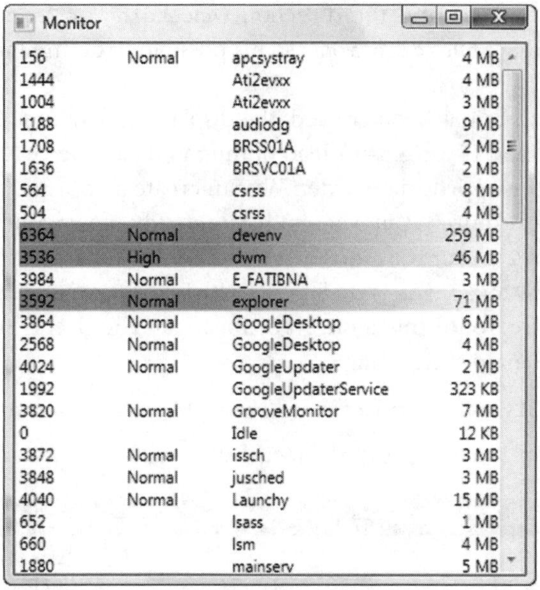

Monitor

156	Normal	apcsystray	4 MB
1444		Ati2evxx	4 MB
1004		Ati2evxx	3 MB
1188		audiodg	9 MB
1708		BRSS01A	2 MB
1636		BRSVC01A	2 MB
564		csrss	8 MB
504		csrss	4 MB
6364	Normal	devenv	259 MB
3536	High	dwm	46 MB
3984	Normal	E_FATIBNA	3 MB
3592	Normal	explorer	71 MB
3864	Normal	GoogleDesktop	6 MB
2568	Normal	GoogleDesktop	4 MB
4024	Normal	GoogleUpdater	2 MB
1992		GoogleUpdaterService	323 KB
3820	Normal	GrooveMonitor	7 MB
0		Idle	12 KB
3872	Normal	issch	3 MB
3848	Normal	jusched	3 MB
4040	Normal	Launchy	15 MB
652		lsass	1 MB
660		lsm	4 MB
1880		mainserv	5 MB

Figure 12.10 The same list, but thanks to the `CollectionViewSource`, the list is now in alphabetical order of process names.

by the process name property, and then provide it to the `ListView`. Figure 12.10 shows the results.

Not too shabby. But, you do need to consider some performance implications. In order to sort, the `CollectionViewSource` has to step through the entire list and hold an ordered set of references. So, even if your original data source is virtual in some way, using the `CollectionViewSource` causes the whole list to be pulled.

Hardcoding a sort order is OK, but there are times when you want to allow the user to choose the order of the data. We'll update the UI to allow the user to choose a sort order, and demonstrate changing the order programmatically.

12.3.2 Programatically sorting with CollectionViewSource

If we were using a proper `Grid` layout, then we'd probably set things up so that the user could click a column header to sort a particular row. But, because we're still stubbornly sticking to our existing structure, we don't have column headers. Even if we did have column headers, though, we'd still need to write some code to make sorting take place—there's no automatic free sort tied into the list view.

Fortunately it's pretty easy to implement dynamic sorting. Let's start by putting a `ComboBox` at the top of the `Grid` with a list of the fields that we want to allow the user to sort by (listing 12.7).

Listing 12.7 Adding an order-by combo

```
<DockPanel>      <-❶ DockPanel to hold everything
  <StackPanel DockPanel.Dock="Top" Orientation="Horizontal">    ❷
    <Label>Sort Order: </Label>
    <ComboBox Width="100" x:Name="sortOrderCombo" SelectedIndex="0"
```

```
                     SelectionChanged="sortOrderCombo_SelectionChanged">  <-- ComboBox for order (3)
      <ComboBoxItem>ProcessName</ComboBoxItem>
      <ComboBoxItem>Id</ComboBoxItem>
      <ComboBoxItem>WorkingSet64</ComboBoxItem>
    </ComboBox>
  </StackPanel>
  <Grid>                                 <-- (4) The original Grid with original ListView
    <ListView Name="listView1">
    ...
    </ListView>
  </Grid>
</DockPanel>
```

As is often the case with layout, there are many different ways to accomplish the same thing. The approach we take is to wrap the original `Grid` inside a `DockPanel` ❶, then put in a `StackPanel` docked at the top, and then our original `Grid` and `ListView` ❹. Because the `Grid` doesn't have docking set, it automatically takes up all remaining space.

Our `StackPanel` ❷ is oriented horizontally so that we can put a label in front of the `ComboBox`. This combo is fairly straightforward ❸—just a list of fields we want to allow to be used for sorting. We're using the exact property names because we're lazy—if this were a better UI, we'd display a friendlier name and map to the property name. (Actually, if this were a better UI, we'd just use a `Grid` and sort using column headers.)

One thing of note about the `ComboBox`: We hooked up an event to the `SelectionChanged` event. We'll use that event handler to do our reordering (listing 12.8).

Listing 12.8 Changing order programmatically

```
private void sortOrderCombo_SelectionChanged(object sender,
                                    SelectionChangedEventArgs e)   <-- ComboBox event handler (1)
{
  SetNewSortOrder();
}

private void SetNewSortOrder()
{
  string newSortOrder =
     ((ComboBoxItem)sortOrderCombo.SelectedItem).Content.ToString();   <-- Gets order name (2)
  SortDescription sortDesc =
     new SortDescription(newSortOrder, ListSortDirection.Ascending);   <-- Creates new SortDescription (3)
  CollectionViewSource src =
     (CollectionViewSource)FindResource("processesView");   <-- Gets CollectionViewSource (4)
  src.SortDescriptions.Clear();
  src.SortDescriptions.Add(sortDesc);   <-- (5) Replaces SortDescription
}
```

Whenever the selection in the sort-order combo changes, our event handler method will be called ❶ which does nothing more than turn around and call a `SetNewSortOrder()` method. We've broken this out to make our lives easier for the next sample.

The `SetNewSortOrder()` method first gets the name of the property to sort by from the `ComboBox` ❷. This would be where a nicer app would do some mapping. We then create a new `SortDescription` object ❸ using the name of the property from the combo. For the example, we're only allowing ascending sorts, but it would be trivial to also support descending ones.

The next step is to get a hold of the `CollectionViewSource`. Because it's defined as a resource, we can use the handy-dandy `FindResource` method to get it ❹. Then, we clear out the `SortDescriptions` collection and add in our new `SortDescription` ❺. Figure 12.11 shows the Process Monitor with our ordering combo in action.

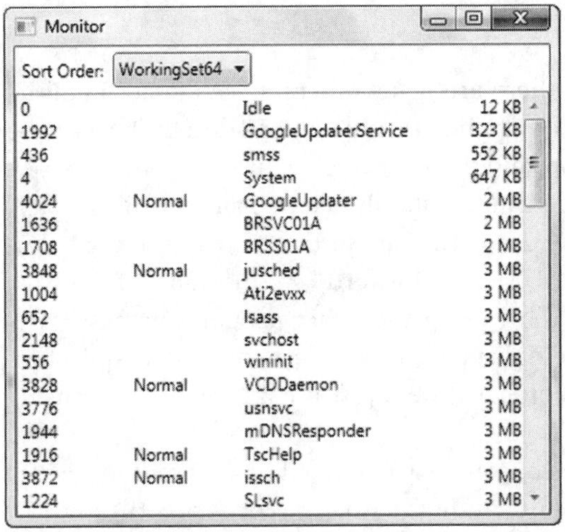

Figure 12.11 When the user changes the sort order in the combo, the list is automatically resorted.

As well as supporting simple sorting, the `CollectionViewSource` also has several additional abilities. It supports grouping (à la report writers) and also, as we'll demonstrate next, filtering.

12.3.3 Filtering with CollectionViewSource

Filtering a list with `CollectionViewSource` is simple. We add a handler for the `Filter` event on the `CollectionViewSource`.

```
<CollectionViewSource x:Key="processesView"
                      Source="{StaticResource processes}"
           Filter="CollectionViewSource_Filter">
```

Then we implement the event handler.

```
private void CollectionViewSource_Filter(object sender, FilterEventArgs e)
{
  Process p = e.Item as Process;
  e.Accepted = (p.BasePriority >= 8);
}
```

The event handler will be called once for each row in the data source. `FilterEventArgs` contain the current item (`e.Item`) and an `Accepted` property. If we set that to `true`, the item will be included. If not, it will be left out. The example here excludes all low priority processes from the list (figure 12.12).

Monitor

Sort Order: ProcessName

564		csrss	8 MB
504		csrss	4 MB
6364	Normal	devenv	251 MB
3536	High	dwm	46 MB
3984	Normal	E_FATIBNA	3 MB
3592	Normal	explorer	71 MB
2568	Normal	GoogleDesktop	3 MB
3864	Normal	GoogleDesktop	7 MB
4024	Normal	GoogleUpdater	2 MB
1992		GoogleUpdaterService	323 KB
3820	Normal	GrooveMonitor	7 MB
3872	Normal	issch	3 MB
3848	Normal	jusched	3 MB
4040	Normal	Launchy	15 MB
652		lsass	2 MB
660		lsm	4 MB
1880		mainserv	5 MB
1944		mDNSResponder	3 MB
8644		MpCmdRun	4 MB
3792	Normal	MSASCui	7 MB
224		MsDtsSrvr	10 MB
1760		msftesql	4 MB

Figure 12.12 We're filtering out all low priority processes via a `CollectionViewSource` filter.

We only lost a couple of processes, but it still shortens our list. By the way, the filtering can only be done programmatically—there's no XAML way of defining a filter. But, our filter can look at other elements to provide whatever functionality we desire. For example, we could add another `ComboBox` to choose how the filtering should be done. We aren't going to show all the XAML, but we've added a `ComboBox` called `priorityFilterCombo` with the following values: All, High, Normal, and Low (figure 12.13).

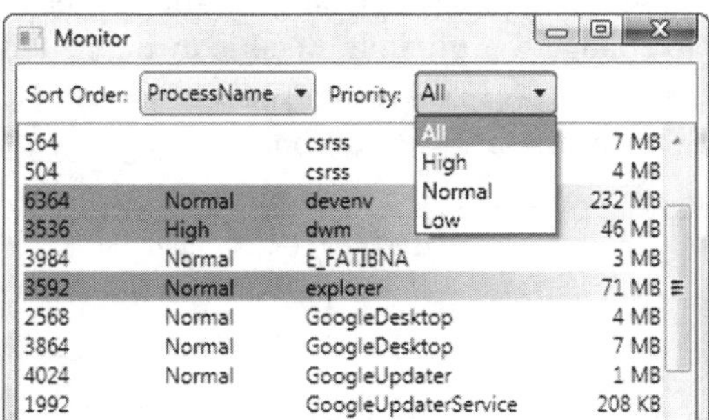

Figure 12.13 We've added a `ComboBox` to let the user choose the shown priority options.

Now we have to change our filter code to take the priority option into account (listing 12.9).

Listing 12.9 Fancier filter code

```
private void CollectionViewSource_Filter(object sender, FilterEventArgs e)
{
  Process p = e.Item as Process;

  int mode = (priorityFilterCombo != null) ?
```

```
                          priorityFilterCombo.SelectedIndex : 0;   <-- Determines selection (1)
  switch (mode)
  {
    case 1:
      e.Accepted = (p.BasePriority > 12);          <-- High priority
      break;
    case 2:
      e.Accepted = (p.BasePriority >= 8 && p.BasePriority <= 12);   <-- Normal priority
      break;
    case 3:
      e.Accepted = (p.BasePriority < 8);           <-- Low priority
      break;
    default:
      e.Accepted = true;           <-- All priorities
      break;
  }
}
```

For reasons of laziness, we're determining the order by the index of the entries in the `ComboBox` ❶. We're also doing a null check because the filter might end up getting called before the `ComboBox` has come into being.

Next, we have a switch statement that determines whether the entry is appropriate for our current filter. `Priority` isn't entirely reliable, so we're using ranges (and, in fact, the ranges aren't reliable either—items with different priorities might have the same base priority value). This isn't a book about processes, though, so we aren't going to worry too much about the workings of the `Process` object.

The only thing left for us to do is to make the list get filtered again whenever the user changes the value in the priority `ComboBox`, but there's no "refresh" method on the `CollectionListView`. Instead, we have to make a change to the `CollectionListView` to convince it that it needs to change. Fortunately, we already have a tailor-made method for doing just that—`SetNewSortOrder()`. We can put a call into that method from the `SelectionChanged` handler for the priority combo.

```
private void priorityFilterCombo_SelectionChanged(object sender,
                                            SelectionChangedEventArgs e)
{
  SetNewSortOrder();
}
```

Now, when the user changes the priority option, the list will be refreshed appropriately (figure 12.14).

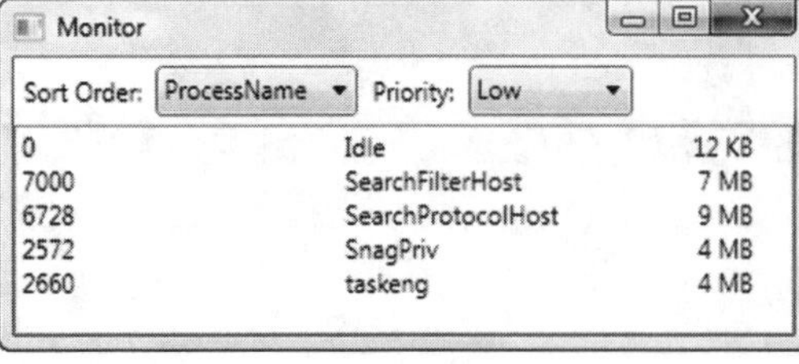

Figure 12.14 When the user changes the Priority value in the combo, the list is automatically refiltered.

We can now sort and filter our list. But, our list still looks like a pretty basic grid. With WPF, though, lists aren't limited to being displayed as grids—we can choose any type of display we like. As we'll show in the next section, we can even make different items in the list display in completely different ways based on some condition.

12.4 Conditional templates

At the moment, the data template for displaying our items is directly inside the `ListView`'s `ItemTemplate` property. But, we could just as easily move it, say, into the `Grid`'s resources.

```
<Grid.Resources>
  <DataTemplate x:Key="NormalTemplate">
    <WrapPanel Name="wrapPanel1">
    <TextBlock Text="{Binding Path=Id}" MinWidth="80" />
    ...
  </DataTemplate>
</Grid.Resources>
```

Now that we've given it a name (NormalTemplate), we can reference it in `ListView`.

```
<ListView Name="listView1"
      ItemsSource="{Binding Source={StaticResource processesView}}"
        ItemTemplate="{StaticResource NormalTemplate}"/>
```

One benefit of moving the template is that it makes it much easier to read the XAML for our presentation. We could even move the details to a standalone resource dictionary, which would improve things even more. It also makes it easier for us to work with different templates.

12.4.1 A more involved template

Now that we've pulled out the template, we can easily replace it with a more involved example. For example, suppose we create a card view template in resources (listing 12.10).

Listing 12.10 A card view template

```
<DataTemplate x:Key="CardViewTemplate">     <— CardViewTemplate
  <GroupBox Header="{Binding Path=ProcessName}" Width="350"
                                          BorderThickness="2">  <—
    <StackPanel Name="stackPanel1">                      GroupBox
      <WrapPanel Orientation="Vertical" Name="wrapPanel1">   for card ❶
        <WrapPanel Orientation="Horizontal">
          <TextBlock MinWidth="80" Text="Id: " xml:space="preserve"/>
          <TextBlock MinWidth="80" Text="{Binding Path=Id}" />
        </WrapPanel>
        <WrapPanel Orientation="Horizontal">
          <TextBlock MinWidth="80" Text="Priority: " xml:space="preserve"/>
          <TextBlock Text="{Binding Path=PriorityClass}" MinWidth="80" />
        </WrapPanel>
        <WrapPanel Orientation="Horizontal">
          <TextBlock MinWidth="80" Text="Name: " xml:space="preserve"/>
          <TextBlock Text="{Binding Path=ProcessName}" MinWidth="140" />
```

```
        </WrapPanel>
        <WrapPanel Orientation="Horizontal">
          <TextBlock MinWidth="80" Text="Working Set:"
    xml:space="preserve"/>
          <TextBlock Name="workingSet" Text="{Binding
              Path=WorkingSet64,Converter={StaticResource numberToText}}"/>
        </WrapPanel>
      </WrapPanel>
      ... We added a number of additional properties. You can add them
          yourself, or download the version that includes them...
    </StackPanel>
  </GroupBox>
  <DataTemplate.Triggers>                    ❷ Priority trigger
    <DataTrigger Binding="{Binding Path=PriorityClass}" Value="High">
      <Setter TargetName="stackPanel1" Property="Background">
        <Setter.Value>
          <LinearGradientBrush StartPoint="1.0,0.5" EndPoint="0.5,1.0">
            <GradientStop Color="White" Offset="0.0" />
            <GradientStop Color="Salmon" Offset="1.0" />
          </LinearGradientBrush>
        </Setter.Value>
      </Setter>
    </DataTrigger>
  </DataTemplate.Triggers>
</DataTemplate>
```

Although this is a much longer template, it isn't significantly more complicated than the other one. The template has a GroupBox ❶ that contains a bunch of label/value items, each bound to an appropriate item in the data source. In fact, we added a bunch more label/value items, but we've excluded them from the code shown to save some space. (We assume we'll sell so many copies of this book that, by excluding one page of XML, we've effectively saved the entire Amazon Rain Basin from destruction.) Here, we also include a trigger that makes our background red for high priority processes ❷.

Now that we have a second template, we can swap out the item template in the ListView.

```
<ListView Name="listView1"
        ItemsSource="{Binding Source={StaticResource processesView}}"
        ItemTemplate="{StaticResource CardViewTemplate}"/>
```

When we run now, instead of a simple list, we get a card for each entry (figure 12.15). Our plan to eventually switch to a card view is the reason we didn't go with a classic grid from the beginning.

We're swapping out the template for the entire list, but suppose we want to *conditionally* choose a template. For example, what if we want a simple one-line entry for small processes, but a card for larger processes?

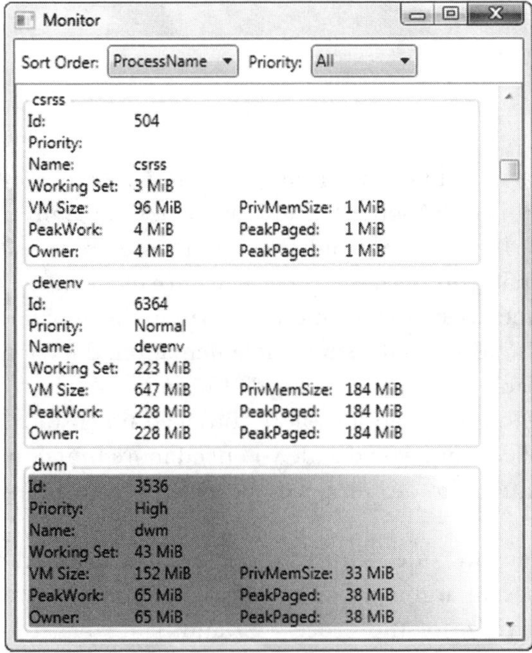

Figure 12.15 The list is now using a different template that provides a card view of each process.

12.4.2 *Conditionally using a template*

To conditionally choose a different template for each item in our list, we can make use of a `DataTemplateSelector`. A `DataTemplateSelector` is a piece of code that, sort of like a filter, is called for each data item. It's passed the item, and asked which template to return. Listing 12.11 shows a selector that returns a different template based on whether the size of a process is above or below a particular threshold.

Listing 12.11 `DataTemplateSelector`

```
using System;
using System.Windows.Controls;
using System.Diagnostics;
using System.Windows;

namespace ProcessMonitor
{
  public class ProcessInterestSelector : DataTemplateSelector      ❶
  {
    public Int64 Threshold { get; set; }                           ❷
    public DataTemplate NormalTemplate { get; set; }               ❸
    public DataTemplate InterestingTemplate { get; set; }

   public override System.Windows.DataTemplate SelectTemplate(object item,
                   System.Windows.DependencyObject container)      ❹
    {
      Process process = (Process)item;

      if (process.WorkingSet64 > Threshold)    ❺
```

❶ Derives from DataTemplateSelector
❷ Automatic property for Threshold
❸ Automatic properties for templates
❹ Selects template method

```
            return InterestingTemplate;

          return NormalTemplate;
        }
      }
    }
```

To create a custom selector, we have to derive from `DataTemplateSelector` ❶. Our derivation is called `ProcessInterestSelector` because it decides which processes are more interesting. To store the threshold ❷ and the templates to return ❸, we're using *automatic properties*. Automatic properties are a new feature of C# 3.0. In the past, we would've created a private member variable and then written the get and set code to set/return the value. But, if we don't put in any implementation, the compiler will automatically generate the variable and the get/set code for us.

Automatic properties are good in situations where you need no custom behavior around your properties; if, in the future, you decide you need more functionality, you can put it in place. We'll get values into our properties when we create an instance in a little while.

The heart of our class is an override of the `SelectTemplate` method ❹. This method gets the current item as an argument and returns an appropriate template. Our logic looks at the memory size of the process ❺ and, if it's big, returns the `InterestingTemplate` (meaning that the data is more interesting). Otherwise, it returns the `NormalTemplate`.

Now that we have our class, we need to create an instance of it. We do that, as per usual, in resources.

```
<Grid.Resources>
  ...
  <local:ProcessInterestSelector x:Key="ProcessTemplateSelector"
           NormalTemplate="{StaticResource NormalTemplate}"
           InterestingTemplate="{StaticResource CardViewTemplate}"
           Threshold="20000000" />
</Grid.Resources>
```

We create an instance of the `ProcessInterestSelector` with the key `"ProcessTemplateSelector"`. In the declaration, we also set our properties for the `Threshold`, `NormalTemplate`, and `InterestingTemplate`. The two templates reference our two existing templates, and the threshold is set to 20MB. The last bit (which is pretty straightforward) is to make the `ListView` use our selector:

```
<ListView Name="listView1"
          ItemsSource="{Binding Source={StaticResource processesView}}"
          ItemTemplateSelector="{StaticResource
  ProcessTemplateSelector}"/>
```

Instead of specifying an `ItemTemplate`, we're now specifying an `ItemTemplateSelector`. When we run, our code will be called for each item—small items will get a single line, and bigger items will get a card (figure 12.16).

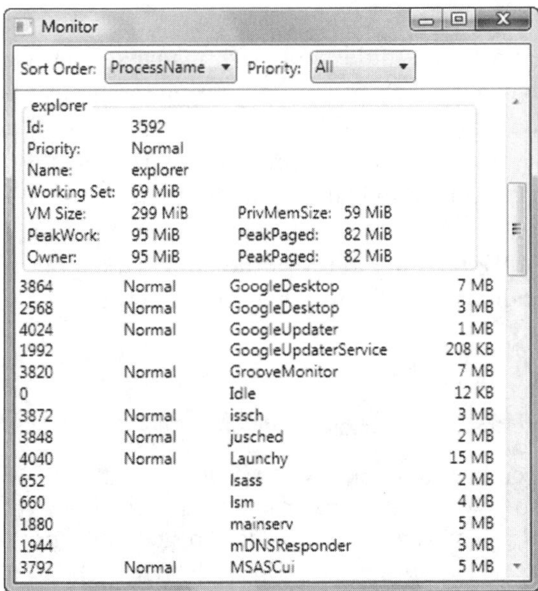

Figure 12.16 The template that is displayed for each item is conditional based on the size of the process. Our `DataTemplateSelector` does the evaluation work.

This isn't, perhaps, the most attractive UI, and it would probably be a good idea to keep your various templates *relatively* similar. For example, displaying a card no matter what, but having more information on the card for the larger processes.

12.4.3 Templates based on type

In our list, all the items are of the same type—`Process`. But, it isn't uncommon to have a list of different types of objects (although usually with a common base). For example, you might have a list that includes both `Directories` and `Files`.

In that situation, you don't need to create a `DataTemplateSelector`. Instead, you can specify a `DataType` for your `DataTemplate`.

```
<DataTemplate DataType="{x:Type io:Directory}">
  ...
</DataTemplate>
<DataTemplate DataType="{x:Type io:File}">
  ...
</DataTemplate>
```

This approach is similar to the use of styles. When a `DataTemplate` is needed for the specified type, the template targeted at that type will automatically be picked up. In fact, another advantage of this approach is that you don't have to specify a template to use at all in your controls (for example, the `ListView`).

We've talked a lot about data templates, and a lot of the little utility capabilities and methods you can use with them. In most of our examples, though, we've been worrying more about displaying data. When the user can enter data back, we then have to worry about whether the data being entered is valid.

12.5 Validators

In the last chapter, we created a simple little bookmark manager that let you add bookmarks and stored the data in a `DataTable`. The application was pretty trusting—it let you type anything you liked in, and assumed it was correct. Ideally, we'd add some code to the application to make sure that the users are entering reasonable data. Conveniently, WPF binding has the concept of validation built in, so we can tie `Validators` to the appropriate places to make sure users are entering reasonable data, as well as provide feedback if they aren't. We're going to revisit the bookmark application now, and add in some validation handling to make sure that the data isn't horribly bogus.

Overzealous over validation

Validation is important to keep the system usable, but...

Be careful of overzealous validation. You certainly want to put reasonable checks in for data; but, if those checks are overly complex, you can make a system unusable. As an example, one of the writers of this book had his zip code changed by the post office. Many online stores have old copies of zip codes and, rather than allowing the entry of a *correct* zip code, the sites would not allow a purchase to be made. Net result? Those sites lost business. This sort of thing happens all the time—a recent survey of e-mail address regular expressions determined that *90% rejected valid e-mail addresses.*

Beyond out-of-date or incorrect validation, another common problem is to require users to fill in a set of information in a particular order and with the correct values—even if the user doesn't yet know how to answer those questions. The developers forget that the software is there to help the user, not the other way around, and the result is that those users find ways to circumvent the system—either by not using it or by picking bogus values to get past the requirements.

That doesn't mean that you shouldn't validate, just that you shouldn't overdo it. If you're doing nothing more than storing a value as a blob, maybe you can warn the user that the value doesn't look valid, but let them enter it anyway. Also, if possible, avoid forcing users to enter data that they don't have.

In an ideal world, your data model is responsible for validating its own data. If an illegal value is entered, it would reject it. Our back-end store for the bookmark application is a simple `DataTable`, but even that can do some basic sanity checking.

12.5.1 The ExceptionValidationRule

If you're following along, bring up the Librarian application. The first thing we want to do is put a constraint on our table—one that prevents the entry of a duplicate title. We can do this by modifying the `CreateDataSource()` method in Library.cs. We want to add one line to the code that creates the bookmarks table.

```
DataTable bookmarks = new DataTable("Bookmarks");
bookmarks.Columns.Add("Id", typeof(Int32));
```

```
bookmarks.Columns.Add("Title", typeof(string));
bookmarks.Columns.Add("Uri", typeof(string));
bookmarks.Columns.Add("Category", typeof(string));
bookmarks.Columns.Add("LastMod", typeof(DateTime));
bookmarks.Constraints.Add("UniqueTitle", bookmarks.Columns[1], false);
```

The last line is the new one. It says is that the value in column 1 (`"Title"`) must be unique for all rows in the table. If you add that and run the application, when you hit add and type in a duplicate name, the value won't get set (figure 12.17).

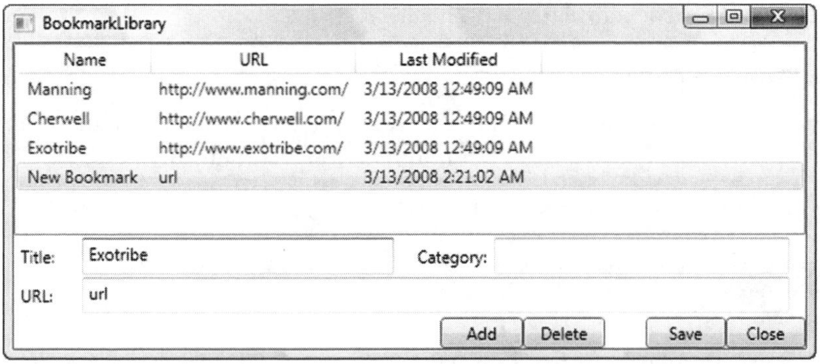

Figure 12.17 Even though we've entered a value for Title and left the control, the `DataTable` won't allow the entry, so the Name stays as the default.

Even though we've tabbed out of the Title control, the Name in the list isn't updated because, when an attempt is made to set a Title to a duplicate value, the `Constraint` throws an exception. This is good because it stops an illegal value from being set; but it's less good that the user gets no obvious feedback—if the list were not displayed, the user would never know that the value was invalid.

Fortunately, there's a built-in mechanism for handling validation and informing the user that an error has occurred. As part of a binding, you can specify any number of validation rules, and there's even a handy one built in for responding to exceptions. We can specify that it be used by updating the binding on our `TextBox`.

```
<TextBox>
  <Binding Path="Title">
    <Binding.ValidationRules>
      <ExceptionValidationRule/>
    </Binding.ValidationRules>
  </Binding>
</TextBox>
```

Now, if the user enters a duplicate name, when the user leave the `TextBox`, the exception validation rule will cause an alternative error template to be defined. The default error template puts a red border around the `TextBox` (figure 12.18).

We have to give kudos to the WPF team for providing some reasonable default behavior here. But, one flaw with the default behavior is that, although it tells you that

Figure 12.18 The Title `TextBox` now has a red border indicating that the value entered isn't valid.

something is wrong, it doesn't tell you *what.* Fortunately, it's relatively easy for us to provide our own error template to do just that.

12.5.2 Custom ErrorTemplates

Somewhere in the bowels of WPF is the resource for a default error template that defines the red-border behavior. That template looks something like this:

```
<ControlTemplate x:Key="defaultErrorTemplate">
  <Border BorderThickness="1" BorderBrush="Red">
    <AdornedElementPlaceholder Name="controlWithError"  />
  </Border>
</ControlTemplate>
```

This is a fairly standard control template. The one thing that is a little special is the `AdornedElementPlaceholder`. This is sort of like a `ContentPresenter`—it's where the element that has the error will be placed—so a red border will be put around whatever has the problem. If we want to create our own—say, to put in a blue border, we can define our own template in our own resources.

```
<Window.Resources>
  <ControlTemplate x:Key="customErrorTemplate">
    <Border BorderThickness="1" BorderBrush="Blue">
      <AdornedElementPlaceholder Name="controlWithError"  />
    </Border>
  </ControlTemplate>
</Window.Resources>
```

Then, we specify that it should be used as part of our binding.

```
<TextBox Validation.ErrorTemplate="{StaticResource customErrorTemplate}">
  <Binding Path="Title">
    <Binding.ValidationRules>
      <ExceptionValidationRule/>
    </Binding.ValidationRules>
  </Binding>
</TextBox>
```

Now, when we run, we'll get a blue border instead of a red one, although, given the black-and-white nature of the book, we aren't going to bother doing another screenshot. Beside anything else, we haven't really improved the situation—a blue border doesn't tell us any more about the error than the red border did. Let's create a more complex template—one that provides a little more information (listing 12.12).

Listing 12.12 A fancier custom error template

```
<Window.Resources>
  <ControlTemplate x:Key="customErrorTemplate">
    <DockPanel LastChildFill="True">
      <TextBlock DockPanel.Dock="Right" FontSize="20" Foreground="Red"
          ToolTip="{Binding ElementName=controlWithError,
          Path=AdornedElement.(Validation.Errors)[0].ErrorContent}"
          Margin="0,1,0,0" >*</TextBlock>
      <Border BorderThickness="1" BorderBrush="DarkRed">
        <AdornedElementPlaceholder Name="controlWithError"  />
      </Border>
    </DockPanel>
  </ControlTemplate>
</Window.Resources>
```

❶ (DockPanel)
❷ Asterisk with ToolTip
❸ Control with red border

The idea behind this template is to put a large asterisk to the right of the control. If the user floats over the asterisk, he gets a tooltip with the error message displayed. To make this work, we start with a `DockPanel` ❶ holding two controls—a `TextBlock` with an asterisk ❷ that's docked right, and our familiar red border with its placeholder ❸. Because it doesn't have docking set, it will take up the remaining available space.

The big scary bit in this code is the way that we get the text for the tooltip.

```
ToolTip="{Binding ElementName=controlWithError,
             Path=AdornedElement.(Validation.Errors)[0].ErrorContent}"
```

The element that the data is coming from is the *adorned element*—the `TextBox` that has the error. Because of the error that's occurred, an attached property has been associated with the `TextBox`. The parenthesis notation references an attached property `(Validation.Errors)`. But, this property is an array, so we need to get the first element out of the array `([0])`; the property we want from the first element is the `ErrorContent`. See, nothing to it! Don't ask us how long we spent figuring it out…

Now, if we run again and enter a duplicate, the application is much more helpful (figure 12.19).

This setup is kind of like the `InfoProvider` capability of WinForms. In fact, if this were a production app, we'd probably use an icon like the `InfoProvider` rather than an asterisk. Also, rather than explicitly assigning our error template to each individual control, we'd use a style—something like:

```
<Style TargetType="TextBox">
  <Setter Property="Validation.ErrorTemplate"
                         Value="{StaticResource customErrorTemplate}"/>
</Style>
```

Figure 12.19 Our new custom error template puts an asterisk at the end of the `TextBox`. If you float over the asterisk, you get a `Tooltip` with the details of the error.

This would make any validated text box use our new custom error template, but this is all based on the idea that the data source will throw an exception when something goes wrong. That isn't always the case.

12.5.3 Custom validation rules

When you have a well-defined data model, the model will always protect itself. But, a well-defined model is often not the case. In fact, our `DataTable` is a good example of where making the model defend itself properly isn't realistically possible—you can set up some simple constraints, but the `DataTable` has no facility for complex rules. In this situation, we need to provide some custom validation logic. We can do this by writing a custom `ValidationRule`.

`ValidationRules` are simple. Like converters, `ValidationRules` take a data object, analyze it in some way, and return a result. The result object contains the result of the validation and, optionally, a description of what's wrong. Ideally, the description should tell the user exactly what's wrong with the input. For example, we allow the user to enter a URI. We might want to make sure that what the user enters is a valid URI. To do that, we'd create a URI validation rule (listing 12.13).

Listing 12.13 A custom URI validation rule

```
using System;
using System.Windows.Controls;
namespace Librarian
{
  public class UriRule : ValidationRule                          <-- 1 Derives from ValidationRule
  {
    public override ValidationResult Validate(object value,
               System.Globalization.CultureInfo cultureInfo)    <-- 2 Validates method
    {
      bool uriIsValid = false;
      string message;
      try
      {
        Uri uri = new Uri((string)value, UriKind.Absolute);     <-- 3 Invalid URI throws an exception
        uriIsValid = true;
        message = "URI is valid";
      }
      catch (Exception ex)
      {
        message = ex.Message;
      }
        return new ValidationResult(uriIsValid, message);       <-- 4 Returns result
    }
  }
}
```

Our new rule is derived from the `ValidationRule` class ❶ and overrides the `Validate` method ❷. The validation itself relies on the `Uri` class, which will throw an exception if an invalid URI is specified ❸. If no exception is thrown, we assume that our URI is okay.

Otherwise, we get the message from the thrown exception. In either case, we wrap the result (success or failure) and the message into a `ValidationResult` object ❹.

Unlike the approach we used with converters, we don't need to create an instance of the class as a resource. To use it, we can reference it directly in the binding's validation rules.

```
<TextBox Margin="0,0,10,0" >
  <TextBox.Text>
    <Binding Path="Uri">
      <Binding.ValidationRules>
        <local:UriRule/>
      </Binding.ValidationRules>
    </Binding>
  </TextBox.Text>
</TextBox>
```

Now, when we run, if we enter a bogus URI, we get an error (figure 12.20).

Figure 12.20 Our custom validator yells at us if the URI isn't legal.

You can also combine `Validators`. For example, if we want to display an error if the URI isn't legal *or* if an exception is thrown, we can add an additional validation rule.

```
<Binding.ValidationRules>
  <local:UriRule/>
  <ExceptionValidationRule/>
</Binding.ValidationRules>
```

Overall, the validation model is pretty flexible, although life is still much simpler if your data model enforces rules! In general, by mixing what you can do with styles, data templates, binding, and validation, you can create very complex applications very quickly. In fact, this approach is at the heart of WPF, and is called *Model-View-ViewModel*.

12.6 Model-View-ViewModel

Before we go into binding any more, we think it might be worth mentioning a new design pattern that Microsoft has put forth—one built around the idea of binding. You're probably familiar with the traditional Model-View-Controller pattern (MVC), as shown in figure 12.21.

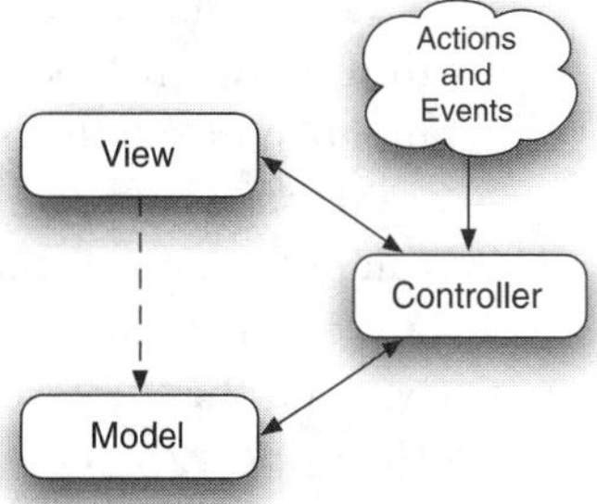

Figure 12.21 In the classic MVC pattern, the Model represents the data, the View represents the UI elements for presenting the data, and the Controller handles events from the user *and* adapts the model as appropriate to the needs of the View(s).

MVC has been around since the late 1970s. The Model is your data source—some set of business objects or even a straight representation of your data—although, ideally, the Model maintains its own data integrity (that is, it doesn't let you set bogus values). The View (or Views) is responsible for the presentation—usually some set of widgets. In theory, there can be any number of views on the same set of data; there could be forms, grids, graphs, and so on.

The purpose of the Controller is twofold. First, it's responsible for taking input from the user (menu commands, for example) and making sure that the UI and the model respond appropriately. Second, it's responsible for mapping between the View and the Model—doing conversions and combining data in various ways as appropriate.

The most important aspect of all this stuff is to keep a clear separation between the Model and the View. It's OK for the View to pull data directly from the Model, but it's strictly forbidden for the Model to know anything about the View (or the Controller, for that matter). The purpose of the Controller is to make this separation possible. Because there are a lot of ways of doing this, there are a lot of variations of the MVC pattern.

In fact, when teaching this stuff, we often find that developers don't really know what the Controller is for; it's like the spleen—everyone has one, and it's important for something, but we aren't really sure for what. There's a reason for this confusion—as the development frameworks have evolved, they've taken on more and more of the responsibility of Controllers themselves—particularly the event and command handling aspects. When you *do* need to do some form of mapping (say, splitting the data from an address field into several different pieces), it isn't always clear where to do it.

The Model-View-ViewModel (MVVM) pattern came out of an understanding of this issue. In MVVM, the Model and the View(s) are exactly the same as in classic MVC. But, rather than there being a single Controller object, the responsibility for what the Controller used to do is split up. For example, many frameworks, including WPF, take care of input and command handling automatically, without requiring a Controller.

And what about the responsibility for converting and massaging data back and forth between Model and View? Well, instead of a single object for that, there's any number of smaller objects that take over the responsibility. These are objects that we've been using all along—`Bindings`. Although a View element (such as a control) can pull a value from the Model, it can also have a `Binding` defined between the two. Although you don't have to explicitly create it, a `Binding` is a real object that exists between the View element and some part of the Model—sort of like a baby Controller (figure 12.22).

The MVVM pattern is only workable if there's a fairly robust binding-like mechanism available—ideally one that does a lot of work automatically, or else you'd end up spending all your time building connectors for everything. In WPF, you just declare the behavior you want, usually in XAML. You only have to write code for specialized situations—when you have to convert the data's format, or combine values, that sort of thing. The nice thing is that the converters that you build can be reused; and, once you have a library of them, you often just have to find the one you need, and you're done.

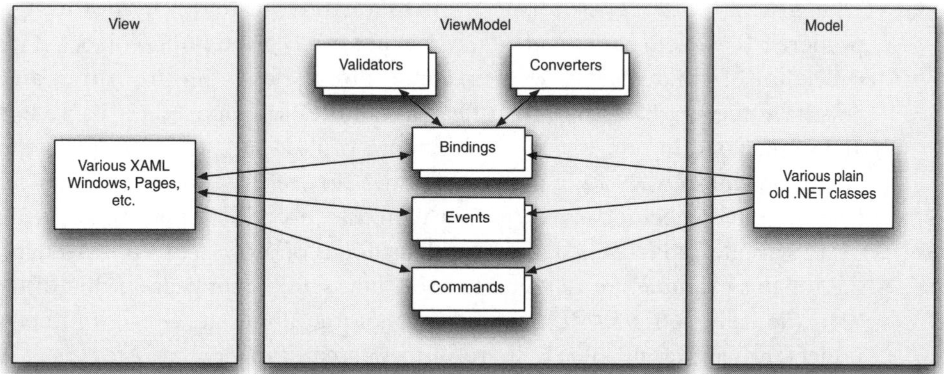

Figure 12.22 In the Model-View-ViewModel pattern, the Model and the View are the same as in classic the MVC pattern. But, the Controller is replaced by a combination of underlying framework support, commands, and a number of "mini" Controllers that provide specific bits of Controller functionality. These mini-Controllers are often `Bindings` that have been automatically created by WPF.

Given the atrophying of the Controller in recent frameworks, but the clear need for a consistent place to mediate between the Model and the View, we think that the MVVM pattern is a pretty good one. The one downside we see with the pattern is that it's somewhat tricky to debug (particularly with the automatically created objects), and responsibility is a little more confusing (OK—two downsides). But, without a pattern like MVVM, the WPF declarative model wouldn't really be possible.

We won't reference the MVVM pattern a whole lot, although we'll be using it. In the next section, you'll see examples of specialized bindings, where the framework provides automatic mediation between Model and View for complex situations (such as with hierarchical binding) or situations where custom mediation is needed (such as with `MultiBinding` and `PriorityBinding`.)

12.7 Advanced binding capabilities

Binding is an incredibly wide topic—which explains why it makes up the two longest chapters in the book. In addition to the powerful binding notations, there are a number of specialized classes for handling specific situations such as when you have hierarchical data or when you need to bind a number of different values to a single control. In this section, we'll explore some of these classes and capabilities.

12.7.1 Hierarchical binding

Data is only useful to the extent to which it can be found. One of the primary ways we find and classify information is through the use of hierarchies. The Windows registry and filesystem are both examples of using hierarchies to classify, store, and find information. XML (and, therefore, XAML) are both storage systems for such forms of information as well. WPF provides for binding to information stored in this way through the use of `HierarchicalDataTemplates`.

HierarchicalDataTemplates differ from flat templates primarily through a single property: ItemsSource. The idea here is that for any given bound object, it may have a collection of child objects. (For example, directories have directories, and registry keys have registry keys, and great fleas have little fleas upon their backs to bite 'em, and so on, ad infinitum.) ItemsSource allows you to specify what property you need to get to the children. By adding this property, HierarchicalDataTemplates can go into a bound data object recursively. Other than that, everything about standard DataTemplates applies, so for this sample, we'll just focus on how to use ItemsSource.

For this example, we're going to use a new sample application that displays some XML (actually, some XAML). If you're following along, go ahead and create a new project called XamlBrowser. In resources, create an XmlDataProvider. We aren't going to load it in the XAML yet, though.

```
<Window.Resources>
  <XmlDataProvider x:Key="xaml" />
</Window.Resources>
```

Next, set up three columns for our traditional "LeftNav" UI. Drop a TreeView on the left column, and a TextBox on the right, with a splitter in the middle (figure 12.23).

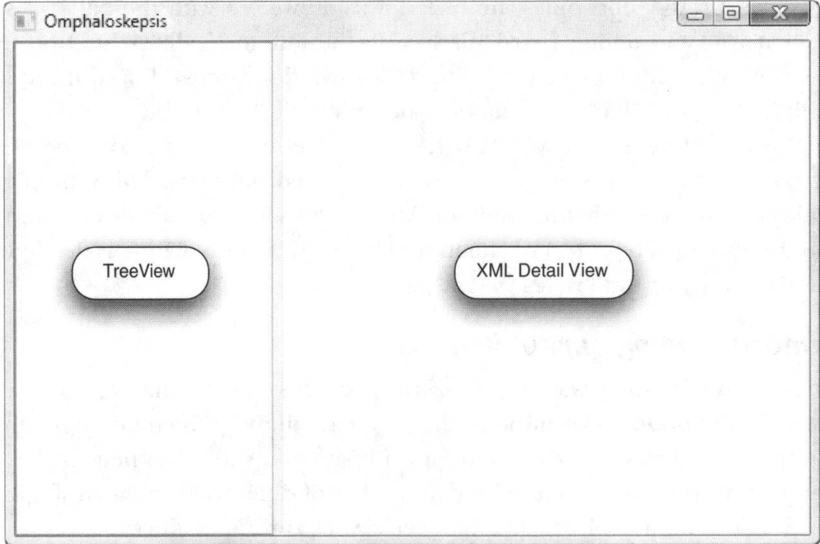

Figure 12.23 Creating a simple "LeftNav" application with a Tree on the left, a splitter in the middle and a TextBox on the right.

Now we need to give the XmlDataProvider some XML. Conveniently enough, our own program is a treasure trove of XML. Double-click the title bar of the window to create a Window_Loaded event, and enter the following code:

```
private void Window_Loaded(object sender, RoutedEventArgs e)
{
```

```
    XmlDocument doc = new XmlDocument();
    doc.LoadXml(XamlWriter.Save(this));

    XmlDataProvider provider = (XmlDataProvider)FindResource("xaml");
    provider.Document = doc;
    provider.Refresh();
}
```

We're just creating an `XmlDocument`, loading our own `Window`'s XAML into it, and then setting the `XmlDataProvider` to our program. Pretty clever, eh?

Now we're ready to populate the `TreeView`:

```
<TreeView Grid.Column="0" Name="treeView1"
  ItemsSource="{Binding Source={StaticResource xaml}, XPath=*}">
</TreeView>
```

The data source for the root of the tree is the `"xaml"` static resource we declared earlier. Because we populated it during the `Window_Loaded` event, it will have data for us. Using the splat `XPath` (*splat* is geek speak for asterisk) selects all the root nodes. You may remember the `XPath` binding property from the previous chapter. Note that the *`ItemsSource`* here is only providing data for the tree. It's the `ItemsSource` that we'll be setting on our template in a moment that's special.

Now that we're tied to data, we need to provide an appropriate template to use. We'll set this directly on the tree.

```
<TreeView.ItemTemplate>
  <HierarchicalDataTemplate ItemsSource="{Binding XPath=*}">
    <TextBlock Text="{Binding Path=Name}" />
  </HierarchicalDataTemplate>
</TreeView.ItemTemplate>
```

The template here is like any other template, *except* for the `ItemsSource`. The tree is bound to an `ItemsSource`, which returns a list of nodes—but how does each node get its children? The answer is that it has its own `ItemsSource`, which knows to pull a set of children of its own. Each child then has its *own* `ItemsSource`, and so on, ad infinitum. Figure 12.24 shows what's going on.

In our example, we're only providing one data template, and that template will be used no matter what the type of child. But, we could also use a `DataTemplateSelector` to provide a different template for different values, and the different templates could get their children in different ways.

We're done populating the nodes for the tree—we're only displaying the node name, but we could have done anything we liked here, making things as ugly as our Process Monitor, for example. But, we also want to display something in the text box on the right. We'll bind that to the outer XML of the currently selected node.

```
<TextBox Grid.Column="2" TextWrapping="Wrap"
  Text="{Binding ElementName=treeView1, Path=SelectedItem.OuterXml,
     Mode=OneWay}" />
```

That's pretty much it. If we run the application now, we've created a perfect navel-gazing application that looks at itself (figure 12.25).

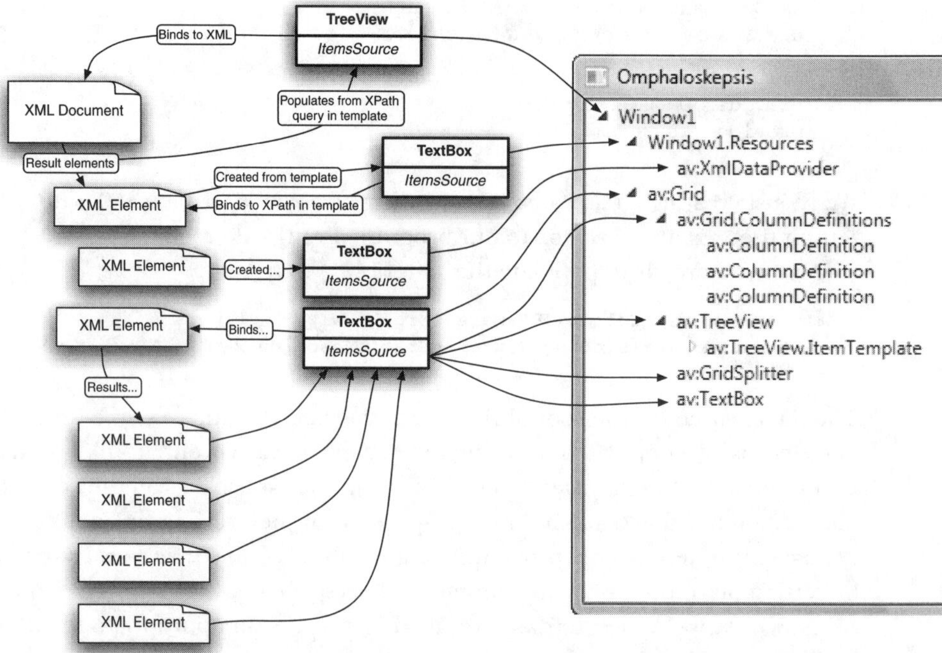

Figure 12.24 Each node in the tree uses a template, which knows how to get its children via the `ItemsSource` property.

The `XMLDataProvider` makes displaying XML extremely easily, and the use of templates allows for a lot of flexibility in the way each node is displayed, as well as the way that children are retrieved. Make sure that you don't point the nested `ItemsSource` at a static data source, though, unless you want to go horribly recursive.

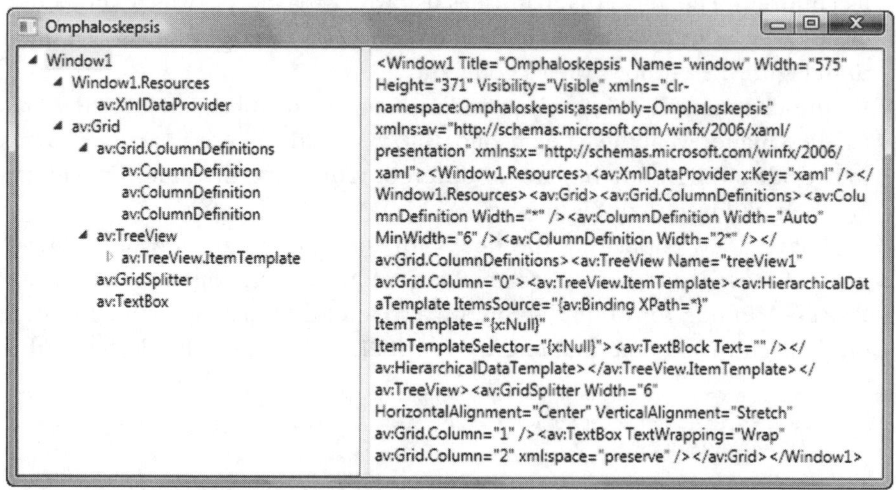

Figure 12.25 The XML browser application looks at its own XAML hierarchically.

Even with hierarchical binding, we're still only binding a single value to a single user. In the next section, we'll show how you can combine a number of values in various ways.

12.7.2 MultiBinding

In the `ValueConverter` examples so far, we've taken a single value (such as a size) and converted it into another single value (such as a color). There are times, though, when you want to use multiple values together. For example, you might have several fields in your data model that represent an address (address 1, city, state, and zip) that you want to combine into a single entry in a grid.

That's precisely what `MultiBinding` lets you do—it lets you take a number of values and combine them (somehow) into a single value. But, when you have multiple values, there's no *default* way of shoving things together. There are two ways of specifying the way to combine the values—by either using a `StringFormat` or by providing a converter that combines the values in some way. The converter is more interesting, so we'll start with that first.

The converter must be derived from `IMultiValueConverter` and is very similar to a converter derived from `IValueConverter` except that, instead of having a single value as an argument, it takes multiple arguments. Let's set up an example. Figure 12.26 shows the basic layout for an application that has three sliders—one each for Red, Green, and Blue. We've put a `Grid` panel at the bottom that will change color based on the position of the sliders.

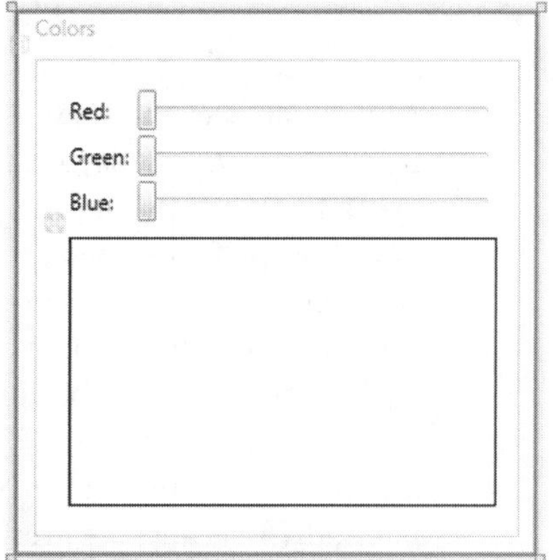

Figure 12.26 The controls for our `MultiBinding` example. The three sliders will allow the color of the `Grid` at the bottom to be changed.

Go ahead and create a new sample application (ours is called ColorConverter), and set it up to look like figure 12.26. The three sliders have minimum/maximum values of 0/255, and are called redSlider, greenSlider, and blueSlider (you get to guess which is which). The `Grid` panel is called colorBlock. You'll see why we used a `Grid` in a while, but for now, it's just a convenient thing whose background color can be changed.

Before we can go much further, we need to create our `MultiValueConverter` that will take the values from each of the three sliders and convert them into a single color. Listing 12.14 shows the code for our converter.

Listing 12.14 `MultiValueConverter`

```
using System;
using System.Windows.Data;
using System.Windows.Media;
```

```
namespace ColorConverter
{
  class ColorMultiConverter : IMultiValueConverter         ❶
  {
    public object Convert(object[] values, Type targetType,
         object parameter, System.Globalization.CultureInfo culture)
    {
      byte R = System.Convert.ToByte((double)values[0]);
      byte G = System.Convert.ToByte((double)values[1]);
      byte B = System.Convert.ToByte((double)values[2]);

      Color newColor = Color.FromRgb(R, G, B);

      return newColor;
    }

    public object[] ConvertBack(object value, Type[] targetTypes,
         object parameter, System.Globalization.CultureInfo culture)
    {
      throw new NotImplementedException();
    }
  }
}
```

❷ **Convert method**

❸ **Retrieves values**

❹ **Converts values**

❺ **ConvertBack method**

As you can see, this class is similar to an `IValueConverter`, except that it's derived from `IMultiValueConverter` ❶ and the `Convert` method ❷ gets an array of objects instead of a single object. The converter assumes that three double values will be passed as the first three arguments of the array ❸. If the binding was done incorrectly, we might not get three doubles—we could get pretty much anything, which would cause this code to crash.

But, assuming the binding is done right, we'll get three values that we convert to bytes and then use to build up a color value ❹. As with most converters, the implementation is pretty simple. Note that we didn't bother implementing the `ConvertBack` method ❺ because we aren't using it. It would be pretty simple to do, though—we'd have to pull the R, G, and B values out of the color passed as the value, and return them as a collection of values.

Now that we have a `MultiValue` converter, we need to create an instance of it in a XAML resource (again, as with a regular `ValueConverter`):

```
<Window x:Class="ColorConverter.Window1"
  xmlns="http://schemas.microsoft.com/winfx/2006/xaml/presentation"
  xmlns:x="http://schemas.microsoft.com/winfx/2006/xaml"
  xmlns:local="clr-namespace:ColorConverter"
  Title="Colors" Height="300" Width="300">
  <Window.Resources>
    <local:ColorMultiConverter x:Key="colorConverter"/>
  </Window.Resources>
  ...
```

We put in the main `Window` tag to remind you to put in the local namespace. Then we instantiate the converter as a resource with a name. Now, we can go ahead and do our multibinding.

```
<Grid Name="colorBlock" >
  <Grid.Background>
    <SolidColorBrush>
      <SolidColorBrush.Color>
        <MultiBinding Converter="{StaticResource colorConverter}">
          <Binding ElementName="redSlider" Path="Value"/>
          <Binding ElementName="greenSlider" Path="Value"/>
          <Binding ElementName="blueSlider" Path="Value"/>
        </MultiBinding>
      </SolidColorBrush.Color>
    </SolidColorBrush>
  </Grid.Background>
</Grid>
```

We're binding to the color of a solid brush for the background of the `Grid`. Instead of a single binding, though, we have a `MultiBinding` element. The `Converter` property takes the reference to our `MultiValueConverter`. The children of the `MultiBinding` element are all regular `Bindings`. The `MultiBinding` will get the value from each binding in turn, put them into an array, and pass that array to our converter, which will return a single value back—a color. If you slide the sliders back and forth, the color in the `Grid` will change automatically (figure 12.27).

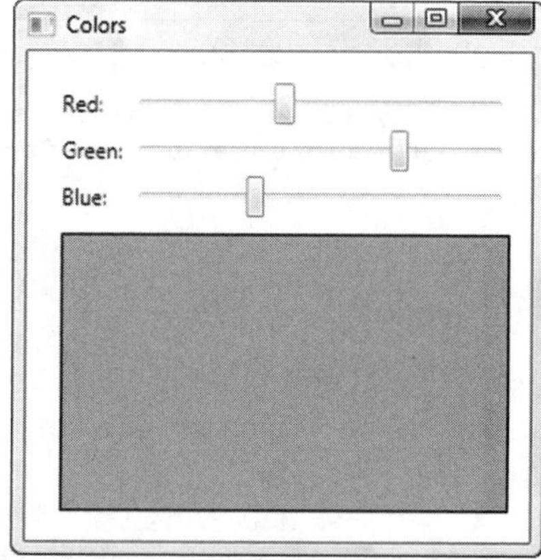

Figure 12.27 When any of the sliders are moved, the multibinding automatically updates the color of the `Grid`.

The converter doesn't care where it gets its values, so we could've easily had text boxes with numbers or any other type of UI. Over time, you'll probably end up with a fairly significant library of `IValueConverters` and `IMultiValueConverters` that you can plug in as needed.

MULTIVALUE PARAMETERS

As with `IValueConverters`, `IMultiValueConverter` can take a parameter to change its behavior. We've come up with a need to do this with our sample—adding a `Label` to the `Grid` to display the color. We've set the label up to be centered and bound its value to the color of the background of the `Grid`:

```
<Label Name="label4" HorizontalContentAlignment="Center"
   VerticalContentAlignment="Center" >
  <Label.Content>
    <Binding ElementName="colorBlock" Path="Background.Color"/>
  </Label.Content>
</Label>
```

Simple enough—but as you can see in figure 12.28, there's a slight problem.

Aside from the fact that we're displaying the ultra-friendly *hex* version of our color, an observant reader might notice a problem reading the text when the text color and the background are the same. To work around this, we could create *another*

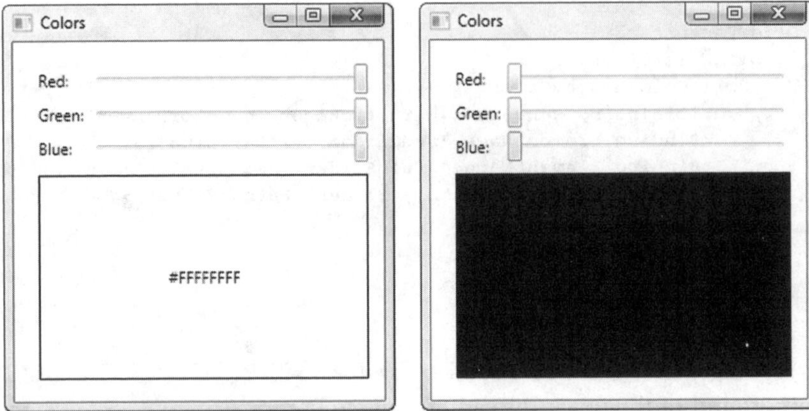

Figure 12.28 When the color is white, we can read the color; but, when the color is black, our display turns ultra-Goth and is completely unreadable.

MultiValueConverter that takes the colors and produces a color that's visible on the particular background, or we could pass a parameter to our existing converter telling it to create an inverse color.

The following XAML binds the foreground color of the label in exactly the same way as the background of our color block—except that it passes a parameter:

```
<Label.Foreground>
  <SolidColorBrush>
    <SolidColorBrush.Color>
      <MultiBinding Converter="{StaticResource colorConverter}"
             ConverterParameter="inverse">
        <Binding ElementName="redSlider" Path="Value"/>
        <Binding ElementName="greenSlider" Path="Value"/>
        <Binding ElementName="blueSlider" Path="Value"/>
      </MultiBinding>
    </SolidColorBrush.Color>
  </SolidColorBrush>
</Label.Foreground>
```

Note the `ConverterParameter="inverse"` attribute in the `MultiBinding` element. Now we have to modify the code in the converter to look for the parameter (listing 12.15).

Listing 12.15 `MultiValueConverter` with parameter

```
public object Convert(object[] values, Type targetType,
      object parameter, System.Globalization.CultureInfo culture)
{                                                    ❶ Checks for parameter
 bool inverse =(parameter != null) &&
         (string.Compare(parameter.ToString(), "inverse", true) == 0);

 byte R = System.Convert.ToByte((double)values[0]);
 byte G = System.Convert.ToByte((double)values[1]);
 byte B = System.Convert.ToByte((double)values[2]);

 Color newColor;                                     ❷ Creates
 if (inverse)                                          inverse color
```

```
    newColor = Color.FromRgb((byte)(255-R), (byte)(255-G), (byte)(255-B));
  else
    newColor = Color.FromRgb(R, G, B);

  return newColor;
}
```

We've added a check to see if a parameter has been passed and if the parameter is the string value "inverse" ❶. If it is, then we invert the color ❷ before returning it. Pretty easy. Now, when we run, we can always read the text (figure 12.29), although sometimes the colors are a little ugly.

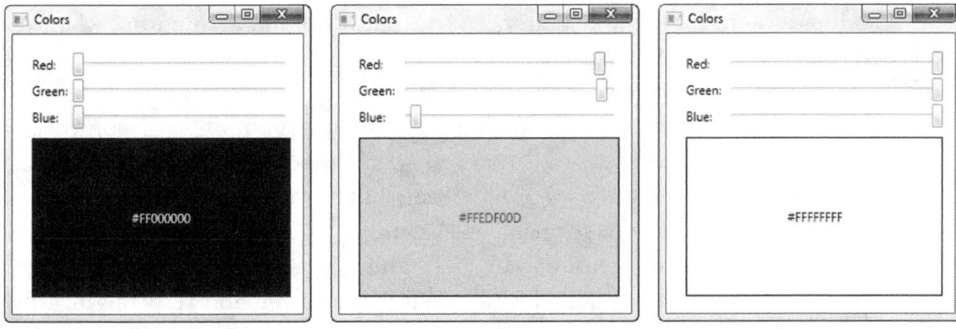

Figure 12.29 Using the parameter of the `MultiValueConverter`, we have the color of our label changing inversely to the color of the background. Better (or at least more diligent) coders might have come up with an algorithm that avoided uglier text colors.

We're passing a pretty simple parameter to get our result, but the parameter could be any value and could be used in any way by the converter.

One flaw with our display is that it's showing an ugly hex value for our color, whereas, for some colors at least, they have real names. (In our book, of course, the names will always be *black, white,* or *gray*—still not bitter about the color thing, though.) One way of cleaning this up is by using a `StringFormat` with our `MultiBinding`.

STRINGFORMAT AND MULTIBINDING

It isn't always necessary to build a converter to combine values in some way. You saw earlier how it's possible to format a single bound value using `StringFormat`;we can do the same thing with a `MultiBinding` (listing 12.16).

Listing 12.16 `StringFormat` with `MultiBinding`

```
<Label.Content>
  <TextBlock>                                         ❶
    <TextBlock.Text>
      <MultiBinding StringFormat="Red={0}, Green={1}, Blue={2}">   ❷ MultiBinding with StringFormat
        <Binding ElementName="redSlider" Path="Value"/>
        <Binding ElementName="greenSlider" Path="Value"/>
        <Binding ElementName="blueSlider" Path="Value"/>
      </MultiBinding>
```

```
      </TextBlock.Text>
    </TextBlock>
  </Label.Content>
```

The code replaces the `Label.Content` block from earlier. The `MultiBinding` should be familiar, except that we've added a `StringFormat` attribute ❷. As with a `String.Format`, the {0}, {1}, {2} values will be replaced at runtime with the first, second, and third values available—our red, green, and blue values.

You've probably also noticed that we put the `MultiBinding` inside a `TextBlock` inside the `Label` ❶. This seems silly, given that we could dump our text inside the `Label`'s content directly. But, there's a problem; `StringFormat` works when we're providing a bound value to a `Text` property, but it doesn't always work when our bound result is being used for `Content`.

`StringFormat` *does* work when used inline for a `Content` property, but we can't put a `MultiBinding` inline, so that doesn't help us. A number of controls, including `Label`, have a `ContentStringFormat` property that allow for the formatting of their content, no matter where it came from, but we can't use this either because the `MultiBinding`, without a format, isn't legal.

There are arcane reasons why `Text` and `Content` behave differently for formatting—which can be explained with much hand-waving and resorting to white boards at late-night Microsoft parties; but, to our limited imaginations, it should be considered a bug that needs to be corrected. And that's probably why we don't get invited to late-night Microsoft parties anymore.

Anyway, the easy way to avoid the problem is to shove in a control that *does* have a `Text` property inside the `Label`—and so we use the `TextBlock`.

Figure 12.30 shows the `StringFormat` in action.

The `StringFormat` could be considered an improvement on the display of the color, but we can probably do better—at least some of the time.

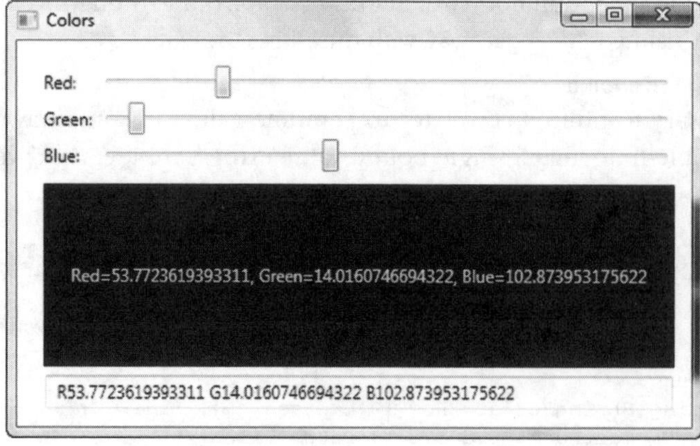

Figure 12.30 Using `StringFormat` to combine the values from a `MultiBinding`.

12.7.3 PriorityBinding

You know how, when you go to a web page, before a picture has been downloaded it first puts in a placeholder for the picture, then displays a brief description, and then finally displays the real image? Think about that as a binding scenario—you have a control that you want to eventually hold a picture. If you already had the picture, then you could bind to that picture and be done. But, because the picture will take a while to download, you don't have that option.

You *could* build some sort of generic store and bind to that and then have your own background code replace the value in that store whenever the data became available. In fact, that's probably the sort of thing that the browsers do. But, it seems that you have to circumvent the binding system to do that, rather than letting it handle things.

What you want is to provide a number of different sources for the item to display—the picture, the caption text, and the default image. If one isn't available, then the code can fall back on the next and so on. This scenario is precisely the type of problem that `PriorityBinding` was built to solve.

Another scenario where `PriorityBinding` is useful is when you have some form of scoping. If the user has specified a value, use that. If not, if the administrator specified a value, use that. If not, then use the default.

As with a `MultiBinding`, you can use a `PriorityBinding` in place of any regular `Binding`. The `PriorityBinding` contains a list of other bindings, which it steps through one at a time, until it gets one that returns data. Because of the underlying Property System, if one of the bindings eventually gets data (for example, the image is loaded), it will automatically update the property.

Because we have already got our color selector, let's use that for an example. Right now we're displaying the color as a hex value, but it would be nice if, when the selected color has a name, we displayed the name instead of the hex. We could build a single value converter that did one or the other, but that would limit us to whatever approach that converter took to format the value. This way we can have any number of converters in place, and the result will be displayed based on the "best" (or, at least, the first) display.

The first thing we'll need is a value converter that can take a color and tell us whether a color is a named color or not. The code in the converter (listing 12.17) is a little ugly because it uses reflection to determine whether a color is named or not; because that isn't really what we're writing about, we can live with a little ugly.

Listing 12.17 `ColorNameConverter`

```
using System;
using System.Collections.Generic;
using System.Windows.Data;
using System.Windows;
using System.Windows.Media;
using System.Reflection;

namespace ColorConverter
{
```

```
class ColorNameValueConverter : IValueConverter
{
  private Dictionary<Color, string> namedColors =                    ❶
                       new Dictionary<Color, string>();
  
  public ColorNameValueConverter()
  {
    PropertyInfo[] colorProperties =                                  ❷

 typeof(Colors).GetProperties(BindingFlags.Static|BindingFlags.Public);
    Color stepColor;
    foreach (PropertyInfo pi in colorProperties)
    {
      if (pi.PropertyType == typeof(Color))
      {
        stepColor = (Color)pi.GetValue(null, null);
        namedColors[stepColor] = pi.Name;
      }
    }
  }

  public object Convert(object value, Type targetType,
        object parameter, System.Globalization.CultureInfo culture)  ❸
  {
    Color col = (Color)value;
    if(namedColors.ContainsKey(col))
      return namedColors[col];

    return DependencyProperty.UnsetValue;  ❹
  }

  public object ConvertBack(object value, Type targetType,
        object parameter, System.Globalization.CultureInfo culture)
  {
    throw new NotImplementedException();
  }
 }
}
```

❶ **Dictionary of named colors**

❷ **Populates dictionary using reflection**

❸ **Convert method**

Unimplemented ConvertBack method

This code populates a dictionary ❶ of colors to names using reflection ❷. The convert method ❸ looks up the color in the dictionary and, if it's found, returns the color's name. If it isn't found, then a special value is returned—`DependencyProperty.UnsetValue` ❹. This value is interpreted by the binding system as "no value available" or, more succinctly, as "dunno." Note that returning `null` wouldn't be sufficient here. `Null` is a perfectly valid (albeit unhelpful) value.

As usual, we need to create an instance of our converter as a resource.

```
<Window.Resources>
  <local:ColorMultiConverter x:Key="colorConverter"/>
  <local:ColorNameValueConverter x:Key="colorNameConverter"/>
</Window.Resources>
```

We add our new converter underneath our multi converter. Now we can finally create our priority binding (listing 12.18).

Listing 12.18 PriorityBinding

```
<Label.Content>
  <PriorityBinding FallbackValue="Unknown">          ❶
    <Binding ElementName="colorBlock" Path="Background.Color"
             Converter="{StaticResource colorNameConverter}"/>   ❷
    <Binding ElementName="colorBlock" Path="Background.Color"/>   ❸
  </PriorityBinding>
</Label.Content>
```

As you can see, we replace single binding for the `Label`'s content with a `PriorityBinding` statement ❶. The `FallbackValue` is the value that will be used if *none* of the bindings in the `PriorityBinding` list return a value, but in our example, this will never happen.

We've ditched the `MultiValueBinding/StringFormat` to save space, although it would have worked if we wanted to keep the `TextBlock`. We've put back our original binding that returns the hex value ❸, but it's listed *second* in the list of bindings. That means that it will only be used if none of the bindings before it return a value. The first binding ❷ passes the background color to our new converter that will either return the name of a color or `DependencyProperty.UnsetValue`. If it returns `DependencyProperty.UnsetValue`, then the old binding will be used. Otherwise, the color name will be used. Figure 12.31 shows the priority binding in action.

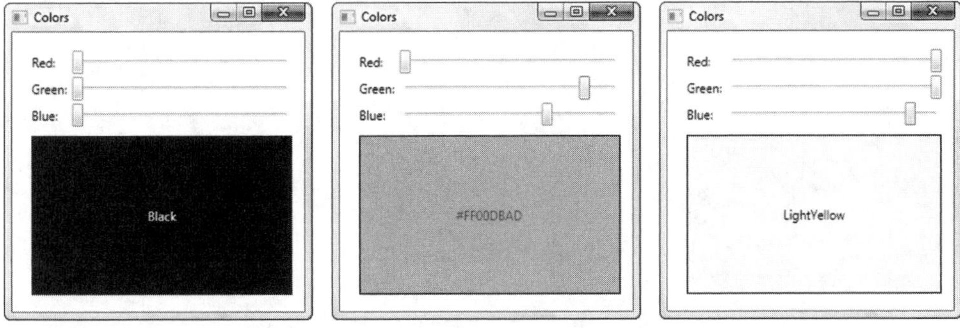

Figure 12.31 When a color is a named color, the highest priority binding, our named color converter provides the name. Otherwise, we fall back to our old hex autoconversion binding.

This example is a fairly trivial one, and obviously we could have done this *without* using a priority binding, but the priority binding makes this type of thing easy. It's particularly useful in the cases where an operation might take a long time—generally with that operation being done asynchronously.

Both `MultiBinding` and `PriorityBinding` are tools that you'll probably only use occasionally; but, when they are needed, they're handy. The binding system is quite thorough in this respect and provides a great deal of flexibility and power. We also like writing little applications for playing with colors, so these samples have been satisfying in that respect as well, but you'll probably be relieved to hear that this is the last topic on binding that we're going to cover (although you'll see binding throughout much of the rest of the book).

12.8 Summary

Binding is definitely here to stay. The benefits of using data binding, particularly in a system such as WPF, are simply too great to *not* make use of it. WPF's data binding is extremely rich and extremely powerful. This comes at a cost—it can sometimes be overly complex. At least in most cases, though, the complexity comes when you're trying to do complex things. Simple to medium-simple things tend to be quite easy to accomplish, once you get the right mindset.

This is good, considering that Microsoft's new model for development—Model-View-ViewModel—is only practical if you have a good binding system to base it on. So far, MVVM seems to be holding its own, although only time will tell if it's here to stay. When implemented correctly, it provides the appropriate separation between model and display and, via the use of data templates, allows for extremely complex presentation of the model.

Using raw data templates isn't your only option for displaying data or making it interactive. There are times when you need to build more complex controls—either by combining existing controls or by building something completely new—which is the topic of the next chapter.

13 Custom controls

This chapter covers:

- Creating user controls
- Creating custom controls
- Changing the template on custom controls
- Making a hyperlink happy and then sad

With Windows Forms, MFC, or even straight SDK programming, you often ended up building custom controls to create a particular look-and-feel or type of behavior that the built-in controls didn't provide. More often, though, you ended up *not* building custom controls, and making do with built-in behavior because building those controls was a royal pain. Building controls was generally all or nothing—either you used all the built-in handling or you built everything from scratch for your control.

WPF changes all that. First, you don't even need to bother building custom controls for most things because the system is so flexible—you can customize the look-and-feel of virtually every aspect of every control, as well as easily changing much of the behavior. Second, if you do need to do something special, you can often do it by combining existing elements (compositing) to get the behavior that you want.

There are still many situations, though, where it's more convenient to build the control once and reuse it, or where you want to do the low-level stuff for some custom behavior. You'll see both approaches throughout this chapter and the next. In the two main examples in this chapter, the `LinkLabel` control and the `ConditionalGroupBox`, we're really just combining existing elements and adding a few properties. In the next chapter, "Drawing," we'll start with this approach, but then build controls that do their own low-level drawing.

It's hard to talk about building custom controls as a standalone topic, because, by taking advantage of the compositional nature of WPF, new "controls" are created all the time. HTML has some similar capabilities via the use of templates, but not to the same scale.

One thing is for sure—WPF is going to change the landscape for third-party control vendors. One of the primary justifications for third-party control libraries is the time and money saved by not having to implement difficult-to-achieve behaviors. WPF lowers the bar for what *difficult-to-achieve* means. Although we know third-party controls vendors aren't going away, they'll necessarily have to start producing much more sophisticated controls by leveraging the power of WPF themselves. Vendors will still add a lot of things. (For example, do a search for WPF grid controls.) In fact, there's now a whole new market for vendors to fill—building nice-looking styles and effects that can be plugged into WPF applications.

Vendors aside, there are lots of situations where developers will want to build custom controls for use in-house. WPF provides three methods to create reusable controls:

- *User controls*—The simplest form of WPF reusability. User controls might also be called *aggregate controls* or *control collections.* User controls are the preferred way of avoiding cutting and pasting identical XAML across your applications. User controls aren't intended for commercial re-use, and are fairly limited. For example, they lack template support, so you may need to implement a full custom control.
- *Custom controls*—Custom controls are more complex to create, but allow for most of the functionality missing from a user control, such as templates and themes. Many of the controls in WPF derive from `Control`, so this approach is generally flexible enough for most uses. In WPF, a proper control has no "look," so controls tend to be focused on behavior. Custom controls also define the command handling (for example, cut, copy, and paste) and dependency properties and events.
- `FrameworkElement` *controls*—Sometimes you need to do something more low-level, where you do your own drawing and interaction behavior. In these situations, the built-in stuff for `CustomControl` or `UserControl` gets in your way. Instead, you can derive from a lower-level class, such as `FrameworkElement`, which still gives you support for things like `DependencyProperties`, but doesn't have a lot of built-in behavior.

In this chapter, we're concentrating on user and custom controls; in the next chapter, we'll demonstrate building a lower-level control that does graphing.

13.1 Composing new user controls

Building new controls from existing controls is the most common form of control reuse. For the next section, go ahead and create a new WPF application called ControlsInAction. This is where we'll test our new controls.

13.1.1 Building a LinkLabel control

The built-in `Hyperlink` class in WPF is nice and all, but sometimes it's a bit *too* flexible. For example, in the context of an XBAP or Silverlight application, it will respond to its `RequestNavigate` by going to a web page, but, in a standalone WPF application, `RequestNavigate` is undefined—which is sensible because we may be navigating within the application, but a hassle when we have to continuously reimplement the event handler every time we use it.

Also, the `Hyperlink` isn't a control, but a `Span`, and so it can't be used in all the places you can use a control. Often (but not always), it has to be hosted in something like a `TextBlock` or `FlowDocument`—also a pain if we only want to shove a link onto a form somewhere. We just want a nice simple control that lets us specify the text for a link and where you go when the link is clicked—we can always use the `Hyperlink` if we need more.

We could implement a `LinkLabel` control in a couple different ways, but the approach we're going to take is to build a user control that holds a *real* `Hyperlink`, but exposes some simple properties to make it easier to use. For our new `LinkLabel` control, we're going to want two properties:

- *`Text`*—The text to display for the link
- *`URI`*—Where to navigate to when the link is clicked

We want both of these properties to be bindable so that we can use the new control in the context of an application data-binding target.

In your new application, right-click your project and select Add User Control. Name the new control `LinkLabel`. In the designer, you'll now be faced with something similar to what you see when you create a new application, but there's no window frame around it (figure 13.1).

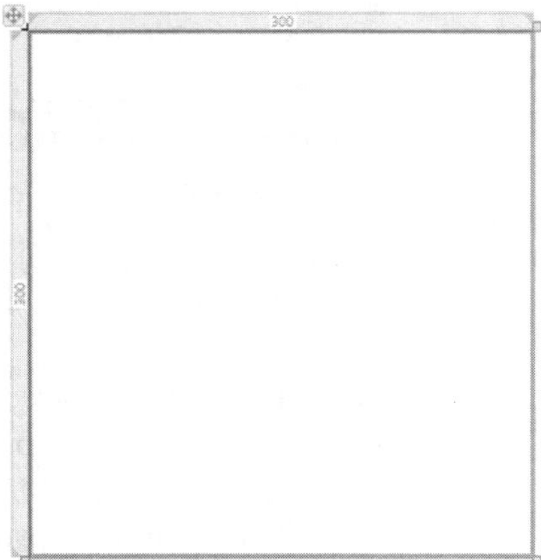

Figure 13.1 Initially the `UserControl` is an empty 300x300 `Grid`, as seen in the designer.

We don't really need the `Grid` at all, and the `Hyperlink` isn't available in the Toolbox, so we need to go to the XAML to set up this control. Most user controls will consist of a number of controls put together with a layout, but ours is just a specialized `Hyperlink` with predefined behavior. Remove the `Grid` elements from the

XAML, and replace them with a Hyperlink. Let Visual Studio help you by creating the event handler when you set the RequestNavigate attribute.

```
<Hyperlink Name="webLink" RequestNavigate="Hyperlink_RequestNavigate" />
```

Next, get rid of the Width and Height of the user control. We want the LinkLabel to take up only the space that it needs to display the Hyperlink. Now your XAML should look like this:

```
<UserControl x:Class="ControlsInAction.LinkLabel"
    xmlns="http://schemas.microsoft.com/winfx/2006/xaml/presentation"
    xmlns:x="http://schemas.microsoft.com/winfx/2006/xaml">
  <Hyperlink Name="webLink" RequestNavigate="Hyperlink_RequestNavigate" />
</UserControl>
```

All you'll see in the designer is a vertical bar with crosses on each end. This is OK because there's nothing for it to display. Now it's all about the code. Right-click the LinkLabel.xaml file and select View Code. Because we want to use this control to bind to URIs, the first thing we'll need are properties for the text of the link and the URI itself (listing 13.1).

Listing 13.1 Adding dependency properties to LinkLabel.xaml.cs

```
public static readonly DependencyProperty TextProperty =      ❶ Establishes custom dependency property
  DependencyProperty.Register("Text", typeof(string),
  typeof(LinkLabel), new FrameworkPropertyMetadata(           ❷ Uses metadata to create callback
   new PropertyChangedCallback(OnTextChanged)));

public string Text     ❸ No backing field
{
  get { return (string)GetValue(TextProperty); }
  set { SetValue(TextProperty, value); }
}

public static readonly DependencyProperty UriProperty =       ❹ URI property
  DependencyProperty.Register("Uri", typeof(string),
  typeof(LinkLabel),
  new FrameworkPropertyMetadata(new
   PropertyChangedCallback(OnUriChanged)));

public string Uri
{
  get { return (string)GetValue(UriProperty); }
  set { SetValue(UriProperty, value); }
}
```

This is rather more involved than the old field with a getter and setter for a property that you might normally write in C#. The complexity is needed for the properties to play nice with the Property System.

Let's look at the Text property in detail—the Uri property is nearly identical ❹. If you look at the Text property declaration ❸, you'll see that getter and setters are calling GetValue and SetValue, rather than returning the value from some private member variable (technically referred to as a *backing field*) such as

```
private string textValue = "";
```

The GetValue and SetValue reference the dictionary of property values held by the object. To look things up in that dictionary, we have to have a key. Now, if the world were a simple place, that key would be a string of the name of the property or something like that, but the world isn't a simple place. The key used by the Property System has to do double duty—not only is it the key, but it also defines a whole bunch of behavior about the property; this behavior is held in an object of type DependencyProperty. By convention, the DependencyProperty is named *PropertyName*Property; in this case, the DependencyProperty is called TextProperty ❶.

Now, in its simplest form, the definition for a DependencyProperty can be *reasonably* straightforward. For example, we could do this:

```
public static readonly DependencyProperty TextProperty =
  DependencyProperty.Register("Text", typeof(string),typeof(LinkLabel));
```

The DependencyProperty key objects are almost always static members of the class that defines the property—they need to be static so that they exist before they're used, and so that the same instance is used by all code that references the property. To create a new DependencyProperty, the minimum we have to do is call the DependencyProperty's Register method and pass the name of the property (Text), the type of data held by the property (string), and the name of the class registering the property (LinkLabel).

But, we want to do one more thing than the minimum—we want to know whenever the value of the property has changed so that we can update our UI. One easy way to do this is to register an event handler with the property ❷. The notation for this is a little odd because the register method doesn't have an overload that takes the handler. Instead, we can pass a FrameworkPropertyMetadata object that describes additional things about the property, including a callback for when the property has changed.

Listing 13.2 shows the event handlers for when the Text and the Uri properties change.

Listing 13.2 Event handlers for property changes

```
private static void OnTextChanged(DependencyObject sender,     <--  Called when
  DependencyPropertyChangedEventArgs e)                             the Text
{                                                                   property
  LinkLabel label = (LinkLabel)sender;       ❷                  ❶ changes
  label.webLink.Inlines.Clear();
  label.webLink.Inlines.Add(new Run(e.NewValue.ToString()));     ❸
}

private static void OnUriChanged(DependencyObject sender,      <--  Called when
  DependencyPropertyChangedEventArgs e)                             the Uri
{                                                                   property
  LinkLabel label = (LinkLabel)sender;                          ❹ changes
  Uri newUri;
  try
  {
    newUri = new Uri(label.Uri);             ❺
    label.webLink.NavigateUri = newUri;
    label.webLink.ToolTip =
```

```
        String.Format("Open a new browser to {0}",(label.Uri));     ❻
  }
  catch(UriFormatException ex)
  {
    label.webLink.ToolTip = String.Format("{0} ({1})", ex.Message,     ❼
    label.Uri);
  }
}
```

`OnTextChanged()` ❶ is the event handler called when the `Text` property changes on our object. Notice that it's a static method—it has to be because the `DependencyProperty` is static. But, the specific instance whose `Text` property has changed is passed as the sender, which we can easily cast to be our `LinkLabel` ❷. The other thing passed to the handler is a `DependencyPropertyChangedEventArgs` object that has, among other things, the old and new values of the property.

At this point, we update the content of the `Hyperlink` to contain the new value of the property ❸. The `Hyperlink` makes us do this by updating its `Inlines` collection (which is part of the reason we decided we needed a custom control for `LinkLabel` in the first place). Note that we're accessing the private members of the `LinkLabel` here—we can do that because we are a static inside the same class.

The `OnUriChanged()` method ❹ is pretty similar. But, we have to do a few extra things to turn the `Uri` *string* of `LinkLabel` into the `Uri` *object* of `Hyperlink` ❺. Notice that we're doing the conversion in a try/catch because, if the UI string isn't legal, an exception will be thrown. We're also setting the tooltip of the link to show the underlying URI ❻, or an error message if it isn't legal ❼.

The last thing we need to do is handle the user clicking the link. You should already have a method defined called `Hyperlink_RequestNavigate`, so all we need is this one line:

```
private void Hyperlink_RequestNavigate(object sender,
                                        RequestNavigateEventArgs e)
{
  System.Diagnostics.Process.Start(e.Uri.ToString());
}
```

The `Hyperlink` control raises the `RequestNavigate` event, and sends a `Uri` along for the ride. This is a bit of a security nightmare because the user could enter any file:/// URI and potentially launch any process on the box. In reality, there are two things we wouldn't do; first, potentially acting upon user data without validating it and, second, making the decision to launch a process in a UI element. In a real-world application, the business logic should receive a command with the request to open a browser and navigate to a page and validate it. When you're developing a control, it's nice to be able to test it outside the context of an application. We'll do that next.

13.1.2 Testing the LinkLabel UserControl

Now that we have our control, we need a place to test it. Fortunately, we already created our test harness when we started the chapter. How convenient. So it's time to try this

Figure 13.2 Setting up a harness to test the `LinkLabel` `UserControl`

control. Open Window1.xaml and drag a couple of `TextBox` controls to it. In the first `TextBox`, set the `Text` property to Manning and, in the second `TextBox`, set the `Text` property to http://www.manning.com. You should now have something like figure 13.2.

Next, we need to add our local namespace to get access to our new `LinkLabel`, so add the `xmlns` line to Window1.xaml.

```
<Window x:Class="ControlsInAction.Window1"
    xmlns="http://schemas.microsoft.com/winfx/2006/xaml/presentation"
    xmlns:x="http://schemas.microsoft.com/winfx/2006/xaml"
    xmlns:local="clr-namespace:ControlsInAction"
    Title="Window1" Height="300" Width="500">
```

And add a `LinkLabel` bound to the test `TextBox` controls.

```
<Grid>
  <local:LinkLabel Margin="63,111,221,129"
     Text="{Binding ElementName=textBox1, Path=Text}"
     Uri="{Binding ElementName=textBox2, Path=Text}" />
  <TextBox Margin="63,51,221,0" Name="textBox1" Height="20"
     VerticalAlignment="Top">Manning</TextBox>
  <TextBox Height="21" Margin="63,81,221,0" Name="textBox2"
     VerticalAlignment="Bottom">http://www.manning.com/</TextBox>
</Grid>
```

Note that the `Text` property of the `LinkLabel` is bound to the `Text` in the first text box, and the `Uri` is bound to the `Text` in the second. We don't have to bind these values; we can also hardcode them.

```
<local:LinkLabel
     Text="Manning"
     Uri="http://www.manning.com" />
```

But, we wanted to demonstrate that the properties are fully *bindable*. When you run, you should now have a `LinkLabel` with the Manning website linked; when it's clicked, it should open your default web browser (figure 13.3).

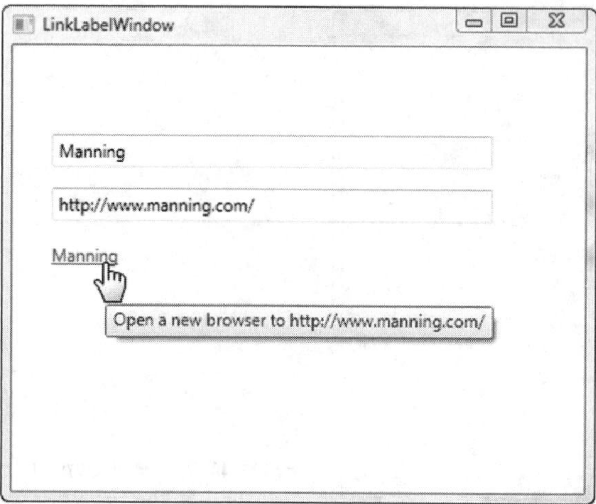

Figure 13.3 The rather ugly, but functional, test harness for the `LinkLabel` control is showing the happy path tooltip.

If you change the URI to simply http://, you can try the sad path tooltip as well (figure 13.4).

That completes our `UserControl`, but there are some issues. First, we can use this control as is, but the XAML behind it is hardcoded. We can't apply our own template to the `LinkLabel` control because it effectively *is* the template. Also, although we can use this control in our test application project willy-nilly, it would be somewhat more useful if it were available to other application projects as well. We can do that by using custom controls.

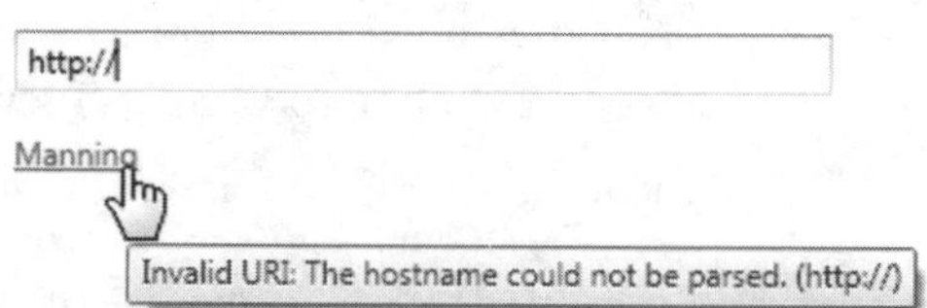

Figure 13.4 The sad path tells the user what's wrong with the URI—for example, if the user enters an invalid URI in a bookmark utility.

13.2 Building custom controls

Once you create new controls, you almost certainly want to make them reusable for other projects. After all, if you're only going to use them once, why even bother? In this section, we're going to create a new control designed to be reused from a library. This new control will be a checked `GroupBox`. In the place where, on a regular `GroupBox`, there's a label, there will be a check box that enables and disables the content of the `GroupBox` (figure 13.5).

As you'll see as we move forward, the way in which the control will be built will not only allow the text of the `CheckBox` and the content of the `GroupBox` to be changed easily but, via control templates, will even allow different controls to be used for the `CheckBox` and the `GroupBox`.

If you went only by the names, it isn't entirely clear why you'd use a `CustomControl` versus a `UserControl`. Technically, there's no class in WPF called `CustomControl`, although you can create a *Custom Control Library*. In the end, all controls are custom controls in that

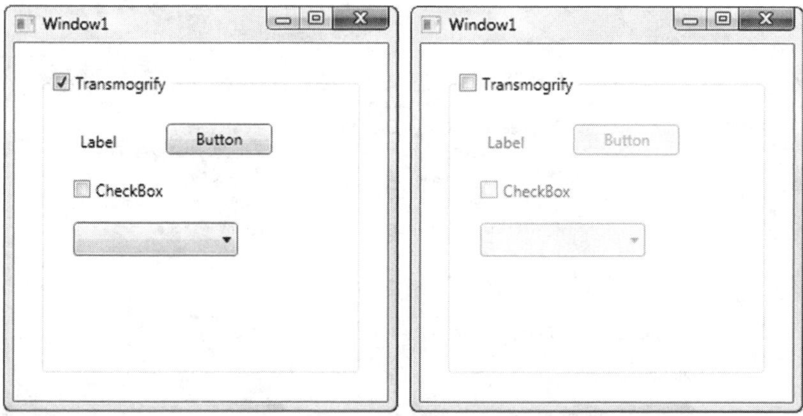

Figure 13.5 The checked `GroupBox` control automatically enables and disables the `GroupBox` content depending on the checked state of the `CheckBox` in the title.

they're customized versions of some other control, whether that be a `ControlTemplate` as applied to an existing control, a new control derived from a `UserControl`, `Control`, `TextBox`, or even a `FrameworkElement`. When we talk about a custom control in WPF terms, we're referring to controls derived from the `Control` class. Many of the built-in controls in WPF derive from this class, so you're getting the same basic control that Microsoft uses, in most cases. The phrase is a bit overloaded, so all you really need to think about are the limitations and allowances that each of the specific classes give you.

At the `FrameworkElement` class level, you have to do a significant amount of work yourself, but that also gives you tremendous flexibility. At the `UserControl` and `ControlTemplate` levels, you can put together existing pieces quickly, but you run into limits a lot sooner.

Before we worry about building the control, let's create a Control Template Library so that we can reference it from multiple places.

13.2.1 Building a control library

Right-click the ControlsInAction solution, and select Add New Project. Select WPF Custom Control Library (as opposed to WPF User Control Library), and name this new project WpfInActionControls (figure 13.6).

We should point out the following things about the project:

- *You don't get a designer.* Yes, custom controls start with code. XAML is still involved, but we'll approach it differently.
- *There's a Themes folder.* In this folder is a file called generic.xaml, which we'll be getting to in a moment. The existence of this folder is highly related to the first point.
- *There's no app.xaml.* This is related to the first and second points. Maybe this was all one point after all...

Now we're ready to create the control.

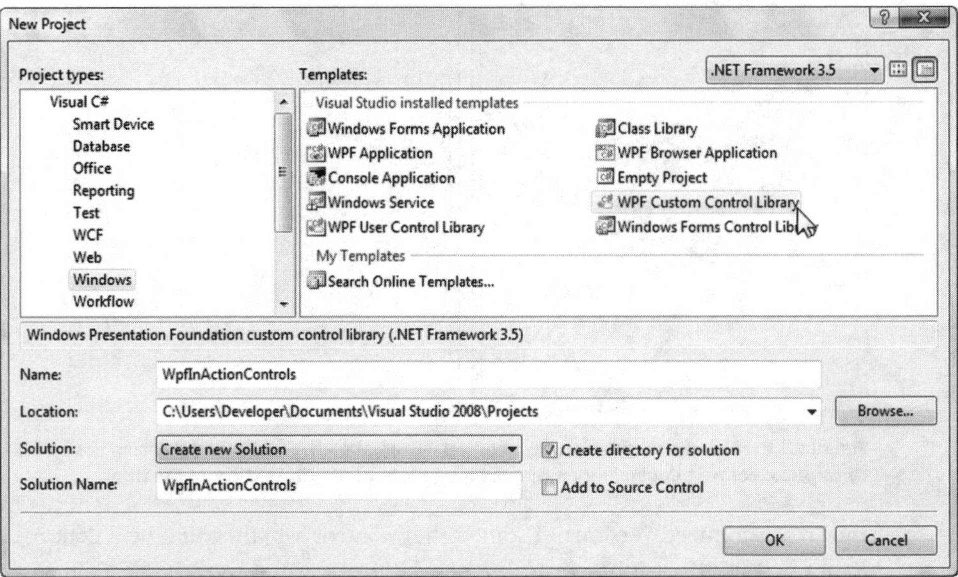

Figure 13.6 Creating a control library

13.2.2 *Create the new custom control*

Before we create the control and give it a name, we should think a little about the nature of the control. One of the reasons for creating a custom control rather than a user control is for the purpose of enabling control templates. In general, we're creating a `GroupBox` with a `CheckBox` in the header. But, WPF allows for a very strong separation of behavior and look, so concentrating on the behavior will help us make a better control. Let's think about what we want from our control in the most general sense:

- Two states for all the contained controls: enabled and disabled
- A way to toggle the state
- An indicator of the grouping of the controls

Given the first point, we should have a property on the control called `IsContentEnabled`. If the property is set to `true`, the content will all be enabled; if it's `false`, it will be disabled (clever, eh?). The second attribute leads us to the check box idea, but we could also use a `ToggleButton`, or even a couple of `RadioButtons`. We don't need anything more than the `IsContentEnabled` property for this functionality, but we do need to be sure that we can hook it up to whatever control happens to be used.

The third quality is purely aesthetic—nesting provides the logical grouping we need. We're assuming a `GroupBox`, but any control that has a header and a place for content would work (for example, the `Expander` control). That being said, we're going to call the control a `ConditionalGroupBox`. This name avoids building in expectations of what sort of control will be used to toggle the state. It definitely *implies* that the grouping control is a `GroupBox`, but giving the control a name like `ConditionalContentHolder` makes us a little queasy because it's so ambiguous.

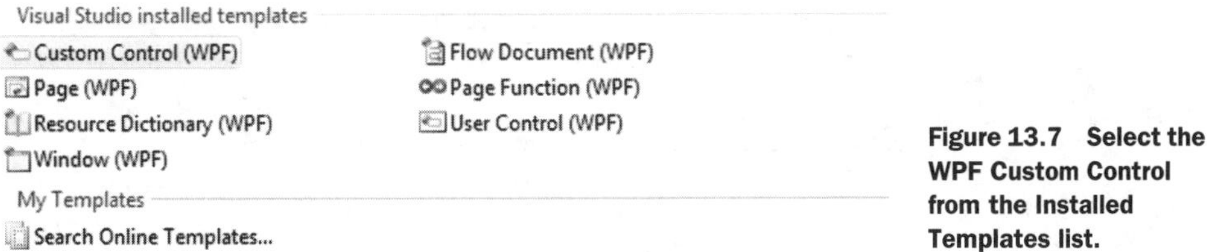

Figure 13.7 Select the WPF Custom Control from the Installed Templates list.

Select Add New Item, and create a Custom Control (WPF) (figure 13.7) called `ConditionalGroupBox`.

You'll be presented with a large comment explaining how to use this control that's from another project. The details of the comment are relevant because Visual Studio 2008 has some limitations that make control reuse a little rough around the edges. We imagine that, in a future version, you'll be able to drag the control from the toolbox, and it will automatically add appropriate namespaces to the XML, enable IntelliSense for it, and all those nice[1] things. Until then, the comment will have to do.

Other than the comment, the file is pretty empty. There's a single static constructor with a call to `DefaultStyleKey.OverrideMetadata`. With all these static properties, this constructor gives us a way to declare that our new class derivation needs its own styling, as well as where to look for the default style. If we were creating a derivation of a `Button` and only adding behaviors, we probably wouldn't override the style key—we'd inherit the styles of a `Button`.

Because we want to host content (other `UIElements`), we technically need to derive from `ContentControl`, but we also have the concept of a grouping mechanism, so we'll end up deriving from `HeaderedContentControl`. WPF has a number of helpful base classes for controls that aren't controls an end-developer would generally use directly in a designer. `HeaderedContentControl` is one of those; it's used for any controls that have some sort of header with some sort of content (like `GroupBox` or `Expander`).

We only need one `DependencyProperty` on this control—`IsContentEnabled`. Add the following code to the `ConditionalGroupBox` class (as we did in the `UserControl`, except this time with a default value of `true`).

```
public class ConditionalGroupBox : HeaderedContentControl
{
  static ConditionalGroupBox()
  {
    ...
  }

  public static readonly DependencyProperty IsContentEnabledProperty =
    DependencyProperty.Register("IsContentEnabled",
    typeof(bool),
    typeof(ConditionalGroupBox),
    new PropertyMetadata(true,
```

[1] And hug it, and pet it, and call the namespace `"xmlns:George"`.

```
        new PropertyChangedCallback(OnIsContentEnabledChanged)));

    public bool IsContentEnabled
    {
      get { return (bool)GetValue(IsContentEnabledProperty); }
      set { SetValue(IsContentEnabledProperty, value); }
    }
  }
```

And now, to set up the control logic for the callback, add the method from listing 13.3.

Listing 13.3 `OnIsContentEnabledChanged` event handler

```
private static void OnIsContentEnabledChanged(DependencyObject sender,
                                    DependencyPropertyChangedEventArgs e)
{
  bool enabled = (bool)e.NewValue;                          ❶ Who sets this?
  ConditionalGroupBox groupBox = (ConditionalGroupBox)sender;

  UIElement content = groupBox.Content as UIElement;
  if (content != null)                                      ❷ Only needed on
     content.IsEnabled = enabled;                              one element
}
```

This method will be called when the `IsContentEnabled` property's value changes. We don't yet know *who* is setting that property, but we also don't care. We get the value from `IsContentEnabled` ❶ from the passed arguments, and then use that value to enable or disable the content of our control ❷—although, again, we don't know what type of control it is. The nice thing is that we only have to enable or disable the main control and all the children in the visual tree will automatically be enabled or disabled.

The control is done! Well, sort of. This is where templating comes in. The control itself *is* technically done—we could use it in an application, but the application developer would have to write the control's template. That isn't very nice. But, we can provide a simple default template for the control through Generic.xaml.

13.2.3 Create the default template for the control

We've made much of the fact that all (or most) controls in WPF are lookless—that is, their look-and-feel isn't tied to the control, and so can be completely customized via control templates. But, when you drag a `Button` (for example) onto a form, it obviously has a *look*, or you wouldn't see anything. In fact, it has a fairly elaborate style that draws the button, makes it change when the mouse moves over, and so on.

The reason for this is that `Button` (and all the other controls) has a default control template that defines the way it should look. We'll do the same thing with our control. For our default template, we'll put a `CheckBox` in the header (our conditional control) and use a `GroupBox` for the, uh, `GroupBox`.

Open the Themes folder and the file Generic.xaml. You'll find that Visual Studio has helpfully started your template for you. It creates a border element and binds it to the parent control's `Background`, `BorderBrush`, and `BorderThickness` properties. We need to create the default template for this control, and we're going to have to do it without any help from a visual designer because it can't currently handle templates. Listing 13.4 shows what the final style should look like.

Listing 13.4 The `ConditionalGroupBox` style from Generic.xaml

```
<Style TargetType="{x:Type local:ConditionalGroupBox}">      ❶ Assigns template to new control
 <Setter Property="Template">     ❷
  <Setter.Value>
   <ControlTemplate TargetType="{x:Type local:ConditionalGroupBox}">     ❸ Creates ControlTemplate
    <Border Background="{TemplateBinding Background}"
            BorderBrush="{TemplateBinding BorderBrush}"     ❹
           BorderThickness="{TemplateBinding BorderThickness}">
     <GroupBox>     ❺ GroupBox to outline controls
      <GroupBox.Header>
       <CheckBox IsChecked=     ❻ CheckBox to enable/disable controls
          "{Binding RelativeSource={RelativeSource TemplatedParent},
          Path=IsContentEnabled}"
          Content=
            "{Binding RelativeSource={RelativeSource TemplatedParent},
            Path=Header}"/>
      </GroupBox.Header>
      <ContentPresenter Content="{TemplateBinding Content}" />     ❼ Directs content to be within GroupBox
     </GroupBox>
    </Border>
   </ControlTemplate>
  </Setter.Value>
 </Setter>
</Style>
```

As with any other template, we're associating this template ❶ to our control. We'd have at least one style entry for each control in this project. We're using a `Setter` to set the `Template` property ❷ on any newly created instances of `ConditionalGroupBox` to our `ControlTemplate` definition ❸.

Visual Studio gave us a nice little `Border` for free ❹, so we're keeping it (but we don't have to). Our template really begins with the definition of the `GroupBox` ❺. A `GroupBox` is a header control; it has header content as well as general content—the stuff in the `GroupBox` itself.

We've put a `CheckBox` into the header ❻. This is where we wire up the behavior that makes everything work. The `IsChecked` property of the `CheckBox` is bound to our custom control's `IsContentEnabled` dependency property. When the check state changes, it will automatically update the property, causing our event handler to be called.

We're also binding the `Content` of the `CheckBox` to the `Header` property of our control. This property is inherited from `HeaderedContentControl`. When someone uses our control, he can set its header, and whatever he sets it to will appear next to the check box.

Finally, we bind the `Content` ❼ specified on the control (also inherited from `HeaderedContentControl`) to present in the `GroupBox` using a `ContentPresenter`. Now we can truly say the control is finished.

13.2.4 Testing the control

Saying the control is finished is nice and all, but we want to see it work before we'll sign any checks. As the comment in the code said, we can't pop this control into the designer and have Visual Studio work out the nuances—we first have to do some prep work. Add a reference to the WpfInActionControl project to the ControlsInAction project. This reference will make the code available. We also have to manually add a namespace to the main `Window` in the test application.

```
xmlns:remote=
    "clr-namespace:WpfInActionControls;assembly=WpfInActionControls"
```

Although "`local`" is a customary namespace for locally defined resources, we know of no standard convention for naming external libraries. At least, once you've typed the opening double-quote, IntelliSense should show the WpfInActionControls namespace and assembly (once the assembly has been referenced). Now add an instance of the control to the `Window` (you'll have to manually put in the XAML), and put a `Grid` inside it.

```
<remote:ConditionalGroupBox Header="Transmogrify" Margin="20,20,20,20">
  <Grid>
  </Grid>
</remote:ConditionalGroupBox>
```

Once you have this in place, you can drag some controls onto the `Grid` for testing purposes.

Our new control acts like a regular `GroupBox`, but also exposes a `CheckBox` to enable or disable the entire `Content` of the `GroupBox`. Have as much fun as you like playing with the busy-box. Figures 13.8, and 13.9 show the application as you click madly between states.

Before we lose you to the fun of playing with the new control, we need to cover one last thing. Remember that the entire point of this exercise is to build a control with full template support, so let's see if we can customize the control by changing its template.

Figure 13.8 All controls are disabled with transmogrify off.

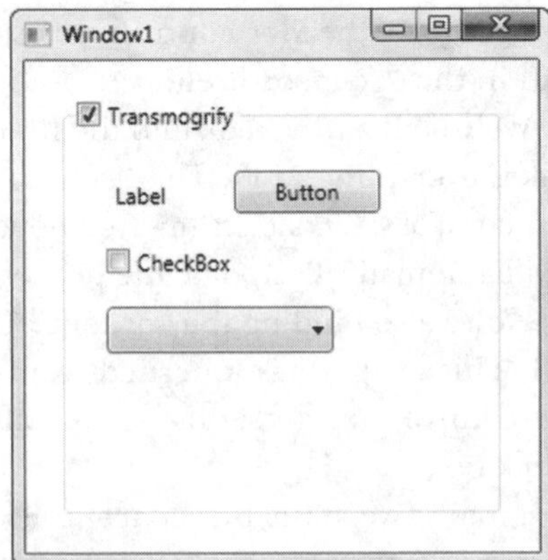

Figure 13.9 All systems are go with transmogrify turned on.

13.2.5 Customizing a custom control with a template

In our default template in Generic.xaml, we created some XAML markup to describe how we wanted our control to look by default. Applying the template is going to follow the same basic pattern, but we'll define the template right here in our application—right where we use the control. Add the following XAML directly after the open tag of the ConditionalGroupBox:

```
<remote:ConditionalGroupBox.Template>
  <ControlTemplate TargetType="remote:ConditionalGroupBox">
  </ControlTemplate>
</remote:ConditionalGroupBox.Template>
```

In the designer, our control just disappeared. When we explicitly set the Template property, we override the Generic.xaml template even if our new template does nothing. That isn't interesting, though, so let's change the CheckBox to a ToggleButton (listing 13.5).

Listing 13.5 Custom template for ConditionalGroupBox

```
<ControlTemplate TargetType="remote:ConditionalGroupBox">
  <GroupBox>
    <GroupBox.Header>
      <ToggleButton                                  <-- ToggleButton instead of CheckBox
        IsChecked=
         "{Binding RelativeSource={RelativeSource TemplatedParent},
           Path=IsContentEnabled}"
        Content="{Binding RelativeSource={RelativeSource TemplatedParent},
           Path=Header}" />
    </GroupBox.Header>
    <ContentPresenter Content="{TemplateBinding Content}" />
  </GroupBox>
</ControlTemplate>
```

All we have to replace from the Generic.xaml template is the element name CheckBox with the element name ToggleButton. Now we have the same behavior and functionality, but with a button (figure 13.10).

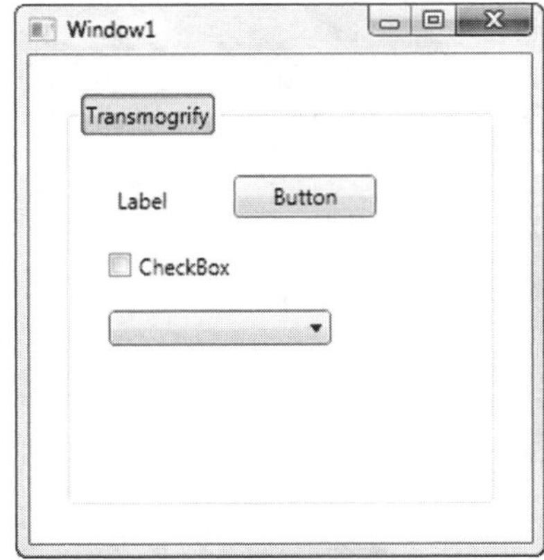

Figure 13.10 The checked GroupBox can easily be changed to a ToggleButton instead.

What makes these controls so powerful and flexible is the absolute separation of look from behavior. By not thinking in terms of assembling controls and, instead, dividing behavior from functionality, we've created a control that can be used and presented in many ways—particularly ones that *we* haven't thought of yet. It would be interesting to give this control to some interaction designers and see what they come up with. Because we didn't put anything in our template that would have tied us strongly to structure or naming of the controls, you can imagine a designer could take a few rules around the template and design something entirely new from it.

13.3 Summary

As you've seen, the amount of work for creating a user control versus a custom sharable control is considerable. Most of the time, you don't need the overhead associated with custom controls, whereas you're likely to create user controls at the drop of a hat. Often you'll just group a bunch of existing controls together, without even adding your own properties—but the ability to do so adds a whole lot of power. Some of the complexity of developing custom controls can be mitigated by prototyping them as user controls first, dividing behavior from appearance, and then splitting your user control into a template and a good old-fashioned C# file.

The next chapter is all about drawing, but we'll do the drawing inside a user control. We'll also demonstrate creating controls that are derived from `FrameworkElement`, which is much higher up in the derivation chain than `UserControl`, and are much lighter weight.

14 Drawing

This chapter covers:

- Drawing with Shapes
- Drawing using direct rendering
- Drawing with Visuals
- Drawing with Geometries
- How to use good pictures to make horrendously ugly backgrounds

It's interesting that, in most applications—particularly business applications—there isn't much straight *drawing*. Yeah, technically, everything is being drawn on the screen, but because of the wealth of built-in controls and third-party controls, you generally don't do too much shoving stuff on the screen yourself.

In Windows Forms, the most common scenarios for drawing (outside of graphical applications) were to create custom controls or to create a custom look-and-feel for an existing control. We (the authors) have done *a lot* of this, and it has been a bit of culture shock to know that, most of the time when we want to customize look-and-feel, we don't have to do low-level drawing code anymore.

But that doesn't mean that you never have to worry about drawing things. For one thing, if you want to customize the look-and-feel of a control, you're generally

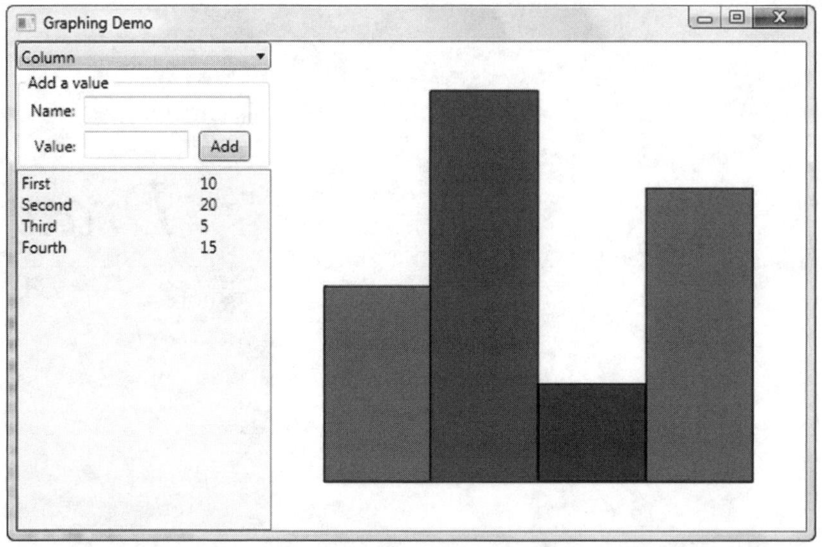

Figure 14.1 One version of the graphing control we're going to build in this chapter. We're going to provide three different versions of the drawing code, each using a different approach to create the graph.

defining a template that uses drawing elements (rectangles, ellipses, lines, and so on) to get what you want. Also, invariably, a few places in even the most staid and boring business application might require some drawing code. For example—in fact, the one we're going to use throughout this chapter—you might want to provide a graph of some data (figure 14.1).

We're going to demonstrate creating this graph not once, not twice, but three times because there are three distinct ways of doing drawing in WPF. And those ways don't even include 3D drawing, which is also somewhat different. Before you start wondering if the WPF team has gone mad, though, there are valid reasons for all three different approaches, and they leverage each other—the developers have just provided flexible wrappers for different scenarios. The three approaches are:

- *Shapes*—The `Shape` class and its derivations (`Rectangle`, `Ellipse`, `Line`, and so on) form a set of classes that work much like controls. You can define them, set their sizes, locations, colors, and so on, as you would with a `TextBox`, and they interact with layout as a control does, supporting styles and events, and so on. We used shapes (`Ellipses` and `Rectangles`) when we were building the UI for the calculator.
- *Direct rendering*—With direct rendering, you take over (sort of) the drawing of your control, and explicitly draw lines and shapes and things directly onto a surface that represents the control. This is the most like classic Windows drawing—with one very big difference that we'll discuss later.

- `Visuals`—With `Visuals`, you build up the way your controls should look using low-level primitives (`Rectangles`, `Lines`, and so on, but simpler versions than the `Shapes` we've already mentioned). `Visuals` don't have all the automatic behavior of `Shapes`, but you can do simple things such as hit tests.

We'll start off by talking about `Shapes`. One note, though: Throughout the book, we've striven to present useful information *without* duplicating the material easily available through MSDN. Likewise, in this chapter, we won't try to provide an exhaustive guide to all the classes and properties available with drawing. Instead, we'll show the primary classes and properties, as well as some of the more interesting things you can do. We figure you can look up the details of each enum as you need it[1] without us repeating it all ad nauseam.

14.1 Drawing with Shapes

Using `Shapes` is probably the simplest way of "drawing" in WPF. In some cases, you can literally drag a `Shape` from the Toolbox onto your window, set a few properties, and voilà, you have a shape. Of course, the situations where this solves a useful programming problem are vanishingly small, but it's still quite useful to be able to manipulate shapes in this manner. Also, the same properties and behaviors apply whether you've dragged a `Shape` onto your designer, whether it's part of a control template, or whether you're programmatically creating and manipulating `Shape` objects.

14.1.1 Shapes in XAML

There are six shape classes in WPF. Figure 14.2 shows an example of them all. Although they all work in more or less the same way, they each have their own different properties and behaviors. When doing any serious graphic work, you're likely to use a combination of the different shapes.

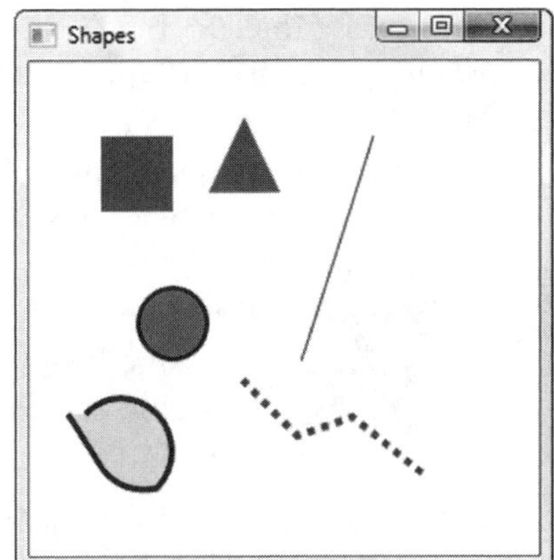

Figure 14.2 There are six shape classes in WPF. It might interest you to know that *Triangle* isn't one of them.

We've created this beautiful application by creating a new WPF app and replacing the `Grid` with a `Canvas`–it's slightly easier to read the properties that way. We're going to run through each shape in turn and show some of the various properties and options. In the Visual Studio 2008 editor, by default, you can only drag a couple of the shapes (`Rectangle` and `Ellipse`) onto the form. But, if you manually add the others to your XAML, you can then edit their properties in the property editor. Also, if you expect to do a lot of work with `Shapes`, you can right-click the Toolbox, select

---

[1] Or do what we do—use IntelliSense and experiment.

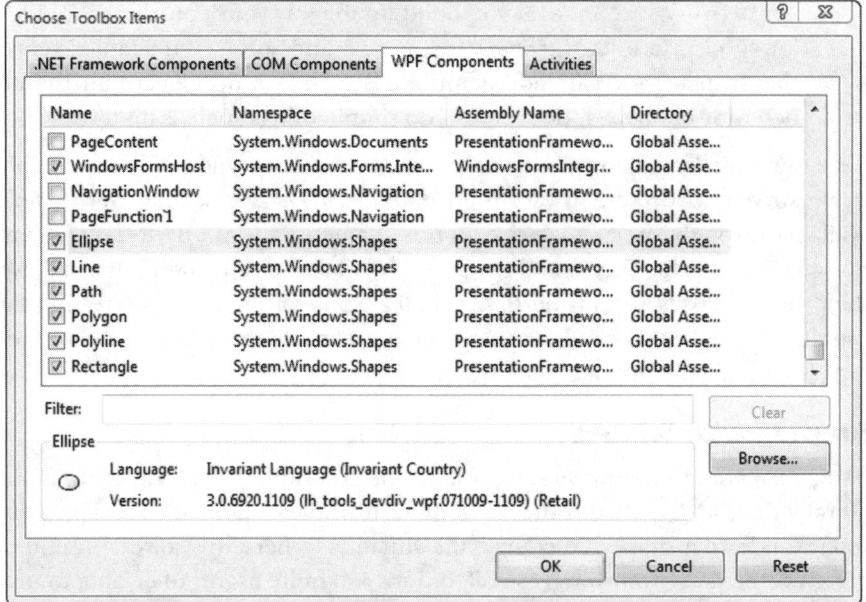

Figure 14.3 You can add the remaining `Shape` classes to the Toolbox by right-clicking the Toolbox and selecting Choose Items... Here you can see the `Path`, `Polygon`, and `Polyline` `Shapes` are now checked. We've also added `Line`, although it's offscreen. `Rectangle` and `Ellipse` are already in the Toolbox by default.

Choose Items…, then switch to the WPF components, and add the other shapes to add to the Toolbox (figure 14.3).

In the real world, it isn't often that you need to be able to drag, say, a `Polygon` onto a form, so it's quite reasonable that the default is to not show all the shapes. Once they are there though, we'd probably never bother to remove them.

RECTANGLE

We hope you learned about this one in kindergarten. Our rectangle has the same height and width, making it a square. You can either enter the XAML or, in the case of a `Rectangle`, drag the thing off the Toolbox. Here's the XAML:

```
<Rectangle Fill="Blue" Canvas.Left = "40" Canvas.Top="40"
      Width="40" Height="40"/>
```

As you can see, the properties are pretty straightforward. The `Canvas.Left` and `Canvas.Top` properties set where the `Shape` goes, and the `Width` and `Height` specify its size. The `Fill` property is the brush to use to fill the shape. If you don't specify a `Fill`, the shape will be invisible. `Fill` can be any brush. For our example, we could use a gradient.

```
<Rectangle Canvas.Left = "40" Canvas.Top="40" Width="40" Height="40">
  <Rectangle.Fill>
    <LinearGradientBrush>
      <GradientStop Offset="0" Color="Blue"/>
```

```
      <GradientStop Offset=".8" Color="Yellow"/>
    </LinearGradientBrush>
  </Rectangle.Fill>
</Rectangle>
```

You could animate this shape, bind properties, catch events, and do just about anything with this shape that you can do with any other `UIElement`, such as a `Button`, although the shape doesn't do too many interesting things by itself. One cool thing is that WPF can automatically round the corners of the `Rectangle` by specifying values for the `RadiusX` and `RadiusY` properties.

```
<Rectangle Canvas.Left = "40" Canvas.Top="40" Width="40" Height="40"
       RadiusX="10" RadiusY="10">
```

Figure 14.4 shows the rectangle with the gradient and with the rounded corners.

Figure 14.4 Rectangle with a gradient and rounded corners

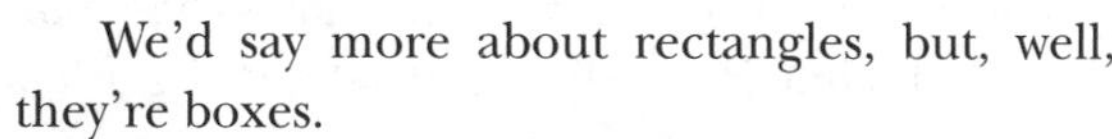

We'd say more about rectangles, but, well, they're boxes.

ELLIPSE

An ellipse is a, well, it's a curvy-roundy shaped thing. The proper definition has all sorts of hard words about multiple foci and such, but all you really need to know is that it's basically a circle or a stretched circle. You define an `Ellipse` in WPF by providing the rectangle that it needs to fit in. Here's the XAML:

```
<Ellipse Fill="Green" Stroke="Black" StrokeThickness="2"
     Canvas.Left = "60" Canvas.Top="120" Width="40" Height="40"/>
```

One thing you might notice is that the ellipse has a border around the edge. We've done that by specifying the `Stroke` and the `StrokeThickness`. `Stroke` is the color of the pen to use to draw the edge and `StrokeThickness` is how big to make it. As you'll see a bit later, there are all sorts of other properties you can specify here, such as making the `Stroke` dashed. And the `Stroke` is a brush, so it can also be any valid type of brush.

POLYGON

No, WPF does *not* have a triangle shape. What it does have is a `Polygon`, where you can specify multiple lines to make up the shape. Here's the XAML for our triangle:

```
<Polygon Fill="Red" Canvas.Left = "100" Canvas.Top="30"
         Points="20 0 40 40 0 40"/>
```

Notice the `Points` property? This is a handy shortcut that XAML allows for specifying a series of values like points. We could have also written this out the long way:

```
<Polygon Fill="Red" Canvas.Left = "100" Canvas.Top="30" >
  <Polygon.Points>
    <Point X="20" Y="0"/>
    <Point X="40" Y="40"/>
    <Point X="0" Y="40"/>
  </Polygon.Points>
</Polygon>
```

This code would do exactly the same thing. Notice that we don't have to close the shape (by adding in the starting point at the end). Polygons are always closed shapes. The `Points` collection *does* show up in the property editor; but, if you use the single-line notation, it isn't editable.

LINE

OK, so this one is pretty obvious, even in this list of pretty obvious things. But, it does have one thing that might be tricky. Here's the XAML:

```
<Line Stroke="Purple" X1="40" X2="0" Y1="0" Y2="120"
        Canvas.Top="40" Canvas.Left="151"  />
```

A line is drawn from the first point (X1, Y1) to the second point (X2, Y2). But, notice that we're *also* setting the `Canvas.Top` and `Canvas.Left` properties. We have two different sets of coordinates to deal with here. The `Canvas` coordinates can be thought of as positioning a rectangular shape, The line is drawn *inside* that rectangle. The upper-left corner of that rectangle is position 0, 0 as far as the line is concerned; as long as no overriding `Width` and `Height` are specified, the rectangle will be as big as it needs to be to hold the entire line.

POLYLINE

A `Polyline` is much like a `Polygon`, except that the shape doesn't have to be closed. As with a single line, the points are relative to a rectangle that's moved by setting the `Canvas Left` and `Top` properties. For our example, we use the verbose notation:

```
<Polyline Stroke="Brown" StrokeThickness="4"  StrokeDashArray="1 1"
        Canvas.Left="119" Canvas.Top="170" >
  <Polyline.Points>
  <Point X="0" Y="0"/>
  <Point X="30" Y="30"/>
  <Point X="60" Y="20"/>
  <Point X="100" Y="50"/>
  </Polyline.Points>
</Polyline>
```

Notice that we specify a `StrokeDashArray` to get the dash effect. The units in the dash array are based on the thickness of the `Stroke`; they say something like "have a dash as long as the line is thick, and then a space as long as the line is thick." If we changed the values to "2 1", that would give us a dash twice as long as the dash is thick (8 pixels) and a space 1 thickness wide (4 pixels). It's an array, so you can do things like "2 1 4 2 8 4" if you have the desire to do so.

You can also specify a bunch of other things, via other `Stroke` properties, about the pen[2] used to draw the lines. You can add end caps to the lines, control what happens at the join points, and so on. Just look at all the Stroke*XXX* properties via IntelliSense.

---

[2] There really is a `Pen` object used for drawing the border. We'll talk about it in more detail later.

If you want to make a Polyline act like a Polygon, you can add a final point that's the same as the starting point. You might not think that you can fill in a Polyline unless you do that, but you can. The fill acts as though that last line exists. You can also control (to some extent) the algorithm used to fill in the shape; this fact matters when you have lines that cross one another. You can control the behavior by setting the FillRule. But, this isn't something you usually have to worry about.

PATH

Just as there's no built-in triangle shape in WPF, there's also no built-in squished lemon. If you want one, you have to create it yourself using a Path. A Path is the most powerful of the drawing shapes, as well as the hardest to use. A Path is sort of like a Polyline, except that the individual segments can be things other than lines, such as arcs and curves. For example, here's the XAML for our shape:

```
<Path Stroke="Black" StrokeThickness="3" Fill="Yellow"
        Canvas.Left="21" Canvas.Top="188" >
  <Path.Data>
    <PathGeometry>
      <PathGeometry.Figures>
        <PathFigure StartPoint="0,0">
          <PathFigure.Segments>
            <LineSegment Point="20 30"/>
            <ArcSegment Size="30,30"  IsLargeArc="False"
                SweepDirection="CounterClockwise" Point="50,40" />
            <ArcSegment Size="10,10"  IsLargeArc="False"
                SweepDirection="CounterClockwise" Point="10,0" />
          </PathFigure.Segments>
        </PathFigure>
      </PathGeometry.Figures>
    </PathGeometry>
  </Path.Data>
</Path>
```

The shape is made up of a series of segments—a straight line and two arcs. Notice that we're filling the shape, even though the shape isn't closed (although there's a property on PathFigure called IsClosed that, if set to true, will automatically close the shape for us).

We're only scratching the surface of Paths. As well as lines and arcs, you can draw Bézier curves, and even full shapes such as ellipses and rectangles. But, we aren't going to go into a great deal of detail here because we'll be discussing the underlying capabilities in a later section.

14.1.2 Stupid shape tricks

One of the cool things about Shapes is that they're UIElements and behave like other things you can drag onto a layout. For example, if we change the layout from a Canvas to a StackPanel, our shapes will line up appropriately (figure 14.5).

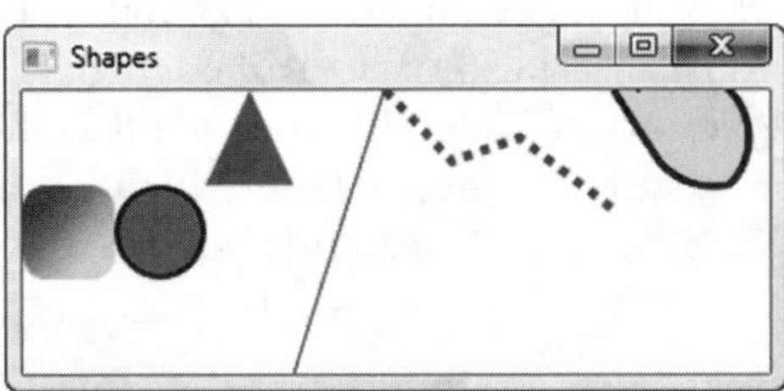

Figure 14.5 The same shapes in a `StackPanel` with the `Orientation` set to `Horizontal`

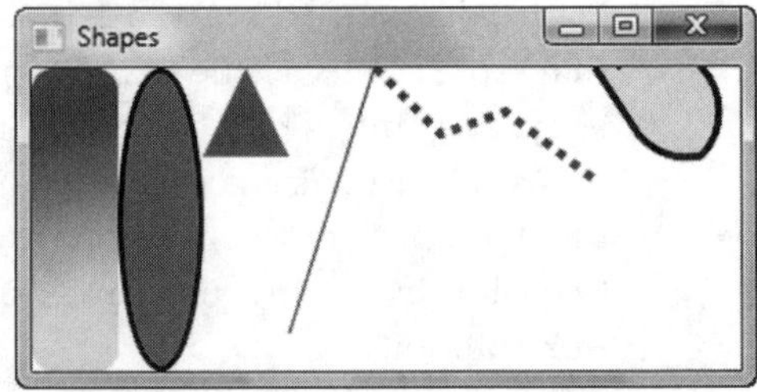

Figure 14.6 By removing the `Height` property from the `Rectangle` and the `Ellipse`, we let the layout control the height of the `Shapes`.

Also, at least for the `Shapes` that don't have explicit points set, you can have the layout control size for you in certain ways. For example, if we remove the `Height` property values from the `Rectangle` and the `Ellipse`, the layout will automatically make the shapes take up all available space (figure 14.6).

`Shapes` also can handle events such as mouse events. For example, we could add a handler to the `MouseDown` event on the `Polygon`.

```
<Polygon Fill="Red" Canvas.Left = "100" Canvas.Top="30"
            MouseDown="Polygon_MouseDown" >
```

Note that we can't catch a `Click` event. Certain controls, such as `Button`, define a `Click` event, but we can get at all the slightly lower-level mouse operations like mouse down, mouse move, and so on. We implement the handler as we would any other.

```
private void Polygon_MouseDown(object sender, MouseButtonEventArgs e)
{
 MessageBox.Show(
     "You clicked on the triangle. Please don't do that again.");
}
```

Figure 14.7 shows what happens when we click the `Polygon`.

The point is that `Shapes` are pretty capable objects. They have all the things that the various controls we've used have, such as binding and layout support, events, and so on, which makes them pretty easy to work with. They also work nicely with control templates, as we demonstrated with the calculator. But, there's a downside to using

Figure 14.7 We add a handler to the `Polygon` for when the user clicks it. We can do this because `Shapes` are full-blown `UIElements`.

Shapes—they're also fairly heavy. If you want to do a complex drawing with dozens or hundreds of shapes, you'll end up putting a lot of overhead on WPF, making your UI memory-intensive and sluggish. If you're going to do more than put a few shapes in a UI, you should probably consider one of the other available approaches.

For the moment, we'll demonstrate using Shapes to create a first version of a graphing control.

14.2 Creating the graphing control

In this section, we're going to create a graphing user control. The control will have a place to enter names and values that will appear in a list and will automatically be graphed as they're entered (figure 14.8). Because of the nature of the graph, we'll be using mostly Rectangle shapes, but we could do line charts using lines or pie charts using ellipses and arcs. In theory, this control could be integrated into the Desktop Wiki application as an alternative type of data to store.

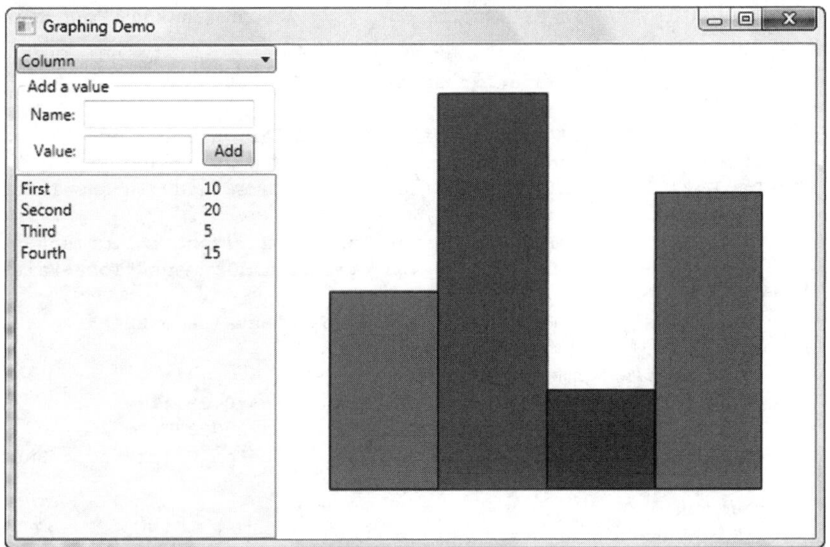

Figure 14.8 We're building the graphing control in a standalone application first. In the online version, we've integrated this control into the Wiki application.

To get started, create a new WPF application, and add a user control called GraphHolder. This will hold the *Add a value* stuff on the left and a swappable control on the right that holds our various graphing displays. The next section will go into the implementation of the control.

14.2.1 Building the GraphHolder control

The UI for GraphHolder has a Grid panel with two columns—one for the list and one for the graph. On the side with the list, there's a DockPanel that holds the ComboBox, a

GroupBox with the Add A Value options, and a ListBox. We've used a DockPanel so that we can have the ListBox easily take up the remaining space. Listing 14.1 shows the entire XAML for the GraphHolder control.

Listing 14.1 The GraphHolder control

```
<UserControl x:Class="GraphingWithShapes.GraphHolder"
    xmlns="http://schemas.microsoft.com/winfx/2006/xaml/presentation"
    xmlns:x="http://schemas.microsoft.com/winfx/2006/xaml"
    xmlns:local="clr-namespace:GraphingWithShapes"              ❶ Namespace for local code
    Height="342" Width="565" Loaded="UserControl_Loaded">
 <Grid>                                                 ❷ Two-column Grid
  <Grid.ColumnDefinitions>
   <ColumnDefinition Width="200" />
   <ColumnDefinition Width="*" />
  </Grid.ColumnDefinitions>                                          ❸ DockPanel
  <DockPanel Name="dockPanel1" Grid.ColumnSpan="1">
   <ComboBox DockPanel.Dock="Top" SelectedIndex="0" Height="21">
    <ComboBoxItem>Column</ComboBoxItem>
   </ComboBox>                              ❹ GroupBox for Add A Value controls
   <GroupBox DockPanel.Dock="Top" Header="Add a value" Height="75"
                    Name="groupBox1" Width="200">
    <Grid Name="grid1">
     <Label Height="23" Name="label1" VerticalAlignment="Top"
         HorizontalAlignment="Left" Width="53">Name:</Label>
     <TextBox Height="21" Margin="46,3,11,0" Name="addValueNameTextBox"
         VerticalAlignment="Top" />
     <Label Margin="2.9,27,0,0" Name="label2" HorizontalAlignment="Left"
         Width="50.09" Height="22.723" VerticalAlignment="Top">Value:</
  Label>
     <TextBox Margin="46,29,59,0" Name="addValueValueTextBox"
  Height="20.723"
         VerticalAlignment="Top" />
     <Button HorizontalAlignment="Right" Margin="0,29,11,0"
         Name="addValueBtn" Width="40" Height="22.723"
         VerticalAlignment="Top" Click="addValueBtn_Click">Add</Button>
    </Grid>
   </GroupBox>
   <ListBox Name="valuesList" Height="Auto"            ❺ List of values
            KeyDown="valuesList_KeyDown"/>
  </DockPanel>
  <local:ColumnGraphCtrl x:Name="graphCtrl" Grid.Column="1"    ❻ Non-existent control for graph
      Height="Auto" Width="Auto"/>
 </Grid>
</UserControl>
```

We're adding a namespace to reference our local code ❶ as you might expect. Also, we've added a handler for the Loaded event because we need to do some initialization. As we said, the UI is a two-column Grid ❷ with a DockPanel ❸ on the lefthand side, which contains a ComboBox for the type of graph (although we're only worrying about column graphs for now) and a GroupBox ❹ for the Add a value controls. We've used drag-and-drop to add a Grid to the GroupBox, and then to position the controls. This is part of the reason why the XAML is so verbose.

The last control in the DockPanel is the ListBox ❺. Because it has no Dock position set, it takes up the remaining space in the DockPanel. In the second column of the Grid, we have a ColumnGraphCtrl ❻. We haven't yet built this control, which will do our drawing, so this won't compile at the moment.

Before we get to the graphing control, let's spend a little time on our ListBox. It's a list—but of what? Let's create a small object that can hold a Name and a Value. Our graph will then be a graph of NameValuePairs. Listing 14.2 shows the NameValuePair class.

Listing 14.2 The NameValuePair class

```
namespace GraphingWithShapes
{
  public class NameValuePair
  {
    public NameValuePair() { }        <-- Regular constructor

    public NameValuePair(string newName, double newValue)     <-- Takes Name and Value
    {
      Name = newName;
      Value = newValue;
    }

    public string Name { get; set; }

    public double Value { get; set; }

    public object Tag { get; set; }
  }
}
```

Not much to this class—it's pretty much a string for a Name and a double for a Value. We've also added a Tag property that holds an object, which we'll use later to reference elements in the graph. One problem, though, is that a ListBox can't display NameValuePair objects. If we add them to the ListBox, then the ListBox will call the ToString() method, and we'll have a bunch of rows that say {GraphingWithShapes.NameValuePair}.

Fortunately, we can provide a DataTemplate for the ListBox telling it how we want it to display each item (listing 14.3).

Listing 14.3 DataTemplate for ListBox

```
<ListBox Name="valuesList" Height="Auto" KeyDown="valuesList_KeyDown">
  <ListBox.ItemTemplate>             <-- 1
    <DataTemplate>
      <Grid>
        <Grid.ColumnDefinitions>
          <ColumnDefinition Width="140"/>     2
          <ColumnDefinition Width="*"/>
          </Grid.ColumnDefinitions>
            <TextBlock Grid.Column="0" Text="{Binding Path=Name}"/>     3
            <TextBlock Grid.Column="1" Text="{Binding Path=Value}"/>
          </Grid>
```

```
        </DataTemplate>
    </ListBox.ItemTemplate>
</ListBox>
```

Just as we can provide a `ControlTemplate` to direct how a regular control is drawn, we can also provide an `ItemTemplate` ❶ for controls, such as `ListBox` and `ComboBox`, to indicate how each individual item in the list should be drawn. We're providing a `DataTemplate` made up of a `Grid` with two columns ❷. In each column, we have a `TextBlock`. We use binding to tell the `TextBlocks` where to get their content ❸. The first one gets the value from the `Name` property, and the second from the `Value` property.

Note that we aren't specifying an object type—just a property. The binding code will automatically search the contained object for a property called `Name` (or `Value`).

Now we can add `NameValuePairs` to the `ListBox`, and they will display in two columns, as you can see in figure 14.8. But, we don't want to only display the list of `NameValuePairs`; we want to graph them as well. It would be convenient if we had them in some sort of collection that we could easily pass to the graphing control. Rather than storing the list in two places (the `ListBox` and a collection for graphing), why don't we use a collection of some sort and bind the contents of the `ListBox` to that collection? That way we won't have to worry about keeping both places up to date.

To hold our collection, we could use an `ArrayList` or a generic collection like `List<NameValuePair>`. The binding code will let us use these collections because they both implement `IEnumerable`. But, when the list changes, we want the `ListBox` to automatically be updated, and neither of these collections is smart enough to tell the `ListBox` when it has changed. Fortunately, WPF has a collection object specifically for this purpose: `ObservableCollection`. We used this same collection in the Wiki application to hold our pages.

`ObservableCollection` implements an interface called `INotifyCollectionChanged`. This is nothing particularly magical. All it does is fire an event when an item is added or removed from the collection. The binding code subscribes to the event and tells the bound control: "Hey, the data you're using has changed; maybe you should do something about this."

We're also doing the binding to the `ListBox` in code, rather than in XAML. We could have declared the list in XAML, and done the binding that way, but sometimes it's cleaner to do that from code. Listing 14.4 shows the declaration of our collection and the code to bind it to our `ListBox` from GraphHolder.xaml.cs.

Listing 14.4 Bindable collection

```
using System.Collections.ObjectModel;          ❶ Goes at top of file

  ObservableCollection<NameValuePair> dataPoints =
        new ObservableCollection<NameValuePair>();     ❷ Creates collection

  private void UserControl_Loaded(object sender, RoutedEventArgs e)
```

```
{
  Binding binding = new Binding();      <-3 Binds
  binding.Source = dataPoints;
  valuesList.SetBinding(ListBox.ItemsSourceProperty, binding);
}
```

Obviously this isn't a complete code listing. The using statement ❶ is needed for `ObservableCollection` and has to go at the top of the file with the other using statements. `ObservableCollection` is a generic collection, so it takes the type of the item we want to collect—`NameValuePair` ❷. We then do the binding in the class's `Loaded` event handler ❸.

What we're doing here is more or less what the XAML compiler ends up doing behind the scenes. We have to create a `Binding` object and specify its source (the collection). Then we call `SetBinding` on our `ListBox`, specifying that we're binding the `ItemSource` property of the `ListBox` to our newly created `Binding` object, which points to our collection.

Now, if we add an item to the collection, it will automatically show up in the `ListBox`.

```
dataPoints.Add(new NameValuePair("First", 10));
```

We want to add an item to the `ListBox` when the user hits the Add button after typing in a name and a value. To handle the operation, we add a handler for the `Click` event on the button and implement it like this:

```
private void addValueBtn_Click(object sender, RoutedEventArgs e)
{
  string name = addValueNameTextBox.Text.Trim();
  string valueAsString = addValueValueTextBox.Text.Trim();
  double valueAsDouble = Convert.ToDouble(valueAsString);

  NameValuePair nvp = new NameValuePair(name, valueAsDouble);
  dataPoints.Add(nvp);

  addValueNameTextBox.Text = "";
  addValueValueTextBox.Text = "";
}
```

To save space, we've omitted the validation code that should be here. In the version on the web, we also have code to edit and remove items, but none of that is related to drawing, so we won't bother showing it here.

Congratulations! If you've followed along, you've now successfully built a control that, uh, lets you add values to a `ListBox`. Your mother would be very proud. Of course, the point of this whole exercise was to demonstrate using shapes to graph our data points. We'll implement that now.

14.2.2 Graphing using shapes

In listing 14.1, we had a reference to a control called `ColumnGraphCtrl` that we hadn't yet defined. Let's go ahead and create it now by adding a new user control. We're going to concentrate on the column chart for the moment. We could take a couple of different approaches here. For example, we could use a `StackPanel`, and then put on a series of rectangles to represent the values. That setup would work fairly well for column or bar charts, but not so well for line or pie charts.

Instead, we're going to use a `Canvas` layout and calculate the sizes and positions ourselves. This may not be the best approach for a column chart, but it will serve us well later when we discuss other drawing approaches. It also means that the XAML for the control will be simple because we're going to drag on a `Canvas` and make it take up the entire available space.

```
<UserControl x:Class="GraphingWithShapes.ColumnGraphCtrl"
    xmlns="http://schemas.microsoft.com/winfx/2006/xaml/presentation"
    xmlns:x="http://schemas.microsoft.com/winfx/2006/xaml"
    Height="300" Width="300">
  <Grid>
    <Canvas x:Name="main" SizeChanged="main_SizeChanged"/>
  </Grid>
</UserControl>
```

We've renamed the `Canvas` as `"main"` and also added an event handler for the `SizeChanged` event. The bulk of the implementation, though, resides in the code file (listing 14.5).

NOTE It can get a little confusing figuring out whether to use `Name` or `x:Name`. Determining which is appropriate is largely driven by the namespace containing the element. But, there's a handy trick—anything that supports `Name` *also* supports `x:Name`; if you always use `x:Name`, you'll always be OK.

Listing 14.5 `ColumnGraphCtrl` implementation

```
using System;
...bulk of using statements omitted...
using System.Collections.ObjectModel;
using System.Collections.Specialized;

namespace GraphingWithShapes
{
  public partial class ColumnGraphCtrl : UserControl
  {
    private ObservableCollection<NameValuePair> dataPoints = null;
    private List<Color> columnColors =
       new List<Color>() { Colors.Blue, Colors.Red, Colors.Green };

    public ColumnGraphCtrl()
    {
      InitializeComponent();
    }

    public void SetData(ObservableCollection<NameValuePair> data)    <-- 1 Collection must be passed in
    {
      dataPoints = data;
      dataPoints.CollectionChanged += new
         NotifyCollectionChangedEventHandler(DataChanged);
      Update();
    }
```

```
void DataChanged(object sender, NotifyCollectionChangedEventArgs e)
{
  Update();
}

public void Update()
{
  Rectangle rect;
  foreach (NameValuePair nvp in dataPoints)
  {
    if (nvp.Tag == null)
    {
      rect = new Rectangle();
      rect.Stroke = Brushes.Black;
      rect.StrokeThickness = 1;
      main.Children.Add(rect);
      nvp.Tag = rect;
    }
  }

  CalculatePositionsAndSizes();
}

public void CalculatePositionsAndSizes()
{
  if (dataPoints == null)
    return;

  double spaceToUseY = main.ActualHeight * 0.8;
  double spaceToUseX = main.ActualWidth * 0.8;

  double barWidth = spaceToUseX / dataPoints.Count;
  double largestValue = GetLargestValue();
  double unitHeight = spaceToUseY / largestValue;

  double bottom = main.ActualHeight * 0.1;
  double left = main.ActualWidth * 0.1;

  Rectangle rect;
  int nIndex = 0;
  foreach (NameValuePair nvp in dataPoints)
  {
    rect = nvp.Tag as Rectangle;
    rect.Fill =
      new SolidColorBrush(columnColors[nIndex++ % columnColors.Count]);

    rect.Width = barWidth;
    rect.Height = nvp.Value * unitHeight;
    Canvas.SetLeft(rect, left);
    Canvas.SetBottom(rect, bottom);
    left += rect.Width;
  }
}

public double GetLargestValue()
{
  double value = 0;
  foreach (NameValuePair nvp in dataPoints)
  {
```

❷ Called when collection changes

❸ Handles changes to collection

❹ Creates Rectangle for each NameValuePair

Does real work

❺ ❻ ❼ ❽ ❾

```
            value = Math.Max(value, nvp.Value);
          }

          return value;
        }
                                                                 ⑩ Catches
        private void main_SizeChanged(object sender,               SizeChanged
                                      SizeChangedEventArgs e)  <┘  event
        {
          CalculatePositionsAndSizes();
        }
      }
    }
```

There's a fair amount of code here, but it's more straightforward than it might seem. The `SetData` method ❶ will need to be called by our owning code to pass in the collection of `NameValuePairs`. We *could* have created a property for this, and done the binding in XAML; but, because we have so much of the rest of the implementation as real code, we might as well just pass it in. When the collection is passed in, we subscribe to the event that says that its content has changed—the same event that the binding code uses! The handler for the event ❷ calls our `Update()` method.

The `Update()` method ❸ steps through the collection and makes sure that there's a `Rectangle` object for each `NameValuePair`.[3] The `Rectangle` is given a 1-pixel-thick black border, and is set as the `Tag` on the `NameValuePair` so that we can find it easily later. We also have to add it to the `Canvas`, or WPF will never bother drawing it.

What's more important is what we are *not* doing when we create the `Rectangle`—we aren't setting its size, its location, or even the fill color. This is all done in the `CalculatePositionsAndSizes()` method ❹. This method is called when the collection is updated, and it's also called when the whole control's size changes ❿ so that the graph remains proportional.

`CalculatePositionsAndSizes()` has a bunch of math in it, but it's only figuring out how big to make each bar. First, we calculate how much of the entire space we want to use ❺. We don't want the chart filling up the entire window because that would be ugly. Then, we figure out how wide each bar should be ❻ and how big each unit of the bar should be, based on the largest value. We get the largest value via a method ❾ that steps through all the values and checks to see which is the biggest; the assumption is that the biggest value will take up the entire space. Note that this method will *not* handle negative numbers.

Next, we step through the entire collection of `NameValuePairs` ❼, get the `Rectangle` that we shoved into the `Tag` property, and set its `Height` and `Width` and the `Canvas`'s `Top` and `Bottom` properties. It's pretty handy being able to set the `Bottom` because this will force all the `Rectangles` to line up properly without us having to calculate the position.

---

[3] In the fancier version of the application that you can download, we also have code here to get rid of `Rectangles` for `NameValuePairs` that have been deleted from the collection.

We're also doing something clever(ish) with the `Fill` color of our `Rectangles` ❽. We defined an array of colors earlier, and we're cycling through that collection, assigning the colors in order to each of the `Rectangles`. We *could* have assigned a color when we created the `Rectangle`; but, if we removed a value from the collection or inserted a new value in the middle, the colors would be wrong.

All that's left is for us to add a call at the bottom of the `GraphHolder's` `UserControl_Loaded` to pass in the collection of `NameValuePairs`.

```
graphCtrl.SetData(dataPoints);
```

And now run the application. If you add a few values, the application should look like the picture from figure 14.8 at the beginning of this section.

14.2.3 Catching clicks

One of the nice things about the fact that each of our bars is a full-blown `UIElement` is that we have support for all the standard `UIElement` behaviors such as `Dependency-Properties` and `Events`. For example, if we want to catch a double-click on a column and display its details, we can do that fairly easily. First, we add a couple of lines to the place where we create the `Rectangles` in the `Update()` method.

```
rect.MouseDown += new MouseButtonEventHandler(rect_MouseDown);
rect.Tag = nvp;
```

We've added a handler for the `MouseDown` event, and we've also set the `Tag` property of the `Rectangle` to point to the `NameValuePair` that the `Rectangle` represents so that we can easily find it. Then, we can implement the `MouseDown` handler (listing 14.6).

Listing 14.6 `Rectangle` `MouseDown` handler

```
private void rect_MouseDown(object sender, MouseButtonEventArgs e)
{
 if (e.ClickCount == 2)     ❶
 {
  Rectangle rect = sender as Rectangle;     ❷
  NameValuePair nvp = rect.Tag as NameValuePair;     ❸

  if (nvp != null)     ❹
    MessageBox.Show(
         "Name: " + nvp.Name + ", Value: " + nvp.Value.ToString());
 }
}
```

`Shapes` don't have a `DoubleClick` event, but one of the properties passed to the handler is the number of times the button has been clicked ❶, so we can easily wait for the second click. You could also implement a triple-click option or, if you *really* hate your users, a quadruple-click feature.

We're using the same handler for all our `Rectangles`, but the specific one that is clicked will be passed as the sender to the handler ❷. We then get the associated `NameValuePair` out of the `Tag` ❸, where we stuck it earlier, and then pop up a functional, if banal, message ❹. Figure 14.9 shows the results.

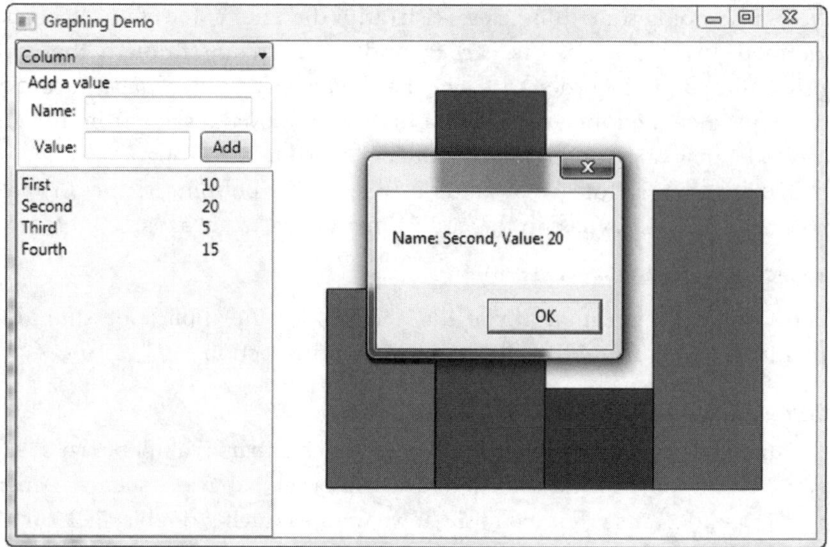

Figure 14.9 Because the columns are full-blown `UIElements`, we can subscribe to events. For example, we can catch clicks on the column.

We could take this further, if we wanted, by allowing the user to drag columns, resize them, and so on.

14.2.4 The downside of Shapes

At the moment, our graph is pretty simple, but we could make it as complex as we liked. We could add axes, labels, a legend, text on the columns, and other nifty things. And we could implement them all as `Shapes` and `Labels`, and so on. But, because `Shapes` are `UIElements`, they have a fair amount of overhead to provide all the support for the `UIElement` features and capabilities. Once the drawing gets more complex (figure 14.10), you might begin to notice some performance issues.

Now, to give the WPF developers their due, you have to add a *lot* of `Shapes` before you'll even notice any slowdown at all. Nonetheless, for complex drawing applications, there are better approaches to take that have much less overhead. In the first half of this chapter, we've concentrated on `Shapes`. Moving forward, we'll look at a couple of lighter-weight approaches. In fact, if you dig deep enough into the code, you'd discover that the `Shape` classes all rely on the lower-level drawing approaches such as *direct rendering*.

14.3 Drawing with direct rendering

Another approach that we can take to drawing is to directly render our graph when it's needed. This approach is the most similar to classic Windows drawing, where you'd catch the `WM_PAINT` message and redraw your application. For this reason, if you've done SDK controls or Windows Forms custom controls, this, in many ways, will feel the most comfortably familiar.

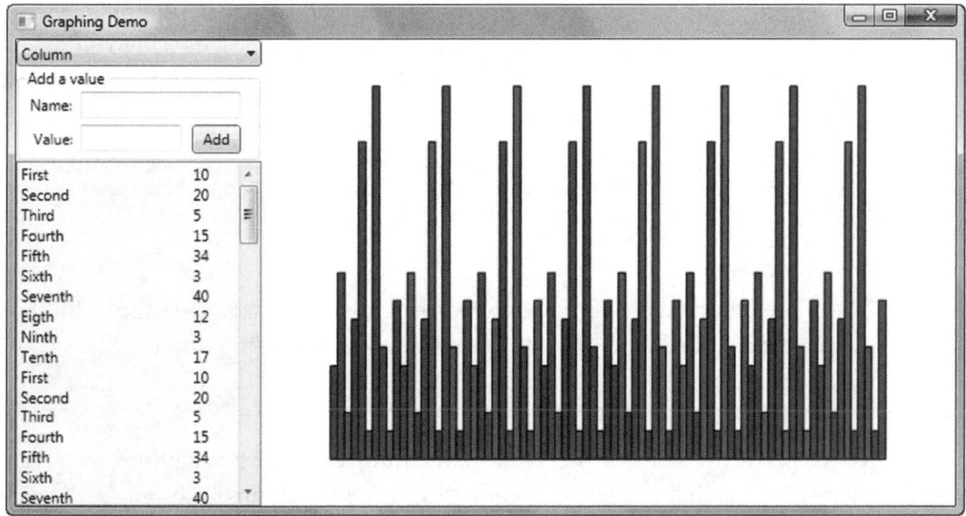

Figure 14.10 When you start adding *lots* of `Shapes`, performance and memory usage will begin to suffer. For example, resizing may get a little sluggish.

But, there's a *major* difference between the WPF approach and the old stuff. In classic Windows drawing, when a section of the screen needed to be redrawn, a message was sent to your `Window`, and you were expected to redraw the screen right away. If a user moved another `Window` on top of your `Window` and then moved it off again, you'd have to re-redraw that bit of the screen. This is referred to as *immediate mode* drawing because you have to immediately redraw everything as needed.

In contrast, WPF uses *retained-mode* drawing. When WPF tells you to draw something, it only tells you once. You then describe your UI to WPF (albeit in a way that seems similar to the immediate-mode approach). The difference, though, is that WPF remembers (or retains) the description of your UI and doesn't ask you to redraw anything when, for example, part of the `Window` is covered and then uncovered. The only time you have to redescribe your UI is if something changes (for example, if the `Window` is resized or if you want to change what it looks like).

Aside from being more convenient for the developer, this approach helps make it possible for WPF to take advantage of graphics card capabilities, handle complex transparency situations, and so on—because it controls the rendering.

14.3.1 Recreating the graph control

To demonstrate direct rendering, let's create an entirely new version of our `ColumnGraphCtrl` called `ColumnGraphRenderCtrl` that, instead of creating `Shape` objects, renders the graph as it's needed. Then we can swap out the controls and see what happens. As with the `Shape`-based graph, we'll be doing almost everything programmatically rather than with the Visual Studio designer. When we were using `Shapes`, if we'd known the `Shapes` we wanted ahead of time, we *could* have dragged them onto our control in the designer. But, with direct rendering, we have no such option; this is fairly normal—if we were using WinForms or MFC, we wouldn't get any designer help either.

The XAML for `ColumnGraphRenderCtrl` is even simpler than for `ColumnGraphCtrl`. We not only don't have to bother with a `Canvas` but we can get rid of the `Grid` as well.

```
<UserControl x:Class="GraphingWithShapes.ColumnGraphRenderCtrl"
    xmlns="http://schemas.microsoft.com/winfx/2006/xaml/presentation"
    xmlns:x="http://schemas.microsoft.com/winfx/2006/xaml"
    Height="300" Width="300" >
</UserControl>
```

That's the whole thing. And we can swap out the old `ColumnGraphCtrl` with the `ColumnGraphRenderCtrl` in the `GraphHolder` control by changing the one line of XAML:

```
<local:ColumnGraphRenderCtrl x:Name="graphCtrl" Grid.Column="1"
        Height="Auto" Width="Auto"/>
```

We've given the control the same name, and we'll have a method in `ColumnGraphRenderCtrl` called `SetData()`, as we did in the old control, so we won't even have to change that. Listing 14.7 has *most* of the code for the `ColumnGraphRenderCtrl`.

Listing 14.7 ColumnGraphRenderCtrl.xaml.cs

```
using System;
...bulk of using statements omitted...
using System.Collections.ObjectModel;
using System.Collections.Specialized;

namespace GraphingWithShapes
{
  public partial class ColumnGraphRenderCtrl : UserControl
  {
    private ObservableCollection<NameValuePair> dataPoints = null;
    private List<Color> columnColors =
       new List<Color>() { Colors.Blue, Colors.Red, Colors.Green };

    public ColumnGraphRenderCtrl()
    {
      InitializeComponent();                       Gets reference to
    }                                              list of values (1)

    public void SetData(ObservableCollection<NameValuePair> data)
    {
      dataPoints = data;
      dataPoints.CollectionChanged += new
         NotifyCollectionChangedEventHandler(dataPoints_CollectionChanged);

      InvalidateVisual();   (2)
    }

    void dataPoints_CollectionChanged(object sender,
                                  NotifyCollectionChangedEventArgs e)
    {
      InvalidateVisual();   (3)
    }
                                          Works the same
    public double GetLargestValue()       as before
```

```
    {
       // Implementation is the same as for the ColumnGraphCtrl
    }

    protected override void OnRender(DrawingContext drawingContext)    ◁┐
    {                                                                  │
       // Implementation will be shown later              The important │
    }                                                          method ❹
  }
}
```

We have a `SetData` method ❶ as we did before, and we subscribe to the `Collection-Changed` event in the same way. The only other thing we're doing is calling `Invali-dateVisual()` ❷. In fact, if you look at the handler for the collection changed event, you'll see that, unlike before, all we're doing here is calling `InvalidateVisual()` ❸. So, what's a `Visual`, and why would we want to `Invalidate` it? In this case, *Visual* refers to the visual representation of our control. There's also a class called `Visual`, which we'll discuss later, but that isn't what we're talking about here.

`Invalidate` is a term left over from the old Windows days. In yon olden days, you'd `Invalidate` a region of the screen, telling Windows that it needed to be repainted. `InvalidateVisual` is similar—it's saying that something has changed, and the visual representation of the control needs to be updated. When the representation is no longer valid, WPF will make a call to the `OnRender()` method ❹ to ask it to render itself again. Notice, by the way, that we don't have any handling anymore for resizing the control because resizing automatically invalidates the rendered version of the control, causing `OnRender` to be called.

IMPLEMENTING RENDERING

How do we *render* a control? (Hint: It does *not* involve big saws and men in bloody aprons.) If you're used to drawing in the Windows SDK or Windows Forms, this will seem spookily familiar (listing 14.8).

Listing 14.8 The `OnRender` method

```
protected override void OnRender(DrawingContext drawingContext)
{
  if (dataPoints != null)
  {                                                   ❶ More boring
    double spaceToUseY = ActualHeight * 0.8;      ◁┘   math stuff
    double spaceToUseX = ActualWidth * 0.8;
    double barWidth = spaceToUseX / dataPoints.Count;
    double largestValue = GetLargestValue();
    double unitHeight = spaceToUseY / largestValue;

    double bottom = ActualHeight * 0.9;      ◁┐  Calculates
    double left = ActualWidth * 0.1;          ❷  the bottom

    Brush fillBrush;
    Pen outlinePen = new Pen(Brushes.Black, 1);     ❸
    int nIndex = 0;
    Rect rect;
    double height;
```

```
        foreach (NameValuePair nvp in dataPoints)        ❹                Gets different ❺
        {                                                                          colors
          fillBrush =
            new SolidColorBrush(columnColors[nIndex % columnColors.Count]);

          height = (nvp.Value * unitHeight);
          rect = new Rect(left, bottom - height, barWidth, height);
          drawingContext.DrawRectangle(fillBrush, outlinePen, rect);      ❻

          left += rect.Width;
          nIndex++;
        }
      }
    }
```

This code looks a lot like the code from our `CalculateSizes` method from before, including most of the same math ❶, although we have to calculate the bottom differently now ❷ because we don't have that handy `Canvas.Bottom` method to do it for us.

We're also stepping through all the `NameValuePairs` as before ❹; but, instead of positioning `Shapes`, we're determining the color to use from our handy little color collection ❺, then determining the rectangle where the column should be, and calling a method called `DrawRectangle()` on the passed `DrawingContext` ❻.

This is where the old Win SDK stuff and the WPF stuff both converge and diverge. In drawing code with the Win SDK, you'd work with something called a Device Context (same initials as a `DrawingContext` even). You'd call methods on the Device Context for operations such as "Draw a Rectangle," "Draw a Line," or "Draw some text." And then the DC would do it. Immediately. Oh, there were a bunch of other things going on, as far as dealing with clipping and converting units and such, but, when you said "Draw a Rectangle," a rectangle would be drawn.

A `DrawingContext` is a little different. When you say "Draw a `Rectangle`," it says, "Uh huh, you want a rectangle, got it. Draw a line, uh huh, I remember." But it doesn't do any drawing. But, it *retains* a list of everything you want drawn. When WPF feels like it, it will get around to rendering the description of your drawing. In fact, the drawing will be done by another thread.

The delay between the commands and the rendering is short enough that it appears as though your drawing is done immediately, but you can do a little test—put a breakpoint in the `OnRender` method. Other than at startup, that breakpoint will only be hit when `InvalidateVisual()` is called *or* you resize the window. Had this been the old immediate-style code, the method would be called continuously to keep refreshing things, particularly as the debugger popped up on top to cover your drawing.

If you run the application now, it will look exactly the same as when we used shapes (figure 14.11). It isn't surprising that everything looks the same because, under the hood, WPF is using the same code to draw the rectangles. All we've changed is how we're providing the instructions.

We want to mention a couple of other things from the example before moving on. For one thing, notice that we're using a `Pen` ❸ to draw the border around the shape, rather than setting a `Brush` and `Stroke` details as we did with `Shape`. This is another

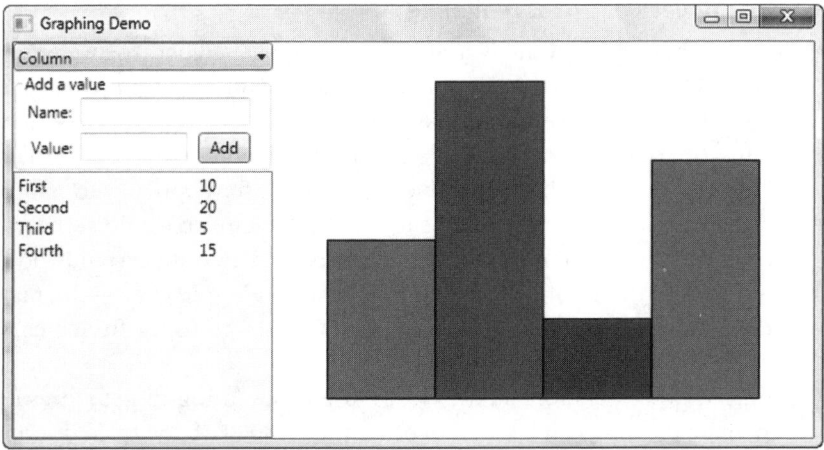

Figure 14.11 We're now using direct rendering instead of `Shapes`, but the graph looks the same.

concept borrowed from the Win SDK. Things like lines are drawn with `Pens`, although the color and content of those lines are defined by a `Brush` (which can be any brush, including gradients). A `Pen` also has properties like `Thickness`, `DashStyle`—in fact, all the properties exposed as Stroke*XXX* on `Shape`. It should come as no surprise that, behind the scenes, `Shape` takes all those properties and creates a `Pen` to draw the outline. `Shape` exposes the `Pen` properties in this way to make binding easier.

In the example, we're only using a single method on `DrawingContext`—`DrawRectangle` ❻. But, there are a bunch of other methods. Table 14.1 shows a handful of the more useful and interesting ones.

As per usual, you can check the doc or use IntelliSense to see all the other available methods.

Table 14.1 Some useful and interesting properties on `DrawingContext`

Method	Description
`DrawRectangle`	Already seen this one. Draws a rectangle.
`DrawEllipse`	Draws an ellipse.
`DrawLine`	Draws a line.
`DrawGeometry`	Draws a complex shape. This can include well-known shapes such as ellipses, rectangles, lines, curves, and so on.
`DrawText`	Draws text.
`DrawVideo`	Yes, you can draw video onto a surface!
`PushTransform`	Adds a Transform to the `DrawingContext`. After the Transform is added, everything added after it will be transformed appropriately (for example, rotated or skewed).

14.3.2 Pluses and minuses of direct rendering

Using direct rendering is definitely faster than using `Shapes` because we've eliminated tons of overhead. Also, in many ways the code seems quite a bit simpler—particularly if, like us, you're comfortable with Win SDK drawing. But, there are some drawbacks.

First, do you remember how easy it was to implement the `Click` handler for `Shapes`? Now that we don't have any objects, we don't have any way to handle that—we're clicking one big picture. This is the same problem we would've had with Win SDK drawing. We have some nice rectangular areas, so we could certainly do the math to figure out where the user clicked, but what if we had a pie chart—the math would be somewhat harder—or some arbitrarily complex shape using Bézier curves? The math would get really ugly really fast.

A second drawback is more subtle. We're used to wanting to get a drawing up on the screen, but a drawing can be used in other ways in WPF. Aside from drawing on the screen, we might want to draw to an image that we can save, or we might want to print. Also, with WPF, we can use drawings as brushes; we might make a design that we want to use, say, as a tiled background or texture. But, if we render everything directly, we can't do any of those things.

What we need is a representation that gives us *some* of the capabilities of a `Shape`—for example, knowing where it is so that we can tell that it has been clicked on, but still keep the fast rendering capabilities. This is where `Visuals` come in.

14.4 Drawing with Visuals

The `Visual` class is the lowest-level class for putting things on the screen. In some respects, it's the WPF equivalent of a Windows handle without all the overhead. `UIElements`, `Controls`, 3D stuff—these are all derived from the `Visual` class.

The `Visual` class itself is abstract, but there's a derivation of the `Visual` class called `DrawingVisual`, which is a lightweight class for handling drawing. In fact, it's so lightweight that it can't even draw by itself—it can be used to describe a drawing, but it needs to be hosted by something else in order to be rendered to the screen—or wherever.

In the previous section, we overrode the `OnRender()` method of our control and painted our UI using the `DrawingContext` passed into that method. To use a `DrawingVisual` we do something similar—except that we get a `DrawingContext` out of the `DrawingVisual`—something like:

```
DrawingVisual vis = new DrawingVisual();
DrawingContext drawingContext = vis.RenderOpen();
drawingContext.DrawRectangle(useful arguments here);
drawingContext.Close();
```

This code leaves us with a `DrawingVisual` object that contains all the instructions to render itself. But, as we said, we need a class to draw the `Visual`. One built-in way is to create a class called `RenderTargetBitmap`. With this class, we can have our `Visual` render itself out, and then put the `Bitmap` into an `Image` object, which can be put anywhere because it's a `Control`. We'd do that like this:

```
RenderTargetBitmap bmp =
   new RenderTargetBitmap(100, 100, 96, 96, PixelFormats.Pbgra32);
bmp.Render(drawingVisual);

Image img = new Image();
img.Source = bmp;
```

We'd then add the `Image` object to a layout, or do whatever we wanted to with it. The downside of this is that we're adding a *picture* (a bitmap) of our rendered `Visual`—the `Visual` itself is lost, so we lose the ability to do hit testing or otherwise manipulate the drawing. Instead, we want something that renders the `Visual(s)` on demand, but doesn't lose track of them.

14.4.1 Control for display Visuals

Unfortunately, there's no built-in class in WPF for rendering `Visuals` in the way described (although there probably should be), but it's pretty easy to build one ourselves. Listing 14.9 shows a class we've created for that purpose.

Listing 14.9 `Visual` Control

```
using System;
using System.Collections.Generic;
using System.Windows;
using System.Windows.Controls;
using System.Windows.Input;
using System.Windows.Media;
using System.Collections.ObjectModel;
using System.Collections.Specialized;
using System.Globalization;

namespace GraphingWithShapes
{
  public class ColumnGraphVisualCtrl : FrameworkElement      ← 1 Derives from FrameworkElement
  {
    private VisualCollection visuals;      ← 2 Collection of Visuals

    public ColumnGraphVisualCtrl()
    {
      visuals = new VisualCollection(this);      3
    }

    protected override int VisualChildrenCount      ← 4 Number of Visuals
    {
      get {return visuals.Count;}
    }

    protected override Visual GetVisualChild(int index)      ← 5 Gets each Visual
    {
      return visuals[index];
    }
  }
}
```

Notice that our new class is derived from `FrameworkElement` ❶. It isn't a `UserControl`. In fact, if you create it as a `UserControl` you'll run into trouble, because

UserControls expect the Visuals that they contain to be a little higher-level than the ones we intend to give it. We've created the ColumnGraphVisualCtrl as a regular class and added the base class reference ourselves—there's no XAML file associated with this control at all.

The whole purpose of this class is to render one or more Visuals, so we need a place to store them. VisualCollection ❷ is a special collection class for that purpose. Notice that we're passing a reference to our class when we initialize the VisualCollection ❸. Because the VisualCollection knows about our class, the collection will automatically do a bunch of housekeeping for us, making sure that the base FrameworkElement class knows about the Visuals in all the appropriate ways.

The Visuals that we add will be considered children of our control. All that we need to do to get WPF to render them for us is override a couple of methods—one that tells the class how *many* children we have ❹ and one that provides each individual child as it's requested ❺.

That's pretty much all we have to do—except to somehow provide the Visuals we want displayed.

To add the Visuals, we're going to add code to this class that does what we did with the other versions of the graphing control for setting and holding onto data. We'll add the same collection of NameValuePairs, and the same initialization and event methods.

```
private ObservableCollection<NameValuePair> dataPoints = null;
private List<Color> columnColors =
          new List<Color>() { Colors.Blue, Colors.Red, Colors.Green };

public void SetData(ObservableCollection<NameValuePair> data)
{
  dataPoints = data;
  dataPoints.CollectionChanged += new
       NotifyCollectionChangedEventHandler(dataPoints_CollectionChanged);
  Update();
}

void dataPoints_CollectionChanged(object sender,
                                   NotifyCollectionChangedEventArgs e)
{
  Update();
}
```

This code should be familiar, except that we're calling an Update() method instead of InvalidateVisual(). The Update() method is where all the work takes place (listing 14.10).

Listing 14.10 Update() method

```
protected void Update()
{
  visuals.Clear();              ❶ Clears existing Visuals

  if (dataPoints != null)
```

```
  {
    double spaceToUseY = ActualHeight * 0.8;          <-- Same old math
    double spaceToUseX = ActualWidth * 0.8;
    double barWidth = spaceToUseX / dataPoints.Count;
    double largestValue = GetLargestValue();           <-- Method copied
    double unitHeight = spaceToUseY / largestValue;        from previous
                                                           implementation
    double bottom = ActualHeight * 0.9;
    double left = ActualWidth * 0.1;

    Brush fillBrush;
    Pen outlinePen = new Pen(Brushes.Black, 1);
    int nIndex = 0;
    Rect rect;
    double height;
    DrawingVisual visual;
    foreach (NameValuePair nvp in dataPoints)
    {                                                  (2) New Visual for
      visual = new DrawingVisual();                  <--   each Column
      using (DrawingContext drawingContext = visual.RenderOpen())     (3)
      {
        fillBrush =
          new SolidColorBrush(columnColors[nIndex % columnColors.Count]);

        height = (nvp.Value * unitHeight);
        rect = new Rect(left, bottom - height, barWidth, height);
        drawingContext.DrawRectangle(fillBrush, outlinePen, rect);     (4)
      }

      visuals.Add(visual);               <--   AddsVisual to
      nvp.Tag = visual;      (6)          (5)  collection

      left += rect.Width;
      nIndex++;
    }
  }
}
```

Much of this code is unchanged from our last implementation. But, we are doing a few things differently. First, we're getting rid of any existing `Visuals` each time the method is called ❶. Unlike with a `Shape`, we can't change the properties of an existing `Visual`.

We create a new `DrawingVisual` for each `NameValuePair` ❷. This `Visual` is what will eventually get rendered for each bar. We *could* put all the bars into a single `Visual`, but if we did that, then we wouldn't be able to tell them apart for things like click-handling. To "draw" into the `DrawingVisual`, we have to get a `DrawingContext`, which we get by calling `RenderOpen()`. Note that we're making use of a *using* statement here ❸; it makes sure that `visual.Close()` is called when we're done. We could have easily called that method explicitly, but this approach is a little safer and more elegant.

We then draw our `Column` onto the `DrawingContext` ❹. Finally, we add our new `DrawingVisual` to our collection of `Children` ❺. Note that we *don't* have to do anything special to make the `Visual` redraw itself. When the `VisualCollection` is updated, it automatically handles that for us. We're also storing a reference to the DrawingVisual in the NameValuePair ❻ so that we can use it for hit testing later.

We need to do one more thing to our control—we need to make sure that our display is appropriately updated when it's resized. To do that, we subscribe to the SizeChanged event, which we can do in the constructor.

```
SizeChanged += new SizeChangedEventHandler(OnSizeChanged);
```

And then we add the handler.

```
private void OnSizeChanged(object sender, SizeChangedEventArgs e)
{
  Update();
}
```

The last step is to update the XAML for GraphHolder to use the new control.

```
<local:ColumnGraphVisualCtrl x:Name="graphCtrl" Grid.Column="1"
                                       Height="Auto" Width="Auto"/>
```

If you're following along, go ahead and run. The application should look just like the direct rendering version shown in figure 14.11, or for that matter, the Shapes version from figure 14.8. But, this version is much lighter-weight than the Shapes version, which would matter more if our display was more complex. Also, unlike the direct-rendering version, we can do things like hit testing, which we'll talk about in the next section.

14.4.2 Hit testing with Visuals

Shapes *are* Visuals, but Visuals are *not* Shapes. (We're going for the profound statement of the year with that one.) The point, though, is that the ability to catch events that exists on Shapes isn't available on our DrawingVisuals, but Visuals *do* support a hit-test mechanism that can tell us whether they've been clicked on or not. This is a much lower-level mechanism, but it is, in fact, the mechanism that Shapes use to expose events.

Our ColumnGraphVisualCtrl is a FrameworkElement, so we can catch the MouseDown event on that class. Rather than subscribing to the event, we can override the OnMouseDown() method on the class to save a step. Then, in that handler, we can use the low-level hit testing to see which (if any) of our Visual children was hit. Listing 14.11 shows the implementation of the OnMouseDown method.

Listing 14.11 Hit testing with Visuals

```
protected override void OnMouseDown(MouseButtonEventArgs e)
{                                                    ❶ Checks for double-click
  if (e.ClickCount == 2)
  {                                                  ❷ Converts point to proper coordinates
    Point pt = e.GetPosition(this);
                                                     ❸ Does hit test
    HitTestResult result = VisualTreeHelper.HitTest(this, pt);
    if (result != null)
```

```
        {
          foreach (NameValuePair nvp in dataPoints)      ❹
          {
            if (nvp.Tag == result.VisualHit)
            {
              MessageBox.Show("Name: " + nvp.Name + ", Value: "
                   + nvp.Value.ToString());
              break;
            }
          }
        }
      }
    }
```

When the user clicks *anywhere on our entire control*, this method will be called. We're first making sure that the user double-clicked ❶. Then we have to convert the point the user clicked into units relative to our control ❷. The real work, though, is done by the static `HitTest` method ❸ on a class called `VisualTreeHelper`. This class has various methods for helping out with `Visuals`. The `HitTest` method looks through all the child `Visuals` of the class to see if the passed point intersects any of the `Visuals` that are children of our control. If one is found, we step through all the `NameValuePairs` to find the one associated with the hit `Visual` ❹. Unfortunately, `Visual` doesn't have a `Tag`, so we can't associate the `NameValuePair` directly with the object. In a more sophisticated example, we'd use some form of dictionary to facilitate quick lookup of the appropriate `NameValuePair`.

That's pretty much it. Again, though, the behavior will look as it did in figure 14.9, so we aren't going to bother with a screenshot.

Handling multiple hits

In our example, our shapes don't overlap, so there's no chance for more than one `Visual` to be hit with the same click, but in other scenarios, it would be quite possible for this to happen. The version of `HitTest()` that we're using will stop as soon as any child is found. But, another overload of `HitTest()` will handle multiple hits. It's a little more complex to use because you have to pass an event handler, which will be called each time a hit takes place. We could rewrite our code to use this overload (listing 14.12).

Listing 14.12 Handling multiple hits

```
protected override void OnMouseDown(MouseButtonEventArgs e)
{
  if (e.ClickCount == 2)
  {
    Point pt = e.GetPosition(this);

    VisualTreeHelper.HitTest(this, null,
        new HitTestResultCallback(OnVisualHit),
        new PointHitTestParameters(pt));          ❶
  }
}

protected HitTestResultBehavior OnVisualHit(HitTestResult result)     ❷
```

```
{
  foreach (NameValuePair nvp in dataPoints)
  {
    if (nvp.Tag == result.VisualHit)
    {
      MessageBox.Show("Name: " + nvp.Name + ", Value: "
          + nvp.Value.ToString());
      break;
    }
  }

  return HitTestResultBehavior.Continue;        ❸
}
```

We're using a version of `HitTest()` that takes a callback method ❶. The method also takes various other arguments that would, for example, let us control the way the hit test takes place, but we aren't going to worry about that right now. The handler ❷ will get called for every `Visual` that's hit. We're doing the same thing here we did before in the `OnMouseDown` method—find the associated `NameValuePair` and display its data.

We can return two different values from our handler: `HitTestResultBehavior.Continue` ❸, which says move on to the next `Visual` that's hit, or `HitTestResultBehavior.Stop`, which would stop looking for any more hits.

Because we have no overlap, we'll only get one hit, so the behavior will be exactly the same. By the way, the reason that the hit test uses a callback instead of, say, returning a collection, is for performance and efficiency. If there were a lot of overlapping shapes, memory would have to be reserved to hold the entire collection and the hit testing would keep going even if the caller was looking for the first or second hit.

14.4.3 Adding labels to our graph

So far our chart hasn't changed its look from implementation to implementation. But, we'd like to add a little bit to this version by displaying the name beneath each column. We want to do this for the following reasons:

- We want to show that a `Visual` isn't tied to a single shape.
- We want to demonstrate that the hit testing is fancy enough to handle complex shapes.
- We want an opportunity to put in another screenshot that *doesn't* look like one we've already done.

As it happens, it's easy to add labels to our chart. In the `Update()` method, directly beneath the `DrawRectangle` call, we add the following:

```
FormattedText ft = new FormattedText(nvp.Name,
                                     CultureInfo.CurrentCulture,
                                     FlowDirection.LeftToRight,
                                     new Typeface("Verdana"), 12,
   fillBrush);
ft.TextAlignment = TextAlignment.Center;
drawingContext.DrawText(ft,
               new Point((left + rect.Width / 2), bottom + 5));
```

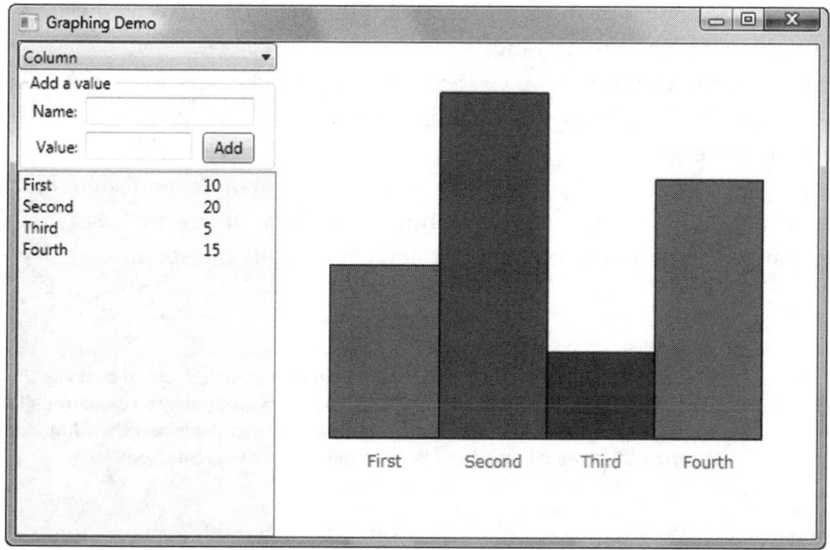

Figure 14.12 We've added labels to our graph, although our implementation won't be quite so pretty if there are a *lot* of rows.

The `DrawText()` method, like the `DrawRectangle()` method, adds something to the `Visual`. The argument that it takes is a `FormattedText` object, which describes the text we want to add, the font to use, the brush, and so on. We're specifying that the text should be drawn 5 pixels below the bottom of our columns and centered on the bar. Figure 14.12 shows the results.

Aside from making our graph a little more readable, we can now demonstrate something pretty cool. Because we've added the labels to the same visuals as the column, clicking the labels will *also* count as a hit on the `Visuals`. If we wanted to do this with the `Shape` implementation, we'd either have to create some `Labels` and handle clicks on those separately, or we'd have to use a `Path Shape` that includes both the column and the `Label`—which would have been quite tricky.

All the drawing that we've done so far has been quite simplistic, which is largely a function of our own artistic abilities (or lack thereof)—and, to be fair, a column chart doesn't inspire our internal muses as much as it might. If we were doing something more impressive, the *approach* would have been the same. And, as you'll see in the next section, WPF will let you do arbitrarily complex drawing.

14.5 Drawings and Geometries

So far we've demonstrated drawing by shoving together some number of elements, such as rectangles, ellipses, text, and so on, in some way that the user can interact with them. This approach works well for the scenarios we've explored so far, but we might want to work with more complex things. For example, we might want to include bitmaps or video clips in what we're rendering. Also, we might want to have more elaborate clip-art-style drawings. In this section, we'll talk about the steps involved in creating and using more elaborate drawings.

Now, with the techniques we've shown so far and with access to the various primitives, we could obviously create complex drawings. For example, suppose we wanted to draw a magnifying glass like the one in figure 14.13. We could write code to draw some ellipses, create some polygons to represent the handle, add some more shapes to fill in the shadows, and so on. By writing the code to draw onto a `Visual`, we could even treat the shape as a whole unit to catch clicks on it, and so on.

Figure 14.13 A drawing of a magnifying glass could be created by using the drawing primitives we've discussed so far. This image was created by a company called Grafile, who has given us permission to use it here. You can download the XAML for this and another 30+ free images from their website at www.grafile.com.

However—and it's a big however—this would be a terrible way of doing drawings. First, artists aren't known for their expertise in procedural code. They want to use drawing tools. Second, code isn't a good transfer medium for drawing. It would be far more convenient if we could define the drawing in XAML, so that it could easily be moved about, referenced, changed without changing code, and so on. Last, we don't want to have to mess with doing the math to resize the magnifying glass (or other images) for different uses—we want the system to handle that for us.

This is where `Drawings` come in. A `Drawing` can define a complex image that can easily be referenced from multiple places. It can be defined in XAML (or in code), and there are multiple tools designed for artists to create drawings, including Microsoft Expression Design, an Illustrator-like tool that exports XAML. The best part is that `Drawings` can be automatically sized and the resized image is very high quality—it isn't just a zoomed-in version of a bunch of pixels (figure 14.14).

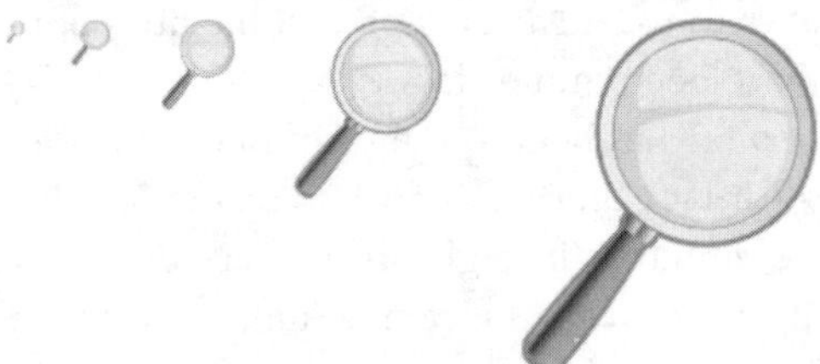

Figure 14.14 `Drawings` can automatically adjust their size, but the quality of the images remains intact. This is the same technology that underlies the high-quality icons used in Windows Vista.

The abstract `Drawing` class in .NET has several different derivations for different purposes (table 14.2).

These different types of `Drawings` can be defined in XAML. For example, an `ImageDrawing` might look like this:

```
<ImageDrawing Rect="0,0,100,100"
           ImageSource="C:\WINDOWS\Web\Wallpaper\Bliss.bmp"/>
```

Table 14.2 Types of `Drawings`

Class	Purpose
`ImageDrawing`	Used to hold a graphic, such as a bitmap. This is the low-level, lower-overhead class to use to hold an `Image`—versus the `Image` class, which has all the event support, layouts, and so on.
`VideoDrawing`	Lets you "draw" a video clip that can be played, started, stopped, and so on.
`GeometryDrawing`	A drawing made up of various shapes such as curves. This is what was used to create the magnifying glass from figure 14.13.
`GlyphRunDrawing`	Lets you draw text with extreme accuracy—you'd use this if you were going to build a typesetting application.
`DrawingGroup`	Groups multiple drawings together.

Note that the details will be different for each type of `Drawing`. But, you can't use a `Drawing` directly—it has to be contained in something. Three different things can hold a `Drawing` (and the first one will blow your mind):

- *`DrawingImage`*—An `Image` (like a bitmap) whose contents are defined by one of the `Drawing` classes. You can use a `DrawingImage` in most of the places where you can use an `ImageSource`, such as in an `Image` class. And, yes, you're reading correctly—you can put an `ImageDrawing` into a `DrawingImage`! Someone at Microsoft was cackling maniacally after coming up with that one. Fortunately, when you're working in XAML, it will yell at you if you try to use the wrong class in the wrong place, so it ends up not being too hard to figure out which class you want. M*ost* of the time, when you are working with drawings, you'll end up using a `DrawingImage` to host it.
- *`DrawingBrush`*—A `Brush` that lets you use a picture to paint things. You can use this brush as you would a solid color brush or a gradient brush. One common use of a `DrawingBrush` is to fill in a shape with a pattern. Figure 14.15 shows our graph using the magnifying glass as a brush.
- *`DrawingVisual`*—A `Visual` whose content is a `Drawing`. As we've covered in some detail already, `Visual` is the base class of virtually everything you can draw on the screen. A `DrawingVisual` is a lightweight representation of a drawing but, as you've seen, you have to have something else to hold onto the Visual. We could, for example, add a `DrawingVisual` directly to our `VisualCollection` in the `ColumnGraphVisualCtrl`, although that wouldn't be a useful thing to do.

The effect in figure 14.15 was accomplished by defining a `DrawingBrush`, setting its `TileMode` to `Tile`, `ViewPortUnits` to `Absolute`, and the `ViewPort` to `"0,0,16,16"`. We then set the `Drawing` of the `DrawingBrush` to the `ImageDrawing` of the magnifying glass.

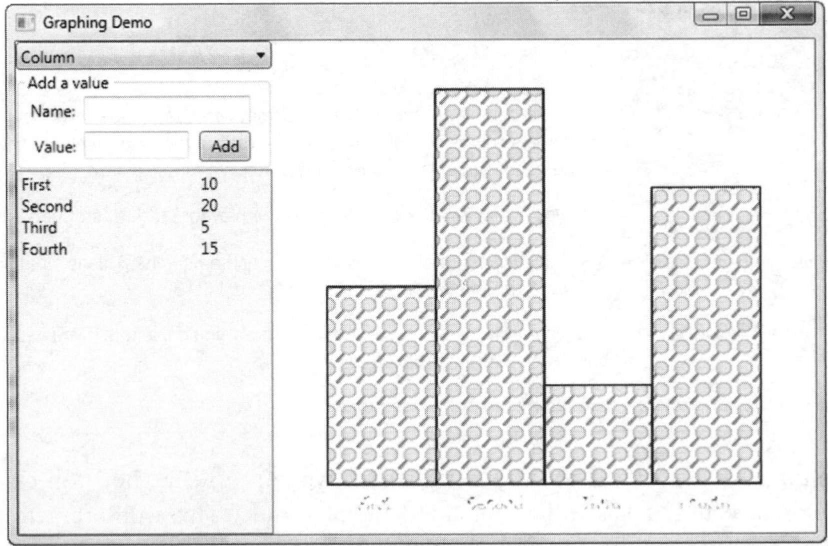

Figure 14.15 Using the magnifying glass as a brush. Notice that we're also using it to draw the text, which isn't terribly readable.

14.5.1 GeometryDrawing

Of the five drawing classes, `GeometryDrawing` is the most interesting because it lets you create arbitrarily complex drawings. A `GeometryDrawing` is made up of a series of `Geometry` elements of different types, such as `Ellipses` and `Rectangles` (sound familiar?). One of the most important `Geometry` classes is `PathGeometry`, which we saw earlier for the `Path Shape`. The `Shape` classes all really just wrap `Drawings` displayed on `Visuals`.

A `PathGeometry` is made up of a set of `PathSegment` classes—`ArcSegment`, `BezierSegment`, `LineSegment`, and so on. You can build a `GeometryDrawing` in code by creating these classes and adding them appropriately, or you can build them in XAML—something like this:

```
<GeometryDrawing>
  <GeometryDrawing.Geometry>
    <PathGeometry>
      <PathFigure>
        <LineSegment Point="100,0" />
        <BezierSegment Point1="100,0" Point2="200,200" Point3="300,100" />
      </PathFigure>
    </PathGeometry>
  <GeometryDrawing.Drawing>
</GeometryDrawing>
```

This is a simple drawing, and there's already a fair amount of XAML. For complex drawings, there could be hundreds of elements, making the XAML very unwieldy. For this reason, there's a shorthand notation defined for geometries that allows them to be specified as long strings of instructions. For example, the previous example could be represented like this:

```
<GeometryDrawing Geometry="L 100,0 C 100,0 200,200 300,100" />
```

You can find the details of both the full notation and the shorthand notation in the MSDN documentation, so we won't bother to reiterate it here; but, to give you an idea of what we're doing, note that L stands for Line and C for Curve. Even with the shorthand notation, complex drawings can be very verbose. For example, the magnifying glass is 95 lines of XAML, even using the shorthand notation. Here's the beginning of it:

```
<DrawingImage x:Key="Horizon_Image_Search">
  <DrawingImage.Drawing>
    <DrawingGroup>
      <DrawingGroup.Children>
        <GeometryDrawing Brush="#FF8D8AA1" Geometry="F1 M 186.689,185.664C
  186.689,125.155 235.918,76.1029 296.648,76.1029C 357.378,76.1029
  406.609,125.155 406.609,185.664C 406.609,246.174 357.378,295.226
  296.648,295.226C 235.918,295.226 186.689,246.174 186.689,185.664 Z M
  209.061,185.664C 209.061,233.862 248.274,272.934 296.648,272.934C
  345.024,272.934 384.237,233.862 384.237,185.664C 384.237,137.465
  345.024,98.3949 296.648,98.3949C 248.274,98.3949 209.061,137.465
  209.061,185.664 Z "/>
        <GeometryDrawing Brush="#FF8D8AA1" Geometry="F1 M 237.133,297.975C
  214.116,334.721 186.581,371.926 154.528,409.579C 152.716,412.254
  145.576,420.27 134.722,416.4C 130.458,414.879 117.658,405.728
  115.005,399.912C 113.265,396.098 111.197,384.04 117.872,378.33C
  143.848,344.773 174.48,311.106 209.75,277.327C 213.31,264.522
  208.849,269.049 220.792,256.186C 230.661,269.312 239.817,274.231
  254.506,281.607C 254.506,281.607 249.67,288.171 247.89,290.352C
  241.554,298.11 242.781,294.211 237.133,297.975 Z "/>
```

...*89* more lines of XAML to follow...

Of course, the artist who created the magnifying glass didn't hand-code this XAML, and it would be very unusual for that to ever be done. Instead, he used a tool like Microsoft Expression Design, and then exported the image as XAML. Expect to see more tools for doing this, as well as more precreated libraries.

14.5.2 Using Drawings

Creating `Drawings` is obviously not trivial, but using them is. The images from Grafile, such as the magnifying glass, are distributed as a XAML resource dictionary, although they could be distributed as a standalone DLL, like the dictionary of Windows styles. The simplest way to use the third-party pictures is to use the `DrawingImage` in an `Image`, like this:

```
<Image Source="{StaticResource Horizon_Image_Search}" />
```

Now you're back to having a `Control` with all its overhead, but it isn't too bad, considering it's containing all the separate elements. If you're doing direct rendering or using `Visuals`, you can get the resource in code, and then draw it to the `DrawingContext`.

```
DrawingImage img =
  Application.Current.FindResource("Horizon_Image_Search") as DrawingImage;
drawingContext.DrawImage(img, rect);
```

This code makes it pretty obvious that the image is being stored as a DrawingImage, but it doesn't have to be—the resource could be the GeometryDrawing. But, that would mean you'd have to wrap the GeometryDrawing, so it's pretty common to go the DrawingImage route. This isn't a major problem, even if you want to use the Geometry in another way. For example, this is how we used the magnifying glass as a brush in figure 14.15:

```
DrawingImage img =
   Application.Current.FindResource("Horizon_Image_Search")
                                                   as DrawingImage;
DrawingBrush drawBrush = new DrawingBrush(img.Drawing);
drawBrush.TileMode = TileMode.Tile;
drawBrush.Viewport = new Rect(0, 0, 16, 16);
drawBrush.ViewportUnits = BrushMappingMode.Absolute;
drawingContext.DrawRectangle(drawBrush, outlinePen, rect);
```

This code extracts the Drawing out of the DrawingImage and passes it into the DrawingBrush. We could also have done that in XAML. This Brush could go anywhere you might put any other brush. For example, we've set the background of the ListBox of NameValuePairs to use the magnifying glass as a brush.

```
<ListBox.Background>
   <DrawingBrush Opacity="0.2"  TileMode="Tile"
     ViewportUnits="Absolute" Viewport="0,0,16,16" Drawing=
     "{Binding Source={StaticResource Horizon_Image_Search},Path=Drawing}"/>
</ListBox.Background>
```

As you can see in figure 14.16, the result is fairly hideous, although we've set the Opacity of the brush to 0.2 to make it slightly less obnoxious.

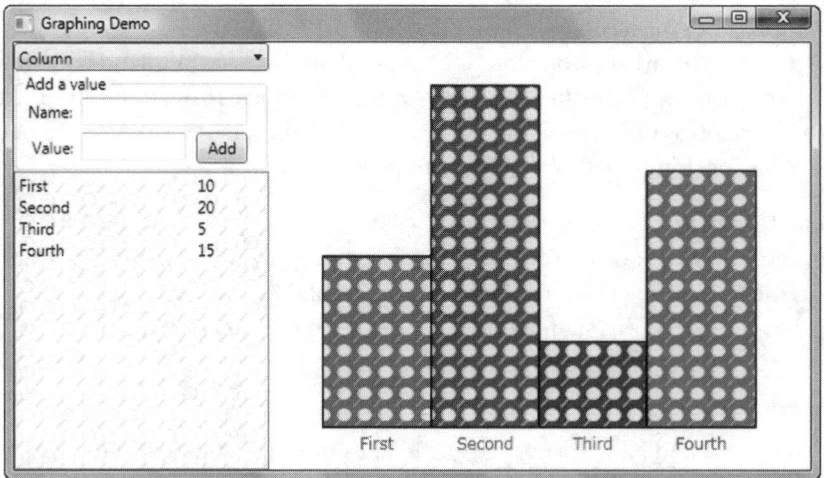

Figure 14.16 The DrawingBrush behind the ListBox was done with XAML. The DrawingBrush in the columns was done in code. If you run this application and then resize the window repeatedly, you'll be hypnotized into going out and buying another 30 copies of this book...

With great power comes great responsibility. Before shipping your application, make sure that you find someone with a modicum of taste. If he immediately passes out from seeing your UI, you should maybe consider going with a solid color. We hope that, in this section (and chapter), we've given you a good feel for the sorts of things that are possible with WPF drawing.

14.6 Summary

All in all, this chapter has been fun to write—we got to play with pretty shapes and colors, and we're pretty easily amused. We were limited by our lack of artistic ability, but managed to work around this by leveraging the work of real artists. This is a core design goal of WPF—to let the artists and the domain experts work independently, but to end up with a unified application. But, as the programmers, we do have the final word on the evil ways in which the artist's work gets used!

Although, in some respects, we've barely scratched the surface of drawing in WPF, you should have enough of an understanding of the framework that you'll know where to go and what to look for. We couldn't possibly cover all the myriad properties of all the different drawing classes without dedicating the entire book to the one topic. MSDN is much better at providing lists of properties, but not so good at the big picture.

We aren't quite done with our graphing application. In the next chapter we're going to explore yet *another* way of drawing our chart—this time in 3D. If nothing else, it will at least look different from the three versions in this chapter!

15 Drawing in 3D

This chapter covers:

- Building a 3D world
- 3D Transforms
- Our ponderings on the thoughts of electronic monks

When we first saw that WPF had extensive support for 3D, we immediately started talking about some of the cool things we expected to be able to do, such as having controls angling off into the distance on a pane to the side of the screen to take up less real estate or creating some really cool 3D transitions.

It turns out that, although it's possible to do these things, it isn't the primary target for 3D in WPF. The 3D support in WPF is reasonably extensive and pretty cool, but it's quite distinct from the 2D world we've inhabited so far. The general approach for 3D is to put a special container into your application and then put 3D content into that. An example would be building a 3D model of your office and allowing the user to fly through it. Adding a maniac with a gun, à la Quake XVII, is an optional extra. When WPF first came out, thinking about anything approaching a Quake-like game would have been unthinkable, but as the technology has progressed, it has become more and more reasonable. WPF still isn't the platform of choice for high-speed games, but it's getting there...

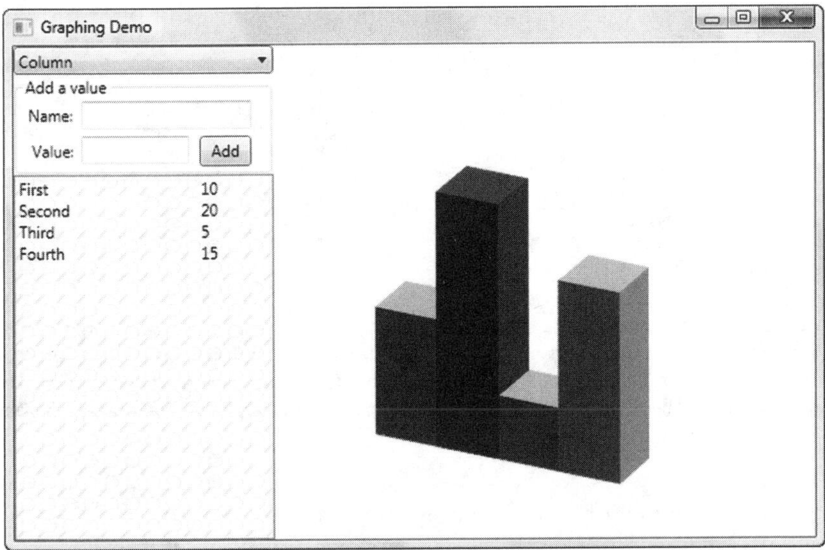

Figure 15.1 In this chapter, we'll re-create the graph from chapter 14 but in 3D.

The 3D support in WPF is a relatively thin wrapper on Direct3D, the 3D portion of DirectX. This isn't surprising, considering that WPF uses Direct3D for pretty much *everything*—most of the 2D stuff uses Direct3D under the hood, although it's wrapped so well that you'd never know it. With 3D, the implementation isn't so well hidden, making it a little more complex to use; it does still use things like XAML and the Property System, so it's not too much of a departure from what you're used to.

Going through all the concepts needed to handle 3D is a book by itself—one with lots of cool pictures and ugly math. The 3D capabilities in WPF, though simple (for 3D implementations), could equally take up another book. In this chapter, we're going to breach the surface of 3D to give a taste of what's possible and how it's approached. We'll take the graphing example from the previous chapter and make a 3D version of the graph (figure 15.1).

15.1 Lights, camera...

Working with 3D is much like working on a movie set. You have to create a simulated world of three-dimensional models that represent the things that you want to show up. You have to position a camera and point it in an appropriate direction to control what you see, and you have to put in lights or you won't be able to see anything. Based on all these things, WPF will create a two-dimensional image that simulates what you'd see if you were looking through the viewfinder of the camera onto the scene.

The viewfinder is represented via the use of a class called `Viewport3D`. `Viewport3D` is another `FrameworkElement` that you can position in your layout like any control. Inside the `Viewport3D` is where all your 3D elements reside. This is one of the biggest limitations of the 3D support in WPF—although you can easily put 3D

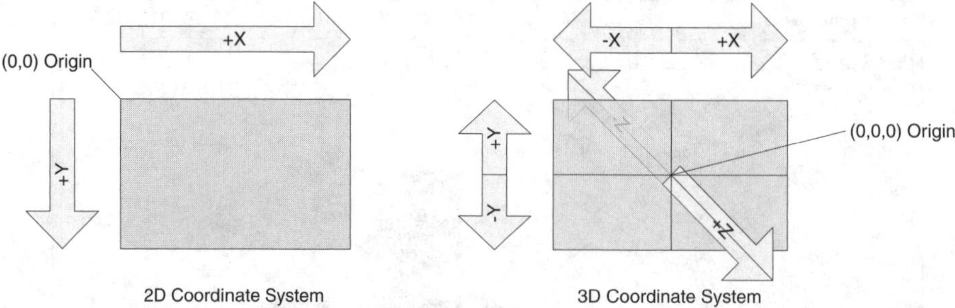

Figure 15.2 In 2D, the coordinates all start in the upper-left corner and go from there. In 3D, the coordinates start at a central point and radiate outward, with right and up being positive, and down and left being negative. On the Z-axis, positive is toward the viewer, and negative is away. This order for the Z-axis follows what's called the *righthand rule*, once again demonstrating the bias against lefthanded people.

content in the middle of your 2D application, the 3D elements are limited to their own sandbox.

In the `Viewport3D` sandbox, the coordinate system is different than what we're used to in the 2D world, as you can see from figure 15.2.

If you were more or less awake during your geometry classes, you should recognize a three-dimensional Cartesian coordinate system; the central point where all the axes cross is 0,0,0, with the values increasing to the right, top, and toward the viewer. Also, like the real universe, but unlike the two-dimensional space, there's no explicit edge based on the width and height of the available space (other than those limits imposed by the numbering system). You can create arbitrarily large or small three-dimensional models, and they will be visible (or not) depending on where and how you set up your camera.

We'll start by creating a model so that we have something to look at. Then we'll set up lighting and cameras so that we can see our models. As with the more low-level drawing in the last chapter, Visual Studio 2008 won't help us out too much, although other tools are often used to create 3D models and scenes and we expect a number of them to support exporting to XAML in the near future.

15.1.1 Models

Models, as in real life, are what we look at in a 3D world. Unlike in the real world (with some very disturbing runway exceptions), WPF models are made up of little triangles because you need a minimum of three points to define a surface in a 3D world, and when you join the three points together, you get a triangle. Once the triangle is defined (by its points) and is covered in some material (say, the color blue), the system can calculate, based on the position of the camera and the available lights, how it should look on a 2D screen.

But, the fact that a model is made up of triangles can make building them fairly tedious, and it's relatively unusual to build models manually. Usually a 3D design tool (such as ZAM3D from Electric Rain) would be used to create the models, just as a design tool would be used to build 2D XAML icons. The design tool would export the model by breaking it down into appropriate little triangles for use by the WPF 3D system.

Curves with triangles?

You might be wondering if *everything* in 3D is done using triangles. For example, if you want to create a sphere, triangles might not seem to be ideal, but even things like spheres are built using triangles. The smoother that you want the curves, the more triangles you have to use. Other 3D technologies, such as ray tracing, work in a different way. With ray tracing, if you want a sphere, you provide the formula for a sphere, and the computer calculates every bit of light intersecting that formula, as well as colors, shadows, and reflections. Whenever you see a detailed 3D computer-generated image with beautiful shadows and reflections, it's almost always done with ray tracing.

Unfortunately, ray-tracing is fairly slow, and the 3D engine behind WPF is more designed for creating 60 frame-per-second animations than really detailed images. It uses triangles and a bunch of tricks to simulate a reasonable facsimile of a 3D image.

Listing 15.1 shows the XAML for a simple (flat) rectangle.

Listing 15.1 XAML for a 3D rectangle

```
<Viewport3D>                                      ❶ ViewPort
  <Viewport3D.Children>
    <ModelVisual3D>
      <ModelVisual3D.Content>
        <GeometryModel3D>                                            Points ❷
          <GeometryModel3D.Geometry>
            <MeshGeometry3D Positions="-2,-2,0  2,-2,0  -2,2,0  2,2,0"
                        TriangleIndices="0,1,2  1,3,2" />
          </GeometryModel3D.Geometry>                            ❸ Triangles
          <GeometryModel3D.Material>
            <DiffuseMaterial>
              <DiffuseMaterial.Brush>
                <SolidColorBrush Color="Blue" />       ❹ Material
              </DiffuseMaterial.Brush>
            </DiffuseMaterial>
          </GeometryModel3D.Material>
        </GeometryModel3D>
      </ModelVisual3D.Content>
    </ModelVisual3D>
  </Viewport3D.Children>
</Viewport3D>
```

We're defining a type of model called a *Geometry* (because it's all geometrical and stuff). A `Geometry` is built by creating a *mesh*, which is sort of like a fishing net. Each place where the line crosses is a point, and there's a line between each point. And all the lines end up making lots and lots of little triangles.

The first thing that we have to specify for our mesh is the points that make it up—this is the set of positions ❶. Figure 15.3 shows the positions relative to our three-dimensional coordinate plane.

Now, you might think that, because we're defining triangles, we'd pass a number of sets of three points to define each triangle, but that would be fairly inefficient because a lot of the points would end up being reused—which would matter a lot for a more complex model. Instead, we pass one collection of points and then another collection of `TriangleIndices` ❷ that specify which points to use from our collection of points to make up the shape we want. In the example, we only have to pass four points, instead of six, because the first triangle is made up of the 0th, 1st, and 2nd points, and the second is made up of the 1st, 3rd, and 2nd points. Figure 15.4 shows how the triangles are defined.

(-2,2,0) (2,2,0)
(-2,-2,0) (2,-2,0)

Figure 15.3 The four points we've defined for our rectangle. Note that the Z coordinate is 0 for all values, so the rectangle is flat.

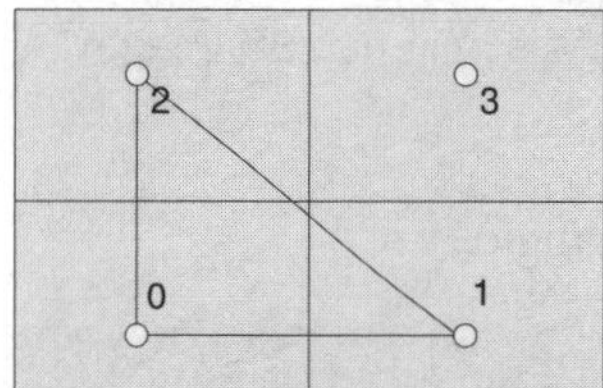

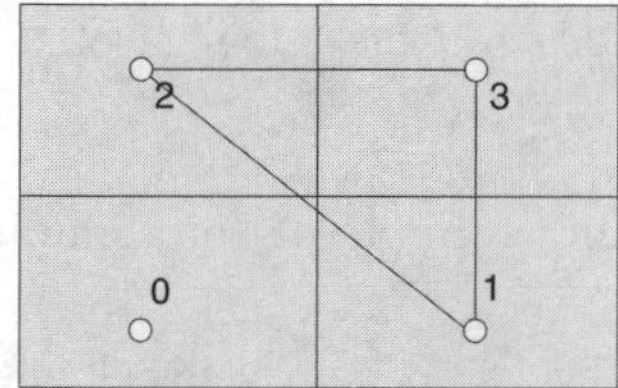

Figure 15.4 Our model is made up of two triangles. One that uses points 0, 1, and 2, and one that uses points 1, 3, and 2.

By the way, you may be wondering if the order that the indices are specified in matters. The answer is yes—from a three-dimensional perspective, the order in which you specify the points can control which way the shape is facing and whether you're seeing its front or its back. We could also specify a collection of `Normals` for each of our triangles to tell more exactly which way the shape is facing and how light should bounce off of it. `Normals` are vectors perpendicular to the surface. The easiest way of thinking about them is as arrows sticking out from the shape in the direction they're pointing. For complex models they matter quite a bit; but, for our simple examples, we can mostly ignore them.

One last thing we need for our shape is a material ❸. The material covers our shape. We're using a `DiffuseMaterial`. A diffuse material is one that, when light hits it, it spreads out evenly. Here's a list of the three options for materials:

- *Diffuse*—Spreads out the light over the whole surface
- *Specular*—Makes the surface reflective and shiny
- *Emissive*—Treats the material as though it has a glow

Beyond specifying that the material is diffuse, we also provide a brush to use ❹. This can be any WPF brush—gradients, images, visuals, and so on—so the approach is pretty flexible. You can also do some fancy things with mapping—for example, positioning an image quite precisely over a model. This is the sort of thing you'd do in a 3D program when creating your model.

When you build a model, you can build it out of a single mesh, but you'll more often build it by combining a series of meshes into a group of meshes. This approach tends to be simpler *and* gives better lighting effects. Usually, in 3D environments, for the environment to provide a collection of primitives—lines, cubes, spheres, and so on. Unfortunately, WPF doesn't ship with any primitives, which is a bit of a disappointment, but this does make it easier for book writers to provide examples that would be silly if you could say, "Give me a cube."

If you took the XAML from our example and dumped it into a layout, you'd see...absolutely nothing. We've built the equivalent of a 2001 monolith—without light, it's a black cube against a black background. But, you have to bring your own apes.

15.1.2 Lights

With 2D, you specify the color or brush you want to use, and voilà, things appear. In 3D, things are more complicated. In a 3D scene, the way in which the model reacts to light helps to make it realistic. For instance, the part of a model directly in a light will be brighter, and the part not in the light will be dimmer, as will parts of the model further away from a light.

Lights are another type of model, so you can put them into your scene and position them like your various other objects. For example, if you create a model of a car, you could put lights in as the headlights, and whatever they hit would be lit as appropriate. WPF currently has the following types of lights:

- *Ambient*—Glows from everywhere. Light comes from all directions equally. This tends to be a fairly boring way to light scenes, although it can be handy to lessen shadows when mixed with other lighting.
- *Directional*—Comes from a particular direction and points in a specific way. This type of light isn't part of the scene per se. It's sort of like having the sun in your scene—it's so far off that it doesn't matter where it is.
- *Point*—Comes from a specific point and glows equally in all directions. This is sort of like gluing Tinker Bell into the scene.
- *Spot*—Comes from a specific point and shines in a particular direction. This would be the one you'd use for the headlight effect.

Listing 15.2 Shows the XAML for a directional light. The XAML would be another child in the `Viewport3D.Children` collection.

Listing 15.2 XAML for a directional light

```
<ModelVisual3D>
  <ModelVisual3D.Content>
    <DirectionalLight Color="White" Direction="-2,-3,-1" />
  </ModelVisual3D.Content>
</ModelVisual3D>
```

We're using a `White` light here, but you can use any color you like. Red is particularly good for horror-movie scenes. The `Direction` is the direction that the light is pointing. The light would be pointing straight back into the scene if we'd used 0,0,-1. By offsetting it slightly, we get some more interesting shadow effects. These values have the light pointing down and to the left, as well as toward the distance on the Z-axis.

The other lights have various other properties and, once again, when you work with a design tool, you can play with the lights easily to get the effect you want.

Now that we have light, you can run our application—and still you'll see nothing…

15.1.3 Cameras

If a tree falls in the forest and there isn't anyone around to see it, does it really fall? In WPF 3D, the answer is no—whatever your local cybernetic Buddhist monk has to say on the issue. You have to define a camera and specify which way it's looking to be able to see anything. WPF has two types of cameras: Orthographic and Perspective. Both show a representation of a scene as seen from a particular place. The Perspective camera foreshortens items—things get smaller as they disappear into the distance. Using this camera makes sense for things like realistic animation. The Orthographic camera puts everything in the right place, but doesn't shrink things into the distance. Using this camera makes more sense for things like graphs or other visual representations of data. Listing 15.3 shows the XAML for an Orthographic camera. The XAML should appear below the `Viewport3D` opening tag, but above the models.

Listing 15.3 XAML for a camera

```
<Viewport3D.Camera>
  <OrthographicCamera Position="0,0,3" LookDirection="0,0,-1" Width="5"  />
</Viewport3D.Camera>
```

The `Position` is the three-dimensional point where the camera is located. The `LookDirection` controls the way it's facing. It isn't a point, but a 3D vector. A good way of thinking about `LookDirection` is to think of a short line from the origin (0,0,0) to a point defined by the vector. In the example, we have a line going straight back from the origin that's 1 unit long. Moving the line so that it starts at the `Position` of the camera gives the way the camera is facing.

The `Width` property controls the aperture of the camera. The bigger the width, the more stuff you can see, but the smaller it will all be.

Now that we have a model, some lights, and a camera, we can unveil our exciting 3D shape (figure 15.5).

Not very exciting. But, to prove that we are really in a 3D world, we can move our camera, changing its angle to something like this:

```
<Viewport3D.Camera>
  <OrthographicCamera Position="3,3,3"
                LookDirection="-1,-1,-1" Width="5" />
</Viewport3D.Camera>
```

And, now, if you run, things are a little different (figure 15.6).

Figure 15.5 We've cleverly created a 3D shape that looks like something we could have done far more easily in 2D. For our next trick, we'll turn water into water.

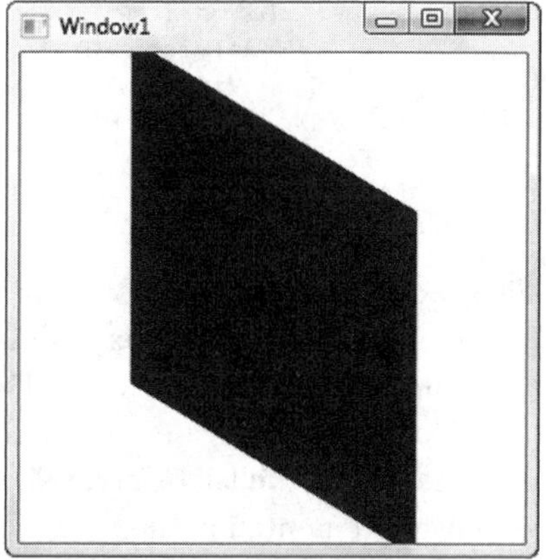

Figure 15.6 By moving our camera, it's suddenly obvious that we're in a 3D world, even though our shape is flat.

It's still not terribly impressive, but you can now see that we can control what we see by moving our camera and that we're undoubtedly working in 3D. In the next section, we'll create some 3D objects that are really 3D.

15.2 Graphing in 3D

In the previous chapter, we showed three different ways of creating the same chart. In this section, we'll add a fourth: a 3D version of our graphing control. The approach is most similar to the `Visual` approach in 2D except that, when the graph changes, we'll create 3D models to represent each column in the chart, instead of a simple visual shape.

If you're following along, open up the graphing sample and then add a new `UserControl` called `ColumnGraph3DControl`. Listing 15.4 shows the XAML for the control.

Listing 15.4 `ColumnGraph3DControl` XAML

```
<UserControl x:Class="GraphingWithShapes.ColumnGraph3DControl"
   xmlns="http://schemas.microsoft.com/winfx/2006/xaml/presentation"
   xmlns:x="http://schemas.microsoft.com/winfx/2006/xaml"
   Height="300" Width="300">
  <Grid>
    <Viewport3D x:Name="main" ClipToBounds="True">        ❶ 3D Viewport

      <Viewport3D.Camera>
        <OrthographicCamera
           Position="0,0,3" LookDirection="-0.5,-0.5,-1" Width="10" />
      </Viewport3D.Camera>                                  Camera ❷

      <Viewport3D.Children>
        <ModelVisual3D>
          <ModelVisual3D.Content>
```

```
            <DirectionalLight Color="White" Direction="-2,-3,-1" />    ◁ Light ❸
          </ModelVisual3D.Content>
        </ModelVisual3D>
      </Viewport3D.Children>
    </Viewport3D>
  </Grid>
</UserControl>
```

First, we add a `Viewport3D` to our `Grid` ❶ to hold our 3D elements. The `Viewport3D` isn't included in the Toolbox by default, so we have to add it directly via XAML, although we could easily customize the Toolbox and then drag a `ViewPort3D` onto the `Grid`.

Next, we set up a camera ❷ and a light ❸. Note that we are *not* creating any models. The models will all be created on the fly in code. Listing 15.5 shows the basic setup of our implementation file.

Listing 15.5 `ColumnGraph3DControl` code

```
using System;
...Rest of standard using statements...

using System.Windows.Media.Media3D;                ❶
using System.Collections.ObjectModel;
using System.Collections.Specialized;

namespace GraphingWithShapes
{                                                              dataPoints ❷
  public partial class ColumnGraph3DControl : UserControl
  {
    private ObservableCollection<NameValuePair> dataPoints = null;   ◁
    private List<Color> columnColors = new List<Color>()
      { Colors.LightBlue, Colors.Red,
        Colors.LightGreen, Colors.Yellow };      ◁ ❸ Better colors!
    public ColumnGraph3DControl()
    {
      InitializeComponent();
    }

    public void SetData(ObservableCollection<NameValuePair> data)     ❹
    {
      dataPoints = data;
      dataPoints.CollectionChanged += new
       NotifyCollectionChangedEventHandler(dataPoints_CollectionChanged);
      Update();
    }

    void dataPoints_CollectionChanged(object sender,
                                NotifyCollectionChangedEventArgs e)
    {
      Update();
    }

    public double GetLargestValue()
    {
       // Code is identical to implementation in the last chapter
    }
```

```
    protected void Update()          ⑤ Does the work
    {
      ClearModels();

      // Details to follow
    }

    private void ClearModels()       ⑥
    {
      ModelVisual3D model;
      for (int i = main.Children.Count - 1; i >= 0; i--)
      {
        model = (ModelVisual3D)main.Children[i];
        if (!(model.Content is Light))
          main.Children.RemoveAt(i);
      }
    }
  }
}
```

Most of the using statements are standard, but we do need to add a using statement for 3D elements ❶, as well as for our specialized collection. We have our usual `ObservableCollection` from the previous chapter ❷ and a `SetData` method ❹ for passing in the collection. When the collection changes, the `Update()` method will be called ❺. We'll get to the implementation of that method in a little while. At the moment, all the method does is call the `ClearModels()` method ❻. We can't clear the entire collection because we don't want to delete our lights every time we re-create our models, so the method steps through the collection and gets rid of any models that are *not* lights.

We've also changed the colors that we're going to use for our graph ❸ because lighter colors tend to come out better in 3D.

Now that we have our new control, we can put it into the `GraphHolder` control in place of any of the 2D implementations. Because it implements the `SetData` method, all we have to do is change the XAML.

```
<local:ColumnGraph3DControl x:Name="graphCtrl" Grid.Column="1"
                                      Height="Auto" Width="Auto"/>
```

If you run now, you *still* won't see any sort of graph because we haven't yet implemented the code to create our columns. Instead of rectangles, each bar will be a 3D shape[1] (figure 15.7).

Listing 15.6 shows the code for the `Update()` method.

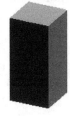

Figure 15.7 Each data point will be represented by a 3D cuboid on our graph.

[1] Officially called a *cuboid* or a *rectangular prism* if you want to get technical.

Listing 15.6 `Update()` method

```
protected void Update()
{
  ClearModels();

  if (dataPoints != null)
  {
    double spaceToUseY = 5;                          ❶ Hardcoded sizes
    double spaceToUseX = 5;
    double barWidth = spaceToUseX / dataPoints.Count;
    double largestValue = GetLargestValue();         Method from previous examples
    double unitHeight = spaceToUseY / largestValue;

    double bottom = -spaceToUseY;    ❷
    double left = -spaceToUseX ;
    double height;
    int nIndex = 0;

    foreach (NameValuePair nvp in dataPoints)
    {
      height = (nvp.Value * unitHeight);
      Color col = columnColors[nIndex % columnColors.Count];
                                                                   ❸
      Model3D column =
        CreateColumn(left, bottom, height, barWidth, 0, barWidth, col);
      ModelVisual3D model = new ModelVisual3D();    ❹ Creates 3D column
      model.Content = column;
      main.Children.Add(model);

      left += barWidth;
      nIndex++;
    }
  }
}
```

A lot of this should look familiar. But, instead of calculating the size of the bars based on the size of the control, we're hardcoding sizes for the available space ❶ because our sizes are relative to the position of the camera and the location of our models. We're positioning our shapes down and to the left of the origin ❷—which will work well with where our camera is positioned.

The creation of the columns is pushed into another method ❸. We are passing the `left`, `bottom`, `height`, and `width` for the column. We're also passing a Z position (0) and a depth (`barWidth`), as well as the color.

The `CreateColumn` method returns a `Model3D`, which we put into a `ModelVisual3D` object in order to add to the `Viewport3D` ❹. `ModelVisual3D` is the 3D equivalent of a `Visual`, except that the `Viewport3D` can handle them directly.

The real 3D stuff is in the `CreateColumn` method (and its helpers), which is shown in listing 15.7.

Listing 15.7 `CreateColumn` method

```
protected Model3D CreateColumn(double left, double bottom, double height,
                       double width, double front, double depth, Color col)
```

```
{
  Model3DGroup modelGroup = new Model3DGroup();        ❶ Group of models

  Point3D p0 = new Point3D(left, bottom, front);                ◁┐ Points for
  Point3D p1 = new Point3D(left + width, bottom, front);        ❷  column
  Point3D p2 = new Point3D(left, bottom + height, front);
  Point3D p3 = new Point3D(left + width, bottom + height, front);
  Point3D p4 = new Point3D(left, bottom, front - depth);
  Point3D p5 = new Point3D(left + width, bottom, front - depth);
  Point3D p6 = new Point3D(left, bottom + height, front - depth);
  Point3D p7 = new Point3D(left + width, bottom + height, front - depth);

  modelGroup.Children.Add(CreateSide(p0, p1, p2, p3, col)); // Front  ◁┐
  modelGroup.Children.Add(CreateSide(p0, p4, p2, p6, col)); // Left    │
  modelGroup.Children.Add(CreateSide(p4, p5, p6, p7, col)); // Back    │
  modelGroup.Children.Add(CreateSide(p1, p5, p3, p7, col)); // Right   │
  modelGroup.Children.Add(CreateSide(p2, p3, p6, p7, col)); // Top     │
  modelGroup.Children.Add(CreateSide(p0, p1, p4, p5, col)); // Bottom  │

  return modelGroup;                                     Creates sides ❸
}
```

Have you ever noticed that, in OO code, you often keep writing methods that don't really do anything, but keep calling into more and more methods? It seems like there's one perfect method at the bottom of every system with two lines of code that does absolutely everything.

Anyway, we're once again doing some setup and then pushing off the real work to another method. In this method, we create a `Model3DGroup` that holds a number of different `Models`—one for each side of the bar ❶. Then we create points that represent each of the eight points that make up each corner ❷—the four corners of the front and back of the shape. Figure 15.8 shows the relative position of the points.

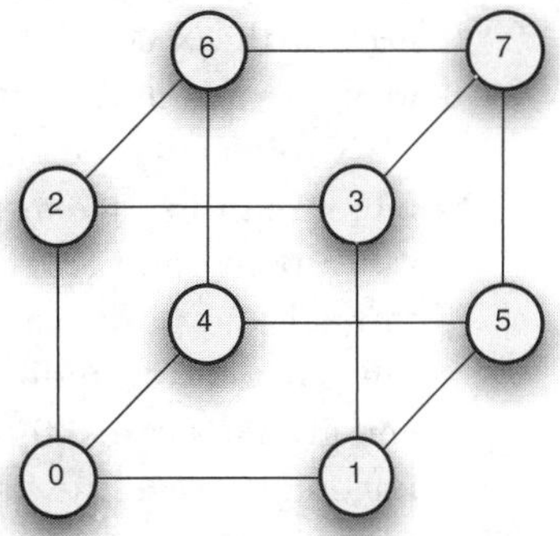

Figure 15.8 The points that make up the cuboid shape

The front of the shape is made up of a rectangle with points 0, 1, 2, and 3. The top uses points 2, 3, 6, and 7. We pass these points on to yet another method (`CreateSides`) ❸ that will *finally* create the side. This method returns a `Model3D` object that we can add to our `Model3DGroup`. The six sides together make up the column. Listing 15.8 shows the code that creates the side.

Listing 15.8 `CreateSide` method

```
protected Model3D CreateSide(Point3D pA, Point3D pB,
                             Point3D pC, Point3D pD, Color col)
{
  GeometryModel3D model = new GeometryModel3D();       ❶ Our model
```

```
    model.Material = new DiffuseMaterial(new SolidColorBrush(col));   ❷ Material
    model.BackMaterial = model.Material;   ❸

    MeshGeometry3D mesh = new MeshGeometry3D();   ❹ Positions
    mesh.Positions.Add(pA);
    mesh.Positions.Add(pB);
    mesh.Positions.Add(pC);
    mesh.Positions.Add(pD);

    mesh.TriangleIndices.Add(0);   ❺ Indexes for triangle 1
    mesh.TriangleIndices.Add(1);
    mesh.TriangleIndices.Add(2);

    mesh.TriangleIndices.Add(1);   ❻ Indexes for triangle 2
    mesh.TriangleIndices.Add(3);
    mesh.TriangleIndices.Add(2);

    model.Geometry = mesh;   ❼

    return model;
}
```

This code does the same thing as the XAML we used for creating a rectangle earlier. We specify a `GeometryModel3D` ❶ and a bunch of points that make up the important positions for the shape ❹. Remember that shapes are made up of triangles that use each of the points. We add the indices for the first triangle ❺, then the second ❻, and then assign the mesh we've created as the `Geometry` for the `Model` ❼. If you look back at the XAML for the rectangle earlier, you'll see that the hierarchy of objects we've created mirrors the XAML version.

Now, you may be wondering why we created 6 different meshes to create our shape, rather than 1 single mesh made up of a bunch of individual triangles (that is, 1 shape with 8 points and 12 triangles). There are two reasons. First, this code is much simpler to read and understand. The second reason has to do with lighting—the lighting works better with individual shapes than it does with complicated meshes. On higher-end graphics cards, this is less of an issue, but with the more complex mesh, the distinction between the sides isn't as clear.

We're setting the material of our side to be a `DiffuseMaterial` in the color passed in ❷. Note that *all* sides are given the same color; but, if you look back at figure 15.7, you'll notice that the different sides are different colors. This is all because of lighting—the sides in the light are brighter and the sides in the shade are darker.

You may also notice that we're setting the color for the `BackMaterial` of our side ❸. This is what the side would look like if you saw it from behind—which is entirely possible in a 3D world. Technically, if we built our shape correctly, the back of each side would be hidden inside the shape, and you'd never see it; but, by setting the back material, we don't have to worry about the order we pass the points or about defining `Normals`—it's one big cheat. Particularly with finicky things like 3D, we like cheats! If you were building complex 3D models, this would be inefficient, and you'd want to make sure the model was correct—but that's something that the 3D modeling software would handle for you, and it's almost certainly better at math than we are.

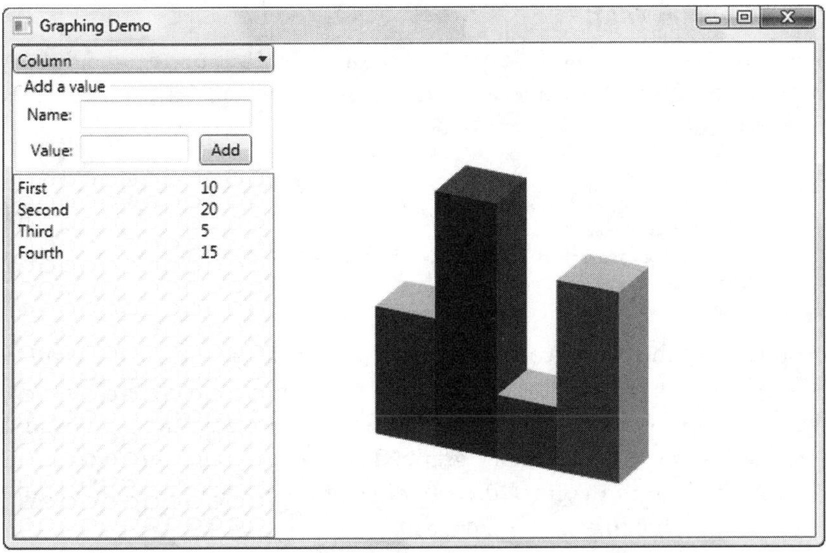

Figure 15.9 The graph is now a 3D model. Adding and removing points works as before.

Anyway, umpteen pages later, we're finally done! We have a 3D version of our graph (figure 15.9).

Depending on your graphics card, the graph may look better or worse—features such as anti-aliasing are controlled by the video card. Our new graph is kind of cool and all, but we'd like to take things a little bit further—perhaps by adding some transforms to our example.

15.3 3D Transforms

As with the 2D world, it's possible to manipulate things in the 3D world via the use of `Transforms`. In fact, `Transforms` play a more important role in 3D—it's pretty inconvenient to modify all the points in a model, but trivial to use a `Transform` to move the model around. Also, the use `Transforms` isn't limited to models—you can move lights and cameras with `Transforms` as well.

The `Transforms` in 3D parallel their 2D counterparts, except that they tend to take rather more arguments:

- *`TranslateTransform3D`*—Moves a 3D object some distance on any of the three axes
- *`ScaleTransform3D`*—Changes the size of a 3D object
- *`RotateTransform3D`*—Rotates a 3D object
- *`MatrixTransform3D`*—Modifies the object via fancy matrix mathematics
- *`Transform3DGroup`*—Combines multiple transforms

A simple example would be to translate the camera along the Z-axis to make the graph bigger or smaller.

15.3.1 A 3D Transform in XAML

Adding a transform to a model or to a camera in XAML is pretty straightforward. For example, to translate the camera along the Z-axis, all we have to do is specify the Transform to use.

```
<OrthographicCamera
      Position="0,0,3" LookDirection="-0.5,-0.5,-1" Width="10"  >
  <OrthographicCamera.Transform>
    <TranslateTransform3D OffsetX="0" OffsetY="0" OffsetZ="4"/>
  </OrthographicCamera.Transform>
</OrthographicCamera>
```

This code moves the camera 4 units forward along the Z-axis. By itself, this would be silly—it would be easier to change the camera position to 0,0,7 and not bother with the Transform. But, with the Transform, we can do some more interesting things. Let's add a slider to the side of our graph. Then we can bind the slider's value to the offset value, and we can control the camera's position. First, we add a couple of columns to the Grid holding the Viewport3D.

```
<Grid.ColumnDefinitions>
  <ColumnDefinition Width="*"/>
  <ColumnDefinition Width="20"/>
</Grid.ColumnDefinitions>
```

Notice that the second column is 20 pixels wide, and the first one (the one that still contains the Viewport3D) takes up the rest of the space. Now add another child to the Grid—a Slider.

```
<Slider x:Name="distanceSlider" Grid.Column="1" Orientation="Vertical"
        Minimum="0" Maximum="10" Value="4" />
```

This vertical slider is in the second column. It has a range from 0 to 10, and defaults to 4 (for no other reason than we think that's a good place for it to start). Now we have to bind our Transform to the value in the Slider. 3D stuff supports binding in exactly the same manner as anything else.

```
<TranslateTransform3D OffsetX="0" OffsetY="0"
         OffsetZ="{Binding ElementName=distanceSlider,Path=Value}"/>
```

Now, if you run, you can move the slider and effectively make the graph appear closer or further away (figure 15.10).

We could easily move in other directions, scaling or rotating the camera in the same way. Rotating the camera would be pretty silly; we'd simply spin the camera until it could no longer see the graph. If we want something to rotate, we should rotate the graph itself...

15.3.2 A 3D Transform in code

Because we've created the graph bars in code, if we want to be able to rotate them, we have to specify the Transform in code as well; if we want to do some form of binding, that also needs to be done in code. If we want to do this the same way that we did the

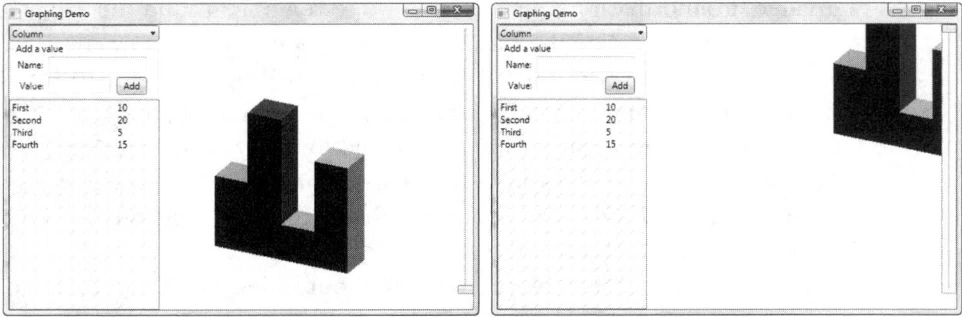

Figure 15.10 Moving the slider moves the camera so that the graph appears to move closer or further away from the viewer. Insert your own Sesame Street bigger/smaller commentary as desired.

translate (with a slider), we can add the slider pretty easily in the designer by adding another row.

```
<Grid.RowDefinitions>
  <RowDefinition Height="*" />
  <RowDefinition Height="20" />
</Grid.RowDefinitions>
```

And then we add the slider in the bottom row.

```
<Slider x:Name="rotateSlider" Grid.Row="1" Orientation="Horizontal"
         Minimum="0" Maximum="360" Value="0" />
```

This horizontal slider has values going from 0 to 360 because we want to be able to rotate the graph 360 degrees. The real work, though, will take place in the `Update()` method. The code in listing 15.9 should go inside the `for` loop in the `Update()` method, right after the model is added to the `ViewPort`'s `Children` collection.

Listing 15.9 Rotation transform in code

```
AxisAngleRotation3D angleRot =
   new AxisAngleRotation3D(new Vector3D(0, 1, 0), 0);          ❶ Rotation type
RotateTransform3D rot =
    new RotateTransform3D(angleRot,
    new Point3D(-spaceToUseX + (spaceToUseX / 2), 0, -(barWidth / 2)));  ◁ Transform ❷
Binding rotBind = new Binding("Value");     ❸ Binding
rotBind.Source = rotateSlider;
BindingOperations.SetBinding(angleRot,
              AxisAngleRotation3D.AngleProperty, rotBind);     ❹ Sets Transform
model.Transform = rot;
```

This looks uglier than it really is, particularly for our simple example. The first thing we have to define is the type of rotation we want. WPF supports two types: `Axis` and `Quaternion`. If you want to know what a `Quaternion` rotation is, you need to find someone smarter than us to explain it. An `Axis` rotation, though, is relatively straightforward. Picture an infinite line going through the shape somewhere. The shape will be rotated around that line. In our case, we're rotating around the Y-axis ❶. We're using a `Vector3D` to define the axis. Again, the easiest way to picture this is to imagine a line going from the origin (0,0,0) to the point used by the vector (0,1,0), and that tells you the direction of the `Vector`. Ours is pointing straight up.

We pass the rotation object we just created to the `RotateTransform3D` ❷, which is the actual `Transform`. We also have to pass a point we want the axis to go through. We're calculating the center of our graph on the fly based on the values we've already calculated.

We want to tie the angle of the rotation to our slider. The next bit of code ❸ creates a `Binding` object tied to the `Value` property of the slider and to the `Angle` property of the `Axis` rotation. Finally, we assign the newly created transform to our model's `Transform` property ❹. Voilà, we're done! Figure 15.11 shows the rotation slider in operation.

Pretty slick, eh? We have to admit to spending some time moving the sliders back and forth. It's strangely hypnotic, as well as a great way to kill time while avoiding working on a book. We highly recommend it.

We could also add another slider to, for example, scale the graph and another to play around with the lights. The techniques for doing this would be about the same as what we've already shown.

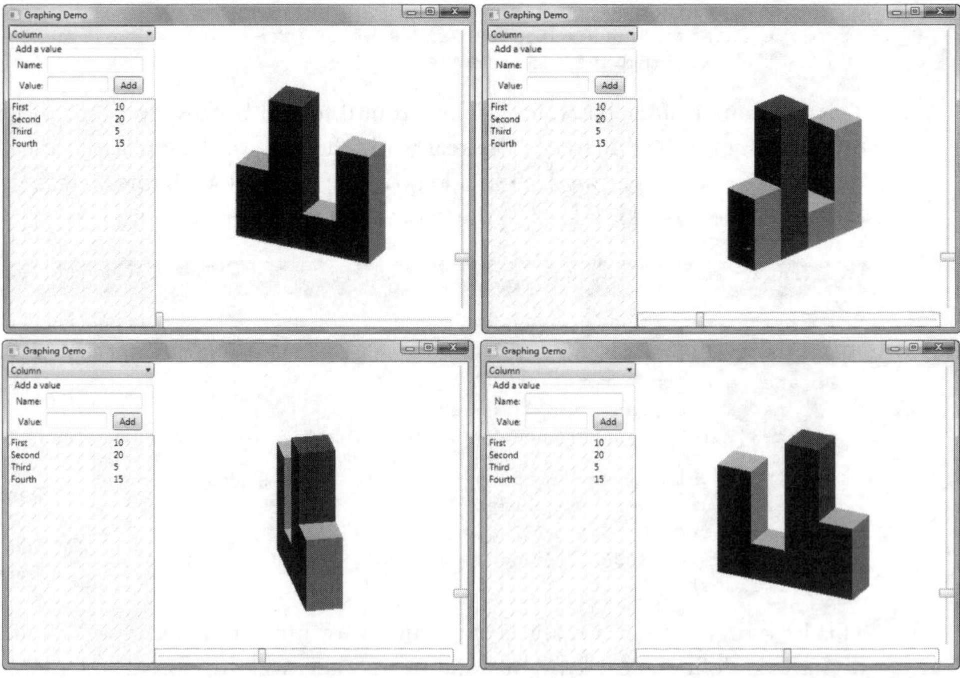

Figure 15.11 We can now use the slider to rotate our graph completely, making it impossible to know which bar represents which data point.

15.4 Summary

Even though we've only scratched the surface of the edge of WPF's 3D support, we think that we've provided enough of an overview as to what is and isn't possible, as well as how to get started with 3D. The 3D support in WPF is fairly nice—for classic 3D applications. If you're so inclined, implementing standard primitives or even building a ray-tracing engine in WPF would be quite straightforward (and we suspect that there will be a bunch of them available in the near future).

One very cool thing added to WPF 3.5 is `Viewport2DVisual3D`. The whole purpose of this class is to allow the 2D worlds and 3D worlds to interact. With this class, it's possible to do some of the things we originally wanted to do with 3D, such as rotating controls in the third dimension while still allowing them to be interactive. It works via some clever math that figures out where the control would be in two dimensions and creates an invisible version of it that, nonetheless, gets feedback. It isn't perfect, but it is pretty cool. SP1 also added a *lot* of things to WPF 3D, including shaders and custom effects and more ways to combine 2D and 3D. This is all, unfortunately, beyond the scope of this book, but it's quite interesting if you like playing with the third dimension! They've also improved performance in lots of different ways.

This is the last chapter on straight "application" development and core WPF capabilities. In the next section, we'll look at some other types of applications and some abilities that can add some polish and finish to your WPF applications.

Part 4

The last mile

In the telecommunication industry, they often refer to the *last mile problem*—it doesn't matter that there's shiny fiber-optic cable run everywhere in the country if the connection between the fiber and your house is a piece of string with a pair of tennis shoes hanging from it.

In development, the distance between getting a basically working application and a finished, shippable application is similar (although perhaps not quite so extreme).

In this section, we'll cover some of the topics that, although not *required* to get an application working, help finish the application or make it available in a different way. We'll start by talking about an alternative type of application that WPF supports in chapter 16, "Building a navigation application." Navigation applications are kind of like browser apps, with back and forward navigation, but they can be standalone. As you'll see in chapter 17—"WPF and browsers: XBAP, ClickOnce, and Silverlight"—navigation applications (and other WPF applications) *can* be run directly within a browser, or they can be deployed over the web via ClickOnce.

Each of the rest of the chapters demonstrates a particular capability that might be necessary for completing an application. Chapter 18—"Printing, documents, and XPS"—demonstrates how to add printing capabilities to an application. Chapter 19—"Transition effects"—demonstrates how to add some snazzy effects to your app. Chapter 20—"Interoperability"—shows how to embed non-WPF controls into WPF and vice versa, and chapter 21—"Threading"—shows some new WPF-specific threading capabilities.

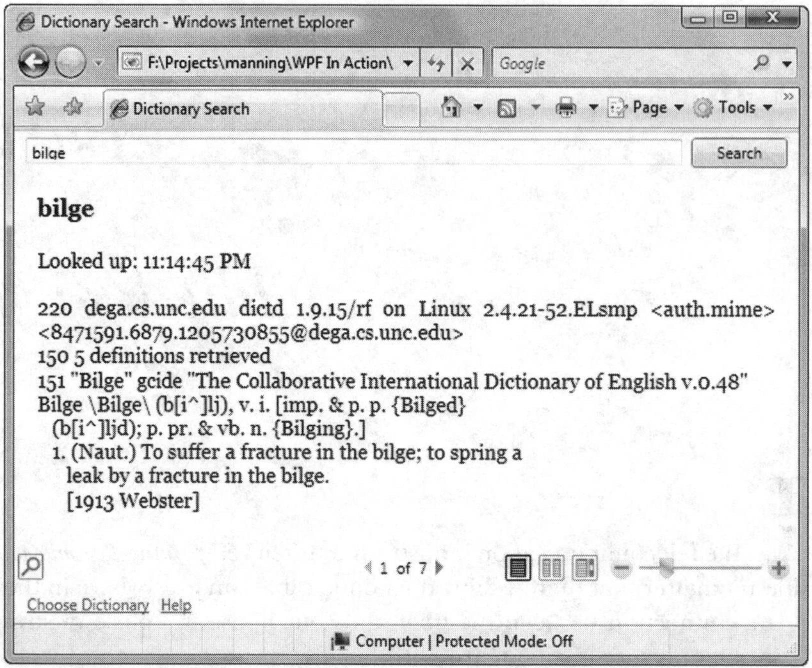

A WPF Navigation application hosted inside a browser

16 Building a navigation application

This chapter covers:

- The purpose of navigation applications
- Building a navigation application
- Page functions
- Finally, a definition for lactucarium

It's one of those strange ironies that, as web browser application developers are doing their best to provide more Windows-like functionality to their applications, Windows application developers are trying to make their apps more "webby." This has led to Windows applications that have back and forward buttons, that never pop up child windows, and that are often quite difficult to use.

The fact is that there are situations where browser concepts fit quite well into Windows applications, just as there are situations where Windows metaphors fit well into browser applications—it all comes down to the purpose of the application. Browsers were designed for navigating content—moving through documents. In such a context, the ability to move back and forward, for example, fits very well. On the other hand, when trying to build a data-entry application in a browser, moving back and forward is, at best, ambiguous, and, at worst, a good way of annoying your customers as their data disappears into the ether.

Microsoft is obviously aware of the desire to build webby apps, and has provided capabilities within WPF for building navigation-style applications. These are applications that operate somewhat like a browser, in that you can navigate between pages via hyperlinks, move back and forward, and so on, but you can also have any WPF controls you like on the different pages. In this chapter, we'll demonstrate building a navigation application—a program that uses the DICT protocol to look up words (and other things) and display their definitions. Before we get to that, though, we want to talk a little bit about when it's appropriate to use nav apps.

16.1 When and where to use navigation applications

In general, there are two situations in which navigation applications are appropriate:

- *Document/data browsing*—If you have interlinked data that you want to be able to easily move through and then back to where you were, this model works well. This should be unsurprising because it's what browsers do best.
- *Inductive user interfaces*—This is the type of interface popularized by applications like Microsoft Money and TurboTax. Users are only doing one thing at a time, often moving step by step (like in a wizard), but they can also jump off to another point if desired. Again, this is much like many browser applications.

It's interesting that Microsoft obviously thought that one of the most common ways you'd want to use a navigation application is by hosting it inside a browser—a technique we'll demonstrate in the next chapter. This is arguably the main reason that WPF has support for navigation applications, but it ends up giving you an application designed to look like a browser application, being run inside a browser (figure 16.1). Strange, no?

As it happens, there's at least one good reason why you'd want to do this. Even with ASP.NET, AJAX, and a whole host of other acronym-powered technology, building browser applications is a pain in the neck; because browsers weren't designed for applications, a large part of making browser applications work is based on hacks and side effects. If there were a clean way of building applications that behaved like browser applications are expected to act (that is, in an inductive manner), and yet had a proper programming model behind it, it would be the best of both worlds.

Unfortunately, this is where it all breaks down. Apparently, in an effort to build a programming model that emulated the inductive style of the web, the developers felt the need to emulate some of the more egregious annoyances from browser-development. For instance, there's no clear control point in the applications, so you end up having to pass information between pages by either forever passing it every time you do something or by storing it in a set of properties, something like session state in a browser. Also, although there are nice clear events for things like `Navigating` to let you know that the user is trying to leave a page, and to give you an opportunity to prevent it, you can't catch these events on the page itself, and you can't easily get to the instance of the page from the places where you can catch it.

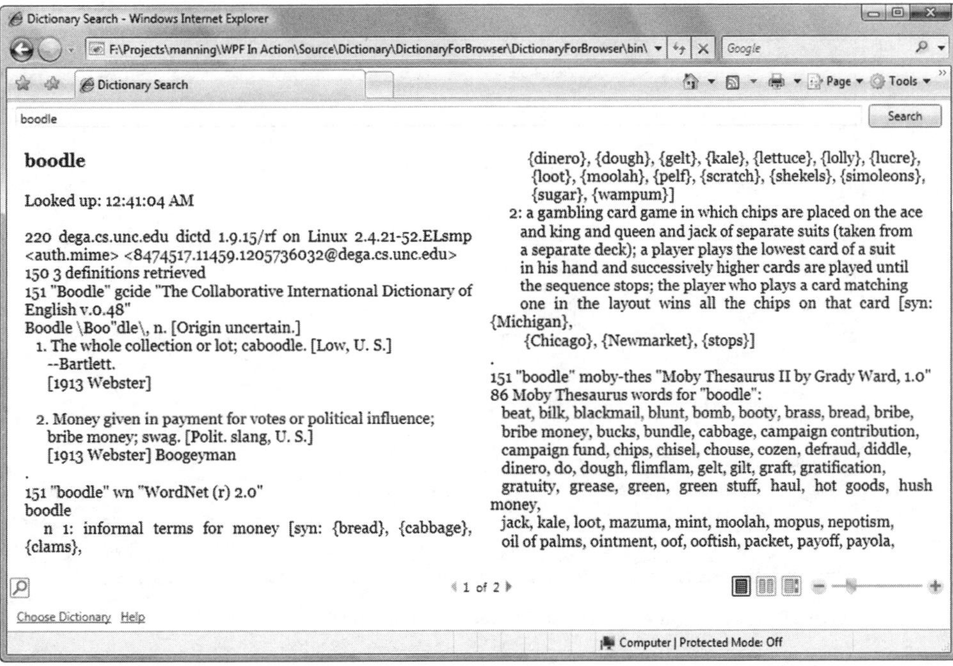

Figure 16.1 A WPF navigation application running inside a browser. The back and forward buttons in IE 7 move between pages within the application.

We can think of no technically coherent reason why these flaws exist, and it's sad because the addition of a very few things would make the navigation application model quite nice.

All that aside, for certain types of applications, the navigation application model does have some useful benefits. In the next section, we're going to develop a dictionary lookup application that uses the DICT protocol to look up definitions for words via TCP over the web. This type of app jibes well with a navigation-style interface because it allows the user to move back and forth among definitions, as well as to double-click an arbitrary word and navigate to its definition. The navigation gives us all the back and forth handling more or less for free.

16.2 Creating a basic navigation application

The first thing we're going to do is create a `Page` that allows us to search for words. A `Page` is much like a `Window`, and we can put in all the various WPF elements that we might want. If you're following along, create a new WPF application (ours is DictionaryPages) and then add a WPF `Page` named SearchPage.xaml (figure 16.2).

The editor, unsurprisingly, looks like the editor for a `Window`, and is already set up with a `Grid` layout panel. We set up the grid with three rows—controls at the top, a `DocumentReader` in the middle, and a space for some links (that we'll add later) at the bottom. We're relying on the automatic pseudo-docking capability that the editor

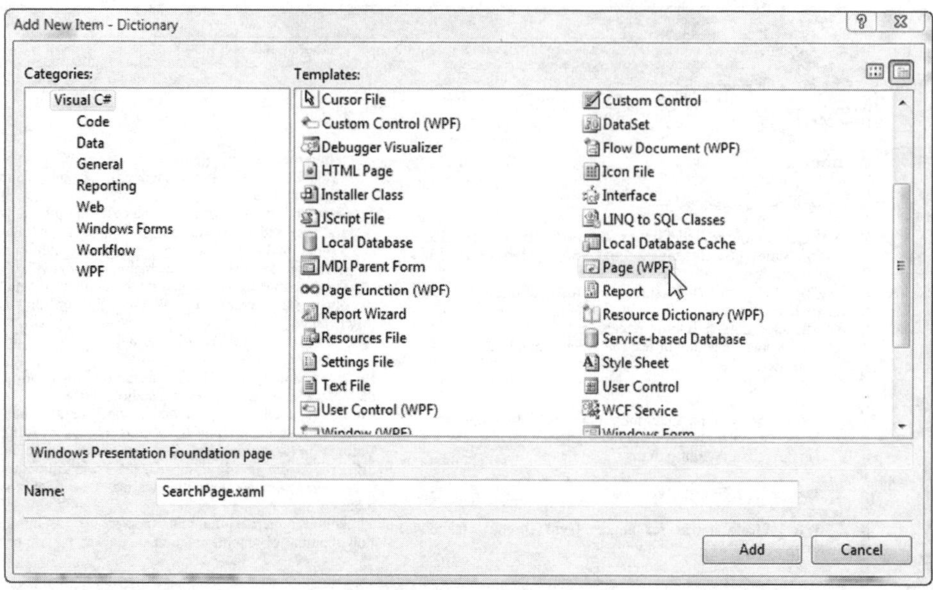

Figure 16.2 Adding a `Page` to the Dictionary application

provides in order to make the controls show up in the right place. Figure 16.3 shows our `SearchPage` in the editor.

Listing 16.1 shows the XAML for this page. It's relatively straightforward.

Listing 16.1 `SearchPage` XAML

```
<Page x:Class="DictionaryPages.SearchPage"
    xmlns="http://schemas.microsoft.com/winfx/2006/xaml/presentation"
    xmlns:x="http://schemas.microsoft.com/winfx/2006/xaml"
    Title="Search"
    WindowTitle="Dictionary Search">
  <Grid>
    <Grid.RowDefinitions>
      <RowDefinition Height="30" />
      <RowDefinition Height="*" />
      <RowDefinition Height="30" />
    </Grid.RowDefinitions>
    <TextBox Name="searchText" Margin="9,5.36,91,5.36" />
    <Button Name="searchButton" Click="OnSearch"
  HorizontalAlignment="Right"
        Width="75" Height="23" Margin="0,3.5,9,3.5">Search</Button>
    <FlowDocumentReader Grid.Row="1" Name="searchResults" />
  </Grid>
</Page>
```

Nothing here is particularly new, except that, instead of a `<Window>` tag, everything is inside a `<Page>`. Also, notice that we've added an `OnSearch Click` handler to the Search button because we know we'll need it. We also set the `WindowTitle` property of the page—this will be used as the main page title when we run.

The next step is to make the application use this page at startup, instead of the default form. We do this by editing the XAML for the application.

```
<Application x:Class="DictionaryPages.App"
    xmlns="http://schemas.microsoft.com/winfx/2006/xaml/presentation"
    xmlns:x="http://schemas.microsoft.com/winfx/2006/xaml"
    StartupUri="SearchPage.xaml">
    <Application.Resources>
    </Application.Resources>
</Application>
```

All we've done is change the `StartupUri` to point to a `Page` instead of a `Window`. When we go ahead and launch the application, though, WPF recognizes the change and automatically adds a navigation framework for us (figure 16.4).

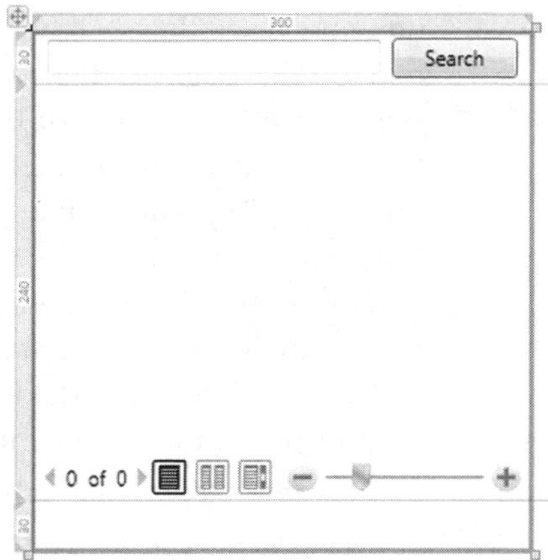

Figure 16.3 The `SearchPage` created in the editor

Notice how we have back and forward buttons, although they're currently disabled because we have nowhere to go back/forward to—WPF automatically created a `NavigationWindow`. The `NavigationWindow` class provides all the basic navigation support. We could also have explicitly created a `NavigationWindow` and told it to navigate to our search page. A situation where you might want to create your own `NavigationWindow` might be a pop-up wizard—wizards generally have back/forward navigation, so you can piggyback on the

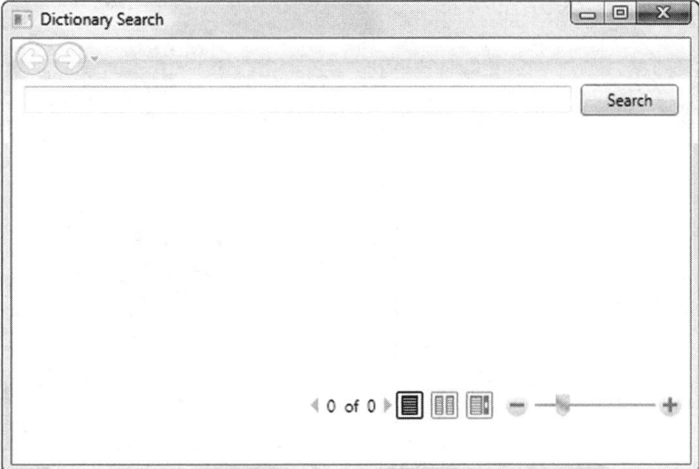

Figure 16.4 By changing the application `StartupURI` to a `Page`, we let WPF know that we want navigation handling.

`NavigationWindow` functionality for the behavior. There's also a lighter-weight navigation class called `Frame`, which you can use to provide navigation inside another control.

Navigation implies that we have somewhere to go; right now, our application is pretty uni-locational. We need at least one more page to make navigation worthwhile.

16.2.1 Adding some navigation

When we hook up the dictionary search, we'll have lots of places to go. Before we worry about that, let's add a simple Help page to our application and put a link to it at the bottom of the page so that we have somewhere to navigate to. If you're following along, create a new page called HelpPage and set it up to look something like figure 16.5.

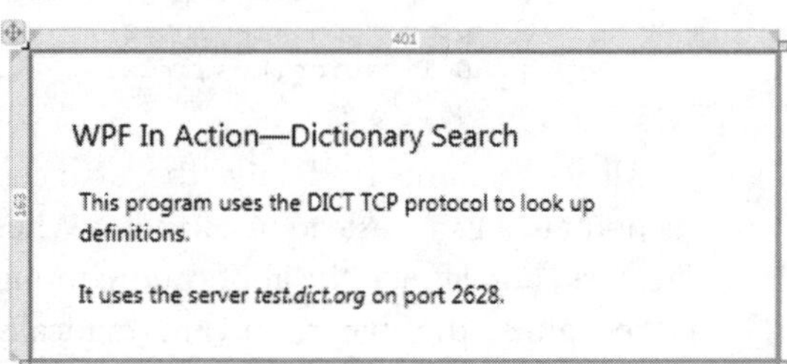

Figure 16.5 Make a `HelpPage` that looks something like this.

Now we need to create a link on our main page to the Help page. With Windows Forms applications, there was a `Hyperlink` control, which could be used like a `Label`. WPF doesn't have a standalone control, but it does have a content control that can be used in places that take content, such as a `TextBlock`. We'll add a `TextBlock` to the empty row of our `Grid` and put a hyperlink in it.[1]

```
<TextBlock Margin="10 0 0 0" VerticalAlignment="Center" Grid.Row="2">
    <Hyperlink NavigateUri="HelpPage.xaml">Help</Hyperlink></TextBlock>
```

Most of this is pretty standard stuff. The interesting thing is the value of the `NavigateUri`—we're referencing the XAML page for our Help page. This is sufficient to tell WPF what we want. Figure 16.6 shows the main page with the link, as well as the Help page after we click the link.

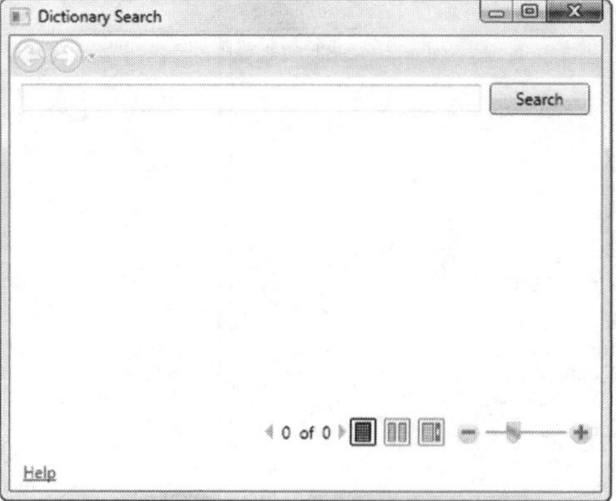

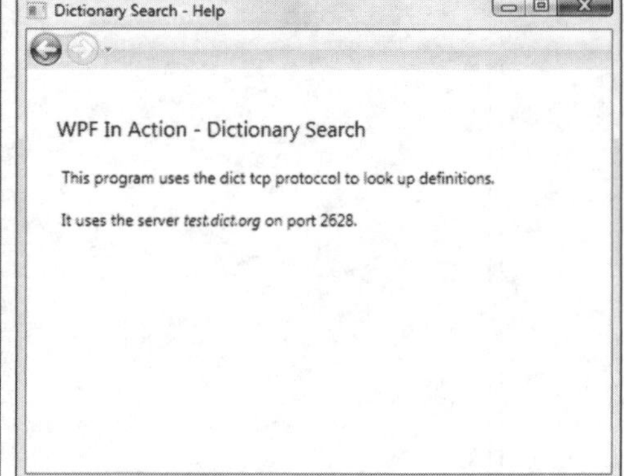

Figure 16.6 Clicking the Help link navigates to another page.

1 If you want to, you could also use the `LinkLabel` control from chapter 13 here.

Notice how the back arrow is now available. Clicking it returns to the Search page. You can also click the little arrow to the right of the back/forward controls to get a navigation history (figure 16.7).

The navigation framework gives us back/forward handling for free—well, almost for free, as you'll see later. First, let's make our search actually do something.

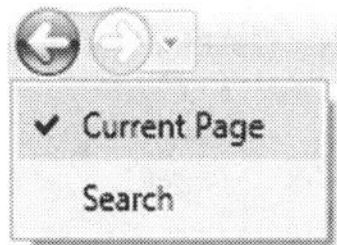

Figure 16.7 We get search history for free!

16.2.2 Implementing dictionary lookup

This is a book about WPF, not TCP, so we'll provide the code for the dictionary lookup with no explanation, other than for some of the WPF-specific items. We're also putting the implementation directly in the Search page. As the dictionary lookup opens and ends its session as part of the process, this isn't a big deal. If this was, say, a database query where there was a held connection, this would be a problem. Unfortunately, the navigation structure doesn't provide any clean way of separating logic, but it would be possible to store a controller object in the `Application`'s properties collection, and then have the pages retrieve it.

Listing 16.2 shows the Search.xaml.cs code in its entirety, including all the code to do the search.

Listing 16.2 Dictionary lookup code

```
using System;
...Rest of default using statements removed for space...

using System.Net.Sockets;      <-- Using statements
using System.IO;                   used by TCP code

namespace DictionaryPages
{
  public partial class SearchPage : System.Windows.Controls.Page
  {
    private Encoding conversationEncoding = Encoding.UTF8;   <-- Various values
    private string defaultServer = "test.dict.org";              for DICT
    private readonly int defaultPort = 2628;                     protocol call
    private const int bufferSize = 4096;

    public SearchPage()
    {
      InitializeComponent();
    }

    protected void OnSearch(object sender, RoutedEventArgs e)    (1)
    {
      Mouse.OverrideCursor = Cursors.Wait;       <-- WPF way to set
      string word = searchText.Text.Trim();      (2) a wait cursor
      if (word.Length > 0)
        DefineWord(word);
      Mouse.OverrideCursor = null;             <-- Restores cursor
    }                                              when done

    private void DefineWord(string word)
    {
```

```
    string command = "DEFINE * " + word;
    string strResult = ExecuteCommand(command);

    FlowDocument doc = new FlowDocument();              <-- ❸ Sets up result text
    Paragraph para1 = new Paragraph();
    para1.FontSize = 18;
    para1.Inlines.Add(new Bold(new Run(word)));
    doc.Blocks.Add(para1);
    Paragraph para2 = new Paragraph();
    para2.Inlines.Add(new Run(strResult));
    doc.Blocks.Add(para2);
    searchResults.Document = doc;
  }

  private string ExecuteCommand(string command)
  {
    StringBuilder response = new StringBuilder();
    using (TcpClient client = new TcpClient())
    {
      client.Connect(defaultServer, defaultPort);
      using (Stream clientStream = client.GetStream())
      {
        response.Append(GetResponse(command + "\r\n", clientStream));
        response.Append(GetResponse("QUIT\r\n", clientStream));
      }
    }
    return response.ToString();
  }

  private string GetResponse(string requestString, Stream clientStream)
  {
    byte[] request = conversationEncoding.GetBytes(requestString);
    clientStream.Write(request, 0, request.Length);
    clientStream.Flush();
    byte[] response = new byte[bufferSize];
    StringBuilder sb = new StringBuilder();
    int currentPosition = 0, bytesRead = 0;
    while((bytesRead = clientStream.Read(response,0, bufferSize)) > 0)
    {
      sb.Append(conversationEncoding.GetString(response, 0, bytesRead));
      currentPosition += bytesRead;
      if (bytesRead < bufferSize)
        break;
    }
    return sb.ToString();
  }
 }
}
```

As we said, most of this code is about using the `DICT` protocol to get a definition, so we won't spend a lot of time on it. The `OnSearch` method ❶ is called when the Search button is hit, and passes the text from the search box to the appropriate methods to do the lookup. Because the operation might take a moment, we're setting a wait cursor ❷. This way is a little bit different than how it was done with Windows Forms—the `Mouse.OverrideCursor` is a cursor that overrides the cursor set on any particular child

WPF elements. Even if elements have particular specialized cursors, we want the whole application to show a wait cursor when the mouse is over it.

The result from the dictionary call is straight text, but we need to format it appropriately for the `FlowDocumentViewer` we're using to display the text (so that we get the nifty, built-in zooming, page breakdowns and searching, and so on). A `FlowDocumentViewer` displays a `FlowDocument`, so we have to create a `FlowDocument` for our text. The `FlowDocument` holds elements like `Paragraphs`, so we create a couple of `Paragraph` objects ❸—one for a title, which is a large, bold repeat of the word for which we searched, and one for the text. Note that `Paragraph` is flexible enough to handle text with carriage returns and the like—unlike, say, the `<p>` tag in a browser.

Now that we have put all this code in place, we should be able to run, type in a word, and voilà (figure 16.8).

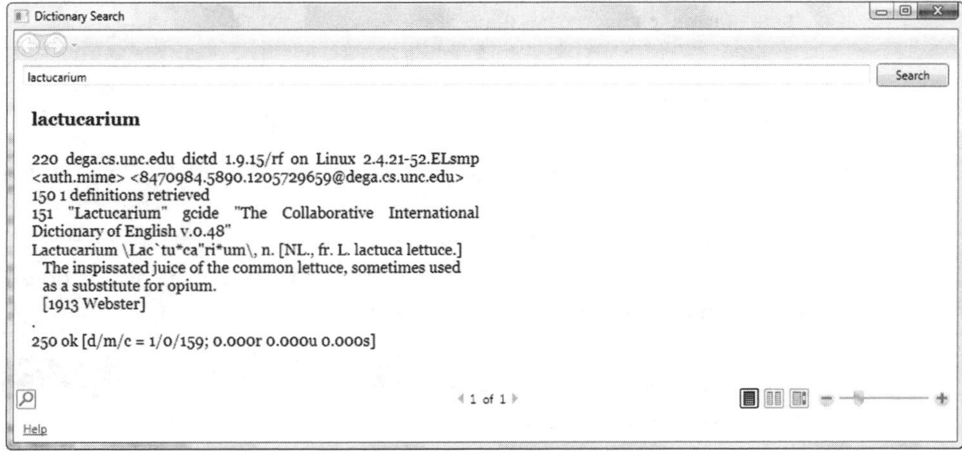

Figure 16.8 Looking up a definition in the dictionary program

So far, so good. But, if you look up a few words, you may notice something—unlike after hitting the Help button, you aren't being given the option to go back. That's because we're just doing stuff within our page. If we want to get navigation behavior, we need to make our search go somewhere.

16.2.3 Navigating programmatically

To build up a search history, we need to make the search button take us to a new page, rather than searching within the current page. This is quite easy. We can programmatically navigate to a page via a URI, or we can provide a specific page to navigate to. The following code would be used to programmatically navigate to the Help page via its URI:

```
NavigationService.Navigate(new Uri("HelpPage.xaml",UriKind.Relative));
```

The `NavigationService` handles all navigation activity. Within a page, we're referencing a property that references the `NavigationService` currently being used by that page. (Note that there can be multiples.) The `Navigate` method takes us to the place where we want to go. We don't want to go to a fixed URL, though—we want to go to a version of the Search page populated with a search for the word we want. Fortunately, we can do that too; we can create an instance of the Search page specifically and navigate to it. We need to change the `OnSearch` method to create the new page and populate it (listing 16.3).

Listing 16.3 New `OnSearch` method

```
protected void OnSearch(object sender, RoutedEventArgs e)
{
  Mouse.OverrideCursor = Cursors.Wait;
  string word = searchText.Text.Trim();
  if (word.Length > 0)
  {
    SearchPage page = new SearchPage(word);
    NavigationService.Navigate(page);
  }
  Mouse.OverrideCursor = null;
}
```

The big change is that, instead of calling the `DefineWord()` method directly here, we're creating a new `SearchPage` and passing the word in the constructor. Then, we call the `Navigate` method on the `NavigationService`, but instead of passing a URI, we pass the page to which we want to navigate. One problem is that `SearchPage` doesn't have a constructor that takes a search word. We can add that easily enough (Listing 16.4).

Listing 16.4 Constructor that takes a word

```
public SearchPage(string word)
{
  InitializeComponent();

  searchText.Text = word;
  DefineWord(word);
  Title = "Search - " + word;
}
```

The constructor has to call `InitializeComponent()` to set up the page. We then set the text in the `searchText TextBox`. We don't have to do this, but it would look odd if the word disappeared after the search is finished. Next we call `DefineWord()`. This method will do the lookup and populate the document with the definition. Finally, we set the `Title` of the page. The `Title` will be used within the search history to identify our location. This is one of several places where the navigation service will look for text for the search history; it's the easiest to set for the moment.

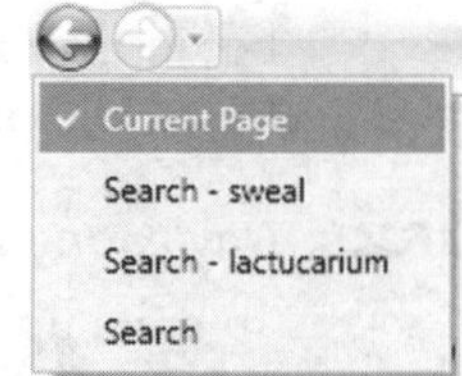

Figure 16.9 Each search now shows up in the search history.

Now if we run and do a couple of different searches, the back arrow will become enabled and, if we hit the search history button, we'll see all our searches (figure 16.9).

Not too shabby. If you hit the back button, you will see the previous pages with their definitions. This brings up an interesting question, though: Is the application holding on to all the pages, or is it reloading them each time? The answer could have a major impact on performance and memory usage. A simple change to our application will make it easy to tell—we'll add a timestamp to our results. If the data is being queried again, then we'll get a new timestamp; otherwise, it will hold the old value. To add a timestamp, we add the following code in the `DefineWord()` method, between the title paragraph and the definition paragraph:

```
Paragraph paraDate = new Paragraph();
paraDate.Inlines.Add(new Run("Looked up: " + DateTime.Now.ToString("T")));
doc.Blocks.Add(paraDate);
```

Now if we run, look up a word, and then go back, we can see more clearly what's happening (figure 16.10).

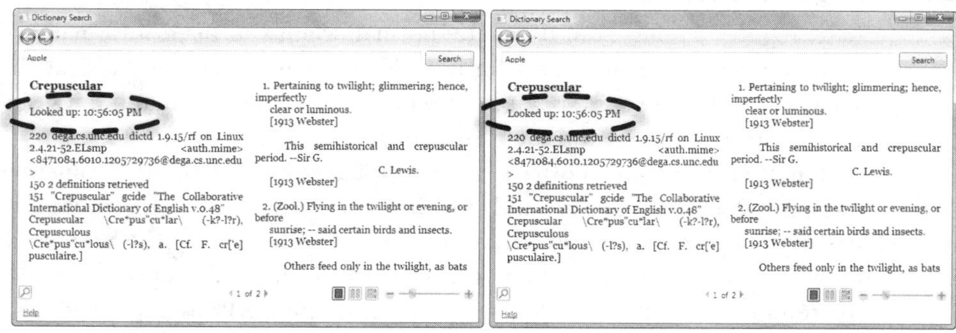

Figure 16.10 When we go back to the page, we can see that the timestamp hasn't changed, so the page hasn't been reloaded.

It probably isn't a big shock, but the matching timestamps demonstrate that this is, in fact, the same page. This makes sense, considering that we never wrote any code to make a page reconstitute itself. In fact, the default caching behavior for navigation applications isn't entirely obvious. If you navigate via a URI, the page is *not* cached by default, and will be re-created every time it's accessed. This behavior can be changed via the use of the `KeepAlive` property. But, if you pass an explicit page, that page is always cached because there's no way to refer to the page.

Re-creating pages could get very painful for a complex application. If you want to avoid caching your pages, you need to write some somewhat involved code, following one of several approaches:

- *You can always navigate via URI and make your URIs contain enough information to identify their content.*
- *You can take advantage of the `Journal` object to create your pages with appropriate state.* The back and forward stacks are made up of `JournalEntry` objects, which can hold state for a page so; assuming you got to a page via a URI, you can

store details of your page to appropriately rehydrate your page as needed. In fact, a number of controls, such as `Textboxes`, will automatically have their states stored in the `JournalEntry` for non-`KeepAlive` pages, so you only have to hold onto specialized data.

- *You can build your own mechanism based on the* `NavigationService` *events.* When you enter or leave a page, a series of events is generated that provides the opportunity to, for example, clean up or re-create your page. But, these events are on the `NavigationService` in general and aren't available at the `Page`, making them somewhat painful to use.

None of these are great solutions, and all are beyond the scope of what we're going to cover. There's one more capability of navigation applications that we do want to cover, page functions.

16.3 Page functions

In a "regular" application, it's pretty normal, when you need information from the user, to pop up a dialog and ask for it. We'd argue that, much of the time, this is a reasonable workflow—you're going somewhere else to get information, it's obvious that you're somewhere else, and then you return.

But, there are some drawbacks to using dialogs. For one thing, it somewhat violates the spirit of an inductive UI (and violating spirits is bad, right?). A more serious issue has to do with deploying applications over the web—one of the many rights that a browser-hosted application doesn't usually have is the right to pop up dialogs. This is to prevent some nefarious ad-ware creator from using WPF to pop up ads all over your screen. We'll discuss security in greater detail in the next chapter.

If we want to add a setting to our dictionary application for the particular dictionary to use, and we don't want to pop up a dialog for options, we can create a Settings page and provide a way to navigate to it. But, we then have to figure out how to get back to where we were. This is a common problem with browser applications—a subroutine has to know a lot about the calling code in order to return.

This problem, at least, is something that navigation applications handle quite well, via the use of page functions. Think of a page function like a subroutine you can call. When you call it, the application navigates to that `Page`, but when that `Page` is finished, you're automatically returned to the calling `Page` without having special logic in the subroutine `Page` and without the back/forward handling being messed up. We'll go ahead and use the Settings page as an example.

16.3.1 Creating a Page function

To get started with our Settings page, we need to create a Settings page function, which is another option on the Add New Item list when we choose to add a new item to our product. Ours is cleverly called SettingsPageFunction. When you create a page function, you get a designer as with any other page. Go ahead and lay out the page something like figure 16.11.

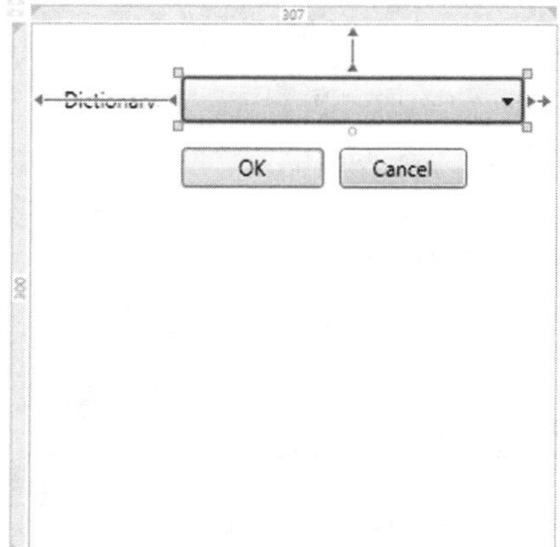

Figure 16.11 The Settings page for the dictionary application

Add a `Click` handler for the OK and Cancel buttons and a handler for the `Loaded` event for the page. Listing 16.5 shows all the code for the Settings page. Note that if you use different names for your controls and handlers, you'll have to adjust the code appropriately. We call our `ComboBox` `dictionaryCombo`, and the `Click` handlers for the buttons `OnOK` and `OnCancel`.

Listing 16.5 Settings page code

```
using System;
...Rest of using statements omitted...

namespace DictionaryPages
{
  public partial class SettingsPageFunction :
                    System.Windows.Navigation.PageFunction<String>     ❶
  {
    private string currentDictionary = "";

    public SettingsPageFunction()
    {
      InitializeComponent();
    }

    public SettingsPageFunction(string strCurrent)     ❷ Custom constructor
    {
      currentDictionary = strCurrent;
      InitializeComponent();
    }

    private void OnLoaded(object sender, RoutedEventArgs e)
    {
       dictionaryCombo.Items.Add("All");            ❸ Some supported dictionaries
       dictionaryCombo.Items.Add("moby-thes");
       dictionaryCombo.Items.Add("vera");
       dictionaryCombo.Items.Add("jargon");
       dictionaryCombo.Items.Add("easton");
       dictionaryCombo.Items.Add("bouvier");
       dictionaryCombo.Items.Add("devils");
```

```
      dictionaryCombo.Items.Add("world02");
                                                    ❹
      if (currentDictionary.Length > 0)          <┘
        dictionaryCombo.SelectedItem = currentDictionary;
      else
        dictionaryCombo.SelectedIndex = 0;
    }

    private void OnOK(object sender, RoutedEventArgs e)
    {
      string value = dictionaryCombo.SelectedItem.ToString();
      OnReturn(new ReturnEventArgs<String>(value));          <┐
    }                                                         ❺

    private void OnCancel(object sender, RoutedEventArgs e)
    {
      OnReturn(new ReturnEventArgs<String>(null));    ❻
    }
  }
}
```

The first interesting thing about this class is what it's derived from ❶. It's called a `PageFunction` because it's a page that acts like a function (profound, no?). And, like a function, the `PageFunction` returns a value. In this case, we're returning a string, and the class uses generics to specify this. The return could be any .NET type, so you could create a custom object to return more complex data.

It's stretching the metaphor a bit, but we also have a custom constructor ❷ that takes the arguments we want to pass to the "function." In fact, we could have set properties on the class, or the class could have retrieved the values themselves, but this works well for us. We're passing in the name of the currently selected dictionary.

In the `OnLoaded` method ❸, we're adding a list of supported dictionaries into the `ComboBox` on the page. In the full version of the application (available on our website at www.manning.com/feldman2), we shove a helper object in with friendly names for the dictionaries, but to save space we're using the somewhat cryptic names that we need to pass to the dictionary service. Then we select the current dictionary ❹.

Finally, we return the selected value to the calling page by using the `OnReturn()` method ❺. `OnReturn` takes an instance of a `ReturnEventArgs` generic instance—one specific to the expected return type, which is string for us. The `OnReturn` method does all the work of returning to the previous page and firing an event on that page to let it know what has happened. We do the same thing for the Cancel button, except we pass back `null` to indicate that the user canceled ❻.

Now that we have the page, we need to call it.

16.3.2 Calling a page function

We need a method to be called to activate our function. For simplicity, we've added another hyperlink next to the Help link at the bottom of the page, inside the `TextBlock`, except, instead of navigating, it calls a method when it's clicked. The XAML looks like this:

```
<Hyperlink Click="OnSelectDictionary">Choose Dictionary</Hyperlink>
```

Listing 16.6 shows the code for the `OnSelectDictionary` method.

Listing 16.6 The `OnSelectDictionary` method

```
private static string dictionaryToUse = "";      <-- Static to hold dictionary name

protected void OnSelectDictionary(object sender, RoutedEventArgs e)
{
  SettingsPageFunction pageFunction = new
            SettingsPageFunction(dictionaryToUse);    ❶
  pageFunction.Return += new
        ReturnEventHandler<String>( OnSettingsPageFunctionReturned);    ❷

  NavigationService.Navigate(pageFunction);    ❸
}
```

Most of the code here is like any other navigation call. We're creating the new page ❶, passing it the currently selected dictionary, and we're navigating to the page using the `NavigationService` ❸. The only different thing is that we're subscribing to the `Return` event on the page ❷. This event will be fired when the `OnReturn` method is called within the other page. Here's the code for the return event handler:

```
protected void OnSettingsPageFunctionReturned(object sender,
                                    ReturnEventArgs<String> e)
{
  if (e.Result != null)
    dictionaryToUse = e.Result;
}
```

All the method does is look to see if the return value isn't `null` (which is how we indicate that the user canceled) and, if not, stores the dictionary. The last change we need to make is to the `DefineWord` method to make it use the selected dictionary. Here's what we've changed:

```
private void DefineWord(string word)
{
  string dictionary = "*";
  if (dictionaryToUse.Length > 0)
    dictionary = dictionaryToUse;
  string command = "DEFINE " + dictionary + " " + word;

  string strResult = ExecuteCommand(command);
  ...Rest of method is unchanged...
}
```

Time to try it out. Run the application, click the Choose Dictionary link, and choose a different dictionary (figure 16.12). Then click the OK button.

Now, when you do a search, only the specified dictionary (in this case, the Jargon File) will be used (figure 16.13).

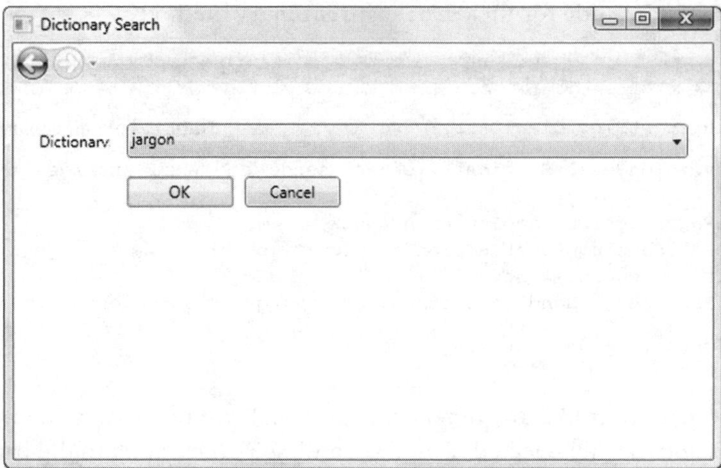

Figure 16.12 Choosing a different dictionary via a page function

The lookup runs against the specified dictionary. Also, notice that the forward button is grayed out—going to the search page doesn't count as a repeatable navigation, an ideal scenario for this type of operation. Overall, the page function capability is one of the nicer features of navigation applications.

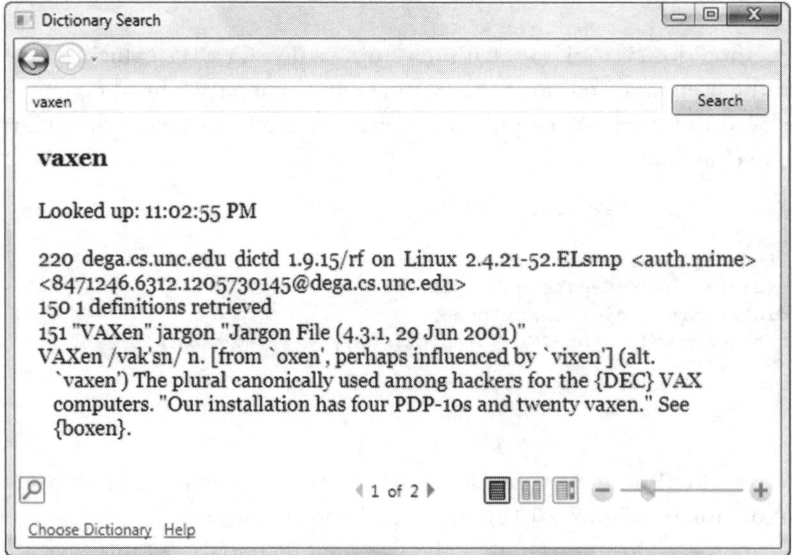

Figure 16.13 Looking up a word in a single dictionary (the Jargon File)

16.4 Summary

You may have picked up a slight bias from us against the navigation application implementation in WPF. (If you didn't, you might want to use the dictionary application to look up Irony and Sarcasm.) It isn't that we don't think that there's a place for inductive UI applications or for document navigation applications, but it seems that the implementation pulled over too many of the problems associated with browser applications for no clear reason.

That doesn't mean that there's no place for these types of applications, and we think that the dictionary application is a pretty good example of where it can be used in a valid way. We're hopeful that the major shortcomings will be addressed in a future version. Also, we have yet to demonstrate one of the cooler things you can do with these applications—running them directly from within a browser. We'll show that in the next chapter. While we're at it, we'll also show how you can autodeploy applications in general.

17

WPF and browsers: XBAP, ClickOnce, and Silverlight

This chapter covers:

- XBAPs
- ClickOnce
- Silverlight
- Our whining about security and why other technologies have cooler names

Although WPF is mainly about building Windows applications, there are many ways in which WPF can be used with browsers. WPF certainly isn't going to replace ASP.NET any time soon, but there are several scenarios where you might want to use WPF when building applications that will be accessed via a browser. Three different technologies in WPF/.NET 3.x provide different mechanisms for accessing WPF applications over the web—XBAP, ClickOnce, Silverlight. We're going to provide a brief summary of each technology here, and then go into more detail throughout the chapter, using the dictionary application as an example.

XBAP

XBAP, short for **X**AML **B**rowser **AP**plication, allows WPF applications to be run directly from within your browser. This is sort of like using ActiveX controls; you can have arbitrary code be downloaded and executed on the client machine inside the browser. The key difference is that, unlike ActiveX, .NET has a robust security model, so it's possible to control what an XBAP is allowed to do. The ActiveX security model had two modes—don't allow or (as one of our colleagues describes it) *party on your hard drive.*

As it happens, the ability to run .NET code within a browser has been around for a while, but WPF makes it *much* easier to create and deploy apps. It's even possible for a browser to automatically render loose XAML files.

In this chapter, we'll take our dictionary application, host it inside a browser, and tackle some of the security issues. While we're at it, we'll also demonstrate some features of navigation applications that lend themselves to being hosted within a browser.

CLICKONCE

ClickOnce is another technology that has been around for a while with .NET, but has been improved. ClickOnce is a deployment technology for automatically shipping out and then updating your applications. The user goes to a website and clicks a link for your application. Unlike XBAP, the application isn't hosted in the browser, but runs as a free-standing application. ClickOnce can even set up desktop icons to run your application again without going to the website. It will also detect changes from that website and automatically download newer versions as they become available.

Almost all the caveats of XBAP exist for ClickOnce as well, although ClickOnce does have the ability to install .NET if required. It does the install via the use of an ActiveX control, so this may not be the best choice in a security-conscious environment.

SILVERLIGHT

Microsoft Silverlight[1] is a new technology designed specifically for building browser components. It's aimed at the same market as Adobe Flash or Sun's JavaFX. Unlike XBAP, it doesn't need to have .NET 3.x installed because it comes with its own (much reduced) version of the runtime, and it's installed, like Flash, as a browser plug-in.

Currently, Silverlight only works on the PC or the Mac, but Microsoft has partnered with the Mono team and Novell to provide Linux support via a project called Moonlight, which is an open source version of Silverlight.[2] For Silverlight to compete with Adobe Flash, it will need to be as ubiquitous, so it's a good thing that it will operate in a number of places.

A number of books are dedicated to Silverlight, including *Silverlight 2 in Action* (Chad A. Campbell and John Stockton), so we aren't going to cover it in depth. Nonetheless, we'll provide a small demonstration later in this chapter. Before we get to that, we'll start by turning our dictionary application into an XBAP.

17.1 Building an XBAP

In the scenarios where it can be used, XBAP provides the best of both worlds—the easy access and deployment of a browser application with a real programming model. But, before deciding on using XBAP, you should be aware of the following limitations:

---

1 See http://silverlight.net for the official details.

2 See http://www.mono-project.com/Moonlight.

- The users have to have .NET 3.0 or 3.5 installed on their machines already. If they have Vista, they already have 3.0. Otherwise, you need to somehow make it available.
- You have to dedicate the remainder of your life to the study of security to get the appropriate permissions for your application configured. OK, this is a bit of an exaggeration, but it *is* a little tricky.

Creating an XBAP application with Visual Studio 2008 is pretty easy. You create a new project of type WPF Browser Application (figure 17.1).

Now, we need to copy all the files from our standalone dictionary application into the browser application and add them as Existing Items. (Right-click the project, and Add Existing—add the xaml files, and the xaml.cs will be automatically picked up.) The last step is to edit the App.xaml file to point to the Search start page.

```
<Application x:Class="DictionaryForBrowser.App"
    xmlns="http://schemas.microsoft.com/winfx/2006/xaml/presentation"
    xmlns:x="http://schemas.microsoft.com/winfx/2006/xaml"
    StartupUri="SearchPage.xaml">
```

Now, go ahead and hit F5 to launch the application. As you can see from figure 17.2, our application is running inside Internet Explorer!

This is real .NET code running inside IE. You can click the Help link, for example, and use the arrows at the top of the window to navigate. Figure 17.2 shows the application running in IE 6. If you happen to be using IE 7, things look a little bit different (figure 17.3).

Something interesting happens when we run inside IE 7—the navigation buttons disappear. IE 7 is WPF savvy and understands navigation applications. The

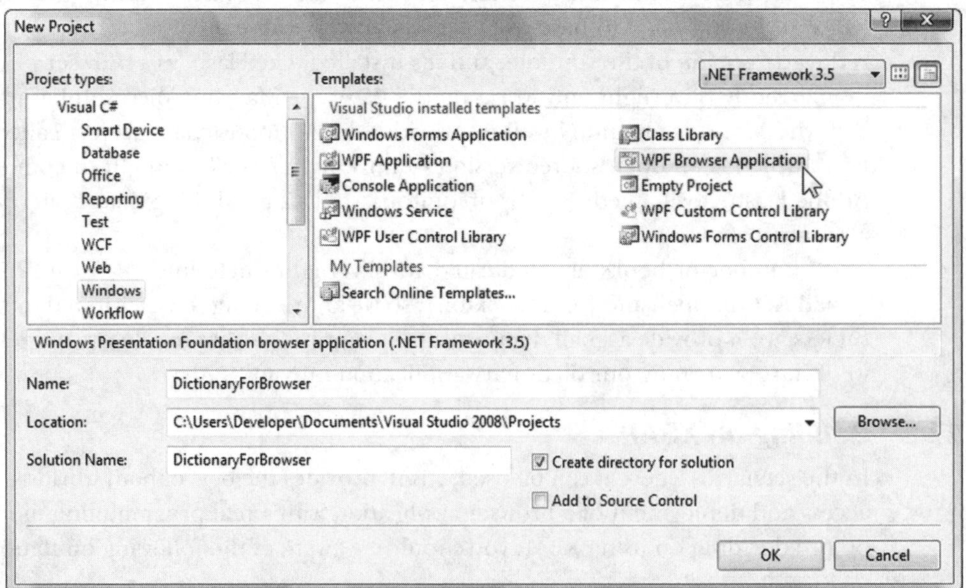

Figure 17.1 Creating a WPF Browser Application

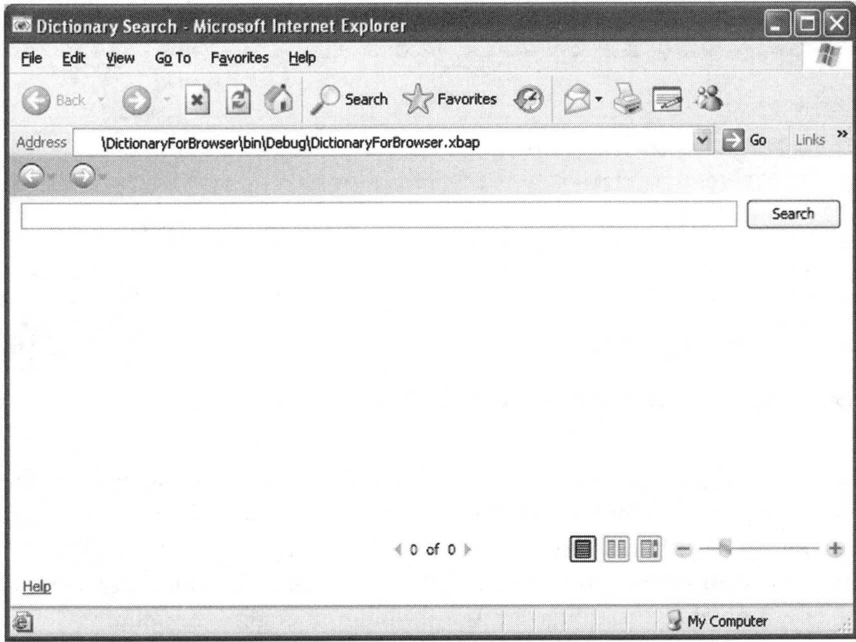

Figure 17.2 The dictionary application, running inside Internet Explorer 6. Looks good, unless you try to search...

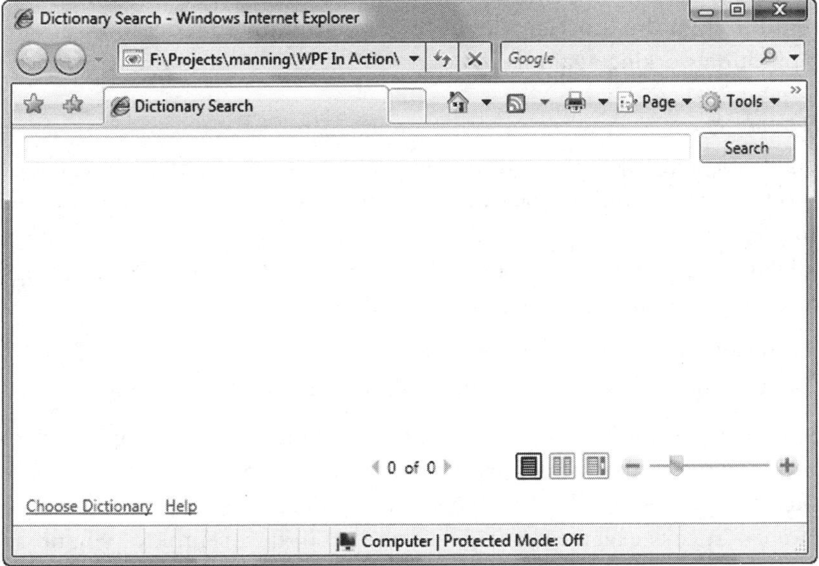

Figure 17.3 The dictionary application running in IE 7. Notice the back/forward buttons have disappeared.

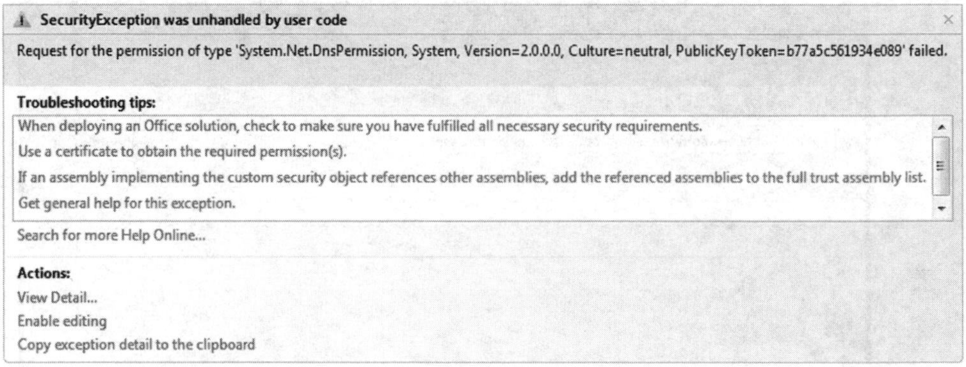

SecurityException was unhandled by user code

Request for the permission of type 'System.Net.DnsPermission, System, Version=2.0.0.0, Culture=neutral, PublicKeyToken=b77a5c561934e089' failed.

Troubleshooting tips:

When deploying an Office solution, check to make sure you have fulfilled all necessary security requirements.

Use a certificate to obtain the required permission(s).

If an assembly implementing the custom security object references other assemblies, add the referenced assemblies to the full trust assembly list.

Get general help for this exception.

Search for more Help Online...

Actions:

View Detail...

Enable editing

Copy exception detail to the clipboard

Figure 17.4 Security exception trying to do a dictionary search

browser's navigation buttons provide the back/forward functionality for the application, so the ones in the browser window are superfluous. You might be wondering if you can end up hitting back right out of your application—well, IE 7's security forces WPF applications to be opened in new windows, in which case over-backage is less of a problem. One thing that is a problem, though, is searching. Go ahead and type in a word, and hit the Search button. Chances are you'll see something like figure 17.4.

On one hand, it's nice to know that .NET security is working well—preventing us from opening a TCP connection from a hosted application. On the other hand, it does tend to limit the functionality of the application. We'll demonstrate how to get the application working again next.

17.1.1 XBAP security

By default, hosted .NET applications are allowed to do certain things, such as put things on the screen and interact with the user, and aren't allowed to do, well, almost anything else. Thanks to pop-up ads, by default a hosted application can't even pop up a dialog (except for some system dialogs like the File Open/Save dialogs). If you want your application to do more, you have to do two things:

1. Indicate to .NET what you want permission to do.
2. Get the hosting system to agree to allow you to do those things.

Asking for permission is pretty straightforward. Right-click the project, select properties, and then switch to the Security tab. You'll see something like figure 17.5.

When this page is first displayed, it shows the default security rights that we'll have. Here we can specify exactly what rights we want. In fact, via the very handy Calculate Permissions button, we can have Visual Studio run through the application and figure it out for us. Unfortunately, when we run Calculate Permissions on this application, it comes up saying that we need Full Trust, which means that users have to give us god-like rights to their systems in order to look up words in a dictionary!

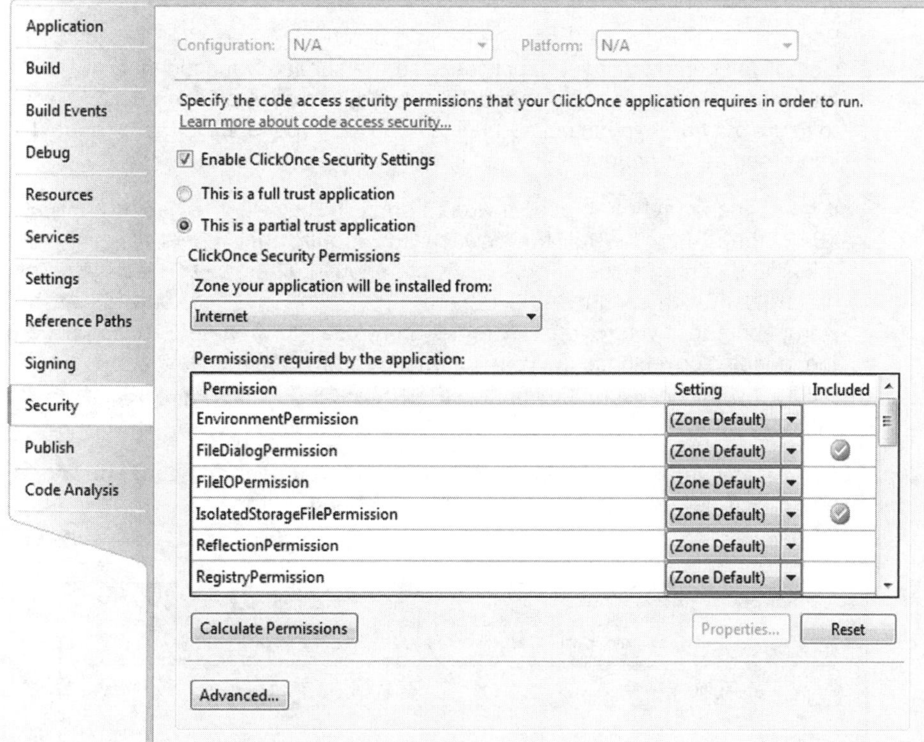

Figure 17.5 Security properties for our XBAP

In reality, we almost certainly do *not* need uber rights, but we'll go ahead and set this up as a full trust application anyway. This isn't because we're lazy (although we are); it's to make a point about security in the sidebar. If you recompile and then run again, everything will now work (figure 17.6).

Cool, eh? But, you may have noticed that we've only completed *one* of our steps—asking for permission. We haven't *given* permission, and yet things are working. The reason is that the built-in web server that Visual Studio uses for debugging ignores all that annoying security stuff and assumes that we have rights to do what we've said we want rights to do. If we want to see what happens in the real world, we'll have to deploy our application.

Security ≠ usability

The world would be a much simpler place if we could just trust one-another. We could pop up a dialog that says, "Is this OK?" and assume that no one would do anything he wasn't supposed to do. Unfortunately, our original specification for Windows security based on the ITOLM (Is This OK? Lan Manager) concept was rejected.

> Security has a big impact on whether it's practical to use XBAP or similar technologies. If you can restrict your application to the subset of functionality available by default, then it's a good fit. If, on the other hand, you need additional rights, you'll need to figure out how to push out certificates and tune your application to request the minimum number of rights.
>
> It's our guess that most people won't bother. If they want to deploy applications via XBAP, they'll flick the full trust switch and require their users to let them do anything. And, if the functionality is desirable enough, users will do just that. This is the big problem with security—it's a pain for everyone involved, and it's easier to not worry about it. If you're in an extremely controlled environment, this may be OK, but the added convenience to your users of easing their install won't gain you any points if your approach ends up frying their systems or letting in someone else to fry their systems.
>
> As with everything else, security is a trade-off. You need to figure out what's appropriate. But hey, we aren't your mother—go ahead, full trust is easy...

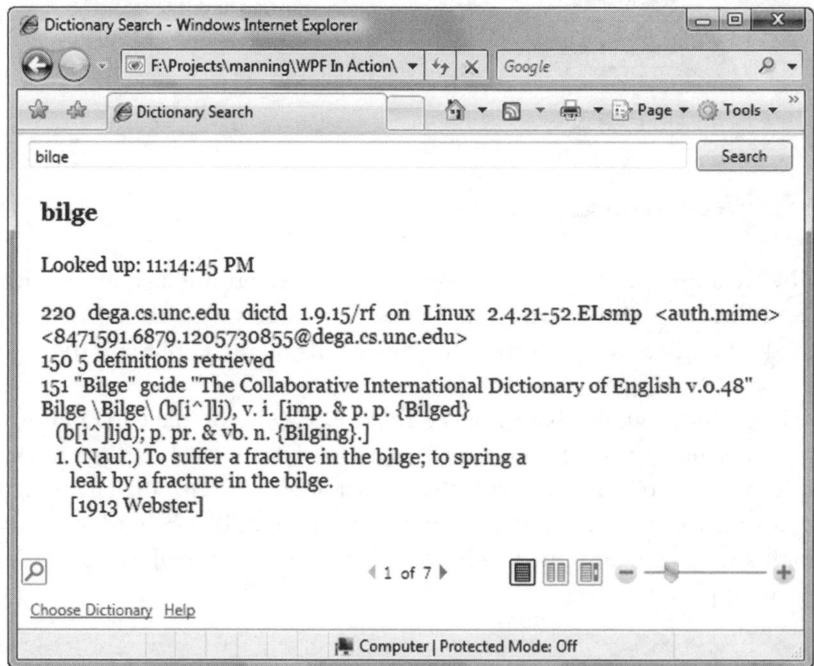

Figure 17.6 We now have appropriate rights to look up words!

17.1.2 Deploying an XBAP

Assuming that you have IIS installed on your system, it's pretty easy to deploy your application. Browse to the bin/debug directory under your project, right-click, and

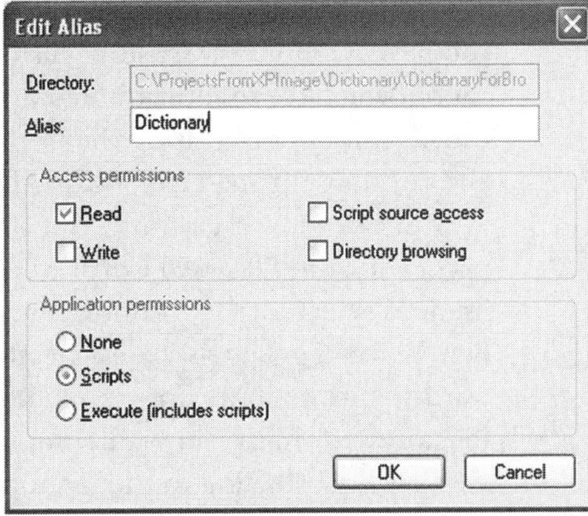

Figure 17.7 Deploying the dictionary. This is much easier in XP (pictured here) than in Vista. With Vista you have to create the virtual directory using IIS.

bring up properties.[3] Then go to the Web Sharing page, click the Share This Folder button, and type in a reasonable alias (figure 17.7).

Now, in your browser, go to the appropriate URI, which will be something like:

```
http://localhost/Dictionary/DictionaryForBrowser.xbap
```

And, voilà—uh, pfft… (figure 17.8).

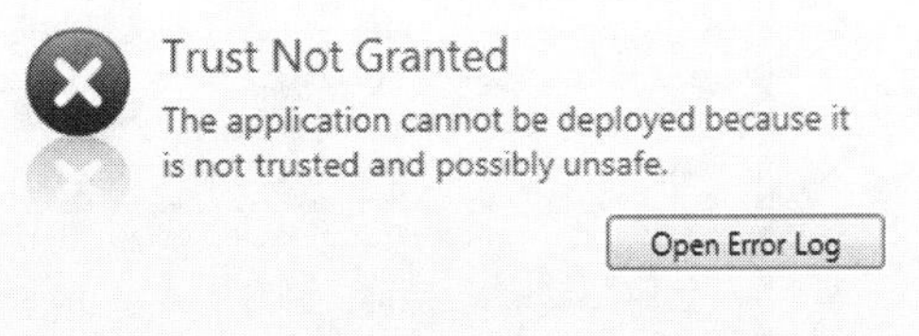

Figure 17.8 The application isn't worthy to be run.

After a brief message telling you that the application is being downloaded, you get the unfriendly (but quite pretty—note the reflection under the X) message telling you that the application is untrusted and possibly tricksy. In the real world, to get around this, you'd have to purchase a certificate from a trusted authority, and then arrange to have it pushed out to your users. But, for testing purposes, Visual Studio 2008 makes life easier by generating a default test key when you create an XBAP.

If you look in the directory for your project, you will see a file with a name like:

```
DictionaryForBrowser_TemporaryKey.pfx
```

---

[3] If you're using Vista, the Web Sharing page isn't available. You'll have to go into IIS and add a new Virtual Directory to the primary website.

This temporary key can be used for testing, but you can't use it for deployment unless you have a lot of very trusting customers. On the machine that wants to run the application, you have to indicate that any applications signed with this key have rights. You can do this either by using the CertMgr tool, or by double-clicking the file in Explorer and running through the wizard (figure 17.9).

You can leave everything as it is until you get to the Certificate Store page. On that page, click the Place All Certificates In The Following Store radio button, browse the list, and select Trusted Root Certification Authorities. After that, click Next and then Finish. You'll get a nasty message about how your filthy certificate is certainly not trustworthy, and what are you thinking about trying to give it rights? Say Yes, and ignore the annoyed sniff from your computer. Hey, your computer works for *you*.

Now, try browsing to the dictionary application again. Not only does it come up in the browser, but, as you can see from figure 17.10, you can look up words again!

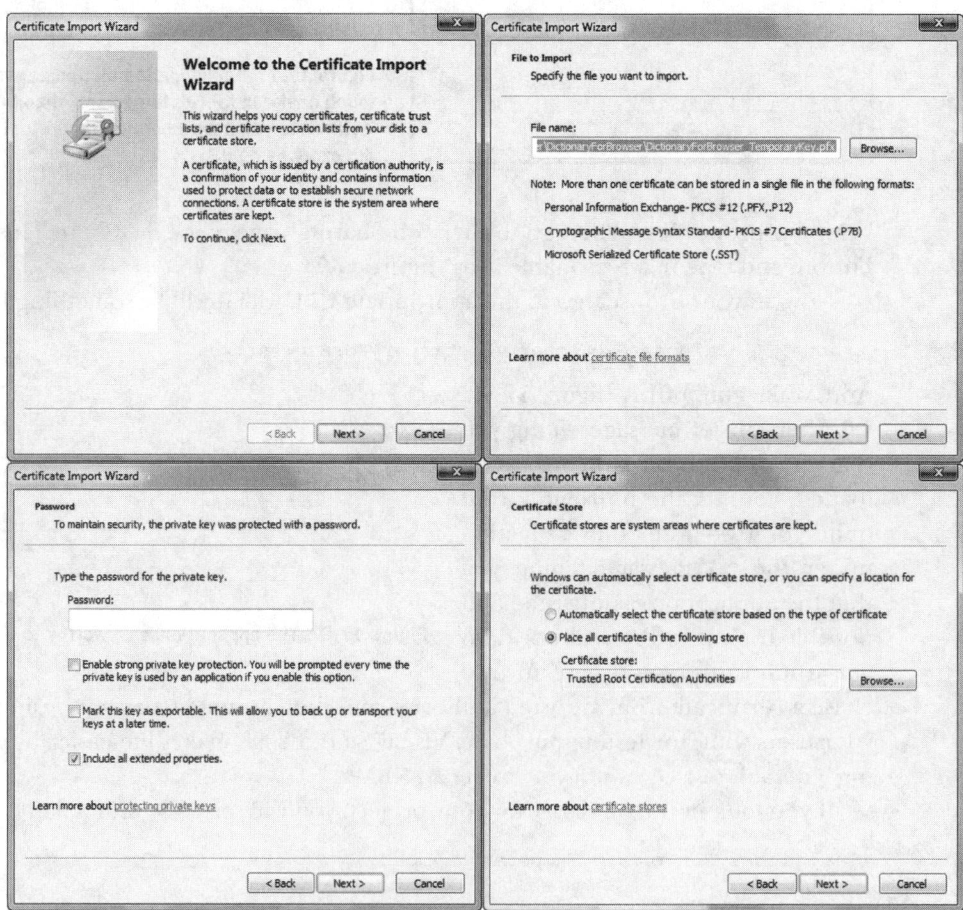

Figure 17.9 The Certificate Import Wizard pages

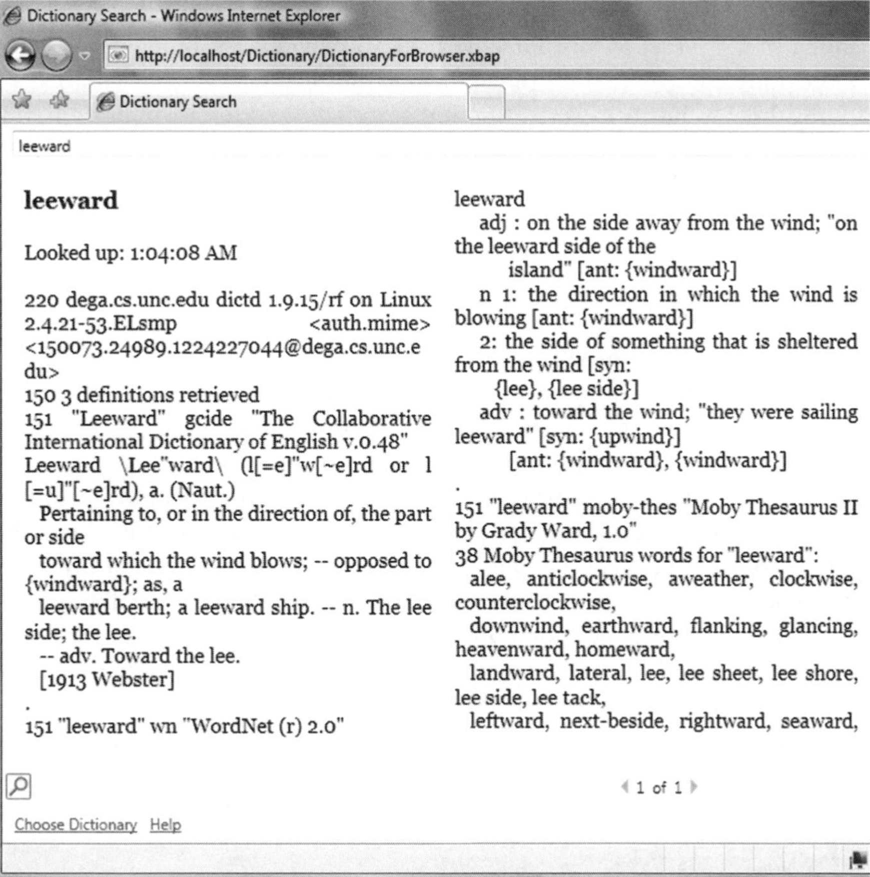

Figure 17.10 The application is now working in a hosted manner.

We've just given anything signed with this key rights to do pretty much anything on the target system, but you can't have everything.

17.1.3 When to use XBAP

Given the security implications of using XBAP, it's worth spending a few moments discussing situations where XBAP is appropriate to use. Assuming that you want to provide rich functionality within a browser, you have two overarching considerations:

- Can you accomplish what you need within the subset of available functionality with standard rights?
- Do you have control over your environment such that you can provide additional rights to users?

That isn't to say that there aren't situations where you might want to sign an application and hope people will trust it; but, in general, if neither of these points is true, we'd recommend against using XBAP.

There's a further consideration: If you *can* live with a subset of capabilities, can you live with a *smaller* subset of functionality? If so, you might want to look at Silverlight. It has more restrictions; but, as we'll discuss later in this chapter, it also has a number of benefits.

By the way, just because we showed a hosted Navigation Application, that doesn't mean that you're limited to only Navigation Applications. WPF will cheerfully let you host any type of application, although all the same caveats still apply. If the goal, though, is to get functionality to users, and you don't particularly want the application to be hosted in IE, you might want to consider ClickOnce.

17.2 Using ClickOnce

ClickOnce isn't new for WPF or .NET 3.x, but it's another way of deploying WPF applications. The biggest difference with using ClickOnce versus XBAP is that the application isn't hosted inside a browser. The idea is that you do *start* inside a browser; you click a link to run your application (see figure 17.11), but once you launch the application, it comes up in its own window. Further, if so configured, the application will now be on the users' start menus for future use. But, if a newer version of the application becomes available, users can be asked if they want to automatically retrieve it.

Publishing a basic WPF application via ClickOnce is almost childishly simple. The tricky part is dealing with additional options and components—and security. In some ways, though, security is a little more straightforward than XBAP. Technically, you'll want to get a proper, authorized certificate and, in a corporate environment, push that certificate out to users as required. But, the default behavior with ClickOnce is to ask the users if they want to go ahead and install. For example, if you click the Install button from figure 17.11, after a brief Downloading dialog, you'll get a dialog like figure 17.12.

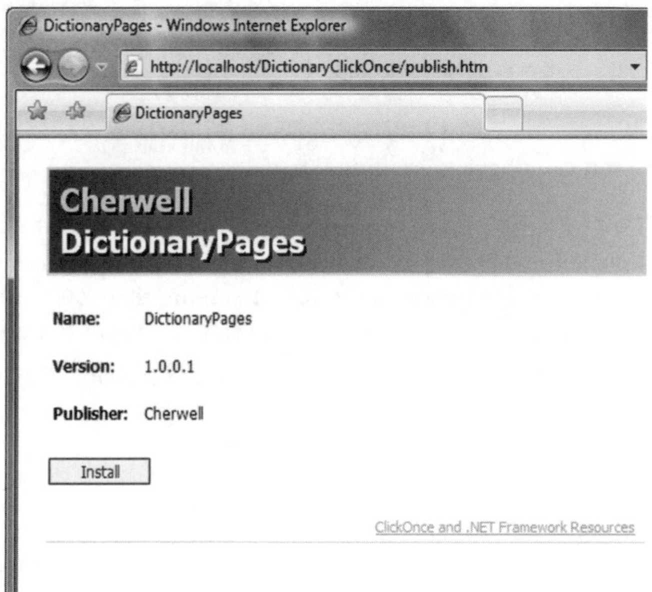

Figure 17.11 The automatically created web page from which the application can be downloaded. The wizard autogenerated this page, but it can be made prettier or embedded within other content as required. Also, if the appropriate version of .NET isn't installed, the option to first install it will also be presented.

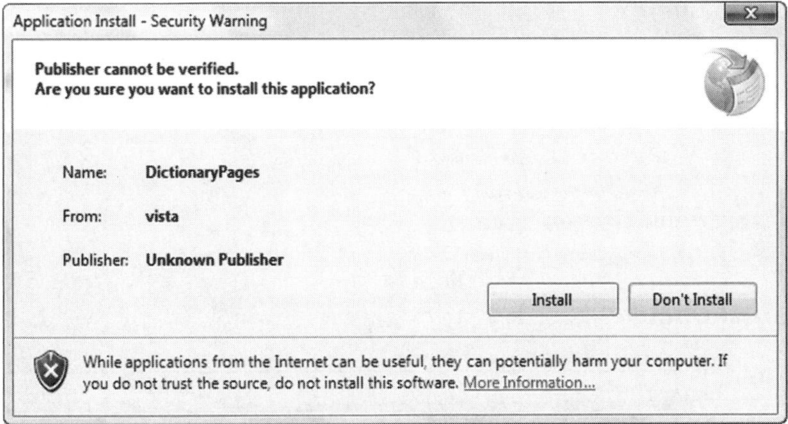

Figure 17.12 Security warning when running ClickOnce. If you click Install, you're implicitly trusting the application.

Notice that this isn't a million miles away from the ActiveX "Trust me?" approach. If, your application limits itself to the same subset of functionality we discussed under XBAP, you wouldn't get any warning. If you go ahead and say Install, the application will be installed (to a special cache location) and then will start up. Further, the application will now show up on the start menu (figure 17.13).

We're a little backwards here, though. We've shown what a ClickOnce deployment looks like, but we haven't shown how you set it up.

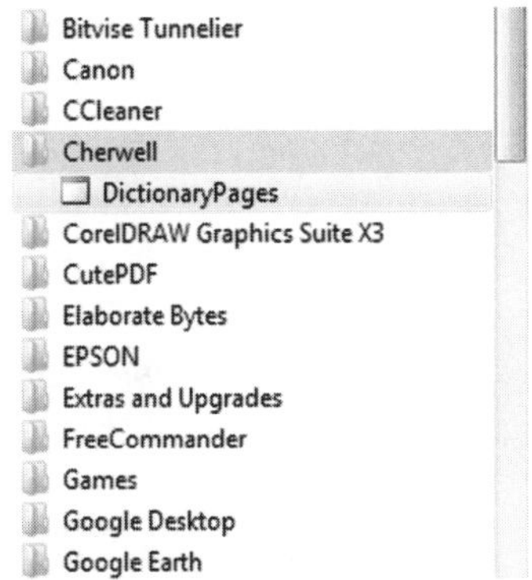

Figure 17.13 ClickOnce can automatically add your application to the start menu. The containing folder defaults to the name under which Visual Studio was installed, but it can be changed.

17.2.1 *Deploying a WPF application via ClickOnce*

We need to go back to the non-XBAP version of the dictionary, and the first thing we need to do is set up security. As with the XBAP, you go to the Security tab on the assembly's properties, and turn on full trust (figure 17.14). Ideally you'd go through and figure out the specific rights, but this will work for our example.

Now, we need to set up a place to publish to. Visual Studio could automatically publish to a website for us; for simplicity, let's create a subdirectory called Dictionary-ClickOnce, right-click to bring up its properties, and, on the Web Sharing page, share the application as DictionaryClickOnce. Believe it or not, this is the hard part. All we have to do now is run through the Publish Wizard, which is available by selecting Publish from the Build menu. Figure 17.15 shows the pages of the wizard with our selections.

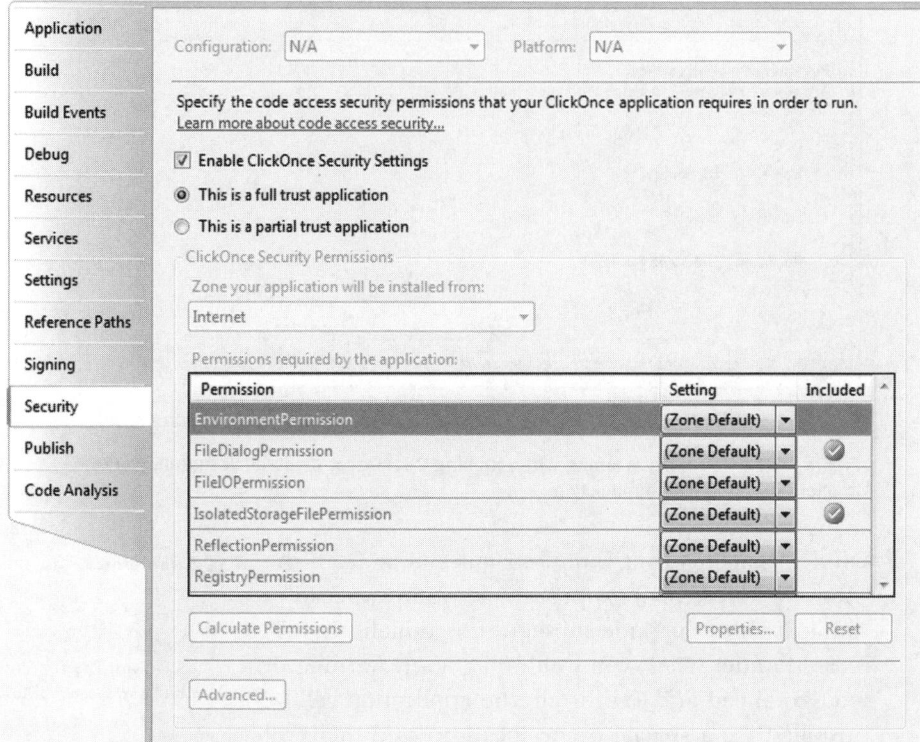

Figure 17.14 We're turning on full trust for the application. This isn't ideal, but even the Calculate Permissions mechanism thinks we need it, and who are we to argue?

Once you've run the wizard, you can go to the appropriate URI and see the web page from figure 17.11. This is pretty much as deep as we're going to get into ClickOnce. The basics are pretty straightforward. Things get trickier when you want to deal with more complex scenarios, such as allowing communication back to your server, pushing out configuration files, and that sort of thing, but none of that's particularly different for WPF as for any other ClickOnce applications.

17.2.2 When to use ClickOnce

Although XBAPs are pretty cool, ClickOnce is arguably more commonly useful. A common reason why ASP.NET is used for complex applications is to avoid having to deploy a rich application. In a better world, the ease of deployment would be balanced against the *much* poorer usability of many ASP.NET applications (even with AJAX and every modern trick). Ah well. In any case, ClickOnce does a lot to level the playing field here. Users can still go to a web page and click a link, but then they get the full experience of a Windows application and automatic updates.

That being said, there are still plenty of caveats. Security is one, although not as severe as with XBAPs. Additional concerns are bandwidth and deployment models.

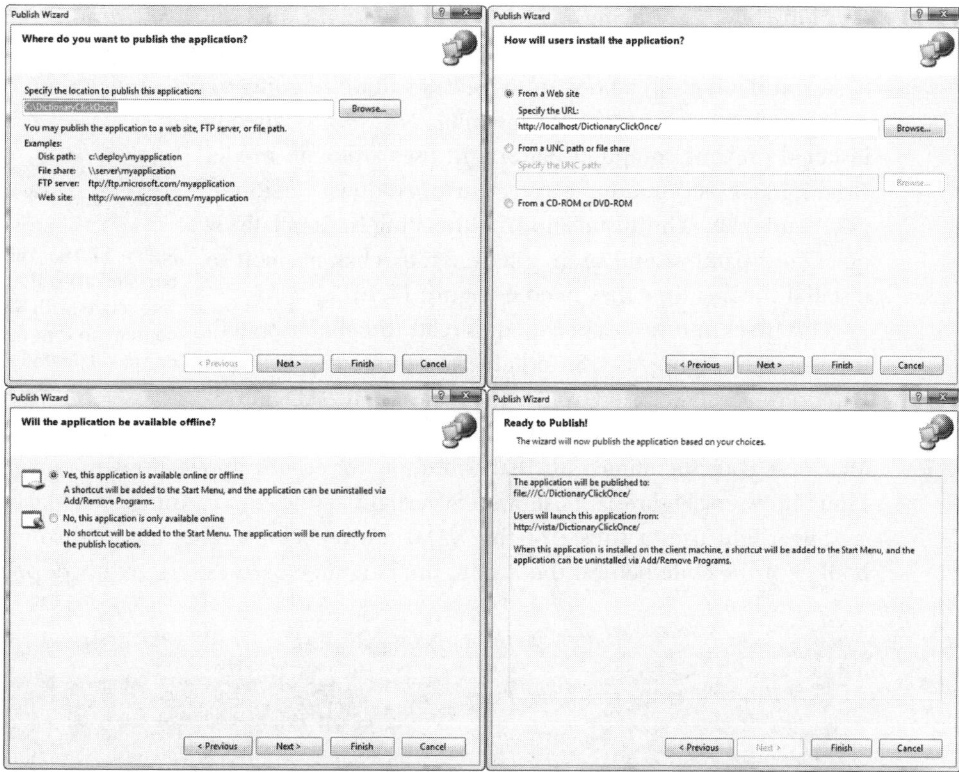

Figure 17.15 The ClickOnce Publish Wizard. For simple deployment situations, the wizard pretty much handles everything. Other than choosing the directory, we've gone with the defaults for everything else.

For occasional-use applications or intensely content-driven applications, such as shopping carts, ASP.NET is a better choice. Also, if users might not have .NET installed, or if the application is likely to be large and users are unlikely to have much bandwidth, ClickOnce loses some of its appeal. On the other hand, if most of your users have good bandwidth, ClickOnce supports a CD deployment model as well, so you can just ship media to the few laggards.

One final caveat has to do with the type of software you're building—if you're building commercial software, and the intent is to install an application on a customer's server that's then deployed to end users at that company, things can get complicated. Things can get particularly complicated if you need to modify the contents of what you're deploying (based on some customer configuration) because this requires resigning the deployment package *when the changes are made.*

17.3 Using Silverlight

In a chapter about WPF running over the web, we couldn't possibly *not* talk about Silverlight. Silverlight is a technology designed for building *rich internet applications,* or RIAs. Silverlight is a head-to-head competitor with Adobe Flash and its successor, Flex.

Many books are being written about Silverlight, including *Silverlight 2 In Action* by Chad A. Campbell and John Stockton from your friendly neighborhood Manning book dealer, and it is really a book unto itself, so all we're going to do is touch on it briefly.

Unlike XBAPs, which assume that .NET 3.x is already installed on your computer, Silverlight uses a plug-in model (again, like Flash) and has a (very) stripped-down version of .NET and WPF. The installation of the Plug-In is relatively quick and painless end users will generally click an icon to install it the first time they need it (figure 17.16).

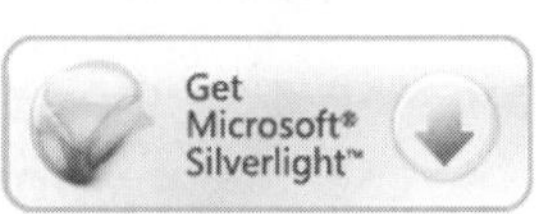

Figure 17.16 This icon (or one similar) will appear on web pages with Silverlight content so that users can download/install the plug-in.

This quick and easy deployment is really the major benefit to using Silverlight. Also, Silverlight isn't limited to Internet Explorer—it will work in Firefox, and Safari on the Macintosh via the appropriate plug-in models. There's an open source project called Moonlight that Microsoft is cooperating with that will allow Silverlight applications to run on Unix/ Linux browsers. Figure 17.17 shows a Silverlight application running on a Macintosh.

Silverlight uses a subset of the XAML we've been talking about throughout the book. For the code behind the XAML, the language used differs greatly depending on

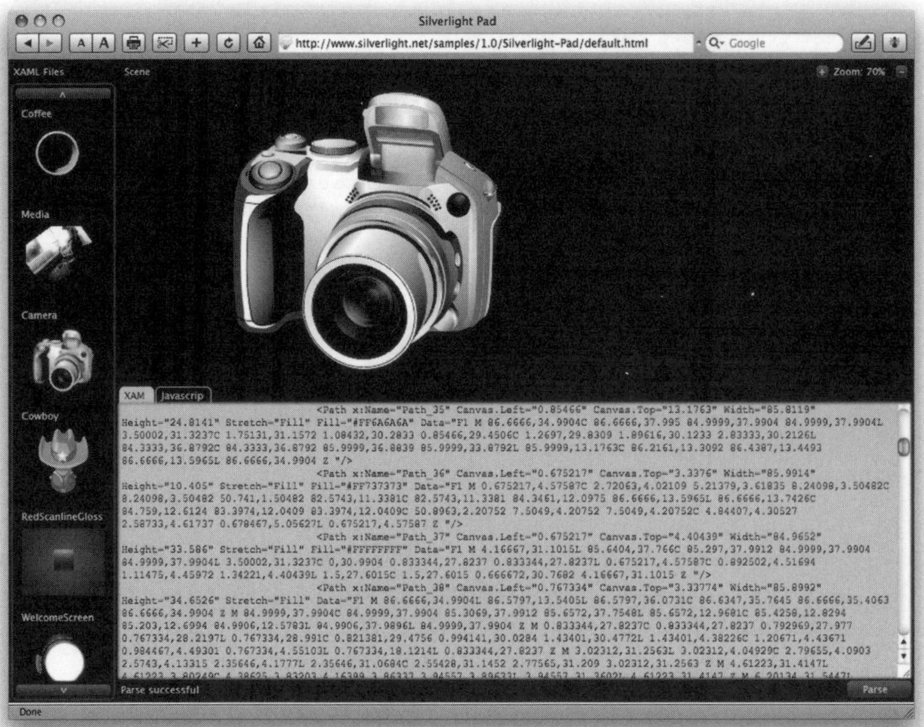

Figure 17.17 This is a Silverlight sample application running under Safari on a Macintosh. Silverlight Pad is sort of like XAMLPad, but for Silverlight. The tab at the bottom shows the rather painful XAML for drawing the camera; this drawing was probably done inside Microsoft Expression Blend.

the version of Silverlight. Version 1.0 only supported Javascript. Version 2.0 allows for any .NET language to be used, including the new dynamic languages IronPython and IronRuby. Although you can build Silverlight applications in Visual Studio 2008 (by installing an add-on to Visual Studio called Microsoft Silverlight Tools), Expression Blend is the primary tool designed for building Silverlight applications—this makes sense, given the graphical focus of Silverlight.

Our one big beef with Silverlight is the name—why did *Avalon* become the intensely boring Windows Presentation Foundation, whereas Silverlight got to be, well, *Silverlight*?[4]

17.4 Summary

It's funny that, in a book about building Windows applications, there's so much to say about working with browsers. WPF has a lot of options for providing functionality in a browser, whether it be through XBAP hosting, Silverlight applications, or easier deployment via ClickOnce.

As technologies converge, it's clear that the line between smart and browser applications will blur more and more—and that security will ever be the biggest challenge to overcome to make the transition a smooth one. We don't know for sure how this will finally play out, but XAML and WPF seem destined to play a part.

We aren't quite done with our dictionary application. In the next chapter, we'll add the ability to print out definitions and discuss printing in general.

[4] We're told that a new marketing head honcho took over and had the previous marketing team's heads stuck on pikes outside MS HQ, but we haven't confirmed the last part.

18 Printing, documents, and XPS

This chapter covers:

- Printing `FlowDocuments`
- Synchronous and asynchronous printing
- Printing `FixedDocuments`
- Saving XPS documents
- Exploring modern art

Do you remember the paperless office? We were reading about it in our flying car the other day and decided that it was one of those concepts that sounded good, but never quite got off the ground. Whether this is because too many people aren't yet comfortable giving up paper or the technology isn't *yet* quite a reasonable replacement, we aren't sure.

The fact is that most applications have to provide some mechanism for printing. Even for applications that eschew paper, there's often a need to provide data in an easily transferable format such as Adobe's PDF format. Yet, we've noticed that most Windows programming guides manage to skirt talking about printing. We think we know the reason for this—up until now, printing from Windows has been a royal pain. Even with Windows Forms, which made things a little better, printing was always one of those tasks to assign to the developer you liked least and who you could then happily blame for your whole schedule slipping.[1]

As with many things in Windows, the reason that printing has been so painful is tied to 20+ year-old technology, in a time where every printing device worked in its own way and Microsoft wasn't big enough to bully hardware companies into consistency.

WPF, in many ways, makes printing simpler—particularly for simple scenarios like printing a document with some data. But, printing has to handle a *lot* of specialized scenarios. Think about the needs of desktop publishing applications that write to high-end typesetters, or printing color-corrected proofs from a drawing program, or even creating a paperless document that can be easily shared à la PDF. Also, even low-end devices now have a whole plethora of options, and the printing mechanism has to handle all of them.

What this means is that WPF has to have a lot of underlying support for different needs, making WPF printing seem somewhat confusing. The trick is to focus on the bits that are relevant to your needs and to know which classes you can ignore. In this chapter, we'll demonstrate a *subset* of the printing capabilities of WPF—a subset because we could easily fill two books the size of this one to do the subject justice.

We'll also discuss XML Paper Specification (XPS), which sits at the heart of WPF printing.

18.1 Printing flow documents

The most straightforward way to print in WPF is to create a document and then send it to the printer (or wherever). Prior to WPF, this wouldn't have been terribly effective, but WPF provides for the ability to build extremely rich documents. Conveniently, our dictionary application already uses a document—the one that displays the results of a search. We aren't doing much with it; it's just a large font title and some paragraphs, but we could easily put in tables, images, built-in or custom controls, or anything else our little hearts desire.

The document in the dictionary application is an example of a `FlowDocument`. WPF has support for two different types of documents:

- *`FlowDocuments`*—Content is added, and the `FlowDocument` figures out how to position it based on the available space and options such as the number of pages to display, the current zoom level, and so on. This type of document is most appropriate for display in applications where you want to get the content out and printed in the most appropriate manner for the display or print device.
- *`FixedDocuments`*—Content is more precisely placed for a particular type of target, such as a specific page format. This type of document is what you would use for printing forms or desktop publishing or for creating transferable documents.

---

[1] One of these days we might be compelled to write a book about the silliness of most software schedules and how to really plan and deliver software. You should call our publisher and tell them you want that book!

Because we already have a `FlowDocument` in our dictionary application, let's look at printing that first.

18.1.1 Setting up to print

The first thing we need to do is provide a way for users to say that they want to print. The easy way is to add another hyperlink to the bottom of the page and hook it up to a `Click` handler. We won't bother showing the details of doing this because it's something we've shown a number of times before. The link should look something like figure 18.1.

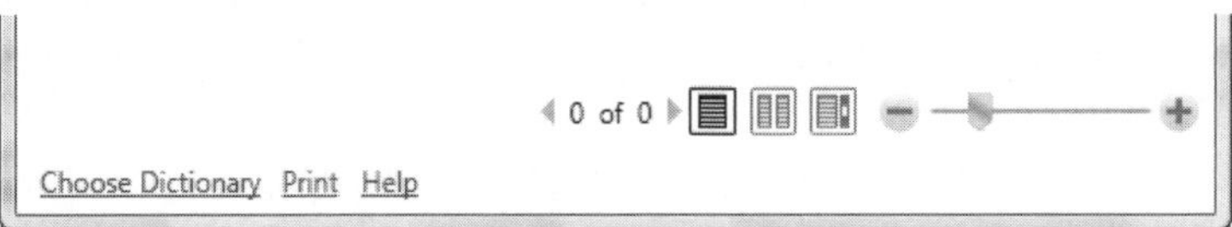

Figure 18.1 We have, very excitingly, added a Print `Hyperlink` to our application. We've also added an `OnPrint` method to the code to handle the click.

Before we can make printing work, we have to add a reference to the appropriate assembly. By default, WPF applications don't reference the `System.Printing` assembly that contains the basic printing support. If you're following along, right-click the References folder under the Dictionary application, and select Add Reference. Then, scroll down until you find `System.Printing`, and say OK (figure 18.2).

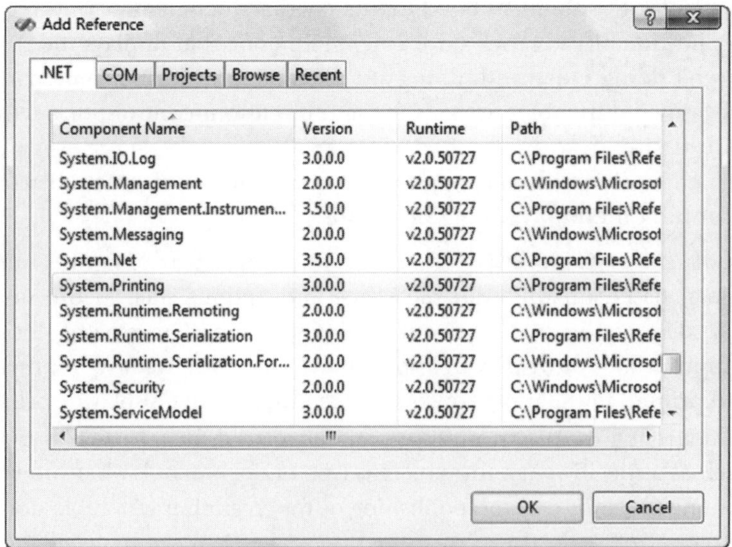

Figure 18.2 Adding a reference to the `System.Printing` assembly. You can get to this dialog by right-clicking the References folder underneath your project in the solution explorer and selecting Add Reference.

Now we need the printing code. Listing 18.1 shows our first version of the printing method. We've shoved the using statement at the top of the listing, but it really goes at the top of the file.

Listing 18.1 Printing code

```
using System.Printing;    <-- Using goes at top of file

protected void OnPrint(object sender, RoutedEventArgs e)
{
  PrintDialog printDialog = new PrintDialog();          <-- (1) Chooses printer and so on
  bool? print = printDialog.ShowDialog();     <-- (2) bool? Why? Why not?
  if (print == true)
  {
    IDocumentPaginatorSource paginatorSource =
           searchResults.Document as IDocumentPaginatorSource;    (3)

    printDialog.PrintDocument(paginatorSource.DocumentPaginator,    <--
           "Dictionary");                                 Does printing (4)
  }
}
```

The first thing we do here is pop up a print dialog (1) to determine the printer we want, the pages to print, and so on. We could have also set some options to customize behavior. Behind the scenes, the print dialog is setting up two important things for us:

- *PrintQueue*—Where we are going to send our print job. It sort of represents the printer, and lets us determine the capabilities of the printer, and so on; but it also represents the queue, so you can do things like cancel jobs.
- *PrintTicket*—Instructions to the printer about how we want our job to be printed, information such as quality, color, and even if we want the printer to put a staple in the middle of the page and immediately jam.[2] The `PrintTicket` is more complex than this because any individual print job could contain multiple tickets (for example: page 1 is landscape, page 2 is portrait, and so on), but this description gets the general idea across.

Because we're using the `PrintDialog`, we don't need to directly interact with either of these objects, but they're exposed as properties off the `PrintDialog` if we need them. Later on, we'll show printing without using the `PrintDialog`, at which time we'll have to be a little more hands-on.

By the way, notice that the `PrintDialog`'s `Show()` method returns a `bool?` (2) instead of a `DialogResult`, as dialogs used to do in days of yore? You may remember that `bool?` is a *nullable* `bool`, which can have values of either `true`, `false`, or `null`. Why a dialog would need to be able to return `null` is unclear—the doc lyingly claims that the dialog will return `null` if the user exits in some way other than clicking `true` or `false`. It won't—it always returns either `true` or `false`. Personally, we think that they

[2] Not supported on all printers.

should have stuck with a `DialogResult` (which was nice and flexible). It's too easy for coders to abuse the nullable return to fake a third option.

Anyway, back to the plot. The next thing we have to do is get hold of a *paginator* ❸, which is responsible for figuring out how to break up our content into pages. This is an example of one of those things that needs to be present for flexibility, but we normally don't care about. The document has hold of the paginator it's using, and we can grab that by casting our document into the interface that knows how to give us the paginator to use.

If we wanted to customize how pages were set up, we'd probably want to create a custom paginator. For example, if we wanted to insert a header and a footer for each page, we'd have to create a custom paginator.[3] Right now, we want to do something simple, though, so we're doing the minimum to get hold of the default paginator, which we get from the cast paginator source (our lowly document) and pass to the `PrintDialog`'s handy `Print` method ❹.

If you go ahead and run, look up a word, and then click Print, you'll get a print dialog that lets you select the printer. Then your document will print (something like figure 18.3).

So far, so good. And, other than having to know one esoteric thing (how to get to the paginator), the code is pretty simple. But, there are some minor issues. For example, we could use some margins, and we'd prefer that the text go all the way across the page.

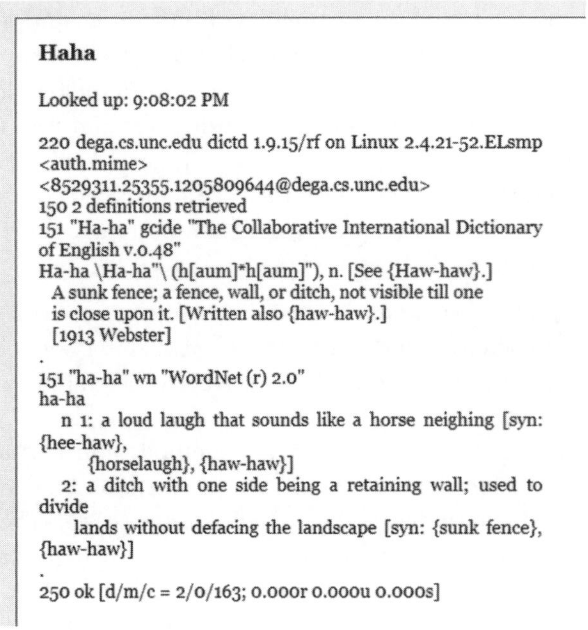

```
Haha

Looked up: 9:08:02 PM

220 dega.cs.unc.edu dictd 1.9.15/rf on Linux 2.4.21-52.ELsmp
<auth.mime>
<8529311.25355.1205809644@dega.cs.unc.edu>
150 2 definitions retrieved
151 "Ha-ha" gcide "The Collaborative International Dictionary
of English v.0.48"
Ha-ha \Ha-ha"\ (h[aum]*h[aum]"), n. [See {Haw-haw}.]
  A sunk fence; a fence, wall, or ditch, not visible till one
  is close upon it. [Written also {haw-haw}.]
  [1913 Webster]
.
151 "ha-ha" wn "WordNet (r) 2.0"
ha-ha
   n 1: a loud laugh that sounds like a horse neighing [syn:
{hee-haw},
        {horselaugh}, {haw-haw}]
   2: a ditch with one side being a retaining wall; used to
divide
      lands without defacing the landscape [syn: {sunk fence},
{haw-haw}]
.
250 ok [d/m/c = 2/0/163; 0.000r 0.000u 0.000s]
```

Figure 18.3 Printout of a looked-up word. Not bad, but it could use some margins and so on.

[3] You could argue that wanting to add headers and footers is so common that it should be handled easily and by default. Unfortunately, that isn't the case. It's likely, though, that code snippets will show up all over the place for tasks like this.

18.1.2 Customizing the output

Because we have a `Document`, we can go ahead and set properties on that `Document`. For example, we could set the margin on the document.

```
searchResults.Document.PagePadding = new Thickness(96);
```

Page padding might *not* be the most obvious way of referring to a margin, but this will work. We're using the value 96 because units are in device independent pixels (DIPs); there are 96 dips in an inch, so we're setting the margin to 1 inch all the way around.

But, there's one problem. We're setting the property on the same document *that we're currently viewing in the application*. This means that our printout will have a 1-inch margin, and so will our document in the application—which won't look very good. Also, if we make any additional changes, they'll also show up in the document, and we don't want that either.

We *could* set the properties, print, and then restore the properties, but that approach is pretty ugly, particularly if we make more and more changes. Also, in a little while, we'll demonstrate printing asynchronously, so that *really* won't work.

Instead, the most straightforward solution is to make a copy of our document and make the changes to that. This approach makes a lot of sense anyway because you often don't want your printout to be *exactly* what you have on the screen. It isn't entirely trivial to copy a `FlowDocument`—we'd prefer a Copy method (hint, hint MS). Listing 18.2 has the simplest code we could come up with for creating a copy of a `FlowDocument`.

Listing 18.2 Copying a `FlowDocument`

```
protected FlowDocument CopyFlowDocument(FlowDocument originalDoc)
{
  string xmlDoc = XamlWriter.Save(originalDoc);

  StringReader stringReader = new StringReader(xmlDoc);
  XmlReader xmlReader = XmlReader.Create(stringReader);
  FlowDocument newDoc = (FlowDocument)XamlReader.Load(xmlReader);

  return newDoc;
}
```

This code writes everything in the original document to a string as XAML and then creates a new `FlowDocument` by reading in the contents of that string. It uses two very useful classes—`XamlWriter` and `XamlReader`. Now all we have to do is change our print code to make a copy and print that (listing 18.3).

Listing 18.3 Printing copy

```
protected void OnPrint(object sender, RoutedEventArgs e)
{
  PrintDialog printDialog = new PrintDialog();
  bool? print = printDialog.ShowDialog();
  if (print == true)
  {
    FlowDocument docCopy = CopyFlowDocument(searchResults.Document);     ❶
```

```
            docCopy.PagePadding = new Thickness(96);
            docCopy.ColumnWidth = double.NaN;

            IDocumentPaginatorSource paginatorSource =
                   docCopy as IDocumentPaginatorSource;
            printDialog.PrintDocument(paginatorSource.DocumentPaginator,
                   "Dictionary");
        }
    }
```

❷ **Setting properties on copy**

This code is pretty similar to the old version. The big difference is that we call our copy method ❶ and then set a few properties on the copy ❷, including the margin and the column width. By setting the column width to "Not a Number", we're saying that we want the column to take up all available space. Everything else is the same—except that we're printing our copy instead of the original. Figure 18.4 shows our page with the nicer formatting.

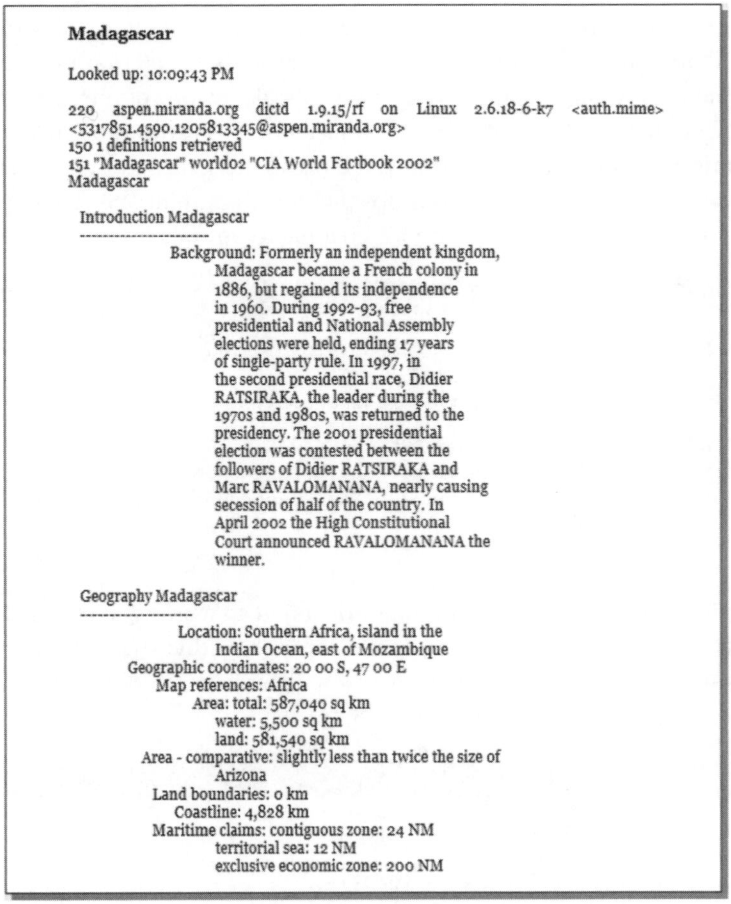

Madagascar

Looked up: 10:09:43 PM

220 aspen.miranda.org dictd 1.9.15/rf on Linux 2.6.18-6-k7 <auth.mime>
<5317851.4590.1205813345@aspen.miranda.org>
150 1 definitions retrieved
151 "Madagascar" world02 "CIA World Factbook 2002"
Madagascar

Introduction Madagascar

Background: Formerly an independent kingdom, Madagascar became a French colony in 1886, but regained its independence in 1960. During 1992-93, free presidential and National Assembly elections were held, ending 17 years of single-party rule. In 1997, in the second presidential race, Didier RATSIRAKA, the leader during the 1970s and 1980s, was returned to the presidency. The 2001 presidential election was contested between the followers of Didier RATSIRAKA and Marc RAVALOMANANA, nearly causing secession of half of the country. In April 2002 the High Constitutional Court announced RAVALOMANANA the winner.

Geography Madagascar

Location: Southern Africa, island in the Indian Ocean, east of Mozambique
Geographic coordinates: 20 00 S, 47 00 E
Map references: Africa
Area: total: 587,040 sq km
water: 5,500 sq km
land: 581,540 sq km
Area - comparative: slightly less than twice the size of Arizona
Land boundaries: 0 km
Coastline: 4,828 km
Maritime claims: contiguous zone: 24 NM
territorial sea: 12 NM
exclusive economic zone: 200 NM

Figure 18.4 First page of our printout using a copy of the document with margins set and the text forced into a single column. This page comes from the CIA's *The World Factbook*, one of the alternative dictionaries.

This certainly looks better. In fact, if you don't set the margins, the defaults will print outside the legal printing area of many printers, cutting off some of the text and looking pretty cheesy.

18.1.3 Printing asynchronously

Now that we have a copy of our document to work with, it would be nice if we could print in the background, instead of making the user wait for the operation to complete. Otherwise, he might get bored and go play Solitaire, hurting the delicate ego of our application.

It's easy to switch to printing asynchronously, but we can't use the `Print()` method on the `PrintDialog` anymore—that's a one-size-fits-one solution. Instead, we have to create an XPS document writer. (We bet you were wondering when XPS would show up—well, keep waiting.) For the moment, don't worry too much about the XPS-iveness of the class, and focus on the writer bit. We create the writer based on the `PrintQueue`; but, before we do that, we have to add an additional using statement.

```
using System.Windows.Xps;
```

Once that's in place, we need to modify the `OnPrint` method (listing 18.4).

Listing 18.4 Printing asynchronously

```
protected void OnPrint(object sender, RoutedEventArgs e)
{
  PrintDialog printDialog = new PrintDialog();
  printDialog.UserPageRangeEnabled = true;        <-- (1) Allows choice of pages to print
  if (printDialog.ShowDialog() == true)
  {
    FlowDocument docCopy = CopyFlowDocument(searchResults.Document);
    docCopy.PagePadding = new Thickness(96);
    docCopy.ColumnWidth = double.NaN;

    IDocumentPaginatorSource paginatorSource =
           docCopy as IDocumentPaginatorSource;
                                                   (2) Creates writer
    XpsDocumentWriter docWriter =
         PrintQueue.CreateXpsDocumentWriter(printDialog.PrintQueue);   <--

    docWriter.WritingCompleted += new
   System.Windows.Documents.Serialization.        (3) Subscribes to completed event
         WritingCompletedEventHandler(docWriter_WritingCompleted);    <--

    docWriter.WriteAsync(paginatorSource.DocumentPaginator);     <-- (4) Prints
  }
}
                                                   (5) Completed event handler
void docWriter_WritingCompleted(object sender,     <--
        System.Windows.Documents.Serialization.WritingCompletedEventArgs e)
{
  MessageBox.Show("Done Printing!","Dictionary");
}
```

By default, the `PrintDialog` doesn't allow the user to print only certain pages. This isn't a big deal, but we thought we'd turn on the option ❶. After that, things are about the same until we're ready to print. Now, instead of calling the `Print()` method on the dialog, we're calling a static method on the `PrintQueue` class that takes a `PrintQueue` as an argument and returns a writer set to print to that queue ❷.

The next step is optional, but nice. We're subscribing to an event to tell us when printing is complete ❸. There's also an event that tells when each bit of the document has been printed, in case you want to update a progress display, or if the print job has been canceled. As you can see, our handler for when printing is completed pops up a message box ❺.

Finally, we call the `WriteAsync()` method to do the actual printing ❹. We could instead called `Write()`, which would have printed synchronously, just as if we'd used the `Print()` method on the `PrintDialog()`.

When we run the code, we get the print dialog as usual, but there's no delay after we click OK. Instead, a few moments later, our message box pops up (figure 18.5). Because we're only printing a couple of pages, the dialog comes up very fast indeed. In fact, you may note that WPF printing is noticeably faster than, say, Windows Forms.

Figure 18.5 Very exciting notification about our background print job being done. We should print something a bit more complex to make the asynchronous approach really show off.

It's nice how easy it is to print in the background. Also, now that we're no longer relying on the `PrintDialog`'s `Print` method, we could, if we choose, skip the dialog altogether and go straight to the default printer (listing 18.5).

Listing 18.5 Printing without using `PrintDialog`

```
protected void OnPrint(object sender, RoutedEventArgs e)
{
  FlowDocument docCopy = CopyFlowDocument(searchResults.Document);
  docCopy.PagePadding = new Thickness(96);
  docCopy.ColumnWidth = double.NaN;

  IDocumentPaginatorSource paginatorSource = docCopy as
        IDocumentPaginatorSource;
  PrintQueue queue = LocalPrintServer.GetDefaultPrintQueue();     <-- Gets default Queue
  XpsDocumentWriter docWriter = PrintQueue.CreateXpsDocumentWriter(queue);

  docWriter.WritingCompleted += new System.Windows.Documents.Serialization.
        WritingCompletedEventHandler(docWriter_WritingCompleted);
  docWriter.WriteAsync(paginatorSource.DocumentPaginator);
}
```

We've dropped all the print dialog code, and, instead got the default queue. You might want to do this if you want your application to operate like MS Word, where the Print toolbar button prints to the default printer, whereas the Print... option from the file menu gives you a dialog and options. You can also step through all the print queues and find the one you want.

18.2 Printing FixedDocuments

So far, our printing has been via the use of a `FlowDocument`, which works well for our particular content. But, often you want a very specifically formatted printout. We mentioned a couple of examples of this earlier—printing a form or doing desktop publishing. For these applications, you want a lot more control over how a page is laid out, and that's precisely what a `FixedDocument` gives—each page is laid out and added independently, and then the whole document is printed.

That isn't to say that you have to lay out each letter in each word—WPF will handle standard things like paragraphs and word-wrapping, but will give you the ability to specify, for example, where the paragraphs will go. And, if you're picky enough, you really *could* specify the exact location for each letter in each word.

A `FixedDocument` is made up of pages, and each page can have any XAML content on it you like; it can use layouts to handle positioning, and any sort of controls you like—although, because this is for printing, you can't interact with the controls, so you really end up with pictures of controls.

We've gone ahead and added another hyperlink to our application—with the label Print Fixed—and then put in a basic implementation. Our first version (listing 18.6) demonstrates putting some items in specific places on the printout. We'll look into adding content from our application in a little while.

Listing 18.6 Printing a `FixedDocument`

```
protected void OnPrintFixed(object sender, RoutedEventArgs e)
{
  PrintDialog printDialog = new PrintDialog();
  if (printDialog.ShowDialog() == true)
  {
    FixedDocument fixedDocument = new FixedDocument();       ❶ Our FixedDocument
    fixedDocument.DocumentPaginator.PageSize = new Size
        (printDialog.PrintableAreaWidth,
         printDialog.PrintableAreaHeight);   ❷

    PageContent firstPage = new PageContent();    ❸ Page of content
    FixedPage fixedPage = new FixedPage();

    Canvas canvas = new Canvas();                 ❹ Needs layout
    canvas.Width = fixedDocument.DocumentPaginator.PageSize.Width;
    canvas.Height = fixedDocument.DocumentPaginator.PageSize.Height;
    fixedPage.Children.Add(canvas);

    TextBlock tb = new TextBlock();    ❺ Adds TextBlock
    tb.Foreground = Brushes.Black;
    tb.FontFamily = new System.Windows.Media.FontFamily("Arial");
    tb.FontSize = 36.0;
    tb.Text = "Hello";
    Canvas.SetTop(tb, 70);
```

```
        Canvas.SetLeft(tb, 70);
        canvas.Children.Add(tb);                      ❻ Adds
                                                        Ellipse
        Ellipse ell = new Ellipse();              <-┘
        ell.Width = 400;
        ell.Height = 400;
        ell.StrokeThickness = 3;
        ell.Stroke = new SolidColorBrush(Colors.Black);
        Canvas.SetTop(ell, 200);
        Canvas.SetLeft(ell, 300);
        canvas.Children.Add(ell);                     Adds page to document ❼

        ((System.Windows.Markup.IAddChild)firstPage).AddChild(fixedPage);  <-┘
        fixedDocument.Pages.Add(firstPage);         ❽ The printing
                                                        bit
        PrintQueue queue = printDialog.PrintQueue;  <-┘
        XpsDocumentWriter docWriter =
                      PrintQueue.CreateXpsDocumentWriter(queue);
        docWriter.Write(fixedDocument.DocumentPaginator);
    }
}
```

This code is quite straightforward. No, really—it's just that `FixedDocuments` are very hierarchical, so we have to create a number of nested objects to hold our content (figure 18.6).

The first thing we have to do is create a `FixedDocument` ❶. We're setting its size based on the printable area of the printer ❷. If we want margins, though, we'll have to make sure that we place our content appropriately (that is, inside the margin). The next thing we create is a `PageContent` object ❸. The `FixedDocument` holds a collection of `PageContent` objects, with each one representing a page. Each `PageContent` object has a `FixedPage` object, which will eventually hold the content. The `FixedPage` primarily deals with breaking the page; it's one of those details that you have to have, but generally don't have to worry too much about.

Now, we have to create the content for our page. This is where the nature of WPF stands us in good stead—we can put just about any WPF content here. We could put in a `Grid` layout, or a `Dock` layout, or some custom layout, and then use that layout to automatically format for us. But, because we're interested, at the moment, in demonstrating fine control, we'll use a `Canvas` layout ❹ so that we can precisely position our content. To start with, our content is a `TextBlock` ❺ and an `Ellipse` ❻, which is somewhat silly. But, we'll put in some more meaningful content in the near future.

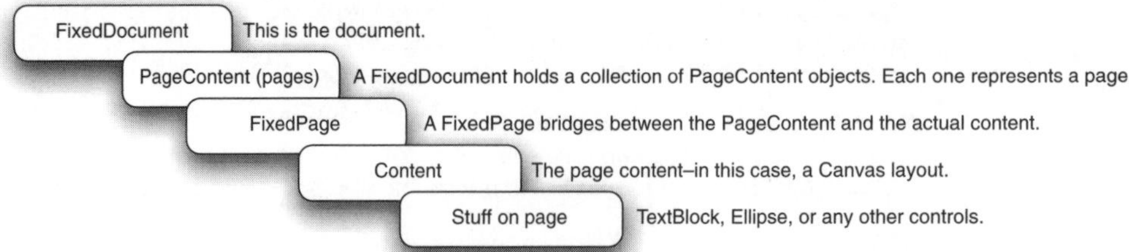

Figure 18.6 The layers in a `FixedDocument`

The Canvas has already been added to the FixedPage. Now we have to add the FixedPage to the PageContent ❼ using a rather inconvenient notation, and then add the PageContent to the Pages collection of the FixedDocument. You can tell this was designed by people thinking about XML. In fact, you can create documents in XAML (or with the designer) and then update the content and print them if you want to.

The last step is the printing ❽. This is no different than printing a FlowDocument, except that the FixedDocument is nice enough to let us have the Paginator without requiring us to do a cast to an interface. Figure 18.7 shows our remarkably lovely printout.

To be complete, let's take some of the text from the dictionary definition, and put it onto our page as well.

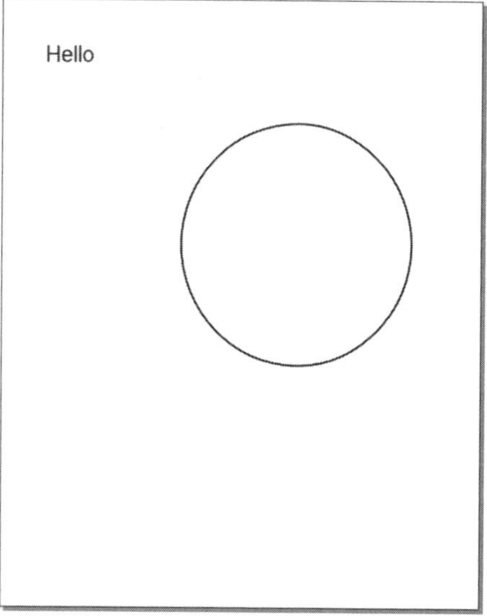

Figure 18.7 It isn't much, but it's ours—a printout of a FixedDocument

18.2.1 Adding some FlowDocument content to our FixedDocument

Because we can arbitrarily add WPF controls to the Canvas in the FixedDocument, one way to put some of our FlowDocument's content onto the page would be to literally dump a viewer on the page with the content. This does work—although you end up with a picture of the search and zoom controls as well! There are also some lighter-weight controls for displaying FlowDocument content, such as the FlowDocument-ScrollViewer and, if we remember to turn off the scroll bars, we can use that to kind of get what we want.

But, these are all pretty ugly approaches—particularly if we're likely to pull out particular pages of content from the FlowDocument. The ScrollViewer will just display the first section of text. If we want to print the second page later, what would we do? Try to figure out how far to scroll? Ick.

The better way is to take advantage of the FlowDocument's own rendering capability to have it break itself into pages. Let's say that we want to put the first page of the FlowDocument's content in a 4x6 inch box on the page. Why would we want to do that? Well, perhaps we're doing some sort of fancy page layout with artistic designs and titles, and we want our content to take up a small area of the page.

Let's start with the box. Adding a box to the form, at least, should be pretty easy. Well, instead of adding a box, let's add a *border.* A Border is a control whose purpose in life is to border things. The nice thing about it is that it holds some content. Listing 18.7 shows the creation of the Border control.

Listing 18.7 Adding an empty `Border`

```
Border border = new Border();
border.BorderBrush = Brushes.Black;
border.BorderThickness = new Thickness(1);
border.Width = (4 * 96);                    <-- What's
border.Height = (6 * 96);                       with 96?
Canvas.SetLeft(border, 96);
Canvas.SetTop(border, 3 * 96);
canvas.Children.Add(border);
```

This code is put into the `OnPrintFixed()` method after the creation of the `Ellipse` and before the print operation. There's nothing very spectacular here, although you may notice the preponderance of values based on the number 96. Although it's, coincidentally, our lucky number, the real reason we use 96 is because the default WPF units are dips, and there happen to be 96 dips in an inch. Our border is 4 inches wide, 6 inches tall, one inch in from the left, and 3 inches down from the top.

If we run the print operation, we'd now get an empty box of the described dimensions. But, we'd like something in that box. Listing 18.8 shows how to get the first 4x6 page of the contents from our definition.

Listing 18.8 Getting a page from a `FlowDocument`

```
FlowDocument docCopy = CopyFlowDocument(searchResults.Document);
docCopy.ColumnWidth = double.NaN;
docCopy.PageWidth = border.Width - 2;          <-- Border, minus
docCopy.PageHeight = border.Height - 2;        (1) space for lines
IDocumentPaginatorSource paginatorSource =
                docCopy as IDocumentPaginatorSource;
DocumentPage docPage = paginatorSource.DocumentPaginator.GetPage(0);   (2)
```

Much of this code should be familiar—we make a copy of the `FlowDocument` and set its size, although we're using the size of the `Border` control to determine the width and height ❶, minus a little bit to make up for the lines on either size. Then we get a paginator as if we're going to print. Instead of printing, though, we ask the paginator for the first page ❷. If we were going to put more content on multiple pages or multiple locations, the paginator could be used to provide the pages as needed.

A `DocumentPage` isn't terribly useful, though. It has virtually no properties or methods, and it can't do very much. We need to get the page into a format that we can put onto our page. An easy way to do this is to draw the page out onto a bitmap, and then put the bitmap on our page. Listing 18.9 shows how to do that.

Listing 18.9 Rendering to a bitmap

```
RenderTargetBitmap renderTarget = new RenderTargetBitmap
        ((int)docCopy.PageWidth,(int)docCopy.PageHeight,96,96,
         System.Windows.Media.PixelFormats.Default);           <-- (1) Creates target

renderTarget.Render(docPage.Visual);          <-- (2) Renders page

Image img = new Image();    <-- (3) Image holder
```

```
img.Width = docCopy.PageWidth;
img.Height = docCopy.PageHeight;
img.Source = renderTarget;
border.Child = img;
```

The first thing we do is create a `RenderTargetBitmap` of the appropriate size and with the appropriate resolution ❶. The whole purpose of a `RenderTargetBitmap` is to make it possible to convert a `Visual` object into a bitmap. As you probably remember from chapter 14, `Visual` is a pretty high-level class that provides basic low-level support for things that need to be able to render themselves (as well as support for hit testing, and so on). `Controls` are, eventually, derived from `Visual`, because they're derived from `UIElement`. If the document page exposed a `UIElement`, we could add it directly to our `Canvas`; but, unfortunately, `DocumentPage` only exposes a `Visual` object, so we have to first render the `Visual` into something else before we can add it.

The `Render` ❷ method on `RenderTargetBitmap` causes the passed object to render itself out to the bitmap or, in English, to draw our page. Then, all we have to do is shove our bitmap into an `Image` control and put the `Image` control inside our `Border` ❸.

We wouldn't say that this is all trivial, but it isn't ridiculously complex either. Figure 18.8 shows the results of all our machinations.

Very avant-garde, wouldn't you say? One thing, though, is that the page we've printed is a little fuzzy—much more so than the *Hello* at the top of the page. The reason

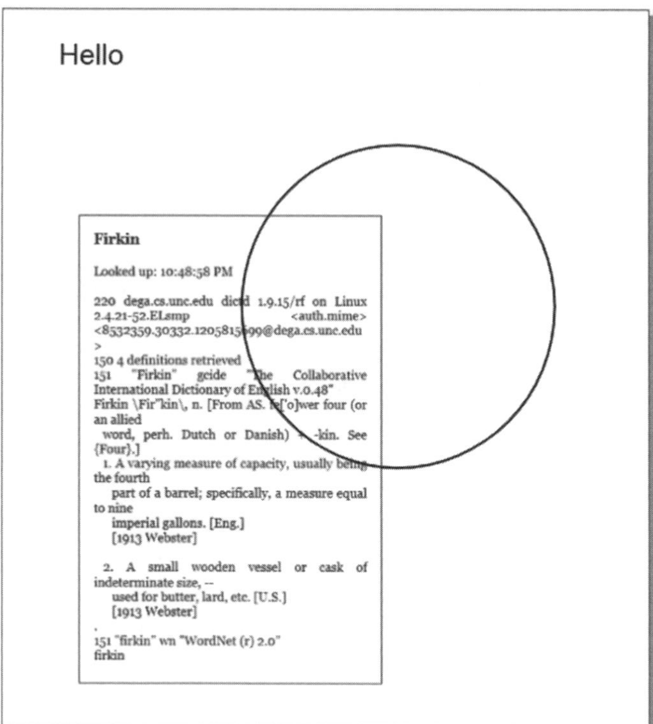

Figure 18.8 We've pulled out a page from our `FlowDocument` and rendered it as part of our printout. The page is a little bit fuzzy—we need to do something about that.

for the fuzziness is the resolution we used for our bitmap. In the next section, we'll improve on this.

18.2.2 Matching resolution

When we rendered the page from our `FlowDocument`, we set the resolution to 96, which is pretty standard for screen resolution. For a printer, though, that's fairly low. Printers these days generally work in resolutions of 300dpi, 600dpi, or higher. Our code should get the resolution that we're going to print at and use that for the bitmap. This is pretty easy, but there's one caveat—the resolution information is stored in the `PrintTicket`, which we have. But, the `PrintTicket` class isn't part of the `System.Printing` assembly; it's part of an assembly called `ReachFramework`. Before we can access members of the `PrintTicket`, we have to add a reference to the `ReachFramework` assembly. Right-click the References node of the project, select Add Reference, and then scroll down until you find `ReachFramework`. Note that it is *not* `System.ReachFramework` or `Microsoft.ReachFramework`—just `ReachFramework`.

> **Why ReachFramework?**
>
> You might be wondering why `PrintTicket` isn't in the `System.Printing` assembly, and why, for that matter, it's called `ReachFramework`. The `ReachFramework` holds various features and functions related to XPS, which we'll talk about in more detail in the near future. XPS is a format for sharing documents and, importantly, is designed to work on a number of different platforms. XPS has to have support outside the normal .NET framework for those other platforms, so it's *reaching out*. Get it?

Once the reference has been added, we have to change the code to use the resolution (listing 18.10).

Listing 18.10 Rendering at right resolution

```
int xPixels = (int)printDialog.PrintTicket.PageResolution.X;     ❶ Gets resolution
int yPixels = (int)printDialog.PrintTicket.PageResolution.Y;
RenderTargetBitmap renderTarget = new RenderTargetBitmap           More appropriate bitmap
     (xPixels * 4, yPixels * 6, xPixels, yPixels,
    System.Windows.Media.PixelFormats.Default);

renderTarget.Render(docPage.Visual);
```

We're getting the `PrintTicket` from the `PrintDialog` ❶, but we could also get it from the `PrintQueue`. The `PageResolution` property holds the resolution that has been set for our printing operation—this isn't specifically the resolution of the printer, but the resolution specified by printer defaults (or overridden values set by the user).

Now we set the resolution of the bitmap and set its size based on that resolution. Now, when we print, (figure 18.9) the text should be sharper.

Firkin
Firkin

Figure 18.9 The text at the bottom was rendered at a higher resolution; it's sharper than the text at the top.

The higher the resolution of your output device, the more noticeable the difference.

18.2.3 Printing Visuals

Throughout this section, we've gone to a lot of effort to create a `FixedDocument` and populate it with pages. It's worth noting that there's a way to cheat. WPF will let you print a `Visual` object such as the `Visual` we got from the `DocumentPage`. But, because controls and layouts are also `Visuals`, we can take a layout and print it directly.

We could simplify our code by eliminating the document, like in listing 18.11.

Listing 18.11 Printing a `Visual` directly

```
protected void OnPrintVisual(object sender, RoutedEventArgs e)
{
  PrintDialog printDialog = new PrintDialog();
  if (printDialog.ShowDialog() == true)
  {
    Canvas canvas = new Canvas();
    canvas.Width = printDialog.PrintableAreaWidth;
    canvas.Height = printDialog.PrintableAreaHeight;

        ...Code to populate the canvas goes here...

    printDialog.PrintVisual(canvas, "Dictionary");      <-- Prints Visual directly
  }
}
```

This approach is really a shortcut method. Behind the scenes, the document is still created. If you run this code, you'll get exactly the same printout as before. So, why do it the hard way? It gives you much more control *and*, if you have more than one page, it handles that too. Still, if you have a fairly simple 1-page scenario, `PrintVisual` is pretty handy. You can also print a Visual to a `PrintQueue` without using the `PrintDialog`

```
PrintQueue queue = LocalPrintServer.GetDefaultPrintQueue();
XpsDocumentWriter docWriter = PrintQueue.CreateXpsDocumentWriter(queue);
docWriter.Write(canvas);
```

Again, for simple needs, this isn't a bad approach—and, if you have to switch to the more complex approach later, it isn't a big jump.

We've now demonstrated printing `FlowDocuments` and `FixedDocuments` and `Visuals` directly. Throughout all of this, there have been little hints of something called *XPS*, in class names if nothing else. It's about time that we explain what XPS is and how it relates to anything.

18.3 XPS

XPS stands for the XML Paper Specification. Although it includes a number of different technologies, it can be thought of as "a way of defining everything related to printing." At the core of XPS is a document format that defines what goes on which pages and where. The fact that this format is tightly related to XAML isn't a coincidence.

In Windows Vista, the whole print queue mechanism now uses XPS. Even if you print from old applications, the output is converted to XPS and sent to the print drivers in that format. The idea is for XPS to replace all the old formats such as WMF and RTF.[4]

There's another format that, arguably, XPS also hopes to replace: PDF. It's very easy to save XPS to a file and then transfer it on. There are XPS viewers available for a variety of browsers now—PC, Mac, and, UNIX flavors. In fact, after installing .NET 3.5, you may have noticed a new printer automatically installed for you—Microsoft XPS Document Writer. If you select that printer, you're prompted for a filename and end up with an XPS document that you can email to your heart's delight, whether or not the application from which you're printing supports XPS.

18.3.1 Saving an XPS document to a file

You might be wondering at this point: If XPS is so important, how come we've waited so long before bringing it up. Well, the truth is that *all* the printing we've done so far has been via XPS. The occasional XPS namespace hinted at this; but, to make it really obvious, let's modify our printing code so that, instead of printing, we save to an XPS file (listing 18.12).

Listing 18.12 Saving XPS document to file

```
using Microsoft.Win32;
using System.Windows.Xps.Packaging;     ❶ Goes at the top!

protected void OnSaveFile(object sender, RoutedEventArgs e)
{
  SaveFileDialog saveDialog = new SaveFileDialog();        Lets user choose file
  saveDialog.Filter = "XPS Document (*.XPS)|*.XPS|All Files (*.*)|*.*";
  if(saveDialog.ShowDialog() == true)
  {
    FixedDocument fixedDocument = new FixedDocument();
    fixedDocument.DocumentPaginator.PageSize =
                          new Size(96 * 8.5, 96 * 11);   ❷

    PageContent firstPage = new PageContent();
    ...The rest of the existing code for creating our document goes here...

    XpsDocument doc =                                    File to save ❸
        new XpsDocument(saveDialog.FileName, FileAccess.ReadWrite);

    XpsDocumentWriter docWriter =
```

[4] There's a point in a sentence when you've reached your third acronym, where you start to wonder if, perhaps, there isn't something seriously wrong with the world.

```
            XpsDocument.CreateXpsDocumentWriter(doc);
        docWriter.Write(fixedDocument.DocumentPaginator);     ❺
        doc.Close();
    }
}
```

❹ Another writer

First, we need to add a couple of additional namespaces to the top of our file ❶. We need `Microsoft.Win32` for the `Save` dialog. The `Packaging` namespace is for packaging up documents as files. Instead of a choose printer dialog, we're now using a choose file dialog.

After that, we do almost exactly the same thing that we did before for printing. The only thing we do differently is to hardcode the page dimensions ❷ (and, later on, the resolution for our image). When writing to a transferable file, we have no particular requirement to have a particular page size or resolution—we can go crazy (although, later, if the user wants to print the file, some conversion would have to take place).

Once we've put together our content, we need some place to write it to. We create a new `XpsDocument` ❸ with the filename provided from the file dialog. Then we get a writer from the document ❹, just as, earlier, we created a writer from the `PrintQueue`. Then we write our content to the writer ❺ again, as before. Finally, we close the file.

The fact that, other than acquiring our writer, the writing process itself is identical is very important. We could, just as easily, have written our `FlowDocument` content or a `Visual`. Writing to an XPS file is no different than writing to a printer. Pretty slick, eh? If we now run, then double-click the file we've created, we'll see our document in the XPS document viewer (figure 18.10).

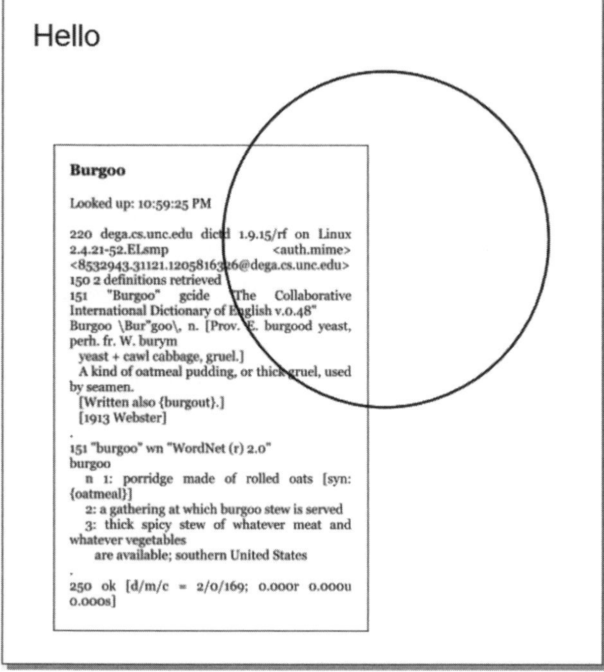

Figure 18.10 Viewing a document in the XPS viewer

And now we could go ahead and print out document from here as well!

18.3.2 The problem with images...

Even though we've designed our output as though we're going to print it, it isn't uncommon to transfer documents around that are generally only read online. One nice thing about the online version is that you can copy the content out of the document for use elsewhere. If you try this with our test document, you can highlight the word *Hello* at the top and copy it to the clipboard. But, if you try to do that with the text from our document, you can't.

We've converted the text into a bitmap, so it's only a *picture* of the text. This is no big deal when we're printing, but it's quite annoying when we're transferring the documents. To fix this, we should ditch the bitmap and use a control that holds a `Visual`, the `Visual` we got out of our `FlowDocument`.

You may remember from chapter 14 that a `Visual` is a low-level class used to represent "stuff you can put on the screen." Further, you may remember that there's no handy container control for holding a `Visual`, but that it's pretty easy to create one. Listing 18.13 shows a `VisualHolder` control that holds a single `Visual`.

Listing 18.13 `VisualHolder` control

```
using System;
using System.Collections.Generic;
using System.Linq;
using System.Text;
using System.Windows;
using System.Windows.Media;

namespace DictionaryPages
{
  class VisualHolder : FrameworkElement
  {
    VisualCollection visuals;           ❶ Collection of Visuals

    public VisualHolder()
    {
      visuals = new VisualCollection(this);
    }
                                            ❷ Property exposing single Visual
    public Visual HeldVisual
    {
      get {return (visuals.Count > 0) ? visuals[0] : null;}
      set
      {
        visuals.Clear();
        visuals.Add(value);
      }
    }

    protected override int VisualChildrenCount     ❸
    {
      get { return visuals.Count; }
    }
```

```
        protected override Visual GetVisualChild(int index)    ❹
        {
          return visuals[index];
        }
      }
    }
```

We're cheating here a little by using a collection of `Visuals` ❶ instead of just holding a single `Visual`. We're doing this because the collection handles some behind-the-scenes stuff for us and also lets us steal the implementation of `VisualChildrenCount` ❸ and `GetVisualChild` ❹ from our sample from chapter 14.

The only thing we really care about is the `HeldVisual` property ❷, which gives us access to a single held `Visual` (that we make sure is the only thing in our collection). Now that we have our holder, we can put our `Visual` in it and, because our `VisualHolder` control is a `FrameworkElement`, we can put it either in our `Border` or directly on our `Canvas`. We can now replace the bitmap code in SearchPage.xaml.cs with the `VisualHolder` (listing 18.14).

Listing 18.14 Using `VisualHolder`

```
VisualHolder holder = new VisualHolder();
holder.Width = docCopy.PageWidth;
holder.Height = docCopy.PageHeight;
holder.HeldVisual = docPage.Visual;
border.Child = holder;
```

This code goes below where we got the `docPage` and replaces all the code to create the `BitmapImage` and the `Image` control. If we run now, the results look just like figure 18.10, except that we can now select text in the definition (figure 18.11).

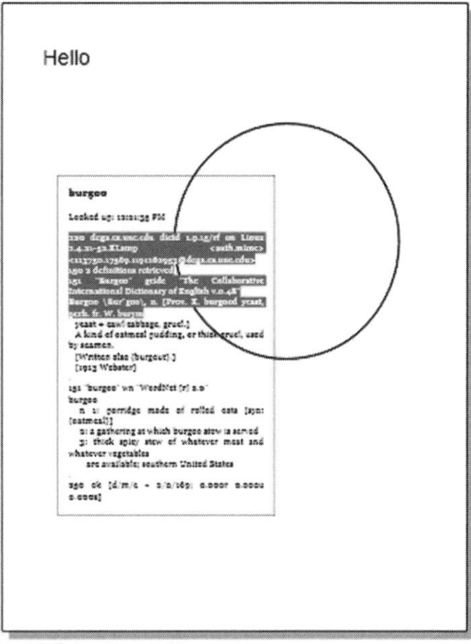

Figure 18.11 Using the `VisualHolder` control. Now the text in our box is selectable.

There's quite a bit more to the XPS format. We could talk a lot about the fact that it can carry with it all the font information it needs, as well as various other information. Also, there's a `FixedDocumentViewer` control that makes it easy to display XPS documents in your own applications. But, we've taken printing about as far as we can reasonably do without dedicating the rest of the book to the topic, and, as you've seen, using the core capabilities of WPF printing is pretty straightforward.

18.4 Summary

Between the two of us, we've probably done printing from just about every scenario: Windows Forms/MFC, writing printer codes to output, even writing custom drivers for obsolete plotters. Looking at printing from WPF, as well as the XPS system, it seems like Microsoft has a good balance between flexibility and straightforwardness—you can do simple things simply and complex things, er, complexly?

Being us, that doesn't mean that we don't want a few changes and improvements. There are some things that should be simple that are tricky (such as adding headers and footers to an existing document), and there should be a built-in control that allows for a `Visual` to be hosted without, for example, requiring its content to be written to a bitmap. Overall, though, for us, we're pretty happy.

Also, we've taken our little dictionary application just about as far as it will go. In the next chapter, we intend to suck out some of the guts of the dictionary (vampire-like) for another purpose. In homage to spy movies, we'll build an application that pulls data from the CIA (really) and uses glitzy transition effects while doing it!

19 Transition effects

This chapter covers:

- Building a cleaner application
- Using the `Application` object
- Lots of spiffy transitions
- Getting as close to a James-Bond-like life as we're ever likely to

There's an old, not very good, joke about a man talking to a genie. "Genie," he says, "make me a sandwich."

"Poof," says the genie, "you're a sandwich."

As we said, it's not a very good joke. Sometimes, though, working with WPF is like that. Unless you get your incantations exactly right, you suddenly find yourself looking out from between two slices of Wonder Bread, wondering what happened.

This chapter is about two things. First, it's about adding some cool transition effects, such as fades and wipes, into your applications. Second, it's about balancing XAML and code, and putting together applications in a way that makes it possible for you to have a shot at getting things to work, while being as understandable and maintainable as possible.

We aren't trying to take a potshot at XAML or declarative programming per se, but we'd like to point out something about the nature of the technology. Via XAML, it's possible to specify incredibly complex behavior with only a few lines. At the same time, XAML isn't strongly typed—even with IntelliSense, it's possible to write and compile XAML that isn't strictly legal, and it's certainly easy to have legal XAML that does things completely differently than what you expect. Add to this the fact that it isn't currently possible to debug XAML—to step line by line as it executes to see what's really going on.[1]

Often, this isn't that big a deal—after all, when you're defining a bunch of controls on a form, it's pretty hard to go wrong. But, when you're trying to create effects, these issues can be extremely frustrating. For this reason, effects often requires a lot more upfront planning and the occasional brain twist. The rewards, though, are worth it. Adding effects to your WPF applications can punch up your UI, and it often takes only a few lines of XAML to do things that previously would have taken massive amounts of code to do smoothly.

Before we get into the really nifty effects, we need a new application to work with. We *could* add effects to one of the existing applications, but we want to build a new application from scratch, this time paying more attention to the details and having a place for logic, separate controls, and so on. We're doing this because one of the points of this chapter is to emphasize the "proper" way to separate out responsibilities within a WPF application. Also, we want an application that lends itself to transitions. Our new application will borrow quite a bit from the Dictionary application—one of the supported dictionaries is the CIA's *The World Factbook*, which has facts about every country (or at least every country that existed when the data was imported about five years ago). The application we're going to build will let us double-click on any country and see the information about that country.

19.1 Building the World Browser application

Before we can add a bunch of effects to our application, we first have to have an application. Figure 19.1 shows more or less what the working application will look like. This application will show a list of countries (broken out by continent) in the left column and the details about the currently selected country in a `FlowDocument` on the right. When we're finished, it will also have a `ComboBox` that allows us to choose the particular transition effect to use when switching between countries.

To get started, create a new solution/project of type WPF Application. Ours is called *World Browser*. The first thing we want to do in our new project is create a class that handles looking up data.

19.1.1 The DictionaryLookup class

In the Dictionary application, we shoved the logic for looking up words into the code behind our Search page. We did this to save time, but it's obviously *not* world-class design. We'll rectify this (at least a little) in the World Browser program by putting

[1] Well, it is *sort of* possible to do this now—you can download the source code for WPF and step through the WPF code to see what's going on, but that isn't the same as stepping through *your* XAML.

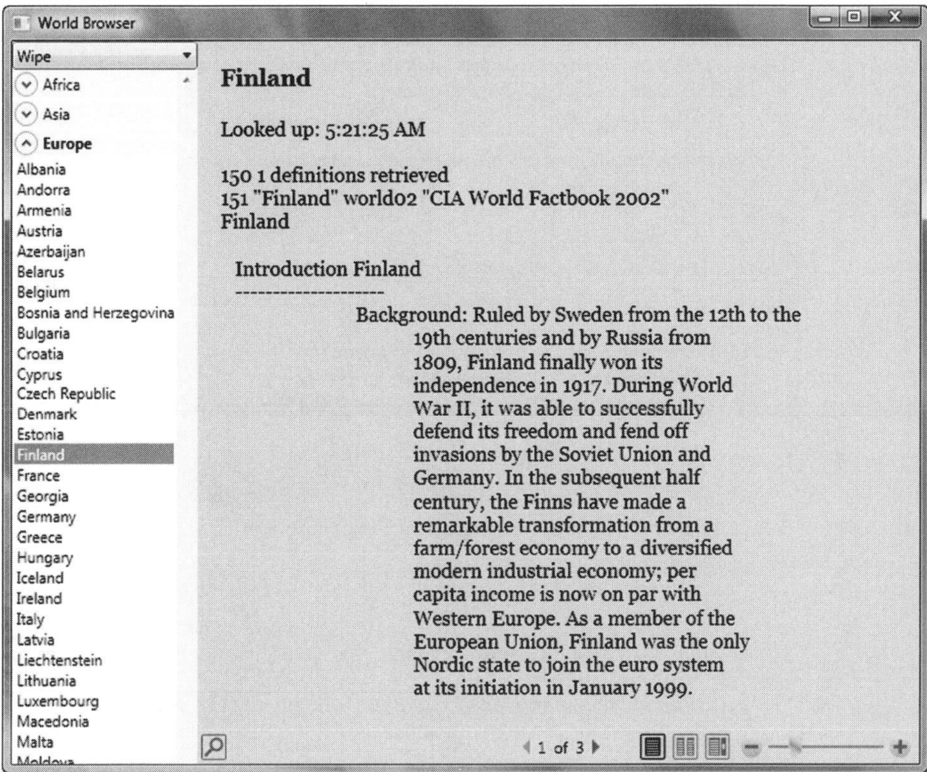

Figure 19.1 The World Browser application lets us look up information on any country from *The World Factbook*.

the lookup code in a standalone class called `DictionaryLookup`. Listing 19.1 shows the code for the `DictionaryLookup` class. But, we've omitted the implementation from several of the methods because they're exactly the same as they were in the Dictionary application.

Listing 19.1 DictionaryLookup.cs

```
using System;
...Additional using statements...

namespace WorldBrowser
{
  public class DictionaryLookup
  {
    private Encoding conversationEncoding = Encoding.UTF8;
    private string defaultServer = "test.dict.org";
    private readonly int defaultPort = 2628;
    private string dictionaryToUse = "world02";     <-- Defaults to The World Factbook
    private const int bufferSize = 4096;

    public FlowDocument DefineWord(string word)     (1)
    {
```

```
    string dictionary = "*";
    if ((dictionaryToUse.Length > 0) ||
        (string.Compare(dictionaryToUse, "all", true) == 0))
      dictionary = dictionaryToUse;
      string command = "DEFINE " + dictionary + " " + '"' + word + '"';

      string result = ExecuteCommand(command);

      return TextToFlowDocument(word, result);
  }

  public FlowDocument TextToFlowDocument
                      (string word, string result)
  {
    FlowDocument doc = new FlowDocument();
    ...Code to build flow document here...
      (was in DefineWord code in the Dictionary application)

    return doc;
  }

  private string ExecuteCommand(string command)
  {
     ...Code is the same as from Dictionary application...
  }

  private string GetResponse(string requestString, Stream clientStream)
  {
     ...Code is the same as from Dictionary application...
  }
 }
}
```

❷ **Code for building FlowDocument**

Nothing in this code should be revelatory—it's about encapsulating the lookup code. Note that we haven't even renamed the `DefineWord()` method ❶ to `LookupCountry()` or anything like that. This way, the code stays a little more generic.

We've also gone ahead and broken out the code that generates the `FlowDocument` into its own method ❷. Now, given that this code isn't related to a particular UI anymore, you could argue that we should be returning the text, and not a UI element. But, a `FlowDocument` isn't *precisely* a UI element, and it's a reasonable intermediary format for us. Probably, in a more formal application, this class would return a structure with information on the results, but we could still argue for this format in a number of circumstances.

By the way, although we aren't showing it, we've done a little clean-up work in the `ExecuteCommand` method—adding some error handling (in case the connection fails) and getting rid of the server-header data—so we end up with only the definition. If you care deeply about this, you can see exactly what we've done by downloading the full version of the application from our website.

Now, because this class is essentially stateless, we *could* either create a new instance of it every time that we need to use it, or make the methods all static. But, it would be better if we have a single instance that we reuse. This way we could, for instance, add caching to the class, or implement a stateful version without breaking the rest of the code. We'll show the best place to put our class.

19.1.2 Working with the Application object

It may not seem worth having an entire section on adding a member variable to the Application class, except that the best way of dealing with application data and objects might not be entirely obvious. The first thing we want to do is to add a handler for the Startup event on the application.

```
<Application x:Class="WorldBrowser.App"
  xmlns="http://schemas.microsoft.com/winfx/2006/xaml/presentation"
  xmlns:x="http://schemas.microsoft.com/winfx/2006/xaml"
  StartupUri="WorldBrowserMain.xaml" Startup="Application_Startup">
```

IntelliSense makes adding this handler pretty easy. If you just start typing Startup, the rest will be filled in for you, and you'll automatically be offered the choice to create a New Default Handler. Once you choose this option, Visual Studio will create the Application_Startup method in the App.xaml.cs file. You can right-click the Startup attribute and select Navigate To Handler to automatically be taken to the method in code.

Listing 19.2 contains the code from App.xaml.cs for the Startup method, including the creation of our instance of the DictionaryLookup class.

Listing 19.2 App class

```
using System;
...Additional using statements...

namespace WorldBrowser
{
  public partial class App : Application
  {
    public DictionaryLookup Lookup { get; private set; }    ❶ Automatic property with private setter

    private void Application_Startup(object sender, StartupEventArgs e)
    {
      Lookup = new DictionaryLookup();    ❷ Creates instance
    }

  }
}
```

Pretty straightforward. We've added an automatic property with a private setter ❶ and initialized it in the Startup method ❷. It's slightly less clear how we've retrieved the property from elsewhere in our code—because creation and navigation to other Windows and Pages is done for us, we can't easily pass a reference to the application around.

Fortunately, WPF solves the problem for us by providing a static member called Current so that we can get hold of the application that way.

```
Application.Current
```

This approach is good, but it returns the base Application object; if we want to access our Lookup property, we'll have to cast

```
((App)Application.Current).Lookup
```

This is a little ugly. Instead, let's add our own static member to the App object that returns the proper type.

```
public static new App Current
{
  [System.Diagnostics.DebuggerStepThrough]
  get { return (App)Application.Current; }
}
```

All we're doing here is adding a property called Current that does the cast for us. Note that we have to use the new keyword because we're using the same name as the static property of Application. Also, we've added the DebuggerStepThrough attribute so that, when debugging, we don't constantly end up stepping into the property. Now, when we want to refer to the Lookup property, we can just do this:

```
App.Current.Lookup
```

Much better. Now, though, we need some UI to make use of our code.

19.1.3 *Our WorldListView user control*

Up until now, we've mostly been creating our UI in the main window. For simple applications, this is fine, but it isn't maintainable or extensible. In this application, we're going to create the bulk of our display in a user control called WorldListView. Why WorldListView? Well, this will provide a list of countries that you can select. Later on, if we want to add, say, a WorldMapView, it would be easy to swap out the view or even allow the user to select between them.

To get started, create a new UserControl (WPF) called WorldListView. We're going to make something that looks like figure 19.2.

You've probably noticed that the list on the left is a little bare. We're going to generate the list programmatically. Listing 19.3 shows the XAML for the WorldListView control.

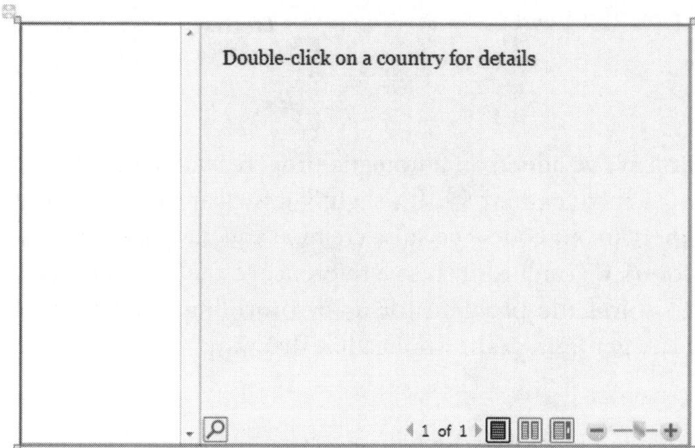

Figure 19.2 The WorldListView user control. We'll add the list on the left programmatically.

Listing 19.3 The `WorldListView` user control

```
<UserControl x:Class="WorldBrowser.WorldListView"
  xmlns="http://schemas.microsoft.com/winfx/2006/xaml/presentation"
  xmlns:x="http://schemas.microsoft.com/winfx/2006/xaml"
  Height="334" Width="551" Loaded="UserControl_Loaded">
  <Grid>                                                    <-- 1 Grid with two columns
    <Grid.ColumnDefinitions>
      <ColumnDefinition Width="150" />
      <ColumnDefinition Width="*" />
    </Grid.ColumnDefinitions>
    <ScrollViewer Name="continentScrollViewer"
                      VerticalAlignment="Stretch"           <-- 2 Place to hold list
          HorizontalAlignment="Stretch" Grid.ColumnSpan="1">
      <StackPanel Name="continentStackPanel" />
    </ScrollViewer>
    <FlowDocumentReader Name="docReaderA" Grid.Column="1"   <-- 3 FlowDocumentReader for content
                          Background="LightGoldenrodYellow">
      <FlowDocument Background="LightGoldenrodYellow">
        <Paragraph>Double-click on a country for details</Paragraph>
      </FlowDocument>
    </FlowDocumentReader>
    <FlowDocumentReader Name="docReaderB" Grid.Column="1"   <-- 4 Another FlowDocumentReader?!
                    Opacity="0" Background="LightBlue"/>
  </Grid>
</UserControl>
```

There's nothing too outrageous here, we hope. The UI is primarily a `Grid` ❶ with two columns. The first column, which will hold our list of countries, has a set width, and the second column takes up the remaining space. For our list, we've put in a `ScrollViewer` ❷ holding a `StackPanel`. We'll populate this list with a series of `Expanders`, but we're going to do this with code. (We'll explain why in a moment.) Next, we have a `FlowDocumentReader` ❸ to hold the details of our country. And then we have *another* `FlowDocumentReader` ❹. Why? One big reason for this application is to demonstrate transitions. To have a transition, we have to have something to transition from and something to transition to. We'll end up switching back and forth between the two `FlowDocumentReaders`.

19.1.4 Populating the country list

As we mentioned before, we're going to populate our list of countries in code. We don't have to do this—we could create a bunch of `Expanders` in XAML and put all the countries underneath them. But, this wouldn't be easy to maintain and update, and it definitely violates any reasonable data versus UI separation.

We should go a step farther than we do; we're still putting the list of countries into the code-behind instead of inside some data provider. Again, from a real-world perspective, we should be reading in this list and providing it to the UI in a data container; it should be obvious by now how that would be done, and so we went cheap to save a little space. Listing 19.4 shows the relevant code from the WorldListView.xaml.cs file.

Listing 19.4 Populating the country list

```
private void UserControl_Loaded(object sender, RoutedEventArgs e)
{
  LoadContinents();    ❶
}
                                                        Abridged list ❷
private void LoadContinents()                           of countries
{
  AddContinent("Africa", false, new string[] { "Algeria", "Angola",
   "Benin", "Botswana", "Burkina", "Burundi", ...rest of countries... });
  AddContinent("Asia", false, new string[] { "Afghanistan", "Bahrain",
   "Bangladesh", "Bhutan", "Brunei", ...rest of countries...});
  AddContinent("Europe", true, new string[] { "Albania", "Andorra",
   "Armenia", "Austria", "Azerbaijan", ...rest of countries... });
  AddContinent("North America", false, new string[] { "Bahamas",
   "Barbados", "Belize", "Canada", "Costa Rica", ...rest of countries...});
  AddContinent("Oceania", false, new string[] { "Australia", "Fiji",
   "Kiribati", "Marshall Islands","Micronesia", ...rest of countries... });
  AddContinent("South America", false, new string[] { "Argentina",
   "Bolivia", "Brazil", "Chile", "Colombia", ...rest of countries... });
}

private void AddContinent(string continent,bool open,
                                        string[] countryList)    ❸
{
  Expander exp = new Expander();    ❹
  exp.Header = continent;
  exp.IsExpanded = open;
                                     ❺
  ListBox lb = new ListBox();
  lb.BorderThickness = new Thickness(0);
  lb.MouseDoubleClick +=
             new MouseButtonEventHandler(lb_MouseDoubleClick);    ❻
  foreach (string country in countryList)
    lb.Items.Add(country);
  exp.Content = lb;

  continentStackPanel.Children.Add(exp);
}
```

First, we add a call to our method for adding the list of continents to the `Loaded()` event handler ❶. You may have noticed in listing 19.3 that we had already included the handler in the definition. `LoadContinents` calls the `AddContinent` method multiple times—once for each continent ❷. If you want to include the entire list of countries, you can download the sample from our website, or get an atlas, or just add your favorite countries from each continent.

The `AddContinent` method ❸ takes three arguments—the name of the continent, whether the continent's display should initially be expanded (open) or not, and the list of countries as a string array. The first thing the method does is create the `Expander` control ❹. We then use a `ListBox` ❺ to hold the individual countries. We also subscribe to the `DoubleClick` event on the `ListBox` ❻ so that we can initiate the lookup when the user double-clicks on a country. Then we add the `ListBox` to the `Expander`, and the `Expander` to the `StackPanel` we defined in XAML.

All that's left is to implement the handler that does the lookup. We aren't going to worry about transitions for the moment—let's set up the code to load the country into our main `FlowDocumentReader` (listing 19.5).

Listing 19.5 Retrieving data

```
private void lb_MouseDoubleClick(object sender, MouseButtonEventArgs e)
{
  Mouse.OverrideCursor = Cursors.Wait;          <-- Could take a while
  try
  {
    ListBox lb = sender as ListBox;        (1)
    if (lb.SelectedItem != null)
    {
      string country = lb.SelectedItem.ToString();
      FlowDocument doc = App.Current.Lookup.DefineWord(country);   <-- (2) Uses Current App property

      docReaderA.Document = doc;
      doc.Background = docReaderA.Background;     (3)
    }
  }
  finally
  {
    Mouse.OverrideCursor = null;
  }
}
```

This code shouldn't be too surprising after the Dictionary application. We get the name of the country from the `ListBox` passed as the sender to our event (1) and then pass it to our `DictionaryLookup` class via the `App.Current` property we created earlier (2). We're also setting the color of the document's background to be the same as the color of our reader (3). We're using colors so that the transitions are a little more obvious. If you want to have a standard white background, then you should explicitly set the background to white here instead of relying on default behavior, which will end up giving a transparent background!

Our `WorldListView` class is finished, but it isn't going to show up anywhere unless we add it to our main window. There are two steps to this. First, we have to add the namespace for our application so that we can reference our user control.

```
<Window x:Class="WorldBrowser.WorldBrowserMain"
    xmlns="http://schemas.microsoft.com/winfx/2006/xaml/presentation"
    xmlns:x="http://schemas.microsoft.com/winfx/2006/xaml"
    xmlns:local="clr-namespace:WorldBrowser"
    Title="World Browser">
```

Nothing new here—we're using the default namespace `local`. We've let IntelliSense do most of the work for us here. The second step is to add an instance of our control to the XAML for the `Window`. Again, it's pretty straightforward.

```
<Grid>
  <local:WorldListView x:Name="worldListView" Width="Auto" Height="Auto"/>
</Grid>
```

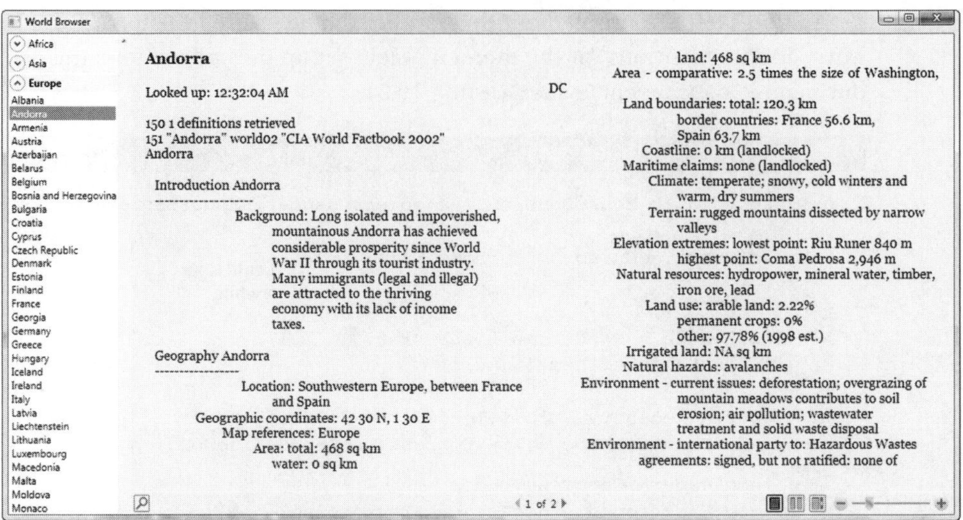

Figure 19.3 First version of the WorldBrowser application. Unless you're somewhat obsessive, you'll probably have fewer countries in your list.

That should do it. If you run the application now, you should get something like figure 19.3.

So far, so good. We have a reasonably well-architected application that provides some useful functionality. But, it's a little boring. In the next section, we'll spice it up a little by adding some transitions—which is, after all, what this chapter is supposed to be about.

19.2 Adding a simple transition

Transitions can punch up the user's interactions with an application, provided they aren't overdone. In many ways, WPF is *really* good at handling things like transitions. Once you tell WPF what you want it to do, it takes care of all the details. On the other hand, it's sometimes quite difficult to tell WPF what it is that you want.

We're going to start out by building a fade transition to switch between our two document viewers whenever a different country is selected. The details of the effect will be written in XAML, but we'll launch the transition manually whenever we change the country to make what's going on a little clearer.

In fact, we're going to build two different transitions: one for fading from document viewer A to document viewer B and one to go the other way. We'll talk a little more about why we're doing this later. Listing 19.6 shows the resource section of WorldListView.xaml, which is where we're temporarily putting our transition.

Listing 19.6 Fade transition

```
<UserControl.Resources>
  <Duration x:Key="animationTime">0:0:0.5</Duration>       ❶ Define a duration we can reuse
  <BeginStoryboard x:Key="FadeInA">                         ❷ Fades from A to B
```

```
    <Storyboard>                       ❸ Fades from B to A
      <DoubleAnimation
          Storyboard.TargetName="docReaderA"
          Storyboard.TargetProperty="Opacity"
          From="0.0" To="1.0" Duration="{StaticResource animationTime}" />
      <DoubleAnimation Storyboard.TargetName="docReaderB"      ❹
          Storyboard.TargetProperty="Opacity"
          From="1.0" To="0.0" Duration="{StaticResource animationTime}" />
    </Storyboard>
  </BeginStoryboard>

  <BeginStoryboard x:Key="FadeInB">     ❺
    <Storyboard>
      <DoubleAnimation
          Storyboard.TargetName="docReaderB"
          Storyboard.TargetProperty="Opacity"
          From="0.0" To="1.0" Duration="{StaticResource animationTime}" />
      <DoubleAnimation Storyboard.TargetName="docReaderA"
          Storyboard.TargetProperty="Opacity"
          From="1.0" To="0.0" Duration="{StaticResource animationTime}" />
    </Storyboard>
  </BeginStoryboard>
</UserControl.Resources>
```

We start by creating a definition for a duration called `animationTime` ❶. We've defined this so that, if we want to change the length of the animation, we don't have to change the value in four different places. You can see how we're referencing the value as a `StaticResource` in each of our animations.

The first storyboard is called FadeInA ❷ and is made up of two different animations. The first of these ❸ changes the `Opacity` (or see-through-ed-ness?) of docReaderA from completely transparent (0) to completely solid (1), taking the amount of time defined in `animationTime`, which is currently set to half of one second. The second animation changes docReaderB from fully solid to fully transparent ❹.

We also have another storyboard called FadeInB that does the exact opposite ❺.

So far, so good. But, we have to execute the animations at the appropriate times for them to be of any use. We also have to make our lookup code populate the proper flow document viewer before the animation starts. To do this, we'll restructure the `lb_MouseDoubleClick` method (listing 19.7). Note that we've omitted the wait cursor code to save space.

Listing 19.7 Launch animation from `lb_MouseDoubleClick`

```
private bool showingA = true;     ❶ Keeps track of current viewer

private void lb_MouseDoubleClick(object sender, MouseButtonEventArgs e)
{
  ListBox lb = sender as ListBox;
  if (lb.SelectedItem != null)
  {
    string country = lb.SelectedItem.ToString();
    FlowDocument doc = App.Current.Lookup.DefineWord(country);
```

```
        if (showingA)    ❷
        {
          docReaderB.Document = doc;                                    Finds
          doc.Background = docReaderB.Background;                   animation ❸
          BeginStoryboard storyboard =
                            FindResource("FadeInB") as BeginStoryboard;
          BeginStoryboard(storyboard.Storyboard);
        }                                              ❹ Launches it
        else ❺
        {
          docReaderA.Document = doc;
          doc.Background = docReaderA.Background;
          BeginStoryboard storyBoard =
                            FindResource("FadeInA") as BeginStoryboard;
          BeginStoryboard(storyBoard.Storyboard);
        }
        showingA = !showingA;                  Switches
      }                                      ❻ current view
    }
```

The code for determining our current viewer is a little ham-fisted, but it works. We have a `bool` ❶ that we swap each time to indicate whether we're showing viewer A or viewer B. If we're showing viewer A ❷, we set the content from our last query in *viewer B* because we want it to be set before viewer B becomes visible. Then we find the appropriate `Storyboard` from resources using `FindResource` ❸. Next we launch the `Storyboard` ❹. This will execute the details that we've defined in XAML.

The rest of the code does the exact opposite if we're currently viewing viewer B ❺ and then switches the current viewer ❻. Now, if we run the application, when we double-click between countries we get a nice fade effect between viewers (figure 19.4).

This is a pretty nice effect, but there some issues. For one thing, the code isn't terribly elegant—we have to go searching for the proper effect to launch. That isn't a big deal when we have a fade; but what if we want to have a few other effects that we can choose between? Also, the effects are tied pretty specifically to docViewerA and docViewerB. If we want to use the effects against, say, a couple of pictures or other content, we'd have to re-create our effects with different targets.

In the next section, we'll present a more generic approach, one where we can arbitrarily plug in different content and different effects!

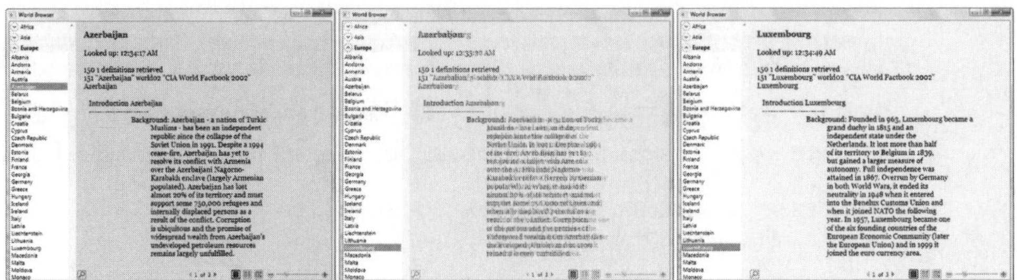

Figure 19.4 Fading from A to B. The transition takes one half of a second to go from one pane to the other.

19.3 Building a generic transition control

XAML is incredibly powerful, but it can also be quite difficult to work with, particularly when doing things like transition effects. For one thing, not everything in XAML is checked at compile time, and so some things often fail—noisily or silently—when you run. Also, there isn't currently any sort of debugger for XAML; when things don't work, you're often reduced to trial and error to figure out why.

Even though it *might* be possible to completely create a framework for doing transitions in XAML, it probably isn't the best approach. In this section, we'll demonstrate a different approach that we believe makes creating and testing transitions easier. We'll build a control that lets us plug in transition effects and the items we want to transition from and to.

We want to separate our implementation into three parts:

- *A transition control*—A control written in C# (or your favorite .NET language[2])
- *Some number of effects*—Primarily written in XAML
- *Binding between content and the transition control*—Written in XAML

In case you haven't guessed by now, this section is going to cover a lot more ground than building some pretty transitions. We'll end up talking about custom controls, defining and working with properties, animation, and a *lot* about binding—this is a little different than the binding we were doing in chapter 11 because we aren't binding to data sources, but are, instead, binding between controls and templates.

We'll start with the transition control.

19.3.1 Creating the transition control

As we showed in earlier chapters, it's possible to create a `Style` for a particular type of control, and then tie things like animations to various property changes on that control. In theory, if we had the right type of control, we could define a control template that used animation to implement our transitions. Further, we could have multiple different control templates with different animations, and could change the current template on that control to switch to a different animation effect.

The control we'd need for this would need to be able to hold two different things that we could transition between. We could probably make use of one of the existing controls, such as the `Grid`, which can hold any number of children. But, that would be awkward—referring to the children within a template would be a nuisance, and it would never be really clear which child was which.

Instead, we're going to build our own control—one that has two clearly named *things* that we can switch between, and one that we can specifically target with our control template. Let's call the control `ABSwitcher`. This is sort of a reference to the old AB video switchers of yore. We then need to figure out what the things are. Technically,

---

[2] If you're interested, there *is* a COBOL.NET...

they're elements, so we'll call them ElementA and ElementB. Then we can set things up to switch between them.

The easiest way to create the `ABSwitcher` class is to add a new item of type `class` and then modify it. Listing 19.8 contains the entire code for the `ABSwitcher` class.

Listing 19.8 `ABSwitcher` class

```
using System;
using System.Windows;
using System.Windows.Controls;

namespace WorldBrowser
{
  public class ABSwitcher : ContentControl          ❶ Derives from ContentControl
  {
    public enum Elements          ❷ Differentiates between elements
    {
      ElementA,
      ElementB
    }

    public static DependencyProperty ElementAProperty;          ❸ Dependency properties
    public static DependencyProperty ElementBProperty;
    public static DependencyProperty CurrentElementProperty;

    public ABSwitcher()
    {
    }

    static ABSwitcher()          ❹ Initializes dependency properties
    {
      ElementAProperty = DependencyProperty.Register("ElementA",
              typeof(object), typeof(ABSwitcher));
      ElementBProperty = DependencyProperty.Register("ElementB",
              typeof(object), typeof(ABSwitcher));
      CurrentElementProperty =
   DependencyProperty.Register("CurrentElement",
              typeof(Elements), typeof(ABSwitcher));
    }

    public object ElementA          ❺ Exposes properties
    {
      get { return GetValue(ElementAProperty); }
      set { SetValue(ElementAProperty, value); }
    }

    public object ElementB
    {
      get { return GetValue(ElementBProperty); }
      set { SetValue(ElementBProperty, value); }
    }

    public Elements CurrentElement          ❻ Properties for convenience
    {
      get { return (Elements)GetValue(CurrentElementProperty); }
      set { SetValue(CurrentElementProperty, value); }
```

```
    }

    public object SelectedElement    ❼
    {
      get {return(CurrentElement==Elements.ElementA) ? ElementA : ElementB;
  }
    }
                                              ❽ Switches between
    public object UnselectedElement   ◁┘        A and B
    {
      get {return(CurrentElement==Elements.ElementA) ? ElementB : ElementA;
  }
    }

    public void Switch()    ❾
    {
      if (CurrentElement == Elements.ElementA)
        CurrentElement = Elements.ElementB;
      else
        CurrentElement = Elements.ElementA;
    }
  }
}
```

We're afraid that this is going to be a fairly lengthy explanation, but we want to be thorough. First, our class, `ABSwitcher`, is going to be a type of `ContentControl` ❶. This will let the class be used like any other content control and will give us, among many other things, support for dependency properties.

Our class has three dependency properties ❸: `ElementA`, `ElementB`, and `CurrentElement`. If these were regular properties, then we'd define the properties, and be done. But, for dependency properties, there's somewhat more work. The benefit of using dependency properties, though, is that we get to participate in the dependency system, and our properties can be accessed from XAML. We start by creating static member variables that will be used to reference our dependency properties ❸, and then we initialize them inside a static constructor ❹ that will only be called once at system startup.

We're passing three arguments to the `DependencyProperty.Register` method—the name of the property, the type of the property, and the type of the class that owns the property. We could also pass additional arguments here. For example, we could register a method that would be called whenever the property's value changes, but we don't need to do anything that fancy for the moment.

The `ElementA` and `ElementB` properties are registered as type `object`—we want to be flexible, and you can't get much more flexible than that. The `CurrentElement` property returns the value from an enum we defined earlier ❷. We *could* have used a Boolean value here because we're swapping between two things; but, trust us, the enum will make the code clearer, and will leave us some flexibility for later.

We also have standard property accessors for our two elements ❺ and for the `CurrentElement` value ❻. If you look at the implementation, you'll see that the get and set methods call `GetValue` and `SetValue`, passing our static `DependencyProperty` variables. These methods access the dictionary of properties for our object.

> **Catching property changes**
>
> A common mistake is for developers to assume that the property code (for example: `ElementA`, `ElementB`) will be called when properties are accessed. The Property System goes directly to the property dictionary without passing go—or your breakpoints. The only time these accessors will be hit is if they're referenced by your code directly.
>
> If you want a guaranteed notification when a property is changed, you have to attach an event to the dependency property. For existing controls, a lot of common properties have a directly exposed event. For custom properties, you have to register a handler when you register the property (or modify the existing metadata). For an example of this, look in chapter 13.

The `CurrentElement` property is the one we'll use for our triggers later. When the current element changes, we'll activate our animation.

The `SelectedElement` ❼ and `UnselectedElement` ❽ are there for convenience. When we update the lookup code, we'll want to make sure that we set our text on the element that is *not* currently visible (the `UnselectedElement`). This way, we keep the code for getting the proper element in our switcher, rather than having to put conditional statements all over the place. The `Switch` method ❾ is likewise a convenient method for switching the `CurrentElement` from `ElementA` to `ElementB`.

Well, that's pretty much all there is to creating our custom control. Now, we have to use it.

19.3.2 Using the transition control

With the one caveat that we have to use a namespace reference, using our new control is just like using any other WPF control. The namespace reference is the same as the one we used in our main application window.

```
<UserControl x:Class="WorldBrowser.WorldListView"
  xmlns="http://schemas.microsoft.com/winfx/2006/xaml/presentation"
  xmlns:x="http://schemas.microsoft.com/winfx/2006/xaml"
  xmlns:local="clr-namespace:WorldBrowser"
  xmlns:system="clr-namespace:System;assembly=mscorlib"
  Height="334" Width="551" Loaded="UserControl_Loaded">
```

Then we replace the content of the `Grid` with our control and two `FlowDocumentReaders` (listing 19.9).

Listing 19.9 Using the `ABSwitcher` in code

```
<local:ABSwitcher x:Name="Switcher" Grid.Column="1" >          ❶
  <local:ABSwitcher.ElementA>                                ❷
    <FlowDocumentReader Name="docReaderA"
                        Background="LightGoldenrodYellow" >
      <FlowDocument Background="LightGoldenrodYellow">
        <Paragraph>Double-click on a country for details</Paragraph>
      </FlowDocument>
```

```
      </FlowDocumentReader>
    </local:ABSwitcher.ElementA>
    <local:ABSwitcher.ElementB>                    3
      <FlowDocumentReader Name="docReaderB" Background="LightBlue"/>
    </local:ABSwitcher.ElementB>
  </local:ABSwitcher>
```

It looks uglier than using a built-in control because of the namespace references, but otherwise it's pretty straightforward. We're inserting an `ABSwitcher` called Switcher and specifying (as we did when we had the `Grid`) that it should be in `Grid.Column "1"` ❶. Then we set the value of the `ElementA` property to be a `FlowDocumentReader` ❷. For our application, this is what we want, but we could put *any* valid XAML element here. We're setting the background to be light goldenrod, and we're putting in a `FlowDocument` with some introductory text in the reader.

We're also setting the value for `ElementB` to be another `FlowDocumentReader` ❸. This one is light blue to make the transitions more visible. We aren't bothering to set any introductory text for this one because it won't initially be visible.

This will compile; but, if you run it, you won't see anything. Unlike built-in controls, there is no default style for how to display an `ABSwitcher`, and we haven't defined one. That will be our next step.

19.3.3 Defining a ControlTemplate for our control

We can define a `ControlTemplate` as just another resource. The template is going to have two jobs. First, it needs to define where and how to display our two different elements: `ElementA` and `ElementB`. Second, it has to contain the definition for how to transition between the elements.

To implement multiple effects, we'll end up implementing multiple control templates; each one will contain both things: the "where to put stuff" instructions and the "how to transition" instructions.

Let's start simply, with a template that makes one control visible and one hidden. Later on, we'll move the resources into a standalone dictionary for easier maintenance; for the moment, we can put them into the resources of the WorldListView xaml file (listing 19.10).

Listing 19.10 Simple transition template

```
<ControlTemplate TargetType="{x:Type local:ABSwitcher}"      1 Template for
         x:Key="SimpleTemplate">                                the ABSwitcher
  <Grid>                                  2 Grid holding our content
    <ContentPresenter Name="ElementAPresenter" Visibility="Hidden"
         Content="{TemplateBinding ElementA}"/>                          3
    <ContentPresenter Name="ElementBPresenter" Visibility="Hidden"
         Content="{TemplateBinding ElementB}"/>
  </Grid>                                                 4 Triggers for
                                                             transitions
  <ControlTemplate.Triggers>
    <Trigger Property="local:ABSwitcher.CurrentElement"
                                         Value="ElementA">      5
```

```
      <Setter TargetName="ElementAPresenter" Property="Visibility"
                                                   Value="Visible"/>
    </Trigger>
    <Trigger Property="local:ABSwitcher.CurrentElement"          ❻
                                          Value="ElementB">    <┘
      <Setter TargetName="ElementBPresenter" Property="Visibility"
                                                   Value="Visible"/>
    </Trigger>
  </ControlTemplate.Triggers>
</ControlTemplate>
```

The `ControlTemplate` that we've defined ❶ has the key `"SimpleTemplate"`, so we can refer to it later, and the target type of `ABSwitcher`. By specifying the target type, we'll automatically have access to all the properties of the `ABSwitcher`.

The main display is a `Grid` layout panel for convenience. If we don't specify any additional properties, our content will automatically fill up all the available space in the one and only cell. In the `Grid`, we have two `ContentPresenters` ❷.

Now, as you might remember from earlier, a `ContentPresenter` is a specialized element that indicates where content should be positioned. In our earlier examples, though, we only had a single `ContentPresenter`, whereas here we have two. This is allowed, as long as we indicate what content needs to be presented. We do this by binding the `Content` property of the `ContentPresenter` to the thing we want to present ❸. `TemplateBinding` is a special type of binding that says "bind to something on the object of which this is a template." In this case, we're binding one of our `ContentPresenters` to `ElementA` and the other to `ElementB`.

You might also have noticed that we've deliberately set the visibility of both `ContentPresenters` to `Hidden`. In theory, neither of them will show up. But, that reckons without the triggers we've defined ❹.

The first trigger ❺ looks for the value of the `CurrentElement` property to be set to `"ElementA"`. When it is, it sets the `Visibility` property of the `ElementAPresenter` to be `Visible`. The second trigger ❻ does the same thing, but for `ElementB`.

By assigning this template to our `ABSwitcher`, WPF will display it as a `Grid` panel with two hidden children (`ElementA` and `ElementB`). But, if `CurrentElement` is set to `ElementA` (which it will be to start with), the trigger will make `ElementA` visible. If `CurrentElement` is changed to `ElementB`, then it will make `ElementB` visible. We don't have to worry about re-hiding `ElementA` because, if you remember the behavior of `Triggers`, once the condition is no longer `true`, WPF will automatically revert the value of the property.

There are still two things left to do before we can run this thing. First, we need to use this template on our `ABSwitcher`, so we set the property on the `ABSwitcher`.

```
<local:ABSwitcher x:Name="Switcher"
               Template="{StaticResource SimpleTemplate}" Grid.Column="1" >
```

The second thing we have to do is to change the code in our `WorldListView` to use the `ABSwitcher` instead of the hardcoded `FlowDocuments`. We'll do that in the next section.

19.3.4 Using the ABSwitcher

Earlier, in the `lb_MouseDoubleClick` method, we had a fair amount of code to set the document on the proper viewer, and retrieve and then launch the animation. We have to update this code, but it gets quite a bit simpler. Listing 19.11 shows the new version of the `DoubleClick` handler.

Listing 19.11 New version of `DoubleClick` handler

```
private void lb_MouseDoubleClick(object sender, MouseButtonEventArgs e)
{
  ListBox lb = sender as ListBox;
  if (lb.SelectedItem != null)
  {
    string country = lb.SelectedItem.ToString();
    FlowDocument doc = App.Current.Lookup.DefineWord(country);

    FlowDocumentReader reader =
                Switcher.UnselectedElement as FlowDocumentReader;    ❶
    doc.Background = reader.Background;
    reader.Document = doc;

    Switcher.Switch();    ❷
  }
}
```

This code starts out the same way—retrieving the appropriate country data. After that, though, it ends up being quite a bit simpler. We first get hold of the control that is *not* selected ❶. This is easy because we've added a property to the `ABSwitcher` for that. We can refer to the switcher by the name we gave it in XAML—*Switcher.* We have to cast the `UnselectedElement` to be a `FlowDocumentReader` because we allow any type of objects to be held by the `ABReader`. Once we have the `FlowDocumentReader`, we set the background of our document and then add it to the reader.

The next step is to call the `Switch` method on the Switcher ❷. Remember that all this does is change the `CurrentElement` property to be either `ElementA` or `ElementB`. The triggers we built in to our `ControlTemplate` take over after that. Now if we run, the transition isn't particularly exciting, but we can tell by the background color change that it worked (figure 19.5).

So far, so good—but pretty boring. In fact, we're moving backwards. We've even lost our fade transition because we replaced our hardcoded effect with our new control. In the next section, we'll add a number of different effects, starting with the fade effect.

19.4 Adding some interesting transition effects

Now that we have a framework for effects, we only have two things to do to change effects—create a new control template, and then change the template on our `ABSwitcher` element in XAML to use it. We'll start by re-creating our fade effect, this time using a `ControlTemplate`.

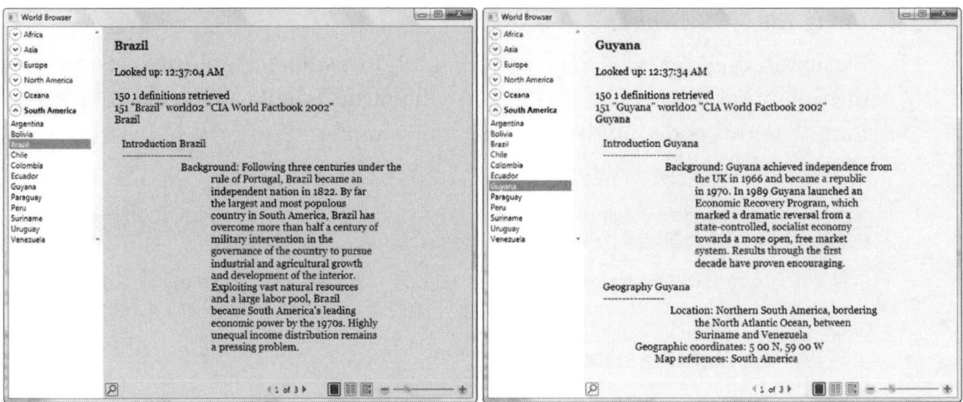

Figure 19.5 We now have a simple transition that changes the visibility of each pane. You can only tell that we've swapped controls because of the different colored backgrounds—given that the book is in black-and-white, you might not even be able to tell at all!

19.4.1 The fade effect

Listing 19.12 shows the XAML for the fade effect `ControlTemplate`. This needs to be put into the resource section of our `WorldListView` control.

Listing 19.12 Fade effect `ControlTemplate`

```
<ControlTemplate TargetType="{x:Type local:ABSwitcher}"
   x:Key="FadeTemplate">
 <Grid>                                                    <- (1) Grid holding content
   <ContentPresenter Name="ElementAPresenter" ContentPresenter.Opacity="1"
        Grid.ZIndex="1" Content="{TemplateBinding ElementA}"/>
   <ContentPresenter Name="ElementBPresenter" ContentPresenter.Opacity="0"
        Grid.ZIndex="0" Content="{TemplateBinding ElementB}"/>
 </Grid>

 <ControlTemplate.Triggers>
  <Trigger Property="local:ABSwitcher.CurrentElement"
                                    Value="ElementA">      <- Fades to ElementA
    <Setter TargetName="ElementAPresenter"
             Property="Grid.ZIndex" Value="1"/>            <- (2) Sets ZOrder
    <Trigger.EnterActions>
      <BeginStoryboard >
        <Storyboard>
          <DoubleAnimation
               Storyboard.TargetName="ElementAPresenter"
               Storyboard.TargetProperty="Opacity"
               From="0.0" To="1.0"
               Duration="{StaticResource animationTime}"
               FillBehavior="HoldEnd" />                   <- (3) Holds on the end value
        </Storyboard>
      </BeginStoryboard>
    </Trigger.EnterActions>
  </Trigger>
```

```
<Trigger Property="local:ABSwitcher.CurrentElement"
                                  Value="ElementB">
  <Setter TargetName="ElementBPresenter"
                      Property="Grid.ZIndex" Value="1"/>
  <Trigger.EnterActions>
    <BeginStoryboard>
      <Storyboard>
        <DoubleAnimation
              Storyboard.TargetName="ElementBPresenter"
              Storyboard.TargetProperty="Opacity"
              From="0.0" To="1.0"
              Duration="{StaticResource animationTime}"
              FillBehavior="HoldEnd" />
      </Storyboard>
    </BeginStoryboard>
  </Trigger.EnterActions>
</Trigger>
</ControlTemplate.Triggers>
</ControlTemplate>
```

Fades to ElementB

Just as with our simple transition template, we have two content presenters in a `Grid` ❶. The slight difference is that we're explicitly setting the `ZOrder` of the controls so that the one in front will allow the user to interact with it. When a control isn't visible, it doesn't interfere with focus in any way, but an invisible control will get mouse and keyboard events if it's in front,[3] possibly confusing the user. To avoid the problem, we make sure that the visible control is in front of the invisible one. In fact, when our trigger is fired, the first thing we do is change the `ZOrder` via a setter ❷.

The rest of the code is pretty much a combination of the simple transition and our old hardcoded fade transition. We trigger on the current element change, and then do our cross-fade animations. One thing we're doing slightly differently, though, is specifying the `HoldEnd` `FillBehavior` ❸. We don't need to do this because `HoldEnd` is the default for `FillBehavior`, but we want to explain `FillBehavior`. `FillBehavior` controls what happens when the animation finishes; it has two legal values:

- *`HoldEnd`*—Instructs the engine to hold the animated value at its final value. In the example, once the `Opacity` reaches 1, it will stick there as long as the animation is active (which is true as long as the trigger expression is `true`). Obviously, in the case of our fade, this is what we want.
- *`Stop`*—Means that, as soon as the animation is finished, the value of the animated value will revert to its original value. In the case of our example, this would mean that the `Opacity` would snap back to 0. This would be pretty undesirable in our situation, but not in all scenarios.

`HoldEnd` doesn't just mean that the last value isn't reset. It means that the value will be *held*. If you have other code that attempts to programmatically set the `Opacity` to another value while the animation is in progress, it won't do anything. The animation will set it back to its hold value. If you want to change the value later, you either need to use a

[3] In fact, there are several techniques for WPF UI development that rely on this.

different type of animation (such as a `Keyframe` animation) or manually stop the animation (programmatically) before changing the value. Just something to keep in mind.

Anyway, the last step is to change our template binding on the `ABSwitcher` to use the fade effect.

```
<local:ABSwitcher x:Name="Switcher"
        Template="{StaticResource FadeTemplate}"
        Grid.Column="1" >
```

Figure 19.6 shows the application in mid-fade.

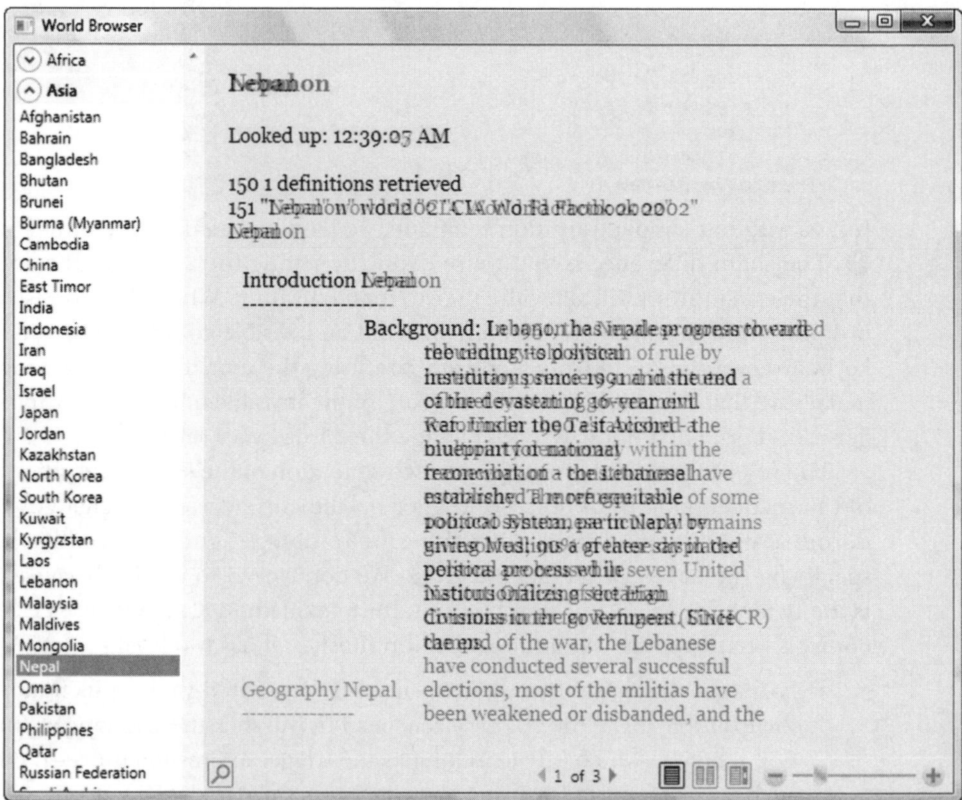

Figure 19.6 Fading from Lebanon to Nepal—the only way to travel

The fade effect is a nice, subtle effect that's pleasing and not too distracting. Our next effect is also relatively subtle—a simple wipe.

19.4.2 Wipe effect

A wipe effect, another common video effect, starts making the second image visible at one edge and then moves to the other edge, making the second image visible as it goes. Listing 19.13 has the XAML for the wipe `ControlTemplate`. As you can see, it's rather more involved than the fade effect.

Listing 19.13 Wipe ControlTemplate

```
<ControlTemplate TargetType="{x:Type local:ABSwitcher}"
  x:Key="WipeTemplate">                                    ❶ Same old Grid with controls
 <Grid>
  <ContentPresenter Name="ElementAPresenter" Visibility="Visible"
            Content="{TemplateBinding ElementA}"/>
  <ContentPresenter Name="ElementBPresenter" Visibility="Visible"
            Content="{TemplateBinding ElementB}"/>
</Grid>                                                    ❷ Wipes from B to A
 <ControlTemplate.Triggers>
  <Trigger Property="local:ABSwitcher.CurrentElement" Value="ElementA">
    <Setter TargetName="ElementAPresenter" Property="Grid.ZIndex"
   Value="1"/>
    <Setter TargetName="ElementAPresenter" Property="OpacityMask" >      ❸
      <Setter.Value>
        <LinearGradientBrush StartPoint="1,0" EndPoint="0,0">
          <GradientStop Offset="0" Color="Black" />
          <GradientStop Offset="0" Color="Transparent" />
        </LinearGradientBrush>
      </Setter.Value>
    </Setter>
    <Trigger.EnterActions>
      <BeginStoryboard >
        <Storyboard>
          <DoubleAnimation Storyboard.TargetName="ElementAPresenter"     ❹
              Storyboard.TargetProperty =                               ❺
               "OpacityMask.(LinearGradientBrush.GradientStops)[0].Offset"
              From="0.0" To="1.0"
              Duration="{StaticResource animationTime}"/>
          <DoubleAnimation Storyboard.TargetName="ElementAPresenter"     ❻
              Storyboard.TargetProperty =
               "OpacityMask.(LinearGradientBrush.GradientStops)[1].Offset"
              From="0.0" To="1.0"
              Duration="{StaticResource animationTime}"/>
        </Storyboard>
      </BeginStoryboard>
    </Trigger.EnterActions>                                    ❼ Wipes from A to B
  </Trigger>

  <Trigger Property="local:ABSwitcher.CurrentElement" Value="ElementB">
    <Setter TargetName="ElementBPresenter" Property="Grid.ZIndex"
   Value="1"/>
    <Setter TargetName="ElementBPresenter" Property="OpacityMask" >
      <Setter.Value>
        <LinearGradientBrush StartPoint="0,0" EndPoint="1,0">    ❽
          <GradientStop Offset="0" Color="Black" />
          <GradientStop Offset="0" Color="Transparent" />
        </LinearGradientBrush>
      </Setter.Value>
    </Setter>
    <Trigger.EnterActions>
      <BeginStoryboard >
        <Storyboard>
          <DoubleAnimation Storyboard.TargetName="ElementBPresenter"
```

```
                Storyboard.TargetProperty=
                  "OpacityMask.(LinearGradientBrush.GradientStops)[0].Offset"
                From="0.0" To="1.0"
                Duration="{StaticResource animationTime}"/>
            <DoubleAnimation Storyboard.TargetName="ElementBPresenter"
                Storyboard.TargetProperty=
                 "OpacityMask.(LinearGradientBrush.GradientStops)[1].Offset"
                From="0.0" To="1.0"
                Duration="{StaticResource animationTime}"/>
          </Storyboard>
        </BeginStoryboard>
      </Trigger.EnterActions>
    </Trigger>
   </ControlTemplate.Triggers>
  </ControlTemplate>
```

This template starts out more or less the same way as the fade—with a `Grid` containing our controls ❶ and a trigger catching the current element change ❷. But, instead of animating the `Opacity` property of the element to go from transparent to visible, we're using an `OpacityMask` ❸. This lets us specify which bits of the element are opaque or transparent, rather than the whole thing. The `OpacityMask` uses a `Brush`; instead of drawing anything, it indicates which bits of the control are visible: If the `OpacityMask Brush` draws something as transparent, then you can't see that bit. If it draws something as black, then you *can* see that bit.

The color isn't really the important bit. Each color has four components: `Red`, `Green`, `Blue`, and `Alpha`. `Alpha` is the alpha channel that controls visibility. An alpha value of 0 means completely transparent, no matter what values RGB has. A value of 255 means completely solid, and values in between indicate relative transparency. We're using black which has a value of 255 for `Alpha`, and values of 0 for `Red`, `Green`, and `Blue`, but we could use any solid color.

More interestingly, though, is that we're setting up an `OpacityMask` as part of a setter ❸. This is more involved than, say, setting visibility, but it's the same concept—when the event fires, the `OpacityMask` property of the presenter will be set to a linear gradient brush that goes from solid to transparent. You may have noticed that the offset for both gradient stops is 0. We're relying on a side effect of the gradient brush to continue the last "color" all the way to the end of our area. For all intents and purposes, we have a gradient brush that goes like this:

- *0*—Solid
- *0*—Transparent
- *1*—Transparent

At the moment, the solid has no effect, and the entire element will have a transparent `OpacityMask`, and so will be entirely invisible. But, we then add a storyboard to animate the gradient stops. The notation to reference the properties is pretty scary ❺.

```
OpacityMask.(LinearGradientBrush.GradientStops)[0].Offset
```

It should be read like this: The `OpacityMask` property needs to be changed. We need to reference the `GradientStops` collection of the `LinearGradientBrush` that's the value of the `OpacityMask` property. We want to reference the first element in the `GradientStops` collection (item 0), and we want to reference the `Offset` property of that element.

This should give you a hint as to the power and flexibility of the binding notation within XAML—although it often will twist your brain figuring out exactly what you need to do, and there are limits to what's possible.

Anyway, we're changing the offset of *both* gradient stops, animating them from 0 to 1, so we have two animations ❹, ❻. At the end of the animation, the gradient stops will look like this (including the implied gradient stop):

- *0*—Solid
- *1*—Solid
- *1*—Transparent

Now the transparent at the end has no meaning, and the entire image is visible. During the animation, different parts of the image will show up. Figure 19.7 shows the effect part of the way through.

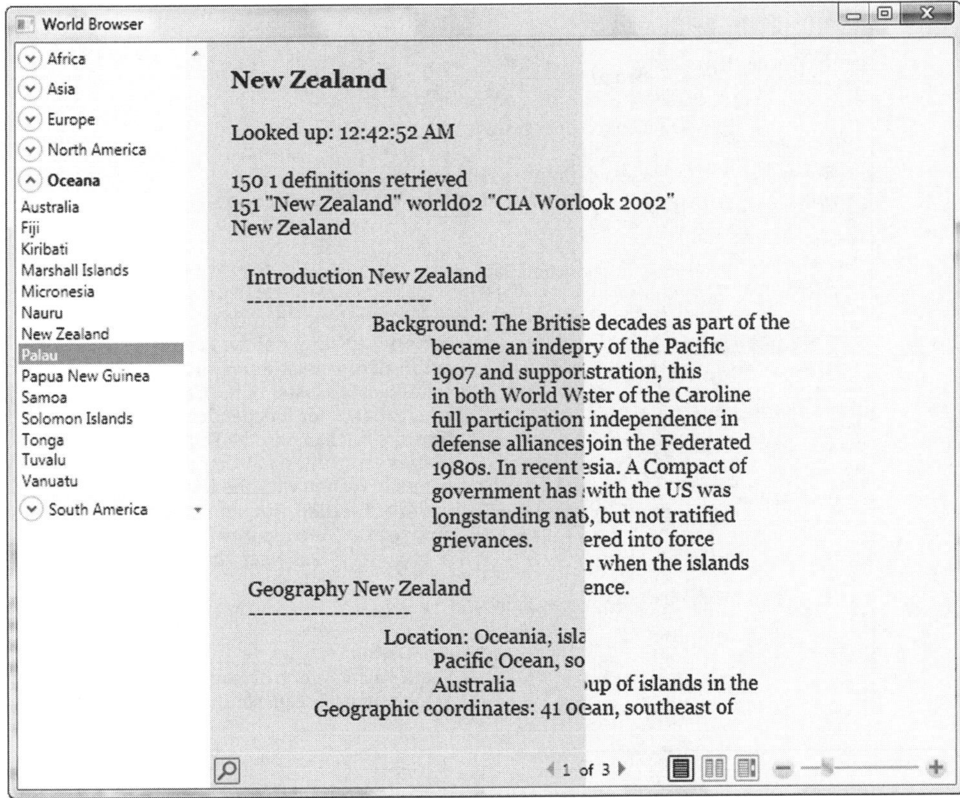

Figure 19.7 Wipe effect. New Zealand is about to be wiped out by Palau. Who would have guessed?

Because we have two animations operating at the same time, we're moving both the solid and transparent gradient stops exactly in sync. But, we can make the effect a little more interesting by offsetting the times a little. We can make the animation moving the solid gradient stop start a fraction of a second later.

```
<DoubleAnimation
    Storyboard.TargetName="ElementAPresenter"
    Storyboard.TargetProperty=
          "OpacityMask.(LinearGradientBrush.GradientStops)[0].Offset"
    From="0.0" To="1.0"
    BeginTime="0:0:0.1"
    Duration="{StaticResource animationTime}"
                                              />
```

By adding in the `BeginTime` clause on the first animation, we're saying that we don't want it to start until a tenth of a second after the other one. This will give us a little bit of a leading edge effect (figure 19.8).

We think this makes the effect look a little bit spiffier. It also demonstrates the giant time hole that WPF can open up as days and days of your previously productive life are spent tweaking effects.

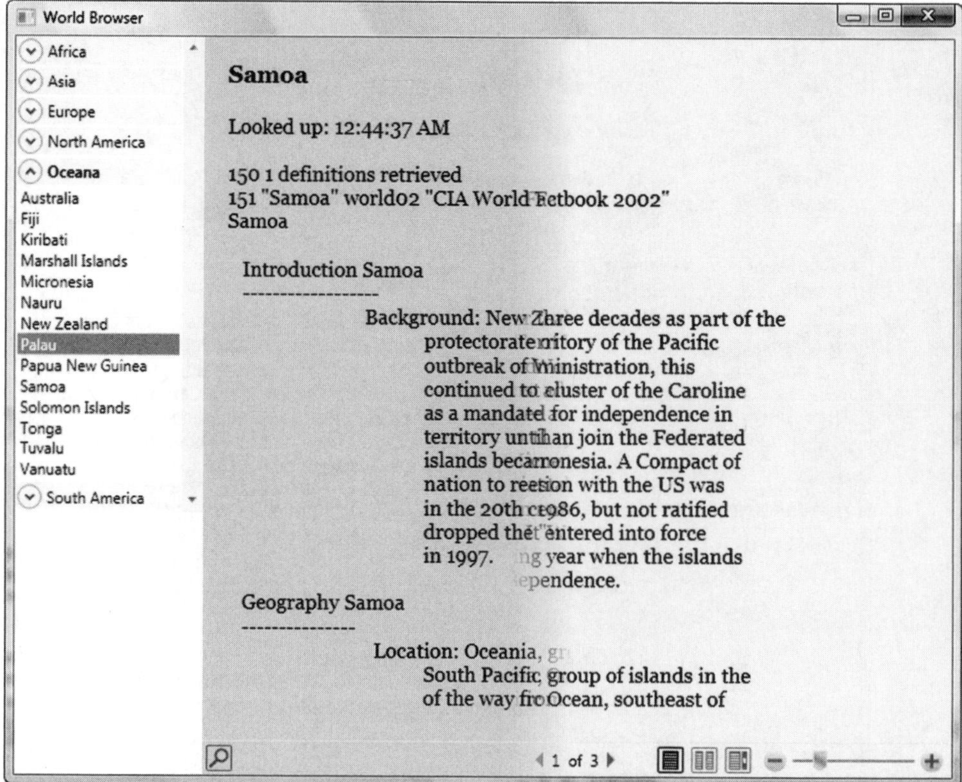

Figure 19.8 Wipe effect with a slight trailing edge. By varying the begin time of the animation, you can alter the size of the edge.

WHY TWO VERSIONS OF THE EFFECT?

In listing 19.13, we have two triggers: one going from `ElementA` to `ElementB` ❼ and one going from `ElementB` to `ElementA` ❷. This dramatically increases the amount of XAML. Doubles it, you might say. Not only that, but if you have to fix something, you have to fix it in two places.

Normally, we'd go to extraordinary effort to be able to reuse the same XAML. There are two different approaches to this:

- *We could modify our `ABSwitcher` so that, instead of having an `ElementA` and an `ElementB`, it had something like a `CurrentElement` and an `OldElement`, and we could bind to those.* The problem with this approach is that, particularly with more complex effects, it gets tricky to make sure that the elements are properly positioned without getting one or the other element to flash up on the screen. If you're *really* good at XAML[4], you could probably handle this, but it does mean that you'll have to handle it for every type of effect.
- *We could store the effect itself as a resource and then bind the appropriate elements within our control template.* The problem with this approach is that it makes the XAML *really* hard to read. Because the goal of combining the effects is to improve maintainability, we think that this is going in the wrong direction.

We've decided that the most maintainable choice is, in this case, to duplicate the effect. We think it's more readable. Also, it gives us the opportunity to vary the back-and-forth effects a little bit. For example, with the wipe, you may have noticed that the `LinearGradientBrush` defined for our B-to-A effect ❸ looks like this:

```
<LinearGradientBrush StartPoint="1,0" EndPoint="0,0">
```

Whereas the A-to-B effect ❽ looks like this:

```
<LinearGradientBrush StartPoint="0,0" EndPoint="1,0">
```

The exact reverse. We wipe in opposite directions each time.

19.4.3 Adding a selector for effects

Now that we have three different effects (and plan to add more), it would be nice if we had a way to choose between them. This might be something that we'd normally configure as a user option; but, for the purposes of this sample, how about if we put in a `ComboBox` that lists all the effects and lets us choose the one we want?

To position the `ComboBox` at the top of the country list, but prevent it from scrolling with the list, we need to put a `StackPanel` in where the `ScrollViewer` is now, put the `ComboBox` at the top, and then the `ScrollViewer` below it. Unfortunately, the designer won't help us much with this, so we need to edit the XAML directly. But, once the controls are in place, we can use the property editor to set the various properties if we like. Listing 19.14 shows the XAML to include the `ComboBox`.

---

[4] Or at least better than us.

Listing 19.14 Adding an effects ComboBox

```
<StackPanel Grid.ColumnSpan="1">
  <ComboBox SelectedIndex="0" Name="TransitionCombo">
    <ComboBox.Items>
      <TextBlock Tag="{StaticResource SimpleTemplate}">Simple</TextBlock>   ❶
      <TextBlock Tag="{StaticResource FadeTemplate}">Fade</TextBlock>
      <TextBlock Tag="{StaticResource WipeTemplate}">Wipe</TextBlock>
    </ComboBox.Items>
  </ComboBox>
  <ScrollViewer Name="continentScrollViewer" VerticalAlignment="Stretch"
        HorizontalAlignment="Stretch" >
    <StackPanel Name="continentStackPanel" />
  </ScrollViewer>
</StackPanel>
```

We could store only strings in the ComboBox, but we're using TextBlocks so that we can store a reference to our templates. As you can see, we've set the Tag property of each item to be bound to the associated ControlTemplate ❶. If we add more effects, we can add more items to the ComboBox. Now, all we have to do is make it so that the effect used is the one selected in the ComboBox. We can do this via binding as well.

```
<local:ABSwitcher x:Name="Switcher" Grid.Column="1"
   Template="{Binding ElementName=TransitionCombo,Path=SelectedItem.Tag}" >
```

This code says that the template to use for the control is the one stored in the SelectedItem's Tag property from the TransitionCombo ComboBox. Figure 19.9 shows the ComboBox in place.

We aren't going to show the implementation for all the other effects, but you can download the full sample from our website. We've included some extensive comments to explain how they work.

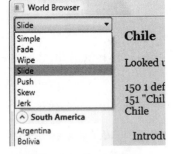

Figure 19.9 ComboBox for choosing the transition effect to use. The downloadable version has a few additional effects.

19.5 Summary

In many ways, we've only scratched the surface of animation effects—we were more interested in exploring the building of a framework to simplify effects than with the effects themselves. (OK, we were pretty interested in the effects too.) Although WPF is pretty new, a number of companies are already producing third-party support; one of the popular things is—you guessed it—transition controls. Page turns, cube rotates, you name it—many of them done by people with far greater artistic ability than us. An example would be Jared Bienz's Transitional project at http://www.codeplex.com/transitionals.

This is a good thing because—we'll let you in on a secret—creating transitions can be a real pain in the neck, particularly using Visual Studio. For one thing, Visual Studio gives you very little assistance, beyond IntelliSense, for building effects. This is particularly an issue when dealing with the binding notation. Microsoft Expression Blend has a built-in bind builder, but Visual Studio doesn't.

A second problem is that it's tricky to debug effects that aren't working correctly, although you do get occasional messages in the Output window (which are worth looking for).

The final problem is that WPF is still fairly new—new enough that not all the kinks have been worked out yet. For example, one of our effects is a push effect (figure 19.10). We like this effect and got it working pretty quickly.

But, when we went to use binding to get the proper width of the page so that the effect started and ended in the right place (instead of hardcoding it), we couldn't get it to work. It turned out, after much crying on our part, that this was because of a bug in WPF—one that Microsoft didn't have a chance to fix before the release.[5] We could work around the problem, but it makes things much more complicated.

The point of this isn't to pick on Microsoft, but to forewarn you that you might run into problems you wouldn't expect. Nor is it to dissuade you from using WPF—the

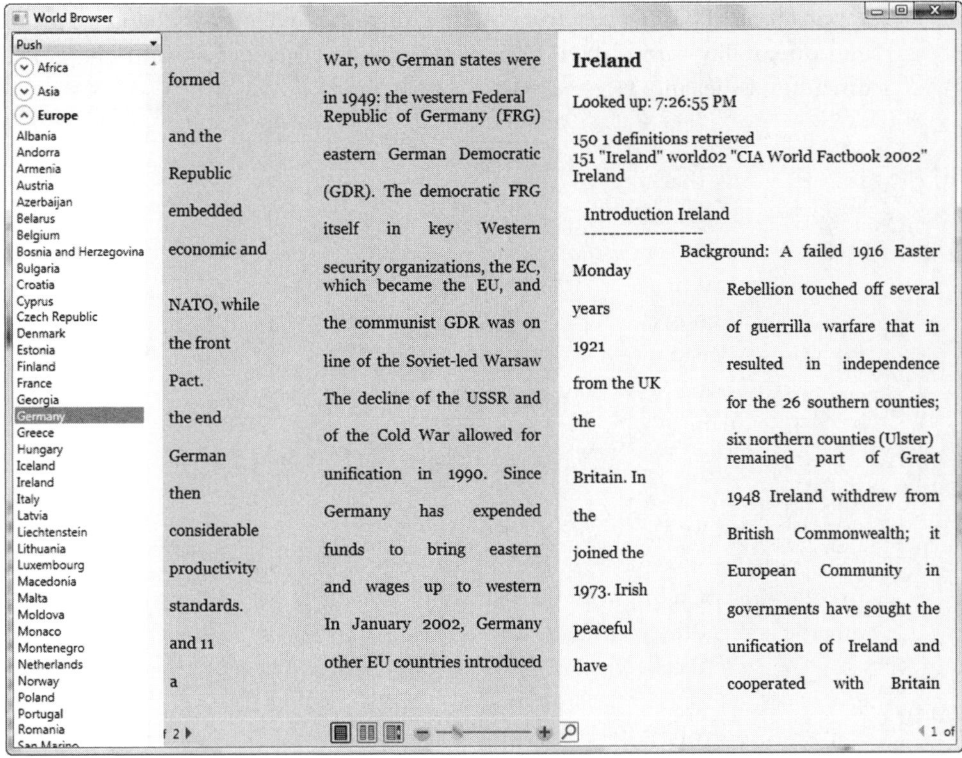

Figure 19.10 The push effect pushes the old page off one edge while the new page pushes in from the side.

[5] Although we have to thank Sam Bent, who is a Dev Lead on the WPF team and who spent two days confirming that this was a bug and that we weren't crazy. (He obviously doesn't know us that well.)

problems we encounter are generally doing things that would be *very* difficult to do smoothly without using WPF. Although it's disappointing that everything isn't perfect for the Visual Studio 2008 and the 2008 SP1 release, we know that the plans for Hawaii[6] will include major improvements to both the tools and the technology. In the meantime, you can do some stunning effects without much effort; and, if you do run into roadblocks, there are a lot of companies rushing to help you out.

This has been a fairly lengthy chapter, but we've accomplished quite a bit. First, we have an application that's put together reasonably "properly"—that is, it isn't a hacked-together example; it has an application object, a separated-out data-access component, and a framework that allows us to easily swap out some cool effects. We won't pretend that this has everything you need for your line-of-business applications, but it isn't bad. In a future chapter, we'll also revisit this application by making it thread-aware.

All the topics in this last section of the book are orphans to a certain extent—they cover topics that don't directly occur along the way to getting started with WPF, but address particular subjects likely to come up when you start implementing real-world applications. This is even truer of the next two chapters. Chapter 20 talks about interoperability—using WPF with WinForms and vice versa—and chapter 21 covers threading issues in WPF.

---

6 Hawaii is the code name for the next release of Visual Studio after 2008 SP1. We have reason to believe that the VS team is hopeful that this will get them a trip to Hawaii when they finish. But, given that they didn't get a trip to Orcas Island when they finished the Orcas release (VS 2008) and they could just about wade there from Redmond, we don't have much hope for them.

20 Interoperability

This chapter covers:

- Using Windows Forms controls in WPF
- Using ActiveX and C++ in WPF
- Using WPF in Windows Forms
- Using Apple *IIe* software via Amiga emulation of a PDP-11

In a perfect world, there would be no legacy. Roving bands of highly intelligent lemurs would rewrite all your code in the middle of the night using the latest technology, and would leave a mint on your chair. To date, though, we've barely managed to train the lemurs to retype the works of Shakespeare. And they keep misspelling Hamlet.[1]

So, here we are. You might want to use WPF for some things, but either you have an old application that's too big to rewrite right now, or you have one or two custom controls that you want to use in our new WPF application. These are the scenarios we're going to address in detail:

[1] We think this is more spite than inability.

- Using Windows Forms controls inside WPF
- Using other stuff (ActiveX, C++/MFC) inside WPF
- Using WPF inside Windows Forms

Aside from the obvious usefulness of being able to do these things, there's another reason why interoperability is important—it makes it possible to start using WPF now, rather than waiting until you can do a full rewrite.

There are other scenarios that we are *not* going to cover here. For example, there are people out there who are probably pretty excited about using WPF inside their MFC applications (or their assembly applications for that matter). Although it's certainly possible (and not *that* difficult) to do that, we think the scenarios are rare enough and complex enough that we've decided that they're beyond the scope of what we would cover here.

20.1 Using Windows Forms controls in WPF

Generally, the reason you'd want to use a Windows Forms control in WPF is because there's something in Windows Forms that WPF doesn't have. Often this will be some custom functionality that you already built—or it might be one of the controls that WPF doesn't have. For example, WPF doesn't yet have a `DateTimePicker` or a `MaskedTextBox`.

We'll start out with a simple example—a dialog that allows the entry of a person's name and birthdate—but we'll use the Windows Forms `DateTimePicker` because WPF doesn't have one.

20.1.1 Using the Windows Forms DateTimePicker in WPF

Go ahead and create a new WPF Application, and set it up something like figure 20.1.

Now we want to get the Windows Forms `DateTimePicker` onto the form. Before we can do that, we need to add a few references to our code. Right-click the References

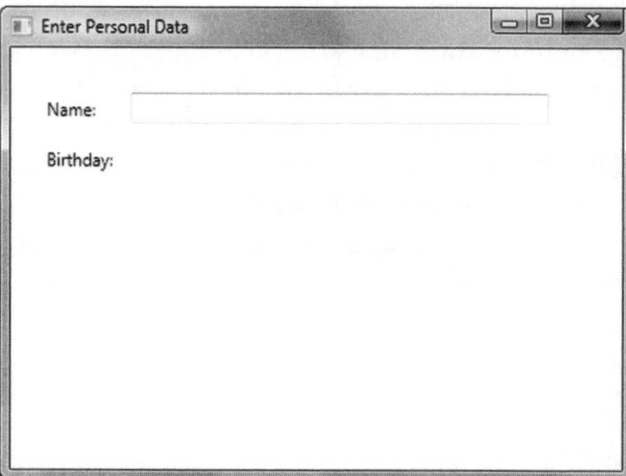

Figure 20.1 Building a dialog that collects some personal information. Unfortunately, WPF doesn't have a `DateTime` control for us to use.

node under your assembly in the Solution Explorer, and add references to the following two assemblies:

- `System.Windows.Forms`—The Windows Forms assembly, which has, among other things, the `DateTimePicker` control in it. WPF applications don't normally bother to reference it.
- `WindowsFormsIntegration`—A new assembly for .NET 3.x that contains the code related to using Windows Forms with WPF and vice versa.

Once `WindowsFormsIntegration` has been linked in, you can drag a handy control off the toolbox—the `WindowsFormsHost`. `WindowsFormsHost` is another one of those classes whose name pretty much says it all—it hosts Windows Forms stuff.

Drag the `WindowsFormsHost` control into position where you want the date control to reside. It will act like any other WPF control as far as things like positioning, margins, docking, and so on, are concerned (figure 20.2).

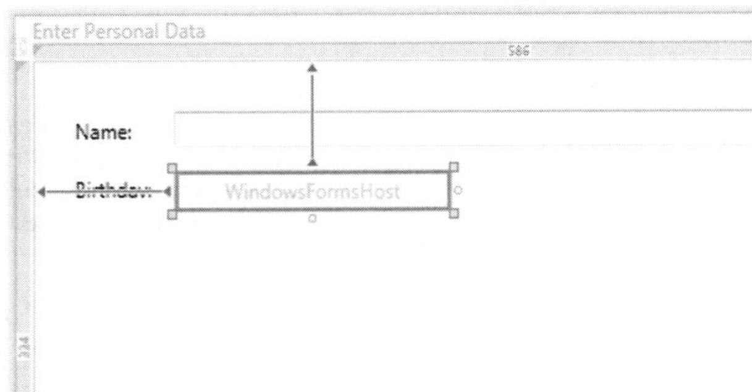

Figure 20.2 The `WindowsFormsHost` control acts like any other WPF control, at least until you put something into it.

To put something *into* the host, we'll have to drop down to the XAML editor; the toolbox isn't smart enough to switch to show us Windows Forms controls here. As per usual, we first have to worry about namespaces. Our XAML doesn't know anything about `System.Windows.Forms` until we tell it:

```
<Window x:Class="Interop3.Window1"
 xmlns="http://schemas.microsoft.com/winfx/2006/xaml/presentation"
 xmlns:x="http://schemas.microsoft.com/winfx/2006/xaml"
 xmlns:wf=
     "clr-namespace:System.Windows.Forms;assembly=System.Windows.Forms"
 Title="Enter Personal Data" Height="300" Width="398">
```

We've added a *wf* namespace that references `System.Windows.Forms`, although we let IntelliSense fill in the details of the reference for us. Now we can add a `DateTimePicker` to the `WindowsFormsHost`.

```
<WindowsFormsHost Margin="85,65,150,0" Height="23"
                                        VerticalAlignment="Top" >
  <wf:DateTimePicker x:Name="birthday" />
</WindowsFormsHost>
```

We're referencing the `DateTimePicker` from the wf space and giving the control a name so that we can refer to it as needed. In earlier CTP releases of Visual Studio 2008, the designer would show you the control you selected displayed inside the `WindowsFormHost`, and you could even edit the contained control's properties in the Properties grid. Unfortunately, this capability obviously caused some problems because, in the final release, all you get is a pretty box with the text `WindowsFormsHost`, which is accurate but not nearly as cool or useful (figure 20.3).

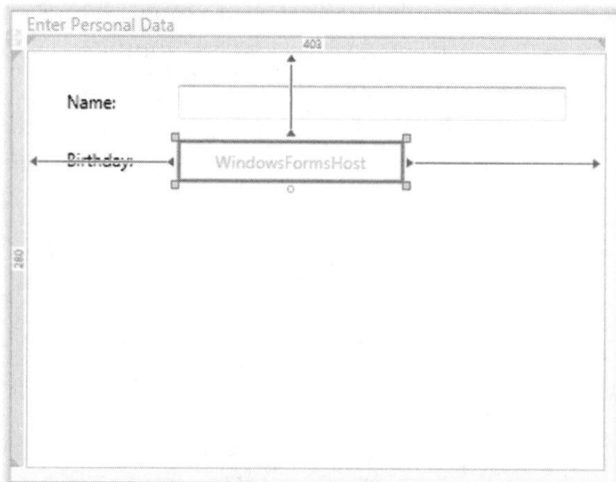

Figure 20.3 The `WindowsFormsHost` doesn't show us specifically what it's hosting in the designer, but the Windows Forms control will show up at runtime.

Even though we don't have the property editor, we can set properties on the Windows Forms controls directly in XAML. For example, we don't want the long date/time format for the control; we want the short date format.

```
<WindowsFormsHost Margin="85,65,150,0" Height="23"
                                        VerticalAlignment="Top" >
  <wf:DateTimePicker x:Name="birthday" Format="Short"/>
</WindowsFormsHost>
```

We're setting the `Format` to `DateTimePickerFormat.Short`. The enum conversion is automatically handled for us. We can also reference our control in code as we would in Windows Forms. For example, if we add a button to our form and then put in a `Click` handler, we can do this in the code (listing 20.1).

Listing 20.1 Referencing WPF and Windows Forms together

```
private void button1_Click(object sender, RoutedEventArgs e)
{
  string name = textBox1.Text;
  DateTime born = birthday.Value;

  MessageBox.Show(name + " was born on " + born.ToLongDateString());
}
```

Note how we're getting the name from the WPF text box and the birthday from the Windows Forms `DateTimePicker` with no special handling. It makes sense that we can

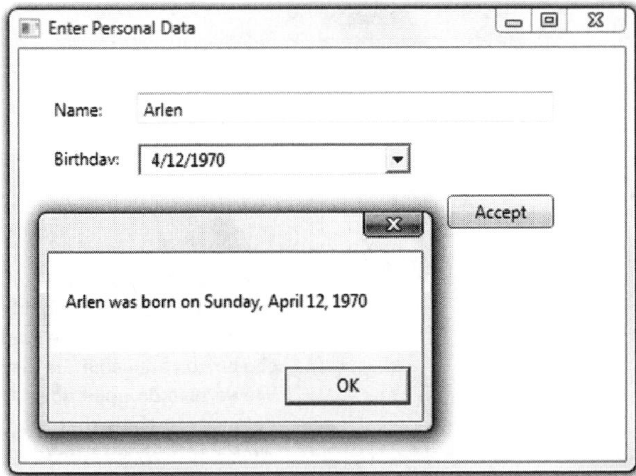

Figure 20.4 Running with an embedded Windows Forms control. Notice that the `DateTimePicker` is using the classic Windows style, rather than the Vista style used by the `TextBox`.

do this because they're both .NET controls. If you want to do data binding, you have to use Windows Forms binding for the `DateTimePicker` and WPF binding for the `TextBox`, but you can still bind them to the same source. Figure 20.4 shows the application running, along with the message displayed after hitting the Accept button.

There's one issue with what we've done that you may have noticed. The Birthday control doesn't look right—it's using the classic Windows look-and-feel, rather than picking up the XP or Vista style. In the next section, we'll rectify that.

20.1.2 Enabling Windows themes for Windows Forms control

The reason that the Windows Forms controls aren't properly themed for the operating system is that we haven't enabled theming. This is something done automatically when you create a Windows Forms application, but WPF applications don't bother because they don't use the operating system theme mechanism at all. But, to enable the theme is pretty easy. We want to enable visual styles at startup, so we add a handler to the `Startup` event in the application.

```
<Application x:Class="Interop3.App"
  xmlns="http://schemas.microsoft.com/winfx/2006/xaml/presentation"
  xmlns:x="http://schemas.microsoft.com/winfx/2006/xaml"
  StartupUri="Window1.xaml" Startup="Application_Startup">
```

And we need to add one line of code to the `Startup` handler.

```
private void Application_Startup(object sender, StartupEventArgs e)
{
  System.Windows.Forms.Application.EnableVisualStyles();
}
```

If you look inside a Windows Forms application, you'll see this same line of code. Now, if we run the application, it will look more like figure 20.5.

Much better. Note that, if we had applied some sort of clever WPF style, the `DateTimePicker` would absolutely *not* use it—Windows Forms controls know nothing about WPF styles.

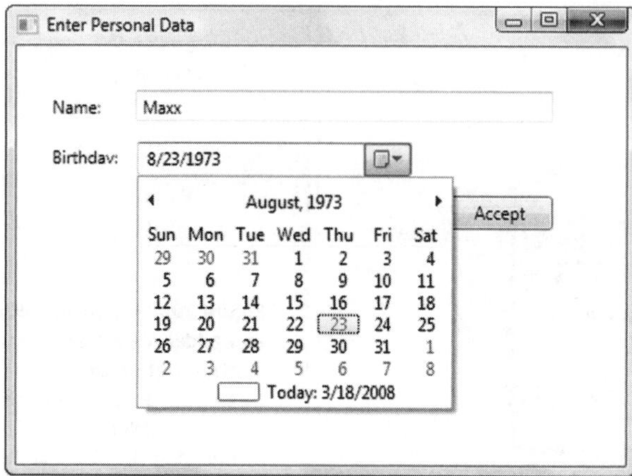

Figure 20.5 Now that `VisualStyles` are enabled, notice the border of the control and the button are using the Vista style. We've also dropped down the calendar to show that the control works entirely as expected.

20.1.3 *What you can't do with embedded Windows Forms controls*

As well as not being able to style controls, there are a few other things that you *cannot* do with embedded controls. For example, *most* transforms won't work. You can't rotate or scale the controls using WPF transforms. Likewise, if you put a Windows Form control into a `ViewBox`, it won't automatically expand—which makes sense, given that the `ViewBox` uses transforms to accomplish what it does.

On the other hand, translate transforms, which move the container *will* work. The control will also play fairly well with layout. In fact, if you resize the Personal Data dialog, you'll see that the Birthday control automatically resizes, even though we haven't explicitly set docking options on the control, because the `WindowsFormsHost` automatically translates that behavior for us.

You do need to be careful about overlapping hosted controls and WPF controls. Windows Forms controls all have an HWND—a handle to a Window. Individual WPF controls don't. From a practical perspective, this means that Windows Forms controls will *always* be on top of WPF controls, no matter how you lay them out.

Also, Windows Forms uses completely different libraries for things like colors and alignment, and you can't mix and match them with WPF's libraries. For example, suppose you want to set one of the color properties on the `DateTimePicker`. You *cannot* do this:

```
birthday.CalendarTitleBackColor = Colors.Blue;
```

`Colors.Blue` is really a `System.Windows.Media.Color` value, whereas the `DateTimePicker` is expecting a `System.Drawing.Color` value. You'd either have to add a reference to `System.Drawing` to your project and do this:

```
birthday.CalendarTitleBackColor = System.Drawing.Color.Blue;
```

Or, if you want to convert an existing color, you'd have to do something like this:

```
Color myColor = Colors.Blue;
birthday.CalendarTitleBackColor =
      System.Drawing.Color.FromArgb(myColor.R, myColor.G, myColor.B);
```

Other things are more of a pain to convert.

> **Fonts and pixels in WPF and Windows Forms**
>
> One thing that might get you in trouble is that WPF and Windows Forms have a different approach for pixels. In Windows Forms, Pixels are device-dependent; in WPF, a Pixel always takes up 1/96th of an inch. This isn't normally a problem; but, if it is, you'll have to do the conversion yourself.
>
> Also, fonts in WPF are based on the 1/96th value, whereas Windows Forms' fonts are based on a 1/72nd value. Fortunately, 72 is precisely 3/4ths of 96, so you can easily convert back and forth by multiplying or dividing by 0.75.

In general, most Windows Forms functionality works fairly well in the host control. Microsoft has done a nice job with this one. Your users can tab between WPF and Windows Forms and back again without knowing that they're doing it. But, embedding Windows Forms (or anything) in WPF does come at a cost—as well as losing some capabilities, there's a performance impact, which can be significant. It's obviously better to stick to a single technology if you can.

20.1.4 *Using your own Windows Forms controls*

In our example, we used one of Microsoft's Windows Forms controls that, all things being equal, we'd expect to work. Using your own (or third-party) Windows Forms controls is just as easy. All you have to do is reference the appropriate assembly, add the namespace, and use the control. For example, we've gone ahead and created an assembly with a (very ugly) Windows Forms user control (figure 20.6).

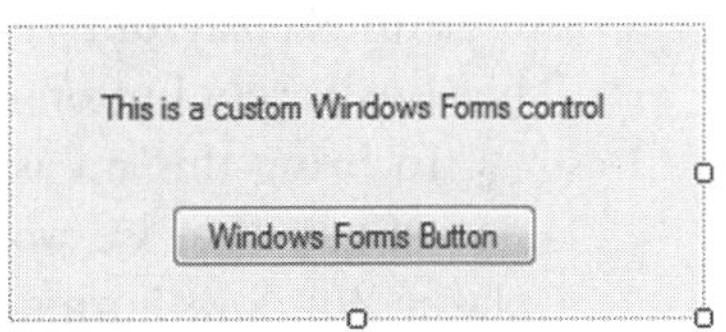

Figure 20.6 This is a classic Windows Forms user control. Obviously, in real life, you'd have some more useful functionality—at least, we hope you would. The control is called `MyWindowsFormsControl` and is in an assembly called `MyWindowsFormsLibrary`.

Now, all you have to do is add a reference to the assembly under References, and add the appropriate namespace in the `Windows` tag:

```
xmlns:mwfl=
    "clr-namespace:MyWindowsFormsLibrary;assembly=MyWindowsFormsLibrary"
```

Then, drag another `WindowsFormsHost` onto the dialog and set its content appropriately.

```
<WindowsFormsHost Height="99" Margin="34,0,99,27"
   VerticalAlignment="Bottom">
  <mwfl:MyWindowsFormsControl />
</WindowsFormsHost>
```

And, voilà, you've embedded a custom user control (figure 20.7).

The `WindowsFormsHost` has even automatically set the background properly.

Figure 20.7 A custom, embedded Windows Forms control

20.1.5 *Popping up Windows Forms dialogs*

Another scenario for using existing Windows Forms functionality is one where you have an entire dialog already set up, and you want to use it in its entirety. As an example, we'll create a Windows Forms `Form` to display our results when the user hits the Accept button (figure 20.8).

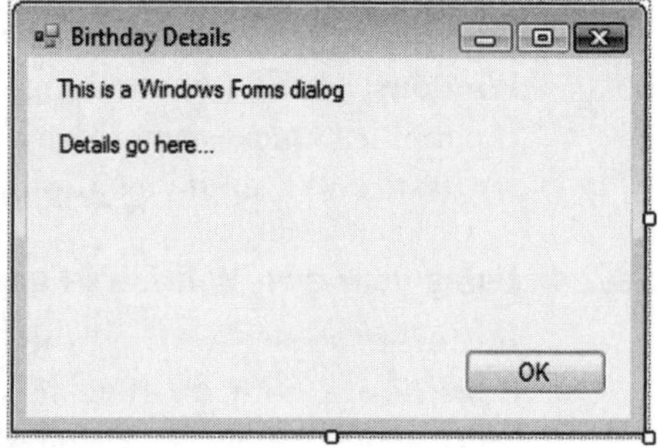

Figure 20.8 An ugly but serviceable Windows Forms dialog

To bring this up as a modal dialog, we do exactly what we would have done in a classic Windows Forms application.

```
private void button1_Click(object sender, RoutedEventArgs e)
{
  string name = textBox1.Text;
  DateTime born = birthday.Value;

  MyWindowsFormsLibrary.BirthdayDetails dlg
            = new MyWindowsFormsLibrary.BirthdayDetails();
  dlg.SetDetails(name + " was born on " + born.ToLongDateString());

  dlg.ShowDialog();
}
```

We've added a method to our dialog called `SetDetails()` to populate the details text. The big thing is that we call `ShowDialog()` and the dialog pops up. It will even automatically stay on top of our main window until we dismiss it. We can also make the dialog modeless by calling `Show()` instead of `ShowDialog()`.

```
dlg.Show();
```

This is more impressive than it sounds. Windows Forms controls need a message pump to make modeless forms works, but this is all taken care of for us. But, there is

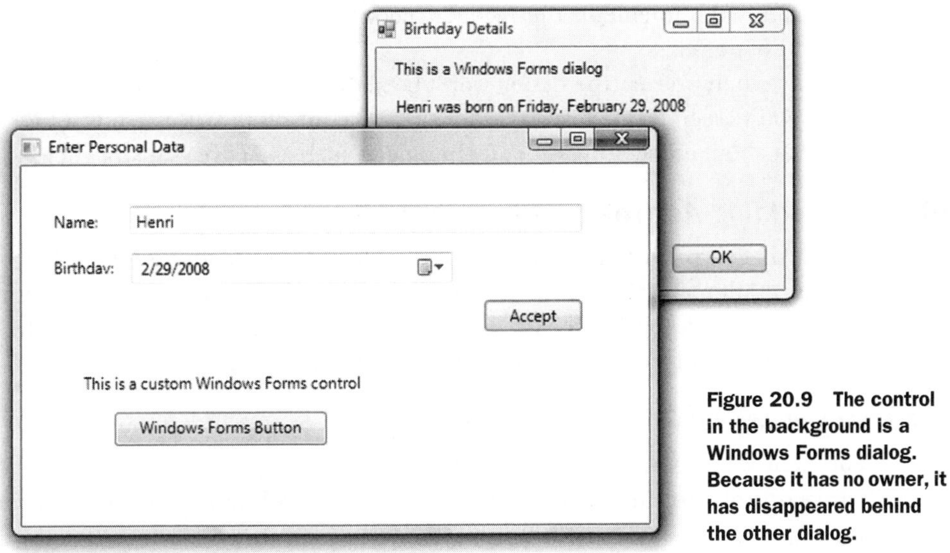

Figure 20.9 The control in the background is a Windows Forms dialog. Because it has no owner, it has disappeared behind the other dialog.

one issue. If we bring up the pop-up dialog and then click back on the main dialog, something like figure 20.9 happens.

As you can see, the Windows Forms control has slipped behind the WPF window. This may be what you want; but, if you want it to always be on top, you have to set the owner of the Windows Forms control. This is tricky because the expected owner is an `IWin32Window`, and we don't have one of those. Fortunately, WPF provides a helper class that will help us solve this problem. Listing 20.2 shows how.

Listing 20.2 Getting parent window from WPF

```
using System.Windows.Interop;      <-- Goes at top of the file

WindowInteropHelper helper = new WindowInteropHelper(this);     <-- ❶ Helper class

System.Windows.Forms.NativeWindow nw =
                    new System.Windows.Forms.NativeWindow();    <-- ❷ Control we can pass
nw.AssignHandle(helper.Handle);

dlg.Show(nw);
```

WPF provides a handy class called the `WindowInteropHelper` ❶ for just this situation. You may remember when we mentioned, about 18 chapters ago, that WPF code does still have *one* HWND running around for each window.[2] The `WindowInteropHelper` lets us get at it via the `Handle` method.

Next we put the handle into a Windows Forms class called `NativeWindow` ❷. The purpose of `NativeWindow` is to provide a simple wrapper for a low-level handle. Most

[2] We're surprised that *we* even remember!

importantly, it implements the `IWin32Window` interface, so we can pass it to the `Show()` method of our class.

Now, when we run, the dialog won't be allowed to go behind our main form.

As you've seen, embedding Windows Forms controls in WPF is pretty straightforward, but what about embedding other technologies such as ActiveX or straight C++ code?

20.2 Embedding ActiveX and C++ in WPF

It isn't that surprising that embedding Windows Forms code in WPF is fairly straightforward. After all, they're both .NET technologies using the .NET runtime. Even though it's a *little* bit harder to embed things like ActiveX (or even straight C++ controls), it isn't *that* much harder—at least for simple cases.

20.2.1 Embedding ActiveX controls in WPF

For many years, ActiveX was the primary technology for interoperability and for third-party controls. For this reason, a *lot* of ActiveX controls are still running around, causing havoc, and people are still using them. WPF doesn't have any direct support for using ActiveX controls. But, Windows Forms *does*; and, as you've just seen, WPF can use Windows Forms relatively easily.

We think you know where this is going…

Yes, we first create a Windows Forms control that contains our ActiveX control. Then we embed the Windows Forms control into our WPF code using the `WindowsFormsHost`. To add an ActiveX to a Windows Forms control is pretty easy with Visual Studio. First, create a new `UserControl` called `SystemMonitorHolder`. Why? Because the ActiveX control we're going to embed is the `SystemMonitor` control, which should already be available on your system.

Next, right-click the Toolbox, and select Choose Items… The dialog takes a while to come up. When it does, switch to the COM Components tab (figure 20.10).

Scroll down in the list until you find the System Monitor Control, check it, and then click OK. Again, it will take a little while, but then System Monitor Control will show up in the Toolbox. Now you can drag it on to the user control you just created (figure 20.11).

We've made the user control a little bit bigger to accommodate the ActiveX control. We've also set the `Dock` property of the control to `Fill` so that it takes up the entire user control. When we put the control into the WPF window, the user control will automatically be sized based on layout, but that won't do us any good if the control *on* the user control isn't set to size with it.

We're halfway there. Now you have to put the control onto the WPF dialog. Again, you drag a `WindowsFormsHost` onto the window, position it appropriately, and then manually set its content in XAML.

```
<WindowsFormsHost Margin="20,130,9,8" Name="windowsFormsHost2">
  <mwfl:SystemMonitorHolder />
</WindowsFormsHost>
```

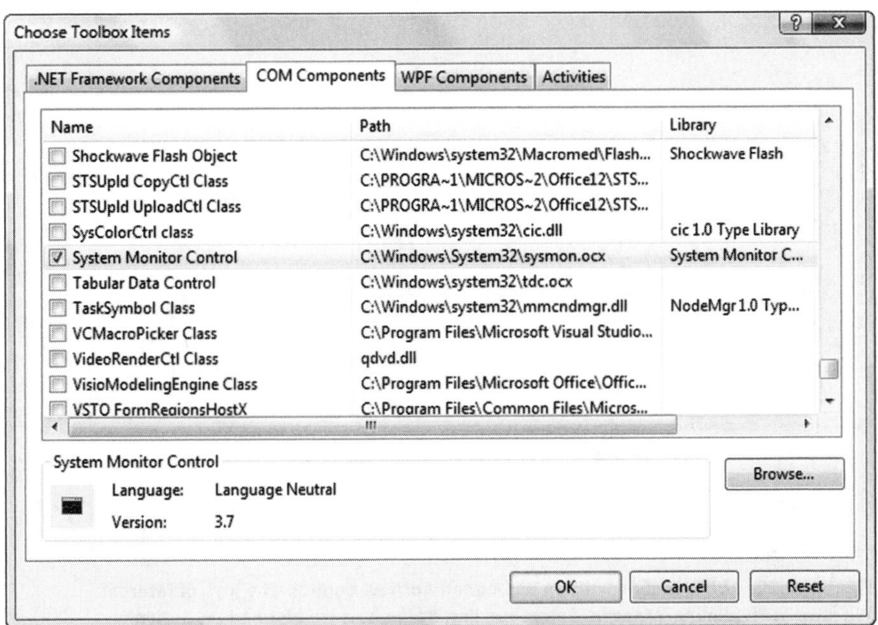

Figure 20.10 Adding the System Monitor Control to the Toolbox. Once you check the item and say OK, Visual Studio will do all the appropriate wrapping for you.

That's it. Now, if you run, you should get something like figure 20.12.

You'll still have to set the properties on your ActiveX control appropriately to be useful, but still, it's pretty nifty. Also, all the Windows Forms caveats still apply, plus any additional limitations related to COM usage. Still, if you're stuck with having to use an ActiveX control, it isn't all that hard.

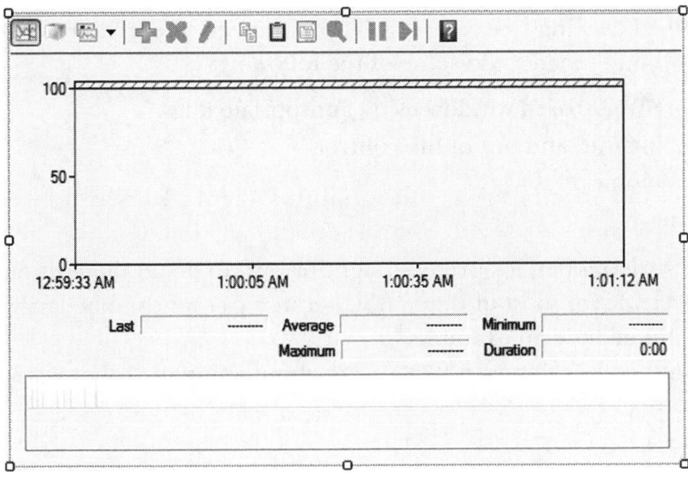

Figure 20.11 The System Monitor ActiveX control on a Windows Forms `UserControl`. Don't forget to set the `Dock` to fill.

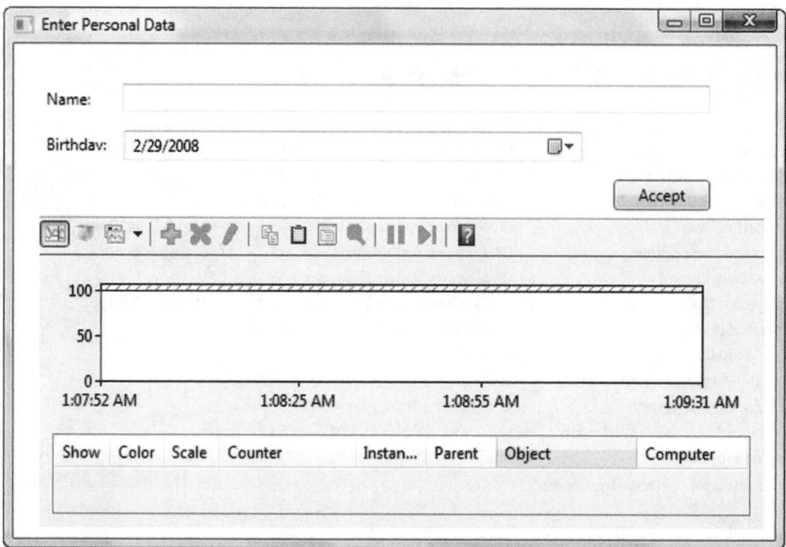

Figure 20.12 WPF window with an embedded ActiveX control. The joys of interop: We have WPF running Windows Forms running ActiveX. If we just had an ActiveX control that was an Apple *IIe* emulator, we'd be over the moon.

20.2.2 Embedding C++ controls in WPF

The last thing we want to talk about is using legacy C++ controls from within WPF. We're only going to talk about the approach, rather than demonstrate it, because we think it's an edge-case; but, at least, this section should point you in the proper direction.

WPF has a class called `HwndHost` whose purpose is to allow WPF to host anything represented by a HWND. `WindowsFormsHost` is derived from `HwndHost`, and adds a bunch of additional functionality to make Windows Forms controls play nicely in WPF. If you want to embed existing C++ code into WPF, you need to derive from `HwndHost`. In your derivation, you'll need to do some of the following:

- Create your HWND-based window using appropriate flags.
- Handle tabbing into and out of the control.
- Handle mnemonics.
- Handle sizing.

For the average C++ developer, it's pretty straightforward to do all these things. There are methods to override for most of them. But, because C++ tends to be fairly verbose, we've decided to not include an example.

So much for using other things in WPF—what about going the other way?

20.3 Using WPF in Windows Forms

Let's face it—unless you're writing something from scratch, it's pretty hard to justify completely rebuilding your UI in WPF. There are some things that are so much easier/better/prettier in WPF, that it would be nice if you could use it for just those things.

Fortunately, providing that you're using Windows Forms, it's just as easy to use WPF in Windows Forms as it is the other way around.

20.3.1 Using a WPF control inside of Windows Forms

Rather than putting together some ugly set of WPF controls, we thought we might as well use something we've already created, so we've taken the calculator application from earlier and converted the calculator to be a WPF User Control. To do this, we first create a WPF User Control Library, and then copy over the Window1 class from the calculator application, and add it. Then we rename Window1 to CalculatorControl and change it from a `Window` to a `UserControl`, and update the namespaces, and so on. We aren't going to show every single change because it would just fill up pages. But here's an example of the types of changes to make.

This XAML:

```
<Window x:Class="Calculator.Window1"
    xmlns="http://schemas.microsoft.com/winfx/2006/xaml/presentation"
    xmlns:x="http://schemas.microsoft.com/winfx/2006/xaml"
    xmlns:calc="clr-namespace:Calculator;assembly="
    Title="Calculator" Height="300" Width="300" Background="Transparent"
    Loaded="OnLoaded">
  <Window.Resources>
  ...
```

becomes

```
<UserControl x:Class="MyWPFControlLibrary.CalculatorControl"
    xmlns="http://schemas.microsoft.com/winfx/2006/xaml/presentation"
    xmlns:x="http://schemas.microsoft.com/winfx/2006/xaml"
    xmlns:calc="clr-namespace:MyWPFControlLibrary"
    Height="300" Width="300" Background="Transparent"
    Loaded="OnLoaded">
  <UserControl.Resources>
  ...
```

Notice that

- `Window` has been replaced with `UserControl` in several places.
- `x:Class` has a different namespace and class name.
- The `calc` namespace has been changed to `MyWPFControlLibrary`.
- The `Title` attribute has been removed because `UserControls` don't have titles.

We also have to update the code in similar ways. For example:

```
namespace Calculator
{
  ...
```

```
public partial class Window1 : System.Windows.Window
{
  ...
  public Window1()
  {
  ...
```

becomes

```
namespace MyWPFControlLibrary
{
    ...
    public partial class CalculatorControl : UserControl
    {
      ...
        public CalculatorControl()
        {
        ...
```

Anyway, you should get the idea. If you can't be bothered to do this yourself, you can always download it from our site or create some ugly set of WPF controls as a `UserControl` for experimental purposes. The important thing is to create the WPF User Control Library with a control in it.

The next step is to create a Windows Forms Application. Once you've done this, you need to add a few references (sound familiar?). The first is to the same `WindowsFormsIntegration` assembly we referenced earlier. The second is to the WPF User Control Library we just created. Assuming you've built the assembly, you can right-click References and then browse for it (figure 20.13). Note that you might also have to add references to `PresentationCore`, `PresentationFramework`, and `WindowsBase`.

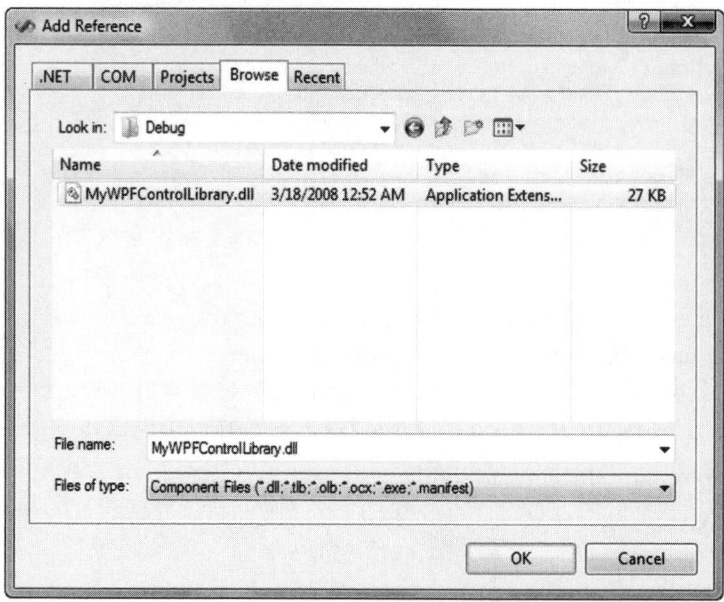

Figure 20.13 Adding a reference to the WPF User Control Library we just created. Because WPF is still .NET, you could also add the library project to your Windows Forms solution and then do a Project reference.

When you created the Windows Forms application, it automatically created a form for you with the clever name of Form1. Go ahead and bring up the editor for the form, and make it a little bigger. Then, from the Toolbox, open the section titled WPF Interoperability (figure 20.14), and drag an `ElementHost` onto the Form.

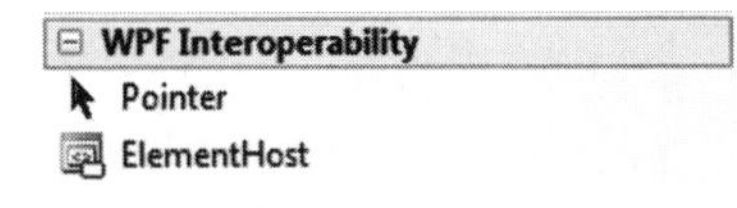

Figure 20.14 When working with Windows Forms, there's now a section on the Toolbox called WPF Interoperability that gives access to the `ElementHost` control.

`ElementHost` is the opposite of `WindowsFormsHost`; it allows WPF elements to be hosted. You can set the host's properties in the same way as any other Windows Form control, such as making it dock, and so on. You can also set the element that it hosts by clicking the little arrow that appears at the upper-right corner of the `ElementHost` (figure 20.15). Notice that the list includes all the user controls in our control library. If you select `CalculatorControl`, it will automatically appear in the `ElementHost`. Now, if you run the Windows Forms application, the calculator will not only be visible, but all its WPF behavior will be intact (figure 20.16).

In some ways, it's even easier to embed WPF inside Windows Forms. The ability to do this is pretty compelling, although, as with going the other way, there are performance issues—and you don't necessarily want to cover a Windows Forms control with a dozen WPF elements.

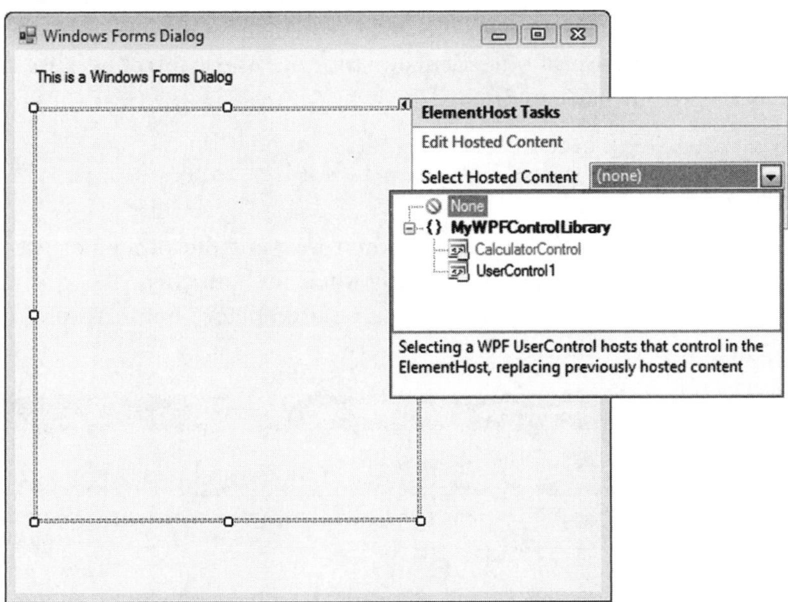

Figure 20.15 The little arrow at the upper-right corner of the `ElementHost` provides a way of selecting the appropriate WPF element to display. The drop-down menu shows all the available elements from referenced WPF assemblies.

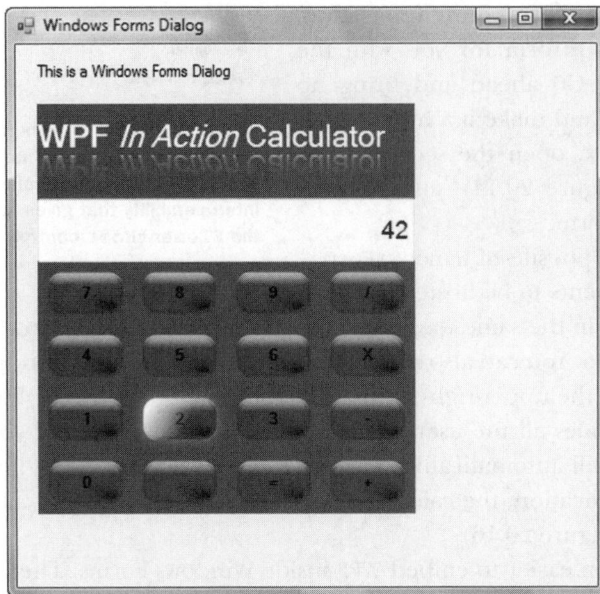

Figure 20.16 The WPF Calculator is now embedded inside a Windows Forms dialog. Everything (including styles and animations) works exactly as it would in a native WPF app.

20.3.2 Popping up WPF dialogs

Just as we can launch Windows Forms dialogs from WPF code, we can launch WPF dialogs from Windows Forms. In fact, the code is virtually the same. For example, to launch the window version of our calculator (not the user control because that can't stand by itself), we only have to do this:

```
MyWPFControlLibrary.CalculatorWindow calc =
                          new MyWPFControlLibrary.CalculatorWindow();
calc.ShowDialog();
```

And this works as expected. But, just as when we went the other way, we do have potential issues with ownership, particularly when the launched dialog is modeless. Fortunately, the same `WindowInteropHelper` we used before helps us solve the problem going the other way (listing 20.3).

Listing 20.3 Setting ownership on a WPF window

```
MyWPFControlLibrary.CalculatorWindow calc =
                          new MyWPFControlLibrary.CalculatorWindow();
WindowInteropHelper helper = new WindowInteropHelper(calc);    ❶
helper.Owner = this.Handle;    ❷
calc.Show();
```

We create the helper, passing the WPF window to it ❶. Note that you'll need a `using System.Windows.Interop` statement in your code somewhere for this to work. Then we set the handle of our class as the owner of the helper ❷ that will become the owner of the window when it appears. Note that the *this* in this case is the Windows Forms Dialog launching the dialog.

All in all, not too difficult. That's all there is to using WPF with Windows Forms. We expect to see a lot of Windows Forms application start sprouting some pretty slick embedded controls in the very near future.

20.4 Summary

Both of us are professional developers and architects, so we spend much of our time justifying our decisions to other people and/or to ourselves. Convincing the powers that be that a new platform should be considered when you have perfectly operational code working in the old stuff isn't an easy sell.

There are times, though, when you know that something you *really* need to do would take two days in the new technology versus five weeks in the old. But, moving your entire legacy app to the new technology might take you two years, so it isn't entirely a good trade-off.

The interop capabilities of WPF and Windows Forms can help out in this situation. You can leave your existing application alone, except for the one bit that needs to be in WPF, or you can build your new UI in WPF, but call into your legacy code for everything you don't have time to replace. It's entirely likely that this capability will be what makes WPF take off in a year or two, instead of in five years.

Our next topic, threading, is something relevant for Windows Forms applications, as well as for WPF applications, but WPF has added a number of useful capabilities for making threading easier.

21 Threading

This chapter covers:

- The Dispatcher
- Asynchronous calls
- Timers
- Making our CIA application more insulting

In Windows Forms, the cardinal rule for threading was that *all* UI operations had to take place on the same thread—or, at least, on the thread that created the window with which you were working. Although the mechanics are a little bit different, the same exact rule applies to WPF.

WPF has two UI threads: the main UI thread and a rendering thread, which does the real rendering, animation, and so on. But, you can almost never interact with the rendering thread; for practical purposes, you can ignore it. In threading situations, you have to make sure that all your UI calls take place on the main UI thread.

There are a several reasons why you might want to use threads within your application. The biggies are:

- *Responsiveness*—So that your application doesn't appear to lock up while operations take place

- *Handling slow operations*—So that users can work on other things while slow ops, such as queries, take place

While discussing threading in general, we'll also demonstrate how to make asynchronous calls with WPF and to use the new `DispatchTimer` mechanism.

For this chapter, we're going to return to the CIA World Browser application. This is a good candidate for threading because, when the application does a query against a DICT server, it can take several seconds, making the application appear non-responsive. If something goes wrong, then it can take even longer. It's conceivable that a lookup could take a much longer time (which we may fake a bit), in which case we want to let the user do other things. To demonstrate the responsiveness issue, we've added a `Thread.Sleep` call inside the `DictionaryLookup` in `WorldBrowser` and then performed a lookup. Figure 21.1 shows the result.

Notice how the application is completely failing to refresh the screen. The main UI, which is responsible for making that happen, is busy doing our query. Fortunately, it isn't hard to move the code to do the lookup into another thread.

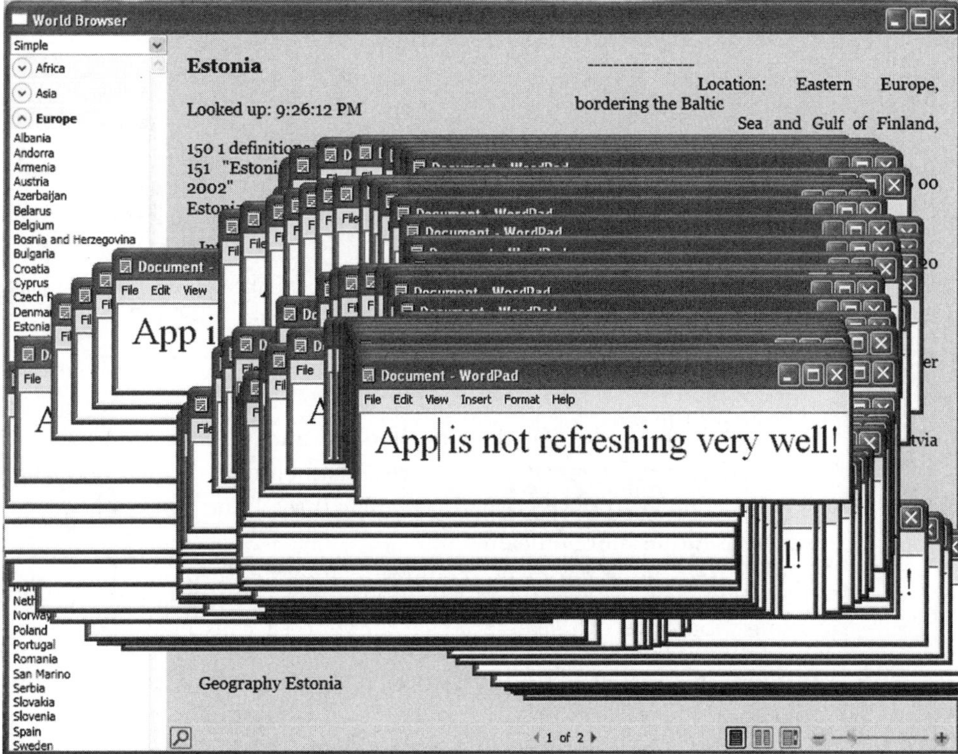

Figure 21.1 While the lookup is going on, the application is completely non-responsive. Note that this is an XP screenshot. Vista handles this a little bit better by putting up a picture of your original application; but, rest assured, your application isn't really responding.

21.1 Moving slow work into a background thread

You may remember from the `WorldBrowser` application that we did the query in the `lb_MouseDoubleClick` method. Anyway, the method in the `WorldListView` class in `WorldBrowser` got the name of the country, looked it up, loaded the document, and then caused the transition animation to get executed—all in a very non-thready way.

If we didn't have to worry about UI code running on the same thread, then we could rewrite the code like listing 21.1 to make it do the work in a thread.

Listing 21.1 First attempt at background lookup

```
using System.Threading;                          // Goes at top of file
using System.Windows.Threading;

private void lb_MouseDoubleClick(object sender, MouseButtonEventArgs e)
{
     ListBox lb = sender as ListBox;
  if (lb.SelectedItem != null)
  {
    string country = lb.SelectedItem.ToString();
    ThreadPool.QueueUserWorkItem(
          new WaitCallback(LookupThreadMethod), country);   // 1 Launches thread
  }
}

protected void LookupThreadMethod(object state)
{
  string country = state.ToString();                          // 2
  FlowDocument doc = App.Current.Lookup.DefineWord(country);  // 3 Does slow work

  FlowDocumentReader reader =
      Switcher.UnselectedElement as FlowDocumentReader;       // 4 Blows up!
  doc.Background = reader.Background;
  reader.Document = doc;
  Switcher.Switch();
}
```

We've taken all the code that does the lookup and UI work and moved it into a method called `LookupThreadMethod()`. We're launching that method using a thread pool ❶. We could also have created a regular thread and done a `Start()`, but the thread pool is rather more efficient.

We've passed the name of the country to the `Thread` method as a state object, which we convert back to a string in the method ❷. Then we do our slow lookup ❸. So far, so good. The application is completely responsive while this is going on—we can move it, resize it, drag things over it to cause repaints, and so on, all with no problems.

No problem, at least, until we try to do something with our result. As soon as we try to get the value from the `UnselectedElement` property ❹, the system throws an `InvalidOperationException` with the descriptive text "The calling thread cannot access this object because a different thread owns it." Although we expected this, it still makes us sad.

In fact, WPF is more stringent than Windows Forms. With Windows Forms, you could usually *get* a value from a property in another thread, although it wasn't recommended. WPF won't even let us do that. We need to make the update take place back on the main UI thread. We can do that using a WPF class called the `Dispatcher` (listing 21.2).

Listing 21.2 Second attempt at background lookup

```
protected void LookupThreadMethod(object state)
{
  string country = state.ToString();
  FlowDocument doc = App.Current.Lookup.DefineWord(country);

  Dispatcher.Invoke(DispatcherPriority.Normal,
               new WaitCallback(FinishLookup), doc);   <- ❶ Invokes method on main UI thread
}

protected void FinishLookup(object state)   ❷
{
  FlowDocument doc = state as FlowDocument;   ❸

  FlowDocumentReader reader =
      Switcher.UnselectedElement as FlowDocumentReader;
  doc.Background = reader.Background;   <- ❹ Blows up!
  reader.Document = doc;
  Switcher.Switch();
}
```

We've have added yet another method, `FinishLookup` ❷, which is designed to be run on the main UI thread. To call this method on the right thread, we have to *Invoke* it. If you did threading in Windows Forms, you may remember the `Invoke()` method that existed on controls. This method forced a call to the control on the thread that created that control.

The problem with the `Invoke` mechanism in Windows Forms was that it was somewhat limited. For example, you could only `Invoke` methods on `Controls`. This may not sound like much of a limitation, but it caused some difficulties—it was not uncommon to have to create an invisible control for no other purpose than for getting a message on the proper thread. WPF, in contrast, allows you to `Invoke` a method on any class derived from `DispatcherObject`. `DispatcherObject` is close to the top of the derivation chain for WPF—several levels even above `Visual`—and it's relatively lightweight, so you can derive from it without too much overhead.

To invoke a method on a `DispatcherObject`, we don't call a method directly. Instead, we use the `Dispatcher` class ❶. It has a number of overloads that support different arguments, but they all come down to forcing a call to be made on the appropriate thread. Notice that we're setting a priority on the `Invoke` call. A nice feature of the `Dispatcher` is that we can specify the importance of the invoke, and have it be high priority, or only get called when the UI thread is idle, or one of a number of other settings.

The `Invoke` method takes a delegate. We're using the `WaitCallback` delegate for no other reason than that it takes a single argument, but we could use any existing or custom delegate that we wanted to here. The argument that we're passing is the FlowDocument returned from the DictionaryLookup class.

So far, so good. When the lookup is complete, the Invoke will cause the FinishLookup method to get called, which will get the document out of the passed argument ❸, and then do the update stuff—except that, as soon as we try to do something with the passed document ❹, we get another exception!

What's wrong this time? Well, we created the FlowDocument on our background thread, and now we're trying to change it on the main thread. That's as forbidden as going the other way!

This is a good reminder about how much thought needs to go into adding threading to an application. The *proper* fix would be to change our DictionaryLookup class to return some sort of structure that holds the data, and then to build our FlowDocument on the main thread. But, a quicker (albeit uglier) fix is to convert the FlowDocument into a string, pass the string to the main thread, and then turn it back into a FlowDocument. If nothing else, this demonstrates the rather cool ability to go back and forth to XAML (listing 21.3).

Listing 21.3 Final attempt at background lookup

```
using System.Windows.Markup;     ❶ Goes at top of file
using System.IO;
using System.Xml;

protected void LookupThreadMethod(object state)     ❷ Converts FlowDocument to XAML
{
  string country = state.ToString();
  FlowDocument doc = App.Current.Lookup.DefineWord(country);

  string str = XamlWriter.Save(doc);
  Dispatcher.Invoke(DispatcherPriority.Normal,
                    new WaitCallback(FinishLookup), str);
}

protected void FinishLookup(object state)
{
  string xamlDoc = state.ToString();   ❸

  StringReader stringReader = new StringReader(xamlDoc);     ❹ Converts XAML back to FlowDocument
  XmlReader xmlReader = XmlReader.Create(stringReader);
  FlowDocument doc = (FlowDocument)XamlReader.Load(xmlReader);

  FlowDocumentReader reader =
      Switcher.UnselectedElement as FlowDocumentReader;
  doc.Background = reader.Background;
  reader.Document = doc;
  Switcher.Switch();
}
```

We need to add several using statements to our file ❶ to be able to do the conversion. Converting the FlowDocument to a XAML string is easy. We pass it to the static Save() method on the XamlWriter class ❷. Then we pass it via the dispatcher and get the XAML string back on the other end ❸.

Getting a `FlowDocument` from the passed XAML is a little more work ❹ because we have to get an `XmlReader` to pass to the `XamlReader`'s `Load` method, but this isn't too bad either. One warning, though: There are limitations as to what the `XamlWriter` and `XamlReader` classes can do. This technique works for a simple control; but, when you start getting control templates with animations, and so on, you'll quickly exceed the serialization capabilities of the classes.

Anyway, now that we've made these changes, everything finally works the way we want. The UI is responsive during the lookup, but the lookup happens, and the documents are updated. We've written the code so that the thread calls back to the UI thread *synchronously*, meaning that the thread will wait until the UI thread is ready to do the work and then will wait while the work happens before it goes on. Because our thread is going to go away when the call is complete, this doesn't really matter, but there are times when you don't want to wait for the target operation to complete.

21.2 Asynchronous calls

When we used the `Dispath.Invoke` method earlier, it was a synchronous call—the code in our thread will sit and wait until the method we invoked is done processing. This is often quite desirable, particularly if you want to get a return result from the method. But, sometimes you just want to tell the UI something and then let the thread get on doing what it was doing. For this scenario, the `Dispatcher` has the ability to do an asynchronous invoke. For example, we could make our `Invoke` from listing 21.3 be asynchronous.

```
DispatcherOperation op =
   Dispatcher.BeginInvoke(DispatcherPriority.Normal,
                         new WaitCallback(FinishLookup), str);
```

Unlike `Invoke`, `BeginInvoke` will return immediately. So, any code after the `BeginInvoke` will start to be executed, but you can check up on how the method is doing via the `DispatcherOperation` object that `BeginInvoke` returns. For example, you can check the value of the `Status` property to see how things are going. Status will return one of three values (table 21.1).

Table 21.1 Possible values of `DispatcherOperation.Status`

Value	Meaning
`Pending`	The method hasn't yet been invoked.
`Executing`	The method is in the process of being executed.
`Completed`	The method has completed running.

Once the operation has completed, you can get the value that the `delegate` method returned via the `Result` property. You can also subscribe to events on the `Dispatcher` so that you get notified when the operation has been completed (or has been aborted).

If you've used the old WinForms Invoke mechanism, you'll see how much more thought-out and robust the WPF mechanism is.

Whether you're working synchronously or asynchronously, the code execution is (relatively) linear—you launch a thread, it does stuff, and then it calls back to the original thread. Sometimes, though, you want things to happen at certain intervals; this is where timers come in.

21.3 Timers

Another scenario that often comes up when discussing threading is using timers to make something happen after X amount of time. Now, in .NET and Windows Forms, there are about a billion different timer classes (OK, three). The timer often used within WinForms controls doesn't use threads at all, but passes messages; it's *very* inaccurate.

WPF has its own, very clean timer model. It uses threads, but takes advantage of the Dispatcher framework, so you know that your code will be called on the proper thread. To demonstrate using the timer, we'll add some code to our class to automatically clear the displayed document after 30 seconds—the data is, after all, from the CIA. Listing 21.4 shows how to set up the timer.

Listing 21.4 Setting up a DispatcherTimer

```
private DispatcherTimer clearTimer = null;    <-- Our Timer object

private void UserControl_Loaded(object sender, RoutedEventArgs e)
{
  LoadContinents();

  clearTimer = new DispatcherTimer(DispatcherPriority.Normal);    ❶
  clearTimer.Interval = new TimeSpan(0, 0, 30);
  clearTimer.Tick += new EventHandler(clearTimer_Tick);

  clearTimer.Start();    <-- ❷ Starting the timer going
}
```

Using a DispatcherTimer is ridiculously easy. By the way, the class is in the System.Windows.Threading namespace. There should already be a using statement in place from the previous example; but, if not, you'll need to add one. We create an instance of DispatcherTimer ❶. We're setting the priority to Normal—we don't need to do this because it's the default, but it shows that the timer class is using the Dispatcher behind the scenes.

We set the interval for the timer (in this case, 30 seconds), provide an event handler to call when the timer should fire, and then kick the timer off ❷. Listing 21.5 shows our event handler.

Listing 21.5 Tick event handler

```
void clearTimer_Tick(object sender, EventArgs e)
{
  FlowDocument doc = new FlowDocument();    <-- ❶ Creates document
  Paragraph para1 = new Paragraph();
```

```
    para1.FontSize = 18;
    para1.Inlines.Add(new Bold(
      new Run("You are not authorized to view this data. Get out.")));
    doc.Blocks.Add(para1);
                                                  ❷ Sets document
    FlowDocumentReader reader =                 <┘
          Switcher.UnselectedElement as FlowDocumentReader;
    doc.Background = reader.Background;
    reader.Document = doc;
    Switcher.Switch();
}
```

All this code does is create a new `FlowDocument` saying that the data is being hidden ❶ and then sets it the same way we would have set it if the user had double-clicked an entry in the list ❷. In more polished code, we would've pulled the setting code into its own method, but you get the idea. Figure 21.2 shows the application after 30 seconds.

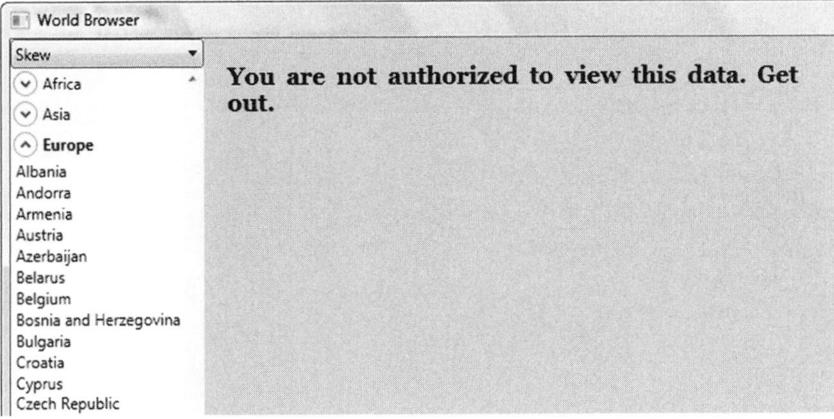

Figure 21.2 After 30 seconds, our timer automatically clears the text displayed by the application.

This is a pretty simple example, but it demonstrates the power of the `DispatcherTimer`. The important thing is that, although the timers use threads to keep time, they invoke your code on the main thread, so you don't have to worry about threading issues when you use them.

21.4 Summary

Obviously, this chapter isn't meant to be an authoritative guide to threading. Threading can be incredibly complex to use correctly, and chances are that two out of every three systems that use threading to any significant degree are doing something that will randomly crash for no obvious reason.

That said, so long as you obey a few simple rules, threading can make your application much more responsive, and WPF has done a good job of making it easy to follow those rules.

Throughout this book, we've tried to give our unvarnished opinion of WPF, even when we know that it will make some of our visits to the Microsoft cafeteria just a tad awkward. It's only fair, then, when something is done really well that we acknowledge it, and we think that the threading support is one of those areas.

Despite some frustrations, overall we really love WPF. We truly believe that, in a year or two, it will be the only serious way to build Windows UI (and possibly UI for other platforms as well). The speed and ease with which you can build spectacular *useful* applications is truly incredible; once the after-market hits its stride with controls, effects, and libraries, it will transform user's expectations and experiences.

index

Numerics

3D 52, 352

A

Accepted property 270
accessibility 50
accordion control 77
ActiveX 10, 390, 458, 466
AddHandler 155
ADO.NET 234
Adobe Flash 43, 391, 403
Adobe Flex 17
Adobe PDF 406
AdornedElementPlaceholder 280
Aero theme 119, 142–143
affordances 140
AJAX 374, 402
AlignmentX 171
almost-standards mode 10
Alpha 450
Ambient light 357
Amiga Datatype system 52
Anchor 96
anchoring 73
Andreessen, Marc 9
animated GIF 165
animation 53, 165–169, 448
App.xaml 392
Apple 12
application 30, 125
  object 431
  services 55
Application tag 31
Application.Current 125, 145, 431
Application.Resources 30
ApplicationCommands 196–197, 200
arcs 321
ArcSegment 348
ARGB Colors 162
Ascender 52
ASP.NET 374, 390
Asynchronous calls 479
ATL 7
attached properties 48, 72–73, 128
audio 52
Aurora 61
automatic properties 276
AutoReverse 168
Avalon 3, 405
AVI 165
Axis rotation 367

B

BackColor 128
background threads 476
backing field 302
BackMaterial 364
bandwidth 402
base services 44, 51
BasedOn 133
BeginInvoke 479
BeginStoryboard 436, 438
BeginTime 452
Berners-Lee, Tim 9
Bézier curves 321
BezierSegment 348
binding 130, 211
  modes 211
  performance 219
  sources 211
Bitmap effects 53
  downside 163
BitmapEffects 163
blink tag 9
Bold 199
Border 311, 417
BorderBrush 121, 126, 129
BorderBrushProperty 129
BorderColor 82
BorderThickness 82
Boulter, Mark 6
BrowseBack 198
BrowseForward 198
browsers 390
Brush 337
brushes 6, 106
bubble up 148
bubble-up events 49–50
bubbling 49
bubbling events 149–151
Business objects 235

C

C APIs 14
C++ 458, 466, 468
Calculate Permissions 394
calculator 101

cameras 358
CancelPrint 197
CanExecute 203
CanExecuteChanged 203
Canvas 67–76, 318
  adding 69
  converting Grid to 69
Cascading Style Sheets 10–11, 131
Center 199
CenterY 172
certificate 397, 400
Certificate Store 398
CertMgr 398
CheckBox 306
Children 66
CIA World Factbook 428
Clark, Jim 9
class events 156
class inheritance 47
classes 6
Click event 26, 113
ClickOnce 34, 55, 390–391, 400
  deploying 401
  publishing 400
  when to use 402
Close 197
CLR. *See* Common Language Runtime
COBOL.NET 439
CollectionListView 272
CollectionView 267
CollectionViewSource 266, 270
Color
  System.Drawing 462
  System.Windows.Media 462
ColorAnimation 166, 169
Column 100
ColumnDefinition 97
ColumnSpan 101
COM Components 466
command binding 195
Command pattern 194
command sources 195
command target 195
CommandBinding 202, 204, 206
CommandManager 208
Commands 154, 191
  built-in 196–200
  custom 201
  disabling 207
  enabling 207
  handling 200
Common Language Runtime 14, 44, 46
Community Technology Preview 60
Component Commands 196, 200
composing 30, 301
composition 148
Composition Engine 53
compostional inheritance 47
conditional templates 273
ConditionalGroupBox 300, 308
conformance 9
content 75, 444
ContentControl 441
ContentPresenter 138, 160, 280, 311
ContentPresenters 137, 444
ContentStringFormat 294
ContextMenu 197
control library 307
Control Templates 159
control templates 119, 136–140
Controller 284
Controls 55
ControlTemplate 307, 443
Convert 222, 259
ConvertBack 222, 259
Copy 197
CorelDRAW 8
CreateXpsDocumentWriter 414, 423
CSS. *See* Cascading Style Sheets
CTP 460
Currency format 256
Current 431
cursor 380
Cursors.Wait 435
Custom Control Library 306
custom controls 299–300, 306
custom validation 282
Cut 197

D

DAL. *See* Data Access Layer
Data Access Layer 236
data binding 56, 209
data converters 254
data templates 253
Data Transfer Object 235
DataContextChanged 249
DataContexts 230
DataSet 211
DataTable 211
DataTemplate 248
DataTemplateSelector 275, 277
DataTriggers 263
DataType 277
DateTime formatting 258
DateTimePicker 458
DateTimePickerFormat 460
DebuggerStepThrough 432
debugging
  bindings 215
Decimal format 256
declarative programming 11, 16, 18, 31, 45, 427
DefaultStyleKey 309
DefaultStyleKey.OverrideMetadata 309
Delete 197
dependency properties 127
Dependency Property System 44, 46
DependencyObjects 211
DependencyProperty 129, 302–303, 440
DependencyProperty.Register 441
DependencyProperty.UnsetValue 296–297
DependencyPropertyChangedEventArgs 249, 304
deployment 55, 402
derivation tree 129
Design pane 24, 35
desktop publishing 407
Desktop Window Manager 54
Device Context 336
device context 6, 8
device independent pixels 13, 411, 418
DialogResult 410
Dialogs
  Windows Forms 464
  WPF 472
DICT 374
DICT protocol 380
Diffuse 356
DiffuseMaterial 356
DIPs. *See* device independent pixels
Direct events 50
direct rendering 316, 332
Direct3D 13, 52, 353
Directional light 357
DirectX 7, 12, 54
Dispatcher 477
DispatcherObject 477
DispatcherOperation 479
DispatcherTimer 480

DispatchTimer 475
DLINQ 211, 250
Dock 85
DockPanel 48, 67, 83–86, 183
document browsing 374
document navigation applications 389
Document Outline 39, 148
document services 44, 56–58
DocumentPaginator 415, 418
DocumentReader 375
documents 406
Document-View 55
dot notation 72
DoubleAnimation 166, 437
DPI 12, 36
DrawEllipse 337
DrawGeometry 337
drawing 51, 315
DrawingBrush 347, 350
DrawingContext 336
DrawingGroup 347
DrawingImage 347
DrawingVisual 338, 347
DrawLine 337
DrawRectangle 336–337
DrawText 6, 337, 345
DrawVideo 337
drop-shadows 163
Duration 166, 437
DWM. *See* Desktop Window Manager
dynamic resource 121, 125–131

E

ECMA 57
EditingCommands 196, 198
ElementHost 471
ElementName 220
Ellipse 138, 319
embossing 163
Emissive 356
EnableVisualStyles 461
EndPoint 161
ErrorTemplates 280
EventArgs 150
EventManager 156
events 49, 132, 147, 192
EventSetter 132
EventSetters
  in derived styles 134
ExceptionValidationRule 278
Execute 194, 203
ExecutedRoutedEventArgs 201
Expander 189
Expander control 81
Expanders 433
Expression 58
Expression Blend 405
Expression Blend. *See* Microsoft Expression Blend
Expression Design. *See* Microsoft Expression Design
Expression Media. *See* Microsoft Expression Media
Expression Web. *See* Microsoft Expression Web

F

façade pattern 244
Fade effect 446
FallbackValue 297
fat applications 4
Favorites 198
Fill 130, 318
FillBehavior 446–447
FillRule 321
FilterEventArgs 270
filtering 270
Find 197
FindAncestor 220
FindResource 124, 270, 438
Firefox 17, 34, 404
FixedDocument 407, 415
FixedDocumentViewer 425
FixedPage 415
Fixed-point format 256
Flash 10, 15
Flex 403
FlowDocument 89–93, 430
  Copying 411
FlowDocuments 407
FlowDocumentScrollViewer 417
FlowDocumentViewer 381
focus 151
FontFamily 182, 415
fonts 6, 463
FontSize 28
FontWeight 133, 135, 162
Foreground 162
FormattedText 345
Framework services 44
FrameworkContentElement 120
FrameworkElement 120, 300
FrameworkPropertyMeta 303
From 167
Full date and time format 258
full trust 395

G

Gang-of-Four 194
garbage collection 14
GDI+ 52
GDI. *See* Graphics Device Interface
General format 256
Generic.xaml 310
Geometry 345, 355
GeometryDrawing 347–348
gestures 202
GetDefaultPrintQueue 414
GetPage 418
GetValue 128, 303
GetVisualChild 425
GladeXML 17
glass 32
glass buttons 158–165
GlyphRunDrawing 347
GNOME/Linux 17
GoF. *See* Gang-of-Four
GPU. *See* Graphics Processing Unit
GradientStops 451
Grafile 346
graphic designer 158
Graphics Device Interface 6
Graphics object 8
Graphics Processing Unit 11
Great Browser War 9
green bits 42
Grid 26, 65, 67, 94, 159
grid layout 26
grids
  nesting 184–190
GridSplitter 187
GroupBox 306

H

Handle method 465
Handled property 151, 201
handledEventsToo 155
Handles to Windows. *See* HWND
Hawaii 456
Header 82
HeaderedContentControl 309
Height 70, 99
Hello, World! 22
Help 200
Hexadecimal format 256
Hierarchical binding 285
HierarchicalDataTemplates 285
History 198

HitTest 343
HitTestResultBehavior 344
HoldEnd 446–447
Homestead theme 141
HorizontalAlignment 28, 79, 187
HorizontalScrollBarVisibility 81
HP 6
HTML 9
HWND 6, 462, 465
HwndHost 468
Hyperlink 301, 378
hyperlinks 374

I

ICommand 203
icons 180, 183
ICustomTypeDescriptor 219
IDocumentPaginatorSource 413
IE 7 392
IEC 260
IEnumerable 251
IIS 396
ImageDrawing 347
ImageSource 347
immediate mode drawing 19, 333
imperative programming 17–18, 45
IMultiValueConverter 289
  parameters 291
inductive UI 384, 389
Inductive user interfaces 374
InfoProvider 281
inheritance 47
InitializeComponent 27, 74, 382
Ink 12, 89
InkPanel 89
INotifyCollectionChanged 243, 326
INotifyPropertyChanged 219, 238
input 49
InputGestures 202
IntelliSense 31, 37, 159, 428, 459
interaction code 25
Intermediate Language 14
Internet Explorer 9, 183, 392, 404
Internet Zone 34
interoperability 457
InvalidateRequerySuggested 208
InvalidateVisual 335
Invoke 477
IsExpanded 189
IsMouseOver 163–164
IsPressed 139, 164
IsSharedSizeScope 108
IsSynchronizedWithCurrentItem 234
Italic 199
ItemsSource 286
ItemTemplate 218, 326
ItemTemplateSelector 276
ItemWidth 87
IValueConverter 222, 259
  parameters 261
IWin32Window 465

J

Jargon File 387
JavaScript 10
Journal 383
JournalEntry 383
Justify 199

K

KeepAlive 383
Kernighan and Ritchie 23
KeyDown 151
KeyEventArgs 154
Keyframe animation 448
KeyGesture 202
KeyUp 151
Kibibytes 260

L

LastChildFill 83, 186
layout 26, 56, 65
layout panel
  types 67
layouts
  nesting 182–186
LayoutTransform 172
Left 70, 199
legacy 457
lights 357
Line 320
LinearGradientBrush 451
LineSegment 348
LinkLabel 300–301
LINQ 40, 250
LINQ to SQL 250
LINQ to XML 250
Linux 404
List 91
ListView 213
Loaded event 74
local 435
localization 107
Long date format 258
LookDirection 358
look-less controls 136
Luna theme 140, 143

M

Macintosh 404
Macintosh OS X 12
Main 181
Main() 30–31
managed code 13–14
Margin 80, 132
MarkupExtension 217, 257
MaskedTextBox 458
Master-Detail Binding 233
Material 364
MatrixTransform 173
MatrixTransform3D 365
MaxLength 132
Mebibytes 260
Media services 44, 51–54
MediaCommands 196, 200
menubars 184
menus 180, 183
merged dictionary 123
MergedDictionaries 123, 145
Message Map 193
message-map model 147
messages 7
Metallic theme 141
MFC 4, 6–7, 34, 147, 193, 458
Microsoft .NET 2.0 42
Microsoft .NET 3.0 42
Microsoft .NET 3.5 42
Microsoft DNA 5
Microsoft Expression Blend 15, 18, 59, 158, 455
Microsoft Expression Design 59
Microsoft Expression Family 59–60
Microsoft Expression Media 60
Microsoft Expression Web 60
Microsoft Money 180, 374
Microsoft Office System 58
Microsoft XPS Document Writer 422

Microsoft.Win32 422
MinHeight 189
MITRE 223
Model 284, 354–357
Model-View-Controller 254
Model-View-ViewModel 254, 283
Moonlight 43, 391, 404
Mosaic Communications Corporation 9
Mouse.OverrideCursor 380, 435
MouseAction 203
MouseEnter 166
MoveToDocumentEnd 198
MoveToDocumentStart 198
MoveUpLine 198
Mozilla 17
MSN Messenger 183
MultiBinding 289
MultiDataTrigger 266
MVC pattern 284
MVVM. *See* Model-View-ViewModel
MXML 17

N

Name 70
namespace 117, 435
NativeWindow 465
Navigate 382
Navigate To Event Handler 31
NavigateUri 232
navigating programmatically 381
navigation application 32–34, 373
NavigationCommands 196, 198
NavigationService 33, 381, 384
NavigationWindow 377
nested grids 184–190
.NET Framework 2.0 24
.NET Framework 3.0 24
.NET Framework 3.5 23
Netscape 9
New 197
New Event Handler 31
normalized spacing 28, 91
Normals 356
NotACommand 197
NTFS 11
Number format 256

O

object initializers 75
ObjectDataProvider 213
object-oriented programming 13
ObservableCollection 238, 243, 326
Office 2007 183
OneTime 211
OneWay 211
OneWayToSource 211
OnRender 335
OnReturn 386
OOP. *See* object-oriented programming
Opacity 161, 437
opacity mask 172
OpacityMask 450
OPC 58
Open Graphics Library 12
Open Packaging 58
OpenGL. *See* Open Graphics Library
OpenType 51
optional inheritance 47
Orientation 87
Orthographic camera 358
OS X 12
Outer glow 163
OverrideCursor 380

P

Padding 71, 76
Page 32, 375
  caching 383
page functions 384
  calling 386
PageContent 415
PagePadding 411
PageResolution 420
Pages 120
paginator 410
paired events 153
Panel 66
Paragraph 91
partial classes 18
Paste 197
Path 216, 321
Path control 39
PathFigure 321
PathGeometry 348
PathSegment 348
PDF 57, 406, 422
Pen 336
pens 6
Perspective camera 358
Photoshop 15, 86
Pixels 463
pixels 19
Point light 357
pointers 6
Polygon 319
Polyline 320
presentation logic 14
PresentationTraceSources 227
preserve 29
PreviewKeyDown 152
PreviewKeyUp 152
PreviousData 221
primitives 357
Print 197, 410
PrintDialog 409
Printing 406
printing 57
  asynchronously 413
  FixedDocuments 415
  FlowDocuments 407
  Visuals 421
PrintPreview 197
PrintQueue 409, 414, 416
PrintTicket 409, 420
PrintVisual 421
PriorityBinding 295
Process Monitor application 254
Properties 197
  catching changes 442
Properties grid 38, 77, 460
Properties window 182
property expression 48
Property System 126, 303
PropertyChanged 231, 241
PushTransform 337

Q

Quartz 52
Quaternion rotation 367
QueueUserWorkItem 476
quirks mode 10

R

RadialGradientBrush 106, 160
ReachFramework 420
Rectangle 29, 318

red bits 42
reflections 169–173
RegisterClassHandler 156
Rehabilitation Act 50
RelativeSource 220, 311
Render 335, 419
rendering thread 474
RenderOpen 341
RenderTargetBitmap 338, 419
RenderTransform 174
Replace 197
RequestNavigate 232, 301–302
resolution 420
ResourceDictionary 121–122, 146
resources 119–131
Result 479
retained-mode drawing 20, 333
Return 387
ReturnEventArgs 386
RGB Colors 162
RIAs. *See* Rich Internet Applications
Ribbon control 180
rich applications 4
rich documents 407
Rich Internet Applications 4, 43, 403
RichTextBox 198
Right 70, 199
RotateTransform 173
RotateTransform3D 365
Routed events 148–154
RoutedCommand 195, 201, 203
RoutedEvent 155
RoutedEventArgs 75, 150
RoutedEventHandler 154
RoutedEvents 193
RoutedUICommand 203
routing strategy 149
Row 100
RowDefinition 99
RowSpan 101
Royale theme 144
RTF 422

S

Safari 34, 404
Save 197
SaveAs 197
ScaleTransform 173
ScaleTransform3D 365
ScaleX 172
ScaleY 172
schema 16
Scientific format 256
scrolling 80
ScrollViewer 81, 433
Search control 38
Section 508 50
security 14, 394–396
SelectAll 197
SelectedItem 230
selecting controls 184
selection controls 39
SelectRight 198
SelectTemplate 276
SelectUp 198
Self 221
session state 374
SetDock 85
SetLeft() 76
SetResourceReference 127
Setter 132, 162
SetValue 128, 303
SGML 9
Shapes 316
SharedSizeGroups 108
Short date format 258
Short time format 258
Shortcuts 202
Show 464
ShowDialog 464
ShutdownMode 30
Silverlight 34, 43, 390–391, 403
Silverlight 2 in Action 391, 404
SizeToContent 109
SkewTransform 173
smart applications 4
SolidColorBrush 105, 120
Solution Explorer 25
SortDescriptions 267
sorting 266
Source 211, 216
Source tab 26
Span 301
sparse property storage 48
sparse storage 128
Specular 356
Split modes 37
splitter 187
Spot light 357
StackPanel 67, 76–83, 189
StartPoint 161
Startup 431, 461
StartupEventArgs 31
StartupUri 30, 33, 181, 377
static resource 121
StaticResource 120, 437, 454
Status 479
StatusBar 186
statusbars 184
Stop 447
Storyboard 166, 438
Stretch 79, 171
StringFormat 255, 293
  MultiBinding 293
Stroke 138, 319
StrokeDashArray 320
StrokeThickness 319
Style 439
styles 56, 119, 131–136
  implicitly applying 135
SyncLINQ 252
System.Drawing.Color 462
System.Printing 408
System.Windows.Controls 66
System.Windows.Forms 66, 459
System.Windows.Interop 472
System.Windows.Media.Color 462
System.Windows.Threading 480
System.Windows.Xps.Packaging 422
SystemColors 129
SystemMonitor 466

T

tablet PCs 12
TabPanel 89
Tag 115–116
Target 211
TargetType 131, 135
TCP 375, 379
template
  binding 138
  default 310
Template property 137
TemplateBinding 138, 311
TemplatedParent 221, 311
temporary key 398
TextBlock 27, 378
TextOut 6
themes 119, 140–146, 307
theming 461
Thickness 76, 411
Thread.Sleep 475
threading 474
ThreadPool 476

timers 480
To 167
ToggleButton 313
ToggleCenter 198
toolbars 180, 183–184
ToolbarTray 186
tools 18
ToolTip 281
TraceLevel 215
Transform3DGroup 365
TransformGroup 173
transforms 171, 173–174
  3D 365
  with Windows Forms 462
Transition effects 427
Transitional project 454
transitions
  generic 439
  simple 436
TranslateTransform 173
TranslateTransform3D 365
TriangleIndices 356
triggers 139–140
trusted authority 397
Trusted Root Certification Authorities 398
TryFindResource 125
tunnel down 49, 148
Tunnel events 50
tunneling 49
tunneling events 151–154
TurboTax 374
TwoWay 211
Two-way notification 46
Typography 51

U

UI Spy 60
UIElements 321
UltraBold 134
Underline 199
UniformGrid 109
URI 383
Uri 304
usability 395
User controls 300
user interface services 44, 55–56
user interfaces, 3
UserPageRangeEnabled 413

V

validation 278
ValidationRules 282
Validators 278
Vector 358
vectors 19–20
VerticalAlignment 28, 79, 187
VerticalScrollBarVisibility 81
VGA 6
video 52
VideoDrawing 347
View 284
ViewBox 462
Viewport2DVisual3D 369
Viewport3D 353
Virtualizing 89
VirtualizingStackPanel 89
Visio 8
Vista 5, 11, 158, 163, 392
Vista Aero theme 142
Vista Theme 461
Visual 171
Visual Studio 18, 60
Visual Studio 2008 18, 22, 34–40, 58, 158
visual tree 129
VisualBrush 171
VisualChildrenCount 425
VisualCollection 340
VisualHolder 424
Visuals 317, 338
VisualTreeHelper 343

W

WaitCallback 477
WCF. *See* Windows Communication Foundation
web 8
web browser 373
Web Sharing 397
whitespace 28
WIC. *See* WPF Imaging Components
Width 70, 97
Wiki 180
Window 32
Window.Resources 120
WindowBrushKey 130
WindowInteropHelper 465, 472
Windows 120
Windows 3.0 5
Windows CardSpace 42
Windows Classic theme 144
Windows Communication Foundation 5, 40, 42
Windows drawing 5
Windows Forms 4, 6–7, 18, 23, 34, 66, 147, 458
Windows Future Storage 11
Windows Imaging Component 52
Windows Presentation Foundation. *See* WPF
Windows SDK 4, 16
Windows themes 461
Windows UI 7
Windows Vista 32, 119
Windows XP 5, 119
WindowsFormsIntegration 459, 470
WindowTitle 376
WinFS 11
WinMain() 30
Wipe effect 448
wizards 374
WMF 422
Workflow Foundation 42
World Wide Web 8
WPF 3, 22
WPF commands 195
WPF Engine 44
WPF form designer 18
WPF Framework 44
WPF Imaging Components 51
WrapPanel 67, 86–88
WriteAsync 413
WritingCompleted 413

X

x:Key 131
XAML 16–18, 44, 427
XAML Browser Application. *See* XBAP
XAML designer 35
XAML pane 24, 36
XAMLPad 16, 60, 180
XamlReader 479
XamlWriter 478
XBAP 33, 55, 390
  building 391
  deploying 396
  security 394
  when to use 399
XLinq 211
XML 27
XML Paper Specification. *See* XPS

xml:space 29
XmlDataProvider 211, 213, 227, 286
xmlns 16, 117
XP themes 461
XPath 211, 227, 229
XPS 57, 406, 422
XPS document viewer 423
XPS document writer 413
XpsDocument 422
XpsDocumentWriter 413, 416, 422
XUL 17

Z

ZAM3D 61, 355
Zoom control 36
Z-Order 240
ZOrder 447
Zune theme 142

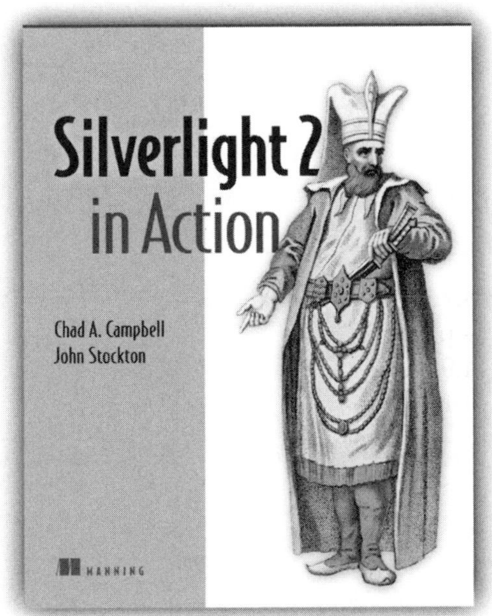

Silverlight 2 in Action
by Chad A. Campbell
and John Stockton

ISBN: 1-933988-42-8
400 pages
$44.99
October 2008

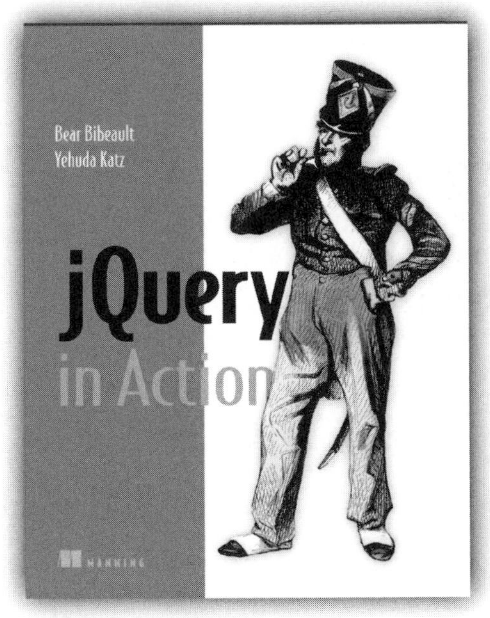

jQuery in Action
by Bear Bibeault
and Yehuda Katz

ISBN: 1-933988-35-5
376 pages
$39.99
February 2008

For ordering information go to www.manning.com

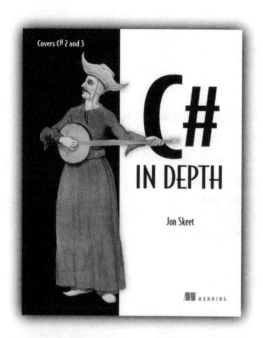

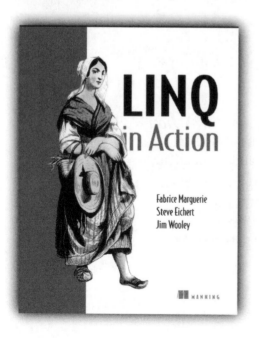

MORE TITLES FROM MANNING

ASP.NET Ajax in Action
by Alessandro Gallo, David Barkol, and Rama Krishna Vavilala

ISBN: 1-933988-14-2
576 pages
$44.99
August 2007

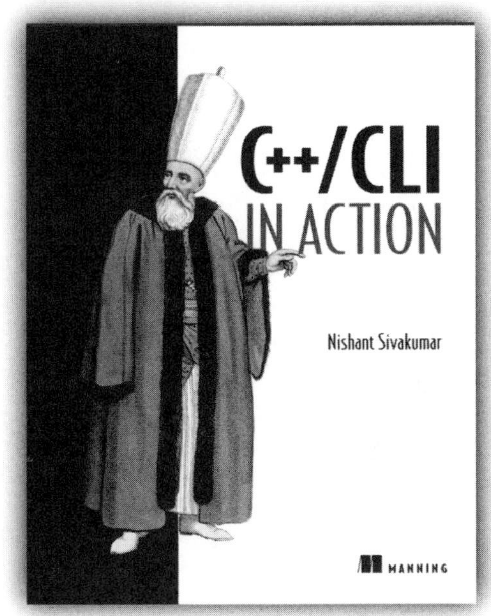

C++/CLI in Action
by Nishant Sivakumar

ISBN: 1-932394-81-8
416 pages
$49.99
April 2007

For ordering information go to www.manning.com

MORE TITLES FROM MANNING

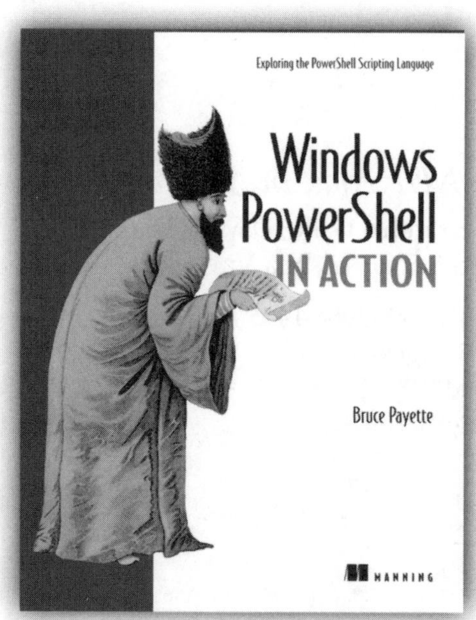

Windows PowerShell in Action
by Bruce Payette

ISBN: 1-932394-90-7
576 pages
$44.99
February 2007

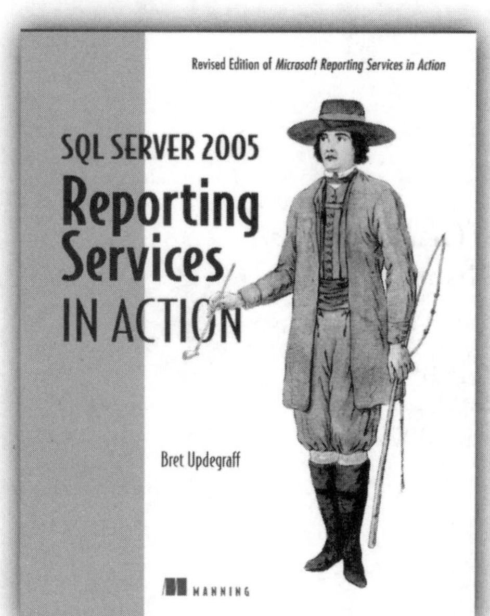

SQL Server 2005 ReportingServices in Action
by Bret Updegraff

ISBN: 1-932394-76-1
600 pages
$49.99
November 2006

For ordering information go to www.manning.com